# A HANDBOOK OF CHILD WELFARE

# A HANDBOOK OF CHILD WELFARE
## Context, Knowledge, and Practice

JOAN LAIRD and ANN HARTMAN,
Editors

**THE FREE PRESS**
*A Division of Macmillan, Inc.*
*NEW YORK*

Collier Macmillan Publishers
LONDON

The Free Press
A Division of Macmillan, Inc.
866 Third Avenue, New York, N.Y. 10022

Collier Macmillan Canada, Inc.

Printed in the United States of America

printing number

1 2 3 4 5 6 7 8 9 10


Library of Congress Cataloging in Publication Data

Main entry under title:

A Handbook of child welfare.

Bibliography: p.
Includes index.
1. Child welfare—United States. 2. Social work with children—United States. I. Laird, Joan.
II. Hartman, Ann.
HV741.H32 1985     362.7'95'0973     84-18769
ISBN 0-02-918090-2

The definitions of group-care settings on pages 618–619 of this book are reprinted by special permission of the Child Welfare League of America, Inc., *CWLA Directory of Member and Associate Agencies, 1981.*

*This book is dedicated to our families, especially to*
*Elizabeth Kathleen Willette*
*Gilbert James Willette*
*and*
*Elizabeth Turner*

# Contents

# Contributors

Jo Ann Allen, M.S.W., is Associate Professor, School of Social Work, at the University of Michigan. An experienced family therapist, she has conducted many workshops and in-service training programs in family therapy, and is the co-author, with Joan Laird, of "Family Theory and Practice" in the recently published *Handbook of Clinical Social Work*.

Stephen Antler, D.S.W., was a participant in several innovative community action programs during the War on Poverty years. He is known for his work in research, policy, and community education and advocacy in the field of child abuse and neglect. Dr. Antler, Associate Professor of Social Work at Boston University School of Social Work, has recently published a book entitled *Child Abuse and Child Protection: Readings in Policy and Practice*.

Florence M. Ceravolo, A.C.S.W., is Project Director and Clinical Supervisor of the Family Day Care Service, Jewish Child Care Association, in New York City. A doctoral candidate at the Hunter College School of Social Work, she is the 1983 recipient of the Distinguished Service Award from the New York Foundling Hospital's Department of Medicine.

WAYNE A. CHESS, PH.D., is Professor of Social Work, School of Social Work, University of Oklahoma. He is currently studying worker and client perceptions of service outcomes and the relationship of job satisfaction and burnout to service outcomes.

ELIZABETH S. COLE, M.S.W., is Director, Permanent Families for Children, Child Welfare League of America. Formerly the first director of the North American Center on Adoption, she also served as Chief of the Bureau of Resource Development, New Jersey Division of Youth and Family Services. In the latter position she helped design that state's subsidized adoption program, launched a mass media campaign to recruit foster, group care, and adoptive parents and initiated regional resource centers and a purchase of service system.

LELA B. COSTIN, M.S.W., recently published a biography of Grace and Edith Abbott entitled *Two Sisters for Social Justice*. A professor in the School of Social Work at the University of Illinois at Urbana–Champaign, she has long been a leader in the field of child welfare. Her widely used text, *Child Welfare: Policies and Practice*, is now in its third edition.

ALBERT G. CRAWFORD, PH.D., is an Administrative Resident at Graduate Hospital in Philadelphia, a Research Associate at the New Jersey School of Osteopathic Medicine, and a Candidate for an M.B.A. in Health Administration at Widener University. He has collaborated with Frank Furstenberg on a number of research projects and articles on divorce and remarriage, family history, and adolescent sexuality, pregnancy, and childbearing.

MARY E. DAVIDSON, PH.D., is Lead Consultant to the Monitoring Commission for Desegregation Implementation of the Chicago Board of Education. Formerly Special Assistant to the Mayor of Boston, she is currently on leave from Southern Illinois University where she is Associate Professor and Chairperson of the Child Welfare Concentration in Social and Community Services.

MILAN J. DLUHY, PH.D., is Associate Professor at the University of Michigan School of Social Work. Professor Dluhy has held various policy and administrative positions with the U.S. Department of Health, Education and Welfare, and in the states of Michigan and Illinois. He is the author of *Changing the System: Political Advocacy for Disadvantaged Groups* and, with John Tropman and Roger Lind, *New Strategic Perspectives on Social Policy*.

GERALDINE ESPOSITO, M.S.W., is Executive Director of the California Society of Clinical Social Workers. She worked in public child welfare as a caseworker, a group worker, and a community organizer. Former director of the Region II Child Welfare Training Center at the Columbia University School of Social Work, she served as a special assistant for human services to Lieutenant Governor Krupsak of New York.

MICHELLE FINE, PH.D., is particularly interested in research on women's experiences of injustice and has recently completed an article entitled "Coping with Rape: Critical Perspectives on Consciousness." Former Research Director of the Industrial Social Welfare Center at the Columbia University School of Social Work, she is currently Assistant Professor of Psychology and Education at the University of Pennsylvania.

FRANK F. FURSTENBERG, JR., PH.D., has done extensive research in the area of teenage pregnancy. Professor of Sociology at the University of Pennsylvania, he is the author of *Unplanned Parenthood: The Social Consequences of Teenage Childbearing*.

CAREL B. GERMAIN, D.S.W., is Professor of Social Work at the University of Connecticut School of Social Work. Dr. Germain has pioneered the application of ecological theory and systems principles to generic social work practice models, and is the author of many articles and books including, with Alex Gitterman, *The Life Model of Social Work Practice*. Her most recent work is *Social Work Practice in Health Care*.

DAVID G. GIL, D.S.W., is Professor of Social Policy at The Florence Heller Graduate School at Brandeis University. Before coming to Brandeis in 1964, he was involved in social welfare practice, research, and administration in the United States and Israel, where he lived in kibbutz settlements. The author of many important studies on social policy and child abuse, he recently completed a study for the United Nations on social welfare policies in the United States. Professor Gil's teaching, research, and practice are concerned with understanding and overcoming forces which obstruct human development, and with liberation, cooperation, and social equality.

JEANNE M. GIOVANNONI, PH.D., is widely known as a researcher and consultant in the fields of family life, child welfare, and mental health. Her most recent book, co-authored with Rosina Becerra, is entitled *Defining Child Abuse* and is a study of the ways in which various professional groups consider and define mistreatment. Professor at the School of Social Welfare, University of California at Los Angeles, Dr. Giovannoni is also the co-author, with Andrew Billingsley, of *Children of the Storm*.

HENRY L. GUNN III, M.S.W., is Director of the Region III Center for Children, Youth, and Families. Formerly Director of Social Services for the State of Virginia Department of Public Welfare, his primary interest is in working with child welfare agencies to identify and devise strategies to eliminate barriers to service. For the past three years he has worked closely with the Philadelphia County Children and Youth Agency to reorganize services and develop worker training programs.

MARK HARDIN, J.D., is a specialist in child welfare law. He is currently Director of the Foster Care Project of the American Bar Association. He is the editor of the recently published volume entitled *Foster Children in the Courts.*

ANN HARTMAN, D.S.W., is Professor of Social Work at the University of Michigan School of Social Work and a staff member of Ann Arbor Center for the Family. For the past five years she has served as Faculty Director of the National Child Welfare Training Center. Professor Hartman has done extensive writing, research, and training in the child welfare and family fields. Her publications include *Finding Families: An Ecological Approach to Assessment and Intervention in Adoption,* and *Family-Centered Social Work Practice,* co-authored with Joan Laird.

SRINIKA JAYARATNE, PH.D., is Associate Professor, School of Social Work, University of Michigan. A noted researcher, he is the author, with Rona L. Levy, of *Empirical Clinical Practice.* He is currently studying the effects of work stress on the family lives of child welfare workers.

JOAN LAIRD, M.S.W., is Associate Professor, Department of Social Work, Eastern Michigan University. On the staff of Ann Arbor Center for the Family, Professor Laird is an experienced trainer, consultant, and clinician in family therapy. Currently working on a doctorate in social work and anthropology at the University of Michigan, she is the co-author of *Family-Centered Social Work Practice.*

JAMES W. LEIGH, JR., M.S.W., Associate Professor at the University of Washington School of Social Work, participated in the Program of Advanced Study at the Smith College School for Social Work. He has pioneered efforts to include ethnic content in practicum instruction as well as content responsive to the service needs of ethnic and racial minority populations in the social work curriculum.

DONALD M. LOPPNOW, M.S.W., is Professor and heads the Department of Social Work at Eastern Michigan University. Under his leadership, the program has built a curriculum particularly strong in the areas of services to families and children. In addition to his interest in practice with adolescents, he is particularly concerned with program development, administration, and in the uses of supervision.

ANTHONY N. MALUCCIO, D.S.W., has authored several important books, was the principal investigator of the Region I (New England) Child Welfare Training Center, and most recently has been appointed the first visiting John Milner Professor of Child Welfare at the University of Southern California School of Social Work. Dr. Maluccio is Professor of Social Work at the University of Connecticut School of Social Work.

EMILY JEAN MCFADDEN, M.S.W., is Assistant Professor of Social Work at Eastern Michigan University where she is also Program Manager of the Foster Parent Training Project. Widely known as a consultant and trainer in the field of foster care and particularly in the area of foster parent training, she has worked in child welfare, served as a Parents Anonymous sponsor, and has authored several articles and developed a videotape series for child welfare education and training.

BRENDA G. MCGOWAN, D.S.W., has served as consultant to numerous public and voluntary child welfare organizations at the local, state and national levels. Associate Professor, Columbia University School of Social Work, she is particularly interested in case advocacy, organizational change, and children's rights and is the author or editor of several articles and books in these areas, most recently, with William Meezan, the editor of *Child Welfare: Current Dilemmas, Future Directions*.

CAROL H. MEYER, D.S.W., is Professor of Social Work at the Columbia University School of Social Work. Widely known for her work in developing a model of practice which both integrates policy and practice and applies systems concepts, she is the author of several books, including *Social Work Practice: The Urban Crisis*, and *Social Work Practice: The Changing Landscape*. Dr. Meyer is currently serving as editor-in-chief of *Social Work*.

MIRIAM MELTZER OLSON, D.S.W., has been a consultant in the fields of health, child welfare, and mental health. She has written and done research on health care and women's issues and, as a Fulbright scholar in England, did research in the field of mental health. Currently Associate Professor of Social Work at Temple University, she has also taught at Columbia and Fordham.

PENNY CALLAN PARTRIDGE, M.S.W., is an adoptee and an adoptive parent who founded the Adoption Forum of Philadelphia. She has recently begun a private clinical practice and is writing the book she wishes she had read as a young adoptee.

PATRICIA L. PASICK, ED.M., is a doctoral candidate in the joint program in Education and Psychology at the University of Michigan. She is interested in the study of child development and parent–child relationships and is co-author of *Affective Education for Special Children and Youth*.

ROBERT S. PASICK, PH.D., is a family therapist and Director of Training and Research at Ann Arbor Center for the Family, where he is exploring the use of play, humor, and drama in work with families and children. He is also interested in the study of the father's role in child development, and in school–family relationships.

RINO J. PATTI, D.S.W., is Professor, School of Social Work, at the University of Washington in Seattle. His most recent book is titled *Social Welfare Administration: Managing Social Programs in a Developmental Context*. Professor Patti is also the co-author, with Herman Resnick, of the book *Change From Within*, published in 1980.

HERMAN RESNICK, PH.D., is Professor, School of Social Work, at the University of Washington in Seattle. Among his many publications is the classic article "Changing the Agency from Within," co-authored with Rino Patti. Resnick and Patti also collaborated on the book *Change From Within*.

ROBERT M. RICE, PH.D., is Executive Vice-President, Family Service America (formerly the Family Service Association of America) where he is responsible for program implementation. He is an expert in the field of family policy and in social agency management and is the author of the widely read volume *American Family Policy: Content and Context*.

NANCY DAY ROBINSON, D.S.W., is Director, Accreditation Program, National HomeCaring Council. The author of several studies of homemaker–home health aides, Dr. Robinson is also a field instructor for the Adelphi University School of Social Work.

DOROTHEA WEND ROSE, A.C.S.W., is a psychotherapist in private practice in Garrett Park, Maryland. She and her husband, Thomas Rose, are the parents of Hannah, age 9, and Aaron, age 2, an adopted child.

THOMAS ROSE, PH.D., is Professor and Coordinator of the Handicapped Assistance Program at Montgomery College in Rockville, Maryland, and is a member of the Maryland Developmental Disabilities Council.

ROSEMARY C. SARRI, PH.D., has wide-ranging research interests in the fields of social welfare and social justice, including the feminization of poverty and organizational responses to deviant behavior. A professor of social work at the University of Michigan, she is co-author of *Women in Prison in Michigan* and an editor of *Alternative Programs for Disruptive Youth*. She has just completed a study of the impact of reductions in AFDC benefits on working welfare women and their families.

BRETT A. SEABURY, D.S.W., has a wide range of interests in social work and child welfare, and has published articles on contracting, space, communication problems, and case advocacy. Associate Professor of Social Work at the University of Michigan, he has recently authored, with Charles D. Garvin, a practice text entitled *Interpersonal Practice in Social Work: Processes and Procedures* and has begun work on a study of cross-cultural healing practices. Dr. Seabury also farms and raises sheep.

VIVIAN B. SHAPIRO, M.S.W., is Assistant Professor of Social Work and Lecturer, Department of Psychiatry, at the University of Michigan. She was, between 1972 and 1980, Senior Social Worker of the Child Development Project, Department of Psychiatry, University of Michigan. Professor Shapiro is currently studying infant and family adaptation in cases of adoption, particularly the relationships between family functioning and certain chronic childhood illnesses.

BENNIE M. STOVALL, PH.D., is Director of Training at the Children's Aid Society of New York. She has done training and consultation nationally and internationally in the area of sexual abuse of children.

GLORIA WALDINGER, D.S.W., is Assistant Dean, School of Social Work, University of California at Los Angeles and is Project Director of the Certificate Program in Leadership Training for Child Welfare Administrators and Managers. Her research interests include the use of adoption subsidy and postadoption services. She is a former Director of the Region IX Child Welfare Training Center.

ELAINE M. WALSH, M.S.W., is a doctoral candidate and adjunct lecturer at Fordham University School of Social Service. She was associated for several years with the New York Foundling Hospital and in recent years has directed and helped develop victim assistance and crime prevention programs.

JAMES K. WHITTAKER, PH.D., is Professor of Social Work and Director of the Social Welfare doctoral program at the University of Washington School of Social Work. He is author of *Caring for Troubled Children: Resi-*

*dential Treatment in a Community Context* and a co-author of *Social Support Networks: Informal Helping in the Human Services.*

KERMIT T. WILTSE, D.S.W., is Professor Emeritus, School of Social Welfare, University of California, Berkeley. He is the author of many articles in the area of foster care, a book, *Children in Foster Homes: Achieving Continuity of Care,* with Theodore Stein and Eileen Gambrill, and most recently a monograph, *Conceptual Statement of Case Management for Family and Children's Services,* with Linda Remy.

MARJORIE ZIEFERT, M.S.W., is Assistant Professor at Eastern Michigan University. She has published several articles and chapters in the area of adolescent abuse, and is the author of a continuing education manual entitled *Adolescent Abuse: Prevention and Treatment.* Professor Ziefert served as consultant to the National Center for Home Based Services.

# Preface

In colonial times, when labor was in short supply and work sanctified, dependent children were indentured. It was understood that such children would earn their keep while learning a skill or trade. Later, when almshouses were developed, children, because they were considered "little adults," were placed in congregate institutions with adults suffering a variety of physical and social ills. In the late nineteenth and early twentieth centuries, a period when education, "habit training," and discipline were prized as the key to the good life, the social planners of the day envisioned a children's institution in every community. Each such institution would rear disciplined, industrious, and literate citizens. And when Horace Greeley said, "Go west, young man," the agrarian myth was in full sway; children were rescued from the urban streets and sent to farm homes in the Midwest.

Thus arrangements made for the welfare of children may serve as a metaphor for society's changing values. It is possible to study important dimensions of social ideology and history by examining the responses to and arrangements made for children in need of care, protection, and control in successive eras. It becomes quickly apparent that such arrangements very much reflect not only current reigning views about children, but also the fundamental values of that society.

Every society at every time must make some provision for its children in need. Preindustrial and folk societies tended to rely largely on informal mutual aid networks and extended family, family-like, or neighborly arrangements. With the growth of the State, and of an increasingly differentiated, complex society, came the formalization and institutionalization of public and private responses to social and family breakdown; thus more formalized arrangements were created for children in need. These arrangements may be considered the Child Welfare system, or the institution of Child Welfare.

In the past few years, Child Welfare, once again, as an institution and as a field of practice, has been experiencing a major transformation, a transformation that some might see as revolutionary. And, although some of these changes may be as yet primarily ideological, located in the discourse or in the language about Child Welfare rather than implemented in program and practice, it is the case that overarching goals, practice assumptions, and planning have all taken a new direction. If funding has been uncertain and some changes halting and uneven in their translation into program and practice, nevertheless the shape of Child Welfare is being altered. Changes can be seen most vividly in the growing emphasis on prevention of placement, in the redefinition of foster care, in the permanency movement, in deinstitutionalization, and in the increased use of citizen, consumer, and self-help group participation in program development and service delivery.

These changes have provided a major stimulus for the conception of this volume. It seemed timely to ask people who are deeply involved in the field of Child Welfare to commit to the written text their views about the changing aspects of the complex Child Welfare scene in the 1980s.

As we observed significant events influencing Child Welfare, reviewed the literature, studied the chapters prepared for this volume, and discussed a range of issues with various authors, we asked ourselves: What are the major assumptions and values, what is the prevailing world view expressed in Child Welfare today? It seemed to us (although we may be overinfluenced by our own biases and reality constructions) that ecological concerns and an ecological perspective are currently shaping Child Welfare theory and practice, just as they are influencing other areas of social concern and other fields of practice.

In 1962, Rachel Carson, in her brilliant and chilling volume, *Silent Spring*, quietly helped to usher in a new perspective. She sounded a warning, bringing national attention to some of the current and potential outcomes of our headlong rush into the modern technological world. Carson described the destruction that was being wrought by thoughtless and radical interventions into natural systems and our failure to attend to the delicate and nurturing balances and life-sustaining connections between living things and their environments that must be protected and preserved. She was followed by others whose work has stimulated a growing ecological enlightenment, by Charles Reich's *The Greening of America*, Alvin Toffler's *Future Shock,* and the work of microbiologist Rene Dubos. And, although many individuals and certainly our large and powerful economic and political institutions continue to ignore the warnings and predictions of such ecologists, it is clear we will never be the same again. Similar to the Copernican Revolution, the ecological revolution has altered our views of our own relationships with the natural world.

Translated into human terms, an ecological perspective leads us to focus on, to protect, to nourish the most vital human connections, to attend to the adaptive balance between human beings and their natural, built, and human environments, to be alert to the transactional patterns in related systems.

This perspective can also provide a framework for understanding and evaluating the nature of the social and institutional responses to children in need of care and protection that define the Child Welfare system of the eighties. In the formal language of current legislation, a central goal of the Child Welfare system is to provide the "least restrictive environment" for each child in need of services. In ecological terms this may be interpreted to mean that environment which is most free from bureaucratic and institutional features such as lack of intimacy and depersonalization, that environment closest to the natural caring system, the biological family. A cornerstone of today's Child Welfare system is the emphasis on the importance of the family and on the need to support and enhance rather than to hinder its capacities and competence, to protect familial bonds, and to maintain children with their families of birth if at all possible.

A second translation of the ecological perspective is found in the growing conviction that, if a child cannot be maintained in his or her own family, arrangements for care should be as close to the natural system as possible. During placement the continuity of familial bonds should be preserved, and return home should be facilitated as promptly as possible. Increasingly, Child Welfare services are focused on the maintenance or rehabilitation of the family system, and careful attention is given to the potential iatrogenic effects of our most well-meaning interventions. When ultimate return home is impossible, adoption, placement with a permanent family, is the goal for all children.

An ecological perspective has made irrelevant the old, contentious argument between those who give priority to parents' rights and those who advocate the rights of children. In Child Welfare, we must be child advocates. In that sense, we may be "child focused," but our practice must be "family-centered" since we know that the welfare and the destiny of children cannot be considered separately from the families of which they are a part.

Finally, an ecological perspective shapes a view of the Child Welfare institution itself, as is demonstrated in the organization of and in the views of practice presented in this volume. The child must be understood and helped in the context of the family, and the family must be seen as part of a larger community and an ideological, social, economic, political, and historical context, as well as within the context of the Child Welfare system. Child Welfare as an institution is itself, of course, continually influencing and influenced by the larger surround.

Thus this presentation of Child Welfare, its context, knowledge, and practice, goes far beyond the interactions between child and worker, or even family and worker. Child Welfare practice takes place at the societal, community, and agency levels as well: all of these system levels are in constant transaction with each other, and the outcomes of these relationships influence profoundly the ultimate welfare of the child and family.

The conception and organization of this volume, then, represent our effort to view Child Welfare, the institution, contextually and as a continuum of practice from larger to smaller system levels and from interventions that are less radical with respect to child and family to those that are more radical.

Within the overarching world view that provides a framework for this volume there are, of course, differences among our authors—in perspective, in emphasis, in definitions of the major problems to be addressed, in theoretical position, and in priorities and preferred strategies for change. The social work profession and the field of Child Welfare encompass a wide diversity in theoretical stances and practice models. Such diversity may at times create confusion, but it is also a source of strength and vitality. This volume reflects that diversity as well as a common concern for the welfare of families and children.

In Part I we begin with the context of Child Welfare, each author examining a portion of that context with the recognition that ideology, history, policy, and institutional arrangements themselves help shape each other.

We then turn, in Part II, to an overview of selected knowledge areas that have special relevance for and furnish substance for practice in Child Welfare. In the first three chapters in this section, prevailing ideas about, respectively, communities, families, and child development are examined, while two additional areas of knowledge highly pertinent to Child Welfare are addressed substantively in the last two chapters, namely, child abuse and neglect and legal issues in Child Welfare.

The following four sections, Parts III through VI, are devoted to program, policy, and practice at various levels of the Child Welfare system. The volume ends with a view of Child Welfare as a world of work and of education and training for practice (Part VII).

The volume also contains, following most of the practice sections, several brief exemplars. Each exemplar explores a particular area in more depth or offers a concrete illustration of program, policy, practice, or research in this field. Our original aim, to include several examples of innovative work in each section, had to be greatly tempered in response to growing concern over size of the volume. Thus the exemplars represent a small sample of contemporary practice in a field in the midst of exciting and meaningful change, a field attracting new interest and attention in education and practice for social work.

Finally, we turn to the pleasant task of acknowledging at least some of the people who have contributed in many different ways to the conception and completion of this volume. First, we especially want to thank the authors themselves for their rich and thoughtful contributions and for their noble patience, as they waited so long to see their work in print. Our respect and sympathy has grown immensely for all those who have in the past or will in the future undertake to construct a volume of this size and complexity. Our original naiveté about the extent and difficulty of the task and our expansiveness has been replaced by more sober understanding of the editing role.

Both of us began our social work careers in public child welfare: Joan in Suffolk County, New York, and Ann in Summit County, Ohio. We particularly want to remember many of our colleagues and friends from those times past who added so much to our thinking; Jane Davis, who understood long before it was fashionable that child welfare had to be family-centered; Abbie Hawk, who fought for high standards of practice and the professionalization of staff in public social services; and Dorothy Gillette, who was willing to listen to a new worker questioning questionable practices.

More recently, Joan's work at Eastern Michigan University, where she develops and teaches family and children's services content, has provided a special opportunity to work with faculty and students in rethinking policy and practice in the family and children's area. Ann's role as Faculty Director of the National Child Welfare Training Center has brought her in touch with leaders in Child Welfare throughout the country. These valuable associations and dialogues have provided a stimulating context for the planning and completion of this project. And both of us wish to recognize how much we have learned from contacts with hundreds of line staff and supervisors in a range of Child Welfare agencies across the country as we have consulted and done training in family-centered practice. But perhaps those people who have taught us the most profound lessons have been our client families, whose courage and resourcefulness in even the worst of circumstances continue to remind us of the resilience of human beings and the persistence of family attachments.

Finally, we must acknowledge the support rendered by our Free Press editor, Laura Wolff, whose ideas and criticism along the way have been intelligent and provocative and who kept us focused on completing what seemed an unfinishable task. Our thanks are extended also to Celia Knight, who has conscientiously guided the manuscript through the production process.

# PART I

# The Context of Child Welfare

How may we describe the context, the "surround," the landscape within which social work practice in child welfare* is embedded? Moreover, how can "context" be conceptualized or portrayed if, when one thinks about it, everything is connected to everything else in one way or another, and the world, indeed the sky, is the limit?

The word "context" from the Latin verb "contexere" means "to weave together." As a noun it is defined as "the whole situation, background, or environment relevant to some happening or personality."[1] How then can this weaving together of the whole situation relevant to child welfare occur?

Our own favored perspective is an ecological one. Human and social systems are constantly engaged in exchanges with their surrounding environment in order to obtain the resources, the supports, the feedback, and the stimulation needed to survive and to differentiate. In the process, both the unit of concern, be it individual, family, group, or larger social organization, as well as the impinging environment, are somehow changed; each must adapt to the other. An ecological perspective adopted as a metaphor for practice implies a concern with the adaptive fit between living systems and their surrounding environments, and a concern with the interdependencies which must be understood

---

*In this volume, we use the term "child welfare" when we are referring to the welfare of all children, and the term "Child Welfare" when we are referring to the institution or field of services to children and families.—Eds.

and altered if the transactions are to be nurturing and sustaining. "A system together with its environment," as Hall and Fagan have said, "makes up the universe of all things of interest in a given context" (1968:84).

The challenge of this opening section, then, is to weave together in some coherent way all things of interest in that context which includes child welfare. This task is complicated by the challenge of defining "child welfare." Each author squarely faces that task. As the editors, our own challenge is to somehow, as family therapists are fond of saying, get "meta" to our distinguished authors, to be able to integrate and then stand outside of their rich conceptions of context to glance at the whole and the relationships among the parts. Here both available knowledge and linear language handicap us, because few concepts and little sound research exist that capture the complexities of ecological environments or the nature of the crucial transactions in any particular context. Visual or three-dimensional models are often more helpful than words in picturing the landscape, but the printed page, unfortunately, is restricted to words and flat diagrams, limiting the kind of picture we wish could rise from these pages.

Bronfenbrenner envisions the ecological environment as "a set of nested structures, each inside the next, like a set of nested dolls" (1979b:3). In his model, the innermost level or ring includes the developing person in the immediate surroundings, or the microsystem, and the outermost ring those overarching patterns of ideology and social institutions common to a particular culture, or the macrosystem. In between are what Bronfenbrenner terms the mesosystem and exosystem levels. The former is constituted by the relationships among major groups or settings that the more intimate parts of the individual's daily life touch, such as family, school, or peer group, while the latter includes other specific social structures that consistently influence the individual, such as local government, community resources, the world of work, or recreation.

Combining Bronfenbrenner's "nested structure" notion with Hartman's (1978; 1979b) eco-map, which was originated to portray family–environment relationships to help workers in child welfare examine the needs of families, our overarching view of the child welfare context is pictured in Figure I–1.

If such a diagram were to be used to help make an assessment in relation to a particular unit of attention, whether child–in family–in environment, child welfare agency–in community, or residents of group home–in community, the salient connections among systems can be characterized by drawing in the lines pictured in the key to characterize various relationships. The completed map, while complex, provides an overall view of the client or agency system in context, helping to locate

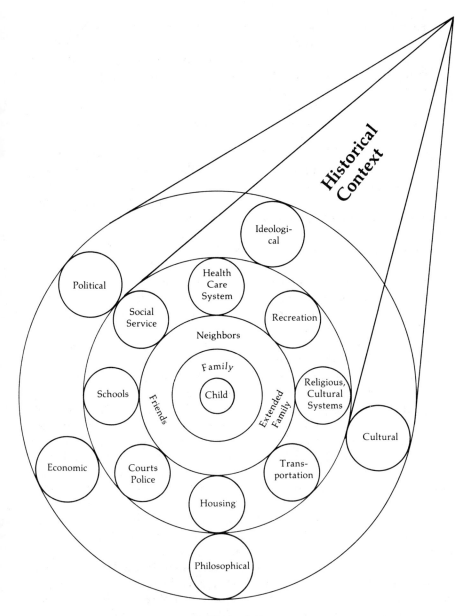

**Figure I–1**

the most significant areas of difficulty and providing a blueprint for guiding change efforts.

Each of the five chapters in this section emphasizes a different dimension of the total context, and each author in his or her own style moves from larger to smaller levels of analysis through space and time, widening and narrowing the boundaries of relevance. Although some overlaps and mergings of content cannot be helped, the reader can envision how these chapters relate to each other and to the diagram of the total context by shading the relevant portions or rings of the diagram. Gil, who perhaps had the most difficult assignment of observing what might be called the suprastructure of Child Welfare as a field of practice and as an arena for the welfare of children, examines the political, social, cultural, economic, and philosophical threads—in short the powerful ideology that helps create and shape the landscape. The implications of his ideas touch every dimension of the context, from the entire population to the smallest child in danger.

In the second chapter, Costin adds texture and depth by describing the most tenacious historical roots, identifying those events, movements, and turning points which have most influenced the shape of the field today. The more intimate and informal environmental opportunities, networks, and sources of support, which add richness and vitality to everyday life and render the difficult role of parenting more rewarding, are of particular interest to Rice, whose contribution surveys the life-world of child and family.

Antler concretizes the ideological, the historical, and the other major forces in the environment of the child welfare world by studying their translation into policies and programs. Here we see the politics of our context in action, as his work moves outward to capture the ideological dimensions and inward to their institutional and family impacts. Finally, Meyer scrutinizes Child Welfare, the institutional context itself, the service structure that seems caught in the middle trying to provide for the welfare of children within the constraints and historical influences of the larger context.

If this overview maps the territory and hints at what the reader will see along the way, it tells us little about the many side trips taken or paths explored. While the focus of each contextual chapter varies, there are common themes and common questions raised throughout. The first is the crucial matter of definition. What is child welfare? This simple enough query turns out to be surprisingly complex, yet these authors achieve a high level of congruence. Gil, for example, describes "child welfare" as a set of nurturing conditions for living in which children "fare well," an environment which offers opportunities and the freedom for children to develop their fullest potential. Child Welfare, on the other hand, is a constellation of public provisions and professional processes which are created to meet the needs of children who do not or have not "fared well."

Rice makes a similar distinction, elaborating his view of each concept and articulating what the public provisions of Child Welfare include, while Meyer expands on the historical and ideological dimensions of Child Welfare as a social institution. Costin, in her portrayal of the historical context, rather than distinguishing between child welfare and Child Welfare, describes a field of action in which humanitarian concerns for the well-being of children are expressed. Her conception broadens the boundaries to include not only child welfare activities, which supplement the family or repair family breakdown, but also such social reform activities as the drive for public education and the fight against child labor.

Historically the field of Child Welfare has had an ambivalent and even competitive relationship with the family. That relationship, mirroring the shifting ideological positions concerning the role of the State in relation to the family's child-rearing function has been, in the wake of renewed interest in the family, once again called into question.

The written and spoken discourse of the Child Welfare system has always held high the primary goal of strengthening the biological family, wherever possible avoiding the separation of family members through child placement. This goal, however, has often been honored more in its breach than in its achievement. From the days of almshouses, foundling homes, and Charles Loring Brace's promotion of the shipment of children by train from the dehumanizing slums of the Eastern cities to the farms of the Midwest, to the eventual growth of the huge system of foster, group, and institutional care functioning today, the placement of children has cornered a far greater share of the human and material resources that comprise the Child Welfare system.

Recently, social observers have begun to note that a virtual revolution might be taking place in the field of Child Welfare, a revolution influenced and shaped by many forces, but most dramatically by an increasing national focus on the "family." This ideological shift, buttressed by a growing body of research questioning the foster care–institutional emphasis, had been slowly gathering strength since the early 1960s.

Several of the authors here directly or indirectly respond to this issue of "focus," juxtaposing child and family, and thus confronting a long-standing and often volatile debate in the field. Rice clearly takes the position that the welfare of children is strongly connected to the welfare of families. He not only outlines what supports and resources families must have to parent, to *not* neglect or abuse children, but he maps a direction for Child Welfare that would place greater emphasis on restructuring the intimate supportive environments for families than on the more residual function of substituting parental roles through child placement.

The interests of children and families both are usually subordinated on the governmental and policy-making levels to those more powerful institutions which are able to speak louder and have more economic and political power, as Antler demonstrates. Of course, the needs and rights of children must often compete with those of other populations and other family members: parents, the aged, the handicapped. Some child welfare experts, however, steadfastly maintain that children need their own advocates, that the focus on their welfare must not be diluted by a shift of emphasis to the welfare of families, that the primary role of Child Welfare should be the provision of services to children whose parents or other caretakers are unable to meet adequately their child-rearing responsibilities. A different view is taken by Meyer, who deplores this residual emphasis as well as the rigid boundaries between such fields of practice as children, family, and mental health. She envisions a unified field of "Family and Children's Services." And Gil argues that *neither* the welfare of the child nor of the family can be assured in a society, such as ours, that stresses competition and sanctifies private gain at the expense of humanitarian goals.

These common themes emerge although each chapter focuses on different aspects of the content of Child Welfare. Each author also explores issues that have special relevance to his or her part of the territory. Gil, in a refreshing approach to discussions of ideology, begins his contribution with a statement of his own ideological position, thus allowing us, the readers, to put *him* in context! He constructs, a strand at a time, a vision of power arrangements that become a veritable spider's web, as an intricate and complex picture of the extent to which people are trapped by the surrounding political, economic, and social forces emerges. Families and children, most notably those caught in the welfare and Child Welfare systems, are among those most helpless. In the process Gil demonstrates how the system of Child Welfare services, rather than attempting to free those most disadvantaged, is generally structured to promote and maintain the status quo and to pacify and control its clientele.

Thus does Gil begin this volume by throwing down a gauntlet. While some readers may be aggrieved, whether or not we agree with Gil's view of reality we must contend with the well-documented evidence concerning what has happened to families and children in a nation rich in resources, espousing humanitarian goals. What other explanations can we provide for the wide chasm between ideology or expressed values and actual practice, for the contradictory and even paradoxical relationship between our social discourse and praxis.

In Chapter 2 we see some of the ideological threads spun by Gil given historical elaboration and more specific applicability to child welfare as Costin summarizes and interprets some of the major historical dialogues in this field. Through her insights Costin demonstrates, in a sense, how the outcomes of ideological, political, and economic controversies become translated into program and practice. These insights are very much evident in her discussion of the struggle between personal rights and property rights reflected in the long battle against the practice of child labor. Costin implicitly supports Gil's argument that it is difficult, if not impossible, to achieve significant improvement in the quality of life for children without transformation of larger and more powerful ideological, economic, and political realities. As she so perceptively points out, in spite of decades of intensive efforts on the part of humanitarian reformers such as Jane Addams and Grace Abbott, only when child labor was no longer needed was concern over the exploitation and abuse of children through atrocious labor conditions translated into meaningful reform legislation.

In Rice's chapter the lens focuses more directly on today's family, its situation, its needs, and the many options and competing demands it faces. For him the satisfaction of the child is profoundly connected to the satisfaction of the parent. No matter what kinds of caring and benevolent bureaucratic supports might be constructed, they can never compete with or replace the familial network. In his view, Child Welfare is a vulnerable social creation that works best when it concentrates on optimizing the regenerative potential for non-bureaucratic, natural, family processes.

Antler agrees with Rice that the family should be the central focus in the enhancement of children's welfare. However, he feels that family supports must, in part, be generated and supported by governmental action. He speculates that such an approach could move the field of Child Welfare to assume a more preventive and universalistic posture rather than the current reactive stance of piecemeal problem-centered categorical responses. Exploring the ideological and political obstacles standing in the way of the development of family-centered policies and interventions, Rice reminds us that groups across the political spectrum fear the potential for the abuse of power which grows when the government gets into family business. The challenge is to develop family policy that emphasizes positive and comprehensive approaches, which enhance and assist families and children without controlling family life or prescribing ethnocentric norms and values.

Meyer crosscuts many of the other rings of our contextual conception as she describes the reverberations which take place between the institutional context of Child Welfare and the institution itself. She takes a hard look at the relationship between the public and Child Welfare, suggesting how that relationship differs from those of other institutions with the public. Reviewing some of the lessons of history, she characterizes the boundaries between Child Welfare and other fields of practice as too rigid. Finally, she examines the relationship between the profession of social work and Child Welfare, highlighting some of the conflicting world views and aims of the school and the field, of education and practice.

What should our priorities be for the future? And what of change? Each of these students of the field has attempted to move back for a moment, to stand outside that context within the larger context he or she explored, to review the past and to take a critical look toward the future.

For Gil, the welfare of children cannot be achieved through professional practice, and prevailing or future child welfare policies have little potential as tools for social change. What is needed is "consistent political practice toward comprehensive transformations of social institutions and consciousness, human relations, and personal lifestyles and values" (p. 32). The human services worker should use his or her position to help free people, to urge people to organize against oppressive conditions. He is calling for major shifts in world views and social and economic structures, yet he ends with a note of optimism.

Costin cautions us against drawing on history as a reliable forecast for what lies ahead and using historical events to justify present day social ills. History, instead, sheds light on current problems and "helps to reduce the risk of parochial thinking" (p. 59–60).

Her work for this volume, however, provides many valuable insights into these historical processes and events whose legacies are profoundly felt, and the heroic ancestors who, as she says, "can broaden one's experience and help lay an authentic foundation for professional identity" (p. 60).

Professional identity, in terms of the professionalization of the field of Child Welfare, concerns Meyer as well. She describes a disengagement between professional social work and public Child Welfare and a history of tension between the focus of education and the needs of the field. Using a very broad definition of "professionalization," which includes not only a practitioner more skilled in direct practice but one who is knowledgeable about the policies that guide practice, this professional will work to achieve a more universal provision of services, will insist on strengthening education and training, and will "seek an improved balance between localized and . . . parochial public interests and rational, research-based recommendations" (p. 115).

Both Rice and Antler urge a focus on the family, although their levels of analysis differ. Rice argues against a substitutive, minimalist approach in Child Welfare. In his view such a strategy "may be unnecessarily alienating children from the possibilities and potentials of their original social environment" (p. 74). A closer synchronization between Child Welfare and child welfare is needed, meaning that the Child Welfare system must emphasize its link to families by restructuring support environments for families, advocating for them, and connecting them to those external resources needed to maximize their potential for adult satisfaction (and thus better parenting) and, when necessary, counseling. Placement, now the center of practice, should be moved to the periphery.

Addressing the same issues on the level of politics and public policy, Antler is hopeful that, although many of the major social reforms of the past thirty years have lost their support in this time of political and social conservatism, it does not mean a passive laissez-faire approach will emerge as a permanent alternative. He predicts, and hopes, that when the American people turn to readdress the nation's social ills, they will not rely on the old incremental style of symptom relief, but rather seek bold and creative approaches to the underlying deprivations and stresses that destroy families and family life.

Is there any hope for meaningful change in any of these directions? Change of any kind seems more possible and more manageable the smaller the system level addressed. Removing a child from a family assaulted by generations of meager resources and hopelessness or from one which is deeply stressed and violent seems more feasible than urging change on a depressed and oppressed family in a hostile environment. Even more challenging is the badgering of that milieu into sharing some of its closely held resources with others less fortunate, particularly in the current ideological and political context. Perhaps some hope of greater professionalization in the field exists in upgrading and expanding services and even forcing a shift toward widening the focus of practice to concentrate on the intimate environment of the family in its lifeworld.

Yet, we are left with the uneasy recognition that each ring is indeed intricately nested in and affected by the others. Just as a small pebble thrown by a child into a polluted pond briefly and gently ripples the surface of the water, so the rehabilitation of one child is not to be discounted and does in some way change the larger environment. But the ecology of the polluted pond is barely shifted; and little shift occurs in the self-perpetuating conditions that rapidly spawn ever more families whose children are in jeopardy.

In later sections of this volume we explore the work of the Child Welfare policy-maker, administrator, and worker, examining the populations with which they work and the knowledge and practice skills needed for such work. This beginning section, we hope, will sensitize the reader to that complex world within which this professional practices.

# CHAPTER 1

# The Ideological Context of Child Welfare

David G. Gil

This chapter examines the ideological context of child welfare in the United States. Differences among scholars, practitioners, administrators, and public officials concerning the meaning of child welfare and of ideology, and concerning value premises and assumptions preclude a simple, "correct" answer to this issue. I shall, therefore, first clarify my understanding of child welfare and ideology, then sketch major ideological themes in relation to the prevailing way of life in the United States, and finally examine implications of that ideological context for child welfare—a condition of child development, and for Child Welfare—a system of services to children, families, and communities. Before proceeding, I should note some of the values and assumptions which underlie my work, to alert readers to possible bias.

I consider all humans to be intrinsically equal in worth, in spite of important differences among individuals and peoples. Hence, all ought to be entitled to equal rights and responsibilities in social, economic, civil, and political spheres. Implicit in this position is a commitment to democratic, socialist, and humanist principles, to cooperative and egalitarian practices and relations of production, exchange, distribution, and governance, and to the protection and conservation of the ecological base of all life. Also implicit in this position is rejection of all forms of exploitation, of domination and discrimination by sex, age, race, social class, or handicap, and of violence, be it social–structural or interpersonal.

Several assumptions underlie this discussion. The first is that organisms are self-propelled toward becoming what they are intrinsically capable of becoming, and that a tendency toward spontaneous growth and development is inherent in humans in the same way it appears to be inherent in the seed of plants. A second is that humans are social beings; their innate potential can unfold fully only when they live in harmonious, mutually supporting relations with their social and natural environment, and when these relations are conducive to the realization of human needs for material necessities, for individual identity and security, for social affirmation and belonging, and for self-actualization. Furthermore, I assume that humans are intrinsically neither "good" nor "evil," that, by nature, they are capable of relating to others lovingly and caringly as well as antagonistically and destructively, and that their specific patterns of relations to others evolve in interaction with particular social, cultural, and historical realities. And finally, I assume that humans themselves, rather than superhuman, creative forces, are the shapers and potential reshapers of their own social, cultural, and historical context which, in turn, shapes their behavior and consciousness.

## Child Welfare: Meanings and Requirements

In the simplest terms, as well as in a most profound sense, child welfare means conditions of living in which children can "fare well," conditions in which their bodies, minds, and souls are free to develop spontaneously through all stages of maturation. To many practitioners, administrators, and public officials Child Welfare, on the other hand, has come to mean an array of legal premises, public provisions, and professional processes dealing with children who, for various reasons, do not fare well. Thus Child Welfare as a field of service and practice, is an index of the absence of child welfare as a condition and process of spontaneous development.

Conditions conducive to child welfare are predicated upon social structures and dynamics, and upon human acts and attitudes which do not inhibit the spontaneous unfolding of the innate physical, emotional, and intellectual capacities of children but rather are compatible with their intrinsic developmental needs. To further clarify the requirements of child development and child welfare, one must identify these intrinsic developmental and existential needs. Though knowledge concerning these needs is still imperfect, many students of human development consider fulfillment of the following related needs a sine qua non of healthy development, and hence of child welfare (Dewey, 1935; Fromm, 1955; Maslow, 1970):

- needs for regular access to life-sustaining and -enhancing goods and services

- needs for meaningful social relations and a sense of belonging to a community in which the potential exists for mutual respect, acceptance, affirmation, care, and love, and which offers opportunities for self-discovery and for the emergence of a positive sense of identity
- needs to participate in meaningful and creative ways, in accordance with one's innate capacities and stage of development, in the productive processes of one's community and society
- needs for a sense of security, derived from continuous fulfillment of one's needs for life-sustaining and -enhancing goods, meaningful relations, and meaningful participation in socially valued productive processes
- needs to become what one is capable of becoming, or, in Maslow's terms, self-actualization through creative, productive work

The quality of life or the level of welfare, and hence, of child welfare, is always a function of the extent to which these fundamental human needs can be realized in given natural and socially shaped settings. In turn, the extent to which these needs can be realized in a society depends on the structures, dynamics, and values of its institutional order, or more specifically on the manner in which:

- life-sustaining and life-enhancing, natural and human-produced resources are controlled, used, developed, and conserved
- work and production are organized
- goods and services, social and civil rights, and political power are distributed
- public issues are decided and society is governed

Interactions among these social processes shape the circumstances of life and the mutual relations of individuals and classes in human societies. It is necessary, therefore, to study the prevailing patterns of these processes when one wants to gain insight into the levels and dynamics of needs realization, the scope of human development or the state of child welfare in a society. Also, it may be necessary to transform radically the established patterns of these processes and social values sustaining them, when enhancing the levels of needs realization, the scope of human development, or the state of child weflare (Gil, 1973).

## Ideology: Meanings, Sources and Dynamics

Webster's *New Collegiate Dictionary* offers several definitions of ideology:

> Visionary theorizing; a systematic body of concepts especially about human life or culture; a manner or the content of thinking characteristic of an individual, group, or class; the intellectual pattern of any widespread

culture or movement; the integrated assertions, theories and aims that constitute a sociopolitical program.

According to *A Modern Dictionary of Sociology* (Theodorson and Theodorson, 1969: 195–196), ideology is:

> a system of interdependent ideas (beliefs, traditions, principles, and myths) held by a social group or society, which reflects, rationalizes, and defends its particular social, moral, religious, political, and economic institutional interests and commitments. Ideologies serve as logical and philosophical justifications for a group's patterns of behavior, as well as its attitudes, goals, and general life situation. The ideology of any population involves an interpretation (and usually a repudiation) of alternative ideological frames of reference. The elements of an ideology tend to be accepted as truth or dogma rather than as tentative philosophical or theoretical formulations, despite the fact that ideologies are modified in accordance with sociocultural changes.
>
>      . . . The concept was given great prominence in the writings of Karl Marx, who defined it as a system of ostensibly logical ideas that in reality are a justification for the vested interests of a particular social class, the most dominant ideology in a society being that of the ruling class. Karl Mannheim used the term to refer to ideas that are distorted by the historical and social setting of individuals and groups.

These definitions and interpretations are useful starting points. What they lack is the historical dimension necessary for dynamic insights into human phenomena and processes. A search for the sources of ideologies reveals them to be products of collective human thought processes. Notions, which are gradually elaborated into seemingly coherent and logical thought structures, are formed simultaneously and in constant dialectical interaction with the discovery, development, and institutionalization of patterns of survival and existence. Accordingly, ideologies are abstract equivalents of concrete patterns of action and social relations of everyday life which they interpret, justify, and rationalize. Throughout history they reflect and legitimate a prevailing, temporary, societal status quo and are, therefore, a potent force in the relative stability and reproduction of social systems as they reflect the interests of those individuals, groups, and classes who benefit from systems continuity in an objective or subjective sense.

Established ways of life with their corresponding ideologies are usually passed on to children as valid and true, through the complex experiential and cognitive processes of child-rearing, socialization, and social control. These processes of intergenerational transmission of culture are usually effective and successful because the consciousness of children in relation to parents and other adults on whom they depend materially, emotionally, and intellectually is largely uncritical.

In the course of history, as the patterns of action and social relations which ideologies reflect and help maintain undergo evolutionary and, at times, revolutionary transformations, so do ideologies. However, in spite of constant interaction between institutional patterns and ideologies, the correspondence between these concrete and abstract dimensions of social life is usually not a perfect one. There are often time lags between changes in practice and changes in ideology, and there are also many contradictions between them. In fact, many philosophers and other students of society have mistakenly viewed these dimensions as separate and independent domains: the world of ideas on the one hand, and the world of action and human relations on the other.

Furthermore, the more complex and fragmented societies became in the course of change and development, the more difficult grew the task of creating illusions of inclusive societal interests or a sense of "national interest," and the less successful the process of ideological integration and indoctrination. Real and perceived conflicts of interests among age groups, sexes, families, clans, tribes, races, religions, castes, and social classes within politically unified social formations gave rise to variations on major ideological themes, to internal contradictions, and to the emergence of counter ideologies.

To conclude this brief analysis of ideology, major substantive themes in all ideological systems need to be noted. Since ideologies are developed in interaction with the evolution of particular designs of social life, they tend to promote, directly and indirectly, particular patterns as "correct." They deal in subtle ways with the essential processes and relations of human existence, such as the control, use, and development of means of survival and production; the division of labor and organization of production; the exchange and distribution of the social product and of human rights and responsibilities; and the design of governance and social control. Beyond these concrete aspects of everyday life, ideologies also usually deal with the social values that reflect and shape the established social design, and with a range of existential and philosophical questions inherent in the human condition and in the human need for answers to unknowable dimensions of existence. These include the sources, nature, and value of life, especially human life; the meaning of death; the nature and origin of the universe, of time and space, and of eternity and infinity. The resolutions one selects to these philosophical questions are usually related in subtle, symbolic ways to one's ideological position on the concrete issues of everyday life.

## Social Reality and Ideology in the United States

Ideologies, as suggested, both influence and are products of the development of social orders, and thus should be studied in relation to particular patterns of life with which they interact. Patterns of life in any society involve a set of interrelated social, economic, and political processes. To get a sense of the life in a society, one needs to examine how its members handle these basic processes. Such an analysis inevitably involves abstractions and simplifications.

## Resource Management

In the United States, a minority of the people, individually or as corporations, own and control most means of production, exchange, and distribution, including land and other natural resources, factories, banks, commercial and service establishments, transportation and communication, and even most of the knowledge and technology. A small fraction of productive resources is owned collectively by all of the people and is administered by government agencies, supposedly in the public interest. In fact, however, administration of the "public sector" tends to be influenced by the interests of individual and corporate enterprises, the "private sector" (Miliband, 1969).

The majority of people do not own or control sufficient resources to survive by working with what they control. They depend for survival on selling their labor, knowledge, and skills to the owners and managers of the means of production, at the discretion and in the interest of those in control of resources. These segments of the population, which include employed persons with high, adequate, and low incomes as well as unemployed and poor persons, differ among themselves: by origin, race, history, and culture; by sex and age; by education, skills, and attitudes; and by occupation and income. These differences tend to divide them as they compete for employment, services, and rights.

Owners and managers tend to use the resources they control toward production of goods and services for sale with the intent of realizing profits. Profits are largely reinvested to expand control over the means of production and markets. The competitive drive among enterprises toward accumulation of capital and control over resources and markets tends to shape the logic of everyday life and to affect the consciousness, behavior, and mutual relations of people (Polanyi, 1957; Tawney, 1920). The quality and quantity of products, the extent to which production corresponds to actual needs of the population, the quality of the labor process, the effects of production on people, communities, the environment, and on the conservation of resources—all these considerations are less important in shaping production decisions than criteria of profitability and accumulation and concentration of capital.

## Organization of Production and Division of Labor

Work and production in the United States reflect the division of the population in terms of control over means of production. Owners and managers rely on the labor of workers who, in turn, depend on employment by individual and corporate owners. In general, the higher the ratio of employment-seeking workers to available jobs, the lower the average level of wages, and the higher the average rate of profits. Owners tend, therefore, to favor an oversupply of workers relative to jobs, forcing workers to compete for scarce jobs.

The inevitable competition for jobs results not only in personal rivalries, but also in intergroup conflicts and discriminatory practices. While these practices have acquired quasi-autonomous dynamics throughout our history, they cannot be eliminated as long as people who depend on gainful employment for their existence do not have unconditional rights to regular work and adequate income. Discriminatory practices are thus intrinsic to the objective reality shaped by the economic, social, and political dynamics of our society.

Competition results not only from job scarcities but also from the pyramidal, bureaucratic organization of work and of corresponding wage and prestige systems. Hierarchical structures, in turn, seem necessary to supervise and control workers who were not prepared for self-direction at work, and who usually lack incentives to maximize productivity, since the fruits of their labor do not belong to them.

Unemployment, which seems a regular feature of our economic system, has many negative consequences. It holds down the general level of wages, depresses the self-image of unemployed workers, and induces insecurity among employed workers who may lose their jobs at the discretion of employers. The effects of unemployment profoundly influence family life and family relationships, causing emotional suffering and material deprivation. Finally, unemployment has consequences beyond directly involved households, since reduced household incomes are reflected in the economic realities of communities and society.

While unemployment is dehumanizing, employment under prevailing conditions can be a mixed blessing, as it may not provide opportunities to actualize one's potential. In efforts to increase efficiency and profits, the tasks of most workers have gradually been reduced to simple routines, each being but a step in complex production processes which those workers need not grasp in their entirety. Workers are, consequently, no longer competent and knowledgable masters of production in their fields. This is the ultimate stage of expropriation, one which deprives workers of their human essence, their sense of integrity and autonomy, and thus completes their transformation into easily marketable and replaceable commodities (Braverman, 1974; Pope John Paul II, 1981).

A further feature of aggregate production in the United States is irrationality. Production tends to be planned, rational, and efficient in terms of profit considerations of individual firms. Yet aggregate production is unplanned, irrational, inefficient, and wasteful in terms of the real needs of the population, the survival and development of communities and regions, and the conservation of resources and the ecology. This internal contradiction of our system of production derives from the fact that individual firms and the economy as a whole are not oriented toward actual needs of people, but toward "effective demand" as reflected in purchasing power and decisions, and toward maximizing profits of competing firms. The needs of people who lack adequate purchasing power are therefore neither considered nor met by production and distribution.

Lack of planning geared to the needs of all people and communities, and waste-induced inflationary practices lead, inevitably, to periodic economic crises to which individual firms and the economic system respond by cutting back production and laying off employees. From the perspective of powerful enterprises and the established economic order, such crises are necessary mechanisms to regulate the economy in the absence of planning. From the perspective of individuals, households, small enterprises, and communities, these crises are usually severe disasters.

*Distribution of Goods and Services, and of Social, Civil, and Political Rights*

An examination of the distribution of wealth and income over time in the United States reveals major inequalities among individuals, households, age groups, sexes, ethnic groups, and social classes (Kolko, 1962; Upton and Lyons, 1972; U.S. Department of Commerce, Bureau of the Census, 1980). The distribution reveals that poverty, defined as income insufficient to secure an acknowledged, minimally adequate standard of living, is built into the fabric of our society, since large segments of the population own little or no income-generating wealth; nor are they assured access to gainful employment.

People who have never secured employment or have lost their jobs, be they young, old, or in between, are usually doomed to poverty. Whatever purchasing power they command derives from government transfer payments or from extra-legal practices such as crime. Transfer payments to poor persons tend to be very low. They usually do not even match the United States government's poverty index, a measure derived from a short-term, emergency food budget, which corresponds to less than two-thirds of the "low-level budget" for urban households as determined by the U.S. Bureau of Labor Statistics. During recent years, nearly 30 million individuals were living in households with incomes at or below the official poverty level, in spite of government assistance. Another 40 million were "near poor" in accordance with a 1980 report of the National Advisory Council on Economic Opportunity (*New York Times*, 10/19/80). "Near poverty" corresponds to 1¼ times the official poverty index. The incidence of poverty and near poverty is significantly higher among children, youth and aged persons; among women, especially in single-parent families; and among racial minorities.

However, not only those individuals who have never secured employment, have lost their jobs, or retired from work, tend to exist in or near poverty. In the United States, many regularly employed workers also live in or near poverty since the minimum wage does not assure incomes above the poverty line, and since the prevailing wage structure generates an income distribution that leaves about one-third of the entire population in or near poverty.

In theory, everyone in the United States is entitled to equal social, civil, and political rights. In reality, however, these rights too, tend to be distributed as unequally as wealth and income, since they are subtly associated with these resources, and with race, sex, age, occupation, education, and social class. The economically powerful, especially white males, tend to acquire disproportionally large shares of social prestige and political influence. Public authorities often treat the well-to-do more politely and more favorably than poor people, especially when the latter are members of racial minorities. Even in courts of law and in the correctional system, wealthy and prestigious individuals and corporations often secure preferential treatment with the help of expensive lawyers.[1]

Access to the communication power of the media to promote views on public issues also tends to be easier for economically powerful and socially prominent individuals and groups. Consequently, freedom of the press and the electronic media seems available mainly to their owners, and to individuals and corporations on whose advertising revenue the media depend and to whose views and interests the media tend to be especially sensitive. Since in this era political influence and power depend to no small extent on access to established media, or on economic resources to create alternative media, those who lack ample economic resources also usually lack opportunitites to acquire political influence.

## Modes of Decision-Making and Governance

The United States claims to be a democratic society in which all citizens are supposedly entitled to equal social, civil, and political rights, liberties, and responsibilities, and to equal shares in decision-making and governance. The foregoing discussion reveals, however, major inequalities among individuals, groups, and classes in the economic sphere, and corresponding inequalities in social, civil, and political rights. How are we to account for this glaring contradiction between the concept of democracy and the actual situation?

While people in the United States have achieved a wider scope of civil and political liberties and rights than people in many past and contemporary societies, our self-designation as a democratic nation seems valid mainly in a formal sense, but not in a comprehensive one. We do hold regular elections and suffrage is nearly universal. Participation in elections tends to be far from universal, however. We are free to organize political movements committed to diverse causes, and to disseminate political views when we can afford the high costs of publicity. Even so, many subtle obstacles exist for organizing minority parties and for their participation in elections. We are also free to assemble, to demonstrate, and to petition our governments.

These and other civil and political rights are certainly important. They were secured after centuries of struggle against feudal, absolutist, and authoritarian systems in Europe and in North America. The achievement of these important rights does not justify the claim that ours is a free and democratic society in the full sense of these terms, rather than in a limited and ritualistic sense. A genuinely free and democratic sociey is one in which all people enjoy equal liberties, are considered and treated as equals in the political sphere, and share effectively in all decisions affecting their lives. Such equality of liberty and political power is incompatible with significant inequalities in social status and economic power. It also depends on free access to all relevant information, and on universal education conducive to the development of critical thinking, to intelligent use of information, and to effective direct and indirect participation in decision-making and governance.

In the United States, most people feel and, in fact, are powerless concerning the major forces which impinge on everyday life and concerning the public policies the government pursues in domestic and foreign affairs. Moreover, most people are uniformed or misinformed on many issues since the government inhibits free access to important, relevant information by declaring it privileged and secret. And finally, most people do not receive education conducive to critical thinking and to intelligent participation in public affairs.

Having sketched major aspects of the prevailing institutional order of the United States, I turn next to an examination of the ideology which evolved in continuous interaction with that order, and which justifies, validates, and yet obfuscates its essence and reality.

## Contemporary Ideology

Central to any ideology are positions on the following related value continua because of their relevance to basic institutional processes:

equality . . . . . . . . . . . . . . . . . . . . . . . . . . . . . . . . . . . . . inequality
affirmation of community
    and individuality . . . . . . . . . . . . . . . . . . . . . . . . selfishness
cooperation . . . . . . . . . . . . . . . . . . . . . . . . . . . . . . . competition
liberty . . . . . . . . . . . . . . . . . . . . . . . . . . . . . . . . . . . domination

Although we tend to deny it, our dominant ideology seems oriented toward the right poles of these value continua. We proclaim that "all men are born equal" but we seem to live by the premise that individuals, groups, classes, and peoples are intrinsically unequal in worth and are consequently entitled to unequal shares of resources, goods and services, and to unequal social, civil, and political rights. We condemn selfishness in our religious and philosophical traditions, but we do not seem to value the lives and individuality of others; we easily disregard community concerns and interests, accepting the pursuit of self-interest as a common sense, guiding principle for everyday life and human relations. We teach children in homes and schools to share and cooperate, but nearly all domains of adult existence are permeated by acquisitiveness and competition. We are enthusiastic advocates of liberty and "human rights" as abstract principles, but we do not seem to hesitate to dominate and exploit other individuals, classes, races, and peoples.

These major values of the dominant ideology in the United States reveal that ideological themes are not always expressed directly and overtly. When everyday practice is in conflict with ancient values, ideological themes tend to be expressed ambiguously or even through overt denial. The flagrant contradictions between the values by which we conduct our lives and human relations and the values we espouse, especially on ceremonial occasions, reflect conflicts between the philosophies of classical liberalism, utilitarianism, Social Darwinism and "welfare state" liberalism on the one hand, and the medieval feudal philosophy of the paternalistic corporate Christian ethic and earlier Judeo-Christian themes, on the other (Hunt and Sherman, 1981).

According to the paternalistic ideology of medieval feudalism, society was a corporate body under God, the father, and his chosen spiritual and secular lords who ruled in his name and by his grace. The sacred scriptures and the writings of the church fathers provided the basis for this social reality and world view. Humans were thought to have reciprocal relations and obligations for one another's welfare as siblings do in families, with the lords' roles and responsibilities corresponding to those of fathers in families. People were supposed to live in accordance with their inherited status, and consequently, there was little social mobility. Aspirations for self-advancement were discouraged. The nobility were considered entitled to the great wealth they controlled as stewards of the community. They were expected to use that wealth in the interest of all the people and to act charitably toward those in need. Selfishness and greed were considered grave evils, while helping neighbors and strangers, virtues.

Crafts and trade were tightly controlled by guilds; craftsmen and merchants were not permitted to profit from their activities but merely to be compensated through a "just price" for the materials and efforts they provided, so that they could maintain themselves at their proper station in life. They were not supposed to acquire wealth and move beyond their traditional status. Charging interest on loans was considered wrongful and was prohibited under religious and secular laws during the feudal period in order to maintain the established order and prevent the creation of new concentrations of wealth and power. Human relations and interactions were shaped by customs and traditions which most people internalized and observed readily. Their customs and traditions were thought to reflect God's will and order. Provisions existed, of course, for external controls and for community sanctions to assure conformity and to punish offenders.

Contemporary ideology in the United States and other capitalist societies is in nearly every respect diametrically opposed to the static and traditional themes of feudal ideology. Contemporary ideology emerged from prolonged political and philosophical struggles between artisan, merchant, and enterpreneurial classes and the secular and religious nobility. The Protestant Reformation, the Renaissance and Enlightenment, a series of political revolutions against aristocracies and absolute monarchies in Europe, and commercial, industrial, and scientific revolutions, led to the establishment of modern, liberal states, dominated by dynamic enterpreneurial classes who promoted an entirely new view of the world, of people, of societies, and of human relations.

According to the philosophers and theoreticians of this new way of life, individuals were to be the masters of their existence. They were entitled to comprehensive civil liberties, to political rights of self-governance, and to uninhibited use of their capacities and property to build their lives and develop themselves as much as they could. Competitive pursuit of material wealth was not only deemed necessary and proper, but was thought to reveal God's favored people. In a complete reversal of the original Christian ethic, according to which it was nearly impossible for a wealthy person to enter the kingdom of heaven, the new Protestant ethic suggested that worldly success foreshadowed spiritual salvation and election into the eternal life. This message was clearly compatible with the emerging requirements of a competitive market economy (Tawney, 1926; Weber, 1958).

Another essential element of the classical liberal ideology was the notion of man's natural right to possessions and acquisitions, the theory of private property. This theory led to the notion of an unchallengeable right to use one's property to one's ends in any way one saw fit, as long as the exercise of this right did not conflict with someone else's property rights. Related to these themes was the principle of laissez-faire, according to which the State must not interfere with citizens' legitimate exercise of sovereignty over their possessions, and their use and disposition of these possessions in a competitive market toward continuous enrichment.

The image of the individual, according to classical liberalism, was that of a separate, independent actor for personal interests, not a member of a community that was larger than the sum of its parts. Society, organized as a state for the convenience of autonomous individuals, was to be limited to the following functions: defense against foreign threats—which often meant elimination or control of competitors for foreign markets and resources; maintenance of internal law and order—which usually meant protection of property rights and enforcement of contractual relations derived from these rights; and provision of essential public services—highways, waterways, or mail services—which private enterpreneurs were reluctant to provide because of high costs or low profits. In general, it was believed that the less government did, the better. The assumption of classical liberal ideology was that production and exchange of goods and services would be most efficient and effective, and would meet the needs of people (and thus serve, indirectly, the interests of society) when each individual and firm pursued selfish material interests. Government intervention with market processes was assumed to result in serious harm to economic activity and social well-being (Smith, 1776).

Underlying much of this ideology was the view that humans were by nature selfish, greedy, pleasure seeking, shrewdly calculating, mean, aggressive, untrustworthy, and lazy. They acted only to attain selfish ends and pleasures, and they were likely to avoid any effort not conducive to those ends. These views led to the conclusion that for humans to work in the interest of others, they would have to be coerced by threats of greater deprivation than that inherent in the work situation. Furthermore, when working under such conditions, they would have to be closely supervised and controlled.

To explain shortcomings in the performance of capitalist markets in satisfying human needs, it was assumed that people who failed in competitive capitalist contexts were by nature less capable and of lesser worth than those who succeeded. Those who revealed, through failing, their inherent inadequacies, deserved their fate and should not be helped, to assure the health and strength of the nation. Aiding the unfit would interfere with nature's self-regulation which assured the selection, survival, and thriving of the fit (Hofstadter, 1955).

These assumptions concerning human nature and innate differences in the capacities and worth of people give rise to the tendency to "blame the victims" of poverty, discrimination, unemployment, and psychological suffering for their own misery, and, by implication, to absolve the social order from responsibility for these phenomena and their consequences (Ryan, 1972). In individual terms, these assumptions result in an impaired sense of identity and a pervasive feeling of self-blame and inadequacy (Sennet and Cobb, 1973). When practice in human services is permeated by these assumptions and tendencies, the results are destructive for clients, service workers, and their relationship (Piven and Cloward, 1971).

The ideological themes of classical liberalism, capitalism, and pluralistic, political democracy sketched here underwent modifications throughout the nineteenth and twentieth centuries in the direction of neoclassical, welfare state liberalism. In ideological terms, these changes did not, however, affect the underlying assumptions concerning individualism, human nature, and property rights. They mainly concerned the role of the State, and the controversial issue of its intervention into the distribution of goods and services when the assumed self-regulation did not bring about satisfaction of basic human needs and, instead, resulted in widespread unemployment, poverty, and misery. State intervention into markets on behalf of disadvantaged and excluded segments of the population gradually came to be considered necessary, not only to meet the pressing needs of large numbers of people, but also to assure the survival of the established social, economic, and political order frequently threatened by radical social movements spurred by economic crises and widespread deprivation.

Welfare state variations on the classical liberal ideology (which eventually came to be known as "conservative" ideology) began with factory inspection acts and length-of-work day legislation in nineteenth century England and culminated in Sweden's comprehensive social democratic programs in the twentieth century. In the United States, welfare state measures appeared after the Civil War with the establishment of the Freedmen's Bureau. In the twentieth century, the Children's Bureau, the New Deal and the Social Security Act, minimum wage laws, the War on Poverty, the Civil Rights Act, the Model Cities Program, Medicare and Medicaid, Social Security Insurance (SSI) and Aid to Families with Dependent Children (AFDC), and many other human services programs reflect the welfare state variation on liberal ideology. It is important to note that though these programs reduced the suffering of the victims of the established social order, they did not significantly change underlying ideological constructs. The relative ease with which the "conservative" administration, elected in 1980, was able to reverse major welfare state policies of earlier administrations provides ample evidence, if evidence is needed, that the core of the dominant ideology has not changed significantly since the times when entrepreneural segments of society gained economic and political power and when liberal and utilitarian philosophers and theorists elaborated the ideological themes compatible with its interests.

I have noted the major contradictions of the fedual system, to wit, the intense exploitation of serfs by the nobility in spite of the Christian paternalistic and corporate ideology. Capitalism involves a parallel, major contradiction, the intense exploitation of poor and working people, and their lack of meaningful liberties and political rights to self governance, in spite of the liberal ideology that declares all people equally entitled to these rights. The major fallacy of the liberal ideology is the fact that civil and political rights and liberties cannot be exercised effectively in the absence of economic rights. Since our competitive and acquisitive economic system tends to deprive large segments of the population of adequate economic rights, it also deprives them indirectly of the civil and political rights claimed for them by the liberal ideology. Having risen over the absolute monarchs and nobility, the entrepreneurial classes have been reluctant to share with working-class, unemployed, and poor people the very liberties they all fought for—just as the nobility had once declined to share privileges with untitled artisans, merchants, and entrepreneurs. Hence the liberal ideology, like the Christian ideology of compassion and noblesse oblige, has remained an illusion and an empty promise for the less advantaged (Dewey, 1935; Polanyi, 1957).

## Implications for Child Welfare

Child development and child welfare are assumed to be related to the extent to which intrinsic human needs are realizable in a society. To discern the consequences for child development and welfare of prevailing patterns of social organization in the United States and of the ideological themes sustaining these patterns, we must examine the extent to which intrinsic human needs are, in fact, realizable in our society. Such an examination serves as an "acid test" for any social order. The fundamental, interrelated needs we are concerned with here were spelled out in the initial section of this chapter. They are needs for (1) basic material goods and services, (2) meaningful human relations conducive to the emergence of a positive sense of identity, (3) meaningful and creative participation in socially valued productive processes, (4) a sense of security, and (5) self-actualization.

1. Analysis of our institutional and ideological context revealed that access to life-sustaining and life-enhancing goods and services is not assured to large segments of the population since they do not own and

control sufficient income generating means of production, and since they do not possess unconditional rights to gainful employment and adequate income. Unemployment, poverty, insecurity, and their massive debilitating, dehumanizing, and alienating consequences are therefore an ever present reality and threat to the satisfaction of material needs of millions of children and households.

2. Next, we found little opportunity for emergence of meaningful, mutually caring human relations conducive to the development of a positive sense of identity, neither in people's homes, nor at places of work and in other public settings. This lack is due to pervasive, structurally induced competition for employment and promotions, and for preferred positions, conditions, and opportunities in many important spheres of existence, all shaped by bureaucratic and hierarchical dynamics. Meaningful human relations are usually not possible among individuals who are unequal in prestige, status, and power, and who continuously evaluate, use, and control one another as means in the pursuit of selfish ends. Also, meaningful relations are unlikely to develop when households and individuals tend to function as separate economic units, each trying to survive as best as possible in a noncooperative way of life. And finally, meaningful relations are often undermined in the private domain, when people's developmental energy is blocked in the public domain through structural violence (Fromm, 1941; Gil, 1979a; 1979b), and when they react to the frustrations of everyday life through interpersonal violence in intimate relations.[2]

3. Meaningful and creative participation in socially valued productive processes is beyond the expectations of most people, when employment is not assured, when most available jobs are designed as fragmented meaningless routines to be performed in alienating, oppressive, and exploiting conditions, and when child care, socialization, and formal schooling result inevitably in massive underdevelopment of innate human capacities.

The transformation of most work into routines requiring little or no initiative, creativity, and intellectual effort, and of workers into uncritical performers of routine tasks within authoritarian work settings, has led inevitably, though subtly, to corresponding transformations of childrearing, socialization and formal education. These interrelated processes in any society prepare the young to fit into established patterns of adult life. If these established patterns of life and work mainly require conforming and apathetic workers, as in the United States, such workers are produced through prevailing modes of life and human relations in homes, schools, churches, and neighborhoods. These destructive consequences of child-rearing, socialization, and formal education do not result from conscious, intentional practices on the part of parents, teachers, and educational authorities but nonetheless, the outcome is massive, differential underdevelopment of the rich innate potential of most children and youth. Much evidence supporting this assertion has been brought to light in recent years and need not be repeated here (Bowles and Gintis, 1976; Gil, 1979c). It suffices to note that most individuals in the United States are not expected, nor do they have opportunities, to use their inherent capacities in everyday life, and that, therefore, many individuals fail to develop fully their capacities. The result is a society in which most people function below their real potential in many spheres of life. This gap may not be static but may increase with time because of the decline in the capacity of culturally and developmentally damaged generations to facilitate the development of those following them. Moreover, ongoing efforts toward further "rationalization" of production and subdivision of labor are likely to intensify the processes which inevitably result in developmental deficits. This trend can be reversed only when people will be expected, and will have opportunities, to use their intellectual, physical, and emotional capacities in an integrated fashion in production and in other domains of everyday life.

4. A sense of security tends to emerge when people's needs for goods and services, for meaningful human relations, and for meaningful participation in society's productive endeavors can be realized. Since these basic needs were shown to be unrealizable in the context of prevailing societal dynamics and values, few individuals can be expected to develop a genuine sense of security. Most are driven by a nagging sense of insecurity to chase after receding mirages of security. Others may escape into addictions, mental and psychosomatic illnesses, crime, or suicide after searching futilely for substitutes for a genuine sense of fulfillment and security.

5. Self-actualization is usually not pursued by people whose material, relational, developmental, and security needs are unrealizable. Hence, based on the foregoing analysis revealing widespread frustration of material, relational, developmental, and security needs, one is forced to conclude that few individuals may be expected to realize their innate need for self-actualization (Maslow, 1971).

When children grow up in environments in which their own and everyone else's fundamental human needs tend to be frustrated constantly, their innate capacities usually do not unfold freely and fully. *Their development is stunted, they do not fare well, they fail to thrive.* As a consequence of the prevailing social, economic, and political structures, dynamics, and ideology, the United States appears to be such a growth inhibiting environment for children, irrespective of the social class position of families. This fact is usually acknowledged with respect to children in poor and low income homes. Paradoxically, it is also true for children in middle income and affluent homes; material adequacy and affluence do not lead directly to the realization of relational, developmental, security, and self-actualization needs, as they do not insulate children from the dehumanizing and alienating effects of inegalitarian, competitive, and exploitative patterns of everyday life.

## Violence

The foregoing analysis of consequences for child development and welfare of the prevailing institutional dynamics and ideology in the United States suggests that our contemporary way of life is permeated by structural violence which, in turn, tends to bring forth "reactive" violence in human relations—especially in people's homes, where they feel relatively hidden from social controls and sanctions (Gil, 1970; 1976; 1979a; 1979b). This conclusion is derived in part from the assumptions concerning human nature and spontaneous human development stated previously. But it also emerges from the view *that violence is a result of those relations, processes, and conditions which obstruct the unfolding of human potential and the intrinsic human drive toward growth, development, and self-actualization; that it interferes with the fulfillment of inherent biological, psychological, and social needs.* Such relations, processes, and conditions may occur between individuals, as well as between individual social institutions and whole societies.

Violence seems thus rooted in, and dialectically related to, socially structure, inequalities in statuses and rights among individuals, sexes, age groups, classes, races, and peoples. For these inequalities did not result from voluntary choices, but from coercion, and, once established, require continuous application of overt or covert force for their maintenance. The presence in a society of inequality maintaining coercive measures inevitably induces diverse manifestations of counterforce and reactive violence—a vicious circle from which humankind has, so far, failed to extricate itself.

Erich Fromm, a noted social scientist and psychoanalyst who studied the sources and dynamics of violence in Europe during the 30s, reached similar conclusions to those suggested here:

> It would seem that the amount of destructiveness to be found in individual is proportionate to the amount to which expansiveness of life is curtailed. By this we do not refer to individual frustrations of this or that instinctive desire, but to the thwarting of the whole of life, the blockage of spontaneity of the growth and expression of man's sensuous, emotional, and intellectual capacities. . . . The more the drive toward life is thwarted, the stronger is the drive toward destruction; the more life is realized, the less is the strength of destructiveness. *Destructiveness is the outcome of unlived life.* (Fromm, 1941: 183–184)

Violence, according to Fromm, is not a primary human tendency but a reaction to a prior blocking of spontaneous, constructive life energy.

Violent acts, relations, and conditions may occur between individuals in their homes and elsewhere and also between individuals, social institutions, and entire societies. Individuals may violate one another's integrity by physical and psychological means or by creating and maintaining conditions which interfere with the development of others through deprivation, exploitation, and oppression. Institutions such as schools, health and welfare systems, and business corporations may, through their policies and practices, disregard developmental needs of people and thus may subject them to conditions that harm their development. Finally, entire societies may, through their values, policies, and laws, evolve and sanction phenomena such as poverty, discrimination by class, race, sex, or age, and unemployment and inflation, which inevitably interfere with the development of many individuals and groups.

Violence resulting from societal conditions may be thought of as *structural violence*, as it is intrinsic to inegalitarian social structures. Structural violence is usually a "normal" condition, inherent in social patterns and legitimate practices, while personal violence involves acts which conflict with prevailing social norms or laws. Personal and structural violence cannot, however, be understood separate from one another. They are merely different symptoms of the same underlying social realities, the same social values, mentality, institutions, and dynamics.

Personal violence, as suggested in Fromm's conclusion, is usually reactive violence rather than initiating violence; it is one way in which people react to stresses and frustrations caused by the structural violence they encounter in everyday life. Personal violence appears to be fed by developmental energy which is transformed into destructive behaviors when blocked by structural violence. Structural violence is, therefore, the source or cause of personal violence which, in turn, may lead to chain reactions as successive victims become agents of further violence. The focus of government agencies and the media on sensational cases of personal violence, and their consistent disregard of the roots of this personal violence in structural violence, disguises the issue, and precludes effective, preventive intervention.

Why does personal violence occur more frequently in homes rather than in settings where people confront structural violence? In modern, industrial, urbanized societies, the family and the home are expected to restore the emotional stability of individuals who encounter unsettling experiences outside their homes, at workplaces and in other formal settings where people are often treated in an impersonal, dehumanizing, and alienating manner. Families function as lightening rods for the stresses of everyday life. They serve as settings for uninhibited discharge of feelings of hurt, insult, frustration, anger, and reactive violence, feelings which originate mostly outside the family, but cannot usually be discharged at their places of origin, since such direct discharge would lead to social sanctions such as dismissal from jobs or arrest and prosecution for unlawful acts. Releasing these feelings in the privacy of one's home is relatively safe, in that behavior in the private domain is hidden from public view, and the risk of social sanctions is usually lower than for similar behavior in the public domain.

A further, subtle link between family life and structural violence is the family's responsibility for preparing children for adult roles and for adaptation to established societal patterns. Accordingly, in societies such as ours, in which submission to structural violence is a "normal" aspect of adult life, families, along with schools, the media, and other agents of socialization, tend to prepare children to adjust to and participate in these practices and experiences. This preparation for living with violence is not intentional but occurs automatically through "normal" child-rearing and educational processes: play, sports, stories, art, cognitive and experiential learning, quality of human relations and emotional milieu, rewards and punishments and especially, an ample measure of corporal punishment. Hierarchical structures, male dominance, and irrational, arbitrary authority are frequent attributes of home life in such societies, all of which contribute to the task of preparing children for adjustment to a lifetime with structural violence.

## Specific Consequences

In addition to the foregoing general consequences of the prevailing institutional and ideological context for the development and welfare of children, several specific consequences should be noted:

• The guiding values of child-rearing and socialization in our society are to prepare children for adaptation to, and for material success in, the established way of life. This preparation involves, inevitably, suppression and atrophy of many innate tendencies of children, with stress on obedience and conformity rather than on initiative, self-direction, and individuality. Since children from different class levels are expected to adjust and to conform to their respective backgrounds, child-rearing philosophy and practice, and especially the degree of control over children's individual tendencies, vary with the social class position of households.

• Children's rights and circumstances of living are shaped largely by the actual life situations of their parents, their economic, educational, and occupational status. This situation exists because in our society people have few rights simply by virtue of membership in society. As noted earlier, rights to material goods and services depend mainly on purchasing power, while social, civil, and political rights are associated subtly with the nature, scope, and sources of one's material wealth and income. Consequently, while wealth and income are protected by laws and the Constitution, the so-called universal human rights of children to development and individuality through realization of basic needs and to integrity of body and mind are nowhere assured through our laws and Constitution, and are not implemented in practice. Under prevailing conditions these rights are nothing but a myth, certainly as far as children in poor and low income homes are concerned.

• Not only are children's effective rights shaped by property and income conditioned rights of parents, but parents, irrespective of wealth and income, exercise nearly absolute authority over children. They are society's primary agents for socializing children in expected directions. Their relations to children are in many ways similar to their relations to property: nearly absolute responsibility, power, and authority. These rights and relations of children and parents, and especially the nearly absolute authority of the latter, have remained relatively constant throughout the history of the United States, in spite of marked changes in many aspects of family life and in social, economic, technological, and cultural dimensions of our way of life.

• The State, through its agencies of government, exercises diffuse and covert, as well as specific and overt functions in relation to child development, child welfare and Child Welfare, aimed at maintaining the established social order. Included among the societal processes which the State influences, are the division of labor, the organization of production, and the distribution of rights. Child-rearing, socialization, and schooling are linked in subtle ways to these key processes.

• "Child Welfare" is a set of specific and overt policies and services sponsored, sanctioned, and carried out by the State and its institutions, when families are unable to carry out normal child care and socialization functions. Child Welfare services are meant to compensate for various objective and subjective shortcomings in the primary systems of child care, socialization, schooling, and social control. Their function is simply to complete and correct the unfinished tasks of the primary systems, namely the adaptation of children to prevailing class determined patterns of life. Child Welfare policies and services are therefore supplementary tools of the State employed in reproducing and preserving the social status quo and its ideology. Prevailing Child Welfare policies and services are not tools toward social transformation, and, verbalized goals to the contrary, they have little to do with facilitating the free and full development of children in their care.

## Epilogue

This outline of general and specific consequences of the prevailing social and ideological context for family life, child development, child welfare, and Child Welfare reveals strong associations between our way of life and our values and ideas on the one hand, and the quality of life of children and families and State policies and services on the other. Such associations are observable not only in our own society, but in any human society, past and present. While it seems possible to enhance the quality of family life, child development, child welfare and Child Welfare somewhat without changing the social and ideological status quo, and while such reforms should be demanded and promoted, it is important to recognize that significant improvements in these domains require prior, radical transformations of the social and ideological context in accordance with socialist, democratic, and humanist principles. Hence, genuine child welfare cannot be attained through professional, technical, and administrative processes alone, but requires consistent political practice toward comprehensive transformations of social institutions and consciousness, human relations, and personal lifestyles and values. We need to ask whether such transformations are feasible or whether we are doomed to perpetuate prevailing dysfunctional and dehumanizing institutions and ideologies. While we cannot know the course of future events, it seems that either of these outcomes is possible and neither is predetermined. The actual course of the future depends on developments of the consciousness and perceptions of interests of large numbers of people, and on their collective actions and commitments, just as history is a product of consciousness, perceptions of interest, and actions in the past.

Social institutions and ideologies are always undergoing changes, although people at any period in history may perceive established patterns of life as permanent and valid. Our present way of life resulted from centuries of struggle by commercial and manufacturing classes against aristocracies and absolute monarchies. Three hundred years ago the very notion of a liberal, democratic, capitalist society would have been considered a radical Utopia. And yet it has gradually become a reality. We are again living in a period of growing political activism with its ups and downs. We have witnessed, in this century, unfinished social revolutions and national liberation struggles. We have experienced liberation movements by women and racial minorities. All over the globe oppressed peoples and classes seem to become conscious of their real conditions and of the forces that obstruct their development. In such situations, individuals everywhere can choose to join movements toward human liberation and development, rather than remain neutral and wonder whether such movements can succeed.

The answer to the feasibility question seems to depend on people's perceptions, choices, and commitments. If enough people come to see their interests as linked with the goals of transformation movements, then new realities can be created to replace prevailing orders. Human services workers have many opportunities to connect their practice with liberation movements. For human service work always has political dimensions: It either supports a societal status quo or it challenges it; it either validates the dominant ideology by blaming victims for their social problems or it helps people discover the roots of their problems in the prevailing social order; it either pacifies frustrated and angry people or helps them organize against oppressive conditions (Galper, 1980; Gil, 1973, 1976, 1979a).

I began this chapter stating my assumptions and values, and I end it realizing that the prevailing social order and ideology have disastrous consequences for child development and welfare, far from the values with which I began. This path leads me to examine the feasibility of radical social transformations conducive to human development and to reach the same conclusion which Antonio Gramsci, an Italian philosopher and activist, reached some fifty years ago in a fascist prison: "Pessimism of the mind—optimism of the will" (Gramsci, 1971). By that he meant that people, working together with a persistent commitment to social justice and freedom, can transform social structure dynamics and ideologies, in spite of resistance by the privileged defenders of established ways of life.

# CHAPTER 2

# The Historical Context of Child Welfare

Lela B. Costin

Social work's concern for the welfare of children and the development of social services for them and their families reflect a long and often slow evolution of ideas and practices. Each professional generation begins its work with a legacy from the history of child welfare, a legacy rich in remarkable personalities and courageous leadership in social reform, commitment to the poor, disadvantaged, and unlucky children of society, and abundant in strategies to advance social justice. That same history reflects controversy, contest, and some decisions that, over time, proved detrimental to children and their families and to the social work profession as well.

This chapter will examine critical periods in the evolution of Child Welfare as an institution, and some of the events, trends, and issues that have shaped its practice. In this country the history of the contemporary child rights movement shows distinct, although often overlapping, organized efforts at reform on the behalf of children. Three of these will be discussed: the child-saving movement, which was focused on the dependent child, the wayward child, and the orphan; the child rescue movement, which was intended to provide protection to severely neglected and abused children; and the child labor movement, through which an end to the exploitation of prematurely employed children was sought. In addition, attention will be given to social inventions of the early twentieth century Progressive Era and of the Depression of the 1930s. This latter focus will highlight the farsighted and innovative advocacy for children represented by the work of the U.S. Children's Bureau. Throughout the chapter, I will attempt to show the links between the history of child welfare and current problems, practices, and public policy issues.[1]

## The Child-Saving Movement

The origins of the child-saving movement can be traced from colonial days, an age when poverty was a sin and work the way to salvation. Except in relation to a few "worthy poor," poverty was believed to be caused by inherent habits or instincts of the individual. Children of the "unworthy poor" had to be saved from developing slothful ways of life that led to idleness and moral degradation. The child-saving remedy included financial assistance to parents in their own homes ("outdoor relief"), the use of almshouses, and other methods that separated children from parents through indenture or placement in foster homes and institutions.

### The Legal Base

The early child savers relied upon two principal sources of authority: the power of the township overseer of the poor, and the power to intervene into the parent–child relationship under the laws of guardianship and the doctrine of *parens patriae*. In the early years of this country as an addition to help extended by neighbors to each other, the colonists continued to employ the English poor law system under which individuals who could not maintain themselves or their children were considered to be the responsibility of the township. The Elizabethan Poor Law of 1601 had grown out of a consciousness of public responsibility for dealing with the problems of poverty. The intent of this reform legislation was to fix responsibility for poor persons upon the local community, thereby to end begging and other manifestations of destitution. In the colonies the local overseer of the poor could supply some form of aid to destitute parents and their children. Some children given aid were orphaned by epidemics and other disasters in the new land. Some showed incorrigible behavior or were physically handicapped. Although overseers of the poor were not necessarily unsympathetic to destitute children, the needs of the particular child seldom formed the primary basis for the child-saving remedy selected.

The power of *parens patriae*, on which American guardianship law rests, was borrowed from English common law developed as part of the feudal system of land tenure. The king as *parens patriae* had the right to assume protection of children in his realm. He exercised this right mainly to supervise a minor child's estate, with the intent of controlling income from the land and conserving it for the ruling class. Given the vicissitudes of frontier life in America, children were at high risk of being orphaned or otherwise left homeless or neglected. Therefore, *parens patriae* came to be more broadly interpreted, providing the justification for intervention into the parent–child relationship in an attempt to enforce parental duty or supply substitute care.

Nevertheless, prior to the beginning of the nineteenth century, relatively few cases of child neglect, exclusive of abandonment or destitution, were acted upon in the courts. Two early adjudications, one in 1675 and another in 1678, are exceptions where children were removed from "unsuitable" homes. In the first instance a father had refused to put his children into service, as the Selectman of Braintree, Massachusettes, had directed. In the other, a father had failed to attend the public worship of God and in other ways had not submitted to authority (Morrison, 1933).

## Relief to Children in Their Own Homes

Public outdoor relief administered by local poor law authorities was looked upon unfavorably. Nevertheless, this remedy gave aid to more dependent children than were provided for by all other special forms of care. The relief given was meager, carelessly administered, and much criticized (G. Abbott, Vol. II, 1938). Probably the best that could be said was that public relief preserved the child's own home. But punitive attitudes toward the poor, especially the able-bodied "unworthy poor," and the belief that public relief increased pauperism made outdoor relief the least accepted form of care. Today's program of Aid to Families with Dependent Children (AFDC), a modern form of outdoor relief, also serves far more children than do alternative forms of care, but as a social welfare program it remains burdened by a legacy of inadequate levels of assistance and restrictive attitudes toward children and families who are poor.

## Almshouses

As an alternative to outdoor relief, dependent children were informally committed to live in dreary, unsanitary almshouses along with their parents and other adult misfits of the town—the mentally ill, the mentally deficient, lawbreakers, the aged, and the infirm. The notion that outdoor relief was the worst method of giving assistance was reinforced in 1823 by the Yates Report (*Assembly Journal*, 1824). In a survey of the conditions of paupers in New York state, Yates reached conclusions that were highly critical of outdoor relief. He urged that every county maintain a "poor house," a recommendation that was widely implemented among the rapidly developing Central and Western states. Children of the paupers who lived in almshouses were to be "educated," and at certain ages sent out for useful labor.

Yates had been enthusiastic about what almshouses would accomplish for children's health, morals, and education. But some thirty years later, publicity about the environment of the poor house and its effects on children led to a demand that children be removed and further placements be prohibited. Implementing the change in public policy was difficult and slow. States had funds invested in lands and buildings. Children could be placed in poor houses all too easily; and new forms of care were not yet fully developed for the large number of children who needed substitute care.

## Indenture

The statutes of many states provided for the apprenticeship of older children. Indenture was a favored practice because it placed the responsibility for the support and care of a dependent child outside the community while also providing training for work. In a period of history when everyone's labor was needed, acquiring skills and an occupation was deemed essential for the continued development of the new country.

Under the indenture system, overseers of the poor in the various towns and counties were authorized to "bind out" to a master workman an orphan, illegitimate child, or any other destitute child old enough to work. They were to be taught a trade and to become a member of the master's household. The children's obedience and labor throughout their minority were considered payment for their keep and training. After the onset of the Industrial Revolution, indenture became less feasible and by 1875 had virtually disappeared (Folks, 1902). Still, it had not been without merit. Despite some cases of cruel masters, the indentured children were on the whole more fortunate than those in almshouses or receiving public outdoor relief. In that sense, indenture was seen as "a forward step in child care" (Thurston, 1930: 10).

## Institutions

During the controversy about outdoor relief, almshouses, and indenture, institutions for children were being established. In areas where the

Quaker influence was strong, institutions for orphaned or destitute black children and for Indian children appeared. Concerned citizens also established institutions as a response to epidemics of cholera and yellow fever or wars between Indians and early settlers which left children orphaned. The states also began to assume responsibility for special classes of children by setting up large congregate institutions: "reform" schools for delinquent children, training schools for blind, deaf, and mentally deficient children, and orphanages for dependent children. These institutions tended to be an improvement over the mixed alms-houses, but too frequently they provided inadequate sanitation, and poor nutritional and medical care, which encouraged epidemics of contagious disease from which many children died. Nevertheless institutions for children flourished, partly because of continued dissatisfaction with almshouses, but also because of the emerging practice of providing public funds to voluntary agencies (Folks, 1902).

Religious groups began to figure largely in the child-saving movement, and many of the new leaders were ministers. Religiously sponsored institutions appeared to provide for the needy children of a particular faith and insure that they were taught that faith. On the whole these programs were characterized by missionary zeal, lack of individualization of children, hard daily work for the children "to inure [them] to hardship and fatigue," and little chance for enduring relationships with individual adults (Thurston, 1930:47). Parents whose children entered institutions were usually required to surrender their parental rights. Many such activities expressed their child-saving intent in the terms: to shelter, educate, and protect the "waifs and strays of the gutter," or "to diminish the victims of the spoiler and save the perishing" (Lundberg, 1947:71).

The nineteenth century orphanages tended to retain children for long periods, sometimes justified by the fact that the public school system was not widely adopted and the institution was a means to secure the proper education of orphan children. Yet many of the institutions made use of indenture for children they did not want to keep. A small proportion of the institutions developed reasonably satisfactory systems of placing orphans. As a rule, though, orphanages that "placed out" made little inquiry into the circumstances of the foster parents and the children were, largely, lost sight of (Folks, 1902:64–65).

## Foster Homes

The foster home movement represented by the work begun in 1853 by a minister, Charles Loring Brace, marks another significant approach to child-saving. Brace was concerned about the high tide of immigration into America, "pouring in its multitude of poor foreigners" who, he said, left uncared for, ignorant, and vagrant children "everywhere abandoned in our midst" (Brace, 1872:91). To this class of children he turned the energy of the Children's Aid Society of New York, an agency he founded. Brace recognized the demand for labor in the rural areas of the expanding country. His child-saving remedy was a bold practice of taking large groups of homeless children from the city to a rural locale first in the North Atlantic states, then into the Midwest and Great Plains where the children were placed in the homes of farmers, "our most solid and intelligent class" (ibid.:225). Brace's intent was to give the needy children work and bring them under the Christian influence of respectable people, thus "relieving the city of youthful pauperism and suffering" (ibid.:227).

To stimulate demand for these dependent children, Brace sent notices to rural newspapers in various states, emphasizing both the children's need for homes, and also that children would pay for their care by their work, basically a renewal of the indenture system. When a village was interested, Brace formed "little companies of emigrants" and with a "competent agent" dispatched them to that part of the country. Upon arrival, crowds of people from the farming community were present to select from among the children. The Society's records indicated that 31,081 children were placed in family homes from 1853 through 1929 (Thurston, 1930:121).

Brace's program attracted both followers and critics. Many children did get good homes, and the program stimulated the placement of children out of almshouses and into family settings. However, there were charges that Brace's program was based on prejudice against immigrants, that many of the children were unnecessarily separated from their parents, and that Brace failed to place children in homes of the same religious faith as that of their natural parents. Most of the children went into Protestant families although they came from largely Catholic, immigrant families. As a result, child-care programs under sectarian auspices expanded, and many states demanded religious matching as one determinant in choosing foster or adoptive homes—outcomes still reflected in today's pattern of child welfare. Concern by child welfare workers was expressed, too, about insufficient investigation of the homes in which children were placed and the lack of follow-up supervision and accurate record keeping by Brace's Society. By the end of the nineteenth century the number of "placing out" societies was steadily increasing and proponents of foster care were giving attention to the necessity to regulate interstate placements and to provide more safeguards in foster home selection and placement.

By the beginning of the twentieth century, foster homes and institutions prevailed as the best developed forms of care for dependent children. However, Brace's program had touched off a century-long debate in child welfare about the relative merits of each (Wolins and Piliavin,

1964). Positions, sometimes extreme ones, had meager support from systematic empirical evidence. Two major studies, one in 1924 and another in 1930, questioned assumptions about the relative merits of the two types of care and suggested less concern with the replacement of one form of care for the other and more attention to the most effective cooperation and coordination of both (Trotskey, 1930; van Senden Theis, 1924).

The foster home versus institution debate gradually subsided and by the middle of the twentieth century considerable harmony prevailed within the foster care system. Adaptations were made in an attempt to be more effective in meeting the individual needs of children. Large congregate institutions were broken up into smaller ones with cottage living; small group homes were developed with attributes of both foster homes and institutions, and "specialized" foster homes were developed as a means of serving the special needs of some children.

A study by Maas and Engler (1959) interrupted the abatement of controversy. This study marshalled alarm about the plight of large numbers of children who were in danger of staying in foster care throughout their childhood years. How to decrease the numbers of these "orphans of the living" was a challenge recognized throughout child welfare practice. Yet almost two decades passed before a movement developed to bring about permanent homes for children, with their biological parents or other permanent parents through adoption, guardianship, or planned long-term foster care. In testimony before Congress, Fanshel noted the relationship of the "permanency planning" development to the child-saving movement.

> . . . The notion that all children should be living with their biological families or adoptive families and that foster care should not be a permanent status has taken on such force in recent years that we face the prospect of a small revolution in child welfare as a result. The first revolution in child welfare was the closing down of the mass congregate institutions and the development of foster family care as a major alternative living arrangement. The second revolution may soon be upon us: a massive effort to make the foster care status a timelimited one" (U.S. Senate Subcommittee on Children and Youth, 1975:77–108).[2]

## The Child Rescue Movement

Another distinct social reform effort for children in the nineteenth and early twentieth century is recorded in the history of the child rescue movement, a large-scale organized response to "cruelty" toward children. In contrast to the religious motives and charity impulses of the child-saving movement, persons active in child rescue relied more upon legal concepts and efforts to advance the rights of children through the application of the law. Like the child-saving movement, however, child rescue was characterized by social distance from its client group and a considerable degree of coercive reform.

## The Legal Base

Although for many hundreds of years history had recorded instances of cruelty to children, prior to the nineteenth century the doctrine of *parens patriae* was little applied outside of child dependency or delinquency. Few cases of parents or other caretakers who were too harsh in disciplining their children were acted upon by the courts. That parents should be allowed to control their children without outside interference was a strong presumption, reflected in a 1646 Massachusetts statute that authorized putting to death any child older than sixteen years where sufficient evidence could be supplied that he was "stubborn and rebellious and will not obey his [parents'] voice and chastisement . . ." (in Bremner, 1970, Vol. 1:101). Given the commonly acknowledged right of adults to use corporal punishment and to determine how severe it should be, achieving progress in protecting children from physical mistreatment posed a particularly difficult problem. Very occasionally, exceptions occurred, such as one in 1655 in which a master severely mistreated his twelve-year-old apprentice. Upon the death of the boy, the master was brought before the Plymouth Colony court, found guilty of manslaughter and ordered to be "burned in the hand" and all his goods confiscated (Shurtleff, 1855:71–72).

Gradually some restrictions were placed upon parent rights in matters of discipline. An Illinois court in 1869 considered a case of "shocking inhumanity" on the part of the parents of a "blind and helpless boy" whom they imprisoned "without a pretense of reasonable cause . . . in a cold and damp cellar without fire, during several days of mid-winter." The court ruled that even though the law gave parents a wide discretion in matters of discipline, parental authority "must be exercised within the bounds of reason and humanity" (*Fletcher et al. v. Illinois*). Fifteen years later in North Carolina where a father was charged with assault and battery of his daughter, the court established "permanent injury or malice" as the test of excessive punishment (*State v. Jones*).

## Societies for the Prevention of Cruelty

Despite the accelerated public interest in cruelly treated children, there were no clear lines of responsibility among voluntary child-saving agencies or public officials for *finding* neglected and abused children. Societies for the rescue and prevention of cruelty to animals had existed for a century in England and for a lesser time in this country. An unusual incident in the year 1874, and the moral indignation that followed, created an opportunity to establish the first organization for the prevention of cruelty to children. A church visitor to tenement homes in New York City was told of a young girl, Mary Ellen Wilson, who was cruelly whipped and left alone for long hours. The thin partition between the tenement apartments let other occupants hear the child's cries and other evidence of harsh treatment inflicted upon her. Concerned occupants of the house had not known to whom to complain or how to get help for the child. The tenement visitor took it upon herself to establish evidence of the abuse and neglect. The man and woman with whom Mary Ellen lived had obtained her from the Department of Charities when she was less than two years old, but no inquiry about her well-being had been made by Charities' personnel during the intervening seven years. The tenement visitor sought advice from child-saving institutions and public officials about obtaining protection for the child. When no one was willing to intervene or seemed to know of legal means to do so, she took her report to Henry Bergh of the New York Society for the Prevention of Cruelty to Animals. This church visitor appealed to him as a humane citizen to use his authority to seek protection not only for cruelly treated animals but also in behalf of the cruelly treated child. Acting as a private citizen of influence, Bergh undertook to effect Mary Ellen's rescue. Elbridge T. Gerry acted as his attorney in initiating court action and emerged as the leader of the new child rescue movement. Within a few months he had founded the New York Society for the Prevention of Cruelty to Children (SPCC), the first such organization anywhere in the world (*New York Times*, December 29, 1874:2; Wheeler, 1910).

The newly organized effort to rescue neglected and abused children was not simply the result of an awareness that children, like animals, merited protection from cruel treatment. Rather, it was an evolutionary step in the movement to protect children from a variety of harms, while establishing their rights. The Mary Ellen case was important in that it dramatized, in a convincing way, the plight of children in a child-saving system where public authority added to the neglect of children by failing to enforce existing legislation, to set standards, and to supervise child placement activities (Thomas, 1972:308).

Interest in the new form of organized protection for children, represented by the New York SPCC, spread. By 1900 more than 250 societies in the United States gave attention to protecting children from neglect and abuse, and others had been established in England and the countries of Europe. In some instances child protection activities were simply added to an already established work of protecting animals. In those organizations with dual responsibilities, when resources were limited, activities on behalf of animals tended to take precedence.[3]

Gerry stated the purpose of the early SPCCs in direct and limited terms: "The prevention of cruelty to children and the prosecution of cruelists. Our object is . . . [to] rescue the child who is being ill-treated, and to deter the brutal from similar acts by bringing to punishment all those who injure children" (1882:129–130). He resisted efforts to ally the cruelty prevention movement with other urgent social questions such as child labor and even the temperance movement although intemperance was continually cited by child rescuers as directly associated with child neglect and abuse. Repeatedly Gerry emphasized that the child rescue movement was not one of almsgiving or other forms of charity, but essentially one of justice and legal protection for children. He proclaimed widely that "at the present day in this country, children have *some* rights which even parents are bound to respect" (ibid).

The early adherents of the movement held their organizations firmly to the symbols of middle-class dominance—that style of life which persons less worthy should pursue as a route to economic and social well-being. Their coercive approach included an acceptance of the principles of a laissez-faire economy and a concern with change in personal characteristics rather than in institutional arrangements. The coercive strain in the movement was nurtured by a cultural context in which the reformers and their involuntary clientele, largely from recent immigrant populations, held contrasting norms.[4] To the reformers, cruelty was of two types: that of "deliberate intention" and that which arose from "passionate habits." A belief in the effects of heredity led the reformers to assume that the blood of a better ancestry had become corrupted through unworthy descendants, and that unless cruelty and neglect were interrupted, they would become an inheritance for future generations.

Lower-class immigrants did not define themselves as they were perceived by the child rescuers, as immoral, of passionate habits, or intentionally cruel. Rather they perceived their reformers as immoral, cruel, dangerous, and tyrannical. From her experiences at Henry Street Settlement on the lower east side of New York City, Lillian Wald described games played by children there: One was "the Gerry Society" in which the children acted out their conception of the SPCC—"the Cruelty," an ogre who would catch them and take them from their homes (Wald, 1915:71).

## Tasks and Remedies in the Prevention of Cruelty

The primary method of the animal protection movement in which Henry Bergh and Elbridge T. Gerry had figured so prominently was to prosecute inhumane offenders against animals. Given the fact that the founders of the New York SPCC came out of the animal protection movement, it is not surprising that the new anticruelty children's agencies saw their primary tasks to be those of investigating reports of serious neglect and cruelty to children, filing complaints against the "cruelists," and aiding the court in prosecuting them. Although these societies were largely private bodies, agents were sometimes given police powers.

The reformers' sense of mission enabled them to resist criticism from the influential segment of the community who believed parental rights should be superior to the rights of the child. The reformers were confident that their strategies were effective deterrents to child neglect and abuse, strategies such as warnings, threats, arrests for nonsupport, playing on parents' fear of losing their children, and swift punishment of child abusers (N.Y. SPCC, 1893). Breaking up families was acknowledged to be "painful, but remedial, and often the only effectual process" (Mass. SPCC, 1902:11). "Moral suasion" was considered to be only minimally effective. Instead, "ignorant and vicious people must be compelled to do what is right by the strong arm of the law." Parents were visited at uncertain hours of both day and night. Society agents often expected children to serve as witnesses against their parents and deemed it of "the utmost importance" to segregate young children from the influence of the parents until they had appeared as court witnesses (American Humane Association [AHA], 1912:20–21, 40; N.Y. SPCC, 1906:20). Often the proper treatment—salvation—for the child was a change of environment and separation from parents; for parents, warning, prosecution, or punishment through the loss of their children or imprisonment at hard labor. The New York Society relied almost exclusively upon placement of children in institutions rather than foster homes, and was influenced in that preference by the fact that "after they are sent away from the City and placed in homes, they do not remain there; . . . they return to their old haunts in the City, only to be again recaptured" (N.Y. SPCC, 1882:8). What complete separation from their parents and loss of liberty meant to children went largely unacknowledged.

The early SPCCs demonstrated another, more positive, method to advance the welfare of children, a method present in the current conception of child advocacy. Law in behalf of children was rooted firmly in the attitude that children were the property of their parents. Society leaders began building a system of legal rights for children by a gradual accumulation of "wrongs-to-children" acts: legislation prohibiting the exploitation of children in dangerous theatrical stunts, in indecent or immoral exhibitions, and in the system where poor parents in Italy sold their young children's services to a padrone who then transported the children to America to work as street musicians and in other forms of begging, all for the profit of the padrone. The Societies also exposed and sought legislation to regulate the notorious "baby farms" where, for profit, unwanted infants were cared for in groups under life-threatening physical and emotional deprivation (N.Y. Sessions Laws, 1883:30–31).

## Conflict in Views

Shortly after the turn of the century a schism appeared among the SPCCs, reflecting a struggle between the social bases and ideologies of the conservative founders and the new progressivism of the early twentieth century. Contests for influence among the SPCCs divided along the lines of the nature of prevention, the proper forms of responding to abuse and neglect, the Societies' relations to other charitable organizations and to the developing profession of social work.

The Massachusetts Society initially followed the pattern set by the New York parent organization, yet, its commitment to the Gerry tenets rested on shaky ground. Massachusetts had never relied so heavily upon institutions as had the New York Society. The Puritan culture was based on the family economy; indenture when dependent children required care suited the Puritan temperament; attaching children to a family was preferred (Lane, 1932).

By the early twentieth century the Massachusetts SPCC was giving more attention to the reformation of parents. "We fully approve the practice of the return of children when the parents reform and establish good homes" (Mass. SPCC, 1902:2). The Massachusetts leaders began stressing the importance of moving from rescue work to remedial and preventive measures and of abandoning the idea that a SPCC was merely a prosecuting agent, "standing alone on a different plane" from other charitable agencies. The Society should play a more active part in all movements directed toward bettering conditions under which the children of the state lived. Especially needed was a stronger effort to discover the causes which made intervention by the Society necessary (Hubbard, n.d.:21).

In Massachusetts a new SPCC general secretary was appointed, C. C. Carstens who, during the thirteen years of his tenure, emphasized remedial action and statewide services designed to strengthen family life, with protective work being only one part of a broader community responsibility. Leadership in some of the other SPCCs also changed and the new social work philosophy was introduced, as in Pennsylvania where the placement of children in homes of relatives or other private families was advocated with a reuniting of children with their own parents "at the earliest possible moment consistent with the welfare of the children" (AHA, 1906:15). The New York Society fought bitterly against the new thought and was supported by the majority of the SPCCs, most of whom "fed" institutions subsidized by public funds (Folks, 1902).

In response to adverse sentiment, Gerry reiterated the exclusive nature of child rescue work and resisted any kind of collaboration with charitable agencies. He was adamant about any intrusion from the new social work philosophy and Mary Richmond's principles of social case-work. He refused to concede any overlapping areas of concern between destitute and dependent children and neglected and abused ones. He opposed legislation for a federal Children's Bureau, terming it an inva-sion of state rights, and a dangerous scheme to exercise jurisdiction over state and local agencies concerned with child welfare (*New York Times*, Jan. 28, 1912:14).

When the Child Welfare League of America was established in 1921, Carstens of the Massachusetts Society was named its first executive. This office greatly widened his arena for influencing a broader definition of child welfare services. In turn the support for Gerry's mold of the SPCC began to erode: In 1922 only fifty-seven such societies remained. Some societies that served both children and animals merged with other charitable organizations to avoid the association with compulsory meth-ods and to acquire an identity with a broader purpose. States, counties, and cities also began to assume more responsibility for protective work (Hubbard, 1922).

The advocacy methods employed in the earliest days of the SPCCs today strike professionals as primitive and poorly thought out. But these leaders and their methods must be understood in light of their times—when the child protection movement began—for example, in relation to the absence of well-developed child welfare agencies and services, the limited knowledge of child development or the causes of serious child neglect and abuse, and the moral attitudes of many persons concerned about the ill treatment of children, such as the need for punishment as a deterrent to repeated child abuse. The early SPCC leaders fearlessly addressed many difficult problems and focused attention on the need to develop legal rights for children and a body of law to govern their affairs. Some of the early leaders were zealous in the cause of suffering children and because of their positions faced repeated heavy censure from a public who feared any semblance of intervention into the affairs of parents. Still, these leaders continued to speak and write about the rights of the child, the child as a citizen, and "not charity, but justice to children." To their credit, a minority of new leaders insisted upon atten-tion to concepts and principles that helped to turn child welfare services toward prevention.

Nevertheless, vestiges of the past are clear in insistent current prob-lems and public policy issues. Both law and social agency practice still reflect an ambivalence in relation to child rights versus parent rights which, in turn, exacerbates the issue of due process and equal treatment under the law for parents and children. Traces of commitment to threat and punishment as a deterrent to cruelty to children can still be identified in the work of child protective services. Gerry's adamant stand against the exclusiveness of child protection versus collaboration with child welfare agencies left a troublesome legacy of resistance to the development of home-based services. That legacy complicated Carstens's efforts at the Child Welfare League and helped to account for the delaying preoccupation with refining techniques in foster care and adoption to the exclusion of new thought and advancement of home-based protective services. The extensive public subsidy system to private child care institutions, which Gerry promoted, accelerated the growth of large congregate institutions that had acquired staunch constituencies who could not be easily abandoned, even when evidence emerged about the advantage of family foster placements or return to children's own homes. Perhaps the most troublesome vestige from the history of child protection is a curious, but continuing, failure to sustain public interest in the prevention of child neglect and abuse through the provision of a range of preventive and remedial services.

## The Child Labor Movement

The employment of children in American industry dates back to the very earliest factories. It was a natural consequence of the Puritan belief in the virtue of work and the sin of idleness, not only for able-bodied adults, but for children as well. Not until the latter part of the nineteenth century did public opinion become enlightened enough to perceive child labor as a pervasive, serious social problem (E. Abbott, 1908:16). Once the child labor movement began, it held the attention of reformers and their adversaries from the 1880s until the 1930s. A look backward makes it clear that "much of the history of modern American reform can be written in terms of the struggle to curb child labor" (Bremner, Vol. II, 1971:601).

### The Legal Base

Many of the child labor reformers had connections with one or more of the social settlements which influenced them to regard the exploitation of children in premature employment as a condition that required a rearrangement in economic relationships. In contrast to the child savers and child rescuers who relied for authority upon the poor law and *parens patriae*, the child labor reformers sought a systematic use of the police power under which the separate states could adopt and apply standards and regulations to industrial employers who wished to hire children. At the peak of the battle for reform, child protectionists sought and obtained federal legislation. Twice the United States Supreme Court ruled federal acts unconstitutional. Then a constitutional amendment offered by Congress failed to be ratified. Not until 1938 was acceptable protective legislation for children in employment achieved as part of the Fair Labor Standards Act, legislation directed mainly toward labor rights for adults. By then large-scale employment of children was no longer feasible for industry nor acceptable to most of the country's citizens.

## Background to the Problem

In the early days of this country, the fast-growing colonies needed almost every individual to augment the general stock of production. The belief that parents had a duty to train children for work, thereby preventing idleness, gradually converted to a belief in a public duty to provide training for children in particular kinds of work that would be profitable to the towns and counties. In the latter part of the eighteenth century, when "domestic manufactories" began developing, the employment of children for commercial gain became general practice throughout the colonies. In 1791, Alexander Hamilton urged that the new industry of spinning cotton "performed by means of machines, which are put in motion by water, and attended chiefly by women and children" be encouraged (Hamilton, 1832).

An argument encountered by the early child protectionists stated that American labor was most profitably employed in agriculture and to take labor away from the soil would be unwise and unprofitable. After all, the argument concluded, the work of the "manufactories" did not require able-bodied men and boys; it "is now better done by little girls from six to twelve years old" (Niles Register, in E. Abbott, 1908:226–227). President George Washington visited a sail "manufactory" in Boston where he saw young girls "spinning with both hands, the flax being fastened to the waist." Each spinner had another child to turn the wheel. He reported on his observations with considerable interest and no apparent misgivings (Bagnall, in E. Abbott, 1908:22–23).

As a result of increased mechanization in industry, the policy of keeping children at work became less and less a question of moral principle, even in New England. "The virtue of industry" was no longer the major concern, but the fact that child labor was a national asset which could be used to further the material greatness of America. Since child labor was believed to be a righteous institution, "when the transition to the factory system was made it was almost inevitable that this attitude toward children's work should be carried over without any questions as to whether circumstances might not have changed" (G. Abbott, Vol. I, 1938:271). With the arrival of the Industrial Revolution, the prevailing belief was that parents and industry had a right to the profitable fruits of children's labor.

The problem for reform was complex. To curb exploitation of working children it was necessary to make concurrent progress in obtaining child labor legislation and compulsory school attendance statutes. The benefits to children of child labor protection would decrease if children were turned out of the factories into the streets and not able to go to school; nor could they be effectively required to go to school if the law permitted them to work. Not all parents understood and accepted the importance of education for their children. Low wages for adults increased their desire for their children to become wage earners. In states where child labor was not prohibited, school officials found little public support for mandatory school attendance. Frequent discrepancies between a state's compulsory education and child labor statutes confused the basis for enforcement.

Employers feared that a reduction of children's hours would lead to a demand for a reduction by adult employees. The early trade unions had mixed interests. While they opposed child labor because it depressed adult wages and could not be unionized, at the same time some trade unionists, like much of the general public, regarded child labor regulation as an interference with parental rights.

Child labor was also an interstate problem. When the textile mills moved from New England into the South where labor was cheap and children's work unregulated, the mill owners fought reform and claimed the same privilege of employing children as the New England states had profited from a century earlier.

## Conditions of Child Labor

The progressive reform climate of the early twentieth century fostered a new interest in children's conditions of employment. Branches of state and federal government, notably the federal Children's Bureau, and voluntary reform groups such as the National Child Labor Committee (NCLC), undertook major inquiries using trained investigators. The findings painted a shocking picture of the physical and emotional hazards under which children were working for long hours, both day and night.

In textile mills, young girls worked in the spinning rooms under strict discipline in humid, lint filled air that irritated the throat and lungs. In urban tenement houses, serving as annexes to the factories, children as young as five worked before and after school hours and on Saturday. Although their work was a relatively simple process, it was repeated endlessly—stringing tags, carding dress fasteners, making artificial flowers with materials containing poisonous dye, picking nuts, tying ostrich feathers. High rates of absence from school were common and in some instances children from seven to fourteen years old, who worked at home, had never attended school. Sometimes "their very existence was unknown to the rest of the children in the house, because they never came out to play" (G. Abbott, Vol. I, 1938:363). Many children worked in their homes manufacturing cigars, a practice which had a serious effect on their health. Shrimp and oyster canneries were another common market for child labor. Young children stood for hours, reaching down into the cars which held the steaming shrimp and oysters which they peeled or opened with a knife, stopping only to take their filled containers to the weighing window, before beginning again. Cuts, burns, infections, and irritations from the corrosive acid and thorns of the shrimp were common. Children were found working in the stockyards of Chicago, in the street trades, and picking cotton in Texas. Boys working in coal mines were in desperate need of protection. With the constant roar of coal rushing down the chute and enveloped by coal dust, they worked in "the breakers," perched high on a scaffolding picking out flakes of slate from the coal on the moving belt before them. Other boys worked underground in the most dangerous sections of the mines, turning ventilating fans by hand. Children worked in the furnace rooms of glass factories, usually at night. Under conditions of extreme heat and air filled with microscopic particles of glass, small boys assisted adult glass blowers hour after hour, darting about with tongs, handling the red hot glass molds and bottles (Bremner, Vol. II, 1970:611–649).

### The Battle for Legislative Reform

For all practical purposes child labor was completely unregulated until after the Civil War. Only a few states passed child labor legislation, which went largely unenforced. By the beginning of the twentieth century, however, most of the progressive states had enacted some kind of protection for children, such as setting minimum ages for employment or maximum hours of children's work. Nevertheless, resistance to enforcement continued to be strong on the part of competing employers.

The conflict grew. Many of the reformers, supported by the Progressive Party in 1912, believed that the evils of child labor could be affected only by a federal law. National interest sparked, the battle continued hot and heavy. From 1890 to the enactment of the first federal child labor law in 1916, public opinion divided as sharply and bitterly over the subject of child labor as it did later over governmental enforcement of the right of workers to organize (G. Abbott, Vol. I, 1938:265).

Federal legislation was first introduced into Congress in 1906; ten years later a child labor act was adopted. Using its power to regulate interstate and foreign commerce, Congress intended to close those channels to the products of child labor. Bitter opponents of the legislation sought relief in the United States Supreme Court. The Court ruled in their favor on the basis that the statute was not a legitimate exercise of Congress's power to regulate interstate commerce. Reformers persisted. Again in 1918 Congress acted to use its taxing power to eliminate child labor. Again the Supreme Court held the law unconstitutional. By that time seventeen states had enacted child labor laws that equalled or exceeded those set by the unsuccessful federal laws. Now the reformers sought and gained widespread support for an amendment to the Constitution specifically authorizing Congress to enact child labor protection. In 1924 an amendment was submitted to the states for ratification. By then it appeared that child labor legislation was no longer a partisan measure. However, proponents of the amendment, and the public generally, underestimated the strength of the industrial opposition, bolstered by conservative groups who feared any federal policy which appeared to encroach upon the rights of parents over children or to limit the freedom of free enterprise over the greater good of society. By 1931 only six states had ratified the proposed amendment (Chambers, 1963).

In the depth of the Depression of the 1930s, the public generally looked to Washington for more guidance. President Roosevelt urged ratification of the amendment and old supporters rallied their efforts again. However, the unflagging opposition repeated the story that the amendment was not a children's amendment but a communistic youth control measure (G. Abbott, Vol. I, 1938:467). Employers took advantage of the cheapness of children's labor, and sweatshops became common again. In Pennsylvania, girls and boys working for starvation wages called attention to themselves, becoming front page news by going on strike against their employers (French, 1933; "Children on Strike," 1933). Regression toward the worst of the old abuses of children's work was checked only temporarily by the administration of the National Industrial Recovery Act of 1933.

The child labor reformers were keenly disappointed in the failure of the states to ratify "the children's amendment." They saw its potential to pave the way for other federal labor legislation and to stand in the Constitution as a clear declaration of child rights, a landmark achievement that could hasten other reforms and benefits for children. To the reformers the amendment was a symbol of social justice for children. Child labor was not perceived by them as an isolated social ill, but one that was inextricably bound to loss of education, depleted health, underdeveloped human potential, and, most of all, poverty. Repeatedly the reformers pointed out that "child labor and poverty are inevitably bound together and if you continue to use the labor of children as the treatment for the social disease of poverty, you will have poverty and child labor to the end of time" (Bradbury, 1956:34). When the time came that it met the interests of industry and labor, and when citizens in general had been convinced of the atrocities committed upon children by exploitative labor conditions, children and young people were given protection in New Deal reform legislation as part of the Fair Labor Standards Act of 1938.

### Implications of Child Labor Reform for Today's Youth

Successful federal legislation for child labor protection and better enforcement of state statutes repudiated the abusive practices in children's work situations. The problem of oppressive conditions in the employment of children is much reduced today, although there are still instances of inadequate enforcement of regulatory legislation and insufficiently protected groups, particularly the children of migrant agricultural workers.

Despite considerable progress, a different but related problem exists today in the number of out-of-school, unemployed youth sixteen years and older who are unable to make or sustain a constructive entrance into the labor market and the mainstream of society. Youth unemployment, both male and female, is pervasive and universally high. Although school and employment problems for today's young people are different from those when the primary need was to protect young children from oppressive and exploitive labor, the underlying economic and political considerations are similar and persistent. Society's current obligation to assure that opportunities for education and employment are available in a form that young people can take advantage of is no less pressing than the school and work challenges faced earlier by generations of reformers.

### The Century of the Child

The progressive era of the early twentieth century provided new leadership and a promising climate for advancing the causes of children. So bright seemed the outlook that child advocates heralded the future as "the century of the child" (Key, 1909). Among the significant social inventions in the new century were the founding of the juvenile court, the staging of the almost legendary Conference on the Care of Dependent Children, the enactment of legislation for mothers' pensions, and the creation of a federal Children's Bureau which marked the first assumption of national responsibility for the well-being of children. The children's provisions of the Social Security Act in 1935 brought substantial gains for certain classes of children, even though limitations of the legislation and continuing change in conditions of national life brought new and still unsolved problems.

### The Juvenile Court

Perhaps no social institution was founded with higher hopes for its contribution to the well-being of children than the first juvenile court, enacted by law in Illinois in 1899. This far-reaching legislation was a product of cooperation among a group of social workers, principally Julia Lathrop and others associated with Jane Addams and Hull House, lawyers from the Chicago Bar Association, and civic leaders from various organizations.

Based on a philosophy of "individualized justice," the purpose of the new court was to provide protection and rehabilitation of the child or youth offender, instead of indictment and punishment. Among the most important benefits was probation service, a practice begun in Massachusetts in 1869, but one that the founding of the juvenile court greatly accelerated. The new legislation was considered a magnificent accomplishment, attained against the heavy weight of tradition. By 1917 juvenile courts were established in forty-five states and the movement had spread to other countries. Jane Addams believed that the new court represented "almost a change in mores. . . . The child was brought before the judge with no one to prosecute him and no one to defend him—the judge and all concerned were merely trying to find out what could be done on his behalf" (Addams, 1935:137). Relatively few persons questioned that the benevolent intent of the state was sufficient to protect children without extending them the full constitutional guarantees of due process of law.

From the beginning, achieving the rewards of individualized justice was seriously hampered by society's failure to provide the court with resources and to enforce standards of court and social agency practice. Most juvenile judges were inadequately prepared educationally in either legal or social considerations. They lacked access to appropriate detention and shelter care facilities and foster homes. Personnel in correctional institutions, as well as probation and social service staffs, too often were improperly trained or not trained at all. Juvenile court judges worked without alternatives to incarcerating children. After a long career as a family court judge, Justine Wise Polier observed that "the lack of appropriate services and facilities for delinquent children and to a much greater extent for neglected children has contributed more than any other single factor to negating the purpose of the court" (Polier, 1964:30).

The informal court procedures were little questioned until the late 1950s and 1960s. Then documentation of the juvenile justice system's failure to protect children's constitutional rights assumed the force of a children's rights movement. Children, it was alleged, were receiving neither justice nor rehabilitation. Subsequently a series of Supreme Court decisions in the 1960s and 1970s and revision of old juvenile court legislation within many states helped to correct some of the basic flaws in court procedures (Brieland and Lemmon, 1977). Still, the problems of inadequate treatment facilities remained acute.

In its time, the founding of the juvenile court was a major step toward social justice, one counter to the prevailing practice of treating children and young people as adult criminals. However, achieving social justice for children is a slow evolutionary process, complicated by conflicts in public opinion, ambivalence in legal theory with respect to children, insufficient resources, and the seriousness of the problems of many children, youth, and families. Historical influences can be discerned in current policy issues involving judicial protection for children. Among these issues are: the practice of "diversion," channeling referral away from the court toward alternative community-based agencies; the thrust toward "deinstitutionalization" as part of a move to diminish disruptive intervention into family life; and the continuing lack of adequate procedural protections for neglected, abused, and dependent children and for minors in need of supervision.

## White House Conferences on Children

Social reformers, recognizing the need for national policy with respect to children instead of local efforts and piecemeal legislation in various states, inaugurated decennial national conferences. Eight White House Conferences on Children have been held since 1909, but none with such farreaching implications for public policy as the first, the Conference on the Care of Dependent Children. This conference was held under the sponsorship of President Theodore Roosevelt who invited over two hundred prominent men and women to meet and discuss the pressing problems of children then coming to the attention of the State. The delegates examined problems and issues, passed resolutions and recommendations, and laid an impressive groundwork for many of the later basic reforms concerning the welfare of children.

Legislation for the founding of a federal Children's Bureau was languishing in Congress and the well-publicized Conference recommendation for its enactment brought new support. The Conference also endorsed the concept of a national voluntary standard-setting agency, which led to the founding of the Child Welfare League of America. Other recommendations included the use of government's regulatory authority to end exploitive child care and to improve living conditions in child-care facilities, and a move toward replacing congregate living with the cottage plan in children's institutions.

The most farreaching and central resolution of the Conference forcefully brought before the nation the subject of the dependent child, an action still timely in view of the current public policy thrust to plan for permanent homes for children. The Conference policy recommendation stated that: "Home life . . . is the highest and finest product of civilization. It is the great molding force of mind and character. Children should not be deprived of it except for urgent and compelling reasons." (White House Conference, 1909:9–10).

The Conference on Child Welfare Standards in 1919 is remembered for the support it received from women all over the country for the controversial maternity and infancy legislation sponsored by the Children's Bureau. The record of the 1930 White House Conference stands as a dramatic portrayal of confrontation between women organized, from all over the country, and the Hoover administration that was attempting to reassign the Bureau's functions to various departments of government, thus denying the importance of the Children's Bureau's purpose to serve "the whole child" (*U.S. Daily News*, 1930). As the succeeding White House Conferences have grown larger and more costly, and as the recommendations have become diverse and global in scope, their general usefulness in affecting public social policy has been questioned.

## Mothers' Pensions

Various factors gave weight to the growing argument for a special form of assistance for mothers whose children were deprived of paternal support. In addition to concern for preserving the values of a child's own home, proposals for mothers' pensions publicly recognized that the contribution of unskilled or semiskilled mothers in their own homes was greater than their financial contributions outside the home; it was a matter of public economic interest to conserve their in-home child-care functions (G. Abbott, Vol. II, 1938). Reaction was also strong against the institutionalization of young children only because juvenile courts had no other way to assist the dependent child of a "poor but competent" mother, thus freeing her to work outside her home. The development of child labor and compulsory school attendance laws was another consideration. A child of nine or ten was no longer free to quit school and work in factories or mines to help his or her widowed mother feed and care for younger brothers and sisters.

Concern about inadequate and punitive methods of public outdoor relief increased. Given reluctantly, relief consisted mostly of unreliable coal or grocery orders or emergency medical care. Social workers were still divided upon the principle of public responsibility for dependent children. The sharp difference of opinion over the merits of public versus private relief accounted for much of the resistance to the passage of mothers' pensions laws in the states. Reformers were also divided over the question of giving assistance to "worthy" mothers versus those of "poor character." Some feared that any semblance of relieving fathers of responsibility for their children's support would weaken family life and promote immorality and dependence. Nevertheless support for the concept of public responsibility for dependent children and the distaste for removing children from their own homes for the sole reason of poverty resulted in the 1911 enactment, in Illinois, of the first statewide mothers' pension law. Ten years after the Illinois act, forty states had enacted such legislation.

Two central problems emerged to plague the effectiveness of the mothers' pension movement. States enacting legislation did not always share fiscal responsibility with local units of government or give other help in implementing the program; and the underlying conflicts about worthy versus unworthy poor confounded the question of which mothers were entitled to public assistance. The concept of "suitable homes" emerged, based on even less objective criteria than were contained in state statutes defining the "dependent child." Eligible mothers usually turned out to be white and to be widows, rather than deserted, divorced, or separated spouses, or most questionable of all, unmarried mothers.

Thus leaders working for children when the Social Security Act was written in 1935 inherited a legacy of purposeful humanitarian effort in behalf of dependent children, as well as inheriting the belief in public responsibility. They also inherited the complicated issue of what was a suitable home and the unsolved problems of shared state and local responsibility for dependent children.

## The Children's Bureau

The origin of the Children's Bureau and its survival under repeated efforts to abolish, control, or subordinate it has become something of a legend. One of the frustrations of the early reformers was the absence of reliable data nationwide about the circumstances of children's lives, their physical, mental, and moral conditions, and their prospects (Kelley, 1905). The idea of a "Children's Bureau" came directly from Florence Kelley and Lillian Wald. According to their account, the spark that ignited their efforts to create a federal children's bureau was a newspaper account of the dangers of the boll weevil and of large expenditures by the Department of Agriculture to exterminate this menace to the South's cotton crop. Wald told a 1909 Congressional committee that reading the account had "brought home, with a very strong emphasis, the fact that nothing that could have happened to the children would have called forth such official action on the part of government" (Goldmark, 1953:96).

Wald, Kelley, and Edward T. Devine (editor of *Charities*), took a proposal for a federal bureau to President Theodore Roosevelt who was receptive to the idea. Thus encouraged, the National Child Labor Committee (NCLC) drafted a bill in 1906 and marshalled support for it. Continuous agitation and promotion by the NCLC, women's organizations, the National Consumers League, the National Conference of Charities and Correction, and the 1909 White House Conference finally brought Congressional enactment, in 1912, of a federal bureau for children. The charge to the Bureau was broad, namely to "investigate and report upon all matters pertaining to the welfare of children and child life among all classes of our people" (Act Establishing the Children's Bureau, 1912).

The first Chiefs of the Children's Bureau were Julia Lathrop from 1913 until 1921, and Grace Abbott, who succeeded her and remained until 1934. Their record of highly competent public administration has come to be referred to as "the glory days" of the Children's Bureau (Steiner, 1976:7). Making no claim to expertise by virtue of being female or possessing special insights common to their sex, Abbott and Lathrop personified the type of reformer who took on the role of professional expert and social engineer. They focused on rational and efficient ways of helping people through the power of the State and preventive legislation. They envisioned public programs that would embrace all the interests of childhood. They believed that the administrative location of the Children's Bureau in the Department of Labor was functionally hospitable to their broad definition of child welfare, a department "interested in securing the welfare of the masses of the wage earners of the country" (Lathrop, 1921).

Early in her tenure, Lathrop gave Bureau priority to two major areas of public concern that had influenced Congress to establish the Bureau. One was child labor, and until federal child labor regulation was achieved in 1938, Bureau resources were turned toward this end. Infant and maternal mortality was a second major focus of attention. Just how many babies died each year was not known with accuracy because unlike other leading countries, the United States had no uniform laws for the registration of births and deaths. Developing and extending registration areas became a Bureau objective. Bureau studies assembled an impressive statistical foundation about the causes of the extraordinarily high rates of death among women in childbirth and of babies in their first year (Meigs, 1917).

Other carefully designed investigations were carried out. They included child nutrition studies; mothers' pension programs in various states and countries; unmarried mothers; delinquency and the juvenile courts; the control of rickets among young children; institutional and community care of dependent and neglected children; and effective practices in foster care, adoption, and in services for crippled children. With the Depression and widespread unemployment threatening family life, Abbott directed studies of the effects of the Depression on children and families, of hunger in coal mining communities, and of the tragic numbers of adolescent transients, for the most part boys, who left home and moved fruitlessly across the country to seek work and relieve their parents of one more mouth to feed.

In all these areas the Bureau disseminated its research findings through easily available pamphlets for parents and other Bureau publications. It took an active role in setting standards with state and voluntary agency programs, and acted as class advocates for children and their parents. One of Lathrop's great contributions was her carefully orchestrated marshaling of support for federal maternity and infancy legislation (the Sheppard–Towner Act of 1921) that made possible the development of state programs to promote the health of mothers and babies. In designing the legislation, the circle of Children's Bureau reformers believed that programs within the states should not imply charity, available only to those unable to pay. They wanted "a community service for all classes" to solve a problem of the gravest importance to the community as a whole. Any less, Lathrop warned, would degenerate into "poor relief" with all its attendant stigma (Lathrop, 1920). The Sheppard–Towner act, as passed, was a declaration of public policy that "the people of the United States through their federal government, shared with the states and localities the responsibility for helping to provide community services that children need for a good start in life" (Eliot, 1962:123).

In administering the Sheppard–Towner Act, the Children's Bureau staff gave special attention to rural areas, where prenatal and postnatal care were generally unavailable. Clinics, which the Bureau termed "conferences" for reasons of political acceptability, reached thousands of women across the country. These conferences, conducted by a physician and a nurse, were held wherever space was available—in churches, schoolrooms, grocery stores, or homes. They were events of great interest to whole families, many of whom would travel over plains or mountains to reach the doctor or nurse there to help them. Pregnant women were examined and instructed; children were examined, weighed, and measured; and the parents were given instruction in normal child growth and development (G. Abbott, 1926:92).

While the Children's Bureau enjoyed widespread support from women across the country and from other reform minded citizens, it also faced bitter opposition. Throughout the first three decades of the Bureau's work, resistance to federal assumption of responsibility for aspects of child and family welfare was strong. Criticism stemmed largely from self-styled groups of "professional patriots," who were former members of anti–woman's suffrage organizations, and from organized physicians and the U.S. Public Health Service who feared any encroachment by a federal agency into the private health field. Much of the opposition from both groups was stridently sexist in its expression.

Without support from President Herbert Hoover, a strong supporter of voluntary social agency over public welfare programs, and as the clouds of the approaching Depression neared, Congress allowed the Sheppard–Towner Act to lapse in 1929. Remaining, however, was a remarkable demonstration of Grace Abbott's competent public administration and her ability to establish a pattern of federal–state relations that facilitated the translation of innovative social policies into effective operations for the benefit of society at large. Her method proved eminently useful to the Children's Bureau in its future administration of children's programs under the Social Security Act.

When, in 1934, President Franklin Roosevelt appointed a Committee on Economic Security to make proposals for a social security program, its Executive Director, Edwin E. Witte, approached the Children's Bureau triumvirate, Grace Abbott, Katharine Lenroot, and Martha Eliot, to learn what they wanted for Children. The programs the three agreed upon and recommended became the children's provisions of the Social Security Act. They were maternal and child health (a revised and extended version of the Sheppard–Towner Act); child welfare services for homeless, dependent, and neglected children and children in danger of becoming delinquent; crippled children's services; and aid to dependent children (based on the experience of the states with mothers' pensions) (Witte, 1934; 1963).

A study of the history of child welfare cannot provide reliable forecasts of what lies ahead, nor does the chronology of past events serve to explain present day problems. However, a study of child welfare history does illuminate many current problems and public policy issues, helping to reduce the risk of parochial thinking. In addition, an understanding of earlier crises in child welfare and how one's professional ancestors confronted similar problems, equal in severity to those of today, can broaden one's experience and help lay an authentic foundation for professional identity.

# CHAPTER 3

# The Well-Being of Families and Children
## A Context for Child Welfare

Robert M. Rice

To consider Child Welfare within a larger society, it is useful to discuss semantics. Child Welfare, a term which denotes a particular field of social work practice, is a title derived from a larger social concept, child welfare. It is not unlike such terms as "public welfare" or "social welfare," terms used to describe broad social concepts or fields of social work practice. Since semantics have a way of molding thought, it is important to examine Child Welfare as it differs from the broader concept of child welfare, all that pertains to a child's well-being.

Child Welfare is part of the world of formal organizations. It is a set of activities usually provided under the auspices of private corporations, usually nonprofit, or through government bureaucracies. As a field of practice, it upholds certain common assumptions about the use of professionals, how professionals and laymen contribute to decision-making, and the proper relationships among administrators, service personnel, and policy decision-makers. Child Welfare represents a division of labor and specialization established in bureaucratic form.

Child Welfare implies specific functions: its traditional services are adoption, foster care, institutional care, and protective services. Child Welfare also includes day care, homemaker services, services to children in their own homes, and other supports, but it provides these services less exclusively, since other fields of practice are often involved. At the center of the concept of Child Welfare is the potential of the field to substitute for and supplement the functions of a natural family environment, which has somehow become disabled in carrying out responsibilities to care for children. Child Welfare services, when functioning well, are strongly connected to the natural environment from which a dependent child emerges for care, and support community capacity for continuing care or return from the Child Welfare system, usually to a family setting. This definition of the child-care task had increasingly become a part of Child Welfare philosophy and is now being mandated in emerging directives of the federal government.[1]

Child Welfare covers a sizable area of functions. It requires the labors of professional and paraprofessional service personnel and support staff, maintains a large administrative structure, and consumes significant monies received from all levels of government, as well as charitable and philanthropic income and fees. Increasingly it reaches out to intervene and support social and family environments of children in jeopardy. With this wide-ranging activity, it is possible to overestimate how Child Welfare affects children. "Child welfare" is a far broader subject area, of which the formalized services of Child Welfare are an infinitesimal part. For the welfare of most children depends not upon Child Welfare, but upon a series of complex, time-honored social arrangements that are basic to the formation of society at large. Child Welfare can be engineered; "child welfare" is subject to all the forces that affect society in a world of myriad variables, where the effects of formal intervention become extremely difficult to trace or control. Yet, somehow, society provides. Any society must offer a modicum of welfare for its citizens or risk revolution or takeover. Safety, a measure of economic security, physical well-being, and nurturing responses to human dependency are some of the basic provisions of any society. Of course, some individuals may fall through the net of social provisions even as most citizens, most of the time, have most of their needs met.

Children are particularly dependent on social provisions, and are vulnerable when such provisions are inadequate. Human beings, with a long period between birth and maturity, must somehow develop a series of controls and supports so that children can become adults. No group within society is more dependent upon social arrangements for care.

## Families at the Core of Child-Rearing

Societies may vary in their social arrangements for children. Historically, some societies have made little attempt to preserve a new generation, but have produced harsh conditions or have been indifferent to the well-being of young children (Aries, 1962). On the other hand, some needs may be met, particularly in an advanced technological society, through an elaborate network of formal organizations. In the United States, considerable care for children is provided through a formalized school system. A variety of recreational, educational, character building, and religious organizations are also active in the process, but it is in informal structures—primarily family and neighborhood—where much of the social experience that trains children to function in society occurs (Bronfenbrenner, 1976). Most complex, most basic, is the family. From the absolute dependency of infancy to the most independent and prosperous of adulthoods, families maintain their influence, even after their members leave them. Ironically, though they are surrounded by laws, they function primarily without them, empowered by highly individualized messages deeply based in generations of social experience. They envelop the lives of people, and despite the difficulty in understanding the process by which it occurs, family experience remains critical to the development of most people's social consciousness (White House Conference on Families, 1980).

Renewed interest in the family as a social structure emerged during the 1970s (Rice, 1979). One of several study commissions activated during this time examined the relationship between the formal social agencies and families, and found that "broadly interpreted, families are like agencies—comparable to the schools, the health and social services agencies—each with authority to do something for somebody else, and yet families themselves have been the major missing ingredient in social policy development" (National Commission on Families and Public Policies, 1978:xi). In effect, this Commission defined families as primary social agencies because it was through families that basic social provisions existed. The point is particularly relevant in considering the social environment for children.

## Family Structure and Function

Arriving at conclusions about the family's role in society is beset with many pitfalls, both intellectual and ideological. One major difficulty having recent political ramifications is the problem of definition. How does one approach the subject of family? Can it be conceptualized as a structure? If so, how does one deal with the pluralism of ethnicity and lifestyle choices which differentiate families from each other? Are there universals?

A certain relativism runs through all this. If one defines family in terms of blood tie, what about adoption? If one identifies the center of the family as a heterosexual conjugal pairing, what about homosexuals, particularly when they function as parents? Is raising children a key? Then what about childless marriages? Does one define family along the lines of immediate nuclear structure, or can "family" include kinship systems and extended families? What about the ethnic differences in our society? How does one include the long-house culture of American Indians, or the fictive kin systems of migrating blacks? Structural definitions tend to exclude groups of people who consider themselves families.

One can also define family in terms of its products or functions within society. Family Service Association of America (1979a; 1979b) and the American Home Economics Association, as service organizations whose clientele include a wide variety of families, have emphasized the functions of families in their own definition, which follows:

> A familial constellation is a person-to-person mutual aid system which intends to provide on a sustained basis for a variety of necessary functions: the provision of emotional support to all its members and the assurance of economical and physical survival of the total constellation. Functional familiar behavior is characterized by intimacy, commitment to the constellation, and continuity and intensity of the relationship over time (FSAA, 1979).

But passionate arguments for a more narrow definition have recently emerged, as some groups, for either political or religious reasons, have become uneasy about uncontrolled free expression in family life. The argument goes that there are limits to what may be sanctioned by a society in the name of families, and that there are reasons to defend against too much variety. One means of doing this is by using a tight structural definition with the force of law, as reflected, for example, in the proposed Family Protection Act (S-1808 and HR-6028).

The issue of definition was a key debate between conservatives and liberals in the 1980 White House Conference on Families. Most of the efforts to define "family" within the Conference failed and only one definition statement, tangential to another issue, was accepted at one regional conference. The difficulty was particularly frustrating because the concept of families was so close to the experience of Conference participants. As was often stated, "Everyone knows what a family is."

Often unwittingly, Conference delegates were reflecting a debate about families in the social sciences that had absorbed the attention of a generation of scholars. Social scientists are only now beginning to come to some synthesis in what has come to be known as the structural–functional debate (McIntyre, 1981). Yet, problems arise with a functional perspective too. People disagree about what are universal functions of families, and, once again, the subject proves difficult because the products of families differ. Even the social mandates for families are open to considerable argument, exemplified regularly in American courts concerned with family law. What are the rights of parents as against the rights of children? Who owes what to whom? Thus, how do families function? Then, there is the question of dysfunction. Not all families carry out their social mandates, nor even their own wishes for themselves. Are they therefore not families? To what degree are families simply collectives of their individual members? Can families be defined separately from their members?

The question of family functions may be seen as having contemporary importance when one considers a recent survey report on raising children (Yankelovich, Skelly, and White, Inc., 1977). In their study of a national probability sample of 1,230 families, a bimodal pattern of raising children emerged. About half of these families, "the new breed," emphasized individual choice, permissiveness, and egalitarian sexual roles with their children. The others, "the traditionalists," emphasized achievement, parental authority, and differentiated sex roles. The United States population is remarkably split about some values in child-rearing, although there is some common ground between the two groups. The study is particularly instructive in demonstrating how some of the cultural value conflict, expressed so vehemently in family policy debates, comes into being.

The functions of some families are not the functions of others. Is it possible to define universals in so pluralistic a society as that of the United States? Moreover, can this universality be expected to remain steadfast when there is so much indication of social change? The family environment is a turbulent one indeed. Yet if families do not function within the larger society, they have little social value. Also the family is in competition with many functions of society. The possibilities for dissonance are great.

Without resolving these many questions, let us suppose that a common function for families is the raising of children, including their physical care and nurture, as well as their socialization and acculturation. In fact, a review of the literature led me to conclude that these are central family functions (Rice, 1977). Let us grant that not *all* families are carrying out this function, either because they are not in the life stage of raising children or because they have not elected this option. Nevertheless, social arrangements continually support the primacy of families in raising children and, in fact, children are usually raised in families rather than in other institutions.

## Stresses and Competing Demands on Families

Families do not function without stress: Many other functions of family life besides raising children compete for primacy and are associated with their own sanctions. The welfare of children is affected by all these factors.

Many observers have traced the development of a "happiness ethic" in American society. Parsons and Bales (1955) described the American trend toward expressionism in family life taking precedence over instrumentalism. Frank (1976) has succinctly described the strain of using hedonism as a guiding ethic in the family. Certainly there are many problems with child raising. No parent can describe the care of children as yielding unending quotients of happiness. Yet, happiness has come to be expected from family life and is a basic motivator for its continuance. Happiness is what most adult family members search for. Without a general sense of happiness in marriage, many divorce.

This is not to say that parents do not enjoy their children. Campbell and his colleagues (1976) have demonstrated in large sample surveys that the reverse is true: Parents do enjoy their children. But there are clearly trade-offs between satisfaction with children and the hard, unpleasant work of nurturing them. Conflicting signals in our society lead parents to interpret what parenting means to them, and whether they are appropriately rewarded for their efforts. Americans are expected to raise their children and be happy too, without a clear understanding about how much happiness is enough. And if not enough satisfaction is derived from the exchange, who is to be blamed? Is it a child's fault, or does a parent interpret that this dissatisfaction means that he or she is a bad parent?

One element of this happiness ethic that has assumed particular dominance in American thought in recent years is the goal of sexual satisfaction. Marriages are supposed to be sexually satisfying, and a newly liberated society has produced a plethora of advice, literature, and educational and counseling tactics, to insure that the right to sexual gratification is duly supported. But children interrupt. They threaten sexual privacy, they physically exhaust, they can absorb parents with unpleasant physical realities—they become ill, they cry, they demand. Children are rarely romantic, nor do they contribute to the exclusiveness of a couple's relationship. I recall attending a lecture on adult sexuality for married couples that advised an hour's cuddling in the marriage bed before starting the day's activities. Parents with children can hardly expect such protected time!

Lasch (1977) has described the family as a haven from other aspects of society. To an increasing extent, parents are engaged in employment outside the home; in fact, the movement of women into the workplace may represent the most significant shift in interpersonal relations within the family since World War II. With the likelihood of both spouses working during their child raising years, a series of complex accommodations and flexibility in social roles may be required, all of which may have a bearing on how children are raised. Moreover, the family is likely to become the second major polarity in adult experience. If work takes up many of a parent's waking hours, then families must in some ways offer release and/or contrast from the experience of the workplace. When much work investment has occurred elsewhere, it can be difficult to be up to the work of raising children. If family is to be a haven, the workload of family life must somehow be experienced differently from simply another demand for production.

Work competes in other ways with family life. Typically, Americans are employed in corporations which utilize a bureaucratic work mode. Rational behavior, where groups of people work together to advance production and are ready and able to regroup when this becomes more practical is emphasized. In other words, relationships are expected to be temporary. On the other hand, families often emphasize emotional connections between people, with an expectation of permanence in relationship. In effect, the general expectations of behavior are likely to be at considerable variance with the workplace. As noted, this variance can be helpful in rounding out life experience, but it can also stretch human resources. Not everyone can function equally well in both modes. Not everyone can appreciate where demands differ and understand what is appropriate within the family as compared to the workplace. Literature and drama which illustrate this point abound (e.g., "Death of a Salesman" or "The Great Santini"). Work demands a style of life which cannot always be easily shed for a style more appropriate to the raising of children.

Family life in general and the raising of children as a particular function of families must compete in many ways with other human functions carried out by family members. The complexity of role performance in a bureaucratic, technological society can make family life extremely fragile. Lifestyles can expand in such a society until, for some, there is an "option glut" (Sussman, 1971:32), a source of confusion more than freedom. Certainly all options are not oriented to the raising of children.

Yet raising children is what families are expected to do—successfully—when children are conceived. Carrying out these functions, while carrying out other competing functions is not an inconsiderable task in a complex modern society. If families are to meet adequately the many competing demands and expectations which currently exist, they will require an environment that supports them.

## Supports for Families

No family can exist in isolation. In fact, kinship systems have historically provided resources to nuclear families and their members. Uncles and cousins and aunts have all served to extend the capacities of the nuclear family long before formal social service networks were ever conceived. While in modern times large extended families infrequently live in single households, many extended family members do live in close proximity and, in addition, modern communications make it possible for connections to be maintained at a distance. Some families nourish their kinship systems and maintain their viability through constant use. Families function throughout society and in business, though often the mediating function of kinship networks is hard to perceive from the outside. Relatives intervene to help their kin get and keep jobs, borrow money, and even care for children. Often, ethnic customs and institutions reinforce the kinship support system.

Viable as the extended family may be for many families, for others it has lost considerable impact. Geographic and social mobility in the United States has been destructive to some kinship ties. In some quarters, preference for small families has meant that kin networks have not had the breadth, and therefore the power, available to others. Or, kinship has functioned more as a sporadic resource for nuclear family members, rather than a continuing, day-to-day experience. Many Americans find it easier to pay a baby-sitter for respite from their child care duties and would find it awkward to call a relative for this task. All children do not experience close relationships with their grandparents.

Some social institutions have worked against kinship ties. Splitting off age groups has been furthered by marketing practices that tend to separate accommodations and amenities among differing age groups, creating segmented markets while decreasing commonalities. Social and technological change has taken its toll; the newly trained find little in common with experiences derived from an earlier time. Technologies have separated contemporaries as well. Work specialities have become pathways to upward class mobility, often substituting for family heritage as the base for social position. Many Americans have found it more possible, and more appropriate, to maintain social distance from their kin, or to dispense with aspects of a given kinship system, picking and choosing relationships on the basis of compatibility. In the process, kinship networks have become less certain resources at times of nuclear family distress. Many households would be hard-pressed to find the time-honored supports of emergency housing, nursing and home care, economic assistance, or even meaningful advice that kinship systems once routinely provided.

A similar fate has befallen another major support system: neighborhoods. Once a universal component of cities and small towns, neighborhoods have often fallen prey to the pace of modern American life. While neighborhoods remain a factor in the lives of many Americans and, once again, may frequently reinforce ethnicity, several observers have expressed alarm about the diminishing viability of neighborhood systems. Economic and political systems have often demolished neighborhoods. Although federal governmental behavior has advanced from policies sanctioning simple demolition of unwanted neighborhoods, as in slum clearance programs, to neighborhood orientations, as expressed in Department of Housing and Urban Development policies, the concern for neighborhoods remains belated and often weak. Artificial means are often utilized to try to recreate the values of neighborhoods, or organize those who live together closely to interpose associations that require years and even generations to develop naturally.

Neighborhoods are important to the child-raising function. Not only are good neighbors helpful to parents, even in some of the ways kinship systems may be, but also viable neighborhoods reinforce parenting by assuring that community standards are met. In a close-knit neighborhood, it is difficult for a child to escape the common interest of the neighborhood and parents in his or her behavior. When neighbors are in close touch with parents, they often act as extensions of parental authority. A neighborly gift of food at a time of illness, assistance with household chores, and friendly advice over a back fence can, and do, bolster the capacities of families. Yet the growing sprawl in the location of Americans' homes, and the rate of change, have all mitigated the neighborhood support system.

Nuclear families need other supports in the larger society. Clearly, they must be connected to the economy. For many, this requires the capacity to be educated or trained for some sort of technological task. But even such training may not be enough, as those who direct job programs have come to learn. The simple experience of work, and the training needed to accommodate the outside workplace in life, often introduced through the family, is a necessary part of acculturation. Families need experience with work to train their children for it, and a tragic pattern is maintained for some generations of families who are not adequately linked with normal work experiences.

As families find support in the economic system, they exercise their options in a complex process of consumption (Nerlove, 1974). This family decision process within the economy is a basic function for the family, and one of the areas where family relations become particularly significant to all members. But the economy must provide well enough to allow for options in a complex process of consumption (Nerlove, 1974). This family decision process within the economy is a basic function for the family, and one of the areas where family relations become particularly significant to all members. But the economy must provide well enough to allow for options; a hand-to-mouth existence does little for the practice of interpersonal relationships, and can deprive family members physically too. Family well-being is deeply dependent in many ways upon the larger society, and perhaps most continually upon economic realities. Not all families have equal opportunities within the economy, nor are they equally rewarded by it. In a complex technological, postindustrial society, families become increasingly dependent on large corporate structures operating outside their control. Capital and production, once centered in the family in the earlier era of cottage industry, now forms outside its boundaries.

In fact, the case can be made that modern American society has weakened support systems for families that once were close, familiar, tangible, and subject to intervention by the family itself. Kinship systems and neighborhoods, as relatively small systems, could be experienced by family members fairly comprehensively. One knows and understands an uncle or an aunt; a next door neighbor is a familiar entity. Opinions and attitudes can be formed through direct observations and interaction, and one can talk to a relative or a neighbor and get direct feedback. Extended families and neighborhoods are within the scope of individual knowledge. But, the family's experience with these primary group systems is often weakened. Supports now come from much more impersonal sources—large corporations, institutions, government. For example, a major and often unappreciated difference exists psychologically in the process of asking a neighbor or relative to baby-sit and making application to a day-care center. The former process appears familiar and thus controllable—the latter may be perceived as giving in to a bureaucracy (Emlen, 1973).

If one considers what families require from their environment in order to survive, it is difficult to ignore the fact that families are dependent upon large and impersonal organizations. After a long study, the Family Service Association, a national organization with a central concern for families, made the following statement:

> Certain social and economic conditions are particularly devastating to family life. These include poverty, unemployment, inadequate education, catastrophic physical or mental illness without access to competent and affordable health facilities, sudden social dislocation, and unequal opportunity. A critical need is the development and coordination of means for preventing, alleviating, or eradicating these conditions (Family Service Association of America, 1979).[2]

If one analyzes these devasting conditions from the viewpoint of social provisions needed to offset them, the necessity for governmental action becomes evident. If one looks further at the origins of these devastating conditions, one thinks of large organizations. Modern poverty and unemployment are closely tied to the dominant structures in the economy, large corporations. Education has become a product of large bureaucracies under government auspices, while services for health and mental health are provided through large systems of professional care.

Disrupting relocations are forced by corporate structures that fail to attend to personal and family needs for stability and continuity. Guarantees against inequality are rooted in recent federal activity. Both cause and cure of these serious disturbances can usually be perceived as products of large, impersonal, bureaucratic, and unresponsive systems. The frequent complaint that these large structures are insensitive to family needs (White House Conference on Families, 1980) attests to the effects of a gradual strengthening of dependency ties between families and large organizational structures and the discomfort many feel with this dependence.

But a decidedly personal aspect to support systems is necessary to help parents raise children. Once basic provisions have been made to avoid calamity, more still is needed. For example, parents need respite from the task of raising children. One potential resource is the baby-sitter, usually hired from outside the family, though often a neighborhood resident. Baby-sitting has been an increasingly significant source of adolescent employment, as parents have become less dependent on kin networks to carry out this task. A parent is seriously deprived when isolated and economically unable to purchase such services. When the parent is without a mate, the problem is even more acute. The need is so great that elaborate barter systems are often developed by parents in poor neighborhoods, and these systems often become some of the most potent of neighborhood and community services to children. A related need is to avoid being overwhelmed by having to respond to too much dependency. Parents with very large families, particularly when children are very young and incapable of helping with household responsibilities, families both raising children and caring for dependent elders as a result of the extended life span, and families where severe handicaps require great attention are all in danger of becoming overwhelmed with child care. Social provisions are needed to maintain the capacity of such parents.

Much of the work of parenthood goes unappreciated. Children expect parents to maintain stable family patterns, and they rarely understand their parents' difficulties and sacrifices. Parents who are isolated, sometimes through single parenthood, sometimes through marital dysfunction, can lose their capacity to function as parents as they become embittered by experiencing relentless need coupled with unappreciative responses. Interrelationships with others who can understand strain, or provide praise, are a necessary support in caring for children.

Adults need to play roles other than that of parent. They need opportunities to be adults, to be students, to be experts, to be employees, and to be dependent themselves. The frequent observation of women entering the work force that they need to be something other than mothers often means that they are using the workplace as a support system for their roles as parents. Whether working or not, parents need to find expression for other facets of their personalities. Parents need recourse to expertise as well. Being a parent is not easy and parents often are eager to utilize media presentations of expert opinion to help them to raise children. Particularly in a society where values are often fragmented, people seek authority and "the right answer." At times a more personal means is needed. Educators who can engage parents, child-care experts who can explain developmental shifts, or other professionals, need to be potentially available to parents. Where more serious difficulties in the parenting process develop, professional counsel, medical service, or special education need to be accessible. Without such resources, dysfunction in the parent–child process can snowball.

Hopefully, parents find a personal network that helps them carry out their tasks in various ways. Some sources may be available within nuclear or extended family life. Others may be available within friendships and neighborhood acquaintances, and still more should be available within the network of organizations which are part of parents' personal lives (churches, clubs, recreational structures, mutual aid groups) or organizations which may be formally structured to help with aspects of parenting (social agencies, clinics, special educational services). Families cannot function as isolated entities, and the social supports necessary for their functioning are considerable. Understanding family strengths as a consequence of support networks is possible since families are so interdependent with those networks. Families, all with their own unique structures of social supports, and each differently dependent upon small primary group attachments and large formal organizations, raise nearly all children in the United States. In this sense, they are more the source of child welfare than any social institution. However, that observation is tempered with recognition of the fact that families are dependent upon a complex and imperfect network of formal and informal social provisions which must support their work.

## Child Welfare in Context

Where does the formal Child Welfare system fit into all this? First, it is important to understand that a relatively small proportion of children are directly dependent upon it. Depending on how the Child Welfare system is defined, and depending upon how numbers are estimated from imperfect statistics, variable estimations of these numbers may be made. In March 1977, for example, based on a carefully selected sample of 1.8 million children, Shyne and Schroeder (1978) estimated that there were 395,000 children in foster care. The Voluntary Cooperative Information Service has reported that on October 1, 1981, there were 274,000 children in foster care and that approximately 425,000 children were in care for at least one day in 1982 (DHHS, 1983). But it is clear that children who enter the Child Welfare system are a very small minority of those in the total population.

Kadushin has made useful distinctions between substitute care services which are "designed to replace the biological parents, temporarily or permanently by a surrogate parent, couple or group," and services oriented to support and supplement family functions. He makes an important case for the need for these substitute services. Reviewing the literature, he writes:

> The warranted conclusion is that supportive and supplementary services cannot substitute for substitute services. Nor is it likely that one kind of substitute care can totally obviate the need for another service. Even if a program of deinstitutionalization were ideally implemented, there would be a residue of children who could not make use of a community-based facility and would require the structure and control that only an institution can make available. (1978a:11)

Kadushin goes on to explicate the difference between a "minimalist" orientation to child welfare and a "developmental" one. The former emphasizes substitute care; the latter a more expansive design which is meant to provide services throughout the total population without being limited only to the most needy clientele.

Kadushin then argues for a minimalist approach as a strategy for the near future:

> Given the reality of limited resources, it may be less visionary but more pragmatic to hold a residual orientation. An "institutional" "developmental" orientation of the child welfare system is too ambitious, less efficient and less equitable than a service targeted toward those who need it most. A universally oriented system does have the advantage of being less stigmatizing. But where services are in short supply, as most child welfare services are, priorities should be given to those in greatest need. The target population of the child welfare system is not all U.S. children, but those who lack adequate care through the usual care-taking arrangements. (*Ibid.*:16)

The approach is reasonable. There is little reason to believe that major new thrusts to enlarge any social service network are immediately foreseeable, and under conditions of shortage, outlining priorities and targets is important. Yet, perhaps the concept of providing services for the needy can be enlarged; difficulties arise in so narrowing the Child Welfare system that its services cannot effectively link with the realities of community life from which their child clientele come. A substitutive philosophy of Child Welfare implies that it is a substitute for failed family function. Kadushin particularly emphasizes institutional care, foster care, and adoption. The latter substitutes the capacity of one family for the failure of another, and makes permanent arrangements to shift parental responsibilities. On the other hand, the maintenance of institutional and foster care requires continuing intervention by the Child Welfare system. Since they are maintenance designs, they often have to be conceived as semipermanent arrangements.

The Child Welfare system has its failings, probably best documented by the child welfare field itself (Mott, 1975; Sherman, Neuman, and Shyne, 1973). A serious problem remains in maintaining adequate monitoring of children in care; children become buffeted by frequent replacements and too shallow adult attachments. But these problems are internal to the system and are subject to improvement by better methods of child welfare management.

Even if the system is improved internally, how does it fit into society in general? More specifically, how does Child Welfare fit into the entire child welfare context? Children emanate from families; most have some connections, however tenuous, with adults, even when families have been practically demolished. Children in foster care will often feel that they have family connections when they are quite distant from them. When severe family problems detach children from relationships with parents, potentials for relationships with extended family members may be possible. When those are not available, linkages with non-relatives or neighborhood people may be important. Well-established systems of fictive kin may carry important functions, particularly within certain ethnic minority groups (Delaney, 1979).

Moreover, *all* families fail at times. We have seen that a variety of supportive functions must be carried out within the natural network of human relations to maintain and strengthen families. Certainly there are children who are entirely cut off from any possibilities of connections with familial experience outside that derived from the Child Welfare system. When this is the case, adoption is often the preferred intervention. When uncertain, but existing, relationships with natural networks do exist substitutive child care provided by institutions and foster care systems may not be the only remedy.

## Directions for Child Welfare

A Child Welfare system which defines itself only as substitutive, or which addresses only the failure of the family and kinship network may be unnecessarily alienating children from the possibilities and potentials of their original social environment. The families of origin, like *all* families, have shortcomings, but for some reason have been unable to overcome them. The Child Welfare system may be a useful addition to support resources for family cohesion in such instances, or it may be a divisive force between a child client and the natural family system.

Recognizing this dilemma, Child Welfare experts are increasingly extending their services so that realistic intervention can include the natural social systems from which children come. Elaborate state and federal legislation has been devised to insure that possibilities for returning children to their natural family networks are used. When this difficult and ambitious goal is attainable, the Child Welfare system becomes a significant and perhaps pivotal component in a support system.

How can the Child Welfare system appropriately intervene with families? Clearly, the technology of interpersonal counseling comes into play. But also, Child Welfare, working as a support for families, may intervene to restructure the support environment, finding and devising supports less divisive than child placement to meet family needs. After all, the support network for families is hardly an organized system. Cohesion between supports offered by such resources as the workplace, the neighborhood, the community, the extended family, the educational system, the church, or social agencies is virtually nonexistent. Our society is complex. Families are supported (or traumatized) by a great variety of influences. Some can be sustained in their child care function by intervention that organizes potential supports within the natural environment. Such family advocacy goes far beyond the process of helping families gain access to social welfare bureaucracies; it is, to a much greater extent, a marriage between family counseling with its sorting out of personal relationships and clarification about what external resources are available.

The support and maintenance of the family is the central expressed goal in the Child Welfare system. However, significant numbers of children continue to move into substitutive care arrangements thought to be unnecessary (Kadushin, 1978b). A high level of interest supports reform of the Child Welfare system, emphasizing building potential links to families (White House Conference on Families, 1980).

Just as demands on the Child Welfare system are merging with internal emphases on reform, cohesion within Child Welfare may be decreasing. For several years, national standards about child welfare have had a decreasing impact for many reasons. The government has tended to emphasize the rights of states to develop Child Welfare systems with diminishing national regulations. Professional social work, once a cohesive discipline within the Child Welfare field, has been weakened by hiring policies which have not insisted on this professional training. Ronald Reagan's "New Beginning" tentatively left Child Welfare standards and financing entirely up to individual states. Under these circumstances, the 1980s will be a crucial period for determining the degree to which Child Welfare, the system, can synchronize with child welfare, the actual well-being of the child. Some trends go in the direction of integrating Child Welfare practice with community support networks, but some demonstrate public disinterest, while lessened funding of all social welfare programs may cripple any extension of the Child Welfare task, ironically renewing emphasis on the relatively expensive process of substitutive child-care arrangements.

Yet it seems unlikely that the Child Welfare system can maintain exclusive and isolating control of the care of its client children. Whatever the fate of Child Welfare reform law, there is a clear direction in recent family court decisions to balance the control of the Child Welfare system with the interests of others. Family law has been moving for several years toward enlarging the list of interested parties in the Child Welfare arena (Goldstein, Freud, and Solnit, 1973). Foster parents have organized and successfully pursued their own rights to become partners in Child Welfare planning. Court review of foster care plans has become more frequent. Parents and extended family members have successfully challenged the rights of placement agencies. Under the circumstances, the Child Welfare establishment cannot afford isolation from other aspects of the environment of the children in its care.

The Child Welfare system is perforce host to many social ironies. Society does not approve of families that abuse, neglect, or are unable to be responsible for their own children. But neither is society willing to abdicate all power for the care of such children to any single institution such as a placement agency. Child Welfare is designed to take the place of the system which doesn't work—but never too completely so. It is a bureaucratic answer to a non-bureaucratic, familial condition and is defended and attacked, often with equal passion. It represents substitution rather than what is preferred, and so it is viewed with ambivalence. Child Welfare systems, then, are vulnerable social creations. They are likely to operate best when they find connections to a larger society, and when they optimize potentials for natural processes to regenerate. To the extent that occurs, Child Welfare can function in the context of child welfare and become strengthened, ironically enough, by becoming one of the many sources that support the task of raising children, primarily in families.

# CHAPTER 4

# The Social Policy Context of Child Welfare

STEPHEN ANTLER

In the final decade of the nineteenth century, progressive reformers, academics, businessmen, municipal officials, and settlement workers successfully argued for a more central government role in the protection of the powerless and the amelioration of social problems. Although the principle of active governmental response to economic and agricultural issues was well established in the United States by the turn of the century, provisions for social welfare had been largely delegated to the private sector under the assumption that government was both ill-equipped to respond to human problems and constitutionally prohibited from developing social welfare programs. Progressive reformers, acting with a strong sense of mission, used research and legislative advocacy techniques to accomplish a veritable revolution in the creation of public programs designed to assist the poor, to protect those unable to fend for themselves, and to insure income sufficiency for the working class. In doing so they created the basis for modern social welfare and established the fundamental procedures, techniques, and values of contemporary social policy (Davis, 1967; Lubove, 1969).

## The Emergence of Social Policy

During the 1890s at the height of the Progressive Era, the little help provided to the poor and working classes came from voluntary charities and limited state and local aid. Few government activities were directed toward what we now call social welfare, and the Progressives, largely centered in the settlement houses and universities of New York and Chicago, were attempting to foster a dramatic shift in public attitudes concerning the responsibilities of government (Lubove, 1968). Through patient data gathering, the extensive, if not extravagant, use of publicity, and aggressive lobbying, men and women such as Jane Addams, Julia Lathrop, Alice Hamilton, Florence Kelley, Henry Moskowitz, Edward Devine, and Frances U. Kellog helped launch what became a long term social movement. Their purpose was to convince the public and the Congress that inattention to issues such as poverty, child labor, maternal and infant mortality, unemployment, illiteracy, and industrial health and safety was both unjust and unwise. In contrast to an earlier generation of reformers which had embraced a decidedly Social Darwinist position that argued for limited government-sponsored reform, the Progressives claimed that a civilized society could seek social improvement through organized government effort and should not fail to intervene when individuals and families were beset by economic and social forces largely beyond their control.

By emphasizing that social improvement could be financed by the normal expansion of the economy, the Progressives succeeded in constructing coalitions composed of academics, business people, workers and social workers that were to prove extraordinarily effective. Recognizing that there were numerous avenues for addressing the problems of businessmen, farmers, and manufacturers, they sought to fill a gap in the political structure by creating federal and state agencies directed toward the concerns of women, children, and workers—and, indirectly, toward their families.

The basic outlines of the program the Progressives sought to create were not to be initiated until the 1930s, after the nation had become mired in a profound economic depression that colored for the remainder of their lives the perceptions of those who lived through it. Not coincidentally, the Depression helped to forge a durable political coalition of workers, ethnic and racial minorities, urban dwellers, and farmers who saw government programs as their primary insurance against economic disaster. With the election of Franklin Roosevelt in 1932 a new era of government involvement in social welfare began, the cornerstones of which were the Social Security Act of 1935 and the employment-generating programs of the Work Progress Adminstration and the Public Works Administration. With these programs the idea that an activist federal government could and would intervene in social relations became firmly established.

The programs of the Depression arose in the context of national and global crisis, setting a pattern for future social legislation that was to heavily influence the character of national social programs. As responses to widespread deprivation and despair the programs were rational, necessary, and pragmatic reactions to a clearly perceived social need. Indeed, though recently under attack by conservative forces, many of the major New Deal programs still exist and retain enthusiastic public support, almost three generations after passage.

## A Categorical Approach to Social Policy

Federal programs subsequent to the Depression—in particular those developed in the crisis atmosphere of the 1960s and early 1970s—although rooted in a tradition of reform that had emphasized the addressing of broad social problems—were designed to combat specific behaviors, such as juvenile delinquency, teenage motherhood, and child and spouse abuse. These "categorical" programs were largely reactive, focusing on narrow deviant behaviors and emphasizing case treatment. They did not, however, address the social context of these problems. Many programs were discovered to have undesirable consequences that were unacknowledged and frequently unanticipated. Child protective programs expanded after the discovery of "child battering," for example, proved to be intrusive, and though well-intentioned, were often ineffective. Although unacknowledged in the discourse, foster care often became a permanent substitute arrangement for many children, generating insecurity in the lives of foster children, their biological parents, and their foster families. Often these programs corroded the relationships between agencies and their clients, escalated costs, and incurred the displeasure of legislative bodies, thereby limiting support and funding (Antler, 1980).

The categorical program approach remains the dominant social welfare mode used in contemporary social service delivery. While some policy analysts argue that there is great efficiency in targeting scarce resources toward relatively well-defined social problems, others note that this choice often reflects public inability to agree on broad social policies and represents political compromises that provide limited social service coverage for the poor. Many analysts, moreover, commenting on the need for stronger, more universal social policies, observe that services designed for the poor often are poor services. Furthermore, these programs tend to blame the victim, to segregate their users, branding them as deviant and implying that large-scale social problems can be remedied by limited case intervention (Ryan, 1971).

In the child welfare area, categorical programs have negative objectives, reflecting public pressure to halt socially undesirable activities, such as child abuse or juvenile delinquency. Yet, it is possible that these programs represent the best possible politically feasible compromise available in the absence of widespread consensus concerning the desired contours of public social welfare activities. The lack of explicit, publicly supported and officially sanctioned social welfare policies, though not uncommon in the Western world, complicates the work of those who seek to understand and change the framework of public interventions affecting children and their families. Since policies are developed by many sectors of government, including the judicial, legislative, and executive branches, and a variety of service fields such as juvenile justice, child welfare or health care, they are often uncoordinated or even conflicting in reference to a specific individual or group.

Planning for changes in social policy requires a synchronized approach that anticipates the impact of broad social changes on the lives and lifestyles of ordinary people. Thus the context for considering social policies for families and children must include not only the existing catalogue of child welfare programs, but also the changing family and its changing needs. That contemporary trends in social policy occasionally seem to develop without due regard for concurrent changes in the family should not discourage the inquiry. Indeed, our analysis may help to illuminate the degree to which contemporary values are in conflict with a nostalgic vision of our recent past, conditioning public dialogue and distorting our capacity to adjust to social changes.

## Distinguishing Social Policies: Boundaries and Sectors

Within the past few decades scholars in the United States from a variety of disciplines have increasingly turned their attention to social welfare institutions and functions as these have assumed greater importance within the total framework of government programs. The emergence of the welfare state in Europe, as well as the United States, has tended to expand the intensity of interest from a small group of scholars to a wider audience of researchers, legislators, administrators, practitioners, and the public.

If we are to influence the shape and direction of policy and program, we must understand both, and the relationships among the central policy areas. There are numerous ways in which the targets of social policy may be defined. They can pertain to fields of practice, such as child welfare, mental health, health, or juvenile justice; to populations, such as the aged, children, the retarded, or families; or to social problems, such as juvenile delinquency, poverty, mental illness, or a specific problem within a sector. Child welfare policy, for example, extends to child abuse, divorce, abortion, or substitute-care programs. Initially, these distinctions appear confusing and complex, yet that is the nature of the world of myriad policies which touch, in some way, on most significant life events. An understanding of social policy thus requires some capacity to tolerate the ambiguous and fluid context in which policy is often described.

One of the ambiguities within the policy field is that concepts referring to different domains are occasionally used interchangeably. For example, the term "social policy" and "social welfare policy" are often discussed as if they were identical, though they refer to different, albeit overlapping, domains. Similarly, the boundaries between child welfare policy, children's policies, and family policies are often unclear since they refer to similar decision areas and social institutions. The differences, however, are important, since the vantage point from which one assesses policy influences the outcome of the analysis. Therefore to regard children's policies as synonomous with policies directed toward families assumes that the interests of children are always congruent with those of their families. This may not always be the case, particularly for teenagers, for abused children, or for those who have special needs resulting from health or mental health problems. Consequently these distinctions, under the broader rubric of social policy, serve the useful purpose of providing different vantage points for assessing social policies and reflecting different or even conflicting interests, leading to the endorsement of different institutions and programs.

## Social Policy and Social Welfare

The concept of social policy evolved to describe the goals and actions of government in regulating or changing social relations. In particular, social policies reflect public choices concerning those programs and services to be provided by government. Such services are not sufficiently accessible or available through the private market. Historically, public activities arose in response to shifts in the social structure stimulated by economic and technological change that encouraged the transfer of certain family functions to public institutions (Schottland, 1967). The education of children, the care of the aged, and economic assistance are examples of social needs, formerly met almost entirely by families, in which government now plays a role. Thus social policies are reflections of and responses to social changes. Moreover, social policies, in turn, can influence the direction of social change by providing incentives for certain functions and discouraging others.

Considerable ambiguity exists as to what distinguishes the "boundaries" between social policy and other public policies. Kenneth Boulding (1967), for example, despairing of finding clear boundaries between economic and social policy, concludes that one must be satisfied with "regions" rather than the crisper and more comfortable delineation "boundary" suggests. He notes that economic policy often intersects with social policy, since government decisions in the economic sphere have important impacts on family life.

Social policy and social welfare policy are occasionally used interchangeably though they refer to somewhat different areas of concern. Social welfare policy generally refers to government policies governing the operations of the social welfare system, namely those social services and programs designed to assist individuals and families and to improve the quality of life (Gilbert and Specht, 1974). Kamerman and Kahn (1976) describe these as "personal social services," incorporating services to individuals and families who are dependent or are incapable of providing for their own needs, as well as counseling, support, and corrective activities.

Social policy, on the other hand, refers to a much larger range of public activities about which there is less specificity and consequently more room for different definitions. Richard Titmuss, for example, suggests that the "study of social policy cannot be isolated from the study of society as a whole in all its varied social, economic and political aspects" (1974:18). Though policy refers to an action plan or a set of agreed upon objectives that guide decision-making, Titmuss argues that to understand social policy one must have a clear conception of the cultural and historical imperatives determining the goals a society establishes for itself, though many of these may be unstated, unclear, or contradictory. Although others would draw the boundaries around social policy differently, there are some unifying themes in virtually all concepts of social policy. Titmuss, with characteristic clarity, describes these: "First, the . . . aim to be beneficent; policy is directed to provide welfare for all citizens. Second, they include economic as well as non-economic objectives; for example, minimum wages, minimum standards of income maintenance and so on. Third, they involve some measure of progressive redistribution in command-over-resources from rich to poor" (1974:27).

These elements, however, suggest a set of beliefs characteristic of social policy analysis that may be unrealistically optimistic concerning the ordering of human affairs. Titmuss reminds us that social policy need not be beneficent; welfare at times might better be described as "ill-fare." The racial policies that guided Hitler's Germany from 1932–1945, as well as contemporary apartheid policies in South Africa or corrections policies in Saudi Arabia, can be mustered as examples of social ill-fare. In our own country the policy toward Japanese-Americans during World War II, the past policies toward American Indians, the newly enacted tax policy designed to stimulate investment by increasing the income of the rich, and the recently discussed notion that government should do nothing to retard the decline of Northeastern cities similarly represent examples of nonbeneficent social policy.

## Child Welfare and the Welfare of Children

The welfare of children, as both David Gil and Robert Rice in the introductory chapters to this book have emphasized, is not synonymous with Child Welfare. Child Welfare policy refers to a specific field of policy activities, namely those policies, programs, and laws which guide the Child Welfare field. The activities subsumed under Child Welfare policy are generally defined as child protection, foster care services, adoption, and institutional care. In addition, most analysts would include various other services designed to supplement or support family life such as day care, homemaker programs, and counseling services directed at child-rearing problems.

It is significant to this discussion of Child Welfare policy, as well as to that of family policy in the next section, that the major public and private institutions of the Child Welfare system evolved in response to the child-rearing difficulties encountered by a relatively well-defined group of poor, extremely deprived families encountering unmanageable family crises. For many generations it has been a relatively rare occurrence, with the exception of adoption, for comfortable working class or middle-class families to utilize the services of Child Welfare agencies. Ordinarily, such families are able to weather the normal life crises most families encounter, either by purchasing the services they need or through the assistance of family members. The poor, who are often less able to absorb shocks to family stability, are more likely to need the help of outside agencies.

In recent years, with the explosion of community interest in child abuse and neglect and legal requirements for action in all states, Child Welfare system priorities have been redirected in response to the growing volume of abuse and neglect referrals. Indeed, the child protective function, which was among the last to join the Child Welfare field since it was viewed as an "arm of the law" rather than a social service, now threatens to overtake in significance many other welfare services (Antler and Antler, 1979).

The scope of government social services directed toward children in need can be highlighted by the traditional Child Welfare categories within the Social Security Act. Federal funding for social services to families resulted from amendments to the Social Security Act of 1956—amendments that were subsequently expanded in the 1960s. Further elaboration of family-oriented programs occurred with the passage of the Economic Opportunity Act and subsequent legislation designed to attack problems of child abuse, teenage pregnancy, delinquency, and runaway youth. Current programs for families and children are largely subsumed under Title XX, Title IV–B and Title IV–E of the Social Security Act, which sanctions funding for most of the basic Child Welfare services. In addition, many states and voluntary agencies supplement the minimum funding provided by the national government. Child Welfare services and policies, since they are primarily directed toward deprived families in the midst of crisis, represent an important and costly, but limited, segment of government-sponsored activities.

The Congressional Research Service provides the following data on the funding levels in 1981 for the major federal programs incorporated in the Child Welfare system.

Approximately 62 percent of Title XX funds are devoted to direct child welfare services; thus the total federal expenditure for such services in 1981 was approximately 2.98 billion dollars. It is estimated that states and voluntary agencies expend an additional one billion dollars on Child Welfare. While other social and economic policies may not center their concern on the welfare of children, nonetheless numerous aspects touch on the lives of children and their families. For example, policies and legislation pertaining to divorce, custody, child support and

**TABLE 4–1  Federal Funding for Child Welfare Programs— Fiscal Year 1981**

| Program | Fiscal Year 1981 Funding Levels (millions) |
|---|---|
| Title XX services | 2,716 |
| Title XX day care | 200 |
| Title XX training | 75 |
| Child welfare services (Title 4–B) | 163 |
| Child welfare training (Title 4–B) | 6 |
| Foster care | 349 |
| Adoption assistance | 10 |
| Child abuse (state grants) | 7 |
| Runaway youth | 10 |
| Adolescent pregnancy | 10 |
| Family planning | 166 |
| Juvenile delinquency | 100 |
| Child abuse research and development | 16 |
| Child welfare research and development | 12 |
| Adoption opportunities | 5 |
| Head Start | 820 |
| Total | 4,665 |

*Source:* Congressional Research Service.

inheritance or economic policies governing employment and working conditions may affect the welfare of children as significantly, if not more, than those policies specifically directed at children's issues. Indeed, the unintended and accidental consequences of policy in widely disparate areas often have substantial effects on children's lives. Since the interests of children and families are usually secondary to other policy goals, such as economic growth, the control of inflation, or urban renewal, these effects should not be surprising. Indeed, it might be observed that children represent an underserved, publicly neglected group, without a voice in the political process through which social and economic amenities are distributed.

## Social Policies and Families

Child Welfare policies, as stated, tend to be residual, categorical, and aimed primarily at poor or dysfunctional families. On the other hand, policies directed toward families (which, of course, also have implication for the welfare of children) often imply a more expansive set of programs and social objectives that are virtually unlimited in their scope and nearly universal in their impact. The family policy question has stimulated broader questions touching upon the relationships between the family and the State, and between the family, community, and church. Also, the discussion of family policy has not only provoked the proposing of various models for government action directed toward families, it has also provided a convenient platform for groups to air their concerns over highly charged issues which relate to changing family life, such as increasing social acceptance of premarital sex, birth control, abortion, high divorce rates, and changing roles of women and men. Child Welfare professionals will be affected by the outcome of this dialogue since virtually all Child Welfare policies derive from government.

In this section the family policy debate will be analyzed in the context of changes that are rapidly altering family life. Three models of family policy will be discussed: comprehensive social planning, limited government involvement, and family impact. These three general frameworks are currently at the center of contemporary controversies about government's role toward maintaining family well-being, and each reflects a particular response to growing public concern about the power of professionals and the possibility of increased bureaucratic control over family life.

Despite common sources of concern, which are largely based on changes in marital demographics, explanations for the changes in family life, as well as the solutions advocated by various observers, differ markedly. Indeed the growing family debate suggests that once the focus of attention shifts from poor and marginal families to middle class, heated dialogue develops that touches upon the deepest social fears and aspirations of many groups. Families are viewed as the basic building block of our culture; they are sanctified and regulated as much by religious conviction as by secular mandate. Few individuals or groups are neutral when it comes to family life, since the experiences, values, and politics of most are at stake. Thus the family debate promises to escalate in a lively contest between political left and right.

American ideology and values have long stressed the inviolability of family life from conscious public intervention, except in extreme situations where families were incapable of fulfilling family responsibilities. The notion of conscious construction of family policies designed to strengthen and support family life has been anathema to policy makers. Not only might such a stance threaten traditional values, but the problems in formulating policies that might meet the needs of all families, regardless of their form, ethnicity, and life stage, are inordinately formidable. Nevertheless, many scholars and policy analysts have attempted to keep the family policy debate alive based on research findings that question the impact of various government policies on families.

## The New Family Policy Debate

In the past two decades, the protection and promotion of family life has been increasingly considered as an explicit, rather than implicit, focal point of social policy. This new policy discussion reflects the growing apprehension, seemingly buttressed by social science data, that the family is in urgent crisis. Concerns about child abuse, sexual mistreatment of the young, runaways, and other issues pointing to social and family breakdown, have contributed to increasing unease about the quality of life in our society. The sense that families are in desperate trouble springs from gloomy interpretations of demographic data and from a growing distrust of government. Policy studies conducted in recent years have supported the general apprehension that indeed, government initiated and directed social reforms may sometimes contribute to family problems rather than lessen them (Donzelot, 1979; Hubbell, 1981). The unprecedented focus on issues of middle- as well as lower-class family life that began in the 1970s derives, at least in part, from this alienation from public institutions.

As individuals have grown more suspicious of the public sector, they have sought security and reassurance in the privacy of the family. However, many believe that the private sphere itself is seriously endangered. Even as public capacity to identify and intervene in many family problems has expanded, the public has grown increasingly critical of the seeming failures of public and voluntary child welfare services to resolve social problems. Media reports of serious abuse not properly managed by protective agencies and well-documented deficiencies in the foster care system contribute to growing disaffection with services to families.

Disillusionment with government programs and intervention has contributed to growing suspicion of the helping professions. The new ethic proclaims that the work of professionals, even when well-intentioned, has iatrogenic or sociatrogenic effects, generating new and more serious pathologies even as they treat those they hope to help (Gaylin, Glasser, and Rothman, 1978; Illich, Zola, McKnight, Caplan, and Shaiken, 1977). Doctors are said to create disease through the misuse of medication or sophisticated scientific technologies, teachers "track" children into inappropriate learning levels, reducing their life opportunities and nudging them into antisocial behavior, diagnoses of pathology are seen as self-fulfilling prophecies rather than steps toward cure. This widespread concern about family life, reflected in popular media and in professional and academic circles, must be seen in the context of the much larger controversy now underway about the contours and purposes of the welfare state itself. In the United States, where popular commitment to social welfare programs has always been fragile because of the high esteem Americans place on values like independence, competition, privacy, and self-sufficiency, the outcome of the debate about family life and family policy will be of crucial importance to the development of future social policies.

## Family Life and the Welfare State

It seems indisputable that massive changes are occurring in the structure and functions of families, changes that have far-ranging implications for the future. These changes seem most apparent in the socializing and nurturant activities of families. Keniston and the Carnegie Council on Children (1977), for example, argue that contemporary families no longer have primary responsibility for the socialization and education of young children. New social institutions, growing professional expertise and hegemony, and the advent of flexible roles for women, they observe, have shifted many familial responsibilities to bureaucrats and professionals, turning parents into "executives" who coordinate and mediate the child's external world and arrange for appropriate interventions from legions of experts. Parents, however, often lack sufficient power or resources to adequately perform these tasks. As Keniston notes, American parents have little influence over the institutions on which they must depend and which have taken over their traditional functions. His solution is to empower them by reducing social disabilities, improving employment and economic status, and making public and voluntary organizations more responsive to parental pressure and needs. Lasch (1977), in a considerably harsher assessment, suggests that the authority and viability of families has eroded almost completely in the face of professional usurpation of family competencies. In his view, the family's confidence has been destroyed and its functions diminished by its being reduced to a consumer of specialized professional services.

In addition to significant changes in family functions, worried observers highlight a variety of recent trends that have transformed the structure of contemporary families. While family historians have, in the past decade, challenged the widely held and nostalgic notion that the extended family form was ever prevalent in our society, new data suggest that the traditional nuclear family may be an endangered species. Structural innovations in family life are now so widespread that few American families conform to the traditional norm of a nuclear family consisting of a working husband, nonworking wife, and two or more children. Replacing it today are a rising number of single-parent families, childless couples, couples with only one child, families with two working parents, homosexual couples, couples cohabiting without marriage, reconstituted families, and individuals living alone.

Though it is clear that roles, functions, and structures of families have changed dramatically in recent years, it is far less certain what these trends signify. Much disagreement can be heard among policy analysts as to whether or not families are in a transitional state shifting to newer, more workable forms, or whether indeed they are actively disintegrating. While some decry the sharp rise in single-parenting, the rate of divorce, and the numbers of working mothers as signaling the death knell of normal family life and wholesome child-rearing, others find in these indices a case for cautious optimism. Bane (1979), for example, notes that despite the rise in divorce, more children are residing with at least one biological parent today than 40 years ago. She notes too, based on recent research, that working mothers may not spend significantly less time interacting with their children than nonworking mothers. Moreover, many studies indicate that more than half the individuals who divorce remarry within five years. Thus, there does not seem to be defection from marriage and family as many claim, but rather changed expectations about the minimum gratifications to be expected within marriage and greater willingness to terminate unsatisfactory unions. Finally, though single parenting does appear to be on the rise, Giraldo and Weatherford (1978) found in their analysis that in 1940 *and* in 1977, 16.2 percent of all families were composed of a single parent and

83.8 percent were composed of a married couple. While divorce rates have risen parental mortality has declined, resulting in no net change in family composition over a 40 year period.

Perhaps the significance of the current debate about the condition of family life in America is demonstrated in the discussion among contending groups. Although concern about family crisis has been a component of American social thought for at least a century, it is only in the present era that this concern has appeared to envelop the entire spectrum of American families—middle-class as well as those of the lower strata—and thus to threaten the very core of American social life. Deviant family structures can no longer be localized in specific classes of families or ethnic groups, but are seen as endemic throughout society. This contemporary vision of families in crisis is a consequence, perhaps, of the fact that the normative standards traditionally used to assess individual and family strength leave little room for experimentation with alternative family forms. The framework of normality that has influenced our perceptions of healthy family life has been a potent, if unconscious, factor in the evolution of policy responses on the part of both public and voluntary sectors. Indeed, the ideal of "normal family life" can be seen as an integrating concept, linking various policy initiatives that do not focus directly on family life and that appear, at first glance, to be vastly disparate in intention and outcome. In considering the future relationship of government to families, the interaction of normative family values with the policy process becomes a crucial determining factor.

## The Development of Family Policy: Competing Frameworks for Action

Though the outlines of the emerging controversy about the appropriate role of government toward families are often vague and indistinct, several major themes can be identified. First, there appears to be agreement among many liberal observers that changes are required in existing policies and programs to make them more responsive to newly emergent family constellations. Problem-oriented, categorical Child Welfare programs targeted at the poor and the deviant are seen as ineffective in resolving the conditions to which they are directed. More importantly, they inappropriately narrow the focus of social welfare concerns to the casualties of a defective society. As long as welfare measures leave out working and middle-class groups, it is unlikely that effective political coalitions which support expanded or reconstituted social programs in areas such as day care or health care will develop. Equally important is the observation that as the lifestyles and structures of an increasing number of families diverge from traditional "normal family" ideals, social supports strengthening the ability these new family groups have to respond to new personal and social stresses are required. While there is little agreement about the specific mechanisms for providing these services, social welfare planners and theoreticians seem to be moving to make them available through public funding, though not necessarily operated by government agencies.

Three competing frameworks have emerged that best exemplify the options for future social policy development concerning families and children. These models are: a national comprehensive planning model; a model stressing voluntarism, pluralism, and minimum government intervention; and a "family impact" model.

Two well-known national policy perspectives are those of the Carnegie Council on Children and of Sheila Kamerman and Alfred Kahn, codirectors of the Cross-National Studies Program at the Columbia University School of Social Work. While the major priorities of the two approaches differ, the basic principles that inform their objectives are quite similar; they focus on the need for programs dealing with income inequality and unemployment and providing universal entitlements to a range of social services.

In a departure from traditional child-oriented social programs, Kenneth Keniston of the Carnegie Council urges a comprehensive approach directed at family life, concluding with the admonition that:

> . . . the goal of public action should be to change the context in which all families live, so that parents and children are freer to exercise their best instincts about the process of growing up. To this end, we propose that the nation develop a family policy as comprehensive as its defense policy. (Keniston, 1977:76)

Focusing primarily on the needs of the poor, however, Keniston places primary emphasis on a national income policy and full employment programs, which would increase the capacity of families to act vigorously in their own behalf in relation to large institutions. Kamerman and Kahn agree with Keniston about the need to deal with questions of income, but are more doubtful about the prospects for comprehensive family policies in the United States which do not take into account ethnic diversity and pluralistic perceptions about the role of government in the lives of families (Kahn and Kamerman, 1975; Kamerman and Kahn, 1978).

Still, in many of their publications, Kahn and Kamerman advocate an expansion of the social welfare sector through more generous provision of income, expanded child care and perinatal health services, and improved social services. In addition, they see the need for rationalizing and extending what they call the "personal social service system." Taking their cue from other Western nations that consciously establish programs to support family life while expanding the rights of individuals, they note the possibilities inherent in a widened view of social services, which accepts them as an important feature of normative family life.

> Recognition of the reciprocity between the family and formal institutions creates interest in the social services as support systems for average families as well as for those with "case" problems giving assistance to the handicapped child or adult while also buttressing the family as a "social service" instrument; providing personal social services to the aged while encouraging adult children in the supportive role and not stereotyping women as home persons or caretakers; offering advice, counselling, education and information to "average" people about everyday experiences, thus filling gaps created by changes in family and community life, and newly emerging norms. (Kamerman and Kahn, 1978:486)

Thus, in extending personal social services, coverage would include the nonpoor, whose periodic need for some kind of material or affective support, not easily available through normal market resources, could be met through easily accessible government funded social services.

In contrast to the explicit emphasis of family policy advocates on expanding public sector services, other more skeptical analysts, who share an abiding distrust of governmental services, urge caution in enlarging the scope of public programs for families. Though many analysts are in agreement that a wider network of services is needed, they recommend decentralization of those organizations closest to families and neighborhoods. The major framework best respresenting this view calls for the development of public policies that respect and strengthen diversity and pluralism while reducing the authority and power of large institutions and professionals. In this system, policy should strengthen voluntary, informal, and religious institutions, utilizing them as "mediating structures" which stand between individuals and the larger institutions of government and industry.

The concept of "mediating structures" as a framework for implementing social policies was suggested by sociologist Peter Berger and the Reverend Richard Neuhaus (Berger and Neuhaus, 1977). Berger and Neuhaus argue that public policy makers ignore the core institutions of American society which encourage independence, provide needed assistance, and protect against alienation. Mediating structures such as families, neighborhoods, churches, and voluntary associations encourage pluralistic identity and stand between the individual and the "megastructures" of society—big business, big government, big unions. These megastructures are "not helpful in providing meaning and identity for individual existence," yet they are an essential element of modernization and growth (Berger and Neuhaus, 1977:2). The dilemma is experienced on the level of the individual who is constantly balancing the requirements of participation in the megastructure—through work, for example—with other needs that tend to be met through the neighborhood, the church, and the family. Professionals, identified primarily with large bureaucracies and big government, tend to be enemies of mediating institutions, since by influencing the affective and nurturant needs of the individual they lobby the State to increase their own authority and thus that of government. In doing so, they reduce the importance of informal associations even as they claim that strengthening these institutions is their major objective.

For Berger and Neuhaus, social policies should encourage mediating institutions to assume more responsibility for the functions now performed by governmental agencies. Consequently, they advocate a less rigid separation of church and state which, while avoiding the establishment of a state religion, does allow public support for church-sponsored education, child care, and social services, as well as the extension of welfare state programs in ways which enhance diversity and pluralism.

These competing frameworks represent mainstream perceptions about the dangers and opportunities of widening the benefit structure of the welfare state. Kamerman and Kahn's view is perhaps most congruent with the post–New Deal historical tradition, which characterizes liberal reform. Their solution, though sensitive to the dangers of extending public services, essentially calls for an expansion of the welfare state, refocused toward family well-being and widened to include the middle class as well as the poor. Their prescription, carried to its conclusion, requires that comprehensive planning, rather than reflexive reaction to problems, should inform implementation of new programs. Berger and Neuhaus, however, see no way out of the destructive effects of programs operated by public bureaucracies except through intermediate institutions which empower new ethnic, racial, and religious groups. While attentive to the psychological need for identity and sociological need for participation and potency, their prescription is inherently conservative. By stripping the federal government of its power to regulate and provide services, they would allow sectarian and regional interests—often prejudicial to the interests of competing groups and to the dictates of an egalitarian society—to determine the structure and content of services. To be sure, their argument has great appeal to those on the left as well as on the right concerned about the misuse of governmental and professional power and the growing distance of public institutions from individual needs.

The third model is perhaps somewhat less controversial since it does not propose to expand government programs for families. The family impact concept, which emerged from the Family Impact Seminar of George Washington University in Washington, D.C., developed out of concern for the vast numbers of government-sponsored programs with direct impact on family life, which were estimated (prior to the Reagan administration) to be 268 federal domestic assistance programs. Family impact proponents suggest that there is no question that government programs affect families; rather the question is: "How do these effects manifest themselves within families?" Their primary objective is to develop a technology for assessing the impact of family-oriented services and laws and providing a system whereby such impacts would be considered by the Congress and executive agencies of government.

Though the family impact concept is appealing and appears to be more politically practical than other approaches for comprehensive family policies, in fact the difficulties in assessing family effects are quite formidable. Ordinarily basic research must precede policy analysis and, while much is known about many existing programs, available data may not be useful in predicting impact. Moreover, translating knowledge about research findings into enactable legislation is no simple matter. The process through which knowledge is translated into program is indeed circuitous—often the actual operations of programs defy the intentions of those who conceived and advocated the intervention. Moreover, the capacity to predict outcomes is far less developed than the ability to measure effects after the fact. These obstacles present a significant challenge to impact studies.

## The Politics of Family Policy

The welfare of children and Child Welfare are both deeply affected by decisions made and directions taken in family policy. But family policy, as is increasingly evident, quickly becomes caught up in ideological and political struggles.

Jimmy Carter, undoubtedly believing that strengthening and supporting the family was an issue around which there would be near universal consensus, made family well-being a central plank of his platform. Rather than consensus, he found a whirlwind of dissension and conflict, which characterized the 1980 White House Conference on Families. The fear of a strong federal presence, which would shape family life through the enactment of policies supporting the family, brought into action groups from almost every segment of our pluralistic society, groups that expressed deep disagreement concerning the state, function, and norms of the family. The conference itself almost foundered on bitter struggles around *defining* the family. Minority groups, feminists, single parents, and gays and lesbians feared that a white, middle-class, normative family model would be supported by federal policy and program, and that people in diverse lifestyles would be penalized. Further, civil libertarians feared that increased governmental intrusion into the private lives of people would increase the potential for social control and the exercise of undue power over dependent or diverse populations.

On the other side of the political spectrum, groups rallied to oppose the broadening of family definitions out of concern that the traditional family structure would be undermined and cherished values subverted. Conservative church groups also feared that increased intervention by an impersonal public sector would erode their authority, both moral and political; such groups tend to favor programs emphasizing informal helping projects and neighborhood-based (and neighborhood-controlled) services. They also support an increased blurring of separation between church and state whereby sectarian service programs are supported by public funds through contractual arrangements, leaving the primary control in the hands of the voluntary or sectarian group.

These political and ideological struggles over the nature of the family and the relationship between the State and the family have implications for the direction of policy and program in the field of Child Welfare. For example, narrow definitions of family that prescribe cultural norms for family life could easily lead to changes in public policy that would have major effects on child welfare. An attempt to shift eligibility rules for families receiving Aid to Families with Dependent Children, for example, might lead to attempts to reduce or eliminate benefits for single-parent or unmarried households. Custody decisions in divorce cases might lean toward the conventional partner, while definitions of neglect might be based on parental lifestyles. Minority families in particular might be confronted with restrictive definitions of child-rearing that could affect their ability to obtain critical social services. Further, concern about the nature and desirability of public surveillance over and intrusion into family life is central in Child Welfare programs and to practitioners, since many of these programs directly and forcefully intrude upon families. Decisions made in family courts, for example, are often based on the observations of social workers. In acting to remove a child from a neglectful home, or for that matter, return a child to the family, there must be a presumption that professionals are competent, non-biased, and fair. The liberal critique, which questions the excessive use of government and professional power, is a reaction to excessive and unjust public actions. Child Welfare is affected since all Child Welfare services depend upon public trust and professional discretion. Reduction of public trust in the efficacy of Child Welfare services could lead to a dramatically narrowed sphere of responsibility as well as an increase in monitoring by the judicial system.

In summary, when welfare state advocates speak of a crisis in the family and promote the notion of government aid to families, deep fears underlying any attempt to develop explicit policies affecting families are unearthed. Changes in values about family life, supported by minority groups and others, and the growth of more or less open alternatives to marriage and childbearing challenge conventional assumptions. Those groups which are more likely to be on the political left, as well as political conservatives, share the fears of some social policy analysts and theoreticians that it is difficult, if not impossible, to construct a policy framework that is neutral to alternative arrangements—one that does not, through penalties and rewards, shape family life.

Lifestyle questions share the stage with traditional ideological concerns about the centrality of the State to personal experience. In that sense, the apprehensions about future expansion of welfare functions, held by the left and the right, are congruent with the concerns of gay groups, feminists, anti- and pro-abortion groups, and others. However, though the debate continues, the overwhelming need for family supports, such as day care, health services, and income programs does not abate. The challenge for proponents of family policies is to develop frameworks that do not ignore the genuine apprehensions of all groups within the society.

## Family and Children's Policy and Legislation: The Current Scene

A brief review of the major thrusts of current Child Welfare policy and legislative initiative illuminates some of the issues discussed in this chapter and illustrates the way in which decisions made around these key issues shape public policy. Implicit in enacted legislation, as well as legislation under consideration, are views about the nature of governmental responsibility in the solution of social ills, where in the government such responsibility should be lodged, and whether the individual child or the family should be the focus of support and intervention.

One theme expressed repeatedly is the disenchantment with and distrust of government, large bureaucracies, and professionals as effective social problem solvers. This theme predates the Reagan administration and may, perhaps, be considered one of the causes rather than a simple effect, of the conservatives' capture of the Presidency. A few examples will suffice.

Most recently America has witnessed and continues to witness massive budget cuts in existing social welfare programs and a shift of responsibility to the states in the social welfare arena. This changeover has resulted in a major dismantling of the federal social welfare bureaucracy and a termination of the federal–local community partnership of the late 1960s and 1970s, a partnership which bypassed the often conservative state houses. Block grants, which replace categorical grants, transfer funds earmarked for expenditure in broad areas from the federal level to the states, without the specific categorical spending requirements that maintain federal direction and control. Although noncategorical block grants could offer the opportunity for better integrated and better coordinated services, the fact that funds have been cut at the same time is likely to stimulate competition for services among clients and providers. Thus, traditional coalitions are being strained and with attention focused on attempting to salvage funding at the state level and with the creation of deep political divisions between institutions usually allied, the moves in Washington to further limit programs and budgets may not receive as powerful and unified a response as would normally occur. (The potential impact of block grants in Child Welfare services is explored in detail later in this volume.)

Interestingly, one of the most important and farreaching pieces of legislation in the area of Child Welfare is a categorical bill, passed during the Carter administration, entitled the Adoption Assistance and Child Welfare Reform Act of 1980 (Public Law #96–272). Through the advocacy efforts of various child welfare interest groups, the bill has survived and has not as yet been collapsed into a block grant. This legislation, an omnibus categorical bill, embodies responses to many of the issues discussed in this chapter. First, implicit in the legislation is a strong family focus, as it is designed to encourage and support the maintenance of children in their own home and, when that is impossible, permanent placement in adoptive homes. The law was enacted, in part, as a response to the discovery that large numbers of children were adrift in the foster care system, moving from home to home with no permanent family ties. The bill paved the way for an increasing emphasis on the delivery of in-home services, the prevention of placement, and an expanded program of subsidized adoption.

Fiscal incentives, which in the past irrationally favored substitute care over in-home services, have been removed, improving agency capacities and funding to offer in-home care. Older children and those with special needs are permitted to receive adoption subsidies as well as medical care.

This bill, through an insistence on a number of accountability measures, also addressed the growing public concern about ineffective or even destructive intervention by the state and by professionals into the lives of people. For example, the act imposes strict requirements on the states for the use of new planning, administrative, and practice techniques that provide management controls, support, and supervision in individual cases. The act also features incentives for the states to develop a state plan for services and information systems that record the number and status of children in care. Further, professional authority is restrained considerably by the fact that the law mandates external, generally citizen or judicial, case review procedures to insure that there is a case plan for each child and that that plan is being used.

The trends to support family life and limit governmental and professional intrusion is dramatically demonstrated in another piece of legislation in the field of Child Welfare, a field which has been criticized for undue public intervention into private matters and the denigration and destruction of the family. The Indian Child Welfare Act (Public Law #95–608), passed in 1978, became law when it came to public attention that some 25 percent of all Indian children were not living with their families and 85 percent of those placed children were in non-Indian situations (Byler, 1976). This act, a major victory for Indian autonomy, returned the jurisdiction over and responsibility for American Indian children to the Indian tribes. However, the same double bind is created in this situation as in block grants when responsibility is shifted, but adequate funds to enable the discharge of these responsibilities are not transferred. Controversy around the Indian Child Welfare Act concerns not only the resource allocation but the sensitive issues of ethnic diversity and of parents', children's and the public's rights (Blanchard and Barsh, 1980; Fischler, 1980).

Family parental rights and family policy became the focal points for conflict and polarization through yet another package of legislation, the Family Protection Act (S–1808 and HR–6028), which has not been acted upon. This legislation also *selectively* expresses the view that government should stay out of family life, but says it in such a way that subtly constrains and shapes the form and nature of family life. The Family Protection Act is the conservative response to federally financed programs for families. First introduced in 1980 by Senator Laxalt of Nevada, the bill proposes to "counter the negative" direction of federal legislation for families by seeking to return power to families, religious leaders, and state authorities in order to discourage the teaching of unconventional values, behaviors, and sex roles in public schools that differ from "traditional family and community values." The Act would prohibit federal reimbursement to states refusing to approve school prayer and would permit the states to set attendance requirements and to regulate the integration of the sexes in school sports. It would remove the jurisdiction of the Supreme Court from these matters as well as eliminate the marriage tax and limit federally funded support for child abuse, spouse abuse, and juvenile delinquency programs. Finally it would redefine child abuse to exclude punishment provided by a parent, require minors to inform their parents before seeking birth control advice or venereal disease treatment, institute sanctions against homosexuals, and prohibit legal services attorneys from assisting in divorce cases. The Family Protection Act manipulates family policy in exactly the way pluralistic and civil libertarian spokespersons have predicted and feared. While the possibility of its passage—in its current form—is questionable, the bill does provide some insight into conservative perspectives on government.

## Conclusions

For the past few generations, rising prosperity and a sympathetic electorate have been associated with a seemingly benign attitude toward those in need, fostering the expansion of the welfare state and the social service system. However, both on the left and on the right, there has been growing disaffection with the programmatic approach of liberal welfare state interventions. Categorical and symptomatic treatment of social ills has led to a proliferation of poorly integrated case services that are increasingly directed toward the poor and the powerless, often without their permission or desire, while limited eligibility requirements for many desirable social services exclude and anger many citizens. The new, powerful conservatism of the current political period reflects a nostalgic, oversimplified vision of our society and is in part a reaction to the failure of aid programs that are often marginal in their impact and occasionally destructive. Loved neither by the rich nor the poor, supported mainly by professionals and bureaucrats who are themselves divided as to their efficacy and effectiveness, the embellished programs of the 60s and 70s are increasingly under attack.

The smoke has not yet cleared sufficiently from the first round of savage attacks on social policy to provide a clear view of the outcome. If there is anything to be learned from the political failures of the 70s and 80s it is that programs must ultimately provide evidence of satisfying the needs and desires of working people, as well as the poor, if they are to earn long-term support in the face of powerful and continuing conservative opposition. Lacking overall policy direction as a guide for legislative initiatives, programmatic approaches cannot address larger systemic questions often at the root of social problems. This requires a larger institutional context, such as the family, which directs attention to broader social conditions and requires consideration of the changing context of family life. Though raising the issue of family life energizes unwelcome constituencies, who demand solutions that are sometimes repressive and retrograde, the ensuing dialogue may eventually permit better resolution of many social policy dilemmas without necessarily compromising a reasonable family program.

Family policy emphasizes positive, planned, comprehensive approaches to family life and to social policy that enhance and assist children and their families, rather than defensive programs targeted to solving the social problems of specific groups, often by deterring deviant or unconventional behavior. Using a family policy model for initiating social policies changes the shape and substance of public discussion, since the dialogue must engage programs of universal applicability rather than those that affect a select few. Therefore, a family policy model opens the way to more radical programs and solutions to contemporary social problems.

In this century the United States has weathered previous periods of conservative reaction after which a consensus was reached about new directions for government and social policy. Thus, the conservative administration of Calvin Coolidge was followed by the emergence of the New Deal and four decades of interventionist government programs. That these programs no longer command the loyalty and commitment of Americans seems patently obvious, but, though they appear to have lost their constituency, there is little reason to believe that the loss is permanent or that the alternative is a passive laissez-faire state.

When the current tide has run its course, social welfare advocates cannot hope to return to the timeworn, incrementalist programs of the past. Bolder ideas, imaginative programs, and wide public dialogue propelled by a humane vision of public responsibility for families must be the core of future efforts in child and family welfare if they are to be of enduring significance. A family policy perspective offers an unusual opportunity for altering Child Welfare policy and improving the welfare of children.

# CHAPTER 5

# The Institutional Context of Child Welfare

CAROL H. MEYER

For a social institution like Child Welfare to be sustained and continuous, it must remain an open system. In times of social change, be that change progressive or regressive, institutions have to be sufficiently flexible and adaptive if they are to respond to and integrate such changes. Institutions have to expand or contract as political and economic systems demand. Sometimes they have to adjust their policy priorities and shift their practice emphases in terms of the populations or areas served to suit new funding patterns; often they have to redesign their services and staffing patterns to carry out new mandates. These are the stresses and challenges to which every social institution must adapt if it is to survive.

## Defining Child Welfare

Child Welfare is probably typical of all lasting social institutions in America. It has adapted to changes in society with sufficient energy to cope with external demands, yet its central purposes have remained essentially the same. Never a radical endeavor since its beginnings in America in the seventeenth century, the Child Welfare system has claimed a maintenance and residual function in the social service domain continually for over 300 years. It has changed its shape and its boundaries, it has redefined its goals and programs, but it has continued to perform in a narrow sector of society, escaping serious public judgments that were either excessively harsh or approving. This is not to say that Child Welfare has always carried out its social mandate, or even that the mandate has been unambiguous. Rather, Child Welfare as a social institution has, over the centuries, met a social need to provide supplementary or substitute parental care for children. This purpose is so necessary to society that, as in the institution of health care, social criticism is always balanced by the need for the continuation of the service. Thus, while Child Welfare has not been able to claim a totally virtuous existence in American history, it has persisted because it has done the job society expected of it.

The care of dependent and neglected children as an informal community activity has biblical roots: some say that Pharoah's daughter became the first foster parent when she scooped up Moses in the bull rushes. Throughout human history, attested to in historical texts, literature, and art, when children's own natural parents have failed them, the community has arranged for some system of substitute care. This activity continues to the present, although the definition of "parental failure" and other reasons for substitute care change, as do the groups responsible for arranging such care. Each era has generated its own concept of causation for child neglect and abuse, whether it has been immorality, poverty, mental illness, ego failure, or family breakdown. The seeming "cause" that has persisted over the centuries is poverty, for the Child Welfare system has always been a poor family's social service. The forms of substitute care have also reflected the knowledge and the social readiness of American communities to recognize the needs and rights of parents and children. Child Welfare services have ranged from almshouses, boarding out, institutions, foster families, adoption, and group care to day care and preventive work with families and children in their own homes.

Since the seventeenth century, these services have been variously provided by town agents, neighbors and relatives, paid child-care staff in institutions, and professional social workers. Although the nature of Child Welfare problems and services has changed over time, their presence remains permanent. As American society has become more urbanized and technical, what once were simple, informal, community-based supports have become professional services provided through social agencies. These represent the major changes: what has not really changed over the centuries is the community's stake in "their children," whatever ways it has delegated that responsibility. In our era social work carries the burden of planning, decision-making, and care.

Child Welfare is not easily defined, as the range and diversity of chapters in this volume suggest. It is primarily a social institution, underwritten by the public to meet certain needs that promote the welfare of children. Without this institution society would have to invent something to care for its dependent, neglected, disordered, and abused children. But child welfare is also an ideology, a commitment with religious, ethnic, and nationalistic features, because every defined group seeks to care for "its own" and to perpetuate itself. Children are seen as "the future" for many groups of people, and thus Child Welfare services can generate fervent commitments which reflect strongly held cultural and political values. The impact of these values on the conduct of Child Welfare services is enormous, making this social institution among the most vulnerable to the public's predilections. As is the case with health care or medicine, institutions with which Child Welfare might be compared, public values play an important role in determining the nature and direction of programs. Yet, in medicine, the presence of scientific evidence and the authority of the doctor can shape public opinion or sometimes prevail over many value preferences expressed by the public. This is not the case in Child Welfare; even though society has allocated responsibility for the welfare of children to a social service community, it has not let go of its direct concern with the ideologies and outcomes of the services.

Child Welfare persists, somewhat anachronistically, in the public's mind as a range of services with nonprofessional characteristics, services that are viewed as familial and extrafamilial, but so "familiar" and "self-evident" that the public continually questions whether special expertise is required or even appropriate in their performance. It is only because of the breakdown of informal arrangements for the performance of Child Welfare tasks that society has—with some ambivalence—permitted social work to assume the major service role. Even so the public, in the role of taxpayer and board member, maintains close surveillance of the Child Welfare enterprise, insuring where possible that its deeply held values govern the conduct of social workers.

Within this public context the profession of social work has defined a field of practice. Understanding the multiple influences of the public will contribute toward the reader's grasp of the uneveness and irrationality of some aspects of this field. Family services and Child Welfare are the only fields of practice in social work that are, for the major part, administered and staffed by social workers. They are primary practice fields for social workers, as opposed to secondary ones where social workers practice as adjuncts to their medical, psychiatric, legal, educational, and industrial hosts. As Child Welfare is a primary field in social work, the profession has the opportunity and the challenge to arrange services and staffing in accordance with "the best" of practice principles. However, as mentioned, social workers do not have a free hand to shape this social institution. Whatever is thought to be "the best" practice—whether derived from empirical study, practice wisdom, or theories of child and family development—it must balance with the public's interest. In Child Welfare, professional work is further complicated and compromised by the fact that its organizations and services are structured through political and legal processes. The professional who works in this field must have the courage to run down a field forested by rigid structures, unyielding policies, and uncertain mandates. The social worker who can manage this institutional and bureaucratic obstacle course, while remaining sensitive to the needs and requirements of the families and children of his or her clientele is the paragon professional.

The field of Child Welfare, like other fields in social work, can be defined by its service structure. Child Welfare is a multilayered structure: Its goals and purposes, the populations it serves, its staffing patterns, and its practices all flow from the interaction of three themes—unresolved issues of the funding, structure, and service focus of Child Welfare. One cannot make practice intelligible in this field without understanding their influence. The themes are: public, voluntary, and quasi-public or purchase of service *funding*; Child Welfare, family, and mental health field of practice *boundaries*; and universal and residual *services*. While these three dimensions of Child Welfare are always present, they achieve different configurations in different locations, and it is the particular configuration that defines and differentiates among the various local, state, and federal Child Welfare services, both public and private.

## Sources of Funding: The Public Sector

A Child Welfare agency totally funded by public taxation is mandated to serve all of the eligible families and children in the state, county, or locality it covers. A voluntary agency totally supported by private or philanthropic donations serves only those families and children whom the agency elects to serve, usually those who are determined as eligible by the board of directors or the funding community. In most American communities public agencies have become overburdened and have offered financial incentives to voluntary agencies to encourage them to share the workload. These incentives are called "purchase-of-service" contracts, and when voluntary agencies participate in these contracts, they maintain their voluntary structures and private funding sources, but assume a new kind of accountability to the public. Voluntary agencies that receive a high proportion of their income from purchase-of-service contracts might be thought of as quasi-public agencies. In some localities public funding may account for over 90 percent of a private Child Welfare agency's total budget.

Beyond the simple provision of money, funding, which is always a powerful tool in legislation, policy, and service delivery, has the potential to control and direct many aspects of Child Welfare. For example, the question whether policy-making and funding powers should be allocated to the federal or state governments attracts support for both sides. The final choice has a strong impact on who will be served, how adequately, and for what purpose (National Research Council, 1976). Proponents of federal funding and centralized authority argue that in a country as diverse as ours, many states do not adequately address the needs of families and children. Tremendous differences exist among the states in terms of the proportion of state budgets allocated to Child Welfare programs. Many social policy experts believe that the inducement of federal funding is needed to achieve equity for children and families.

When it comes to costly public endeavors (especially those that are primarily concerned with the poor), it seems that the closer the relationship between the service and the funding appear in the taxpayer's view, the more critical and niggardly the taxpayer becomes. Perhaps the competition for funding and personnel among public services—police, fire, sanitation, health, education, and welfare—is felt most keenly when the taxpayer is aware of concrete programs and expenditures for *others*, particularly any which might be intended to benefit the poor. While most public services are defined as meeting everybody's health and social needs, Child Welfare is conceived of as a service for poor and poorly functioning segments of the population. Support for federal funding derives partly from the concern that without federal support, Child Welfare programs would not be funded. On a more philosophical level, supporters of the idea of federal funding believe that children's welfare is a national responsibility, one that must be located in the Congress and executive arms of government to assure coverage in spite of local political, economic, or racial tensions.

On the other side, those who view the states as the appropriate source of policy and funding in the area of social services resist a strong federal role in the Child Welfare system, feeling that each state should take responsibility for service provision only within their own borders and that the citizenry should not be burdened with the social and economic problems of distant people. Further, those who advocate a strong state role hold the conviction that political power should be decentralized and the scope of the federal bureaucracy diminished. State funding, although decreasing the power and control of the federal government, does not necessarily promote local participation more than does federal funding, as was demonstrated in the innovative programs of the '60s and early '70s.

Another theme in American ideology concerns the location and control of social programs. Along with competition between federal and state governments for the control of service provision, there has been a recurrent belief, since colonial days, that the location of social programs under local or community control is desirable. Whether the community is defined by geography, ethnicity, race or religion, this heterogeneous country has always sought to locate Child Welfare services as close to the "neighborhood" as possible. Two quite different viewpoints underlie the notion of local control. The first viewpoint is that local communities, since they are closer to the conditions to be remediated and closer to people in need, can structure services more congruent to the diverse lifestyles, needs, and values of their populations. The second view favors local control and responsibility, based on the necessity of careful monitoring, in order to insure that resources are well spent and well used in situations of genuine need. This second perspective tends to promote the outcome described above, that the closer the connection between the funder and the recipient, the more cautious and critical the funder will be.

The Kennedy and Johnson administrations attempted to resolve the dilemmas inherent in funding decisions in another way, through the granting of federal funds directly to local communities, by-passing the state and, in many cases, even city and county governments. The "New Frontier" and the "Great Society" programs, which distributed the financial burden nationally but delegated control to small, local, often extra-governmental units, are now history, swept away by ensuing administrations that returned power to the states and terminated most federally supported local program efforts.

## Voluntarism and Program Support

The other sources of funding and locus of control of Child Welfare and other social service programs are found in the tradition of voluntarism which runs deep in American social thought. This tradition is expressed, particularly in the older states, in a parallel service system governed by citizen boards and exclusively supported, until recently, by voluntary contributions. The "community" in Child Welfare services may be variously defined, but can frequently be characterized as a group of people sharing a common interest. Although the vicissitudes of group interests can be played out in federal, state, and local structures, the most direct expression of group interests in Child Welfare programs is to be found in voluntarism, as groups of people with a shared interest found and support child-care programs which express and further those interests.

Religious fervor and the socialization of piety gave rise to the voluntary movement in the eighteenth and nineteenth centuries, and in child-caring programs the nature of the religious upbringing of children in care was a central issue. Religion formed the core around which many Child Welfare programs developed, and sectarianism and voluntarism continue to be strongly associated to the present day. The parallel structure of voluntary social services is particularly evident along the Eastern seaboard and in some of the older cities in the Midwest, where such agencies were entrenched before the exclusive development of public responsibility for social programs. The existence of these parallel service structures has important consequences for today's complex institutional context within which Child Welfare services are delivered.

Many of the voluntary agencies have long histories and established reputations that are well-known by the public and by professional social workers. Further, their religious affiliations have generated a kind of political power in local communities, especially with large religious federations of Catholic, Protestant, and Jewish agencies. To the extent that these federations, or agencies with commitments to particular ethnic or racial groups, remain supported solely by private, philanthropic funding, they present no ethical or professional issues to be addressed. On the contrary, in a heterogeneous society like America, the freedom to create private organizations to meet the needs of a particular population is highly valued. Those families and children who are fortunate enough to have behind them the supports of organizations of like-minded folk—based on neighborhood, religious, ethnic, or racial ties—reap the benefits of a support system not unlike an extended family. Controversy arises when these organizations do not have sufficient monies available and when they then seek public funds through purchase-of-service contracts. These contracts are allocated by the public agencies so that their own staffing and program resources can be supplemented by the voluntary agencies. Such a purchase-of-service arrangement, then, is a mutually agreeable system where each type of agency needs the resources of the other. In the case of the voluntary agency, its services are offered to the "public agency's children" in return for funding. The public agency, having received funds from the State to carry out certain Child Welfare programs, can use some of this money to supplement its often sparse services with the voluntary agency's services.

Controversy often occurs when the amounts of public funding are so large as to define the voluntary agency as a quasi-public agency, but without the accountability measures required of the regular public agency. Controversy and tension may also occur when the "public agency's children" are of a different race, religion, or ethnic background than the auspice of the private agency. These differences can lead to accentuated social and cultural distance between clientele and agency staff and policy-makers and to a lack of sensitivity on the part of agency personnel and programs to the culture and values of this new clientele.

In light of the existence of three types of funding of services—public, voluntary and quasi-public—each community in the United States can create its own configuration of service delivery. Recalling the impact of the public at large in the conduct of Child Welfare affairs, the public's role is often clearly expressed in the power arrangements of voluntary vis-à-vis public Child Welfare agencies. For example, in some states and localities, the salaries of the voluntary agency staff are higher than those of the public agency even though both agencies receive funding from the same public source. In such situations funds from private sources may be used in the voluntary sector to increase salaries. In other communities, the public agency plays a more significant role and that salary scale may be higher than in the private agency. Salaries account for a large portion of Child Welfare budgets because social services are highly labor-intensive. Furthermore, salary levels tend to be directly related to the quality of staff employed in the agency. Professional M.S.W. staff cost more than B.S.W. staff, and nonprofessional B.A. or A.A. staff cost the least of all. Therefore, the relationships between public and voluntary agencies, expressed by, among other features, differential salary levels, will then differentiate the level, type of preparation, and education of staff as well.

No model provides "the best way" to relate the public and voluntary agencies to each other. Depending on the community involved and the regard it has for the status of both public and voluntary agency, the two kinds of agencies might work out a truly supplementary arrangement, where overflow cases from the public agency, or particular cases in which the voluntary agency has particular expertise, are referred. In some communities research is carried out in the public agencies, while in others research takes place in the voluntary agencies. In some communities, the public agency dominates the definition of Child Welfare services system and practices, while in other communities the voluntary agency influences this definition. Unfortunately, in those communities where there has been a long tradition of voluntarism, a certain amount of "creaming" of cases takes place. For example, a more politically and professionally powerful voluntary agency may offer services that attract families that are easier to work with, while the public agency is left with a residual caseload. In communities where "creaming" of both staff and cases takes place, a serious service deficit can result. Some Child Welfare functions, such as protective services, must be kept in the public sector for reasons of legal accountability. In instances where the voluntary agencies have absorbed the highest quality staff and the highest public and professional regard, the public agency is left with less qualified staff and a poor reputation to work with the most difficult caseloads. With no planning and with no professional or public effort to raise the level of the public agency's work, a second-class system of services is perpetuated. This dual system of Child Welfare services has a very strong impact on practice.

In addition to issues of staffing difference, the ways in which communities arrange and emphasize public–private organizational relationships and particular services greatly affects both the nature and quality of those services. In the case of highly specialized agencies, the greater risk always exists that the definition of the family's issues and needs will be described in terms of the services valued by the agency rather than in terms of what would be most appropriate for the family. Assessment is, of course, a key aspect of all practice formulations; it is the process of understanding a problem or need and determining what can be done about it. But even this crucial part of the practice process is influenced by the nature of the service structure which is, in turn, a reflection of institutional interests. As so often happens in voluntary requests for service, a family can reach a specific agency by various paths: by accident, by word of mouth, by an inappropriate referral, or by chance because there are waiting lists at some agencies and not others.

To take a hypothetical situation, let us assume that a family with a behaviorally disturbed ten-year-old child is overwhelmed with extended family stresses and child-care responsibilities and is experiencing marital conflict. Agency A in a large Midwestern community offers foster care as its primary service, while Agency B in that community offers an array of family and children's services—foster care, adoption, homemaker, family counseling, and day care. In either case, family and worker may arrive at a common assessment, one which identifies a number of needs and difficulties and suggests ideas concerning the sources of those difficulties and potential resources to better meet them. The family seeking the service of the placement Agency A may well find the need for placement interwoven into its assessment, while the family approaching Agency B may find that placement can be prevented, because other services which may help meet the family's needs are available in or easily accessible to that agency. Child Welfare workers are all too familiar, for example, with the ways in which child and family needs are reinterpreted in court situations when it becomes apparent that the kind of residential placement recommended is not available.

What is the professional task in such situations? The social worker must "stick to one's guns," once having correctly assessed the family's need. The nature of the service should serve the family; the family should not have to define its need in terms of the nature of the service. If change must take place to bring need and service together, change efforts should be addressed to the service arrangements, not the assessment. Only in this way will practice in the field of Child Welfare become more professional.

While there is no model arrangement to follow, there are social and professional values that can guide choice. One can envision, under forward-looking social policy, the existence in every community of a well-staffed and highly regarded public child welfare agency offering a total range of services to families and children. Its size would be manageable, its staff would be professional, and its practices would be of the highest quality. In this model, the voluntary agency would supplement the public agency's services, would experiment with innovative services for which the public agency is not funded, and would play a complementary role with the public agency.

This analysis of the institutional context of Child Welfare began with, among other things, an examination of the impact of funding sources on the ways in which policy and practice become intimately entwined. To some extent, states arrange service delivery in their own ways, locating direct services on a statewide, countywide, or municipal basis. Sharing the field with voluntary and quasi-public agencies, public Child Welfare agencies are governed by federal legislation and statutes, funded in some programs by federal sources, and in the current era, increasingly by state sources. Maintaining a balance of authority and purpose among these often competing interests uses a great deal of professional and bureaucratic energy. Each level of government and each locus of service delivery commands its own public, so the practice of Child Welfare takes place in a staggeringly complex institutional environment.

## Boundaries among Fields of Practice

As other chapters have emphasized, Child Welfare is both a field of social work practice and a concept. As a concept it, of course, includes the notion of welfare. Conceptually, the welfare of children is not separate and apart from the welfare of their families. But discussing the field of Child Welfare and its relationship to family services is quite a different thing from the conceptually rational notion of family and child welfare joined in theory and purpose.

Given the child-saving history of the field of Child Welfare and the long preoccupation with protecting children from their parents, it should not be surprising that Child Welfare and family services have maintained rigid boundaries between each other. Their purposes, traditions, structures, funding sources, policies, and practices have always been different, and despite the current interest in family expressed in legislation and in agency policies, they remain apart. As the history of these two fields indicates, their roots had different sources: Services in the one field were often intended for "intact families" and in the other for placement of children. Over the decades the separateness of family-centered and child-centered practice become exaggerated as these two parallel emphases became institutionalized. One notable modern expression of the separateness of the two fields is the inability of the Family Service Association of America and the Child Welfare League of America, the two national service organizations identified with these fields of practice, to join forces. In the federal government, the interests of the field of Child Welfare, as well as those of children, have been largely identified with and represented by the Children's Bureau since 1912, while only briefly was there a Bureau of Family Services in the organizational structures antecedent to the current Department of Health and Human Services. When family services were highlighted in the federal structure it was mainly to deal with economic assistance programs, while the Children's Bureau always had a strong social service focus.

Aid to Families with Dependent Children (AFDC) is a prime example of a program in which public concern for families is expressed and located in the arena of public assistance. This program has been one of the most significant public ones on behalf of families, but, belying the title of the program, the field of Child Welfare has never included AFDC within its boundaries. The program has been considered a family or income maintenance program. In 1956 efforts were made to separate income maintenance from (family) service in public welfare agencies with the hope that quality supportive and rehabilitative services could be offered families without the subtle coercion implicit when such services are linked to income maintenance. But the expected expansion of these services never took place, with the result that throughout the country scant and uneven attention is paid to professional services to families not defined as Child Welfare services. Today, most public agencies continue to separate their Child Welfare functions from their general or family service programs, partly because of the unfortunate fragmentation in family and children's legislation and funding. When Title XX of the Social Security Act replaced Titles IV–A and IV–B, which addressed Child Welfare, there was some hope that child and family welfare rights might be integrated. However, public and agency interests in child welfare are institutionally bound, and the field of family services has not as yet come to a clear determination of its particular function, making the more specifically articulated Child Welfare provisions more observable in the political and professional arenas.

The ideal model (and name) for this field would be Family and Children's Services, as professional knowledge and principles seem to suggest. As observed, though, fairly rigid boundaries persist between the two fields of family and children's services, perpetuating a dysfunctional structure of services for both families and children.

When the Child Welfare field is looked at in relation to the field of mental health, the situation is equally problematic and the boundaries even more rigid. As in the case of families and child welfare, separating a mental health focus from a child welfare focus is very difficult. All social work practice concerns itself with mental health, as it does with families, but when it comes to definitions of *fields of practice*, differentiation among the fields becomes a political and economic issue, despite theoretical and conceptual affinities. As is the case in the fields of family and child services, mental health also springs from its own roots, psychiatry and child guidance. Mental health has its own funding sources and hospital and clinic service structures; even its purposes are defined differently from Child Welfare and from family services. In view of these separate features, the populations served probably tend to be different and service arrangements, policies, and practices pursue yet another separate course. Even though conceptually the welfare of children is inseparable from the welfare of their families and the welfare of both may involve issues and services in the mental health domain, institutional requirements suggest that the three fields of practice will remain separate from each other through the perpetuation of many kinds of boundaries. The field of social work itself, influenced by the public's desires and by governmental structure and funding, is seeking forms of specialization. It is unlikely that social work will adjust its structural boundaries, but no political or economic barrier interferes with the melding of professional concerns when it comes to considering the mental health focus or the family as the center of Child Welfare practice itself. In practice, families, children, and mental health have to be welded into a single focus.

As in the case of funding, the issue of boundaries among fields whose concerns impinge on each other adds complexity to the analysis of Child Welfare. Expressed purposes and latent intents pervade every field of service and every profession. Yet, central to the enhancement of functioning of social work practice in the field of Child Welfare is the integration of particular knowledge and skills that cross institutionally-defined barriers. Boundaries that artificially separate practice with the child from practice with the family must be removed.

## Focus of Services

As discussed in Chapter 3, the definition of Child Welfare as a field that should be concerned with the welfare of all children or only those most in need determines the general contours of program and practice. Funding, service structures, policies and practices are governed in significant ways by the kinds of populations served and vice versa; even the purposes of Child Welfare practices are reciprocally shaped by whether the services shall be considered universal and developmental or residual. Institutional services respond to the public's definition of those needs viewed as universal in an advanced, urbanized and technical society. What does everyone need that society must offer, without reference to particular eligibility factors beyond that of a status defined by the service? Public education for all children is an example, as is social insurance for defined groups of citizens such as the elderly or disabled. No such universal services are provided by the field of Child Welfare; the field has always been defined selectively and residually, usually meaning that families and children must be poor and unable to find their own resources, and children must be dependent, neglected, abused, or delinquent to receive services. Protective and other social services become available only after these life conditions are evident: They are not preventive (Jenkins, 1974).

One can imagine what universal or institutional services could be like if, in this country, we did not presume that Child Welfare was only for the poor and needy. One envisions accessible and available neighborhood transient housing for young people, respite resources for overburdened mothers, planned parenthood services, publically supported child-care services, and even family recreation and vacation opportunities. Were families thus supported through such universal services, in addition to family allowances, adequate housing, and opportunities for meaningful employment it is fairly safe to say that the need for residual child welfare services—services to meet those needs unmet after universal services are used—would decrease significantly.

The residual character of Child Welfare, which concerns itself primarily with the poorest and neediest families, may well have contributed to the prevalence of what has been called paternalistic attitudes toward clients in need of services. Services for the poor tend to be poor services, and traditionally the poor are viewed as recipients of benevolence, rather than as citizens with rights for services. It is a cycle not likely to be broken given the current conservative trend toward privatization of services, return of federal programs to the states, and ungenerous public attitudes to the poor.

## Patterns of Staffing and Education

Social institutions like Child Welfare are subject to the public's political will (or whim) and thus their nature and structure are politically inspired. In a society that does not engage in social planning, but rather leaves to chance or political pressure the development of service programs, the system—or non-system—of services can become nonrational. Child Welfare practice may be based on theoretical and traditional wisdom, but without recognition of the political realities or the institutional context of the field, the practitioner can fail to be effective. The themes and issues described—funding, boundaries, and the service focus—determine the content and outcome of Child Welfare programs. As we have seen, unevenness and lack of rational planning exist in the development of services, and change will not come about readily. Social workers in Child Welfare will continue to practice in this flawed milieu, but it is encumbent upon them to comprehend the political, social, and economic forces which shape the context in which they practice.

The effect of differential funding structures on staffing as one of the most crucial variables in provision of quality services was briefly mentioned previously. In view of the range of ways that the fifty states organize their services, the unfolding of specialization as a feature of the social work profession, and the uncertainties attendant on the Reagan administration and its focus on the most residual of all policies, the "safety net," or services for those who are excluded from all other services, it is not possible to describe the way staffing is or should be. The phrase most helpful under these conditions of fluidity and downward drift of Child Welfare programs is "it depends. . . ."

In a rational system, even with moderate funding, one could plan, accommodate to existing realities, and make many adaptations in staffing as well as in other program efforts. In a situation of uncertainty and outright governmental hostility toward social service programs and the people who use them, our discussion must, necessarily be theoretical.

In considering the nature and experience of the staff operating within Child Welfare, yet another aspect of the institutional context must be examined, albeit briefly, and that is the profession of social work and social work education. Child Welfare has been, for over a century, a social work enterprise and there has been a long, but unsuccessful, effort by some to "professionalize" the field, to staff Child Welfare agencies with professionally trained social workers and to infuse social work degree programs with the knowledge and skill that would support child welfare practice. Ideally, the model of staffing in agencies would be congruent with the model of social work education, and, as there are three degree levels, doctoral, M.S.W., and B.S.W., the tasks and functions necessary to carrying out child welfare services would be allocated in accordance with the educational preparation and practice skills of each of these levels. The fact is, however, that although leadership positions in the Child Welfare system are likely to be held by professionally trained social workers (National Child Welfare Training Center, 1982), a high proportion of line and supervisory staff, at least in public agencies, are unlikely to hold a social work degree (Shyne and Schroeder, 1978c). In fact, there is evidence that, until recently, the proportion of professionally trained social workers in public Child Welfare has been declining. The press toward the declassification of positions in the public sector has both reflected and hastened this trend.

Recently, in the professional community, in social work education, and in federal and local Child Welfare agencies, interest in enhancing education and training for Child Welfare practice has been expressed (National Child Welfare Training Center, 1981; 1983).

The situation in the voluntary sector is somewhat different in that the proportion of B.S.W. and M.S.W. staff is greater (Haddow and Jones, 1981) and professional interests are more likely to be expressed.

Many factors contributed to the disengagement between professional social work and public Child Welfare, a disengagement that perhaps reflects uncertain mandates offered by the public and, to some degree, ambivalence on the part of professional social workers concerning the job of a Child Welfare worker, particularly in the public sector. Furthermore, although in the early years social work education offered specialties, among which was Child Welfare, recent decades found graduate programs avoiding special focus on fields of practice. This tended to leave students less prepared in terms of the special knowledge and skill required for the delivery of Child Welfare services and also failed to stimulate their interest in entering this field.

Further, inevitable tension is found between schools and agencies, particularly because schools are future-oriented, as they must be in the education of students for lifetime careers. Agencies must be concerned first with maintaining their programs, and their goals will at times conflict with those of the professional school. Other tensions stem from the necessity in professional education to teach students to think critically about the content and purposes of their profession. The hard truth that confronts a traditional, political field like Child Welfare is that professional graduates challenge policies and practice of individual Child Welfare agencies, as well as the system itself.

Some changes developing in social work education, however, may develop greater complementarity between "town and gown" in Child Welfare. Increasingly, M.S.W. graduate programs are characterized by content concentrations, notably centered on fields of practice, of which Child Welfare, of course, is one of several. Many B.S.W. programs are enriching their offerings in this area or are considering a Child Welfare focus within their general programs (National Child Welfare Training Center, 1983). As the movement toward field of practice concentrations and increased attention to Child Welfare continues, it is likely that in a few years at least some M.S.W. and B.S.W. graduates will have a respectable grasp of this field and will set their professional goals within Child Welfare, and might at some future time have a greater professional impact on its conduct.

At the present time, however, inservice training remains the major educational device for line public welfare staff. This has important implications for the nature of the institutional context and potential for change. Staffing arrangements and training models, developed within an agency to serve that agency without input from the professional or educational community, tend to perpetuate existing structures, programs, and conceptions of practice. Further, this piecemeal approach perpetuates the non-system of Child Welfare services, because the practice is then defined agency by agency and locality by locality. Barring a strong federal presence and a professional curriculum that could define the job, the actuality is that child welfare services are whatever they happen to be, as determined by the local public service agency.

## Conclusion

Child Welfare as a field of practice has an institutional connection to every level of political organization from the federal government to the smallest community. Child Welfare services are engendered in the Congress and in state legislatures as well as by extragovernmental groups and citizen-inspired movements in public, voluntary, and quasi-public social agencies. Because of the exceedingly strong connection between the practices in the field and the public's values about children and families, Child Welfare has always been a field shaped by those values. Attitudes toward the poor, toward child neglect and abuse, and toward delinquency and teenage pregnancy influence the laws, policies, and service arrangements governing the conduct of this field, and rarely are public attitudes toward the potential Child Welfare clientele as socially advanced as are professional values. Yet, in this socioeconomic-political milieu the profession of social work has assumed a primary role.

In a short period of time, measured in decades as compared with the three centuries of child welfare services in this country, the professional community of practitioners and academicians, with the support of the Children's Bureau, has attempted to professionalize this field. In this instance, "to professionalize" means to be cognizant of policies that affect practice, to broaden the focus of services to make them more universal than residual, to seek an improved balance between localized and (necessarily) parochial public interests and rational, research-based recommendations, to upgrade staff, and to strengthen education and training for Child Welfare practice. The balance between public and professional interests and viewpoints must be maintained in this system of services that is so visible and so close to the heart of the public. That is the special challenge of workers in Child Welfare. This field, old as it is, is still pioneer country to professional social workers, and that fact alone, in a technical society such as ours, is an attraction to those social workers who seek to have an impact upon a field of service that is deeply rooted, but still maturing.

# PART II

# Knowledge for Child Welfare Practice

The topography of the complex world of Child Welfare has been charted in the preceding section. We now examine in more detail the major systems that command the attention of the practitioner in Child Welfare, that is, the community, the family, and the child. In doing so, we will explore some specific areas that have particular salience to this field, including research on child abuse and neglect and the workings of the legal system as it pertains to children and Child Welfare.

As the title implies, this section will present the reader with information and facts needed by every knowledgeable Child Welfare practitioner. Our title contains an assumption that we have some notion about what that necessary knowledge is and where to find it. The title also assumes that there must be some general understanding of what *knowledge* itself is—that is, what information exists that may be distinguished from theory, from value or preference, or from purpose. Neither of these assumptions is defensible. Not only would it be both naive and presumptuous to specify the necessary knowledge for Child Welfare, but, we believe, it would be appropriate at this stage to question prevailing assumptions about what knowledge itself is. The key distinction, which is widely accepted in social work and perhaps most articulately made by William Gordon in a now-classic article, is one between knowledge and value. *Value,* according to Gordon, concerns what is preferred or wanted, whereas knowledge "denotes the picture man has built up of the world as it *is, a picture derived from the most rigorous interpretation they are capable of giving to the most objective sense data they are able to obtain. . . .* Thus knowledge refers to what, in fact, *seems to be,* established by the highest standards of objectivity and rationality of which the human being is capable" (Gordon, 1965:34).[1]

The assumption generally made is that knowledge has to do with ideas or propositions that can be verified or confirmed, while value has to do with what is wished for or desirable. Compton and Galaway make a further distinction between knowledge and *theory,* proposing that knowledge consists of "discrete facts" while theory "is a set of related and logical propositions that orders and relates facts into some sort of meaningful whole" (1979:41). Theories, then, are cognitive maps for making sense out of what is objectively measureable.

Recently there have been stirrings of a meaningful debate in the social work literature over the epistemological stance taken in social work and social science research.[2] Some practitioners are questioning the prevailing positivist epistemology, which spawns research models noted for their objectivity and rigor and which assumes that natural science offers us our best models for understanding human and social phenomena. This paradigm or world view is dominated by an empirical stance; knowledge or "truth" is defined as that which can be observed, that which is derived from sensory experience. In this world view, seeing is believing, and mathematical symbols, rather than human interpretations or meanings, most accurately represent reality. Rarely is it acknowledged that a commitment to an empirical, positivist, truth-seeking stance is in itself a way of interpreting the world, a way of constructing and making sense out of an experienced reality that cannot be separated from what is studied.

There are, of course, very powerful consequences derived from one's epistemology, which influence what is defined and accepted as knowledge. One's epistemology shapes what one chooses to try to understand or "know" about human behavior and the social environment, what one sees as the causes of behavior, indeed what assumptions one makes about human nature. It guides *what* questions are asked and *how* the questions are posed—that is, what one chooses to look at and what it is one chooses to find out about it. The "measurement" criterion which dominates the quest for social work knowledge, in our view, while valuable for seeking some kinds of understandings, has tended to dichotomize thought from action, emotion from reason, and subject from object, reducing human beings at times to sets of isolated functions in turn isolated from the environment around them. Current models of research tend to separate the knower from what is to be known, making sharp distinctions between the data (clients) and the data gatherers (us, the professionals).

In our view, the so-called scientific method is itself a construction of reality, a second-order concept which makes its own limited models of things and which itself has become a model of the world which is assumed to represent reality. We tend to agree with Berger and Luckmann (1968), who argue that much of reality is not objective, but rather exists outside of science and cannot be separated from the subjects who continually construct what Weber has called "webs of significance." Man indeed, says Geertz (1973) is suspended in these webs which he himself has spun and continues to spin as we watch. Much of human reality is symbolic, and thus the study of humankind requires that we move behind a search for laws of function and structure to an interpretation of meaning.

What is needed are methods of seeking knowledge which foster understanding of the interconnectedness of the personal and social, of class and culture, of history and the present, and particularly of the meanings events have for those who participate in them. The requirement that concepts be defined in quantifiable terms or that approaches to helping can be experimentally validated has meant that those theories of human behavior which are broad, comprehensive, inclusive, and transactional, thereby difficult to "test" or validate, are often viewed as inferior or unacceptable. This state of affairs, argues Heineman (1981), is an example of using methodology to beg substantive questions. Perhaps we are, once again, coming full circle, getting ready to concentrate less on the distinctions than on the similarities between knowledge, value, and meaning; we should not be so quick to apologize for our lack of distinctions and we should propose that knowledge cannot meaningfully be distinguished from the values and purposes which make social work practice unique. What is accepted as knowledge is shaped by those values and purposes. Therefore, we need to welcome complexity, to include, not exclude, to find ways to interpret "wholes," not parts, and to recognize that there is no such thing as an inner or an outer, but only some shifting experiences between the two. Our dichotomies and partitionings, however scientifically rigorous, distort rather than explain or interpret.

Clearly our own world view has influenced how we defined and drew the boundaries around the complex of the child and the family in Child Welfare, which in turn influences the parameters of the knowledge and theory considered relevant for practice and the choice of thinkers presenting their interpretations of that knowledge. Knowledge which supports practice is taken from a variety of sources. It is borrowed from the social sciences, particularly from psychology, sociology, social psychology, and, to a lesser extent, anthropology. It is drawn from other professions, from medicine, particularly psychiatry, clinical psychology, economics, and law. It is also gleaned from the profession's own experience, its history, practice, and research and thus includes knowledge about social work practice, policy, and programs and about those special populations and social problems that have been of particular concern to social workers.

Each of the authors turns the lens to magnify one or another dimension of the child and family-in-environment complex; they are comprehensive, open, and transactional in their thinking and look to many ideas and sources to understand multilayered phenomena.

In this volume, we can only present a sample of a much more complete body of knowledge for the Child Welfare worker.

In the first three chapters, Carel Germain, Jo Ann Allen, and Patricia and Robert Pasick discuss the major systems of concern to the Child Welfare practitioner: the community, the organization, the family, and the child. Although each is authored by a different contributor, the chapters share an ecological perspective as they collect and integrate information from a wide variety of sources. Throughout, each of the authors adopts a transactional perspective, attempting to clarify the dynamics of his or her own focus for the others and for the larger society. Thus, although these systems are presented separately, a common ecological perspective places the child as an integral part of the family, and the family in the larger context of the community and the organizations which with these systems are connected.

Germain coins an acronym, CARE, which describes both the outcome and the ingredients of the creative, mutually adaptive, "goodness of fit" processes that take place between people, systems, and the larger environment. CARE symbolizes the four concepts of competence, autonomy, relatedness, and esteem for self. Communities and organizations can be CARE-ing and can support CARE-ing qualities in small groups, families, and individuals. Germain outlines some of the major concepts essential to the understanding of communities and organizations and brings these to life through examples from practice.

The CARE-ing potentials of families are also central in Allen's presentation of the family in its role as the primary provider of social services. Beginning with the important issue of the definition of the family, Allen presents an overview of the state of the family in the ecological environment of today's America, a stressed, yet adapting, coping, and remarkably resilient system. She then trains her sights on the family itself, drawing upon knowledge and theory from many family theorists to teach us various ways of understanding this unique system.

An ecological and developmental perspective shapes the Pasicks's discussion of the child. Considering the latest research on child development, the Pasicks avoid the either-or arguments that have long plagued theory in this area and adopt a view that characterizes the development of the child as emerging from circular processes involving many variables, such as nature and nurture, parents and child, family and environment, and the child's cognitive and emotional characteristics. Their presentation includes examples of transactions that have major significance for Child Welfare practice and programs, such as the finding that the social support of a mother by close others (father, extended family) is the best predictor of secure mother–infant attachment.

The final chapters in this section draw together information about two different, but intimately connected, areas that are particularly salient to Child Welfare practice. First, Giovannoni explores the issue of child abuse and neglect on the societal, institutional, and familial levels. She examines how children suffer from systems which fail in their CARE-ing functions and how the economic and social arrangements in our society have discriminated against poor children and children of color and their families. In examining familial neglect and abuse, she first tackles the complex value issues that underlie definitions of mistreatment, then reviews societal and social service responses to abuse and neglect. She ends with an examination of research that contributes to our understanding of the complex social phenomenon of child mistreatment, of epidemiological trends, possible causative factors, and the relative efficacy of different interventive approaches.

In the final chapter in this section, Hardin, who comes to these issues from his position as attorney and child advocate, spells out in concise and practical terms the legal processes that ultimately determine the destiny of families and children and describes both the Child Welfare agency's and the practitioner's role in those processes. Although coming from a different perspective, this chapter is highly relevant to the two which preceed it since, in the final analysis, families are permanently separated or reunited through action in a court of law. Family continuity is maintained or disrupted. Family membership may be altered. Further, definitions of neglect and of abuse ultimately are operationalized on a case-by-case basis by court decision. Throughout, Hardin emphasizes the grave responsibility of Child Welfare agencies and workers in these legal processes, particularly in the thoughtful gathering and reporting of information.

# CHAPTER 6

# Understanding and Changing Communities and Organizations in the Practice of Child Welfare

CAREL B. GERMAIN

The welfare of children must be considered a public or community, as well as a family, responsibility. While we rely more and more on institutions outside of the family to meet our needs for health, education, and well-being, little attention is paid in the child welfare field to the role of the community and its institutions in the abuse and neglect of children. In fact, relatively little of the practice literature in child welfare addresses either community work or organizational innovation by line staff.

In situations of child abuse and neglect, attention is largely directed to natural parents on the assumption that the source of the problem is in the psychopathology of the parents or other caretaking perpetrators. Gil (1975) pointed out that such an emphasis obscures the etiological functions of other levels of human organization in the social problems of child abuse and neglect. Such levels include institutions and formal organizations, social and economic policies that neglect the health and well-being of millions of children, and societal and cultural values, and media systems that support the use of violence and force in family and national life and in the management of international conflict.

If social work's historical concern for social justice and a caring society is to extend to the nation's—and the world's—children, then all social workers must become their advocates. For the Child Welfare worker in particular, community work, including efforts to introduce organizational and institutional innovations and to influence public policy on behalf of children and their parents, must become a central concern of practice.

This chapter is a beginning attempt to redress the imbalance in Child Welfare practice—between a strong focus on personal change and a weak one on environmental change—with particular attention to the community and the organization. Three assumptions underlie the discussion. First, practice tasks related to community and organization require a shift from an emphasis on particular individuals and families to a particular population. Second, ecological ideas can help social workers reach toward a more useful balance between personal and environmental characteristics and between personal and environmental interventions in practice. And third, commonalities in concepts, principles, and skills exist across practice with individuals, families, groups, communities, and organizations. The first and second assumptions will be examined in the next two sections. The third will be explored in the sections on community work and organizational innovation.

## Population as the Unit of Concern

To undertake community work and organizational innovation, the practitioner must be able to shift focus as needed to a particular population without losing sight of the individual or primary group. For practitioners educated for and/or experienced in face-to-face practice with individuals, families, and formed groups, a shift of concern to the facelessness of a larger population may be difficult. In the same way, of course, practitioners educated for and/or experienced in practice with large populations may find it difficult to shift focus to particular individuals and families.

The concept of population in an ecological perspective refers to a human aggregate in which the individuals comprising it share one or more characteristics (Hawley, 1950:77–79). In the case of child welfare, several popularions can be specified ranging from the totality of persons receiving service and providing service within the Child Welfare system to just the children, just the biological parents, all families, or all substitute caretakers receiving Child Welfare services. Such populations may be expanded to include, or may be distinguished from, persons in those four groups who need, but are not receiving, Child Welfare services because they have not entered the system. Various population segments can be further specified, such as all abused or neglected children, all foster children, all adoptees, all single mothers, all one-parent families, or all minority foster parents. For purposes of this chapter, emphasis will be placed on that segment, within the Child Welfare population, consisting of biological parents and their children, whether practice is geared toward goals of keeping children and family together, maintenance of parent–child involvement during placement, or re-unification. Nevertheless, many of the practice principles regarding community work and organizational innovation are applicable to other segments or the Child Welfare population, including foster parents, adoptive parents, teenage and adult adoptees, and child-care staff.

What are the characteristics of this segment of the Child Welfare population? A review of Child Welfare statistics (Pelton, 1978) estab-lished that the vast majority of the biological families in the Child Wel-fare population live in poverty. While child abuse and neglect are found in all levels of society, they are more prevalent among the poor and most prevalent among the very poor. It is also likely that other reasons for children's entry into the Child Welfare system, such as parental illness or death, financial factors, and other stressful situations, are associated with poverty as well. Middle-class parents are able to purchase services that all families require for raising children, especially during times of stress. But many poor parents consistently face a lack of needed ser-vices, or may not be eligible for services until after trouble comes. Help is often rendered too late to prevent further stress or even family breakdown.

Pelton's review also revealed that child neglect is twice as prevalent as child abuse; within the category of neglect, leaving the child alone or unattended occurs in 50 percent of neglect cases. He also asserts that leaving a child alone in a poverty environment, rife with hazards, is much more dangerous to the child than being left in a middle-class environment. For minority children, the Child Welfare system presents additional hazards. Keniston (1977) reports that in South Dakota, Amer-ican Indian children are ten times more likely to be placed in foster care than other children. "Where other types of data are available, they show the same trends: for example, minority children enter foster homes in disproportionate numbers, and they are more likely than their white counterparts to remain in the care of the state without being returned to their families or adopted" (ibid.:33).

Most children and their parents in the Child Welfare population are living in or near poverty with the attendant conditions of poor nutrition, dangerous housing, deteriorating neighborhoods, inadequate schools, and poor systems of health care. Children have little or no political and economic power, hence their rights are rarely a matter of national in-terest or concern. Most parents in the Child Welfare population also lack power—as well as social respect and access to the opportunity struc-tures of society—because of discrimination based on ethnicity, sex, and poverty. Powerlessness surfaces as a characteristic of this population, then, suggesting that a focus for community work and organizational innovation is empowerment at individual and group levels (Germain, 1985; Solomon, 1976).

## Ecological Ideas

Before proceeding to the analysis of intervention at the community and organizational levels, it is necessary to examine certain ecological ideas and their assumed pertinence to such interventions. Ecology is the science that studies the relationship between organisms and their environments. As a metaphor for practice designed to replace the disease metaphor or deficit model, its concepts have been discussed elsewhere (Germain and Gitterman, 1980). The emphasis in this chapter is on the reciprocal nature of such person–environment relationships, on stress and coping, power and powerlessness, and on such positive outcomes of person–environment exchanges as competence, autonomy (self-directedness), relatedness to others, and self-esteem or sense of identity.

Exchanges between people and their physical and social environments go well when there is a good fit between people's rights, needs, goals, and capacities, and the qualities of their environments. Such a fit permits optimal growth, health, and social functioning and also promotes the growth-supporting capacities of the environment (Dubos, 1968). Among the positive outcomes of past and present exchanges when the fit is good is the development of such human characteristics as competence, autonomy, relatedness, and esteem for self—or what will be referred to henceforth as CARE-ing qualities of individuals, families, communities, and even organizations (Germain, 1979a).

### Stress

When the exchanges or relationships between person and environment do not go well people's growth and functioning may be impaired. Environments too may be adversely affected by those various technological, social and cultural processes, characterized by the seeking and abuse of power and by insensitivity to human and environmental damage, thereby further undermining people's growth, health, and social functioning. A poor person–environment fit leads to emotional, physiological, and/or social stress. Stress is generated by a discrepancy between a perceived demand (or a harm or a loss) and one's perceived internal and external resources for dealing with the demand (Cox, 1978; Lazarus and Launier, 1978). What will be experienced or perceived as a stressful demand depends on, in addition to the nature of the environment, such personal factors as age, sex, culture, past experience, vulnerabilities, physical and emotional states, and the personal meaning attributed to the demand. Stress therefore differs from challenge in that challenge is a demand associated with anticipation of mastery. Challenge, associated with positive feelings, may even be sought, whereas stress is associated with such negative feelings as anxiety, depression, helplessness, low self-esteem. Stress, then, expresses a particular person–environment relationship; there is a poor fit between people's needs, rights, goals, capacities, and the qualities or properties of their environments.

Stress and the coping capabilities for dealing with it are significant variables in Child Welfare practice. Most parents and children enter the Child Welfare system because they are experiencing demands that exceed their personal and environmental resources, or because institutions or individuals in the environment have been stressed by the parents' or children's behavior or by indications that children's needs are unmet. In the latter circumstance, service is usually mandated and often unwanted, adding to the family's stress. Stressors common to members of the child welfare population are: poverty; institutional oppression based on color, ethnicity, social class, gender, and age; and systems of work, no-work, or undervalued work (including child-rearing). Society generates these stressors that require intervention on the level of public policy. Other stressors, such as social isolation and lack of external resources, can often be diminished by intervening at community and organizational levels.

Social isolation characterizes many biological parents and their children in the Child Welfare population. Most poor families withstand the stresses of living in impoverished, harsh environments, partly because they are connected to strong mutual aid systems and informal helping networks (Stack, 1974; Valentine, 1978). But many biological parents in the Child Welfare population lack connectedness to relatives, friends, or neighbors, perhaps because of one or more of the following circumstances: frequent moves and transience; lack of work and hence of workmates; the alienating circumstances of life in high rise public housing and the absence of physical arrangements to support network formation (Germain, 1978); as well as low self-esteem, fear, and suspicion. A low degree of relatedness often stems from (and contributes to) a lowered sense of competence, autonomy (self-directedness), and esteem for one's self. Low CARE-ing qualities are associated with powerlessness, but they can be buttressed by an empowerment orientation to intervention—at individual, family, community, and organizational levels.

## Coping

The subjective experience of stress evokes coping efforts. And coping expresses a person–environment relationship because it requires both personal and environmental resources for effectiveness. The almost infinite variety of coping strategies are said to fall into four general modes (Lazarus and Launier, 1978) which are directed either to changing the person–environment relationship or to managing negative feelings aroused by the stress that may interfere with successful coping or both. They may be focused on the self, the environment, or both, and may be oriented to present or future demands, or both. The four modes are: information seeking, direct action, inhibition of dangerous or impulsive action, and drawing on intrapsychic resources.

Each mode represents a person–environment relationship or exchange. For example, information needed by a person for dealing with the stress must be provided by the environment. Taking direct action requires that the environment provide adequate time for planning and trying-out strategies; it must also provide opportunities for making decisions and taking action on one's own behalf in important matters. The important action of turning to others for help, for example, requires the presence of social networks, natural helpers, self-help groups, or mutual aid systems, as well as the formal network of services and resources— income support, employment, health care, or transportation—for meeting such needs.

Inhibiting dangerous or impulsive action (such as the self-destructive use of alcohol or drugs, or family violence) depends in part on incentives, rewards, and the restraining structures provided by social and emotional supports in the environment. Throughout all systems, natural or informal support networks act as buffers in mediating the experience of stress and as aids to coping activities (Cassel, 1974). Among people exposed to high and prolonged stress, those embedded in natural support systems tend to have lower levels of physical and emotional symptomatology than their counterparts without such connections. Cobb (1976) attributes this effect to the fact that network figures convey to the stressed person that she or he is esteemed and valued and is part of a system of exchange.

When coping activities are effective, the demand will be met fully or partially, and the stress will be reduced, eliminated, or mastered. The usual person–environment fit is restored or even enhanced. However, when coping activities are ineffective because of insufficient personal or environmental resources, then stress is likely to continue and even intensify. Marked, unrelieved stress can lead to physical illness, emotional disturbance, or social disruption in family and community life, including child abuse and neglect. Such outcomes of stress and insufficient coping resources create further stress, increasing negative feelings and lowering self-esteem still more, in a circular feedback loop. Stress begets stress, and coping failures reduce coping resources and lower self esteem, increasing anxiety, guilt, depression, rage, and a sense of powerlessness. These feelings lead to behaviors which elicit negative responses from the environment that then intensify the negative feelings, leading to an increase of the behaviors that ultimately bring the family into the Child Welfare system.

*Practice Implications*

Intervention must be directed to removing or reducing the stress and/or strengthening the internal and external resources for coping with it. Circular feedback loops or "vicious cycles," must be interrupted and supplanted by benign cycles of self-confidence, competence, self-directedness, and relatedness, eliciting new favorable environmental responses that then bolster the changes in behavior in a reciprocal or circular manner. Work at community and organizational levels, as presented in later sections, can help with this task.

In summary, the paradigm of stress and coping suggests that the Child Welfare practitioner's interventions with children, biological, foster, and adoptive parents, and child care staff are oriented toward (1) removal, reduction, or amelioration of stress; (2) supporting the problem-solving function of coping by teaching such skills as parenting, negotiating environments, assertiveness, and interpersonal relationship development; (3) help in managing negative feelings and elevating self-esteem through empathy, supporting adaptive defenses, and easing maladaptive ones in the context of a trusting relationship; (4) providing information about child development, environmental resources, or other information a family may lack; (5) furnishing opportunities for decision-making and action within an adequate time frame; (6) helping to inhibit dangerous action through consideration of consequences, the development of alternatives, and, where needed, by limit-setting; (7) restoring connections to relatives, friends, neighbors, church and other groups, if the person or family is interested; and (8) helping to obtain needed resources from the formal network of services. Such individualized helping efforts, where engaged in jointly with clients, can enhance CARE-ing qualities.

Helping efforts oriented to achieving the outcomes defined above, while necessary, are not sufficient. In addition to such work with individuals and families, efforts must be made to ensure that the community and the Child Welfare organization alleviate, rather than exacerbate, stress and support, rather than undermine, coping efforts. Both the community and organization are salient elements of the environment affecting, at every turn, the processes of stress and coping.

## The Community

One can define the community in many ways. In this chapter community is defined as a geographic locale, "a relatively small unit of territory," and "the structure of relationships through which a localized population provides its daily requirements" (Hawley, 1950:180). An urban community therefore might be defined as a neighborhood, a housing project, a block or two of apartment houses, or an elementary school district; a rural community might be considered a village or small town, including persons living in the countryside but dependent on the village or town for resources and social connectedness (Cox, 1979).

The community consists of aspects of the natural world (especially in rural areas) and of the built world of urban and rural structures of different kinds and purposes. Thus the community is a physical, as well as a social, environment. A neighborhood possesses a culture or subcultures of its own which may or may not be congruent with the culture of the larger environment in which it is embedded. It possesses a web of norms and values, and knowledge and belief systems which may be somewhat homogenous, as in an ethnic enclave, or may be quite heterogenous and even seriously conflicting, given the patterns of migration in and out of communities and neighborhoods in today's mobile world. Rural and some urban communities may also be units composed of residents having a sense of common identity and belonging to a recognizable collective life that has a recognizable geographic boundary.

## Community Development in a Rural Setting

The following case example illustrates community work on behalf of families and children through which a rural community and some of its stressed members enhance their CARE-ing qualities. This case is reported by a worker in the State Division of Welfare in rural New England, who participated in the entire process.* Clearly her starting point was her concern not only about her own particular clients, but the county's entire population of biological parents whose children had been placed in foster care because of abuse or neglect. She states:

> In over 75% of all abuse and neglect cases in the county in 1979, professional counseling for the natural parents had been ordered by the district court. Only one family followed through on a weekly basis, but any learning or insight the family gained was not transferred to the parenting tasks. Court-ordered referrals seemed useless. Most parents feel bewildered, and they cannot initiate comfortably a new relationship with yet another authoritarian bureaucracy. For them, the mental health center is a "foreign place" and there is a perceived threat to parental rights and privacy. Their dignity is further assaulted because they equate the required counselling

---

*I am grateful to Marilyn Fraser for so generously sharing her work with me.

with "being crazy." Such a system is a good example of clients having to fit their problems into existing agency structures and processes instead of the other way around. My own agency operated on a traditional base of making single home visits and continously recommending "professional counselling" for abusive, neglectful parents. It assumed that non-MSW social workers who comprised the child welfare staff were not qualified to provide "intensive insight counselling" (Fraser, 1980).

Here a need affecting the population of abusive, neglectful parents was identified: The lack of *appropriate* services made it difficult for such parents to ready themselves for the return of their children. Individual troubles were raised to a public issue. The worker's concern for this population was shared by her colleagues on the interdisciplinary Suspected Child Abuse and Neglect (SCAN) team. Several alternative solutions might have been considered, such as an advocacy effort with the community mental health services for outreach programs designed for the specific needs of these parents, taking into account their fears, an intra-agency change in the district office of the state welfare department to redefine the social worker's role as one of providing guidance and instruction in parenting and homemaking skills, and mobilizing and strengthening natural or informal helping systems. In this case the third solution was selected; not only was it viewed as the most feasible but it was considered to be more beneficial to the population involved because of its potential for their empowerment and because it represented a shift away from the deficit model. With a clear definition of need and a potential solution in mind, interested members of SCAN formed an independent task force, the Rural Community Resources Group (RCRG) to initiate a community process. RCRG was composed of the state placement worker, an outreach worker from the local mental health center, a social worker from Child and Family Services, two nurses from the Visiting Nurses Association (VNA), and the Director of Volunteers in the Protective Services Program. The worker further describes the project:

> Because our practice had already taught us the value in natural helpers serving as primary familial supporters and role models, we decided to assist communities in developing their own informal resources. The specific resource to be developed would be decided upon by the community itself. Two communities were selected, and I was designated to work with the rural town of Pittsfield. There were several reasons for choosing Pittsfield. Although it has only 2617 inhabitants, it has one of the highest percentages of low income and AFDC families in the county. It also has one of the highest referral rates for child abuse and neglect. Furthermore, in 1979 the teenage pregnancy rate was 10% higher than that of the county as

a whole. Statistics obtained from the State Bureau of Vital Statistics showed that the number of teenage births had risen dramatically:

| Year | Births |
|------|--------|
| 1975 | 27 |
| 1976 | 34 |
| 1977 | 44 |
| 1978 | 46 |
| 1979 | 63 |

In spite of these striking figures, support services for parents were not available. There were no group day care centers, parents' groups, training courses at the high school level, or family planning services. The only service available for parents was a monthly well-child clinic conducted by the Visiting Nurse Association. All other formal services are twenty miles away in the nearest small city, but the lack of transportation is a formidable barrier. Residents also recognized these lacks. For example, several protective services clients had repeatedly expressed a desire for periodic relief from parenting tasks. In a mothers' discussion group recently sponsored by the VNA, all the mothers expressed an interest in further opportunities to meet together around shared concerns. The family nurse practitioner at the local physician's office, when contacted, attested to the needs for respite services and for improved parenting skills which were felt by her clientele as well (Fraser, 1980).

Several steps were taken simultaneously. Ten mothers, including some from the VNA group, and some protective service clients, met weekly with the RCRG during May and June. There was immediate agreement on the goal; a drop-in parent–child center, perhaps a cooperative, where children could be cared for a few hours a day or week and where mothers could seek information and find a sympathetic ear. Both respite and improved parental functioning were seen as desired outcomes.

Many suggestions were offered by the mothers: organizing a clothing or toy swap, a toy and book lending library, the enlistment of elderly residents as volunteers, and teenagers for child care experience with high school credit, or building experience for shop students. Mothers and the RCRG together decided on a needs assessment in order to canvass and engage as many community members as possible in the project.

The mothers volunteered to canvass the residents in a door-to-door approach, using a questionnaire. (See Form 6–1.) Other questionnaires were left at the two grocery stores, the free swimming pool, and the physician's office. Posters were made and distributed by several mothers, and a news article was written and published in the local free newspaper. (See Form 6–2.) Inquiries by interested parents were directed to the VNA in order to capitalize on its positive image, while keeping a low profile on the State Department of Welfare and the Community Mental Health Center. This would also help to avoid defining any participants as clients, especially as protective service clients. The overall aim was to plan with the community residents, not for them, and to identify and support the natural leaders. We spoke at a meeting of the Pittsfield Advisory Council, to a group of influential residents and secured their support for the center. The director of Community Development was contacted and he assisted us in locating four vacant sites. We hoped to make final arrangements on a visible and accessible site by September so that the program could begin. We undertook a search for seed money as we anticipated the eventual need of a coordinator, supplies, and building maintenance. Various community residents were helping with this task, some approaching the trustees of a local trust fund, others approaching the officers of the local bank and businesses and civic clubs for donations. I approached the State Welfare Division which has a new grant for direct services in rural areas, and administrators agreed to accept a proposal from us (Fraser, 1980).

The center for mothers and their preschool children was opened in the fall and was located in the fellowship hall of a local church. A grant of $25,000 was received from the Governor's Comprehensive Children's and Youth Project to support this and another center. The centers are open one morning a week, providing self-planned programs and discussions for parents, child care, and transportation services. The programs will be extended to two mornings a week as interest grows (Fraser, 1982).

Six practice principles and strategies appropriate to community work can be drawn from this rural illustration. First, the unit of concern is conceptualized as the Child Welfare population in a given community, not the individual client(s) of a particular worker. Second, relationship building was informal and took place in the course of task-focused activities, as the worker attended meetings, engaged in informal discussions, and generally made herself known in the community. She developed an atmosphere of trust, and talked of community strengths rather than weaknesses. Third, assessment included a range of variables. She familiarized herself with the physical layout of the community, its social structure, demographic composition, and norms and values. She secured documentary evidence pertaining to teenage pregnancy, and child abuse and neglect. In urban areas more data might be necessary and could be obtained from such sources as Census materials, maternal and child health services, morbidity and mortality rates, and school dropout rates.

Fourth, community members directed and shaped the project. Alternative solutions were considered, and the most feasible was selected by the members of the Child Welfare population and by other parents. They were engaged in defining the problem, considering alternative solutions, selecting the goal, planning the timetable for tasks, and carrying out those tasks. The Child Welfare worker and her colleagues on the RCRG served as advisors and resources to parents and other community residents.

Fifth, the community itself participated in the assessment process. A needs assessment was considered necessary by all concerned to gather the data needed for engaging the support and participation of the influential members of the community and for seeking grant support. Plans for program monitoring and evaluation were devised for the same reasons and to insure that the program remained responsive to the needs and interests of the mothers.

Sixth, as many segments of the community as possible were enlisted: informal leaders, officials, business and civic persons, clergy, the physician, and the press. Informal and formal systems of support in the community were skillfully linked, enhancing the positive image of the VNA among the population and in the total community.

## The Outcome: CARE

The outcome, a needed respite and support service, was a beginning step in a longer process of empowering the mothers—and empowering the community itself by creating a more nurturing environment for its residents. Solomon defines empowerment as the ability "to manage emotions, skills, knowledge and/or material resources in a way that effective performance of valued social roles will lead to personal gratification" (1976:16). Grosser and Mondros (1985) state that participation in community action by individuals who are isolated, unaffiliated, and without knowledge or influence, leads to their personal growth, skill acquisition, and to institutional and political accountability.

Personal growth includes the enhancement of self-esteem and competence and the increased energy and power that comes through joining with others with similar interests and concerns. Citizenship skills that may be acquired include group decision-making, the building of constituencies, and taking and utilizing leadership. Such community organization activities also teach participants about the structure of communities and the processes through which they operate and can be changed. Such skills and knowledge become sources of personal power, enhancing a mother's ability, in this case, to increase the responsiveness of her environment to her needs, rights, and goals. Yet another outcome, that of bureaucratic accountability, will be addressed in the next section.

In addition to enhancing the CARE-ing qualities of the mothers in the programs, the same qualities were strengthened for the community. Competence has been defined as effective interaction with the environment (Maluccio, 1980; White, 1959), including the ability to change the environment for oneself and others. A competent community "is one in which the various component parts of the community (1) are able to collaborate effectively in identifying the problems and needs of the community, (2) can achieve a working consensus on goals and priorities, (3) can agree on ways and means to implement the agreed upon goals, and (4) can collaborate effectively in the required actions . . . a community that can provide the conditions and generate the capabilities required to meet the above performance tests will be competent to cope with the problems of its collective life" (Cottrell, 1976:197).

Elements of such competence include commitment to the community, which develops when people see that what the community does and what happens to it affects their lives and values, when they have a recognized role in the community and when they see positive results of their efforts to participate.

Total community autonomy does not really exist in contemporary society. But communities do differ in the degree of control they exert over their own affairs and the degree of interdependence they establish with the larger environment to secure needed resources. Autonomy, or self-regulation, is also reflected in the ability of the community to make use of social workers and other resource people by retaining the decision-making function and acting to achieve community goals.

Relatedness refers to the sense of caring and social respect provided by component parts of the community to one another. Relatedness also involves the strength of social networks, the presence of natural helpers, and the extent of mutual aid systems. Many impoverished communities are laced with informal support systems (Keefe, Padilla, and Carlos, 1979; Stack, 1974; Valentine, 1978). Such community strengths make it possible for people to survive the conditions of poverty, unemployment, and other inexorable stressors of a harsh environment.

Esteem for one's community or a sense of community identity may already be present, or it may need to be generated. The sense of identity may be a negative one, as in some urban housing projects (Germain, 1978) or single room occupancy hotels (Shapiro, 1970), or it may be a fractured one in communities where migration patterns have led to conflict among age, ethnic, or religious groups or to transiency. Participation in successful community action can create among its participants a sense of esteem for and pride in their community.

In working at the community level on behalf of a Child Welfare population, the practitioner must assess the CARE-ing qualities of the community. Their absence means that the helping process must be carried out in a way that fosters their development. Their presence makes the practitioner's tasks easier and the family's burdens lighter. In the case of relatedness, for example, neighbors or relatives nearby may be available for needed foster care, thereby maintaining biological and social continuity for the child and reducing the pain of separation for parents and child (Laird, 1979).

## Community Development in an Urban Setting

In the next illustration, the community is a housing project in an urban ghetto where fear and suspicion prevail, and hostilities, deprivations, and conflicts characterize the residents' daily lives. Glaser (1972) developed the concept of stairwell societies in his work in a Boston housing project whose CARE-ing potentialities had been stifled by the nature of the physical setting and the social environment. "A stairwell society simply consists of all those families who share a common entrance and exit in the public housing project" (1972:160). The author's examples focus on the resolution of interpersonal problems among the stairwell families and of their shared concerns regarding maintenance and recreation. Nevertheless, the concept lends itself to engaging residents receiving child welfare services and their neighbors in a participatory process of mutual aid and environmental change. Taking successful action together on common needs and problems, with the support of the Child Welfare worker, can lead to the positive outcomes mentioned in the previous section. Such needs and problems might include security, safety (traffic, or screens for windows), school relations, child care, park clean-up, transportation, health care, and welfare arrangements.

Techniques suggested by Glaser are applicable to other kinds of urban communities, such as trailer courts and blocks of tenements, or to rural environments, such as migrant labor camps. He advocates the use of the home visit to each family to learn what concerns they have about their shared life space and to engage their interest in meeting with neighboring families around such issues. These meetings should take place in the community in a participant's home and it is important that the worker does not lead the process, but serves primarily as resource person. In this role, the worker helps the residents identify needs, set priorities, select goals, and initiate action. The projected goals should be attainable within a specific time period.

Full participation in the problem-solving tasks is encouraged. Role play, modelling, and direct teaching can be utilized to strengthen problem-solving and communication skills. The focus is on strengths, not deficits. Such powerless groups, who may feel both helpless and hopeless, are empowered when their options are increased and they are able to take some control over their environment. Among the child welfare population, these experiences can lead to greater confidence, a sense of mastery, and a feeling of connectedness to others. As passivity decreases, the achievements may be generalized to family relationships and parenting patterns as well.

With prevention in mind, Pancoast (1980) and Collins (1980) describe community work finding and working with natural helpers in neighborhoods. These neighbors are enlisted to help in the prevention and treatment of child abuse and neglect by working with families in at-risk situations. Pancoast suggests how such neighbors can be located, enlisted, and then linked to the families. In such community work, the Child Welfare worker matches resource to need, attempting to extend the neighbor's scope of helping through sensitive consultation and support.

Collins (1980) describes how this is done in a series of illustrations. She believes that such consultation enables the natural helper to handle similar problems that may arise in the future without further need for consultation. In addressing the issue of increasingly limited financial support of services, Collins points out that partnership with natural helpers extends services in an economical way.

Help by natural helpers and mutual aid systems, mobilized and supported by the Child Welfare worker's community work, reduces isolation; gives recognition to parents; encourages parent–child activities; provides information about children, neighborhood, services, and resources; encourages the exchange of resources among neighboring families; and enhances parenting capacities (Cochran and Woolever, 1980). Viewing the community and neighborhood as social contexts and as sources of help enables the worker to consider how they can be used to buffer stress and enhance coping among the Child Welfare population. Indeed, helping to build collective strength and social connectedness where none existed before may be the most important help the Child Welfare worker can provide.

An inevitable question is how can the already overburdened Child Welfare worker spare the time that community work requires? Fraser, whose work was described earlier, reports:

> The first problem I encountered was how to convince my immediate superiors that any time involved would eventually be worthwhile for our clients. There has only been intervention on one level, after the fact of abuse or neglect, and preventive services are non-existent. The Division of Welfare has never hired a community worker nor a group worker, and any deviation in traditional services would require a series of administrative approvals. However, my student status, requiring new learning experiences, won the day (Fraser, 1980).

This experienced worker made good use of her student status. But practitioners may find the challenge more difficult, especially in times of fiscal constraints. Some workers undertake community work in addition to their assigned case responsibility. For example, a Child Welfare supervisor in urban New Jersey developed a three month program working in her district office with biological mothers receiving protective services, after ascertaining their interest through home visits, telephone and mail contacts, and consultation with their workers. The mothers, of several different racial and ethnic backgrounds, decided on a combination of lessons in sewing and ethnic cookery and discussion groups on other shared interests related to child-rearing. The mothers planned and carried out the program themselves. The worker served as a resource for making community arrangements, providing a meeting place, gathering information, and she also obtained a small fund from her agency to cover food costs. The mothers later reported that their feelings of loneliness had been reduced. They had made friendships which they felt would continue (Zucconi, 1975).

Other practitioners, understandably, may feel that their limited resources of time and energy are insurmountable obstacles to undertaking community work. A Child Welfare worker who helped organize a community coalition, Parents and Children Together (PACT) providing prevention and treatment programs in child neglect and abuse, experienced the demanding nature of community work (Griffith, 1979). But she had anticipated this and had persuaded her agency beforehand to allow her the needed time away from her other duties. She succeeded in interceding with her own agency to initiate an innovation that would benefit the Child Welfare population and others in at-risk situations. This example leads us to consider the Child Welfare organization not only as an element in practice, but as target of change as well.

## The Organization

Bureaucratic organizations are social structures designed to get tasks done through a rational division of labor and a hierarchical structure of authority which operates in the interests of efficiency, objectivity, and fairness. In business and industrial organizations, the tasks are geared to the goals of production and profit, but in welfare, health, and educational organizations, the tasks are geared toward service, resource provision, and/or behavioral change. Over time and as a function of their large size, these latter organizations may develop the very problems they were designed to correct. The number of levels of the hierarchy may increase to the point where decision-making is slowed. Because of size, huge organizations may need to substitute written for face-to-face communication, and the organization may be awash in a sea of memos that no one has the time or inclination to read. Staff and staff–client relations may become depersonalized. Policies, procedures, and job descriptions may become increasingly rigid. Consequences include the dehumanization of clients and staff alike, a subversion of the original service goals as they are gradually replaced by goals of organizational maintenance, and even abuses of power and insensitivity to human need. The question is, then: How can the line worker influence the organization to change its behaviors, technologies, or structures, if its service function is being carried out inadequately (Brager and Holloway, 1978)?

## Change within the Organization

Traditionally, organizational innovation has been initiated by those in authority, to be carried out by those in face-to-face contact with the users of the service. Sometimes line staff resist imposed change, especially if it conflicts with personal or professional values and commitments, but often, unfortunately, in a passive way, which doesn't improve services. Sometimes staff may bend a rule, by-pass a policy, or invoke a favor from another, quid pro quo, in order to meet the need of a particular individual, family, or group. The strategy is often effective for that client, but does nothing for the population of clients who may be suffering from the effects of the same rule or policy. This rule bending may even obscure organizational ineffectiveness.

Loyalty, fear of the employing agency's response, unwillingness to see negatives in a system of which one is part, all make locating service problems in agencies other than one's own easier. It is also easier to undertake advocacy for a client with some other organization, such as the housing authority, school, hospital outpatient department, or the social security office. Social workers in Child Welfare perform that kind of case advocacy very well, and it is important that they continue to do so. But it is also necessary that they act to reduce service problems affecting groups of clients in their own agency. "Bucking the system" without the knowledge and skill required can be self-destructive and can lead to repeated failures and feelings of helplessness and hopelessness. However, in the 1980s, perhaps in part out of past failures, the profession has amassed the knowledge, skill, and experience to achieve modest, and perhaps incremental, change by agency staff members at lower levels of the organization.

KNOWLEDGE. Understanding how bureaucratic organizations work is a prerequisite to helping them work more effectively. Organizations, like people, are embedded in social and physical environments with which they must maintain adaptive relations if they are to grow (a typical organizational aim, not necessarily "good"), let alone survive. The environment shapes the goals, structures, policies, and functioning of the organization and, reciprocally, the organization has an impact for good or ill on elements of its physical and social environments. Societal belief systems regarding families and children, as well as local norms and values, affect the level of public support and interest in the work of Child Welfare organizations. Public attitudes in the community may reflect an ongoing concern and interest in program effectiveness. Or interest may be ambivalent, only emerging in response to a tragic incident of parental abuse or the revelation of scandalous conditions in a child-care institution. Typically, interest subsides when an investigation is scheduled.

Legislative and judicial processes at federal, state, and local levels affect directly the financial support available for service provision, staff training, and program development, and the structures, policies and procedures adopted by the organization. Regulatory bodies, such as state departments of health or welfare, federal granting institutions, accrediting bodies, such as the Child Welfare League, professional groups such as National Association of Social Workers (NASW), and advocacy groups such as the Children's Defense Fund, can be potent forces in the organization's environment. For example, the Connecticut Child Welfare Association, an advocacy group of concerned private citizens and professionals, had considerable impact on that State's public and private Child Welfare agencies through testifying before legislative groups, contributing to the development of model laws, and heightening public awareness of the needs of children and the incidence of neglect and abuse in the state. During the 1970s, with grant support from the federal Office of Child Development, the Association, led by the Board of Directors and the executive director, a social worker, carried out a number of demonstration projects that were instrumental in improving Child Welfare practices in the public sector. Service gaps, however, continued to exist.

In order to address the problem, this advocacy group designed an unusual project as a small part of an overall effort to achieve coordination among seven state departments mandated to serve children. A new governor had replaced the commissioners of five of those seven departments, and the new commissioners had had little opportunity to become acquainted with the other departments. Moreover, the seven staffs had long complained about the lack of communication and coordination among the seven child-serving departments.

On the assumption that elementary and obvious devices are frequently overlooked and that "breaking bread" together is a base for communication, the Association decided to host a series of six monthly luncheons for the seven Commissioners. All accepted, and most came regularly. The Commissioners had been assured that their attendance would have "no strings attached," no publicity for the program would be sought, and no formal agenda would be presented. Two Association Board members served as hosts each time, rotating members across the six luncheons, but no staff members were present. The Commissioners had been advised at the outset that an evaluation interview would be held with each of them at the end of the series. The evaluations revealed that five of the seven rated the series as "very helpful" and two rated them as "fairly helpful." Five felt that an agenda would have been helpful. The Commissioners commented that they had learned about other services, ironed out some problems, and were able to engage in frank and productive discussions. (Dille and Warkov, 1975)

Groups of a more informal nature, such as Parents Anonymous, foster parent associations, and associations of adult adoptees, have varying degrees of influence on the organization. The presence of competing agencies serving the same general Child Welfare population may stimulate more effective functioning or may stifle the organization's efforts to provide responsive services by draining off staff and resources directly or through turf struggles. The demographic composition of the community with respect to ethnicity, race, religion, age, and its formal network of services, shapes the perceptions and expectations exerted on the organization.

The development of new technologies in Child Welfare may serve as a positive force toward organizational change or may induce a defensive and rigid process of protecting the status quo. Local and national media may be supportive or critical of the organization's programs and staff, or of Child Welfare efforts in general. For the most part, the media is characterized by its neglect of Child Welfare issues except at points of crisis as mentioned above, and rarely reports on an agency's or the field's achievements. Finally, and most importantly, the condition of the economy and the political climate have profound effects on the day to day operations of the organization and the level of support on which it can count.

It is often difficult for a member of the line staff, particularly in a large, complex agency, to comprehend the nature of these and other environmental forces that exert pressure on the administration to move in one direction or another or not to move at all. Yet such awareness is essential since environmental conditions will affect the organization's receptivity to proposed change. Just as the organization must maintain an adaptive balance with its environment, it also must maintain an adaptive balance among its internal elements. In a large agency these might include the various departments, specialized units, and occupations and professions, all of whom compete for scarce resources of funds, space, power, and status. Buffeted by these internal forces, administration may make decisions based upon factors not always visible to or understood by line workers. Again, understanding these internal factors is essential as they too affect receptivity to innovation since they involve values, interests, preferences, and attitudes.

These internal elements comprise the social structure and its formal and informal systems of operations. The formal refers to the *arrangement of roles,* usually pyramidal in shape although sometimes flattened, with authority centered at the top. Information is expected to flow upward so that decision-making can be based on it, while directives for task performance and role behaviors flow downward. A dimension of this formal arrangement is *power* and its centralization (Hage and Aikin, 1970). The formal system also refers to the codified policies and procedures that govern the operations of the organization, including its external and internal relationships. A second dimension of the formal system is its *rules.* The formal system is also characterized by *status*—having the power to distribute rewards including promotion, pay raises, office location, and other perquisites and amenities. Knowledge of these and other dimensions of the formal system reveals potential barriers and potential access points for introducing and implementing organizational change.

Side by side with the formal system exists the informal one, with its parallel dimensions. Informal influence corresponds to the dimension of formal *authority* and, like *authority,* it yields *power.* Informal *customs, traditions,* and *norms* correspond to the dimension of formal *regulations.* They, too, are forceful rules regarding job performance and other organizational behaviors. Informal *prestige* corresponds to formal status, and has its own rewards of deference and respect. Knowledge about how the informal system operates reveals the presence of previously unrecognized resources for the line worker interested in organizational innovation. Influence and prestige—garnered through professional competence, commitment to the service ethic, interpersonal skills, and the exchange of professional favors—are essential to a successful change effort. Informal traditions and customs, including reciprocal support in staff relationships, can be drawn on throughout the change effort.

SKILLS. What is involved in influencing the organization to increase its responsiveness to clients' rights and needs? Part of the answer lies in acquiring politically-oriented, influencing skills that are different from helping or therapeutic skills (Brager and Holloway, 1978; Patti and Resnick, 1972; Wax, 1971; Weissman, 1973) although such helping skills as empathic communication and supportive measures may also be brought into play in organizational innovation. But the success of the change effort also rests on phases and processes that parallel those involved in working with individuals and families. Further, as is the case in working with clients, workers attempting organizational change must be aware of their own motives, values, beliefs, and attitudes toward the organization. This knowledge will help insure that they are acting on objective assessment of client need and organizational functioning and not out of personal issues regarding authority, territoriality, or anger at adminstrators for perceived insults. Effort to maintain self-awareness also permits workers to "hear" the content of objections to the change voiced by the opposition. Brager and Holloway (1978) observe that sometimes such content points to important potential negative consequences of the change not otherwise considered.

PREPARATION.  In the beginning phase, preparation starts with the identification of a service problem for one or more of one's own clients. The assumption that the problem exists for many other clients of the agency must be validated and documented. Documenting the existence of the problem may be done through examination of case records, reports by client groups, and exchanges with other staff about their practice experiences. Once the extent of the problem is established, the worker considers possible alternative solutions or change goals, possible ways to achieve each of them, and the feasibility and potential consequences of each. The most feasible is then selected as a tentative goal with a tentative plan for attaining it. Brager and Holloway note:

> Since changes in people often occur without appreciable effect on other elements in the organization, when all other things are equal, people-focused change has the least impact. It is, therefore, most appropriate as a short-term intervention in a longer-range change effort rather than as the ultimate objective of a change. Changes in technology, on the other hand, are likely to affect a myriad of other factors; interpersonal relations, staff work load, authority arrangements, communication patterns, and the like. And since in one sense the structure *is* the organization, changes in one aspect of structure are potentially able to impact every other aspect of the organization. (1978:23)

An example of people-focused change is a staff workshop on group work skills. In the absence of structural changes to encourage and support the use of groups, such training may be ineffective. An example of technological change is the introduction of a team approach in work with biological families. The team consists of trained volunteers, homemakers, nutritionists, and social workers on call to the family twenty-four hours a day. An example of structural change is the moving of the social work staff out of the administration building in a child care institution and into an individual office in each treatment cottage as a way of improving cottage life (Peterson, 1980). Also, the introduction of a parent organization project for parents of children in substitute care provides them with roles of planner, collaborator, informed consumer, and educator (Carbino, 1981). Which one of the three types is selected will depend on the problem definition and feasibility.

Assessment of the problem is helped by considering its latent and manifest functions (Merton, 1957). In organizational life, *manifest* functions (policies and procedures set up to achieve the manifest goal) may have unplanned and unrecognized consequences or *latent* functions. These may have a negative impact on clients and line staff, and yet serve the *latent* goals of the organization. The worker who examines the history of the service problem and its lack of resolution may discover its latent functions. Knowing what organizational needs and latent functions are being served by the continued existence of the problem provides clues about potential resistance and where it will appear. Such knowledge may make it possible to disarm the resistance in advance by redefining the problem or reframing a solution. For example, absence of group services for foster parents may be attributed to the lack of appropriate space, but the latent function may be to protect administration from a perceived threat of excessive demands on the agency by group members. The worker who believes that group services can improve the responsiveness of the organization may recast the problem and solution. The problem becomes one of dwindling resources, and the solution is the provision of group foster parent studies as a means of initial screening that will conserve agency resources. Once this service is in place, demonstrating the value of group approaches, it will be easier to advance group services for other segments of the Child Welfare population, such as adolescents in foster care, a technological change (Lee and Park, 1978).

Assessment must also include an analysis of the external and internal forces described earlier and their impact on the organization. This analysis helps in evaluating feasibility and also suggests means for supporting pro-change forces and neutralizing anti-change forces. Such means or strategies also rest on an adequate assessment of preferences, interests, and commitments of the decision-makers and other participants. Adequate assessment must also include an evaluation of the worker's own resources for the influencing effort.

Entry. Next, the worker will need to create receptiveness to change. Brager and Holloway (1978) suggest three methods: practitioner positioning to maximize resources for influencing, the inducement and management of stress, and structural positioning. Practitioner positioning was described earlier in terms of the worker's influence through professional and personal attributes. Positioning is also aided by acquiring knowledge and expertise pertinent to the service problem, lending legitimacy to the worker's efforts.

There must be some tension among staff if change is even to be considered. The stress must be felt enough, so that when reduced people will experience the proposed change with relief, perceiving it as a solution to their discomfort. If concern about the problem is absent, the worker may need to arouse it by making the problem visible by invoking professional norms and commitments. Professional guilt about the problem can be mobilized by pointing to the discrepancy between the organization's avowed goals and the realities of the service, or between professional values and those realities.

Structural positioning is also used to insure receptivity. It requires decisions about where (i.e., which agency structure) and to whom (i.e., which agency group) the service problem and change goal are to be introduced.

ONGOING PHASE.    With these tasks of the beginning phase completed, the worker must now decide on strategies for influencing, to whom they should be directed (i.e., key figures who will have to support the change effort if it is to succeed), who is to undertake the effort, how it should be carried out, and in which forum of the agency it should take place. The assessment will have revealed who are the key decision-makers, or the facilitating persons around them who must be approached first, and how best to influence them. Also, the assessment has pointed the way to sources of support, so that now alliances can be formed for added strength and plans made for disarming anticipated resistances among those likely to oppose the change. At this time also, the worker will need to decide whether or not he or she is the best person to make the change effort. If, for a variety of reasons, the worker is not, then someone else with more credibility may be enlisted.

In considering the range of influencing strategies usually available, one should begin with that one which requires the least amount of effort and resources and proceed toward more difficult ones as needed. Collaborative strategies are used where it is likely the key decision-makers will agree with the goal: joint exploration and problem-solving, program demonstration, information sharing, alternative examination, and friendly persuasion. Where collaboration does not work, or no agreement on the change goal exists, then campaign strategies can be used. These include deliberately selective and more forceful persuasion, negotiation, and bargaining. Escalating change efforts to include adversarial activities, such as petitioning, picketing, use of the media, or litigation, is rarely used in one's own agency unless the violation of client rights warrants the use of such coercive measures (and the risk of job loss).

There are probably more opportunities for the use of collaborative approaches than practitioners may think. This is especially true as the worker becomes more skilled in defining problems and solutions in terms congruent with the adaptive needs of the organization, and more adept in the use of alliance building and persuasion.

An additional issue is client involvement in the change effort. Potential benefits are similar to those gained from participation in community work: empowerment, with concomitant enhancement of competence, autonomy, relatedness, and self-esteem. But there are also potential dangers: possible backlash or retaliation, the effects on self-esteem of a failed effort. Each situation needs to be considered in its uniqueness, but in all instances, client groups invited to participate must be provided with all the information available regarding positive benefits and potentially negative consequences.

ENDING. Once the change goal has been adopted, the task of implementing the new policy, procedure, structure, or service remains. This task is accomplished by obtaining and monitoring the continuing commitment of the key decision-makers and the continuing cooperation of the staff directly involved in carrying out the innovation. Regular reporting back to all staff on the progress and status of the change effort can aid in this task. The worker may need to devote time and energy to motivating, clarifying, providing information, and otherwise supporting those involved. When the change is no longer experienced as a change, but is perceived as "the way things are," then the worker knows the innovation has been institutionalized. Before that point, however, the change as implemented should be evaluated to see if it *is* meeting its goal, if any unanticipated negative consequences have appeared, and, if so, what needs to be done about them.

## The Organization as a Work Environment

Thus far, the organization has been regarded as a service environment in which operations are directed to meeting the rights and needs of the Child Welfare population. The assumption of this chapter is that when the agency is responsive in that way, it will reduce rather than generate stress in those who use the service and will enhance rather than undermine their coping efforts. Among the positive outcomes of such adaptive exchanges between the agency and clientele will be the enhancement of the CARE-ing qualities of those served.

However, as is discussed in greater detail in the final section of this volume, it is possible also to consider the agency as a work environment for staff members as they go about the social work business of serving children and parents and other segments of the Child Welfare population. The work environment and the service environment shape and influence each other. The administration's tasks include developing reciprocity between the two environments, and, as in Alice's looking-glass world, the social work staff's tasks in the work environment are the mirror image of their tasks in the service environment. That is, the staff seeks to support the CARE-ing qualities of their clients through empowerment. But at the same time, staff, often without power themselves, must enhance their professional competence, professional autonomy (self-directedness), professional relatedness with clients and colleagues, and professional esteem or pride in being a social worker.

To return to the ecological perspective described early in this chapter, it must be remembered that the Child Welfare worker delivers services in the context of an agency system that shapes the practice of that worker and defines the services to be delivered. Further, the agency itself is embedded in and greatly influenced by the community and the larger social, political, and economic environment.

The position has been taken in this chapter that the relationships between worker and organization, and between worker and community, should be reciprocal, one in which the worker, in concert with others, also influences and shapes the agency and the community. The ability to assume this practice position depends on the mastery of a body of knowledge and skill often not included in education and training for Child Welfare practice. Such knowledge and skill is needed to enhance the competence of and to help empower the worker to participate in decision-making, policy formulation, and program planning.

The agency and the administrator must at the same time be willing to relinquish some authority and power in favor of a more collaborative model that recognizes the worker as a competent professional leader-among-peers. Such a model holds promise of overcoming the staff alienation, apathy, fatigue, and loss of idealism and commitment that are the consequences of powerlessness. The same concepts, principles, and skills for intervening to influence the organization's service environment can be used by staff as steps in achieving a CARE-ing work environment.

**FORM 6–1**

## Rural Community Resource Group (RCRG)
## Parent Questionnaire

Being a parent is a difficult job. There is no question that everyone welcomes sharing common parenting experiences and having child care opportunities available. We, the Rural Community Resource Group, comprised of interested human service agencies and Pittsfield residents, are interested in helping the people of Pittsfield develop some resources to help in living day to day with children.

1. Do you have any children under 18 years? ____ Yes ____ No

   a. How many? ____
   b. What ages? _____

2. Are you employed outside of the home? ____ Yes ____ No
   ____ Full Time ____ Part Time

3. Do you have child care arrangements while working outside of the home? ____ Yes ____ No.
   Is it available when you're not working? ____ Yes ____ No

4. Is this arrangement working out for you? ____ Yes ____ No

5. Would you be interested in any of the following: (check those that interest you)
   ____ A play group where mothers and children meet together with a leader for activities and games
   ____ At home babysitting service where qualified babysitter comes into your home
   ____ Group child care at a central location where you would sign up a week in advance to leave your child 1–3 hours
   ____ A babysitting co-op at a central location where you could trade babysitting services with other mothers at no cost
   ____ A drop-in center where mothers can get out of the house for a few hours for coffee and talk and child care provided
   ____ A parent training group where mothers meet to share ideas about discipline, frustrations, children fighting, nutrition, etc.
   ____ An activity group for mothers, such as:

| | | |
|---|---|---|
| ____ Arts and crafts | ____ Day trips | |
| ____ Exercise or yoga | ____ Diet | |
| ____ Sports | ____ Other: _____ | |

   ____ Other areas of interest you may have: _____

_____

6. Are there specific times when you would use these most?

_____

7. If something was set up, would you really use it? ____ Yes ____ No
   Would you need transportation? ____ Yes ____ No

8. Do you wish there were more activities for school age children?
   ____ Yes ____ No
   Like what? _____

9. If something is developed in the Pittsfield area, would you like to be on a mailing list? ____ Yes ____ No
If so, fill in below:

Name: _____

Address: _____

_____

## FORM 6–2   News Release to Local Papers

Have you ever had a day of the "blues," neither your children's demands nor your headaches ever cease, and you yearn, perhaps dream, for some relief—maybe a cooperative play group where you could leave your children for a few hours, with some extra benefits, too, such as adults to converse with. Sound like fantasy? Well, maybe not.

A group of interested human service agencies and Pittsfield citizens have been meeting together on a weekly basis to determine whether or not there is a need for some type of children's center in Pittsfield—maybe such a facility could operate on a cooperative basis, with some additional highlights such as a parents' discussion group, a toy–clothing exchange, etc. Are there other needs for parents and children that you could suggest?

A survey is presently underway in town. All volunteers will be wearing identifying badges and they will be canvassing the community for your ideas and suggestions. If a volunteer does not visit your home, questionnaires can be found at the pool, the doctor's office, Denis Market, and IGA!

If there are any questions about the questionnaire or any related matters, please call the Pittsfield Regional Visiting Nurses Association, Inc. Ask for Barbara.

# CHAPTER 7

# Understanding the Family
## A Central Concern in Child Welfare

Jo Ann Allen

The purpose of this chapter is to explore the family as a complex social system existing in space and time. After reviewing some of the issues which emerge in attempts to define it, the family will be examined in terms of its contemporary and ever-changing structures and functions. The family will also be viewed as a developmental unit with a life cycle of its own, and intergenerationally, as a social system which evolves over time. The internal life of the family, as it is understood in terms of its structure, communication, rule patterns, and boundaries, will be explored. Throughout the chapter, as we draw implications for the field of Child Welfare, we will emphasize the diversity of family life in American society.

## Defining the Family

An essential task in any discussion of the family is that of defining what is meant by the term "family." The definitional process implies making decisions about what components are considered essential before a group can be said to constitute a family. This process can quickly lead into some hotly contested value issues about social arrangements and lifestyles, issues that have important implications for Child Welfare policy and practice.

Some believe that family life is in danger of crumbling, and with it, incidentally, the whole fabric of American society. They consider that the only acceptable form is the traditional nuclear family constructed by legal heterosexual marriage. This circumscribed vision of the well-functioning family includes a father, usually the only wage earner, a mother, and at least one child. All other forms of family life are considered incomplete, deficient, dysfunctional, or deviant. It is as though the nuclear structure is somehow sanctified, as a universally desired ideal. The notion of the nuclear family structure as the only correct, healthy form has not been limited to the lay person. Arlene Skolnick writes:

> For family textbook writers, many social scientists, and the American public "the family" is the nuclear family—a married couple and their children. Society seems to be divided into nuclear-family groups, each living in a home of its own. Any deviation from the parent–child unit living together is not quite a family and needs explanation. It may be a "broken home" or some other variation from the expected pattern. (1973:6)

This model of the family has its proponents in all of the social sciences and certainly is implicit in many of the theories that social workers and other family-centered practitioners draw upon for understanding human behavior.

While many social scientists make a strong case for the universality of the nuclear family, there also seems to be wide variation in what is encompassed by that term. In some societies, including our own, the concept of the nuclear family refers to a group consisting of husband, wife, and children who live together as a unit, distinguished from the rest of society. In other societies, the nuclear unit may not necessarily live together, may be embedded in a large kin group, and may be part of a polygamous family arrangement.[1] Even if one argues that a nuclear unit can be found in all societies and thus is the basic building block of all family structures, one must be impressed with the great variety of family organization around the world.

The argument for the universality of the nuclear family loses some of its persuasiveness when one realizes that in many societies the functions usually associated with the family are not actually performed by the nuclear unit. Often, for example, the production of needed goods and services, socialization of the young, and caretaking tasks are the legitimate concern not only of the nuclear unit but also of the extended kin network, including grandparents, uncles, aunts, and cousins. The notion of the isolated and self-sufficient nuclear unit is clearly not a universally accepted form.

Another issue in defining the American family concerns the fact that there is much confusion and mythology about both contemporary and historical family structure. It has been assumed that the history of

American family structure proceeded from the extended family, which was thought to be adaptive for agricultural societies, to the nuclear family, which was thought to be suited to industrial societies. Both the extended and nuclear family in its turn has been idealized and sentimentalized. Actually, the idyllic picture of the American family of the past, consisting of many extended kin is largely a myth according to many family researchers. Hareven, for example, after surveying recent research, concludes:

> The "great extended families" that have become part of the folklore of modern industrial society were rarely in existence. Households and families were simple in their structure and not drastically different in their organization from contemporary families. (1982:448)

Similar myths exist about the nuclear family of today. There is widespread belief that the nuclear family is isolated from the larger kinship system, is more adaptable to the demands of modern society, and, in fact, is the natural consequence of industrialization. The self-sufficient nuclear family is portrayed as the dominant family form and superior to other forms. Many researchers challenge these notions. Moroney concludes "not only that families of all social classes tended to function in extended kin networks, but that the support included physical care, financial support, assistance in household tasks, and counseling" (1980:31).

It is much more likely that the dominant family structure is not nuclear, but what has been called "modified extended." Litwak describes this structure as follows:

> The modified extended family structure . . . consists of a coalition of nuclear families in a state of partial dependence. Such partial dependence means that nuclear family members exchange significant services with each other, thus differing from the isolated nuclear family, as well as retain considerable autonomy (that is, not bound economically or geographically), therefore, differing from the classical extended family (1965:291).

Mounting evidence supports the idea that families may be housed in nuclear units, but actually function in extended networks. Citing two recent surveys, Moroney (1980) points out that in contrast to the picture of families as isolated and self-sufficient units, a high rate of intergenerational contact, mutual aid, and support is present in today's families.

One of the reasons for such myths and misconceptions has to do with the tendency to equate the family unit with the dwelling unit or household. This clearly assumes that one criterion for being considered a family is that members share a common residence. In some societies, members of a nuclear family unit never form a common household. In our own society, there are many situations in which extended kin may not live together, but are deeply involved in each other's lives and consider themselves a family. Members may be absent from a household for long periods of time for a variety of reasons but are still very much a part of the family. To insist that members share a particular space in order to be considered family is to gloss over much of the meaning and reality of family life. In Child Welfare practice and in planning for children in need of care, such limitations can cut off many potential resources.

Leaving aside the issue of what families should be like, if we are to define what the family *is* like, we must probe behind the prevalent myths, ideology, and idealist notions. The past twenty-five years have seen social changes that have had a great impact upon American family life and have relevance in any discussion of family definition. These changes include an increasing number of one-parent families, women working outside the home, more men sharing in child care and household tasks, and larger numbers of remarried families.

One of the most significant changes in American family life in recent years has been that of wives and mothers entering the job market. For the first time in our history, it is more the norm than the exception for a school-age child to have a mother who works outside the home. In 1978, 57 percent of married women with children from ages 6 to 17 were in the labor force (White House Conference on Families Report, 1980:178).

The number of one-parent families has increased considerably in recent years. From 1970 to 1978, there was an increase of 8 percent with one-parent families representing 19 percent of all families with children present (ibid., 177). It is estimated that four out of every ten children born in the 1970s will spend part of childhood in a one-parent family. Most of these will be in households headed by women, although there has been an increase in the last decade of one-parent families headed by men. It is interesting to note that if one abided by the narrow definition of nuclear family stated earlier—mother/homemaker, father/breadwinner, and their children—only about 13 percent of American families would qualify.

In addition to these changes, recent years have witnessed a proliferation of lifestyles that are very different from the traditional nuclear family. There are more married but childless couples, heterosexual couples living together but not married, homosexual couples living together and bringing up children, and communal living arrangements. Almost 20 percent of all households today consist of a single adult living alone. For some, these changes support the belief that the family as an institution is dying. Others, however, simply see these changes as evidence that the family is highly adaptable, arguing that "the family is not dying. It is diversifying" (Toffler and Toffler, 1981:8).

No matter how one judges these social changes, they must be considered in defining family life today. Actually how one defines a family might be only an academic exercise were it not for the consequences of such a definition. Jerome and Arlene Skolnik point to those consequences, stating: "In our own society, the nuclear model defines what is normal and natural both for research and 'therapy' and subtly influences our thinking to regard deviations from the nuclear as sick or perverse or immoral" (1971:12).

The implications of this statement are obvious. If, for example, a Child Welfare worker is guided by a nuclear family ideology, such a view can shape his or her judgments concerning the potential and viability of children's biological families as well as whether certain families are appropriate for foster or adoptive placements. Such thinking has delayed the use of single adults as resources for children and automatically labeled single-parent families as deviant or dysfunctional.

Another major problem in endorsing a narrow definition of family is that such a definition tends to conform to white, middle-class American values and, to some extent, to describe the population more typically than other segments. If this group is taken as the cultural "ideal" by researchers who study family life, it follows that many ethnic and racial groups who deviate from that ideal will be judged as deficient or pathological. A recent study identifies the following as two of the similarities common to people of color: (1) patterns of close involvement with kin, including frequent interactions and exchange of help; and (2) close relationships with extended family members, which often include close friends who become fictive kin (McAdoo, 1982:16).

The adaptive quality of the extended network for the survival of these families has been documented by many writers (Hill, 1972; Stack, 1974). Yet, measured against the nuclear family ideal, such families have often been judged as dependent, weak, pathological, and chaotic. And in Child Welfare, foster home placement decisions and plans are often made without regard for the resources available in extended or fictive kin.

Another important consequence of definition emerges on the level of social and family policy. Moroney points out that most policies assume a nuclear family structure; that definition then is used "to include or exclude families from services, to penalize or benefit certain families" (1980:47). In effect, families are then coerced to organize themselves in particular ways and to behave in accordance with someone else's image of what a family ought to be. Although practice is changing now, foster care and adoption provide good examples of the impact of definition on policy. Until relatively recently, it was only the "normal" nuclear family that was judged adequate to care for children. Wives were discouraged from working outside the home and placement of a child in a one-parent home was extremely rare. As a consequence, many children, particularly so-called hard-to-place children, were denied permanent homes and many families were denied the right to foster or adopt a child.

The foregoing discussion leads to the conclusion that our definitions and notions of family must recognize and attend to the strengths and needs of the rich variety of family forms flourishing in our society today.

Definitions should be flexible and linked to purpose. The purpose of this chapter is to review current knowledge about the structure and function of the family, upon which family-centered models of practice in Child Welfare can be built. With these purposes in mind and with the awareness that Child Welfare administrators, policy makers, and line workers are concerned with people living in a variety of ways, it makes sense to opt for a definition such as the one developed by Hartman, which states that "a family consists of two or more individuals who define themselves as a family and who, over time, assume those obligations to one another that are generally considered an essential component of family systems" (1981:8).

## The Family as a Service Delivery System

While we do not know exactly how long it has existed, it seems safe to conclude that the family has a very respectable endurance record. As Margaret Mead phrased it: "The family is, as far as we know, the toughest institution we have. It is, in fact, the institution to which we owe our humanity" (1953:4). Why has the family as an institution survived for such a long period of time? And why, in spite of the fierce debates over form and direction, do most writers predict that it does have a future?

Does the family as an institution have some intrinsic value that somehow insures its survival in spite of change? The family, certainly, is one of the major institutions found in all societies—along with government, an economic system, some form of education, and religion. Leslie states:

> The fact that certain institutions are found in all known societies suggests that societies may not be able to exist without them. Or, to put it differently, the major social institutions play a very large part in accomplishing those basic functions which are essential to society's survival. (1979:7)

From this point of view, the family is one of the essential components in the arrangements societies make for the carrying out of those minimum tasks requisite to survival.

A variety of views persist concerning the social functions special to the family. These functions usually include:

(1) the physical maintenance and care of family members; (2) the addition of new members through procreation or adoption and their relinquishment when they have matured; (3) the socialization of children for adult roles, such as those of spouse, parent, worker, neighbor, voter, and community member; (4) the social control of members, which refers to the maintenance of order within the family and groups external to it; (5) the maintenance of family morale and motivation to ensure task performance in the family and in other social groups; and (6) the production and distribution of goods and services needed to support and maintain the family unit. (Zimmerman, 1980:196)

This list suggests that the family is charged with extremely important tasks, although the extent and the particulars of that charge may vary from society to society. The implementation of prescribed family functions may vary, too, with class, economic, and ethnic differences. Despite variation in the nature and implementation of functions, it is clear that the family is traditionally charged with the survival, development and well-being of its members. In a very real sense, it can be described as a major, if not primary, service delivery system in every society as it fulfills its caretaking and protective functions. As such, it serves not only the needs of its members, but also those of the larger society.

## Family Functioning Today

In examining how the American family is faring today in carrying out its functions, it is important to consider the cultural and ethnic diversity that characterizes American society. This rich diversity is attributable to the long tradition of large-scale immigration of peoples from all over the world. Thus, the way in which the family in America addresses its tasks is influenced by the heterogeneity of the various racial, ethnic, and cultural groups which make up the population. Further, one cannot ignore the changes that have occurred as American society moved to industrialization and urbanization from predominantly agricultural and rural origins. Families undergo change as they must adapt to a changing world. Moreover, the family is currently struggling with the impact of rapid technological changes which many foresee will usher in a postindustrial society which is likely to bring with it social upheaval in all sectors of our society.[2] The adaptive quality of the family is being, and will continue to be, tested as it tries to keep pace with the technological and social changes of the future.

Another major concern of those who study contemporary family life in America is whether those functions traditionally associated with the family are being stripped away from it by other institutions. Keniston believes that of all the developments in family life in the past two centuries, "the most important is a shift in the functions of families" (1977:13). He points out that three centuries ago almost all families were largely self-sufficient agricultural units. He goes on to state: "The most important difference between these early American families and our own is that early families constituted economic units in which all members, from young children on up, played important productive roles within the household" (ibid.). Large families were valued since children, as well as adults, were necessary to the family enterprise. Socialization of children and even formal education were primarily the responsibility of the parents, although there were a few schools at that time. The sick were cared for at home by the family. In most important respects the family was considered the major producer of goods and services and certainly the major service delivery system.

Is it true, then, that the family has lost most of its functions in today's society? A brief look at how the American family is faring in relation to its traditional family functions may shed light on that question.

## The Family and Work

A critical result of the Industrial Revolution was the separation of the economic function from the family as a unit. The home ceased to be the primary worksite and production a family enterprise as family members went to work for wages in the factories, a shift which had tremendous impact upon the family (Harevan, 1982). Over the decades the home increasingly became glorified as a domestic retreat, and in fact an ideology of domesticity developed that "relegated women to the home and glorified their domestic role. The roles of husbands and wives became gradually segregated; a clear division of labor replaced the old economic partnership, with the husband now responsible for economic support and the wife's effort directed toward homemaking and child rearing" (ibid.:453–454). Women became caretakers of the "retreat" and men became separated from wives and children for much of the day. Privacy and individualism replaced earlier values based upon collectivity and cooperation. It is well to note that this "cult of domesticity" was largely a middle-class phenomenon that gradually generalized to a kind of cultural ideal, influencing all segments of society. However, in many working-class and ethnic groups, a view of the family as a collective economic unit, in which all members contribute to the general well-being, persisted. In some groups, notably blacks and recent immigrants, it was common for women to work outside the home and for children to contribute to the economic well-being, while housework and child care continued to be valued as economic contributions.

Given the larger society's ideological view of the home as a retreat, and of woman as the nurturing wife and mother, it is easy to understand why the fact that large numbers of women have entered the labor force in recent years has caused widespread concern. Women of all ages and backgrounds have entered the labor force and, in 1979, comprised 42 percent of all workers. Working wives accounted for nearly 25 percent of the entire labor force (ibid.). As noted earlier, it is now the norm for a school-age child to have a mother who works outside the home. What seems at stake here is not whether women shall work but how their place in society is viewed. "What has changed is not the fact of women's work, but the institutional arrangements, occupations, and settings in which they work" (Levitan and Belous, 1981:83). Regardless of the consternation experienced by some in American society, working women are an established fact of life; it is highly unlikely that women will return to the home and to former roles.

The advent of the working wife and mother has been both beneficial and problematic for families. Obviously, a family's economic resources are enhanced with two wage earners. Women are likely to achieve personal satisfaction, more power within the family, and a greater sense of control over their own lives—factors which may affect positively their self-images, individual functioning, and ability to parent. The effects on marriage are more debatable. Some have suggested that the rising divorce rate is due, in part, to the fact that women, now able to support themselves, are more likely to abandon an unsatisfactory marriage.

Unquestionably, many families have been stressed as women have joined the labor force either out of necessity or personal choice. For example, even though most women still carry a greater share of responsibility for the home, their work schedules have often necessitated shifts in male–female roles and shared arrangements for child care and housework. When both parents work outside the home, extrafamilial help with child care is required. Of particular concern to Child Welfare is the development of adequate personal and institutional programs and supports for the care and supervision of children of all ages, appropriately structured for developmental stage.

At the present time, however, what child care is available is often expensive and not readily accessible to many families who need it. The lack of reasonably priced, accessible child care poses a particular problem for many single-parent families, with no spouse to share responsibility, and there has been considerable concern for so-called latch key children, who spend much time alone while the parent (or parents) works. In spite of the obvious stresses and potential problems, norms concerning family work roles seem to be evolving, and the phenomenon of the working woman has had considerable effect on the way the family functions economically and socially.

Clearly, while the family still is invested with an economic function, the way in which it carries out that function has changed and is still changing. Nevertheless, it is still the family that has the responsibility for obtaining the necessary goods and services its members need. There seems to be general agreement that today the family is primarily a unit of consumption rather than production. There are those, however, who contend that if the current system of economic accounting took into account in-kind family transfers, the family would still be considered as performing an important role in production (Burns, 1975). It is fascinating, too, that some futurists predict a return to the family as the major productive unit in postindustrial society. Toffler (1981), for example, visualizes a future in which work is transferred back to the home as a response to advances in high technology and the rapidly increasing costs of commuting to centralized workplaces. One may speculate on the impact the return to "cottage" industry could have on the welfare of children.

## The Family and Children

One of the main functions of the family has always been to produce and to nurture society's next generation. It is this function that is most salient when a family becomes known to the Child Welfare system. A number of social conditions and changes in recent years have made an impact upon the role of the family in these areas. Demographic data indicate that the fertility rate has been declining steadily for the past 100 years until at the close of the 1970s, it was roughly at the zero population growth level. The economic character of a pre-industrial, rural society called for large numbers of children, spaced over many years, since they were needed for family work and the care of younger and aging family members. In today's society, children are not as necessary to the work of the family, and child-rearing has become an increasingly expensive endeavor. With improved birth control methods, and greater acceptance and legalization of abortion, it is now possible for families to plan for desired family size. A consequence of these major social changes, which has altered Child Welfare practice, is that it has become very difficult for infertile couples to have the opportunity to become parents of infants through adoption.

While more people may be choosing to remain childless, and there is a trend toward smaller family size, there does not, according to current research, seem to be a major trend toward childlessness (Rice,

1977). A reduction in the size of the average family may well result in improvement of the quality of life, since available resources, both material and emotional, need not be spread so thinly among family members (Levitan and Belous, 1981).

Of major social concern regarding the care of children is the increasing number of one-parent families formed as a result of separation, divorce, or single parenthood. There is particular cause for concern about the physical well-being of children in such families because fewer material resources are available to them. Most one-parent families are headed by women, who tend to be in lower-paying jobs than men or who have to rely upon public assistance or uncertain child-support payments for income. Given adequate resources, however, there is nothing inherently dysfunctional for children in the one-parent family structure, and the single-parent family may, in fact, have some special advantages and strengths.[3]

## The Family and Socialization

Socialization of the young in this society was once almost the exclusive domain of the family. Today, the family is still charged with great responsibility in this area but has experienced diminished power and control over those institutions with whom it shares this function. Keniston (1977), for example, suggests the advent of compulsory, free public education has made great inroads on the traditional roles of the family as educator and socializer. Schools tend to take over the job of teaching good work habits, essential skills, and character building. Also, in recent years, parents have had to compete with television as a powerful influence in the lives of their children.

Socialization, however, is a complex phenomenon, which takes place over the course of a lifetime. It may be useful to distinguish between primary and secondary socialization. "Primary socialization is the first socialization an individual undergoes in childhood, through which he becomes a member of society. Secondary socialization is any subsequent process that inducts an already socialized individual into new sectors of the objective world of his society" (Berger and Luckmann, 1966:130).

Much of what we consider primary socialization is still located in the family; the emotional attachments that exist among family members facilitate social learning and internalization of values and attitudes. However, much of the secondary socialization function, which builds upon primary socialization, has become the province of specialized agencies such as public schools and universities. Certainly the family is sharing the socialization function in this increasingly complex world and it may be that the parent has become a "weakened executive" (Keniston, 1977:17), responsible for seeing that children are educated and socialized, responsible for coordinating the activities of the many experts involved, and yet quite limited in power over those who teach children. In spite of the fact that other institutions share in this function, it is still the family that is held accountable.

## The Family and Physical Well-Being

Traditionally, the family has been charged with the health care of its members, although it has gradually become much more dependent on outside medical expertise and care. Part of this change has to do with the advances in medical science, which put health care decisions more in the hands of doctors and hospitals. But the family still plays an important role in monitoring the health of its members and in obtaining medical care. Moreover, much evidence shows that the family is still highly involved in the care of the sick, elderly, disabled, and handicapped (Moroney, 1980).

Many families experience serious obstacles in their attempts to carry out the health care function. Poor families, more dependent upon the public sector, are less likely to get consistent and quality health care (Keniston, 1977). Levitan and Belous (1981) report that one-parent families and households headed by elderly individuals have more health-related problems than other groups and fewer resources to cope with them. Actually, rising medical costs could pose a serious financial threat for any family today.

## The Family and Emotional Well-Being

The role of the family in fulfilling the emotional needs of all of its members has become more important. The family has come to be thought of as a retreat from the impersonal, highly competitive outside world. "The modern family, in losing some of its earlier functions, has emerged as an agency specializing in emotional services for its members. It provides adults with an escape from the competitive pressures of the market while at the same time equips the young with the necessary resources to master these pressures" (Moroney, 1980:27).

While the family may be able to perform this function at least in part, the responsibility it carries for emotional satisfaction and fulfillment can be a source of stress. Unrealistic expectations for closeness and emotional gratification place a tremendous burden on family relationships, leading to disappointment and dissatisfaction. For example, many question whether this phenomenon has not contributed to the rising divorce rate. Further, the notion of the family as a very private retreat may have other consequences. Such a view may well lead to the development of increasingly opaque family boundaries, and to the expectation that the personal and intimate lives of family members must be limited to relationships inside the family system, while the obtaining of gratifications outside the family is somehow disloyal. Also, the high expectations placed upon the family for intimacy and emotional fulfillment may also have the function of lowering expectations and demands on other institutions, contributing to a withdrawal from more public or community systems. As Harevan points out, "the tendency of the family to shelter its members from other institutions has weakened its ability to affect the structure of or to influence the programs and legislation that public agencies have directed at the family" (1982:461).

One of the problems with trying to decide whether the family has indeed lost much of its purpose and function in today's world is that we are blinded by myths and hampered by linear thinking. Keniston (1977) writes of the norm of self-sufficiency, for example, which has deep roots in American society. Well-functioning individuals and families were defined as independent and able to care for all of their needs without outside help. Families in need of help from the community or others were often thought of as weak or deficient. Our judgement of how well today's families are doing is measured against this ideal of self-sufficiency. The belief that one institution in a society can perform its roles without being influenced by the others is to underestimate the interdependent nature of social institutions. Changes in one central institution affect all of the others. The family should not have to compete with other institutions; the emphasis should be on facilitating cooperation and coordination between the family and those other societal institutions with which it shares its roles and exchanges resources. Further, as many writers have urged, it is time to recognize the family for the major social service role it plays (Hartman, 1981; Keniston, 1977; Moroney, 1980). Given that acceptance, one could, as Moroney did, raise the following question: "What is the most desirable, effective, and feasible division of responsibility between the family and extrafamilial institutions in meeting the needs of individuals, and in what ways can these institutions relate to each other to maximize benefits?" (Moroney, 1980:15). The answer to this question may become even more critical in a postindustrial society in which the family may have an even more expanded role.

The extent to which families, in all their varied and changing forms, are able to meet and carry out these functions in concert with other institutions in society has profound impact on the welfare of the nation's children. Clearly, the family cannot carry these burdens alone and, as has been discussed in other chapters, the nature of the relationship between State and family and the availability of supportive resources in the environment are major variables in predicting how well children—and families—will fare.

When families are insufficiently supported, when family and/or environmental resources are lacking, when families are stressed through death, illness, or other events, when families are having difficulty performing those tasks related to the nurture and care of their children, they are likely to become known to the Child Welfare system. Although the focus of this chapter is on the family itself, the family may only be understood within the context of its environment. It is frequently the relationship between the family and its social environment that becomes the area for intervention by Child Welfare workers in their efforts to support families, prevent placement, or help families toward reunification.

## The Family Life Cycle

The challenge of the family, as can be seen from the functions with which it is charged, is to insure both the survival and the healthy development of its members, and to reproduce itself. As Hoffman so colorfully phrases it:

> The individuals making up a family are growing (at least partly) according to an internal biological design, but the larger groupings within a family, the subsystems and the generations, must endure major shifts in relation to each other. The task of the family is to produce and train new sets of humans to be independent, form new families, and repeat the process, as the old set loses power, declines, and dies. Family life is a multi-generational changing of the guard. (1981:160)

Families are not static but evolving systems that are required, from time to time, to make organizational and relationship changes to accommodate the changing, developmental needs of their members. The family system proceeds through a life cycle with identifiable stages, each of which presents it with developmental tasks that must be mastered before it and its members can move on to new challenges. In working with a family, a Child Welfare worker must recognize the particular life stage the family is traversing and understand the specific characteristics and demands of that period in the family's life.

Most readers are familiar with the formulations of Erik Erikson (1959) concerning the life cycle of the individual. In recent years, family theorists and family therapists alike have recognized that the family as a whole is faced with developmental stages that parallel individual life stages and tasks. These are, in fact, interactional in the sense that the individual members and the family as a whole must complete the tasks to insure the continued growth of both. For example, as Carter and McGoldrick point out: "adolescence happens to a family, not just to an individual" (1980:14). The young adult cannot successfully manage all of the physical and emotional issues connected with leaving home unless the family itself can negotiate the "letting go" process.

The life stages of a family are associated with the usual, predictable events that occur in most families. These events include such transitions as marriage, birth or adoption of children, children entering school, adolescence, children leaving home, middle and old age, retirement, and death. Each of these events is associated with a transitional period in which the family as a unit is forced to reorganize its roles, change its rules, and redefine relationships. For example, the advent of the first child in a family means that the adults must assume the role of parent, agree on a new division of labor and methods of child care, and expand their relationship to make room for the child. The ease with which a family manages these adjustments varies a great deal, but it seems clear that a certain amount of normative stress accompanies each transition. Although the stress and escalation of conflict, experienced in many families at these turning points, should not necessarily be viewed as pathology, it is at these particularly demanding times that families whose resources are already taxed to the limit may be at risk of becoming overwhelmed. For example, any couple may be stressed by the addition of their first born child, but consider how much more likely to be at risk is the unmarried teenager, expecting a child, unable or unwilling to involve the father, and living with her family, which itself may be overburdened and lacking resources. These are the kinds of life cycle crises that come to the attention of the Child Welfare system. Preventive programs in Child Welfare can be made available to families at these particularly stressful points and families at risk identified through considering the variable of developmental life stage, as well as the availability of family and environmental resources.

Several formulations of the family life cycle are based on predictable life events, and most of them suffer in that they primarily depict the white, middle-class American family. Such conceptions generally presume a nuclear structure consisting of husband, wife, and children, and do not take into account events such as divorce and remarriage, or the diversity of family structures and lifestyles. Most formulations also lack a cross cultural perspective, resulting in poor applicability to families whose patterns and values may differ from others around them. Therefore, although such schemes can stimulate Child Welfare workers to consider life cycle issues, they should give careful attention to adjustments and alterations that must be made to adapt life cycle concepts to families with different structures, lifestyles, and stresses.

Recognizing that no one family life cycle scheme will accurately describe the stages and tasks for all families, Carter and McGoldrick (1980) have formulated one that is useful as a beginning framework.

These stages reflect those times in family life when entrance into and exit from the system are at issue. It is also clear that there is an attendant and characteristic emotional process to be negotiated at each stage. If these processes are dealt with successfully, the family moves to fundamental shifts in relationships and a new organizational level. This shift represents a basic or second order change in the family system.

However, since most of the life transitions are associated with adding or losing family members, and altering relationships, responsibilities, and roles, it is little wonder that the adaptive balance—the "goodness of fit"—is often disturbed. It is understandable that many families experience stresses in relation to these transitions. Most families are able to weather the difficulties, make the necessary changes, and move on, without outside help. Other families get "stuck". As Haley (1973:42) says: "Symptoms appear when there is a dislocation or interruption in the unfolding life cycle of a family or other natural group. The symptom is a signal that a family has difficulty in getting past a stage in the life cycle."

Since all life transitions pose adaptive tasks for families and their members and are stressful to some extent, what factors moderate stress and what factors hamper successful completion of the developmental tasks? Carter and McGoldrick (1980) discuss what they call stressors, important determinants in the ease with which a family copes with the demands of life transitions. Vertical stressors are those factors that are passed down through generations and include the very powerful family patterns, myths, attitudes, legacies, and issues that influence the meaning attributed to a given life event, such as the birth of the first child. If past generations have experienced unresolved conflict or tragedy in connection with a transition, the residue of attitudes and feelings is likely to be transmitted to the current nuclear family. Family anxiety and difficulty around a specific life stage can be rooted in past generations. On the other hand, the experience of past generations can be quite facilitative to growth when the event has been associated with joy and good feeling. Some Child Welfare workers have made use of the genogram and take careful family history to gain an understanding of the intergenerational sources of family strengths, anxiety, or pain.

On another level, the family life cycle process can be disrupted by unpredictable events that frequently occur in family life. These are all of those events which everyone knows can happen but does not really plan

**TABLE 7–1  The Stages of the Family Life Cycle**

| Family Life Cycle Stage | Emotional Process of Transition: Key Principles | Second Order Changes in Family Status Required to Proceed Developmentally |
| --- | --- | --- |
| 1. Between Families: The Unattached Young Adult | Accepting parent–offspring separation | a. Differentiation of self in relation to family of origin<br>b. Development of intimate peer relationships<br>c. Establishment of self in work |
| 2. The Joining of Families Through Marriage: The Newly Married Couple | Commitment to new system | a. Formation of marital system<br>b. Realignment of relationships with extended families and friends to include spouse |
| 3. The Family with Young Children | Accepting new members into the system | a. Adjusting marital system to make space for child(ren)<br>b. Taking on parenting roles<br>c. Realignment of relationships with extended family to include parenting and grandparenting role |
| 4. The Family with Adolescents | Increasing flexibility of family boundaries to include children's independence | a. Shifting of parent–child relationships to permit adolescent to move in and out of system<br>b. Refocus on mid-life marital and career issues<br>c. Beginning shift toward concerns for older generation |
| 5. Launching Children and Moving On | Accepting a multitude of exits from and entries into the family system | a. Renegotiation of marital system as a dyad<br>b. Development of adult to adult relationships between grown children and their parents<br>c. Realignment of relationships to include in-laws and grandchildren<br>d. Dealing with disabilities and death of parents (grandparents) |

*(continued)*

**TABLE 7–1** *(Continued)*

| Family Life Cycle Stage | Emotional Process of Transition: Key Principles | Second Order Changes in Family Status Required to Proceed Developmentally |
|---|---|---|
| 6. The Family in Later Life | Accepting the shifting of generational roles | a. Maintaining own and/or couple functioning and interests in face of physiological decline; exploration of new familial and social role options <br> b. Support for a more central role for middle generation <br> c. Making room in the system for the wisdom and experience of the elderly; supporting the older generation without overfunctioning for them <br> d. Dealing with loss of spouse, siblings and other peers and preparation for own death. Life review and integration |

Table taken from E. Carter and M. McGoldrick, *The Family Life Cycle*. Copyright © 1980, Gardner Press, New York, New York. Reprinted here with permission.

for: sudden death, miscarriage, major illnesses, birth of a handicapped child, separation and divorce, or a major change in socioeconomic status. Any of these can stress a family to the point of crisis. Such events will place new demands upon the family, often requiring role and relationship changes to "modify the normative momentum of the family unit" (Terkelson, 1980:41).

Frequently families approach or are referred to Child Welfare agencies at the time of such unanticipated stressful events. The illness or death of a single parent or the birth of a handicapped child to a family with limited resources are events which may very likely require Child Welfare services. In assessing families, it is important for workers to distinguish between chronic deteriorating situations and acute crises, and to identify the stressors and the situational variables that rendered the family particularly vulnerable.

*Family Survival versus Individual Development*

In order to understand more clearly the problems and stresses associated with life stages, it is imperative to recognize that the family must address two fundamental orders of need throughout its life cycle. These are described by Terkelson as needs pertinent to survival and needs pertinent to development. The former pertain to physical security, health, food, and shelter, while the latter refer to the cognitive, emotional, and spiritual development of family members. Survival, obviously, takes precedence over everything else; thus, as Terkelson concludes, "a family unit will address developmental needs of members only if survival needs are actively and sufficiently met" (1980:28). Poor families are often severely stressed in trying to meet their material needs. However, income level is not necessarily the major determinant of how well developmental needs are met. Physical security and well-being can be threatened in many ways as described above. When a family believes its survival is at stake, energy and resources must be channeled toward maintaining the family. Developmental needs, which by their very nature are oriented toward growth and change, must often be "put on hold" which can hamper, delay, or thwart orderly progression through the life stages.

Even though many low or marginal income families do well, many are severely disadvantaged—to the point that physical survival is the major issue in the family most of the time. In effect, the environment is not supportive enough so that developmental needs can be met within the family. Aponte speaks of the multiproblem poor family as "underorganized," drawing this conclusion regarding developmental issues:

> Families who are poor, and therefore powerless, friendless, and excluded from the vital operations of society, do not have the kind of institutional and community supports necessary for their ongoing development as organizations in their own right. This factor contributes to denying the individuals in the families the optimum context within which to develop their own personalities. (1976:448)

These families often comprise a large portion of the Child Welfare worker's caseload.

Another point about families who live in poverty is that "the life cycle of poor families seems more truncated than that of middle-class families" (Colón, 1980:355). In many respects, the poor family lives in a much more dangerous world than the middle-class family. The association between poverty and the neglect of children has been well documented. Such neglect may take the more easily observable form of physical deprivation of needed medical care, nutrition, or adequate housing, or may be found in the deprivation of those resources needed for maturation and healthy personality and social development.

## Cultural Variations

Most family life cycle models do not sufficiently take into account variables associated with race, ethnicity, class, and religion. While some roles and events, such as procreation, child care, sex roles, coming of age, and intergenerational relationships are presumably common to most families, the meaning of each life stage, its expectations and values, and the rituals that mark it vary widely. To cite just one example, Falicov and Karrer (1980), in their discussion of the life cycle of Mexican-American families, point out that these families are more clearly three-generational in life stage patterns than are Anglo-American families. Extended family members, friends, and neighbors play strong roles in family life. Older members tend to be highly respected. Families are protective and cooperation for the good of the family unit is prized. Ideas about when and under what circumstances young people leave home are quite different from middle-class American families. Such developmental tasks are of course particularly complicated for young persons placed in foster or institutional care, whose opportunities to leave home in appropriate, culturally sanctioned ways have been short-circuited.

As Falicov and Karrer stress, in relation to Mexican-American families: "Not only do the content and themes of the different stages vary with race, class, religion, and ethnicity, but also the original family structures, the developmental tasks, and the mechanisms by which changes take place may differ" (ibid.:384). These same points may be made about many of the varying ethnic families in our society, thus it is essential to view the family life cycle in its sociocultural context.

## Intergenerational Themes and Patterns

Although it is not always clearly recognized by the current participants in the life of a family, they are strongly linked to and influenced by past generations. "One would think that with removal by death, past generations could not possibly affect those of the present. Past events do, however, cast long, historical shadows. Ideas set in motion by past generations influence present generations. The linkages are symbolic, but this characterizes much of human ways. We are all creatures attuned to imagery and symbolization" (Koller, 1974:8). This quotation stresses that, through the transmission of patterns, themes, myths, values, and rituals, past generations are very much alive in current families. Students of the family have long been aware, too, of the powerful impact of carefully guarded family secrets—perhaps a suicide, an affair, or a criminal act—on individuals of the current generation. Toxic events in a past generation, such as an untimely death or desertion, may influence the life course of current family members.

For example, a young father who severely beat his ten-year-old daughter for staying out too late had been abandoned by his mother when he was ten. This father had been investing considerable energy in anxiously monitoring the movements of both his wife and daughter, who had learned to avoid and evade him. The Child Welfare worker was able to help him reunite with his mother and, for the first time, to learn of the circumstances which had led her to leave and her thwarted efforts to keep in contact. These interventions helped alleviate the tension in his nuclear family.

Boszormenyi-Nagy and Spark (1973) conceive of a kind of family ledger through which debts and obligations are passed from one generation to the next. In this view, it is not uncommon for certain individuals in the current generation to be sacrificed in the interest of this multigenerational balance sheet.

In the previous section of this chapter, it was noted that "vertical" stress, passed from one generation to the next, is a powerful determinant in how well the current family negotiates life cycle issues. Most family-centered practitioners today include at least three generations in their thinking about family systems, accepting the notion that in any family "the operative emotional field at any given moment" includes at least three generations (Carter and McGoldrick, 1980:9). Murray Bowen (1978), a leader in the field of family therapy, believes that most of the interpersonal and interactional problems experienced by individuals have their roots in unresolved intergenerational emotional issues. He proposes that there is a "family projection process" through which the relative lack of differentiation or emotional growth is passed from the parents to one or more of their children.

Child Welfare workers frequently encounter such intergenerational issues and themes: the abandoning parents who were themselves abandoned as children, or the daughters of fathers who abused their mothers finding themselves resigned and hopeless in the face of their husbands' cruelty and abuse. On the other hand, positive sources of identity may also be available: the family heroine, a powerful great grandmother who, in spite of overwhelming hardship through hard work and resourcefulness successfully raised her children alone, keeping the family together.

The notion that families are truly intergenerational entities and that past generations influence present generations is not so surprising, nor should it be considered in a negative light. Patterns, myths, values, and rituals, passed from one generation to another, contribute to a sense of continuity of family life and to a sense of identity and belonging. Reiss speaks of the "active conservation of culture within family generations" through which cherished traditions are transmitted from one generation to another (1981:171). He adds, though, that each family originates its own culture and, in essence, changes and adds to that which has come from the past. "These cultures, intrinsic to each family, can only be shaped and then transmitted to the next generation by an active, resilient process within the family" (ibid.: 172). While continuity is of great importance, families are not necessarily passive recipients of their heritage; they can and do leave their own marks on the family history. Thus Child Welfare workers need to be sensitive to the integenerational themes which may be influencing family behavior and parent–child relationships.

## The Family as a Biopsychosocial System

One of the things that makes one family different from another, and thus contributes to a sense of both family and individual identity, is a shared history. The family is a biological unit in that members share a genetic history and a multigenerational history of people and events. Out of this history comes an important sense of kinship, rooted in the past and including a vision of future generations.

> Kin ties are powerful and compelling and the individual's sense of identity and continuity is formed not only by the significant attachments in his intimate environment but also is deeply rooted in the biological family—in the genetic link that reaches back in the past and ahead into the future. (Laird, 1979:177)

While patterns from the past may be incorporated into the ways in which a family is organized, its role structure, its communication style, its values, and its rules for behavior, how can we understand the current operation of these processes? In the last twenty-five years family researchers and practitioners have turned increasingly to systems theory and the field of cybernetics for help in understanding families (Laird and Allen, 1983).[4] It has, in fact, become commonplace to hear the phrase, "the family as a system." But what are the implications of viewing the family as a system? Observation of families has led students of the family to conclude that a family unit is much more than a collection of individuals; one cannot understand family dynamics by studying each member individually. Families have emergent qualities, as the family takes on a meaning and a life of its own above and beyond the individuals who comprise it. There are patterns, processes, and sequences of behavior outside the conscious awareness and control of individual family members that are automatic and compelling. The members of a family are interrelated and interdependent components of an organizationally complex system, and their interaction has a circular, reciprocal quality. What happens to one affects all of the others. Family systems are not closed mechanical systems, but are open, living, adaptive systems evolving over time.

In a sense, every family system faces a dilemma in providing emotional and physical security for its members through a certain steadiness over time, while remaining flexible enough to respond to the expected and the unexpected events of life in a way that promotes the growth and development of its members. On the face of it, it would seem that family systems contain two opposing forces—one directed toward maintaining a steady state and the other directed toward change. In fact, they are complementary since living systems need constancy and integrity along with stimulation, growth, and change in order to survive. Like any living system, if a family lacks input, it tends toward disorder and dissolution; too much input and change, however, may result in loss of identity and coherence.

## The Family as Stable and Governed by Rules

The need for stability is achieved primarily through the development of rules that govern the behavior and the relationships of family members. Over a period of time the family works out rules of living together, sets limits on the behavior of its members, and devises ways of regulating that behavior. A kind of homeostasis is established and mechanisms to restore the equilibrium are triggered if a member deviates too much from the norms.

Family rules are both overt and covert; they help define the relationships of members with each other and of the family to the outside world. There are rules about closeness, conflict, communication style, power, and even rules about rules, which are called meta-rules. One family may have an operating rule making it impossible for anger to be expressed openly, while in another an open display of affection is discouraged. Largely, the rules depend on what the family perceives as necessary for the stability of the system. The rules may not be easy for an outsider to detect or for a family member to articulate. They can, however, be observed in repetitious patterned sequences of interaction among family members.

The feedback loop is a key concept in understanding the rule-governing process of a family. This is a "process by which a system informs its component parts how to relate to one another and to the external environment to facilitate the correct or beneficial execution of certain system functions" (Kantor and Lehr, 1975:12). The family rewards those behaviors that are in line with the norms and has ways of correcting or discouraging behaviors that are too far out of line. These negative feedback loops, activated by errors, inhibit change and are associated with maintaining constancy in a family system. The process by which a family maintains stability has also been called "morphostasis" (Wertheim, 1973; 1975).

### Family Change

The family as a system may be said to have a certain built-in conservatism, though a capacity for change in response to internal and external pressures is essential to the well-being of the family. Earlier discussion pointed to the necessity for basic structural change throughout the life cycle to meet the needs and demands of growing family members and in response to environmental change. The process associated with change and variety in family life has been termed "morphogenesis." As negative feedback loops encourage constancy in families, positive feedback loops amplify deviation and encourage change.

There are times in the life of a family when stability does not serve it well. As a matter of fact, to stay the same, to insist on living by the same rules and patterns, may lead to breakdown in the family. At times, the developmental needs of the family members, unexpected events, or environmental changes may demand new ways of doing things. The problem-solving mechanisms that worked before are no longer effective. The family must allow "newness" and variety into its patterns and processes or become incapacitated by the dysfunction of one or several members, perhaps to the point of serious disorganization in the entire family. Families that do not have adequate capacity for change can become "stuck" in their normal progression through the life cycle, with serious developmental consequences for the members. Clearly, the mechanisms promoting change are just as essential as those maintaining stability.

A natural tension exists between morphostatic and morphogenic forces which often creates stress in families during times of change. Also, as Hoffman has pointed out in applying an evolutionary framework to family systems thinking, families "do not change in a smooth, unbroken line but in discontinuous leaps" (1981:158). The family must shift or transform itself to a new level or organization. The stress that is experienced should not necessarily be construed as pathology or permanent dysfunction. The family is struggling toward a new balance and the resulting anxiety may even help to move the family to a new and necessary developmental level. A family may experience anxiety and conflict as an adolescent moves away from the family unit, but it is that same upset that may finally help to make appropriate changes in rules and relationships.

If stress can be seen as a natural part of transition, individual problems and symptoms can be viewed as both attempts to stabilize the system and as signals for change. For example, the outcome of a boy's delinquent act or running away may be to unite the family in their anxiety and concern, while a sixteen year old's pregnancy may provide her depressed mother with a new lease on life. This kind of event, although seemingly disruptive and painful, may eventually lead a "stuck" family to real change in the way the system operates—a second order change. The relative ease with which a family negotiates change depends upon many factors, among them are: the meaning the family ascribes to the change, the resources for meeting change, and the level of family reorganization required.

## The Family as an Organization

The family can be thought of in organizational, as well as in systems, terms. The family is a hierarchy which organizes around interlocking and interdependent roles to carry out its functions. After all, every family has to work out ways of carrying out the daily tasks of child care, household work, wage earning, and decision-making. Role organization and expectations vary a great deal from family to family and are influenced by such factors as culture, ethnicity, one's own family of origin, and composition of the family. No one right, acceptable way to organize a family exists.

Families differentiate and carry out their functions through subsystems according to generation, sex, common interest, or function. Rules are developed to define who participates and what the nature of that participation will be in each of the various subsystems, as well as how members will interact across subsystems—how parents and children relate to each other, for example (Minuchin, 1974).

The rules regulating the distance between and the nature of the interaction among subsystems tend to serve as invisible boundaries whose function it is to protect the differentiation of that system. According to Minuchin, adequate family functioning depends upon clear, distinct boundaries, defined well enough to allow the various family subsystems to carry out their functions autonomously, at the same time allowing for contact between the members of the subsystem and others.

Minuchin has proposed that families can be located on a continuum from enmeshment to disengagement in terms of subsystem relationships. In between these two extremes are those families with clear but open boundaries. The enmeshed family, characterized by blurred boundaries, tends to be overly protective and overly reactive and tends toward fusion of individual identities. The disengaged family is characterized by rigid boundaries, insufficient availability of one subsystem to another, inadequate support alliances, and underreactivity to each other (Minuchin, 1974:54).

The family also has an external boundary that sets it off from other systems, a boundary which may be defined along a continuum from tightly closed to almost nonexistent. One might speculate that the enmeshed family is more likely to maintain a closed external boundary, cutting itself off from relationship options outside the family, perhaps experiencing input from the outside world as threatening. The members of a disengaged family, on the other hand, are more likely to turn to the outside world for support and to have a wide variety of individual connections.

When assessing a family, the clarity and consistency of the organizational arrangements, rather than a normative prescription concerning the design, of a family is important. Many of the families that come to the attention of the child welfare system are underorganized (Aponte, 1976; Colón, 1980); that is, rather than being stuck in rigid rule systems, there are few established rules, and expectations are unclear or constantly shifting. Boundaries between people and limits defining the use of time and space are non-existent or vague. On the other hand, many families that appear to be underorganized or disorganized to an outsider may, in fact, be operating within a very complex series of rules and arrangements, which are well understood by each family member. Frequently, a Child Welfare worker who was raised in a tightly organized, small nuclear family system will experience a large extended family as chaotic. Such a family may have a clear and consistent pattern of organization, but the worker is not privy to the family's game plan.

## Family Communication

One of the most important processes in any family, of course, is the communication system. Kantor and Lehr (1975) discuss the family system as an information processing system. They believe "that family systems seek to attain their goals by continuously informing their members what constitutes a proper or optimal distance" among the members and between members and the outside world (ibid.:112). In this sense, communication can be said to be focused primarily on the regulation of distance.

All behavior is communicative; it is impossible *not* to communicate (Watzlawick, Beavin, and Jackson, 1967). The communication system parallels the relationship system and communicates about the nature of that system. Communication is also both verbal and nonverbal. Satir (1967) and Bandler and Grinder[5] who have written extensively on the topic of family communication, emphasize the importance of congruence between verbal and nonverbal messages in order to avoid ambiguous and contradictory communication. That is, it is important that what is said is not disqualified or contradicted by behavior. Finally, it is important to be aware of the extent to which communication within a family system is open or closed. In a family with open communication, it is possible for members to reveal their needs and wants without fear of unresponsiveness or invalidation from other family members.

## Power, Harmony, and Conflict

Power and decision-making arrangements persist in all families. Normally, one expects power to be vested primarily in adult members of the family, yet there is great variation in how power is distributed and used. It is important that all members "have enough power in the family to protect their personal interests in the family at all times, while keeping the well-being of the other members, and of the family as a whole, in mind" (Aponte, 1976:436–437).

Family harmony tends to be equated with family stability, perhaps as a result of the emphasis on the family as a retreat and source of all emotional satisfaction. A number of family scholars question that notion. Sprey, for example, rejects "the implication that stability, the fact of family continuity, is somehow normal and incompatible with the presence of conflict and disorder" (1969:699). The point to be made here is that conflict itself is not the major cause of family disorganization, but that unresolved strife can lead to disintegration of family life. Conflict is to be expected in the highly charged emotional atmosphere of families. Problems are often worked out through a certain amount of conflict. What is essential is that families possess adequate conflict resolution mechanisms in order to minimize unresolved grievances that hamper family relationships.

*Ethnicity and the Family*

"Common to the ethnic group is a shared feeling of peoplehood and a common sense of past and future. This sense of belonging often connotes cohesion, solidarity and a basis of identity" (Devore and Schlesinger 1981:6–7). In a pluralistic society, as American society surely is, every aspect of family life must be studied in the context of "the ethnic reality."[6] Although an effort has been made throughout this chapter to stress the impact of ethnicity on family life, it is well to highlight it once again.

Ethnic factors are a significant determinant of individual and family behavior, values, goals, and of the world views people use to interpret events. The ways in which the life cycle is played out differ with each ethnic group. The rituals that mark life transitions, and prevailing attitudes and expectations for each life stage may vary greatly. Families with strong ties to ethnic groups may have strictly defined sex roles and, of particular importance to Child Welfare practice, may subscribe to child-rearing methods that are at variance with the larger society. Ethnic roots and current ties are of great personal significance in the life of a family and its members. As McGoldrick has said in writing about ethnicity: "It involves conscious and unconscious processes that fulfill a deep psychological need for identity and a sense of historical continuity" (1982:400).

Strong ties to an ethnic group—including here those groups defined by race, religion, and national origin—can be a source of identity, pride, support, and comfort to a family and its members. As assimilation or changing ideas confront the family, these ties can also be a source of stress and conflict and can affect the ability of a family to meet the needs of its members. Many individuals get caught between the ethnic tie and the larger society. Children from ethnic groups are often misunderstood or labeled as deviant because the family's teachings, behavior, and values contrast with the dominant group in schools or other organizations. Young people and adults may find that they are pulled toward the ways of the dominant culture in order to survive or to advance, albeit at the price of loyalty conflicts and distancing from the family of origin.

Wide diversity in family life should be expected in a nation largely composed of immigrants and their descendants, and one might think these differences would be valued for contributing to the richness and vitality of life in such a country. As McGoldrick points out, there has instead been a marked inability to tolerate differences in American society. "The desire to obscure cultural variations and develop homogeneous 'norms' dominates our culture. This has led to stress and conflict which is always most evident in the cultural group with the least 'seniority'" (1982:400). As a consequence, those groups that do not emulate the model of family life of the dominant Anglo-Saxon culture have often been judged dysfunctional and have been devalued.

Those families who belong to racial minority groups, perhaps due to their high visibility, have suffered most from this situation. They have been stereotyped and labeled in ways that suggest pathology, deviance, lack of initiative, and even lack of intelligence. The opportunity structure of the larger society has often been systematically closed off to members of these groups, making it extremely difficult for minority families to meet the needs of their members. While some progress has been made in recent years, life is still more dangerous and difficult in the families of these groups, which contain a disproportionate number of poor and which are heavily represented in the Child Welfare system. Much research remains to be done in the area of ethnicity and the family. This research should consider both the special strengths and the particular vulnerabilities of minority families. Many researchers conclude, as Staples and Mirandé do, that "while there is no validity to the idea that the family system of a given minority is pathological, there also is little credibility to a philosophical school that assumes that all aspects of minority family life are strong and healthy and that no weaknesses of any kind exist" (1983:514). It is the task of the Child Welfare system to recognize and build on those strengths and to offer support and preventive intervention in areas of vulnerability. What is quite clear at this point is that ethnicity has great impact on family organization and functioning and needs to be looked at, not from a "cultural deviant" or "deficit" perspective as it often has been in the past, but from a "cultural variant" or "nondeficit" approach.

The position taken in this chapter is that the family, far from being sick or dead, is a highly adaptive, durable, and essential institution in American society. The diverse but functional forms that the family takes contribute to a richness of life in this society. The family is indeed a major service delivery system, fulfilling important caretaking and protective functions; however, it is often sorely stressed by lack of supportive connections with other systems of society. Given the fundamental importance of the family in the growth and development of the individuals who comprise society, those who are interested in child welfare must focus their efforts on the welfare of the family. Child Welfare practice must be informed by an understanding and appreciation of the family as the most important and influential unit to which anyone ever belongs. Child Welfare workers must move toward an approach based on a thorough knowledge of family theory and practice. Practitioners at all levels, from direct service delivery positions to policy making positions, must view their actions and decisions in terms of how they may be supportive of families in their struggle to fulfill their functions.

# CHAPTER 8

# The Developing Child

Patricia L. Pasick
Robert S. Pasick

The emerging adolescent bears a striking resemblance to the status of child development as a discipline. Both are changing at a rapid pace, struggling with complexity and ambiguity, motivated by the challenge of new experiences and discoveries, seeking to incorporate past knowledge and influences, increasingly in revolt against previously held assumptions, and—most acutely—trying to forge a single identity from a multitude of influences. That identity is partially captured by Scarr (1979) who, in describing several themes prominent in contemporary child psychology, implores us to consider that (1) it is necessary to study children's behavior in context by understanding the settings in which children live and develop; (2) child psychology is imbedded in its own social-cultural-historical context; and (3) developmental changes occur not only in children but continue throughout the entire life cycle.

Throughout the twentieth century, Child Welfare workers and educators have shared with psychologists a keen interest in the formation of a scientifically-based body of knowledge about the developing child, particularly in its application to the welfare of children. When faced with a clinical or placement issue about a child, it is difficult to make an assessment, to sort out the salient data from a bewildering array of apparently conflicting sign posts: recent and past knowledge from child psychology and family development; shifting social policy stances which bend to winds of political and economic change; and individual, familial, and sociocultural patterns—all of which are alleged to determine the ultimate course of a child's development. The questions that face today's Child Welfare practitioner about the developing child are staggering in their importance. Can placement at an early age in a day-care center cause irreparable harm? Should abused children be removed from their families? Will an unwanted child grow up to be an unhappy child? Can early intervention make a difference in a child's overall development? Should parents raise children permissively or strictly, singly or together? Does psychotherapy help a disturbed child? If so, should it be individual or family therapy?

While it is beyond the scope of this chapter to specifically answer these and the other crucial questions about the developing child, the aim is to summarize the current status of some aspects of child developmental psychology within a context that may be useful for informed practice.

## The Historical Perspective

Several historical and cultural trends have influenced the Western view of the developing child. Philip Aries, in his monumental work tracing childhood from the twelfth to the eighteenth century in Western Europe, points out that childhood as we know it today is a relatively new invention. Before the seventeenth century medieval people did not see childhood as a period of existence important to society. He notes that a child who had passed the age of five or seven was immediately absorbed into the world of adults:

> In the Middle Ages, at the beginning of modern times, and for a long time after that in the lower classes, children were mixed with adults as soon as they were considered capable of doing without their mothers or nannies, not long after a tardy weaning (in other words at about the age of seven). They immediately went straight into the great community of men, sharing in the work and play of their companions, old and young alike. (1962:411)

In the nineteenth century the Child Welfare movement led to changes in the upbringing of poor, handicapped, and delinquent children as institutions were developed in the United States and Europe to provide for their care. Later in that century the field of psychology began the formal study of the developing child. Kesson (1979) in "The American Child and Other Cultural Inventions" identifies several "determining spirits" that have had impact on our view of child development. Behavioral psychologists from John Watson to B. F. Skinner have provided a learning theory perspective on the child's socialization and acquisition of knowledge. Cognitive theorists from William James to Piaget have studied how children sense, perceive, think, and solve problems. Furthermore, biologically oriented scientists have been rooted in the evolutionary and genetic aspects of behavior.

Two other influences on developmental theory have been central in the shaping of Child Welfare practices. One is deeply imbedded in the significant cultural change that occurred as the United States developed from an agricultural to an industrialized nation. With this transition came the separation of the domain of work from the domain of home. Children continued to be cared for at home by women while men worked in other settings. As a result, according to Kesson (1979), a basic principle emerged that has dominated the thoughts of Child Welfare workers, pediatricians, psychologists, and educators for the past seventy years, namely that children need home and mother to grow as they should grow. Only recently has this premise been challenged (see Kagan, Kearsley, and Zelazo, 1978; Rapoport, Rapoport, Strelitz, and Kew, 1980). Emerging cultural changes now direct our attention to the role of fathers, the effects of extrafamilial care, the diversity of current parental situations, and the dynamics of the family as a system.

Finally it is well accepted that psychoanalytic theory has been highly influential upon Child Welfare and clinical practice. Freud, the first scientist to produce a comprehensive theory of child development, focused on early psychosexual experiences as crucial to subsequent adult adjustment. For the past fifty years his writing and that of other psychoanalysts including Anna Freud, Karen Horney, and Margaret Mahler have had a powerful impact on the contemporary view of the developing child. Until recently, the prevalence of the psychoanalytic framework led to a stronger emphasis on childhood fantasy and instinctual drives than on environmental factors in the treatment of emotional disorders of children.

## Current Assumptions in Child Development

As a discipline, child development (like the adolescent, to carry forward the earlier metaphor) has the beginnings of a distinct identity that can now be of some use to the practitioner. This identity is shaped by some widely held—if still debated—assumptions regarding the psychological growth of children. These assumptions are based on several decades of longitudinal research, clinical and normative studies of development, cross-cultural investigations, as well as some theoretical formulations. In total, they reflect a trend toward a more complex, less extreme, and, ultimately, a more optimistic view of development. What is outlined here is certainly not a comprehensive picture of "the state of the art," but a highlight of some recent assumptions that may have particular relevance for Child Welfare workers.

ASSUMPTION 1. *Human development is the result of a dynamic interaction between genetic–constitutional and environmental factors over the entire course of development.*

The combination of nature with nurture to produce an individual has long been recognized in child psychology, with the traditional debate centering on which factor has predominance in development. Increasingly, however, the emphasis is shifting away from *how much* each sphere of influence independently contributes and instead, to *how they interact* to affect individual psychology. This trend has led some psychologists to articulate a model of development that directly addresses interactional processes.

The interactional or transactional model was described initially by Sameroff and Chandler (1975). Strong support for the model came from the New York Longitudinal Study of temperament and behavior disorders in children from infancy to adolescence. Thomas and Chess (1980) and others (Anthony, 1974; Bell, 1979; Kagan, Kearsley and Zelazo, 1978; Meisels and Anastasiow, 1982; Sameroff, 1980) have provided more recent elaborations of interactionist theory.

What is the theory and what are its implications? The notion is that development at any point in time is the result of a constant interplay between a child's biological and constitutional status on one hand, and the larger environment on the other. The implications are numerous. Most importantly, an interactional model dictates that no single factor alone has predictive value for a child's future. Rather, as Segal and Yahraes (1978) note, children are affected by a "mosaic of forces." Moreover, since this schema is a dynamic one, a person continues to affect and be affected by the environment—for better or worse—throughout the life cycle.

A major implication drawn from an interactional model of development is the importance of early childhood experiences. New strands of evidence have surfaced, stating that early experience is important but not decisive or all-determining for later functioning; early experience is not a critical period beyond which a substantial change in cognitive and personality structures is impossible. This controversial view is presented most strongly by Clarke and Clarke (1976). Their collection provides some evidence for the ability to reverse and to recover from adverse early experiences, such as separation, hospitalization, and institutionalization through interventions which alter the child's caretaking environment in early and middle childhood. Rutter (1976; 1979) hypothesizes that early separation per se may not be harmful. Yet, when separation is in association with family discord (as in divorce) or general family disruption (as in hospitalization) or poor environmental conditions, problems in development may occur. Kadushin summarizes a follow-up study of older adopted children (ages 5–12) and concludes that the present—especially when it provides a different environment, social class, and neighborhood—"is a constant, countervailing force upon the past" (1976:204).

While Clarke and Clarke agree that the limits of personal change are not the same throughout development, they remind us that the effects of increasingly wider experiences available to a growing child after early childhood may assist to "self-right" the child. Caution is voiced by Sroufe (1979) who remarks that while children's early and later experiences make a difference, the lasting consequences of early inadequate experience may be subtle and complex and become manifest only when a child attempts to establish intimate adult relationships or engage in parenting.

Implicit in Clarke and Clarke's view and in the interactional model itself is the belief that the human organism—whether it be parent or child—has potential for change. However, when some major aspects of development do *not* change, like certain caretaking practices, aspects of child temperament, or particular socioeconomic factors, it is easier to make predictions of future development. In short, anything that remains relatively constant over time has a more enduring effect upon development.

For example, the impact of low socioeconomic status on child development has held the attention of educators and psychologists for at least two decades. Several prospective, longitudinal studies of social status and perinatal conditions, for example, have concluded that while an interactional process is at work, the socioeconomic status of the caretaking environment plays a central role in predicting developmental outcome from birth onwards (Broman, Nichols, and Kennedy, 1975; Rubin and Balow, 1979; Werner and Smith, 1977). Logically, it is not difficult to understand why. First, social class is a broad variable, subsuming such factors as: economic resources and opportunities; nutrition and health; cultural and ethical standards and expectations about children and parenting; levels of parental education; and some index of family stress and stability. Second, social class is a complex and continuing experience that affects children's daily interaction with their environments.

In a broader sense, any caretaking environment that is not adaptable to children's individual needs may constitute a risk factor (Sameroff, 1980). In summary, from an interactional perspective on the developing child, clinicians need to: (a) understand how inner and outer factors are in mutual interaction with each other; (b) assess the adaptiveness of both child and environment (family, neighborhood, school, culture, and society); and (c) anticipate how new influences, developmental needs, and competencies will affect the coping capacities of family and child.

What follows is a brief description of other assumptions within current developmental theory; assumptions derived particularly from the interactional model outlined above.

ASSUMPTION 2.  *The child is an active (versus passive) participant in development.*

As Kagan, Kearsley and Zelazo (1978) so clearly outline in their review of infancy, the art and science of child development has moved far from Watson's view of the child as a "blank slate" upon which environment makes its mark. More than a decade of research (Bell and Harper, 1977; Lamb, 1978; Lewis and Rosenblum, 1974) has shown that the child is not a passive recipient of environmental influences but actively seeks to influence his or her world. As Bell (1971) and others (Brazelton, 1973) have demonstrated, this is never quite so clear as in infancy when the newborn's state (cry, sleep–wake patterns, feeding patterns) evokes essential caretaking by significant adults. Furthermore, this process occurs differentially in families, with some infants possessing more "sending power" or clear cues than others, and some caretakers more able to read those cues than others (Brazelton, 1973; Goldberg, 1977). Traditionally investigators and clinicians have studied the "product" (the child) as one "produced" by the parents, without looking in any detail at the process by which the child's current status has been obtained. Bell and Harper's position, which is finding wide acceptance in the developmental community, is:

> The child plays a substantial role in shaping the process by which any particular end state is reached. In a nutshell, the love-oriented, permissive parent and the sweet little child who is obediently doing chores may have done some real shouting and hair pulling before you appeared on the scene to observe their currently peaceful truce (1977:213).

In other words, throughout childhood, it is assumed that children are both architects and products of their environment.

ASSUMPTION 3. *Significant individual differences in children affect their development.*

Much interest in child development continues to revolve around normative structures and processes which show a different organization at different development points. However, more attention is now being paid to individual characteristics and how they may contribute to children's vulnerability or invulnerability to later difficulties.

Differences in early temperamental characteristics, for example, have been linked to the development of later behavior disorders. Thomas, Chess and Birch's New York Longitudinal Study (NYLS, Thomas and Chess, 1977; Thomas, Chess and Birch, 1968) reveals that 70 percent of children characterized by "difficult" temperament (a constellation which included irregular, nonadaptive and withdrawal behaviors in combination with negative mood of high intensity) had later behavioral disturbances in middle childhood. Terestman (1980), using NYLS data on three- to five-year-old children, concludes that teacher and observer ratings of mood quality and intensity successfully predict later behavior problems. Recent investigations of parent–infant interaction describe how an infant's readability, predictability, and responsiveness have important effects on parental self-confidence (Goldberg, 1977). Emde (1978) notes that an infant whose constitution reflects a narrow range of behavioral variability has few opportunities for "matching up" with any given caretaking environment. In contrast, some characteristics such as high adaptive ability (Murphy and Moriarity, 1976) may help children remain relatively invulnerable to some caretaking disorders, particularly when they have the benefit of a positive adult model (Anthony, 1974).

New attention to constitutional dimensions of behavior has derived, in part, from a growing concern about abused children. Some studies of child abuse have substantiated that characteristics of certain children in a family, such as low birth weight (Klein and Stern, 1971), prematurity (Klaus and Kennell, 1976) or an infant's perceived difficult temperament (Morse, Sahler, and Friedman, 1970), may elicit selective abusive behavior from parents who are preconditioned to abuse from their own childhood histories.

Some debate persists about whether the passage of time diminishes differences in temperament among children (Kagan, Kearsley, and Zelazo, 1978; Sameroff, 1979) and some question remains about whether temperament is only a parental perception that has little objective reality (Bates, 1980). Nevertheless, there is a general consensus that children are born with certain constitutional differences, that these can be measured with some degree of objectivity (Carey, 1973), and that they may—in interaction with parental attitudes, values, and caretaking practices—have a relatively enduring effect on development.

ASSUMPTION 4. *Cognitive and emotional development are interdependent.*

The foundation for this assumption can be traced, on the one hand, to Freud, who described affect (an id function) as a primary source for cognitive activity (an ego function) and, on the other to Piaget's (1981) notions that the energy of affect combines with cognition to focus the individual's interest on an idea. Recently, Yarrow and Pedersen (1976) have begun to draw attention to the concept of mastery motivation—a blend of competence and confidence—in infant psychology. And, Cicchetti and Sroufe (1976) point out that emotions are cognitive, as well as affective, events and that the intellectual assimilation and understanding of environmental events is mediated by affective states such as mood and temperament.

## Developmental Tasks: An Ecological Perspective

Over the past decade the study of the developing child has moved away from a perspective of the child as a self-contained, independent being toward a broader, more ecological view which integrates family systems theory and ecological psychology. The family systems perspective, represented in part by Minuchin (1974), emphasizes the need to understand family structure in order to thoroughly appreciate the complexities of a developing child. According to this view, a child develops within a unique social system that has evolved its own set of rules, boundaries, roles, forms of communication, and power structures. This system is constantly changing through the reciprocal interactions of its members who respond as well to external influences of society.

Urie Bronfrenbrenner (1979a; 1979b), an ecological psychologist, stresses the need to look beyond relationships *within* the family (the microsystem) to a consideration of how these relationships are affected by people, social institutions, and events *outside* of the family (the exosystem). For example, employment patterns dictate whether a father or mother can be home as a child ends the school day, and the quality of a neighborhood affects decisions about children's autonomy during play hours. Other powerful influences in the exosystem include schools, government rules and regulations, and social welfare agencies.

The overriding cultural beliefs and values of the society (the macrosystem) also have an influence on the developing child, according to Bronfrenbrenner. These values (which are often transmitted through media) contribute to many pressures and problems which children and families face daily. For example, Belsky (1980) goes as far as to suggest that the cultural fabric of society contributes to the high incidence of child abuse. He cites such influences as high levels of violence in America, the sanctioning of physical punishment as a means of controlling children's behavior, and the belief that children are property to be handled as parents choose.

### Prenatal and Infancy Period of Development

In no other period of development is the salience of an ecological perspective as clear as in the prenatal period. Our increasing knowledge of environmental hazards on a growing fetus has been demonstrated with evidence of the negative effects of maternal age (as in teenage pregnancy), alcoholism, drug abuse, smoking, poor nutrition, and prolonged maternal stress on intrauterine growth. Low birthweight—often the developmental outcome of these hazards—is itself a hazard. Some preterm babies must endure an early prolonged hospitalization which separates them from parents who must cope with the sudden appearance of a small, sick baby. Other children in the family may become symptomatic and the marital relationship becomes strained as well. All of this may result, at least for the short term, in impaired parent–infant interactions, particularly if the family is also stressed socioeconomically. In summary, it is clear that child welfare concerns begin before birth.

During infancy (0–2 years), many developmental tasks are accomplished through maturational forces which assure that competencies occur, such as walking, perception, concept of the permanent object, and beginning utterances. By age two, the infant has passed through the "sensorimotor stage" (Piaget, 1952; 1954) and now has some knowledge and ideas about how the immediate world *works*. Throughout infancy, social experiences with caretakers are of great importance. Through mutual interactive patterns, the infant obtains satisfaction of basic physiological needs, is provided with opportunities for exploration and language development, and is granted increasing autonomy. Freud's and Erikson's (1963) elaborations of this period remind us that developmental child-rearing issues, especially around feeding, elimination, and autonomy are *differentially* resolved by babies and their parents—some with more success than others. Kohlberg and Turiel's (1971) expansion of Piaget's (1948) earlier work on moral development is instructive about how highly egocentric the infant is. Before age two, for example, a baby, while fearing punishment, possesses no moral concepts about right or wrong.

Caretakers provide not only a resource for the infant's physical and explorative needs, but also provide the basis for an emotional relationship or affectional tie embodied in *attachment*. The most prominent view of attachment comes from Bowlby (1969) who has recently expanded the concept into adulthood (Bowlby, 1980). His definitive foundational theory, derived from observations of caregiver–infant proximity, has been explored by Ainsworth (1964) and her colleagues (Ainsworth, Blehar, Water, and Wall, 1978), with other elaborations by Sroufe (1977) and Sroufe and Waters (1977).

The basic features of the Bowlby–Ainsworth concept of attachment imply that a securely attached infant is one who is able to use the caregiver as a base from which to explore the environment and who utilizes the comfort of the primary caretaker under stress. The insecurely or maladaptively attached infant, it is argued, is unable to find comfort under stress or resume exploration upon reunion with the caregiver. It is hypothesized that when a secure attachment relationship between infant and caretaker is not established within the first year, there are social, emotional, and cognitive developmental consequences. Some preliminary data point to the possibility that maladaptive or insecure attachments constitute a risk factor in infancy, at least for the short term.

Patterns of insecure and anxious attachment at twelve to eighteen months have predicted reduced curiosity and poor adaptation in problem-solving situations a year later (Main, 1977; Matas, Arend, and Sroufe, 1978) and difficulties in peer relations at age 4½–5 (Waters, Wippman, and Sroufe, 1979). In addition, tentative findings show that a group of lower socioeconomic mothers under significant stress tend to have infants who are less securely attached (Vaughn, Egeland, Sroufe, and Waters, 1979).

Proponents of attachment theory point out that secure attachment need not be established within a critical period. As Vaughn et al. note: ". . . infant–mother attachments arise from interaction; they continue to develop even after an affective bond has formed, and they are responsive to changes in the behavior of either partner" (1979:975). Furthermore, another view is that attachment is not the same as a symbolic love relationship between preschoolers and their parents, which depends on children's perceptions of the degree to which their parents value them. In other words, emotional bonds can develop without a prior attachment (Kagan et al., 1978).

The concept of attachment is closely allied to notions about maternal *bonding*, the emotional tie of the mother to her infant. The view that early mother–infant bonding within the first week is necessary for a child's healthy psychological development (Klaus and Kennell, 1976) has been a force for recent hospital policy changes regarding routine postnatal mother–infant separations. However, the theory has not been wholly upheld by subsequent research (Leiderman, 1978; Rode, Chang, Fisch, and Sroufe, 1981). It is now felt that very early bonding may *facilitate* attachment rather than be essential to future adjustment. Finally, from an ecological perspective, it has been recently demonstrated (Crockenberg, 1981) that social support of mothers by fathers, older children, and others within the extended family/neighborhood network, is the best predictor of secure attachment, particularly for mothers with irritable babies.

## Early and Middle Childhood

From ages two to approximately twelve, the child gradually emerges as a remembering, thinking, problem-solving, and imagining individual—Piaget's preoperational and concrete operational child, well known for the ability to "classify" and "conserve." This is also Erikson's initiative-taking and industrious explorer and Freud's Oedipal child, who becomes, in middle childhood, a latent repressor of those Oedipal strivings.

The developmental tasks of this age period are a reflection of an ever widening world of extrafamilial caretakers, peers, schools, and media characters, and ever increasing demands for socially appropriate behavior, task performance, and control over aggression. Parents remain key influences in this period. However, recent research interest in children's friendships (Asher, 1978) and social cognition (Selman, 1976) point to an increasing understanding of the role of peers in middle childhood. It is felt that as the child's experiences broaden and his or her cognitive abilities become more organized, the child is better able to make judgments of others' behavior. What is of particular importance about this age, at least from the perspective of helping professionals, is the child's development of self-concept or self-esteem. The set of perceptions and feelings a child has in relation to himself or herself are continually developed in relation to *experiences*—developing competencies at home, success in school, and ability to establish peer relationships. Closely allied to self-concept is the developmental task of sex role identification.

An ecological perspective on the child in this age period is an important one. The rapid pace of social change in the last decade has created some difficult stresses for parents. First, the rise of dual career families has generated needs that, on the whole, have not been met in the workplace or in schools: both institutions set inflexible hours which inevitably conflict. The impact of out-of-home or extrafamilial care upon development is still under debate. Suffice it to say that parental uncertainties regarding the kind and quantity of non-parental child care, combined with societal structures that remain out of step with dual career work patterns, have been a great source of anxiety for families. Second, the isolation of many nuclear families from a network of support and from an extended family has been well documented by sociologists. "Reaching out to touch" a faraway family member by phone provides little solace when a working mother or father faces lost wages in order to nurse an ill child. Furthermore, as Bronfrenbrenner (1979b) reminds us, the neighborhood, once filled with companionable at-home supports for child caregivers, is often filled instead with empty houses: Children are at school or in day care while parents are at work.

While Freud's characterization of middle childhood is one of "latency," referring to a period of suppressed Oedipal strivings in children, the *family* during this time is anything but latent. Change is a virtual constant in early childhood, as the task is to create a viable family structure to accommodate one or more new members. As middle childhood approaches new challenges emerge. Parental careers may be on the rise and result in one or more relocations. Economic pressures are greater, and, in many cases, issues arise about the retirement, illness, or death of elderly family members. In short, families face a multitude of challenges as their children grow. It is a tribute to their strength that children develop as well as they do.

*Adolescence*

Most persons intimately acquainted with an adolescent—including the adolescent—are not sufficiently prepared for the suddenness with which this age period begins. It is, some parents will say, as if a stranger is now among them. To some extent, they are right. Adolescence is marked by the rapid emergence of new physiological and psychological structures and these often give rise to behaviors which set a young person apart from adults. The impact of new sexual characteristics upon children has been well documented (Blos, 1962). Not only is there a new sexual awareness but a strong sense of physicality as well. In fact, the adolescent's self-image is built, to some extent, upon the physical images of others, resulting in the well known "look-alike" phenomenon among some groups of young people.

Relationships with peers take on a new personal and sometimes sexual *intimacy*. Increasingly throughout this period, the ability to empathize with others is apparent, paving the way for the formation of strong identifications with peer culture and adult role models. This period is one of heightened emotionality as well. Feelings run deep and wide and seem unmediated by rationality, especially when appeals for reason come from parents.

It is well accepted that many of these social and emotional changes in adolescence are part of a shift in psychological structures. As Piaget made clear, the young person, at least by late teens, is capable of new levels of abstract thinking. With the ability to conduct what Piaget termed "formal operations," the adolescent can establish a personal philosophy of life, an individual view of the world, and a set of guiding moral beliefs. For some, these are well-formulated ideas. For others, adolescence is at least a time for questioning previously held beliefs. In fact, as Kagan et al. (1978) note, awareness of the discrepancy between the actual and the possible helps make the adolescent a rebel, giving force to the alienation some young people experience with adults and adult-led institutions. As Erikson described, this life stage is one that is preoccupied with identity or "who am I" issues. To answer that question, the adolescent experiments with a variety of identities.

Despite the increased influence of peers and a growing day-to-day independence from parents, the reciprocal nature of the parent–child relationship continues to be important in adolescence. One task of the family during this period, according to Carter and McGoldrick (1980), is to increase the flexibility of family boundaries to include teenagers' independence, while maintaining an acceptable power hierarchy relative to parental values. While on a daily basis the average adolescent no longer "needs" care, the need for a stable home that is safe and comforting remains important.

From a family perspective, adolescent struggles are not unidirectional, not simply the cause of family tension. As Rapoport et al. (1980) note, the salient issues of midlife for parents as people often surface during their children's adolescence, adding strain to an already disrupted family. For example, parents may feel caught emotionally between the demands of aged parents and rebellious children. Facing an "empty nest" or perhaps as part of career planning, some women return to work. This re-entry process affects all family members—negatively and positively. In addition, midlife is a period when many adults take stock of their lives. This process may be accompanied by depression or by a re-energizing toward new goals. Many parents want time away from the mainstream of family life for some long overdue reflection or to pursue personal interests. The inventory-taking process may include an assessment of marital satisfaction which, for some, precipitates difficulties in the relationship.

Aside from midlife concerns, the presence of sexually aware, career-aspiring, and nearly grown young people may spark some unresolved adolescent issues within parents, especially regarding sexual freedom and career choices. In summary, for many parents a variety of their own separation, vocational, sexual, and even identity issues are present during their children's adolescence. These interweave—or interlock—with similar issues within teenagers themselves. The result is an entanglement that, at worst, provokes disturbances within individuals and the family system, and, at best, provides a rich context for new growth and development.

Among the first to describe adolescence was social scientist G. Stanley Hall in 1904 in his wide-ranging book, *Adolescence: Its Psychology and its Relations to Physiology, Anthropology, Sociology, Sex, Crime, Religion and Education*. The title hints at the variety of societal structures that influence—and are influenced by—adolescents. Today's macrosystem has much effect upon youth. For example, the need for advanced education and training has meant that children assume adult roles much later than was true thirty years ago. Some young people do not leave home until their 20s, and some require financial support for higher education until their 30s. As a result identity formation, in the Eriksonian sense, takes place much later.

Some societal factors may produce troubled youth, according to Bronfrenbrenner (1979a). He indicts the isolation of today's children from a larger society through the deterioration of extended family networks and neighborhoods, occupational mobility, television, and other factors which "abandon them to a world . . . ruled by the destructive impulses and compelling pressures of the age-segregated peer group and the aggressive and exploitative television screen" (1979:161–162).

School and school-related activities often dominate a young person's hour-by-hour adolescence. Oddly, however, the impact of educational settings has not drawn much attention in the psychological literature, compared to the effects of parental influence. Since identity issues often center around academic success and failure, it seems logical that the adolescent's "place" within this complex educational, vocational, and social institution be considered a major influence upon development. (See discussion by Morse, 1975.)

Erikson's (1963) explanation of identity formation includes two components: (1) the individual's consolidation of a 'self-structure' or identity, and (2) society's affirmation of the newly emerging individual. Today's Western society has not yet decided when, ideally, that affirmation should occur. Puberty is often unwelcomed, given society's difficulties with promiscuity and teenage pregnancy. High school graduation often is not viewed as a milestone, but as a stepping off place to college or vocational training. Similarly, graduation from college, especially when employment is not immediately forthcoming or graduate study is in sight, brings forth a less thunderous applause than it did thirty years ago. Even marriage, an obvious adult marker, does not automatically evoke societal recognition of adulthood, perhaps because it is an increasingly short-lived phenomenon among young adults. Only stable employment that sustains an individual independently from outside financial support seems to mark a young adult's rite of passage. For growing numbers of people, that status is not attained until the late 20s or early 30s. In light of macrosystem influences, then, adolescence is a longer, more complex period than Hall or Freud described. It is certain to capture the attention of an increasing number of developmentalists. (See a recent review by Conger, 1978.)

Scientific inquiry about how a child develops began in earnest during the twentieth century. Perhaps the greatest accomplishment of this massive research endeavor has been the discovery of how much more we really need to understand before we can answer the basic question: "How do we get to be the way we are?" Our incomprehension is an advance in itself. No longer are we smugly able to conclude that we know absolutely what is best for all children. Except in the most extreme cases any one event or factor in a child's life does not unalterably control that child's development. As Segal and Yahraes note in *A Child's Journey,* "It is rarely mother alone, father alone, schools alone—any one factor alone—that shapes the destiny of the child. From birth onward, children are affected by a mosaic of forces" (1979:303).

What has begun to emerge is the conception of developing children as resilient beings who play an active role in the course of their own development. Born with certain constitutional features, they are constantly engaged in a complex process of interaction where they are influenced by and in turn have an influence upon their environment. It is clear that no one perfect environment exists for raising children, that no one critical time determines their destiny, and that no one ideal genetic composition can insure a child's success. Decisions made in the best interest of the child require an understanding of the complexity of not only the child, but of the family and society in which the child will be raised.

# CHAPTER 9

# Child Abuse and Neglect
## An Overview

JEANNE M. GIOVANNONI

"Child abuse" and "child neglect" are terms that are applied to a diverse set of phenomena. Indeed all aspects of abuse or neglect, when broadly conceived, transect all of the other subjects dealt with in this book, and one may approach an analysis of the topic from many perspectives. We have chosen to structure our discussion around the various sources of abuse or neglect: societal, institutional, and familial. Different definitions and types of harm to children will be addressed in the discussion of familial abuse and neglect.

Abuse and neglect of children can be conceived as stemming from various levels of social organization, from the larger society itself, its specific social institutions, nonrelated individuals, and family members, especially parents and caretakers. This chapter will be primarily concerned with the latter, that is familial child abuse and neglect, for the simple reason that this form of mistreatment has captured the most attention in the field of child welfare. Nonetheless, both societal and institutional abuse are considered first because they serve as an essential context for the understanding of familial abuse and neglect. Abuse of children by unrelated adults is not discussed, since ordinarily such abuse concerns only the criminal justice, not the Child Welfare, system.

## Societal Abuse

Just as child welfare, broadly conceived, can be construed as consisting of the sum total of a society's efforts to enhance or deter the development of its children, so also can societal abuse and neglect be conceived as the sum of that society's actions, beliefs, and values that impede the healthy development of its children. Of course, when it comes to specifying either that which impedes development or that which constitutes healthy or optimal development, social values play a key role. Ultimately optimal child development produces the kinds of adults who are valued by a society. In a pluralistic society, such as ours, no consensus exists about just what constitutes that desirable adult; therefore, designating "societal abuse" or "neglect" is problematic.

Nevertheless, despite disparate values concerning optimal child development, American society is clearly responsible for the abuse and neglect of large segments of its child population. For ours is a society that permits children, who have no control over the matter, to become victims of the circumstances under which they happen to be conceived. The chances for actual survival are not equal among our children, as several social indicators attest. For example, infant mortality is considerably higher for nonwhite children (Keniston, 1977) and the gross disparity in educational opportunity for children documents the differing chances that await them because of the circumstances of their birth. Children of Hispanic descent, for example, are often particularly disadvantaged by the failure of educational institutions to develop bilingual programs or to appreciate cultural and value differences (Jenkins, 1981).

At the root of these and other disparities that demonstrate the gross inequality of opportunity for poor children and children of color is a fundamental value stance running through the fabric of American life. America places a higher value on the maintenance of a socioeconomic structure predicated on individualism and competitiveness than it does on the well-being of all of its children. What else can account for the fact that there are so few national resources or any major social policies directed toward equalizing the life circumstances and opportunities of children? Whether one believes that the circumstances of the parents are due to their own inadequacy or to factors generated by the socioeconomic structure is irrelevant to the value choice made in refusing to mediate these circumstances for children.

These societal factors concerning social and economic inequality are integrally involved with child abuse and neglect. As will subsequently be discussed, the conditions of poverty, which reflect this inequality, are highly correlated with the incidence of child abuse and neglect. How directly contributory such conditions are is not well-established. Nonetheless, that our society permits these conditions to exist suggests, at the very least, that societal factors play some part in the occurrence of abuse and neglect nominally considered to be familial in nature. The very fact that we have no minimal standards of child care, or any national distribution of resources to enable the meeting of such standards, indicates the measure of societal responsibility that must be considered in all child abuse and neglect.

Many analysts also agree that another contributing factor in child abuse is a relatively high tolerance for violence in our society (Gil, 1970; Straus, Gelles, and Steinmetz, 1980). For example, the acceptance of corporal punishment throughout society, without any clear sanctions against its excessive use, or even any clear distinctions between how much is acceptable and how much is excessive, can be seen as a source of potential child abuse rooted in societal values.

Finally, a third societal source of child abuse concerns the relationship between sexual abuse and our sexual mores and the generally devalued position of women. Although the incest taboo is clearly enunciated in our society, other values concerning sexuality are confusing and contradictory. A double standard for male and female sexual behavior, for example, persists. The extent to which societal conflicts over sexuality and its proper expression may contribute to child sexual abuse is debatable. Less debatable, however, is the ambivalent social stance taken in relation to sexual abuse. Just as female rape victims are often disbelieved, so are the accusations of small children, especially little girls, against their male caretakers. Children involved in such situations can be further victimized by the very processes intended to rescue them. As a result, they may bear the burden not only of the initial assault, but also guilt and confusion about their part in the sexual abuse and the familial and societal reactions to it.

In sum, what one conceives of as societal child abuse and neglect is inseparable from very fundamental values of what the good society is, what the good adult is, and what circumstances of child-rearing will produce both. What is suggested here is, at the very minimum, that there are three ways in which societal abuse has direct bearing on particular aspects of child mistreatment. These are the conditions of socioeconomic inequality that pervade society, the general attitude toward violence, and the contradictory attitudes concerning sexuality and sex role behavior.

## Institutional Abuse and Neglect

Closely linked to societal abuse and neglect and, in fact, a direct reflection of societal values, are abuse and neglect perpetrated on children through society's institutions. Indeed, all social institutions and the ways they function reflect those values. With respect to child abuse and neglect it is well to separate two kinds of institutions: the more general institutions developed by society with specific child-care functions and the institutions integral to the Child Welfare system, including those directly concerned with abused and neglected children. Further, the forms of abuse and neglect that may be engendered through social institutions can be divided into those generalized practices harmful to children and direct assaults on children perpetrated by these institutions and their personnel.

Three major systems of social institutions are involved with children: the legal system, the educational system, and the medical care system. Within the legal system, including the laws and the courts empowered to uphold those laws, the situation of children is, at best, ambiguous (Katz, 1971). To begin with, just what age demarcates childhood from adulthood is not at all clear. States vary even in their definitions of "child" for purposes of designating child abuse and neglect. Efforts to impose a uniform age of eighteen have still not been successful and in some states abuse and neglect refer only to children sixteen and under. There are numerous other examples of this lack of uniformity across states, and even within the same state, concerning the age delimitation of childhood in relation to voting, the obligation of parents to support, the right to purchase alcoholic beverages, the definition of statutory rape, the obligation of the public schools to educate, and the accessibility to contraception. Such ambiguity in our laws promotes unequal treatment of children by the legal system and variation in the rights and protections accorded them under law. Apart from this confusion, children, however defined by age, simply do not exist as legal entities. At the present time the best that can be said is that children who are accused of crimes share most of the protections that adults, similarly accused, do. Other children coming before the courts, including abused and neglected children, have no specified, uniform rights within the legal system. How children are treated within the judicial system presently varies with the social labeling of their particular situations, and the ways in which given states have decided to deal with children so labeled.*

Observations have already been made about the inequality of treatment children receive within our educational system. That system's failures with respect to children reflect the broader societal devaluation of some children. Since "educational neglect" itself is a type of child mistreatment, the burden of responsibility that schools bear for such mistreatment must be considered. Although educational neglect is com-

---

*Editors' note: This topic is elaborated on in Chapters 10 and 18.

monly treated as a form of familial mistreatment, the educational system itself must take some responsibility for the failure to educate children or even to keep them in school. If expulsions and suspensions can be partially attributed to the educational system's inability to cope with some children then indeed such practices can be considered forms of institutional neglect. Another way in which the educational system harms children is by the misclassification and misplacement of students on the basis of tests that may be inappropriate or invalid. Even when such tests are valid, many educational systems lack the resources to assist the children so classified. A final, and perhaps the clearest, way in which the educational system contributes to child abuse is through the use of corporal punishment. Such practice is indeed controversial but, at the moment, it is a right of educational institutions, upheld by the United States Supreme Court, to physically chastise students. *When* such chastisement becomes excessive is as unclear in the case of school personnel as it is with parents. Insofar as the schools themselves serve as societal models for the proper upbringing of children, at the very least one can say that their use of corporal punishment is certainly no deterrent to familial child abuse.

The health care system is another social institution in which poor and minority children do not fare well (Keniston, 1977; Steiner, 1976). The individually oriented entrepreneural model which characterizes most of the medical profession has retarded efforts to achieve a more equitable distribution of its services (Keniston, 1977). Further, the refusal of many physicians to treat Medicaid patients and the abuse of Medicaid by still others are some examples of the ways in which the medical profession contributes to poor quality care for some children. However, perhaps most central to the topic of child abuse, including sexual abuse, is the continued evidence that many physicians refuse to cooperate with their own state reporting laws and protective agencies. Beyond the medical profession, hospital care systems indulge in practices that may be harmful to children both physically and emotionally. Of particular note here are obstetrical and pediatric practices that unnecessarily separate children from their mothers for the hospital's convenience.

These examples of mistreatment of children by the major systems that deal with them only illustrate the many ways in which major social institutions may harm children, directly or indirectly. We turn now to more specific forms of child abuse and neglect that may be perpetrated by Child Welfare institutions. These forms of mistreatment have been receiving considerable attention of late, especially since the federally sponsored National Center on Child Abuse (NCCA) brought some of its resources to bear on the subject through research and demonstration grants. The data are not all in, but they substantiate that children are physically and sexually abused and often neglected both emotionally and physically in foster homes, in group homes, and in larger institutions, including jails. Ironically, many of these children have been sent to these placements due to their parents' mistreatment of them. Others are there because of their own behavior or disability. What has long been apparent within the Child Welfare field is that no satisfactory mechanisms have been developed to insure that the very people to whom children are entrusted in substitute care will protect them. Licensing continues to be based largely on adequacy of physical environment and gross kinds of personal criteria. In addition to the inadequacy of licensing mechanisms, the problem of insufficient supervision of staff and substitute caretakers remains chronic.

Beyond the direct and even intentional mistreatment of children by individuals in foster homes and institutions, other less direct forms of mistreatment also occur. Of major concern are the effects of repeated separations of children through movement from one placement to another and of unplanned, long-term lingering in "temporary" foster care. These issues are now in the forefront of Child Welfare concerns, embodied in the establishment of new legislation which emphasizes reunification and permanency planning. Yet it must be underscored that at this point these goals remain ideals. For the forseeable future millions of children will be at the mercy of the substitute care system, and constant vigilance over their proper treatment should be a priority equal to that of reunification and permanency planning.

## Familial Abuse and Neglect

We shift our focus now to familial abuse and neglect. In this section, definitional issues are presented, the development of social and legal responses to the problems are discussed, and the current body of knowledge, gleaned from research on abuse and neglect, is reviewed.

### Definitional Issues

Familial abuse and neglect refer to the mistreatment of children by their own families, especially by those entrusted as primary caretakers—parents or parent substitutes. This type of mistreatment has been the principal interest of the Child Welfare system. Because of the special nature of the relationship between parents and their children and between the family and the State, familial abuse presents particular problems that do not arise in situations of institutional abuse or in abuse inflicted by individuals unrelated to the children. For this reason we have deferred discussion of more precise definitions of "abuse" and "neglect." Such definitions cannot be attempted without consideration of the specialness of the relationship of the family to the rest of society. While child abuse and neglect can be defined in the abstract, out of the context of that relationship, for all practical purposes such definition is meaningless. Child abuse and neglect are defined through the identification of the circumstances within which the society and its agents are empowered to interfere in family relationships, in this case those between parent and child. The term "interference" is used here to include the allocation of societal resources to the family, as well as curtailment or even termination of parents' rights to rear their child autonomously. Hence, any definition of such mistreatment must always be considered in the context of the implications of State intrusion into family life. Ultimately, the boundaries set in determining situations of mistreatment must always be set according to the seriousness of the mistreatment relative to societal willingness to intrude on the family's autonomy. Indeed one operational definition of child abuse or neglect might simply be parental behavior that warrants State intervention. If the criteria for such intervention are based on the harmful impact of such mistreatment on children, then it might be said that child abuse and neglect consist of parental behaviors considered sufficiently harmful to children that suspension of parental rights to autonomy is deemed warranted.

Such a definition, however, bypasses many problematic issues that contribute to the confusion surrounding a clear delineation of abuse. The first concerns the establishment of conditions known to be harmful to children, either immediately or more slowly over a longer period of time. In part, ambiguity stems from lack of knowledge concerning the impact of parental treatment on child development. There is relatively more certainty about the impact of physical care of children on their development, especially that of young children (Giovannoni, Conklin, and Iiyama, 1978). There is much less certainty about the impact of parental treatment on emotional and psychological development.* Moreover, the lack of definitive knowledge is compounded by the problem of conflicting social valuations about parental behavior. Lack of agreement about parental roles, including both rights and obligations, impede the establishment of clear definitions of familial abuse and neglect. With respect to societal willingness to intervene, apart from the issues of impingement on parental rights, there is the equally important aspect of the State's willingness to assume responsibility for the care and nurturance of children through the allocation of societal resources. At the present time no widely accepted resolutions of these issues are available. Rather, only a relative consensus about the seriousness of various kinds of mistreatment and the degrees of seriousness of any

---

*Editors' note: Please refer to Chapter 8 for an excellent summary of current research on child development.

particular kind exists (Giovannoni and Becerra, 1979). Thus, while it is possible to circumscribe various forms of child mistreatment in the abstract, the ease of application of any of these definitions to particular situations remains a relative matter.

Many subcategories of child abuse and neglect can be delineated. These include physical abuse, sexual abuse, various forms of neglect of parental responsibilities including physical neglect, educational and medical neglect, lack of supervision and protection, and emotional mistreatment. Added to these direct failures of parents in nurturing and rearing their children are those concerns that involve parental behavior in other, more tangential areas, such as their sexual mores or criminal activity outside the home. The definition of such behavior as child mistreatment, in the absence of any other kind of direct mistreatment, is very controversial at present.

## Development of Social Responses to Child Abuse and Neglect

Although child abuse, or at least public attention to it, is considered by some to be a relatively new phenomenon, that is not the case. Historical review of the circumstances under which parents have lost their children or their autonomy over them indicates that since colonial times, such circumstances always have occurred and some form of community sanctions employed. Present day arrangements for dealing with child mistreatment—both legal and social service responses—have roots in the nineteenth century. Impingement on parents' rights has called for legal responses, while removal of children from mistreating parents has called for social service responses to substitute for the parents' care.

The legal apparatus empowering states and localities to remove children from their parents' custody first arose in situations where the children's own behavior brought them into conflict with the community. Children, formally accused of no crime, could be removed to the reformatory and their parents held legally responsible. The doctrine of *parens patriae*—the State is the ultimate parent of children—means that the State's rights supercede those of individual parents; this doctrine was invoked as the legal base on which such intrusion into family life could be justified. In time these statutes were amended to include parental failure that did not necessarily manifest itself in children's delinquent behavior. At first the preoccupation was with the moral failures of parents and with physical abuse. Physical neglect of children was gradually incorporated into the law toward the end of the nineteenth century, while only in recent decades has their emotional mistreatment been considered. Children adjudicated under these laws could be sent to orphanages or to foster homes, rather than to reformatories. At the turn of the century, juvenile court was established in counties across the nation as the legal institution for handling child abuse and neglect as well as juvenile delinquency. Previously, children's cases were handled either in criminal or probate courts. It should be noted that throughout this time a parallel legal system, the poor laws, which regulated the dispersal of public relief, empowered local authorities to remove children from their parents as a means of and as a condition of granting relief from economic destitution. The philosophy underlying this practice changed early in the twentieth century, but it was not until the initiation of federal involvement in poor relief, through the AFDC program, that the actual practice has slowly eroded. Although less directly, poverty continues to be a major cause of family dissolution.

Along with the evolution of legal responses to the problems of child mistreatment, the social service response has developed gradually. Child Welfare, as it relates to abuse and neglect, has generally consisted of two parallel and often poorly integrated systems, one concerned with child protection and the other with the provision of substitute care. Until very recently, the functions of practice in child protection were to investigate and validate complaints of child mistreatment and when so validated to see that the situations were adjudicated and, if necessary, the children protected through removal from their parents. Return of those children to their parents was not considered an integral function of child protection. Rather, once children passed into the substitute parental care system, management of their lives, including return to their parents, was delegated to the foster care system. Although the provision of social services to forestall or eliminate the need for removal of children has for many decades been an ideology of child protection, the actual provision of such services has been ambiguous and haphazard.

The roots of this dichotomy are found in the historical development of child protection throughout history, in both the private and the public social service sectors. In the private sector, the Society for the Prevention of Cruelty to Children was established in 1874 in New York City and by 1900 existed in 161 communities. For many decades the function of this agency was essentially a law-enforcement one, stressing investigation of complaints of child abuse and advocacy promoting the development and enforcement of child protective legislation. Gradually, the philosophy changed and the functions of the SPCC were extended to include social service efforts to prevent both placement and court involvement in cases of child mistreatment. The present day concept of child protective services as a "preventive social service" (preventing the placement of children, not preventing the initial mistreatment) emerged from the work of that organization. The SPCC's involvement in direct services began to decline in most communities in the late 1950s and early 1960s as their functions were taken over by the public sector. Today the national successor organization, the Children's Division of the American Humane Society, remains an important influence in child protection.

Parallel to these developments were those in the public sector. With the establishment of juvenile courts and their social service arm, probation, the investigation of mistreatment, and any concomitant social services, were delivered through probation, albeit often by probation officers with a social service, rather than a law enforcement, orientation. The shift in the provision of public child protective services from juvenile court and probation to public Child Welfare services, spurred largely by federal Child Welfare policies as directed in amendments to the Social Security Act, has been accomplished only in the last decade. This shift, along with the nationwide interest devoted to the problems of child abuse in recent years, focuses on issues regarding the role and function of protective services, as well as those relating to the training and practice expertise of social workers rendering protective services. Of particular note are issues concerning the combination of legal authority and investigative functions with therapeutic missions (Giovannoni and Becerra, 1979).

Presently the most typical service arrangement for the management of child abuse and neglect is the juvenile courts and public departments of social services. In addition, local law enforcement carries an investigatory role, since some instances of child abuse or neglect are also criminal acts. Protective services units within public social services are responsible for investigation of complaints of child mistreatment, for determining whether court action should be sought, and, if so, for making recommendations to the court as to disposition. In lieu of court action, or in addition to it, social services to restore adequate parental and family functioning may be provided. If the recommendation to the court is for placement of the child, continued services to both the child and the family are typically offered by units within the department dealing with placement and continued services. Also, the resources of other community agencies may be used for the family.

The ideologies underlying the handling of abuse and neglect have changed and are best encapsulated in Public Law 96–272 passed in 1980. In this law manifestations of family dysfunction affecting children, including mistreatment, are considered best handled through resolution of the difficulties without removal of the children. In this way, family autonomy and integrity are better maintained and children spared the trauma of separation from their families. If such family maintenance is not possible because the home environment is deemed too unsafe, then an effort to restore the family unit through "reunification services" is extended while the children are in placement. If these efforts should fail within a reasonable time, the ideology dictates that efforts should be made to terminate parental rights and to find alternative permanent plans for the children, preferably through adoption.

This legislation represents the culmination of many movements

within the Child Welfare system. With respect to child abuse and neglect, it is an expression of the long held preference for a treatment and
rehabilitation rather than a punitive approach to parents and a belief in
their rehabilitative potential. The philosophy itself, however, is ahead of
the means to implement it—with respect to the provision of adequate
resources and the development of both the optimum array of services
and the organizational arrangements to facilitate them. Not the least of
the organizational problems is the full integration of protective services
into local Child Welfare networks and the insurance of continuity of
services and service providers from the point of investigation through
ultimate reunification or termination of parental rights.

While juvenile courts and public social service agencies are the core
institutions for managing problems of child abuse and neglect, other
public responses to the problems are worthy of mention. First of all,
there are three kinds of relevant statutes. There are those laws usually
contained in the civil codes of states which empower the State to take
jurisdiction over children declared to be "dependents" of the courts and
to terminate parental rights. Next, of more recent vintage, are the reporting laws that came into being in the 1960s. These laws mandate
certain persons to report situations of child abuse or neglect to agencies
authorized to accept, keep, and investigate such reports. Finally, in the
criminal codes of all states, various statutes exist that establish the conditions under which perpetrators of child abuse or neglect may be crimi-
nally prosecuted. All of these laws vary from state to state and across
laws even within the same state with respect to the definitions of child
abuse or neglect incorporated, the ages of children under their jurisdiction, the persons mandated to report, and the agencies authorized to
receive the reports. The functions of reporting laws may be multiple: to
trigger investigation, to provide a central registry so that repeated abuse
may be detected, and to provide uniform statistics on the incidence of
abuse and neglect. The first is not problematic, but the keeping of central registries has stirred controversy about the rights of privacy and the
noxious effects of labeling people.

While abuse and neglect have long been recognized as legal and
social service problems, the growing national attention paid to the issues
in the past twenty years was originally spearheaded by pediatricians
(Antler, 1978). The work of Helfer and Kempe, reported in *The Battered
Child* (1968) and based on their pioneering work with physically abused
children, gained widespread public attention via the media. Their research gained momentum from advances in radiological technology
which could reveal old bone injuries in children, indicative of abuse
(Robin, 1982). Subsequently, public and professional concern extended
to other forms of mistreatment, and, by the end of the 1960s, most states
had passed child abuse reporting laws, mandating physicians, nurses,

social workers, and other professionals working with children to report suspected abuse and neglect.

Continued concern about the problem, spurred by pediatric leadership, led to Congressional action in 1973 and the creation of the National Center for Child Abuse and Neglect within the United States Children's Bureau. The future of this federal agency is uncertain, but to date considerable activity has been generated through research and demonstration projects devoted to all aspects of child abuse and neglect. This activity in turn has stimulated more public interest in the problems, both in the private and public sectors and among both professional and lay persons. Child Abuse and Neglect Resource Centers, in each of the ten federal regions, were established as part of the ongoing work of the National Center, serving as both information clearinghouses and as stimulants to states and communities in program development. For example, child abuse coordinating councils, involving a variety of interested parties, were established in many communities.

Paralleling the work of the National Center, the National Committee for the Prevention of Child Abuse, a voluntary organization engaging in a variety of activities aimed at preventing child abuse, now has chapters in several states. A self-help group, Parents Anonymous, founded in the 1960s by an abusive parent with the help of a small group of professionals, now has chapters throughout the country. Its aims are both to prevent child abuse as well as to assist parents in stopping abusive practices. In sum, the 1970s have seen a national movement that has brought the problems of child abuse and neglect into public consciousness. How long-lived this movement will be remains to be seen, as does the long-range institutional impact of these diverse and multiple efforts. It is important to remember that the problems themselves are not new, nor are the basic social and legal institutions for handling them. The only true barometer of the adequacy of societal response to child abuse and neglect is the viability and adequacy of these institutions in the total Child Welfare system. There are few who would agree now or in the forseeable future that the resources allocated to those institutions reflect the goals of a society that cares about and protects its children. Indeed, in spite of the vast attention paid to the problems in recent years, probably not a county in the country has any greater or even equal the amount of investment in its public Child Welfare services than it did before the growth of public and professional awareness.

## Factors Associated with Familial Child Abuse and Neglect

Our knowledge about child abuse and neglect comes from many sources. First, there is the knowledge derived from the direct experience of practitioners. This knowledge includes clinical impressions about possible precipitants of abuse and neglect and, until recently, most of the information was of this kind. More recently information has been accumulated based on more systematic research. These two sources of information are not mutually exclusive, since much of the research itself has either been initiated by clinicians or has been based on their clinical formulations and embodies principal concepts included in the clinical literature.

Questions about child mistreatment have been explained in three kinds of research. (1) Epidemiological research seeks to establish the incidence and distribution of child abuse and neglect; (2) Etiological research attempts to identify the precipitants, concomitants, and dynamics of abuse and neglect; and (3) Evaluation research tries to establish the efficacy of ameliorative or preventive interventions. Although any given research project may be classified under one of these three categories, data from any given category have implications for the others.

As with many other social problems, such as delinquency and mental illness, a common mind set, borrowed from problem solving in the physical sciences, has been an assumption that through research, the "causes" of the problems of child abuse and neglect can be established and, once so established, both the means of reversing the situations, as well as of preventing them, can be achieved. But child abuse and neglect, like other human problems, defy any such simplistic formulations. To begin with, the definitional problems already detailed crop up. For any given research study a particular definition has been used, but differences among definitions in various studies make comparisons difficult—especially when the only "definition" of mistreatment is the presence of children in a designated agency's caseload, since the selection criteria of different agencies are known to be different. Related to the problem of definition is the fact that child abuse does not connote a unitary phenomenon, despite the underlying common base of bringing harm to children. Certainly there is no good reason to assume that the precipitants of diverse situations such as physical injury, sexual abuse, or improper feeding of children are the same unless that commonality is conceived of as something so broad as "family dysfunction," which is of little practical import. Hence, the search for a "cause" of child abuse is in reality a search for the "causes" of multiple and diverse effects. Added to these complexities is the fact that given the variation in children's development, child mistreatment must always be linked to children's ages. For example, it seems reasonable to assume that the physical abuse of an infant is different in nature from that of an adolescent.

Given these complexities with respect to research in child abuse and neglect, it must be understood that while a body of work with some broad common aspects may be the basis for discussion, in actuality the relevance of investigation of one type of mistreatment to those of another may be very weak, even though they may have common research purposes. The result is that while we have had much greater research effort devoted to child mistreatment in the past decade, research related to specific entities is, in fact, sparse. Consequently, we can only look to the research for limited answers and certainly nothing so global and profound as a common cause or causes. At best we can begin to identify what some common factors appear to be in the contexts in which various kinds of mistreatment have occurred in selected populations. The interpretation of these data, and the theoretical explanations that they serve to support, are still best thought of as speculative.

## Epidemiological Research and Incidence of Child Mistreatment

How widespread is the problem of child mistreatment in the United States? How many children are affected? Are there demographic characteristics of mistreated children and their families distinguishing them from those in the general population? Two important national studies have addressed these questions. The first, by David Gil, focused only on reported cases of physical injury (Gil, 1970). The second, conducted for the Department of Health and Human Services, investigated all forms of mistreatment, including cases reported to Child Protective Services and those known to some other agencies, but not so reported (U.S. DHHS, 1981).

Gil conducted his study in 1967 and 1968. His research staff screened more than 13,000 reports of select cases that met his criteria of child abuse: deliberate injury inflicted on children by a parent or other caretaker aimed at harming the child. Analysis of these reports led to an estimate of a nationwide reporting rate of 8.4 children per 100,000 in 1967 and of 9.3 children per 100,000 in 1968. With respect to the sex and age of victims, boys were somewhat overrepresented among abused children under twelve, and girls among those over twelve. Nearly half the children were over six, indicating that child abuse is not limited to very young children. With respect to the families, about 30 percent were female-headed, a fact that suggests that while such families were overrepresented, abusive families were more likely to consist of two parents. Compared to all United States families, poor families were greatly overrepresented. Forty-eight percent of the abusive cohort had incomes below $5,000, as compared with 25 percent of families overall. This association with poverty was more pronounced among black abusive families (53%) than white (40%), and most pronounced among Puerto Rican abusive families (76%). Gil found nonwhite children to be overrepresented among his abused children. Reporting rates for nonwhite children were 21 per 100,000 and for white children, 6.7 per 100,000.

The second study, which was federally funded by the National Center on Child Abuse and Neglect, was conducted in 1979–1980 in a nationally representative sample of 26 United States counties (USDHHS, 1981). Cases were drawn from all reports to Child Protective Services (CPS) in those counties and from other sources, such as law enforcement, probation, and other community agencies, as well as public schools, general hospitals, and mental health facilities. Thus, both officially reported and unreported cases were included. All forms of mistreatment were included and were categorized under one of the following: physical assault, sexual exploitation, emotional abuse, physical neglect, educational neglect, and emotional neglect. All cases were screened to meet study criteria, which were quite precise but too complex to repeat here, save to note that they were weighted toward the more, rather than less, severe types of mistreatment. Within these broad categories there were a total of 21 subcategories. The following are some of the highlights of the reported results of that study.

Overall, the estimate of the rate of children mistreated in some way, both reported and unreported, was 10.5 per 1,000. For the specific types of mistreatment the rates calculated were 3.4 per 1,000 for physical assault, 0.7 per 1,000 for sexual exploitation, 1.7 per 1,000 for physical neglect, 2.2 per 1,000 for emotional abuse, 1.0 per 1,000 for emotional neglect, and 2.9 per 1,000 for educational neglect. Of all studied mistreated children only 33 percent had been reported to Child Protective Services. These figures must always be taken as conservative estimates of the actual number of children mistreated, including those not known either to CPS or any other agency. The type of mistreatment varied by the sex and age of the children.

The data on income and ethnicity of mistreated children also varied by the type of mistreatment. Among higher income groups incidence rates were essentially the same for white and nonwhite children. Among white children, all mistreatment incidence rates were much higher for those in low-income groups. Among nonwhite children this association with poverty was noted only for neglect but not for abuse. Overall black children were found to be underrepresented in all mistreatment categories except educational neglect.

Clearly there are some discrepancies between Gil's data and the DHHS study. Such differences do not necessarily tarnish the validity of either study. In fact, great caution should be used in comparing the two studies at all. Given that each used different definitions and sampling procedures and were conducted over ten years apart, such comparison may be futile. The presence of conflicting data does mean, however, that interpretations of either set must be considered speculative, especially with interpretations of why some people are more likely than others to mistreat their children. Without evidence to support the idea that they actually do, such interpretation is indeed meaningless. Unfortunately in the area of child mistreatment we often have had more interpretations than we have had facts to undergird them.

## Etiologic Research

Large-scale epidemiologic studies like the two just described are useful in delineating the magnitude and distribution of child mistreatment. However, they are limited in explaining what etiologic links might exist between mistreatment and the various factors associated with its distribution, such as poverty or family structure. Further, the magnitude of the associations themselves suggest their limited utility in establishing such connections. Some population groups are overrepresented among mistreating families. However, such overrepresentation by no means suggests that mistreatment is typical or modal among these groups. The association between poverty, for example, and mistreatment does not tell us why some poor families mistreat their children, while the vast majority do not, and clearly offers us no clues as to why some affluent families also mistreat their children. The answers to those questions are sought in studies smaller in scope but more intensive in the depth of information gathered. Some highlights of that research will be covered here.

First let us start with what has not been found. As the curtain went up on the recent spate of research into child mistreatment those already engaged in the field were said to be polarized to either the psychological or sociological approaches, that is either seeking explanations in the psychodynamics of individuals (Kempe and Kempe, 1978; Polansky, Borgman, and DeSaix, 1972; Spinetta and Rigler, 1980), or attributing mistreatment to dysfunctions of the broader socioeconomic structure (Steinmetz and Straus, 1974; Straus, Gelles, and Steinmetz, 1980). A middle ground was also established by some researchers who attributed child mistreatment to an interaction between factors resident in individuals and those reflecting their position in the broader socioeconomic structure (Gelles, 1973; Giovannoni and Billingsley, 1970; Young, 1964).

No psychological profile unique to abusing parents has been found to distinguish them from other parents. Nonabusive parents have been found to have personality and other psychosocial characteristics attributed to abusive ones (Starr, 1982). Further, extreme psychopathology, evidenced by a diagnosis of psychosis, has been estimated to occur in only about 10 percent of abusive parents.

With respect to purely socioeconomic explanations, of particular importance are the data concerning income and ethnicity. Some have rejected outright any connection between poverty or ethnicity and mistreatment as simply a reflection of bias in a reporting system that favors the white and more affluent (Parke and Collmer, 1975). Others have accepted the information as valid and interpreted the data as a reflection of the noxious effects on parenting of poverty and racism. Still others have sought to find associations between differing cultural values and child-rearing practices and the occurrence of child mistreatment. This kind of argument splits into two camps. One would maintain that some subcultures actually condone child-rearing practices considered to be harmful to children. At least for gross kinds of mistreatment, such as breaking children's bones or sexually assaulting them, there is no evidence that any subculture in America condones such practices. The other argument maintains that some culturally acceptable child-rearing practices, such as physically disciplining children with an instrument, put children at greater risk of injury—an injury that is not culturally sanctioned (Gil, 1970). The information from studies of cultural differences in disciplinary practices is conflicting, and to date does not substantiate this viewpoint (Erlanger, 1975). The best that can be said is that poverty, extremely low income, does bear a consistent relationship to the occurrence of child mistreatment (Pelton, 1981). The relationship between its occurrence and ethnicity is much more ambiguous. In any event, no evidence suggests that any overrepresentation of poor and minority families is attributable to culturally sanctioned mistreatment of children. Opinion and attitude surveys of low-income and ethnic minority groups report repugnance on their part of abusive and neglectful acts (Giovannoni and Becerra, 1979; Polansky, Chalmers, Buttenweiser, and Williams, 1981). The fact that a majority of reports of mistreatment originate with private individuals, relatives, and neighbors, corroborates the unacceptability of mistreatment among them. These data suggest that even if some overrepresentation does exist among certain socioeconomic groups, mistreating behavior among them is far from the norm and is considered deviant.

Citation of the failure to find clearly delineated psychological or sociological factors acting as etiologic agents in child mistreatment does not mean that both do not play a part. As other research indicates, they do, but in an interactive way, suggesting that mistreatment cannot be explained solely as a psychological, sociological, or economic phenomenon.

Growing from recent empirical research, an ecological approach to understanding child mistreatment has probably gained wider credence than any other. If one examines the various studies done, one finds that psychological, social, and economic factors all have been found to bear some relationship to situations of child mistreatment (L. Allen, 1978).

Factors resident in the child, the parent, the family interaction, the neighborhood, and even the broader community have all been noted as associated with the occurrence of child mistreatment. One formulation of how this myriad of factors may interact to precipitate child mistreatment emphasizes the relationship between family stresses and family supports (Garbarino, 1977). The stresses and the supports to be considered include the intrapersonal, interpersonal, familial, and environmental, those of both a tangible and material nature, as well as the intangible and symbolic. For example, the stresses of poverty—material deprivation and social and personal frustration—unless mediated by intrapersonal resources in conjunction with environmental supports and supplementation can result in situations of child mistreatment. What this formulation suggests is that explanations of child mistreatment will be more fruitful when examining total situations of mistreatment. As yet, we do not have any satisfactory typology or classification of what these myriad situations might be, limiting the practical utility of the formulation. We do not know, for example, which, if any, are more closely associated with particular kinds of mistreatment, although we know more about some than others. We know, for example, that situations of physical neglect are more likely than other kinds of mistreatment to take place in situations of extreme poverty, in female-headed households, and perhaps in the presence of a depressive state in the mother. On the other hand situations of both physical and sexual abuse suggest a much more diffuse pattern. Further, we know that a good proportion of cases coming to public attention involves multiple forms of mistreatment, including physical neglect, physical abuse, and sexual abuse. Therefore, the formulation of a typical situation unique to a particular kind of mistreatment must be limited in scope. In addition some variables seem to be associated with all kinds of mistreatment. These variables involve social isolation and to a much lesser but still significant extent the presence of parental drug and alcohol abuse. The pervasiveness of poverty in all kinds of mistreatment also must be underscored.

It would be a mistake in any discussion of the precipitants of mistreatment to leave the impression that somewhere underlying child abuse and neglect a unique set of pathological conditions exists, setting abuse and neglect apart from other manifestations of family dysfunction. In medical terms, child abuse and neglect are, at best, symptoms of disorder. They are not disease entities. The very designation of child abuse and neglect as social problems, worthy of public attention and the expenditure of public resources, is a matter of social policy and the values that underlie it. So also is the research effort to uncover their etiology. Indeed, child abuse and neglect can and often do exist side by side in the same families with other problems including delinquency, mental illness, marital disharmony, and under and overachievement in school. Designating such families as suitable subjects for research in child abuse and neglect is arbitrary.

What does the knowledge about child abuse and neglect learned from empirical research imply for the practitioner? First it suggests that no pat formula, however tempting, is likely to supplant the individualized treatment of each family. The ecological approach does suggest that in attempting interventions into situations of child abuse and neglect, a broad scanning of the possible points of intervention is warranted. Such intervention might include the provision of environmental supports, both tangible and interpersonal, and interventions targeted not only at the internal family system, but at its external environment as well. But such decisions are not in the hands of individual practitioners. They cannot harness resources that do not exist for their clients. As most experienced practitioners are all too sadly aware, more often than not vital resources such as child care, better housing, and supportive community organizations are not available for their clients. As the following review of child abuse intervention evaluations indicate, the paucity of extrafamilial resources may account for the less than impressive record of success.

## Evaluative Research

The largest quantity of data on the success of ameliorative intervention into situations of child abuse and neglect comes from the evaluation of the treatment demonstrations funded by the federal government in the past decade (Cohn and Collignon, 1979; Layzer and Goodson, 1979). As demonstration projects they cannot be considered as fully representative of the usual ongoing treatment resources available. If anything, demonstration projects usually have more resources. This makes these results even more discouraging. Using recidivism as the basic criterion of success, it appears that treatment interventions were successful in nearly half the cases treated. Other data from longitudinal studies of abusive families who had received services corroborate this discouraging observation (Sudia, 1981).

Two pieces of information mitigate a state of hopelessness about the rehabilitation of abusive families. First, these demonstrations also found that those families who had fewer problems and shorter histories of mistreatment showed significantly less recidivism than those enmeshed in chronic situations. Hence, early intervention does appear to hold a greater promise of success. Unfortunately, in times of severe budget limitations, such intervention is most likely to be eliminated. The other information that mediates hopelessness about these families concerns the kinds of interventions that were most typically offered them. Despite the assumed repetoire of services available in the demonstration projects, the most common form of intervention was individual counseling by a single professional. The use of a professional and nonprofessional together as a team was found to be more effective, indicating that this kind of supplementation of counseling by an individual worker could have observable beneficial results. These data on the kinds of services usually offered to abusive families are corroborated by other surveys of protective services clients. Child-centered environmental supports, such as day care and homemaker services, are the exception, and assistance with housing, employment, and basic subsistence the very rare exception (Sudia, 1981). Yet these were the very kinds of help that the clients sought most.

Given what we know about the situations of abusive and neglectful families it would seem premature to dismiss them as hopeless on the basis of the recidivism rates. The information on the services rendered would more appropriately suggest that they were never given a chance to succeed. To cite the apparent inefficacy of individual counseling with the majority of these families is not to disparage it entirely, but rather to cite its limitations when unaccompanied by other forms of intervention.

Based on the results of these evaluation studies and others it would appear that a practice model predicated solely on the efficacy of individual counseling is not likely to succeed. The ecological model, derived from empirical research, offers another alternative. Yet, that practice model cannot be instituted without fundamental changes in values. As long as our social policies continue to be predicated on a belief that child mistreatment and other forms of family dysfunction are simply manifestations of individual aberration, an unsupplemented individual treatment model will continue to be used. At the core of the discrepancy between empirical fact and policy orientation there is public ambivalence concerning community and societal responsibility for the rearing of children. As long as families, in keeping with the basic values of individualism, are seen as totally responsible for the rearing of the young without corresponding obligations on the part of the society to provide a nurturing milieu in which those responsibilities can be optimally carried out, neither the treatment nor prevention of child abuse is likely to be enhanced. In one sense it would seem that the doctrine of parens patriae has been only partially invoked in the societal response to child mistreatment. If the State, the community, is the ultimate parent of the child, does the responsibility of such a parent cease with the usurpation of familial parental rights? Or does it not also include the responsibility to support children's development before their parent's rights are denied?

# CHAPTER 10

# Families, Children, and the Law

Mark Hardin

## Working with the Legal System

It is important for agencies and social workers to reflect carefully on their methods of dealing with attorneys and also to think analytically about the effects the legal system has on their practice. Agencies need to understand how to use the legal system in a positive manner, both to improve case results and to help reform deficiencies in legal services and legal decision-making. Too often, social workers find themselves drifting into negative, passive, or manipulative means of dealing with the legal system, methods which neither yield positive legal results nor improve the overall decision-making process.

### The Importance of the Law in Child Welfare Cases

Court systems and Child Welfare legislation are indispensable components of Child Welfare practice. Without laws authorizing the agency, police, and courts to intervene on behalf of abused and neglected children, society would be powerless to become involved in child protection. Indeed, in earlier times, the authority of the State to protect abused children was extremely limited. Child protection laws establish guidelines and procedures, thereby helping to insure a degree of consistency, fairness, and impartiality concerning when and how the state intervenes to protect children. One can imagine the terrible power to intimidate and control families that Child Welfare agencies would have if they were empowered to intervene and remove children without a legal hearing or trial. While most Child Welfare officials and workers would no doubt continue to operate with professional care, good faith, and minimal bias, a few would be free to use their authority in less benevolent ways.

When courts operate properly, they provide an orderly and meticulous decision-making process, which is not duplicated by the Child Welfare agency. Court rules, procedures, and standards of evidence mandate a highly exacting sifting and evaluation of information before making decisions critical to the family. While juvenile courts do approve agency recommendations and sustain agency petitions in the vast majority of juvenile cases, the legal process also shapes and disciplines agency fact gathering and decision-making.

Finally, the courts make key decisions which determine the direction of agency practice in individual cases. Courts decide whether a child will be removed from the home, whether the child will be placed in foster care, whether the child will be permanently placed in a substitute home, and many other matters. Although the court often leaves the agency with broad responsibility over the case, and although there are often substantial time gaps between court decisions, Child Welfare practice must be oriented toward satisfying legal requirements.

## Law-Related Skills Needed by Social Workers

While individual differences among lawyers and judges do affect legal decisions, the Child Welfare agency also has an enormous influence on juvenile court proceedings. The quality of day-to-day practice, the thoroughness and precision of fact gathering by the worker, and communication of information from the worker to the attorney largely control the ultimate outcome of cases. Workers must take the major responsibility for the preparation of juvenile court cases. Workers who take the position that "case preparation is the attorney's job" are doing a disservice to the child, particularly when the tasks in question clearly are not being done by the attorney. In fact, the worker is responsible for the majority of information available to the attorney and presented to the court, one of the principal reasons why social work practice skills have such a great bearing on courtroom success.

An area of expertise essential to the Child Welfare practitioner is that of investigation. Workers must be capable of meticulously observing and reporting the conditions and circumstances surrounding the abuse or neglect and of obtaining social, medical, and other information important to a full understanding of the situation. In severe abuse cases, it may become necessary to collect physical evidence, to carefully interview others who may have important information regarding the abuse or neglect, or to arrange for the taking of photographs or written statements. Workers must be capable of recognizing and following leads to further information and knowing when and how to involve the police if they are needed for protective purposes. In some cases the worker may be blocked from gathering necessary information and should know how to draw upon the authority of the court to gain access.

A closely related skill is that of documentation. This involves the recording of case activities as a matter of routine, including what the client does and says, what services are provided, the directions given by the agency to the parent, case plans, and other important information. Critical documentation skills include the ability to focus on concrete observations of fact rather than vague impressions or generalizations. Proper documentation also requires a knowledge of which records need to be gathered, at what times, and how to use the court process, especially for collection of information from out of state. Documentation is not only crucial to obtaining equitable court decisions, but to the helping process itself. Work with families and children is greatly enhanced when it is based on specific, concrete observations rather than on impressions or unverified facts.

Another important law-related skill has to do with preparation and presentation of information to the attorney. The worker must have a sense of which facts are important to the legal proceeding and must be capable of organizing that information in a manner useful to the attorney. Since the attorney is the funnel through which case information reaches the attention of the court, ineffective communication with the attorney makes positive case results far more difficult. The worker must be organized, tactful, and assertive in communicating with legal counsel.

Finally, workers need to gain a better understanding concerning how their work with the family affects the legal case. A principle example concerns the impact of visitation policies on decisions by the court. Where visitation is greatly restricted or denied without the most thorough justification and documentation, the court is likely to conclude that any breakdown in the parent-child relationship has largely been caused by the agency itself rather than due to parental inadequacy. In general, workers need to gain a sense of what case plans and agency efforts on behalf of the family are most likely to sell in court proceedings.

## Role of the Parents' Attorney in Child Welfare Cases

A good parents' attorney is not passive and uncritical of agency practice. The diligent parents' attorney will perform an independent investigation, will conduct discovery through the court process, and will consult independent experts. The job of the parents' attorney is to advocate the will of the parents. Nevertheless, the parents' attorney often does perform a constructive role that also ultimately benefits the child. Since the juvenile court focuses on the interests and welfare of the child, the parent's attorney may advise the client to make specific improvements or to cooperate in order to create a favorable impression with the court.

Competent parents' attorneys help objectify Child Welfare decision-making. By criticizing and attacking information adverse to the client, the attorney imposes more structure on the court proceeding. This presupposes, however, a reasonable balance between the quality of advocates on both sides. Just as the skilled parents' attorney can sometimes exclude important information concerning mistreatment of the child, a superior agency attorney sometimes can successfully prosecute a case against a parent, even though the case may be based on a haphazard investigation and erroneous conclusions.

Often, parents' attorneys cause delays in the juvenile process, particularly if they are appointed late in the proceedings and are unprepared at the time of the trial. When the child is already in the parents' custody or when parents are thought to need time to make a favorable impression on the court, the attorney is likely to seek delays. On the other hand, parents' attorneys are sometimes strong advocates of speedy court proceedings, particularly when the child has been taken from parents and the attorney sees a good chance of regaining custody at the time of the forthcoming court proceedings. A good attorney realizes that the longer the child remains in the custody of a particular party, the more difficult it is to reverse the situation.

Another important way in which parents' attorneys seek to influence court proceedings is by creating a favorable record of the facts in the case. For example, an attorney may seek to obscure the original record of the child abuse or neglect in the court proceedings, because of their potential impact on later proceedings. For this reason, a parents' attorney, who views the chances of winning as poor, may offer to agree to placement of the child in foster care without a contest, in exchange for a court record which is not damning to the client. This practice is sometimes justified as a means to maintain a "positive relationship" between client and agency.

## Role of the Guardian Ad Litem or Attorney for the Child

Considerable variation persists at the state and local level concerning who, if anyone, represents the child. While in some places an attorney will be appointed to represent the child in every case, some jurisdictions use lay persons to represent the child; others use lay persons with access to attorneys, and still others assume that the child will be represented by the Child Welfare agency or its attorneys.

Not only are there differences in who represents the child, but in the perceived mission of the person doing the representation. Some children's representatives see their role as strictly representing the wishes of the child, while others believe they should represent their own independent decision on behalf of the child. The predominant view is that the child's attorney or guardian *ad litem* should advocate for the child's best interest, while informing the court of the views and preferences of the child. An exception is often made in the case of the mature adolescent, whom many attorneys and guardians *ad litem* view as a client whose wishes must be represented. Clearly, to investigate and represent the best interests of the child, the attorney or guardian *ad litem* needs expertise and training, as well as access to independent consultants.

The child's attorney or guardian *ad litem* who passively and uncritically accepts the facts of the case as presented by the agency is not performing professionally. Rather, the child's representative should conduct a thorough review of records, interview the parties, carry out a follow-up investigation when called for, and arrange for independent experts when needed. The thoroughness of such an investigation and consultation will depend in part on the apparent thoroughness and sufficiency of work already done by the agency.

Many social workers ask why it is necessary to have a special representative for the child, when the agency itself is charged with the child's protection and supervision. This question is reasonable. If an independent advocate is really needed, some interest of the child must not be already fully represented or protected, some gap in agency representation or flaw in agency case work must exist. The fact is that the agency itself is an interested party in the case and its own practices will frequently come under scrutiny.

The primary value of the independent child representative is that this representative is substantially free of any constraints except concern for the child. The agency attorney may feel constrained from pointing out limitations in agency policies and services, deficiencies in resources, or needed improvements in practice. On the other hand, often the child's representative is an important ally to the worker. The representative may push the case forward where the agency attorney is less responsive. The child's representative may also be especially credible to the court.

## Role of the Agency Attorney

There is even greater variation in who represents the Child Welfare agency than in who performs the role of the child's representative. Local agencies might be represented by district attorneys, state's attorneys, county counsel, corporation counsel, city solicitors, city attorneys, or even private attorneys. The significant distinction, however, is not the title of the attorney, but whether specific attorneys are assigned to Child Welfare cases on a long-term basis. Many urban agencies are represented by a separate unit of attorneys working within the city or county office, while some rural agencies are represented by a particular attorney who consistently handles neglect or abuse cases. Many agencies are represented by attorneys employed by the state who are either directly employed by the agency or work for the state attorney general. Among states whose agencies are represented by the attorney general's office, individual attorneys may have mixed assignments, rotating in and out of fulltime juvenile work, or hired on a long-term basis to handle juvenile matters.

Finally, hybrid arrangements exist in a number of states, where agencies are represented by local attorneys in some matters and by state attorneys in others. For example, in one agency local attorneys handle juvenile court cases, while an attorney working for the state provides advice on policy. Unfortunately, this particular state attorney is said to lack experience in abuse and neglect cases and has no special expertise to contribute to policy development. In another state, however, the attorney general has hired several fulltime attorneys to provide back-up to local prosecutors. These attorneys, in addition to assisting local prosecutors where there is a backlog or a complicated case, provide training to workers and help the state agency formulate policy.

An important issue in the representation of Child Welfare agencies concerns who makes the decision when an attorney and social worker disagree on how to handle a case. Many take the position that the attorney should decide clearly "legal" issues, while the social worker should have a say in "social work" concerns. Unfortunately, issues in juvenile court cases do not neatly divide into purely legal and purely social concerns. This is especially true when workers and attorneys cannot agree on whether to take a case to court. Agency workers may feel that a case is so urgent that it is worth initiating legal proceedings even though the attorney advises that the documentation of abuse or neglect is inadequate. The attorney may feel that bringing the case to court will undermine agency credibility with the court.

In some agencies, the final decision whether to file a case in court is made by the attorney. This is often the situation, for example, when the agency is represented by a deputy district attorney and the district attorney is independently elected. In such cases, the district attorney sometimes regards the job as representing the "public interest" as he or she sees it and, therefore, is not bound by agency decisions. On the other hand, in some areas, agencies regard the decision whether to file the prerogative of agency staff, particularly where attorneys are employed by the agency. In a few states, independent "intake officers" make the decision whether to file petitions.

In most agencies, however, neither the attorney nor agency staff is clearly given final control over how court cases are handled. A few have worked out specific procedures, whereby workers or attorneys can take such disputes to supervisors or convene a committee to resolve the issue. It is particularly important that cases not be settled in chambers without advance consultation between the attorney and social worker concerning the precise terms of the settlement. Perhaps the best attitude toward who should make decisions is that the agency should have the prerogative to decide whether a case should be filed as long as the case is not legally frivolous. The attorney, however, should have some control over the timing of the case and should perform a supervisory role concerning case preparation. In many agencies Child Welfare agency attorneys are insufficiently utilized. This sometimes, but not always, occurs in jurisdictions in which parents are denied, or receive insufficient, representation themselves.

Differences in the scope of participation by agency attorneys appears in three areas: the lawyer's presence at trial, trial preparation, and the lawyer's involvement in case planning while litigation is inactive. Child Welfare workers are generally not expected to appear unrepresented in termination of parental rights cases or contested proceedings alleging abuse or neglect, although in a few agencies workers sometimes have to represent the agency in court alone even when the parents have their own attorneys. Attorneys are often not present at emergency shelter care hearings or foster care court review proceedings.

Agencies need to have specific procedures regarding trial preparation. For example, one agency uses a detailed check list, which its social workers follow in preparing written information for the attorneys. The written information is submitted before a petition is filed. The attorney then must review the information and contact the worker before drafting a neglect or termination petition. Later, a conference between the worker and attorney must be scheduled at least five days before a contested trial. At the conference, the worker and attorney determine which witnesses must be supoenaed. The attorney meets with and prepares the witnesses at least a day before trial.

This kind of process is no more than normal trial preparation in other types of legal practice, but many Child Welfare agencies receive relatively lax preparation. In some agencies, petitions are drafted by workers, who usually fill in preprinted forms. In some agencies workers can obtain the help of court liaison workers or intake officers in planning the case or drafting the petition. However, the court liaisons generally have not received legal training and usually work independently from the attorneys representing the agency. In some agencies attorneys, unfortunately, first speak to social workers and witnesses on the day of the trial, sometimes less than an hour before trial. Obviously, more preparation is needed to assure that all pertinent facts come out at trial.

Some agencies consistently consult with attorneys even in the interim while the case is not in court. This practice is required, for the following reasons: workers need legal advice concerning long term case strategy, including the immediate steps necessary to insure complete documentation when the case later comes to court. Also, the attorney can check for specific problems that can cause substantial delays later, such as failure to notify fathers of hearing dates or even the fact that parental rights may be terminated, or failure to maintain records needed for later court proceedings. In some agencies, an attorney is consistently present during periodic agency case review meetings. Some agencies require a strategy session with their attorney whenever agency staff tentatively decide that a child should be returned home. In most agencies, workers are free to telephone or make appointments with attorneys to obtain advice on case strategy, although the average case worker does not often call the attorney, except regarding imminent litigation. This may be due to difficulty in obtaining access to the attorney, tension between the two professional groups, a lack of confidence in the attorney, or simply a lack of knowledge concerning what information might be obtained from the attorney. Whatever the reason, however, it is important for agencies to improve their communications with legal staff.

Agencies need to involve attorneys not only in legal training for practitioners, but in the development of law-related agency policy. Ideally, states should develop comprehensive legal training curricula for workers, including a legal manual which is periodically updated, training for new workers, annual refresher training for all workers, and information on recent changes in the law and legal procedures. All workers should be provided with updated state statutes and should receive regular bulletins from agency attorneys, outlining the legal policies of the agency.

In terms of agency policy development, legal input is critical in several areas. Among these are: establishment of clear criteria and steps for deciding whether to initiate court cases, techniques of investigation, and compliance with state and federal legal requirements. In spite of the recognition by agencies of the increasing importance of legal services, agencies are too often inappropriately passive in their attitudes toward their own counsel. Agencies accept long delays in the filing of petitions in court proceedings without attempting to remedy the problem, even to complain to the attorney or court. Because the quality of legal counsel is so critical to the success of Child Welfare practice, agencies need to concentrate on both improving their own cooperation with their attorney and getting better services from their attorneys. However, special problems can exist where the attorney is ultimately accountable to someone other than Child Welfare agency executives. Difficulties also can arise because of the special expertise of attorneys and the unfamiliarity of Child Welfare agencies with legal concepts and procedures or because attorneys lack knowledge concerning the roles and expertise of the Child Welfare worker and agency.

Still, many agencies have made successful efforts to insure good legal representation. For example, one agency set up a meeting with their attorneys and local judges to help alleviate delays in getting cases heard. One ironic outcome of the meeting was to isolate a major source of delays within the agency which had incorrectly been attributed to the legal system. The judges and attorneys were also able to explain how cases were docketed, and they decided to set aside a special day and time to hear periodic reviews. This helped minimize the time workers needed to spend in the court room. Another agency successfully supported a legislative appropriation for more attorneys, arguing the great financial and human costs of the hundreds of children remaining in foster care for lack of attorney time to handle cases. Another persuaded the district attorney to stop rotating attorneys in and out of juvenile court and also critiqued the various attorneys representing them.

## The Juvenile Court Process: Neglected and Abused Children

The following section describes the key stages of the juvenile court process in proceedings brought for the protection of abused and neglected children. This section proposes policy and practice suggestions for Child Welfare workers at each of these stages.

Before proceeding to the specific stages of the legal process it is helpful to consider two basic principles that should guide the agency at every stage. First, the juvenile court process is best understood as a series of decisions concerning the future of the child, each of which flows from and logically follows the last. That is, each hearing and decision must be handled both in light of its immediate and long-term consequences. Second, Child Welfare agencies need to be conscious of how they affect the speed of the court proceedings. Unwarranted delays in court proceedings create paralysis and delays in case planning and generally contribute to the problem of foster care "drift."

### Emergency Removal

Emergency removal proceedings are those in which the court first decides whether to authorize removal of a child from the home under emergency conditions, based on an immediate harm or danger to the child. An emergency removal means the placement of a child into foster care before the opportunity for a full trial. State law may permit a child to be removed without prior court approval in limited circumstances, but generally a court order is required unless there is no time to obtain it prior to removal. If the child can be removed without a court order, there may be a short time limit within which court approval must be obtained.

In nearly every state, an emergency hearing must also be held within a short time of removal of the child, usually between one and three days. Such hearings tend to be very brief and informal. Often emergency hearings are conducted without attorneys. The central issue at the emergency hearing is whether the child should be held in foster care pending the trial of the case, whether the child may be safely returned home, or whether the child may be temporarily placed with a familiar relative or caretaker. In deciding whether the child can safely remain at home, the court may take into account the availability of services and supervision in the home that might be provided to the family.

Agencies should involve the parents in the legal proceedings as rapidly as possible after removal. This involvement limits the traumatic effect of separation where return is possible and speeds the legal proceedings where it is not. Rapid involvement of the parties requires diligent and immediate efforts to locate the parents, to notify them that the child is in custody, and to advise them as to the time and place of the next proceeding.

Rapid appointment of counsel for the parents and for the child (where required by law) helps to speed the neglect or abuse trial. While it is generally permissible and reasonable for Child Welfare workers to interview parents prior to appointment of counsel for noncriminal abuse or neglect proceedings, it is inappropriate to intentionally hold up the appointment of counsel until complete and satisfactory interviews can be concluded.

Documentation of the circumstances surrounding the emergency removal is essential, not only for the neglect or abuse trial, but often for later court proceedings. A vivid and accurate account of the circumstances compelling removal of the child can set the tone for the case throughout the juvenile court process. Accordingly, agency policy and practice should demand that workers prepare factual and precise descriptions of what they saw and heard to convince them to remove the child; should require them to take written or recorded statements from important witnesses at the time of the removal; should require the preservation not only of names and addresses of witnesses, but also means of contacting the witnesses should they change address; and should specify procedures for taking photographs and preserving physical objects that are important evidence in the case.

Given the traumatic effects of unplanned and unprepared for separation and the significance of the circumstances of removal as evidence in the case, it is particularly important not to remove a child prior to trial unless the danger or emergency is significant and genuine. Although it is not possible to blueprint the precise circumstances in which any child can be removed, agency policy should give guidance and support to their workers by providing an outline of the types of evidence of physical danger or emotional damage that do and do not justify immediate removal.

## Adjudication

The adjudication, which is also sometimes referred to as the "fact-finding hearing," or "jurisdictional hearing," is the trial where it is decided whether the child has in fact been abused or neglected. The adjudication is based on facts or circumstances stated ("alleged") in the petition, the legal document outlining the State's case against the parents. Testimony and documents submitted at the adjudication generally must conform to relatively strict rules of evidence. If the court finds that the facts which are alleged in the petition are accurate, the court can assume "jurisdiction" over the case. This means that the juvenile court has the power to review and determine the plans for care and placement of the particular child, a power that the court does not have over children in the general population.

Agencies and their attorneys should exercise extreme caution when entering into compromises concerning the allegations of mistreatment of the child. That is, the petition and findings of the court should accurately reflect how the child was mistreated, the dangers confronting the child, and why it is necessary for this court to intervene. This final report is critically important, because subsequent agency work with and planning for the family will be evaluated partly in terms of how well they address those family problems proved during the adjudication.

The following example should illustrate the pitfalls of negotiating about the court record. Jennifer, 5, came into care as the result of severe burns on her left hand and upper arm. Jennifer's aunt reported that the burns were a result of the mother holding the child's hand against a hot clothes iron, as a punishment. At the urging of the defense attorney and to avoid a contested trial, the agency filed a petition alleging the child to be "in need of care and services that the mother is unable to provide." No written statement was ever taken from the aunt, who later recanted the story under pressure from the mother.

After Jennifer was placed in care, her mother secured a steady job, found suitable housing, but consistently refused to cooperate in any training or therapy to examine her relationship with Jennifer and to enhance her mothering skills. The mother visited Jennifer as permitted by the agency, but Jennifer remained distant and withdrawn from her mother. One and one half years after Jennifer was removed, the agency remained afraid to return her to her mother, but did not know how to prove that the mother caused Jennifer's burns. Because of the agency's failure to make an accurate record of the abuse in the original court proceedings, not only did case planning go awry, but it became difficult to free the child for adoption, condemning Jennifer to long-term "temporary" care.

To create a strong record, the agency attorney should draft petitions, stating the nature of the abuse and neglect as accurately and completely as possible. If the initial petition proves to be inaccurate and incomplete, generally it can be amended. At the close of the trial, it may be possible to convince the court to enter helpful findings of fact. When a detailed petition has been filed, it is easier for the court to enter their findings, based on the petition. In addition, important photographs and other evidence should be retained after the adjudication. Also, it is very important that both parents be given formal notice in advance of the proceedings and made parties to the adjudication, including parents who have lost legal custody after a divorce proceeding, as well as unmarried, absent fathers.

Involving the noncustodial parent or unmarried father in the adjudication protects the absent father's rights and is an important way to avoid long-term case delays. If the parent is first brought into the case long after the child has been placed in care, and after the agency has finally given up work with the custodial parent, then work with the new parent must begin from scratch. But when parents are involved from the beginning, agencies can reach a final decision concerning the child more rapidly. Most important, noncustodial parents may sometimes be a resource for the child, and involving them early may make foster home placement unnecessary.

Special problems may be created when there is a question of paternity or when the noncustodial parent lives out of state. In these situations, it is sometimes unreasonable to delay the adjudication until the question of paternity can be legally resolved or the out-of-state parent can be given proper legal notice.

In the case of the out-of-state parent, legal notice should be given as soon as possible. If notice is given after adjudication, the parent should have the opportunity to reopen the proceedings and to seek custody of the child. With regard to the putative unmarried father, if he has had some substantial role in the child's life he might be made a party to the original adjudication. Alternatively, he may be given the opportunity to participate in or reopen the proceedings after the issue of paternity can be legally resolved. In either case, the agency needs to bring the issue of legal paternity to the courts promptly.

## Disposition

Disposition is the stage of the juvenile court process in which, after adjuciation, the court determines whether the child may be placed in foster care, determines who will be awarded the authority to care for and supervise the child, and, in some cases, sets the conditions under which the child is placed. The exact timing of disposition depends on both state law and the practice of the particular court. Disposition may occur at a separate hearing some time after adjudication or be determined at a hearing immediately following adjudication. Sometimes the court simply enters a dispositional order at the close of the adjudication. While disposition typically occurs within several weeks of removal in some courts, in others it may occur many months later.

The issues at disposition are different from those at adjudication. Therefore, the agency has the right, in most states, to present additional evidence on disposition after the adjudication has been completed. State law does distinguish between the adjudication and disposition in all but a few states, although sometimes different terminology is used. In many states, the rules of evidence at disposition are less strict than at adjudication, although opposing attorneys generally have the right to cross examine the authors of disposition reports submitted to the court.

The predisposition report needs to be made available to the parties at least several days in advance of the dispositional hearing in order to give them the opportunity to analyze and critique the agency's recommendations. Agency policy should rigorously require such a practice, so that the report can meaningfully contribute to an intelligent dispositional decision.

Agency workers and their attorneys should plan for and conduct dispositional proceedings with great care and attention. Not only does the court make the critical decision of whether to place the child in foster care, but an important record can be created. In most agencies, preparation for disposition begins with the writing of a predisposition report. This report should focus the dispositional proceeding. Through the report, the agency worker should articulate the family problems and suggest a direction for planning and work with the family. It is then the task of the attorneys and the court to critique, refine and, hopefully, improve on the original product. Workers should not feel defeated if the recommendations of the disposition report are not accepted untouched, but should view it as an achievement if the dispositional report has served as a good working draft to develop a precise and appropriate dispositional order.

The dispositional report need not be a family history per se, but it should include recommendations for disposition and an explanation of reasons for the recommendations. For example, if removal is recommended, the report should outline how the child is likely to be harmed if left in the home; what services were provided to keep the child at home; and what should be done after removal to minimize the adverse affects of the family's separation. Among other things, this report should include recommendations on visitation and contacts between parents and child.

The report should also include, to the extent practical, an outline of what the parents and agency should be expected to do to remedy the problems causing the State to intervene in the case. But, while it may be possible to present goals and tasks for parents and worker at disposition in one case, it may only be possible to set forth the broadest outline of a plan in another.

Agencies should be aware of both the benefits and risks of submitting a detailed case plan to the court at the time of disposition. To the extent that a court order specifies what the parent and agency are expected to do, there is less room for disagreement and misunderstandings between them as to what is expected. The court order can also resolve possible conflicts between parents and agencies, such as disputes concerning services, tasks, visits, or medical examinations. Specified goals and tasks also establish momentum for later court proceedings; it is often easier for a judge to resolve a case decisively where there has been a court-ordered case plan in effect. That is, a judge is able to rely on a case plan that was considered by all parties in open court and sanctioned by a judge. Also, the court may possibly improve the plan.

The risks involved in submitting a detailed case plan and disposition can also be substantial. To the extent that a plan may be premature or circumstances may change, the parties may be "locked in" until there is an opportunity for a subsequent court hearing. There is also the risk that the court may inappropriately modify a plan submitted to it.

Fashioning a good dispositional order is a high art which requires balancing the need for a flexibile framework within which to work with the family against the need for a court record and the need to resolve disputes hampering case progress. If a case plan is completed prior to disposition, it might be attached to or incorporated into the predisposition report. The report can also be an appropriate place to present a description of the efforts and services provided by the agency to prevent removal of the child or to reunify the family. In fact, to claim federal matching funds for a child in foster care the court must find that there have been reasonable efforts to prevent placement or to reunify the family.

## Court Review

The term "court review" refers to proceedings that take place after disposition at which the court examines case progress or determines whether to modify existing court orders. This review might take place on a periodic basis or it might be initiated by the parties or the court. Although in some jurisdictions the court reviews the case by simply reading written reports or by listening to information presented by the agency alone, such practices are of questionable constitutionality. Court review should occur in open court where the parties have notice of the time and place of the proceedings and in which it is possible for the parties to make statements and introduce evidence.

While nearly every state requires some form of judicial review, there are substantial differences in their requirements: how often the review must take place, the issues at review, and the procedural details. One important distinction in court review proceedings is that the court must attempt to make an ultimate decision in the case within a particular time period. In California, for example, if a child is not returned home after twelve months from the date of the original placement and is unlikely to return within six months, the court must elect another permanent option for the child. Specifically, if the child cannot return home, the court must select one of the following alternatives in this order of preference: adoption, guardianship, or long-term foster care with specified foster parents.

A number of other states also require specific decisions at certain review hearings, to comply with federal requirements. Federal law requires a hearing within eighteen months of placement, which shall determine whether the child is returned home, should be continued in foster care for a specified period, should be placed for adoption, or should, because of the child's special needs or circumstances, be continued in foster care on a permanent or long-term basis.

Court review proceedings often build upon earlier reviews conducted by the Child Welfare agency or by citizen review boards. Federal law requires a review every six months conducted by a court, an agency, or a citizen review board. The federally mandated eighteen-month hearing, by comparison, must be conducted by a court or by a court-appointed or approved body.

In many ways a good court review should be similar to a good disposition. A prereview report submitted to the parties in advance serves the same basic purpose as the predisposition report, and many of the same benefits and pitfalls exist at disposition and review when seeking a court-ordered, detailed case plan. However, some differences do arise between disposition and review, because review takes place later in the case. Where the disposition report may recommend a case plan, review should update the previous plan, and make recommendations for changes.

Review proceedings provide a special opportunity to make a record of how the case has progressed since the last court hearing. Since both parties may still be working toward a common goal of family reunification, a full and frank disclosure of how the case is progressing may be much more possible than in a later and more adversarial proceeding, such as in a hearing for termination of parental rights. Among the information the agency may wish to place in the record are what services it has offered to the family since the last court hearing, what efforts and progress, or lack thereof, the parents have made to respond to such services, what strengths the family has demonstrated, and what problems remain within the biological family.

Since the case may have gone on for a long time by the time of review, fewer risks are taken when asking the court to approve a case plan. After the agency has exercised responsibility for the child for an extended period, it should be possible to specify detailed tasks and goals to be met by the parties and to specify the consequences of failing to do so. In many cases, the judge will not only endorse the case plan, but state that termination of parental rights should be initiated should the plan be unsuccessful.

Not all courts are willing to specify goals, tasks, and services for the parties as part of the court order. In some cases, state law may limit what the judge can order. If the judge is unwilling or feels unable to order the parties to follow a case plan, agency attorneys may request that the judge urge the parties to comply. Such a recommendation can be reduced to writing and included in court documents. When parents are working toward reunification, such recommendations may carry considerable wieght with them and their attorneys.

## Termination of Parental Rights

The termination of parental rights is a grave decision with extremely important implications for the child as well as the family. Such termination involves a separate legal proceeding to sever completely a parent's legal rights and responsibilities to the child. In some states, termination is referred to as "permanent commitment" or "permanent guardianship" with the right to consent to adoption. Whatever term is used, this legal action severs the parents' rights to visit or communicate with the child and removes the right to make any decisions concerning the child. It also eliminates the need for parental consent as a precondition for the child's adoption. Termination is generally the most formal of legal proceedings in child protection cases, even more formal than the adjudication. In many states, termination is heard in a different court than prior child protection proceedings.

Preparation of a contested termination case involves putting together a detailed and focused case history. In the course of the termination proceeding, the worker will need to demonstrate the original problems or maltreatment causing the child to be placed in foster care, the efforts of the Child Welfare agency and others to resolve the problem and unify the family, the response of the parents to agency efforts to help, and the current needs of the child and the child's relationship to the parents and other caretakers. The success of the case will depend on the worker's preparation of a case summary, gathering of documentation, case recording, and identification of potential witnesses.

The most basic issue in a termination of parental rights proceeding is whether a reasonable likelihood exists for the child to be safely returned to the parent. Although the grounds for termination of parental rights set forth in state law do vary and must be carefully adhered to, the chief focus of termination cases concerns whether the child cannot or should not be reunited with the parents.

Five basic types of indicators show that a child should not return home. When the facts are strong enough one indicator alone may be sufficient to demonstrate that a return is unlikely, but more often, a combination of indicators will apply in a particular case.

First, the child may be unable to return because the parent has demonstrated an extreme lack of interest or commitment toward the child. Key examples of extreme lack of motivation and concern are a parent's failure to visit or communicate with the child while the child was in foster care, and a pattern of needlessly leaving the child with others for prolonged periods of time and then failing to pick up the child as agreed. When such behavior has extended over a period of time and the agency has been liberal in assiting the parent to maintain contacts and a relationship with the child, parental disinterest can be a strong basis for termination. In many states, parental disinterest comes under the legal heading of abandonment, though abandonment grounds can be more or less strict depending on the particular state.

Second, the child may be unable to return because the parent has failed to make necessary adjustments to prepare for the child's return, in spite of help from the Child Welfare agency. This is the most common and basic ground for termination of parental rights. In short, the agency must prove that a child is unable to return by demonstrating that it has tried everything reasonable and possible to reunify the family, but the parent is still not ready to care for the child. To present proof of this type, the agency should be prepared to demonstrate that the court and the Child Welfare agency formulated a program for the parent, designed to alleviate the problems that caused the continued parent–child separation. The agency also needs to prove that it diligently attempted to follow through with its program of assistance, and prove that the parent persists in conduct that prevents the return of the child. Proving this particular basis for the termination of parental rights is specifically centered around the history of the parent's problems and behavior toward the child, as well as on the agency's involvement with the family.

Third, return may be inappropriate because of the severity or repetition of abuse or neglect. Parental mistreatment of a child may be so chronic or severe that continued work with the parents may be inappropriate and prompt termination needed. In one case, for example, a father abused his child, causing an escalating series of injuries. Eventually, the child was hospitalized and placed in foster care after suffering from serious burns and broken ribs. The agency first learned of the case as the result of the hospitalization. While the child was in foster care, a younger sibling died as a result of the father's abuse. In this case, no further efforts to work with the father were appropriate as a precondition to a termination of parental rights, since unacceptable danger was involved in returning the child. Even in less extreme cases, where it is necessary to show efforts to work with the family, the severity and persistence of mistreatment is important in determining whether termination is supportable.

Fourth, return may be impractical because a diagnosable condition may make the parent unable to assume care of the child. Parental "condition" refers to incapacities so severe that the parent cannot care for the child, such as intractable mental illness, mental deficiency, alcohol or drug addiction, or in rare cases, extreme physical disability. Cases of this type should be provable without reference to parental fault. A diagnosis made by an expert is usually critical proof in "condition" cases.

If a parent suffers from a condition that renders him or her totally unable to care for the child, it should not be necessary to show that the agency has attempted to work with the parent. However, where the agency has made futile efforts to help the parent, such efforts can help demonstrate the intractability of the condition and reinforce the prognosis of the expert witness. Further, in the many cases where the parent is partially incapacitated, a combination of evidence of incapacity and unsuccessful agency efforts to work with the parent may be required.

Fifth, return may be inappropriate because, as a result of the parent's past behavior, the child is unalterably averse to return. Return home may trigger a harmful reaction in a child due to past experiences in the home. Even though the parent may now be capable of providing appropriate care for the child, traumatic memories or new relationships may make return profoundly painful or frightening.

This basis for termination, ironically, is often underemphasized and unpersuasive to the courts, in part because it is difficult to prove precisely why and how return home will harm the child. In some cases, however, such proof may be readily available. A dramatic example might be a child who, upon being visited by a natural parent, retreats into a corner of a room, coils into a fetal position and rhythmically knocks his head against the wall. Medical testimony indicates that such behavior illustrates severe danger of the child's extreme and even irreversible regression should there be a forced return to the parent. In this case, return may be inappropriate no matter how rehabilitated the parent.

Less dramatic examples will probably not stand alone as the sole basis for a termination of parental rights case. However, in every termination case there should be evidence focusing precisely on how return home will affect the individual child in the proceeding. This issue needs to be given considerable thought by the worker and should be reflected not only in testimony, but also in the arguments of the agency attorney.

In addition to demonstrating that a child is unable to return home and to satisfying the specific statutory grounds for termination, it is important to be prepared to demonstrate that termination will actually result in an appropriate permanent placement for the child. Usually, this means offering evidence that the child actually will be adopted within a reasonable time. While most judges do not require that a specific adoptive home be selected before granting termination, many do expect testimony from adoption specialists indicating that the particular child can be adopted. Other judges deal with the issue by terminating parental rights, but retaining jurisdiction and periodically reviewing the case to be sure that the agency is conducting an adequate adoptive search and is not excluding suitable adoptive parents.

## Alternatives to Termination of Parental Rights

In a small number of cases where children are unable to return home, adoption may be inappropriate or unfeasible—possibly a child is old enough to block adoption legally and does not want to be adopted in spite of the agency's best counseling efforts. Or, perhaps, a long-term foster parent with whom the child should remain may be unwilling to adopt. The possibility of adoption subsidy should be thoroughly explored in such cases, as well as the possibility of adoption without a change of name. If adoption is not possible, it may be necessary to consider alternatives, such as long-term foster care, permanent legal custody, and guardianship.

These alternatives often have disadvantages compared to adoption in that there may be further court battles over custody, state supervision may continue, the new parent may not have undivided responsibility for the child, and, in some cases, without subsidy or other economic supplement, the financial impact on the new parents may be devastating. It is important for the agency not only to understand the implications of such alternatives fully, but also to learn to utilize them in a way most likely to make them permanent and secure. Changes in state law may be needed as well, such as the provision of limited "open adoption" option, in which it is possible to continue parental visitation rights along with a legally secure and permanent adoption.

## Division of Rights and Responsibilities: Children in the Child Welfare System

When the juvenile court and Child Welfare agency assume control and responsibility concerning a child, the result is both an erosion of parental responsibilities and a fragmentation of control and responsibility concerning the child. This is one of the problems of foster care. The following section will describe the transfer of rights concerning a child as the result of court proceedings.

Figure 10.1 graphically shows some of the kinds of legal statuses regarding children in the Child Welfare system, and the parental rights and duties attached to each. While illustrating the variations in the legal status of biological parents, this figure does not show the fragmentation of control between the juvenile court, public and private welfare agencies, and foster parents.

Column 1 shows the situation where all parental rights are left untouched—some of the basic rights that parents in our society have in regard to their children. The parents retain full custody, and the children are not subject to the jurisdiction of the juvenile court.

Column 2 illustrates protective supervision, the situation in which the juvenile court has determined through a formal proceeding that it has jurisdiction over a child not receiving proper care.

Protective supervision means that the juvenile court has jurisdiction over the child, but the child remains with the parent by court order. The child cannot be removed without a further court hearing, but the parent must cooperate and submit to the supervision of the Child Welfare agency as specified in the court's disposition order. In many states, the juvenile court may set forth specific conditions that the parents must meet while the child remains in their care. The Child Welfare agency ordinarily may clarify or add to such conditions, depending upon the wording of the court order.

Column 3 illustrates the situation in which, after jurisdiction has been established, the court has granted legal custody to the Child Welfare agency, which has determined that the child should be left at home for the time being. In some states, the agency can remove the child from the parents' home without a further hearing. This situation contrasts with the situation in protective supervision, where a hearing is necessary before the child is removed. However, permitting the removal of a child without a hearing may well be unconstitutional, and federal law

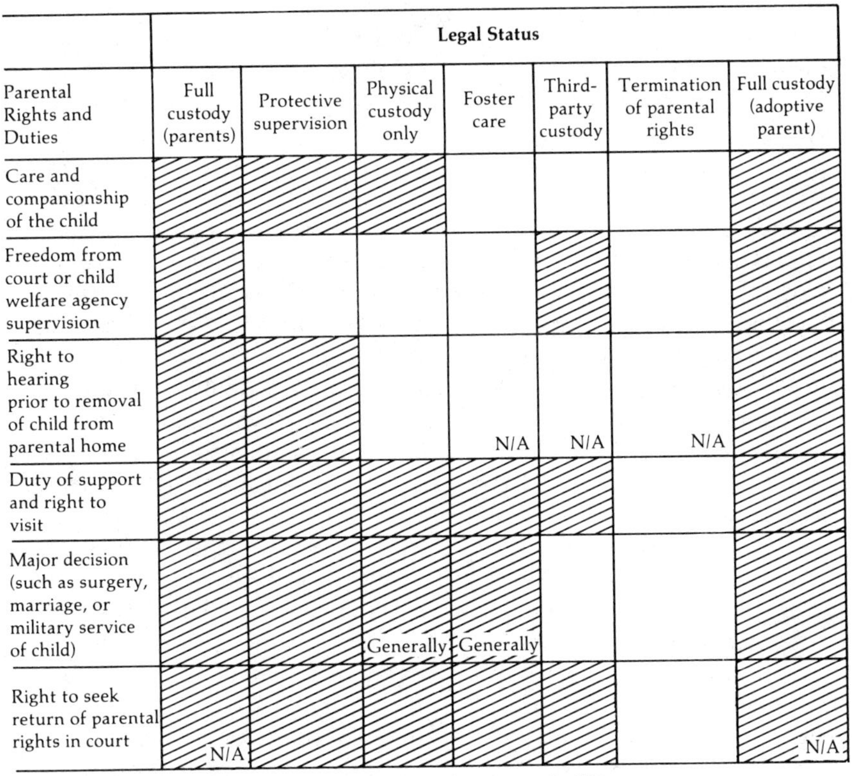

| | Legal Status | | | | | | |
|---|---|---|---|---|---|---|---|
| Parental Rights and Duties | Full custody (parents) | Protective supervision | Physical custody only | Foster care | Third-party custody | Termination of parental rights | Full custody (adoptive parent) |
| Care and companionship of the child | ▨ | ▨ | ▨ | | | | ▨ |
| Freedom from court or child welfare agency supervision | ▨ | | | | ▨ | | ▨ |
| Right to hearing prior to removal of child from parental home | ▨ | | | N/A | N/A | N/A | ▨ |
| Duty of support and right to visit | ▨ | ▨ | ▨ | ▨ | ▨ | | ▨ |
| Major decision (such as surgery, marriage, or military service of child) | ▨ | ▨ | ▨ | Generally | Generally | | ▨ |
| Right to seek return of parental rights in court | N/A | ▨ | ▨ | ▨ | ▨ | | ▨ N/A |

N/A indicates that the right or duty is inapplicable
Shaded area indicates rights and duties exist
A black space indicates that the right or duty is lacking

**Figure 10–1**  The Erosion of Parental Rights

*Source:* Hardin, M., "The Erosion of Parental Rights," in S. Downs and K. Taylor, *Permanent Planning for Children in Foster Care: Resources for Training* (Washington, D.C.: U.S. Government Printing Office, DHHS Publication No. [OHDS] 81-30790, 1980).

requires "procedural protections" to the parents in any situation in which a child is removed from their home.

Column 4 shows the status of foster care. This status occurs when a court either orders foster care placement or grants the Child Welfare agency legal custody and the agency places the child. In either case, parental rights and duties are the same.

With foster care biological parents cannot live with the child but, normally, are permitted to visit and required to pay support. The parents retain the right to request that the court return the child to their care and to share in planning the visiting and support schedules. This status is different from the situation in which parents voluntarily place their children in foster care and no court proceeding is brought. Parents generally lose less legal authority over the child through a written foster care agreement than through court proceedings, although the fact of foster care will certainly have a bearing if a hearing does subsequently take place.

Biological parents of children in court-ordered foster care generally retain a degree of power and responsibility concerning the child beyond those of visitation and support. As a general principle, biological parents retain whatever rights have not been taken from them: For example, biological parents sometimes have the rights to be consulted concerning educational decisions, other legal proceedings affecting the child, major medical care, driver's licenses, enlistment in the armed services, or marriage. Courts sometimes, but not always, have flexibility whether biological parents should retain such rights short of termination of parental rights, but in many cases neither the court decision, state law, nor agency policy actually clarifies exactly what powers are enjoyed by biological parents of children in foster care.

The legal control and responsibility for a child is most fragmented in the foster care situation. First, the juvenile court itself assumes a control and responsibility for the child which is far greater than that of other courts making decisions affecting children. Other court proceedings affecting children, such as suits for damages on behalf of injured children, suits for government benefits—social security or welfare—and divorce cases in which the custody of the child is at issue are far less intrusive upon the family. Even in a divorce case, the court does no more than to assign custody and visitation in a contest between two private contesting parties.

In a juvenile court proceeding, as described earlier, the court assumes a supervisory function and may set conditions on placement, review case progress, or even consider the appropriateness of the case plan. Furthermore, juvenile court proceedings are considered ongoing, while the custody decision in a divorce decision is generally regarded as final.

When the court authorizes foster care, substantial responsibility for the child is given to the foster care placing agency. This authority generally includes selection of the placement, supervision of the foster home, and responsibility to plan and provide services for the child. These responsibilities are not only split among employees of the agency, but may be divided between a public and private agency, when the court awards custody to the public agency which in turn assigns responsibility to a private placement agency.

In the case of foster family care, day-to-day care of the child is delegated to foster parents. Many legal constraints exist as to how foster parents' responsibilities can be exercised. Foster parents must meet licensing standards, comply with the rules of the agency, adhere to the terms of the contract entered into between the agency and foster parents, and must accept supervision by the worker. This situation is in striking contrast to the ordinary legal position of the family in our society operating with a far greater degree of autonomy.

Since it is the foster parent who spends the time with the child, and the social worker is often dependent on the foster parent for information about the child's daily functioning, the foster parent has a strong influence on important decisions affecting the child. Still, the foster parent often must obtain agency permission to make many routine decisions, such as securing particular services for the child or dealing with schools. An increasing number of agencies have created special categories of foster care parents who are delegated special authority and responsibility for the child. Particularly notable are the categories of permanent foster parents and specialized foster parents, who have special training and expertise to deal with the particular handicaps or problems of the individual child.

Column 5 refers to the situation in which a child is placed in third party private custody or guardianship. Although it is seldom done, a child is sometimes withdrawn from juvenile court jurisdiction and custody or guardianship is assigned to a private individual or couple. The rights of the parent in this case are usually basically the same as those of an out-of-custody parent after a divorce. Private guardians or custodians may be relatives, family friends, or, sometimes, foster parents who change to this more permanent status.

All significant decisions regarding the child are made by the guardian or custodian, who is also responsible for the daily care of the child. Neither the juvenile court nor the Child Welfare agency have responsibility over the child or guardian. The parent can seek return of the child, in roughly the same way that an out-of-custody parent can sue to regain custody after a divorce.

Column 6 refers to the situation after termination of parental rights. At this point, the biological parent has permanently lost all rights and responsibilities for the child, including the right to ask the court to change its decision. Since the child is usually still in foster care at this point, responsibility for the child remains fragmented between the court, agency, and foster parents, but excluding the biological parents. Termination of parental rights is normally ordered in contemplation of a subsequent adoption by new parents.

Column 7 refers to the authority of the adoptive parents. The person who adopts the child obtains essentially the same rights to care and control that originally were the biological parents'. (Compare Columns 1 and 7.)

Since the legal process and Child Welfare practice must be closely integrated, social workers and attorneys need to become more familiar with and sensitive to each others' functions. In a sense, Child Welfare workers must become somewhat more like lawyers, and Child Welfare lawyers must acquire some of the skills and knowledge of social workers. Interprofessional differences and misunderstandings can no longer be permitted to contribute to the plight of foster children.

# PART III

# Child Welfare Practice on Behalf of Families and Children

For too long, the tendency has been to define Child Welfare practice almost exclusively as direct practice with families and children. Yet, Child Welfare services are delivered through organizational structures that must be administered or changed. Also they are delivered within the context of laws and public policies that give them shape and direction. However, the role of the Child Welfare practitioner in program analysis, development, administration, in the creation and passage of legislation, and on all levels of advocacy on behalf of families and children, has tended to be ignored. Further, the role of social work education in the preparation of practitioners to assume administrative, program development, and policy-making roles has been minimal. A recent survey of staff in public and voluntary Child Welfare agencies revealed that 83 percent of state administrators of Child Welfare programs, and 75 percent of a stratified random sample of local agency directors had completed graduate studies in social work (National Child Welfare Training Center, 1981). Despite this fact, agency and program administrators, M.S.W. and B.S.W. Child Welfare faculty, and field instructors, when ranking the importance of forty-four content areas in preparing for practice in Child Welfare, consistently ranked items related to administration, policy development, planning, and supervision as much less important than knowledge and skills related to direct service delivery. Further, content areas that would support the direct practitioner's efforts to affect the delivery system itself also received low rankings (National Child Welfare Training Center, 1984). In the same survey, a review of in-service training received by staff revealed that content on practice with large systems was not generally offered and agency staff, even those in middle management positions, did not identify such content as a training need. To complete the picture, continuing education programs only occasionally offered programs focused on the enhancement of knowledge and skill for macro practice.

In this section we turn to this neglected area in Child Welfare and focus on the administration, analysis, and change of larger systems. We make no pretense of comprehensive coverage of these broad and varied areas for practice; the chapters here represent and exemplify such practice in Child Welfare.

Strategies and processes for influencing social policy and legislative change are described in Chapter 11 by Brenda McGowan and Elaine Walsh. After defining policy and identifying the determinants that give it shape and direction, the authors present an agenda for Child Welfare legislative and policy change. They then go on to detail how Child Welfare practitioners at all levels, as professionals and as advocates, can influence the direction of policy formation, legislative enactment, and implementation.

Noting the shift of responsibility to the state levels, these authors focus particularly on how state law is made, emphasizing the opportunity decentralization offers for local influence. They lay out in a concrete and practical way the steps Child Welfare practitioners may take and the roles they may occupy to influence policy-making and the legislative process. Child Welfare workers, even those in direct practice, are encouraged to become involved in the political process. McGowan and Walsh cite research demonstrating that once a social worker takes one step toward bringing about policy or legislative changes, he or she tends to continue to take further action.

Rino Patti and Herman Resnick shift to the service organization itself as target for change. After defining the steps toward planned change, these authors, whose earlier work on organizational change has been influential in social work, identify different leadership styles which may be employed to bring about organizational change. They then develop a matrix which portrays the interaction between leadership style and procedures for change. Patti and Resnick do not advocate one or another leadership style, but take the position that different contingencies require different approaches, recommending that a skilled professional should be flexible, able to make an assessment, and able to adopt a leadership style appropriate to the situation. The chapter ends with a presentation of force field analysis and its use in selecting appropriate change strategies.

In the next chapter, the nuts and bolts of day-by-day administration are presented by Henry Gunn, who was for several years the chief administrator of a state public welfare system. In what is almost an open letter to a fledgling administrator, the author, out of his own experience, describes how to survive and even to succeed as an adminstrator of a bureaucracy. The administrator must be able to assume a wide range of roles, from fund raising to advocacy, and must be able to communicate effectively with both internal staff and external public representatives and groups from the local to national levels. Gunn, too, deals with the issue of internal change and reorganization on a highly practical level. Like most of the contributors to this volume, he takes account of resource issues and budget constraints as they affect program implementation.

The section ends with two exemplars of policy or program analysis, both of which demonstrate the analytical process and suggest some of the challenges faced by Child Welfare practitioners as they are influenced by policy enactments that affect service delivery. First, Milan Dluhy gives us a succinct and lucid analysis of a major change in social welfare policy—the growing change to block grant funding, reminding us that the shifting of responsibility for social welfare programs to the states has been developing for several years. Dluhy outlines the impact this shift is having and will continue to have on social welfare, the dangers inherent in the increasing competition among state programs, and the politicalization of social welfare that comes with block grant funding.

Mary Davidson challenges Child Welfare practitioners at all levels to examine their own and their agencies' practices to make certain that programs and procedures are not in violation of Title VI of the Civil Rights Act of 1964. Reviewing the litigation that has taken place around violations of Title VI, the author reveals how, without malicious intent, arrangements in many areas of agency functioning can lead to less appropriate or inadequate service to minority groups. She demonstrates how to assess the discriminatory outcomes of agency arrangements and suggests that practitioners at every level need to be attentive to both the letter and the spirit of this law.

# CHAPTER 11

# Social Policy and Legislative Change

Brenda G. McGowan
Elaine M. Walsh

This time is a difficult one in which to address the topic of influencing Child Welfare policies and programs. Certainly the need for social work participation in the ongoing debate about social policies and provisions is probably greater now than in any previous period within the career span of the most senior members of the Child Welfare community. Yet the likelihood of our having a significant impact on this debate is probably less now than at any earlier point in the last fifty years. Not only are the methods and strategies for achieving traditional social welfare objectives under attack, but also the very values and premises underlying these objectives are being questioned and undermined at every level in the political arena. Consequently, it is no longer possible to assume even a begrudging social consensus regarding the State's obligation to protect the welfare of all children.

This development imposes a serious constraint on the expectations that can realistically be maintained for significant change in the Child Welfare system. But it also makes it imperative for practitioners—many of whom have formerly been content to leave such matters to the "experts"—to begin to address the question of how they can influence the policies and programs shaping the nature of Child Welfare practice. Therefore, this chapter has two major objectives: (1) to examine the ways Child Welfare policies are developed and changed and (2) to identify potential roles for Child Welfare workers in the essentially political process of policy development and implementation.

This introductory section reviews the major determinants of Child Welfare policy and analyzes some of the dilemmas that must be faced by social workers engaged in efforts aimed at influencing policies and programs in this field of practice. In the second section we shall present our views regarding policy issues and problems in the Child Welfare field that should, despite a negative political climate, command priority attention from professional practitioners. The third section analyzes potential advocacy roles for practitioners. In the final section we shall discuss strategies for effecting legislative change.

## Determinants of Child Welfare Policy

Discussions of social policy, in general, and Child Welfare policy, in particular, are frequently blurred by a lack of distinction between two dominant views of public policy. Some define public policy as an abstract set of principles designed to promote behavior and activities oriented toward the achievement of specific objectives. Others suggest that public policy must be perceived as a set of legislative and regulatory opportunities and constraints, all of which influence the behavior of relevant actors in ways that determine the degree to which ideal goals can be attained. These two distinct yet complementary views highlight the frequent gap between formulation of policy objectives and implementation of policy directives. This gap contributes directly to many of the problems in the Child Welfare field because practice is ultimately shaped by policy that is put into action, not by policy that is theoretical. Therefore, although it would be interesting to consider the competing forces contributing to the formulation of policy objectives, the primary focus in this chapter will be issues related to Child Welfare policy as it is implemented in practice.

Seen in this context, one can identify at least five major determinants of Child Welfare policy: federal and state laws, administrative regulations and guidelines, court decisions, funding allocations, and program decisions.[1] First are the federal and state laws that deal directly with Child Welfare services, as well as those which affect families and children who may come into contact with this system. These laws not only define the objectives, boundaries, priorities, and funding arrangements for Child Welfare services, but also prescribe the grounds for governmental intervention in family life, the rights and responsibilities of the various parties involved in the Child Welfare system, and the State's obligations regarding the welfare of dependent children.

Second are the administrative regulations and guidelines developed by the federal and state agencies responsible for the implementation of these laws. Administrative regulations often have the force of law and do much to elaborate, clarify, and refine broad legislative mandates. Although administrative guidelines do not have the force of law, they have a significant impact on the way policies are defined and implemented in practice. Agency policy manuals and procedural manuals, for example, essentially outline the ways in which workers are expected to carry out the intent of the law and can serve to preserve or subvert broad policy directives.

Judicial decisions interpreting the intent of laws impinging on the Child Welfare system are the third major determinant of Child Welfare policy. Although courts are expected to determine only whether or not the actions of responsible parties meet the intent of specific laws, and judicial decisions of the lower courts technically apply only to the parties directly involved in cases presented to the court, administrative agencies are often quick to assess the implications of significant court decisions for their own policies and procedures and to issue guidelines reflecting the policy directives inherent in these decisions. Moreover, rulings of the United States Supreme Court are often couched in terms that have direct and broad policy implications. For example, the famous *Stanley v. Illinois* and *In re Gault* decisions have both had a significant impact on Child Welfare policy, the first by granting unmarried fathers, under specified circumstances, the right to be heard before plans can be made for their children, and the latter by guaranteeing specific due process protections to youth at delinquency hearings and suggesting the potential need for similar due process protections in other types of hearings affecting the lives of children.

The degree to which the courts should be involved in social change via the issuance of decisions and opinions that constitute a reformulation of public policy has been a long-standing debate among judicial scholars. But despite this controversy, the courts have, in fact, contributed heavily to much of the social change that has taken place in American society in recent years. Although the impact of individual lawsuits is limited, rather significant changes have resulted from sustained litigation campaigns, such as those surrounding school integration and the right of institutionalized persons. This has been due in part to appellate rulings affecting not only the parties involved in a particular lawsuit, but also all those in similar situations. However, sustained, well-publicized litigation campaigns have also served to influence social policy, no matter what the ruling in specific cases, by stimulating public debate and concern and encouraging administrative reform as well as the passage of new legislation.[2]

There are two other derivative determinants of Child Welfare policy, both of which offer opportunities for practitioners to help shape the process of policy implementation. Perhaps the most important of these is the availability and allocation of funding for various programs. Although funding decisions technically are expected only to reflect the policy directives embodied in law, limited fiscal resources necessitate careful allocation of public funds among competing interest groups; the programs which lose in this political funding process are unlikely to achieve their alleged objectives. To illustrate, Title IV–B of the Social Security Law has historically been viewed as the most progressive federal Child Welfare legislation. If funded and implemented properly, this Child Welfare Services Program could have enabled the federal government to assist the states in providing comprehensive, adequate public services for dependent children and their families. However, until 1980 appropriations for this program had never exceeded $56.5 million, although Congressional authorization had reached $266 million, and the federal agency responsible for administration of these funds had never provided the strong leadership necessary to insure that even these limited funds were targeted appropriately. Hence the policy objectives inherent in this law have been repeatedly undermined by funding decisions (Children's Defense Fund, 1978). The Adoption Assistance and Child Welfare Act of 1980 (Public Law 96–272) was designed, in part, to increase funding allocations for services oriented toward achieving the policy goal implicit in Title IV-B of insuring permanency planning for all children. But only vigorous lobbying efforts by a wide range of child advocacy groups have saved the provisions of this bill from incorporation in block grant funding of social services, a move which certainly would defeat the original intent of this legislation. It is still too early to assess the ways in which other funding decisions may enhance or inhibit other efforts to implement the objectives of this law.

Finally, the program decisions made by federal and state administrative and regulatory agencies also have a significant impact on the ways in which Child Welfare policies are implemented. As suggested, the regulations and guidelines issued by these agencies serve to refine broad policy objectives and specify procedures for their implementation. In addition, administrative decisions regarding the program priorities, allocation and training of staff, use of discretionary funds, and the application of sanctioning powers all contribute to the process of policy implementation. Although at first glance there would seem to be considerable overlap between administrative regulations and program decisions, we believe these must be viewed as two distinct determinants of Child Welfare policy. The regulations and guidelines issued by federal and state administrative agencies are ordinarily subject to extensive external discussion and review before being promulgated in final form, whereas the program decisions made by these same agencies, which may have an equally important impact on policy implementation, seldom receive any public notice or scrutiny.

In sum, we are suggesting that there are multiple components and determinants of social policy, all of which deserve serious attention from practitioners hoping to shape the framework for Child Welfare services. Although policy can be defined theoretically as a set of principles that governs a specific field of action, has been adopted by a legislative body, and is expected to guide activities in this area, in practice policies usually reflect an emerging, somewhat uneven consensus about the objectives that are to be pursued in a particular service sector. Moreover the means by which these policies are to be implemented may be interpreted very differently by the various interest groups responsible. Consequently, practitioners attempting to achieve specific social change objectives must participate in and monitor developments at each stage of the policy formulation and implementation process.

## Dilemmas in Child Welfare Policy Analysis

Several dilemmas are inherent in the task of analyzing potentials for change in Child Welfare policies and programs. First is the confusion about what is encompassed by the field of Child Welfare. This term is sometimes used to refer to all policies and programs designed to enhance the welfare of children, and at other times to refer to a specialized field of social work practice organized to serve children at risk because their parents are unwilling or unable to fulfill all or part of their child-rearing functions. (See Chapter 3 for further discussion of this issue.) The primary focus of this chapter is Child Welfare as defined in the latter sense—a specialized field of social work practice. However, social policies can never be examined in a vacuum. Discussion of potential changes in the policy framework for Child Welfare services necessarily involves consideration of broader social policies affecting all families and children. For example, a change in the age at which children are expected to accept criminal responsibility for their actions or a modification of the eligibility requirements for income transfer payments or family support services could significantly alter the size and nature of the population entering the traditional Child Welfare system. Therefore, we shall at times have to consider the policy framework for Child Welfare services in the larger sense of policies relating to all families and children.

A second dilemma inherent in addressing the topic of influencing Child Welfare policy is that the traditional objectives and policy framework for this field are changing very rapidly, in some ways in the direction that practitioners would advocate, and in other ways, in quite an opposite direction. This dilemma is reflected, for example, in the passage of Public Law 96–272, the Adoption Assistance and Child Welfare Act of 1980. This law very much supports the goal of permanency planning for children at risk of long-term placement in foster care, a goal that professional workers certainly would support. But the restructuring of the federal and state roles in Child Welfare services mandated by this Act significantly reduces the autonomy traditionally granted to practitioners to make individualized, professional judgments about the service needs of children in care. The enormous monitoring and accountability requirements attached to the receipt of federal funds under this Act can necessitate a reduction in the proportion of staff time allocated to direct work with families and children, perhaps an unintended, but clearly an undesirable, outcome. It is still too early to make any assessment of the impact of this legislation or of related state statutes on Child Welfare services. Therefore, although these laws have set the policy stage for Child Welfare practice in the foreseeable future, it is impossible at this point to delineate those areas in which change may be both desirable and feasible.

A third dilemma deserving discussion is that the recent activities of various legal rights, advocacy, and professional groups have led not only to greater recognition of the problems in the Child Welfare system and to some limited reform efforts, but also to the widespread perception that Child Welfare workers are themselves the source of many of the deficiencies in this field. Practitioners are expected to preserve family integrity, protect the welfare of children at-risk, and insure permanent homes for all children—despite an ambiguous social mandate, inadequate resources, and funding patterns that undermine the very goals they are attempting to achieve. When they inevitably fail in some of these efforts, workers are blamed for what are essentially the consequences of faulty social policy. The introduction, for example, of citizen review boards or improved management information systems alone can do little to redress these basic structural problems, and recent reform efforts have been directed primarily toward monitoring practitioners' activities more closely and reducing their professional decision-making responsibilities.

This scapegoating process should provide a strong impetus for practitioners to be active in change efforts aimed at resolving the basic problems in the Child Welfare system. However, those who advocate change risk being accused of acting in a self-serving manner. Therefore, workers must recognize the very real need for mechanisms to insure accountability and protect clients' rights in any system that holds significant power over the lives of its service recipients and one in which some degree of professional incompetency and misjudgment is inevitable. Practitioners' energies should be directed toward highlighting and changing dysfunctional social policies, not toward fighting the somewhat futile reform efforts of those who ultimately share their goal of enhancing the quality of Child Welfare services.

A final dilemma that must be confronted by social workers engaged in any form of child advocacy is the conflict that frequently arises between the needs of different interest groups. Controversies regarding the rights of parents versus children, the community's need for protection versus the need of severely disturbed youth for normalizing experiences, or the proportion of resources that should be devoted to the developmentally disabled versus the physically handicapped are more easily resolved by lawyers and other members of advocacy groups publically committed to protecting the interests of specific client populations. But practitioners in the Child Welfare system are mandated to help carry out the State's responsiblity for protecting the rights of all parties to any particular conflict and guaranteeing equal treatment to all. This delicate balancing act must be handled repeatedly; as King Solomon discovered long ago, the resolution of such painful conflicts defies any simple or final solutions. Unfortunately many practitioners resolve this tension by abdicating responsibility for decision-making and action. By leaving matters related to policy formulation and implementation to the legislature, courts, and state administrative agencies, workers can feel relieved of any personal responsibility or guilt. But such an approach can result in even more serious violations of clients' rights because it eliminates the influence professional knowledge should bring to bear on the resolution of questions that may otherwise be defined merely as political issues.

## Assessing Priorities for Change: A Proposed Policy Agenda

There is certainly no shortage of policy and programming issues for Child Welfare practitioners to address. The problems and dilemmas in this service system have been documented repeatedly. (See, for example, Billingsley and Giovannoni, 1972; Children's Defense Fund, 1978; National Commission on Children in Need of Parents, 1979; Schorr, 1974.) Any two experts in this field of practice could undoubtedly construct different lists of action priorities; other chapters in this book describe service issues and deficiencies that the reader may well find more disturbing than those identified here. However, in this section, we would like to discuss briefly a number of recent policy developments impinging on Child Welfare practice—policies which we view as most problematic. We will also suggest some of the areas in which we believe change is urgently needed.[3]

### Reconceptualization of Federal Role in Service Provision

The Reagan Administration's efforts to redefine the concept of social need, reduce funding for all social programs, and reverse the trend toward expansion of social entitlements for all people in need have had a less severe impact on programs for the traditional Child Welfare population than on many other social programs. For example, funding allocations for special categorical programs such as the Child Abuse Prevention and Treatment Act of 1974 and the Adoption Assistance and Child Welfare Act of 1980 have been separated from the monies designated for social service block grants to states, thereby permitting Child Welfare agencies to maintain at least their most residual services without participating in the inevitable losing battle for a fair share of the limited social service funds to be distributed at the state level. This apparent effort to preserve Child Welfare services, at least at a superficial level, is not difficult to understand, given the strong historic social consensus that children whose parents are unable to provide adequate care need special protection. The perception is clear that this population, perhaps more than any other, must be provided with the "safety net" now being touted as the justification for reducing more universal costly social programs.

However, Child Welfare advocates can take little comfort from the protections currently being extended to traditional services. All of the recent efforts to expand the boundaries of the Child Welfare system, enhance the quality of care for children in their own homes and communities, and protect the rights of parents and children are being threatened by the proposed additional moves toward reducing the social and economic benefits available to low-income families, relaxing affirmative action efforts, as well as the governmental protections designed to insure equal opportunity for women and minority groups, and delegating to the states the responsibility for establishing and monitoring service standards. These trends can only result in (1) a reduction of the capacity of agencies to provide the services necessary to maintain children in their own homes, (2) an increase in the proportion of children requiring out of home care, and (3) a diminishment of standards for the quality of service provided to children in and out of their own homes. Consequently, it would seem that efforts to reverse the trend toward redefining the concept of social entitlement and reducing the federal role in the provision of social services should be high on the social action agenda of those who are concerned about developing and maintaining public policies that support the delivery of comprehensive, equitable, quality Child Welfare services.

## Deprofessionalization and Devaluation of Child Welfare Services

A second major problem area that deserves consideration is the trend—rooted in developments of the late 1960s and early 1970s—toward devaluing the role of professional social workers in the Child Welfare system. The efforts of social welfare leaders to establish a framework for the development of a comprehensive, public social service system that could diminish the dysfunctional separation between family and Child Welfare services and meet the service needs of all low-income families (Wickenden, 1976), combined with repeated attacks on traditional casework services as unresponsive to the needs of the poor, led to major reorganizations of public social service agencies in the past decade. These changes resulted in increasing employment of paraprofessional staff for the provision of Child Welfare services and gradual reduction of the "elite" status formerly accorded the professional Child Welfare worker.

On a theoretical level, no one would argue the need for broadening the base of Child Welfare services, providing services on a more efficient, rational, and equitable basis, as well as developing mechanisms to insure service integration. However, the unfortunate result of efforts in these directions has been a reduction in the organizational visibility and coherence of Child Welfare service within state human service departments (Children's Bureau, 1976). This means that in the same way that the reorganization of the U.S. Department of Health, Education and Welfare in 1969 led to the virtual decimation of the Children's Bureau, thereby limiting opportunities for leadership at the federal level by those experienced in and committed to Child Welfare services, so the reorganization of state human service departments has decreased opportunities for leadership by those with expertise in Child Welfare. As such leadership declines, the priority and resources allocated to children's services at the federal and state levels diminishes. The inevitable result of this devaluation of Child Welfare services is a reduction in the proportion of talented young professionals interested in entering this field of practice.

This deprofessionalization of Child Welfare services has been occurring at the same time that this service system is being asked to take increased responsibility for children with special physical, emotional, and behavioral problems and to provide more intensive preventive and protective services to families with multiple problems. Consequently, questions are now being raised as to whether current staffs in Child Welfare agencies have the knowledge and skills necessary to provide the range and quality of services required (Jenkins, Schroeder, and Burgdorf, 1981; Children's Bureau, 1976). Neither a strong policy framework nor a superb accountability system alone is sufficient to insure the provision of adequate services to families and children in need; the quality of any service is also determined by the competency and commitment of the practitioner providing that service. Therefore, it is essential that those hoping to influence the political process, which shapes the nature of Child Welfare services, give some priority to the development and maintenance of standards for professional practice and to securing the funding necessary for agencies to hire and train competent staff.

## The Accountability Mystique

A third area in which we believe practitioners should attempt to effect some change relates to what can only be termed a national obsession with developing accountability mechanisms designed to rationalize the delivery of Child Welfare services. Little doubt remains that the somewhat haphazard organization of services in this system has often resulted in children being lost and perhaps injured while in care. The inadequacy of accountability systems was dramatically revealed in 1975 when it was discovered that the public Child Welfare agency in New York City responsible for some 28,000 foster children was still using 5-by-8-inch index cards as the primary mechanism for tracking the movement of children in care;[4] and when the records of a sample of 2,511 children were subpoenaed for a major lawsuit, the responsible city officials were able to locate records for only 1,590 of these children (McGowan, Knitzer, and Nishi, 1976).

On the national scene the picture does not get better. Given the major advances in computer technology during the past two decades, it is somewhat mind boggling to realize that it is still impossible to obtain an accurate national count of the total number and demographic breakdown of children in care and/or of those receiving other types of Child Welfare services. Therefore, the recent emphasis on developing improved management information systems, accountability mechanisms, and various procedures for monitoring the activities of Child Welfare agencies reflects an understandable and needed social initiative. Yet, this emphasis poses some serious risks.

The potentially negative consequences of this emphasis on technology and monitoring are as follows. First, it creates the illusion that all decision-making and service provision in a field charged with resolving the complex social, emotional, and value dilemmas inherent in all parent–child conflict can be reduced to a series of technical problems, all of which can be resolved by the application of a series of scientific decision-making and action strategies. Second, this focus on monitoring workers' activities, no matter whether by court review, community boards, or regulatory agencies, diverts attention from the many more serious deficiencies in the Child Welfare system. As indicated earlier, some degree of professional malfeasance (or misfeasance) must be expected in any large human service system, hence, it is essential to develop mechanisms to protect clients' rights and insure public accountability. However, the perception that Child Welfare workers and agencies per se, rather than the social, economic, and familial conditions which create the need for Child Welfare services, are the cause of the many deficiencies in this service system can only be destructive in the long run.

Therefore, we would urge that professional practitioners concerned about the quality of Child Welfare services take more of a proactive stance in response to this trend. Rather than simply defending themselves against the many fair—and unfair—allegations to which they are exposed, workers should attempt to educate the community and lawmakers alike about the complexity of the family situations with which they are expected to deal, the limits of current knowledge and technology, and the need for broadening the base of responsibility for families and children at-risk. Little change can be expected in the policy framework for Child Welfare services until the Child Welfare population is viewed as part of a continuum of families and children in need of various types of social supports, and until public responsibility for the provision of these supports is assumed by all segments of the community.

## The Myth of Prevention

The concept of prevention has attracted much attention in recent years in all fields of human service. But it has held special interest for those concerned about the severe human and fiscal costs incurred as a result of the Child Welfare system's failure to provide adequately for large numbers of dependent and neglected children. Consequently, a great deal of discussion by social planners and practitioners alike takes place about the need to develop preventive service programs for families and children at risk, and those in a position to develop and influence public policy have been quick to latch on to preventive service strategies. At both the state and federal levels, effort has been made to shift funding from substitute care to preventive services, while a number of public and voluntary agencies have attempted to develop preventive service programs.

However, the concept of prevention is very difficult to put into operation. The goals of the Child Welfare system are so global and ambiguous, there is relatively little consensus about the specific threats to child development that preventive service programs are expected to eliminate or reduce and even less agreement about how such efforts should be carried out. Although the early advocates of prevention in Child Welfare originally envisioned the provision of a broad range of services designed to enhance family functioning, these aspirations have eroded as pressure has mounted to reduce the number of children in foster care. Increased publicity about the number of children left adrift in foster care at enormous costs to themselves and the community has led to the widespread perception that foster placement poses an inherent threat to child development. As a result, the conceptual focus of preventive service programs has narrowed from the provision of services intended to prevent all forms of family dysfunctioning and to expand opportunities for the development of children at risk to the implementation of strategies designed primarily to reduce the number of children in foster care.

This development serves as a clear illustration of the goal displacement that frequently occurs in the human service sector. Attention shifts from the social needs that a particular program (in this case, foster care) was designed to address to the unanticipated costs and negative consequences of this intended solution. In other words, what was originally planned as a social good gradually becomes perceived as an evil, and, in this process of goal displacement, public concern is diverted from the real sources of social problems, such as poverty, racism, sexism, and intolerance of individual differences. The current emphasis on prevention of foster care closely parallels the recent deinstitutionalization movement and poses similar risks.

Although entry into foster care is harmful to some families and children, relatively strong research evidence shows that temporary placement is beneficial for most at-risk children (Fanshel and Shinn, 1978; Kadushin, 1978b). Foster care is a needed social resource for a number of families in which children are at risk. Therefore, we urge that practitioners strongly oppose efforts to refocus the concept of preventive Child Welfare services. Services, which are limited to children at imminent risk of placement or who are already in placement, as, for example, in the administrative regulations governing implementation of the New York State Child Welfare Reform act of 1979—an act initially viewed as providing a model for other states—can only be defined as tertiary, or at best secondary, prevention. Such a shift clearly signals abandonment of the original goal of providing primary and secondary preventive services and indicates a return to a residual model of Child Welfare.

Given a conservative political climate, we suggest that practitioners may temporarily have to accept this residual approach to service provision. But rather than participating in the move to decimate needed foster care services under the rubric of prevention, Child Welfare workers should fight to insure that high quality standards are maintained for the limited services they are now able to provide. And practitioners should begin to establish a data base so they will be ready to demonstrate—when the political climate is more receptive to the introduction of legislation designed to provide a statutory base and funding—the need for what should perhaps be termed developmental, rather than preventive, services for families and children at risk.

## Potential Roles for Child Welfare Practitioners

The effort to engage in advocacy activities designed to influence social policies and programs has long been a part of the social work tradition, especially in working with children. Early leaders such as Florence Kelley, Lillian Wald, Julia Lathrop, and Grace Abbott provide excellent role models for Child Welfare workers of today who recognize the constraints that social policies can and do impose on their practice. The Code of Ethics of the National Association of Social Workers provides a clear mandate for professionals to participate in social change efforts (Ad Hoc Committee on Advocacy, 1969).

Despite this tradition and mandate, the influence of the professional Child Welfare community on social policy developments during the past fifty years has been relatively limited. Many different explanations have been offered for practitioners' failure to address social policy issues or to have any significant impact when they do become engaged in social change efforts. These explanations include: the professional's tendency to have limited goals and to become preoccupied with technical problems (Steiner, 1976); the historic polarization between segments of the profession involved in direct service and social reform activities and the traditional perspectives on social policy and clients' rights held by many direct service practitioners (Grosser, 1976; Scurfield, 1980); the organizational constraints imposed on the activities of agency-based workers (Ad Hoc Committee on Advocacy, 1969; McGowan, 1978); and lack of knowledge and technical skills necessary for effective political action (Grosser, 1976; Wolk, 1981).

No matter what the current explanation for lack of effective social change efforts by Child Welfare workers in the past, there are now several converging forces which should lead to increased practitioner participation in social policy formulation in the future. First is the development of the child advocacy movement during the past decade. Although leadership for this movement has been provided primarily by citizen groups and members of professions other than social work, and the initial expectations of what might be attained far exceeded its actual accomplishments, the very existence of this movement has served to legitimize an advocacy role for the human service professional and to expand the practitioner's knowledge about effective advocacy strategies.[5] A second major force leading Child Welfare workers to have an increased interest in social policy formulation is the relatively recent development of a systems perspective on social work practice, as well as the formulation of integrated practice approaches which force a redefinition of the practitioner's unit of attention and an expansion of the roles assumed by direct service workers (Germain and Gitterman, 1980; Meyer, 1976; Pincus and Minahan, 1973). Finally, if history can serve as any predictor, then as the impact of the regressive social policies introduced by the Reagan administration is felt more widely, social workers will be aroused to return to a concern with cause rather than function[6] and to fight for the reformulation of a policy framework supporting the values and service goals to which they are committed.

Given the assumption that Child Welfare practitioners will become increasingly involved in efforts to influence social policy, a number of potential roles can be identified for professionals in the political change process. It is, however, important to distinguish between the roles a Child Welfare practitioner may assume as a citizen, as an agency employee, and as a professional. Those functioning in a professional social work capacity must face certain limitations. They are seldom in a position to define public issues since this requires unusual leadership and charisma, as well as a broad constituency and strong power base. Also, when assuming a public position as a professional, social workers are expected to uphold specific values and to be guided in their actions by the NASW Code of Ethics. Although this code does not prohibit engaging in civil disobedience or other types of direct action campaigns, such as sit-ins or boycotts, the obligation to maintain professional standards of behavior raises questions about the use of various covert tactics and the trading of interests often necessary to achieve certain political objectives.[7]

On the other hand, professionals can help to influence the definition of public issues by their involvement in larger political bodies and movements. Furthermore, they can help to shape the solutions proposed for different social problems by collecting data to substantiate need, offering illustrative case examples, identifying the policy implications of different research findings, providing technical consultation to legislators, participating in the development of administrative regulations, and carefully monitoring the ways in which laws are enacted and their effects on different client populations.

The type and extent of political activity engaged in by workers is often determined by the nature of their agency position. For example, as might be expected, a recent study of political involvement by a sample of social workers in Michigan found that those in macro-level positions, such as administration and community organization, were more active than those in direct practice. This finding is quite understandable since political activity is usually defined as a part of the job function of persons in such positions. It should be noted, however, that this same study found that social workers as a group, regardless of their organizational role, are more likely to be politically active than the general population and are as active as other professionals in general. Another interesting finding was that political activity on the part of social workers tends to be cumulative. In other words, if a social worker had provided legislative testimony, he or she was also likely to have contacted legislators, participated in an election campaign, attended political meetings, and contributed money to political efforts. But if a worker had not, for example, attended political meetings, he or she was unlikely to have campaigned, contacted legislators, or provided testimony on any public policy issues (Wolk, 1981).

These findings suggest that, as a group, social workers are willing to engage in activity designed to influence policy and that as they begin to get involved in political activity, their participation is likely to increase. Therefore, it seems important to identify potential roles for beginning Child Welfare practitioners, as well as for those in higher-level positions. Certainly those in direct practice are ideally situated for collecting case data that may be used (in disguised form) to influence legislative deliberations, to educate clients about their rights and to help them organize consumer advocacy groups, and to monitor the implementation of various laws. Although their case responsibilities may not permit them to spend time conducting careful analyses of proposed laws, regulations and budgetary changes, preparing testimony, or providing technical consultation to legislators, they can provide case and program illustrations that will help those in macro-level positions carry out these tasks. The National Association of Social Workers' Educational Legislative Action Network (ELAN) and Political Action for Candidate Election (PACE) both provide excellent opportunities for direct service practitioners to become more actively involved in the political arena on a volunteer basis.

As will be discussed in the following section, social workers who hope to influence and shape the legislative framework for Child Welfare services must engage in a range of change strategies. However, some fundamental principles of effective advocacy should be followed by all practitioners, no matter what their specific professional role. Once these principles are mastered, workers should be able to adapt more easily to the different advocacy roles they may wish to assume as environmental circumstances change and they move into different organizational positions.

The first essential step is to assess differential needs and identify priorities for action. Often this principle is difficult for practitioners to accept because they are so aware of a wide range of needs and tend to want to address them all simultaneously. Yet, because of the nature of our political system, effective advocacy must be focused on issues, and this demands the establishment of priorities. A second important step is fact gathering. Data must be collected to support whatever policy the practitioner wants to advance. Third is a careful assessment of the political situation, permitting the advocate to identify the sources of authority governing the problem under consideration and to analyze the potential forces for and against change. Such an assessment should naturally lead to the establishment of realistic objectives and the identification of an appropriate target and strategy for change.

Once the practitioner has developed a strategy for effecting the change desired, he or she should begin to mobilize support by reaching out to groups likely to favor the position being advocated, building coalitions of consumer and professional groups and other potential allies, and making careful use of the media to educate the broader public about the particular issue. At this point the advocate should be ready to orchestrate the various activities and tasks which must be carried out to implement the change strategy devised. Finally, if the practitioner is successful in achieving the policy change desired, it is essential that plans be made to insure ongoing monitoring of the way in which the proposed policy is actually put into action. Many alleged policy changes are little more than paper victories because the advocate fails to follow through and monitor the impact of the change on practice.[8]

## Strategies for Effecting Legislative Change

As suggested earlier in the discussion of determinants of Child Welfare policy, practitioners who wish to effect policy changes must consider a number of potential target systems. Choice of a particular target and strategy for change is usually determined by the nature of the problem being addressed, the resources available to the practitioner, the constraints imposed by the worker's agency base, and external political forces that may impinge on the change desired. Although responsibility for the formulation of public policy ultimately rests with the legislative branches of government, the courts are frequently asked to interpret laws and in so doing may significantly shape policy. Moreover, the executive office and administrative agencies at both the federal and state levels are responsible for implementing legislative changes. As all practitioners know, administrative regulations can do much to advance or undermine the intent of the policies they are expected to implement. Consequently, the courts and federal and state administrative and regulatory agencies may be as significant targets for change as Congress and the state legislatures.

Since a discussion of strategies for working with all of these potential target systems is impractical, we shall focus primarily on strategies for influencing social policy by legislative change. The emphasis will be on legislative action at the state level because the current trend toward returning responsibility for social service provision to the states suggests that this arena will become increasingly important for advocacy activity.

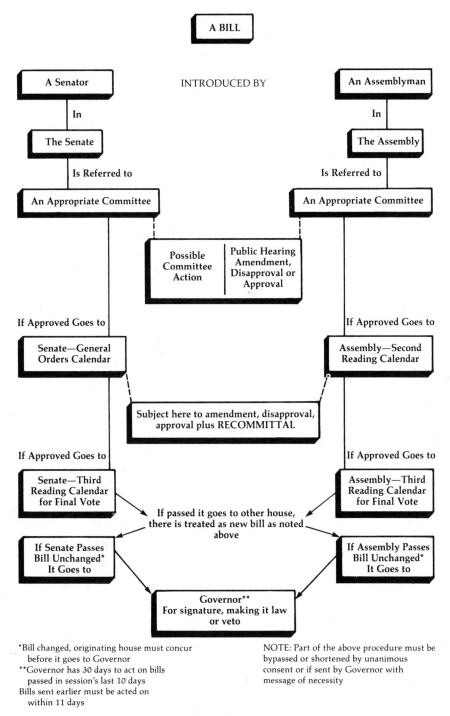

**A BILL**

INTRODUCED BY

A Senator — In — The Senate — Is Referred to — An Appropriate Committee

An Assemblyman — In — The Assembly — Is Referred to — An Appropriate Committee

| Possible Committee Action | Public Hearing Amendment, Disapproval or Approval |

If Approved Goes to

Senate—General Orders Calendar

Assembly—Second Reading Calendar

Subject here to amendment, disapproval, approval plus RECOMMITTAL

If Approved Goes to

Senate—Third Reading Calendar for Final Vote

Assembly—Third Reading Calendar for Final Vote

If passed it goes to other house, there is treated as new bill as noted above

If Senate Passes Bill Unchanged* It Goes to

If Assembly Passes Bill Unchanged* It Goes to

Governor**
For signature, making it law or veto

*Bill changed, originating house must concur
  before it goes to Governor
**Governor has 30 days to act on bills
  passed in session's last 10 days
Bills sent earlier must be acted on
  within 11 days

NOTE: Part of the above procedure must be
bypassed or shortened by unanimous
consent or if sent by Governor with
message of necessity

**Figure 11–1**   How A Bill Becomes A Law

*Source:* New York State AFL–CIO Legislative Department.

## The Legislative Process

We have noted that many practitioners are reluctant to engage in political activity because they feel overwhelmed by the seeming complexities of the legislative process. Therefore, before discussing strategies for effecting legislative change, we shall review briefly the relatively straightforward process by which a bill becomes a law.

For purposes of illustration, we shall describe the legislative process in the New York State Legislature as a typical process by which a bill becomes a law in Congress and in other state legislatures. With the exception of Nebraska, federal and state legislatures are composed of two chambers, a senate and a house of representatives (Kleinkauf, 1981). In New York State these bodies are called the Senate and the Assembly. As illustrated in Figure 11–1, a bill can be introduced by a member of either the Senate or the Assembly. It is immediately referred to an appropriate committee for action. If approved—with or without amendment—it is sent back to the originating body for a second reading. At this point, the bill can be amended, disapproved, or recommended for action by another committee. If approved, the bill is calendared or scheduled for a third reading and final vote. If passed, the bill is then sent to the other house where it goes through an essentially parallel process. When introduced in both houses at the same time, the bill may go through these processes simultaneously.

If the bill is amended before passage in the second house, it must go back to the originating house for ratification before it is sent to the governor. A joint subcommittee may be asked to reconcile differences when the two houses pass different versions of the same bill. After final approval the bill is sent to the governor. If the governor signs the bill, it then becomes a law. If the governor vetoes the bill, it is returned to the originating house. This body then reviews the governor's objections; and if consensus is obtained regarding desired modifications, an amended version of the bill is again sent through the same legislative process as described.

A governor's veto can be overriden by a two-thirds vote of the members of both houses. A bill can also become a law if the governor does not return it to the originating body with a list of specific objections within a prescribed number of days after it has been forwarded for signature. However, if the legislative session has been adjourned, the governor cannot return the bill for further action. Consequently, if it is not signed, the bill does not become a law. This action is called a "pocket veto."

Although the process by which a bill becomes a law is quite straightforward, the influence of numerous forces on the legislature makes the

**EXHIBIT 11–1    Steps for the Practitioner in Effecting Legislative Change**

*Preliminary Activity*

1. Meet with legislators
2. Learn positions of legislators
3. Develop legislative alliances
4. Identify key aides
5. Develop ongoing relationships with aides
6. Provide support and assistance on relevant issues
7. Supply updates on issues and programs via reports, flyers, newsletters
8. Invite legislators to public meetings and to visit agencies
9. Provide informal consultation on child welfare issues
10. Identify issues or problems that can be addressed by legislative change

*Introduction of Bill*

1. Specify problems and objectives clearly
2. Gather supporting data
*3. Seek multiple sponsorship from influential legislators
*4. Have bill introduced early in session (if not before)
5. Function as educator and/or facilitator
   a. Work with legislative aides (local and in capital)
   b. Assist in drafting bill
   c. Provide lists of potential support and nonsupport groups
*6. Obtain sponsorship of majority party and, if possible, bipartisan sponsorship

7. Begin to organize professional and community constituents by holding educational meetings, forming telephone trees, establishing coalitions
*8. Seek support of governor and relevant state agencies
9. Provide information on bill's potential impact, cost–benefit analyses
10. Use personal influence

*Committee Hearings*

*1. Press for open hearings
*2. Provide expert testimony
3. Make contact with Committee Chair
4. Lobby committee members and their staffs
5. Obtain support of state agency responsible for child welfare services
6. Build coalitions
   a. To provide testimony
   b. To delineate priorities and resolve differences that may arise during committee deliberations
   c. To mobilize support for bill
7. Obtain media coverage
8. Hold rally
9. Provide additional data as needed
10. Facilitate communication between committee members and constituency
*11. Use amendatory process to obtain favorable outcome (Requires negotiation and compromise tactics)

*(continued)*

## EXHIBIT 11-1  *(Continued)*

*Floor Action*

1. Contact and lobby key legislators
2. Mobilize community support
   a. Organize letter writing campaign
   b. Mobilize telephone tree
   c. Obtain media coverage
3. Pressure for support and action from relevant state agencies
4. Provide data and case examples for debate
5. Provide consultation to bill's sponsors, committee chairs, other legislators
6. Monitor legislative response
7. Provide feedback to professional constituency and community groups about bill's progress
8. Utilize amendatory process

*Executive Action*

1. Obtain governor's support of bill
2. Use personal influence of coalition leaders, board members, campaign contributors, local political officials, governor's close associates and advisors

3. Have support of majority and minority leaders
4. Apply amendatory process
5. Be available as consultant
6. Monitor and publicize governor's action

*After Passage*

1. Acknowledge those who supported bill via newsletter, media coverage, individual letters (especially assistance of key aides at each step)
2. Maintain relationships with legislators
3. Monitor implementation of law
4. Provide feeedback
   a. Update legislators on law's impact, problems
   b. Update constituency on law's impact
   c. Suggest needed modification, amendments
5. Function as informal consultant re implementation problems
6. Keep legislators and community informed on other issues

*In a study of committee action on health and social services bills introduced in the 43d and 44th sessions of the Washington State Legislature, these advocacy tactics were found to be especially effective (Dear and Patti, 1981).

The steps outlined are merely suggestive, not prescriptive. The selection of particular tactics should be guided by the specifics of the legislative situation. And much further research and exchange is needed to determine which tactics are most effective under which circumstances.

process of effecting legislative change rather complex. It demands that practitioners engage in a number of different, yet overlapping change activities and use a range of change tactics. We have divided these into five major areas, each of which involves numerous tasks. These areas include: (1) developing legislative contacts, (2) building coalitions and mobilizing support, (3) providing education and consultation, (4) providing testimony, and (5) lobbying. As illustrated in Exhibit 11-1 the practitioner may have to engage in some of these activities repeatedly at each decision point in the legislative process.

## Developing Legislative Contacts

An essential task for all professionals hoping to influence social policy is to develop working relationships with various members of the legislature and their staffs. Social workers are sometimes skeptical about the possibility of building alliances with legislators, either because they are not sure politicians can be trusted or because they cannot imagine that legislators would be interested. Yet, asking a member of the legislature to sponsor a bill, to offer an amendment, to schedule hearings, or to vote a particular way is much easier if a prior relationship has been established. If one contacts a legislator only when help or support is needed, then one often is too late to have any real impact.

Because legislators cannot possibly be experts on the subject of every bill they are asked to consider, they are usually quite eager to develop relationships with professionals on whom they can rely for accurate data and reasoned policy positions on different issues. In the best circumstances, practitioners can use their professional expertise as a base for building relationships with different legislators. Also, practitioners should try to sustain these relationships by providing periodic updates about issues and programs they are concerned with and by developing a reputation for reliability in delivering information, support, or consultation on a particular issue.

As practitioners work to develop legislative alliances, they must try to obtain as much information as possible about the inner workings of the legislature. For example, they should learn the best timing for introduction of a bill; the attitudes of the heads of key legislative committees toward Child Welfare issues; how various legislative offices are staffed; who should be approached to insure that a hearing is scheduled; the interest groups to which different legislators are likely to respond and so forth. By building a base of information on such matters, practitioners can begin to develop more effective strategies and use their limited energy and resources more fruitfully.

## Building Coalitions and Mobilizing Support

Practitioners acting *alone* are seldom able to have any significant impact on legislation because elected officials who want to remain in office are primarily concerned about representing the interests of their constituents. Therefore, it is essential that workers persuade the legislators they are hoping to influence that the position they are advocating is supported—or at least is not opposed—by their constituents or other significant interest groups. To do this, practitioners should attempt to mobilize support and, if necessary, organize coalitions around specific legislative issues.

Since many issues of concern to Child Welfare practitioners, such as subsidized adoption or external review of children in foster care, are of little interest to the larger community, it is often possible to obtain legislative support for Child Welfare bills advocated only by professional and consumer groups. In such cases, the practitioner should work primarily toward developing consensus among the interested parties about the proposed legislation to insure that enough support is expressed to persuade legislators of the importance of this bill. When professional and consumer groups are in disagreement about the specifics of a proposed bill, legislators are inclined to let the bill die so they can avoid taking a position that might alienate one group or another. To prevent this from happening, practitioners must do their homework and try to get differences resolved before the legislation is introduced.

This discussion is not meant to imply that the general public should be excluded from debates on Child Welfare policy, but rather that given limited resources, practitioners should focus their energies on achieving consensus within the smaller professional arena. Yet, with an increased use of block grants for social services, Child Welfare practitioners may have to devote more attention to influencing public decisions regarding the allocation of funding at the state and local levels. For example, in New York City, the local community planning board can be an important ally or foe in the effort to secure adequate funds for Child Welfare services. Even at this time, some bills of potential concern to Child Welfare practitioners such as those expanding homemaker or day-care services for families at risk, granting specific rights to children in care, or requiring the establishment of group homes for deinstitutionalized populations clearly attract the attention of larger segments of the community. In these situations, it is imperative that practitioners attempt to mobilize broad-based support for the legislation by speaking to various community groups, obtaining media coverage of the issue, and developing coalitions with church groups, unions, business people, and representatives of different citizen action groups. Professionals usually cannot manage successful lobbying campaigns alone. They need the support of volunteers and professionals identified with other interest groups in order to find spokespeople who "have the ear" of key legislators, to develop persuasive testimony, and to demonstrate that the bill being advocated is supported by a significant number of voters.

Building coalitions can be especially important in situations in which the practitioner's own representatives and/or key legislative leaders are opposed to a bill. In such cases it may be possible to identify one or more legislators from other districts who would be willing to sponsor the bill, and other members of the coalition may have more influence with key persons in the legislature.[9] Because of the trading of favors which characterizes the legislative process in this country, legislators often respond to pressure from their colleagues. Consequently, by developing a coalition which can demonstrate widespread support for a particular bill, practitioners may be able to persuade legislators who were initially opposed to the bill to change their position. Issue-oriented coalitions can also be used to mobilize support for legislators who may fear that their position will be jeopardized because of their stance on an unpopular bill. In other words, legislators and coalitions may work in a *quid pro quo* manner to insure that their mutual interests are protected.

## Providing Education and Consultation

Professionals acting alone can seldom bring about specific legislative change. But by providing information and expert consultation to legislators about Child Welfare issues, they can often have a gradual impact on the legislative process. Political leaders are sought after by numerous interest groups and asked to take up many diverse causes. Yet it is not humanly possible for them to stay well-informed about all the issues they are asked to consider or even to give equal consideration to these issues. Consequently, they are likely to be most responsive to advocates on whom they can rely to provide facts about a specific area of concern, realistic suggestions for action, substantiating data to support any legislative proposals, and information about the potential political and fiscal consequences of any contemplated change.

This need suggests a number of potential roles for practitioners interested in influencing social policy. One of the most important, especially for those in direct practice, is data collection. Direct service practitioners are in an ideal position to collect both quantitative and case data about what is happening to people and to make suggestions about how legislators might better respond to the needs of their constituents. Sometimes they can provide this information directly to their representatives; at other times it may be more effective to contribute to a case data bank that can be used by professional colleagues who are developing legislation, providing testimony, or lobbying on a specific issue.[10]

Another potential educational role for practitioners is that of informal consultant to key legislators or legislative committees. For example, one of the authors served for several years as member of an advisory committee to the New York State Assembly Committee on Child Care. In this capacity she was asked to review all major bills introduced relating to Child Welfare and to make recommendations for action. This advisory group was established because the chairperson of the legislative committee was eager for professional input and had a social worker as one of his chief aides. In other, more typical situations, practitioners may not be able to act in this semiofficial capacity. However, it is often possible for professionals to develop an informal consulting role with one or more legislative aides covering Child Welfare issues and to provide ongoing feedback regarding general concerns in the field and specific legislative proposals.

Practitioners also are often able to provide technical assistance to legislators interested in introducing legislation related to some Child Welfare issue. Because political leaders usually lack intimate knowledge of the field, they may identify some problem but not be certain how it should be addressed. In these situations, practitioners may be asked to help develop a bill, review various drafts, make recommendations regarding the feasibility of implementing different potential solutions, comment on proposed amendments to the bill and so forth. In order to be in a position to be asked to provide this type of technical assistance, professionals must endeavor to establish ongoing relationships with key legislators and demonstrate that they follow through when asked for assistance.

## Providing Testimony

All legislatures have a number of standing committees in both houses. These committees, which are usually structured to correspond with the major administrative functions and departments of the federal and state government, perform the major work of the legislature. They review all bills that could affect policies and operations in the corresponding departments (Kleinkauf, 1981). They also consider in a broad fashion issues touching on the work of these departments. For example, they may hold hearings on a general topic such as adoption although they are not reviewing any specific legislation on this topic.

One of the primary ways that committees obtain information about the issues they are asked to consider is to hold hearings. Therefore, practitioners hoping to influence the legislative process should call for hearings on bills they are interested in and try to make certain that convincing testimony is presented at each hearing. Although testimony provided at public hearings may have less impact on legislators than personal contacts, informal consultation, or other lobbying tactics, hearings do offer an opportunity to draw public attention to an issue that may otherwise be dropped. Moreover, there is some evidence that informed testimony can be persuasive, especially to legislators who are wavering, or to those seeking information to reinforce an unpopular position on an issue (Dear and Patti, 1981). For example, Representative George Miller, Chairperson of the House Select Committee on Children, Youth, and Families, recently commented that testimony provided at Committee hearings regarding the success of specific programs had a significant impact on the Congressional decision to increase appropriations for a number of children's programs for the fiscal year 1984.[11]

From a legislator's perspective, committee hearings can serve several functions. They can stimulate interest in a particular topic or bill, provide an opportunity to acquire information and learn the opinions of those who are experts in a particular area, and offer a means to test public attitudes and to assess constituents' views on the issue under consideration. Although legislators are elected by a majority of those who voted, they are very aware that they do not necessarily represent the views of a majority of their total constituency. Consequently, they are usually eager to learn how their constituents view different issues and often must try to balance expert and constituent opinion when reaching their own position on a particular bill. When providing testimony, professionals should remember the many functions the hearing may be serving and the tension committee members may feel regarding discrepancies between expert and constituent opinions.

Practitioners who are asked or who decide to testify at a particular hearing may do so in several different capacities. Prior to making a commitment to testify, the worker must determine whether to appear as a private citizen who has independent professional knowledge and opinions or whether to represent the views of his or her agency or professional group. When functioning in either of the latter capacities, the advocate should obtain clear sanction to represent an organizational position; it is advisable to obtain a letter requesting testimony from the hearing body as a protection against any objections from funding sources. In such situations it is also important for the agency or professional group to determine who will be able to provide the most persuasive testimony. To illustrate, although the direct service practitioner may be best able to collect data and prepare testimony, a person with administrative authority and some public stature may be more effective in giving testimony. It may be felt that consumers of the service will be listened to more closely, making the practitioner's task to help clients prepare testimony and perhaps rehearse them to answer the questions they may be asked.

Generally, relatively short notice is given prior to public hearings. Therefore, practitioners must be ready to act quickly in regard to obtaining necessary clearances if they plan to represent an organizational position; deciding who can present the testimony most effectively; discovering who else will be providing testimony; reaching some consensus, if possible, with other allied groups about the position to be taken and how specific points will be made; gathering the data necessary to support the position advocated; and learning about how this particular committee functions, the composition and positions of its membership, and the legislative history, if any, of the issue under consideration. It is also essential to determine as clearly as possible why this particular hearing is being held, what specifically people are being asked to testify on, and what questions are likely to be raised by the legislators.

Oral testimony is usually limited to three to five minutes, but it is often possible to submit written statements in which the position being advocated can be discussed and substantiated in more detail. The key points for practitioners to remember when providing testimony are: to identify clearly who they are and what interests they represent; to present their views in as brief, specific, and factual a way as possible; to cite case examples; to consider negative and positive consequences of the action proposed, as well as any cost factors; to speak in an articulate, warm, open, and knowledgable manner; to answer questions nondefensively; and to get back to the hearing committee as quickly as possible with any additional information that is requested.[12]

Although public hearings are usually called by legislative committees or government agencies to hear feedback on proposed actions, it is sometimes effective for consumer or advocacy groups to call a public hearing to highlight specific concerns. For example, a group of day-care centers might organize a hearing on the impact of proposed budget cuts and ask legislators, as well as other public officials, to testify or to preside while consumers and practitioners present their testimony. This strategy offers a means of drawing legislative and public attention to a policy issue not currently being addressed in the political arena.

## Lobbying

The term lobbying usually conjures up the image of the paid professional lobbyist who represents the interests of an influential interest group by engaging in extensive wheeling and dealing with public officials; in fact much lobbying is carried out in this manner. However, many professional, consumer, and citizen groups also engage in lobbying by trying to use outside influence to carry a bill through the legislative process.

Nonprofit organizations are prohibited by their tax-exempt status from spending a substantial part (usually interpreted as no more than 5–10 percent) of their budgets on lobbying, and government employees are quite restricted as to the type of political activity they can pursue. Consequently, most practitioners functioning as agency employees are not permitted to engage in any real lobbying. Even top administrators and community organizers whose job responsibilities include keeping contact with legislators usually endeavor to maintain this contact by informal means including arranging to be asked to testify or to provide consultation rather than openly lobbying for specific bills. However, social workers functioning as professionals or citizens rather than as agency employees are able to lobby through the National Association of Social Workers' ELAN committees, as well as through various citizen groups.

The strategies employed by lobbyists are generally quite similar to those suggested in this chapter for practitioners hoping to effect legislative change by other means. The key difference between lobbying and, for example, providing consultation or testifying at public hearings, is that when lobbying, the practitioner is taking the initiative and essentially asking for a favor whereas when engaging in these other activities, the practitioner is responding to a request from the legislature. Given this difference, two tactics practitioners should keep in mind when lobbying are to seek bipartisan, multiple sponsorship of legislation and to mobilize as much community support as possible for the position advocated.

Tactics such as letter writing, telephone campaigns, and petitions have generally been viewed as somewhat futile. However, the political climate has changed radically since 1980 and increasing numbers of right-wing groups opposed to basic social welfare provisions have learned to use mass mail campaigns very effectively. To illustrate, several members of Congress contacted social workers with whom they had worked on other issues during a recent battle over block grants for social services to ask that groups be organized to write in opposition to this proposal. They explained that since their mail was coming in so strongly in favor of the proposal, they would be hard pressed to vote against it unless they could say that they had some strong constituency support in favor of their position. Although the effort to defeat this proposal was not successful, we believe this incident illustrates the importance of practitioners using every possible strategy, including mail campaigns, to influence legislation. This example also highlights the need for increased numbers of practitioners to become engaged in legislative change efforts if they want to sustain and build a policy framework that supports family and child welfare.

At the same time it should be noted that recent proposed regulations from the federal Office of Management and Budget prohibit the use of federal funds for any lobbying or related activities, including grass roots organizing.[13] Regulations regarding federal and state funding, as well as the tax codes governing nonprofit organizations, are likely to change over time. Therefore, readers should be cautioned that it would be advisable to obtain legal consultation before engaging in any official activities that could be construed as political in nature.

Having highlighted the need for practitioner involvement in efforts to influence social policy and having discussed a range of strategies for effecting change, we would like to underscore our position that active engagement in this change process does not justify laying aside professional knowledge and values. Participation in the political game can be a very heady experience, demanding that practitioners exercise skills very different from those required in direct practice. But as professionals, Child Welfare workers have a responsibility to remain very clear about their objectives and not to compromise their values in order to achieve temporary gains.

We realize that some of our views may sound rather quixotic, especially given the regressive social climate of the last few years. However, history has demonstrated that with knowledge, patience, and persistence, individuals can help to effect change. We believe that practitioners who are willing to learn the political process and to mobilize others—clients, colleagues, and citizen groups alike—to join in their efforts can begin to have a more significant impact on social policy. As Child Welfare practitioners become more involved in political change efforts, we would hope that they will also attempt to document their experiences. Although there is some knowledge about how social workers operating from a practice base can influence policy, much more is to be learned. As the social work profession develops a larger data base on effective strategies for change and ways to engage others in change efforts, it will enhance its opportunities for developing a sound policy framework for family and children's services.

# CHAPTER 12

# Leadership and Change in Child Welfare Organizations

RINO J. PATTI
HERMAN RESNICK

Child Welfare agencies, like all human service organizations, are being buffeted by a host of political, economic, and social forces that are requiring adaptation and change. The most obvious and immediate of these forces are the substantial cutbacks in governmental support for social programs (Terrell, 1981), but others which may ultimately be as significant are changes in family form and composition, the declining birth rate, the increased divorce rate, and the increased numbers of women in the labor force. These forces are not new, but it does appear that they have been significantly augmented in recent years and that their implications for the survival and effectiveness of Child Welfare agencies have never been more clear.

While there is a good deal of attention directed at the substance of the changes that may be required of Child Welfare agencies, there is relatively little in the human services literature regarding how leaders can best administer such changes (Davis, 1978; York, 1977). This chapter is concerned with the process of planned organizational change and the approaches to leadership that might be employed by managers in Child Welfare agencies who are seeking to modify policies, programs, or practices, or to promote the adoption of innovations. Our purpose is to provide a framework which will be helpful to Child Welfare administrators in assessing the contingencies that exist in a change situation and their implications for the type of leadership that might be employed.

## A Model of Management-Initiated Change

The model of management-initiated change discussed contains two major dimensions: steps or phases in the change process; and styles of leadership available to the manager. After describing each of these dimensions and their relationship to one another, we shall turn our attention to situational variables (contingencies) that managers should consider in deciding on an appropriate leadership approach in a given change project.

### Steps in the Change Process

The change process is conceived as containing seven steps or phases which, taken together, include all the action in an organizational change project from the inception of the original idea, to its implementation, and eventual institutionalization into the organizational structure (see, for example, Greiner 1967). We assume that although the administrator of the Child Welfare agency is responsible for initiating the change, he or she can share much of the responsibility for change goals and processes with the staff. A second assumption is that management initiated organizational change can be a guided and directed process and that thinking through the goal and process questions can increase the effectiveness of the manager's change efforts.

THE PROBLEM SITUATION. The first step in the change process is the selection of a problem situation that is detrimental to agency functioning. A problem exists when the manager, his or her superiors, subordinates, or authoritative bodies in the task environment, identify a gap between what is presently occurring in the agency and some desirable level of functioning. Some problems are largely indigenous to the organization. For example: levels of output or outcome may be less than anticipated; rates of employee absenteeism or turnover rise to a level that is disruptive to operations; workers fail to comply with policies and procedures; interunit coordination suffers because of poor communication or conflict; employee morale declines and leads to uncooperative behavior; or, the adolescents in a group home increase their acting out behavior. Other kinds of problems are mainly exogenous to the agency:

the budget for the coming fiscal year is significantly reduced, resulting in the need to reallocate resources; a new law is passed that requires the program to modify policies and procedures; the agency director or board changes priorities so that some services are de-emphasized in favor of others. (In the latter case the discrepancy between current and desirable levels of performance is created by externally imposed demands.)

PROBLEM ANALYSIS.   Whether the impetus for change is internal or external the manager must acquire an understanding of those conditions which stand as barriers to reducing the discrepancy between current and desired levels of performance. For example, the problem regarding acting out behavior in the group home may have many causes and could be understood differently depending on the vested interests of those analyzing it. Its impact may be experienced differently by staff and by administrators and so its salience may depend upon who is calling it a problem, their location in the organization, their treatment theory, and their distance from the psychological and social effects of the problem. A therapist treating an adolescent in his or her office may see the young person's behavior as normal for this developmental stage, whereas a child-care worker in a residential unit may see the behaviors as threatening or disruptive to group life.

Analyses of an organizational problem may be conducted in several ways, which need not be mutually exclusive. First, the manager may unilaterally define the problem and the causes of it, drawing upon whatever data are already available as well as his or her own personal observations. Second, the manager may resort to a more formal analytic approach to problem analysis. Surveys, program evaluations, administrative audits, or operations analysis are among the techniques that can be employed (Epstein and Tripodi, 1977). These modes of analysis, which often require considerable resources and the use of external expertise, are ordinarily reserved for situations in which the problem has major implications for the agency and the manager requires a detailed, technical understanding. A third approach to problem analysis draws principally on the information and ideas of program participants, especially subordinates. Typically, staff who are most involved with the problem are brought together to share information and perceptions regarding the nature of the difficulty, as well as any factors that may be contributing to it. (For an example of this approach, see French and Bell, 1973.) Staff meetings, retreats or workshops often provide the forum for staff involvement. This approach is probably most useful when subordinates believe that the administrator is open to new information and that input can be provided without fear of reprisal. These approaches to problem analysis, which may be used in some combination, will normally generate a fuller understanding of the problem and the alternative courses of action that might be followed.

DETERMINATION OF CHANGE OBJECTIVE.   The third step in the change process involves a description of the situation with the problem reduced or eliminated. It entails projecting the specific behaviors, activities, or events that need to be changed. The purpose here is to provide some end state toward which the change effort can move, and around which some judgment can later be made about whether the change project was completed and how well it was done. Using the example of the high frequency of acting out behaviors of adolescent residents in a group home, a change objective could be the reduction of destructive incidents, from nine such incidents per day to two or three per day, within a month's period of time. This kind of change objective provides the participants in the project with specific goals to keep in mind as they proceed.

SELECTION OF COURSE OF ACTION.   The fourth phase in the change process is the selection of a strategy—a sequence of action steps—which appear to have the greatest probability of achieving the change objective (Kotter and Schlesinger, 1979; Powells and Posner, 1976). This strategy may be selected as a result of a search of the literature describing similar problem situations and successful strategies used by others. It may also involve efforts to determine if other organizations are experiencing similar problems and finding effective strategies. Finally, it is often useful to seek help from one's colleagues, for example, from the board or the staff, to hear their ideas about which strategies may best ameliorate the problem. Depending upon time and resources available, administrators typically engage in all of these search activities to discover the most feasible and "best fit" strategies. An example of strategy alternatives with respect to the problem of acting out behavior in a group home might be to: 1) develop a training program for staff to increase their skill in dealing with difficult youngsters; and/or 2) to change the client composition of the group home to include fewer acting-out teenagers. The strategy selected should be related to the analysis of the problem situation so that, for example, if the analysis yielded the understanding that the residents were acting destructively because staff were not sufficiently skilled to handle them, then the strategy might be to enhance the staff's skill through a long-range training program. However, if the analysis suggested that the youths were exploiting a lack of communication in staff–staff or staff–administrator relationships, then a completely different strategy might be in order, for example one which involves team building or communication.

START-UP PERIOD. These four steps comprise the planning work that precedes the actual implementation of the change project. What generally follows is a period during which the organization begins to put in place the strategy—the action steps—that have been selected. Three basic tasks are generally necessary to get the change project off the ground: communication, allocation of roles, and provision of resources.

Administrators who have participated in a planning process which has led to some agreement on the basic elements of a change project, that is, on an organizational problem to be worked on and on a solution to this problem, now have to communicate these decisions to relevant staff members. To do this effectively a number of questions should be dealt with:

1. What information will be passed on to the staff? In how much detail? Whether to emphasize the selection or the solution of the problem or background to either are decisions administrators must make. *Too little* information, and the staff may feel cheated and mistrusting; *too much* information, and staff may feel bored or overwhelmed.

2. How should the information about the change project be transmitted to staff? Should it be written or verbal or both? If verbal, should the format be in small groups or large meetings, or both? What norms should be operative in these sessions? A crucial ingredient for successful discussion at these meetings is the receptivity of those conducting the meetings to criticism of the change project. Encouraging and allowing criticism at these sessions serves the twofold purpose of bringing real weaknesses and limitations of the change project to the surface at an early stage, so they can be modified appropriately, and reducing resistance by encouraging both criticism and suggestions for improvement.

3. Who shall present the information to staff? Administration? Staff? Or some grouping of both? A judicious and honest use of leadership staff to participate in presenting some or all of the information often goes a long way to reducing the staff's first resistances to a change project.

4. When the information about the change project should be passed on to the staff is another question with which administrators need to contend. Too early distribution of information which may not be completed or cogent can result in misinterpretations, because the full picture has not been made clear. With too late distribution of information, distrust ensues because some people will have obtained some information earlier and

others will not, leading to bad feelings and misapprehensions on the part of staff.

The second activity in the start-up phase has to do with who does what. What tasks are involved in this change project and what kinds of groupings with what kinds of leadership should be made? It is critical that administrators be clear about the levels of responsibility and authority they assign to specific staff members in these task groups. Failure to provide a staff group with leadership can sometimes lead to confusion and a jockeying for power, both of which are detrimental to the group's effectiveness.

The third activity is the provision of resources to implement the strategy. Resources should be broadly defined; they include, among other things, expertise, time, funding, reasonable expectation, psychological support (for example, access and recognition), and space that might be needed for a particular task force. Recognizing that staff are usually overcommitted when they volunteer for, or are assigned to, a change project task force, the stress and fatigue generated by the extra work of such a task force may lead to a reduction of commitment and motivation of members to the task force objectives.

IMPLEMENTATION. After a period of transition in which the strategy and even the change objective itself may be modified to reflect unanticipated problems and constraints, the organization begins the process of consolidating new modes of operation. Additional fine tuning of the problems, procedures, or behaviors is likely to occur during this period as staff seek an accomodation between personal goals, group norms, and work pressures, and the demands imposed on them by the changes introduced. Among the issues that may arise at this point are the reluctance of staff to invest the energy required to implement the strategy or a gradual modification of the strategy so that it begins to look quite different from what was originally intended. In the example of the group home for adolescents, let us say that one of the changes introduced to reduce the incidence of destructive behavior was a policy which called for social workers to spend a number of hours each week observing the behavior of children in the residential setting and interacting with child-care staff. Let us further suppose that as social workers began to spend time on the units, they were received coolly by the child care staff. Given the press of other duties and perhaps a preference for using their time in individual therapy sessions, some social workers might choose to spend less time on the residential unit than was originally planned. If several social workers began to reduce their time or invest less energy in making these visits productive, the new policy could quickly become a dead letter. Identifying and correcting these problems as they occur is often critical to the successful implementation of the change strategy.

EVALUATION.   The final step in the change process is evaluation. In a more or less formal way the manager and/or staff assess whether the strategy for change has been implemented as initially intended, the modifications that may have occurred in the process of implementation, and any unintended benefits or problems that the strategy may have created. At some point there is also likely to be an assessment of whether the change objectives have been achieved, for example, in determing whether the incidence of destructive behavior on the residential unit has decreased to the desired level. An evaluation of the change strategy or outcome may consist of nothing more than observations or verbal reports, or it may involve more systematic evaluative efforts. In either case the feedback is likely to be used to determine whether the change strategy will be maintained, modified, or abandoned.

## Leadership Styles

Assuming the change process described above, a crucial decision about which leadership style should be employed by the management team to initiate and engage in this change process needs to be made. Leadership styles may be viewed on a continuum ranging from unilateral action (with little or no input or consultation with subordinates) to the delegation of decision-making authority to subordinates (Tannenbaum and Schmidt, 1973).

For purposes of our model, we shall refer to leadership which falls on one end of the continuum as *directive* and that at the other end as *delegative.* The middle of the continuum we will call *participative* leadership. When employing a directive style, the management team identifies the problem to be worked on, makes an analysis, determines the change objectives, and devises the strategy to be employed in achieving the change objective. Implementation is typically handled by subordinates but the directive style is typically characterized by close and continuous monitoring by superiors. In the delegative style of leadership, staff are given responsibility for all or most of the steps in the change process. Staff take a central role in deciding which problems the Child Welfare agency will work on, analyzing those problems, and determining both the strategy and change objectives to be pursued. The manager sets parameters for staff decision-making and may exercise considerable influence by virtue of his or her information and control of resources, but the staff (or some component of it) is ultimately responsible for decisions at each stage. Typically in the delegative style, the staff is responsible not only for planning change, but for implementing it as well.

In the participative style the manager elicits the ideas, information, and preferences of subordinates in making major administrative decisions, delegates decision-making authority to workers and subordinates in areas where they carry responsibility, and allows practitioners to exercise some discretion in choosing the means for carrying out decisions made at a higher level. Participatory management does not require that all decisions be delegated or that staff be consulted in all matters. In some cases, the decisions to be made are relatively routine and participation is not necessary. In others, the options are severely constrained so that everyone recognizes that a participatory process is not worthwhile. In general, however, the participatory style proceeds on the assumption that when decisions affect subordinates, they should have an opportunity to contribute to, and exert some influence on, the decisions made.

## The Change Process and Leadership Style

These two dimensions of the management-initiated change model are depicted in Table 12–1. In each of the cells proceeding vertically down the matrix we have indicated the managerial behaviors characteristic of a type of leadership style in a given phase of organizational change. Thus, in the column under directive leadership are listed the behaviors that typify this kind of leadership style in each step of the organizational change process. Two parts are important to note. First, the manager who uses a type of leadership at one point in the change process need not use that same style in successive steps. A manager may be directive with regard to determining whether a problem exists and requires corrective action, participative in analyzing the causes of the problem and the change objective, and delegative with regard to strategy selection and implementation. Another way of putting this is that at each step of the change process a manager has a choice to make regarding the kind of leadership that is the most appropriate at that point in the change project.

Second, while leadership may vary in each stage, it is probably true that managers find it easier to move from directive to more employee-centered styles, than vice versa. The use of either participatory or delegative behaviors in the early stages of a change project, establishes (at least implicitly) a degree of subordinate ownership over the nature and direction of the change process. To take unilateral control, after power has been shared with staff, is likely to be seen as a breach of faith unless, of course, subordinates decide that directive management is required. On the other hand, managers who are directive in the early stages of change, may either retain that control or share it with subordinates as the change process proceeds. Staff may resent having been denied ear-

**TABLE 12-1  Styles of Leadership in the Organizational Change Process**

| | STYLES OF ADMINISTRATIVE LEADERSHIP | | |
| --- | --- | --- | --- |
| PHASES IN THE CHANGE PROCESS | DIRECTIVE | PARTICIPATIVE | DELEGATIVE |
| Problem identification | Manager identifies problem and defines parameters. | Manager senses problem, seeks input from subordinates, then defines parameters. | Manager senses problem, works with staff group to define parameters or delegates this task to them. |
| Problem analysis | Manager solicits information he or she considers salient to understanding the problem, completes assessment. | Manager structures the analysis. Seeks involvement of subordinates in formulating problem analysis, uses information to complete assessment. | Staff group structures the analysis and formulates an assessment, manager accepts assessment. |
| Determination of change objective | Manager determines change objective. | Manager solicits ideas regarding a proposed change objective or seeks ideas regarding objectives, then decides. | Staff group determines change objective with broad guidelines laid down by manager. |
| Analysis of alternatives and selection of course of action | Manager solicits information regarding alternatives, and chooses a course of action. | Manager seeks involvement of subordinates in identifying and evaluating alternative courses of action, then decides. | Staff group evaluates alternatives, then decides on a course of action. |

*(continued)*

**TABLE 12–1** (*Continued*)

| PHASES IN THE CHANGE PROCESS | STYLES OF ADMINISTRATIVE LEADERSHIP | | |
| --- | --- | --- | --- |
| | DIRECTIVE | PARTICIPATIVE | 'DELEGATIVE |
| Implementation planning and start-up | Manager monitors closely, makes most decisions regarding tasks, roles, timelines, resources, etc. | Manager delegates responsibility for planning to staff group, monitors periodically, signs off on major decisions. | Staff group does implementation planning within timelines and resources that are agreed to with manager. |
| Implementation | Manager monitors progress, detects early deviations from plan, makes decisions regarding corrections and refinements. Maintains control over means and ends. | Manager is informed of *major* problems, solicits input from staff regarding corrections and refinements, then makes decisions. Allows latitude regarding means, mostly concerned with progress toward objectives. | Staff group determines corrections and refinements needed in plan. Manager is consulted. |
| Evaluation | Manager determines nature and content of the evaluation. | Manager delegates responsibility for evaluation to subordinates within broad guidelines. | Staff group determines the nature and content of the evaluation. Manager is consulted. |

lier involvement, and may even see their participation as token involvement, but in either case they tend to see their lack of participation as a less serious management error than a promise to share power initially, only to withdraw it.

## Choosing a Leadership Style

To this point, we have attempted to describe stages in the organizational change process and the continuum of leadership styles that are potentially available to managers engaged in change. We turn now to the question of *choice,* or rather the contingencies that should be considered as the manager decides on an appropriate leadership style. Two assumptions underlie this discussion. First, we assume that there is no single best way for managers to effect change in organizations. The belief that change only occurs when it is mandated and closely supervised by superiors is no more tenable, in our view, than the notion that change can only occur when subordinates have fully participated in the process. In other words, we do not assume the intrinsic superiority of one approach to change. The issue is, rather, what style is likely to be most effective in achieving sound decisions about the change objective and the successful implementation of means to this objective, given environmental and intraorganizational circumstances. In this spirit, we will argue that none of the leadership styles discussed above are inherently more desirable than others. Each is a tool which can be used to good advantage given a particular set of contingencies.

Secondly, we assume that most managers, given self-awareness and proper training, can develop a behavioral repertoire sufficiently large to permit a purposeful selection of a management style best suited to a given instance of change. There is some debate on this matter. Fiedler (1977), for example, has argued that leaders are inherently predisposed to one or another set of leadership behaviors and are not capable of great flexibility in this regard. Others contend that leaders can acquire an array of leadership styles for use in varied circumstances (Vroom, 1977). In what follows, we assume the latter view, while recognizing that individuals vary greatly in the ease with which they can flexibly adopt various leadership stances.

What factors, then, must a manager consider in deciding on an appropriate leadership style? Three clusters of variables, or contingencies, appear particularly important in this regard: contextual circumstances, staff resistance or receptivity, and desired impact on staff. We will discuss each of these contingencies and their implications for leadership.

## Contextual Circumstances

Contextual circumstances are relatively fixed conditions that predate or surround the change project and serve to constrain or influence the manager's choice of leadership style.

TIME. Administrators are sometimes confronted with problems that must be resolved immediately. Some examples are practice strategies or program arrangements which are clearly injurious to clients; fiscal crises which pose a threat to agency survival or necessitate immediate program curtailment; or, a new law or court decision which dictates change in agency policy or procedure and orders immediate compliance. These and similar problems occur with some frequency and often leave the manager with few options, but to act quickly and unilaterally, with a minimum amount of input from subordinates. The meaningful involvement of staff in analyzing a problem and weighing alternative solutions is necessarily time-consuming. Under severe time constraints, it may not be possible to do justice to the participatory process and still accomplish the required change objective in the allotted time. In this situation, the urgency of the problem and the prohibitive costs entailed for clients or agency in not responding within a designated period outweigh the value of staff participation or staff-led change. The manager who has a strong preference for participatory leadership may, in this situation, move to involve the staff at later stages in the change process (for example, during start-up or implementation) after the change objective and strategy have been determined.

NATURE OF THE PROBLEM. In some situations, the problem that prompts the need for organizational change is easily defined and understood and the solution to it readily apparent (Vroom, 1977). Assume, for example, that an agency must routinely supply information to a contractor regarding the number of clients served and the services delivered, in order to be accurately reimbursed. The agency is committed to providing the contracted service and is assured that client confidentiality will be protected. However, the agency has no systematic means of retrieving, analyzing, and reporting the information needed. Extensive participation of the staff in analyzing the problem and determining objectives would seem both artificial and inefficient in this circumstance. Indeed, there may not even be the need for staff involvement in selecting a course of action because the decision regarding means is relatively straightforward (that is, collecting additional information from direct service staff about clients and services). As the change moves into implementation planning, however, the manager may well want to consult closely with staff (or even delegate the task to them) on how to obtain the information since it is they who will be responsible for generating the data.

Conversely, when the problem is ambiguous and the manager lacks the necessary information to understand it or choose an objective, participatory leadership is probably the strategy of choice from the outset. Take the example presented above, but imagine that the contracting agency is requesting information that might potentially violate client confidentiality. Assume further that the contractor's reimbursement formula prevents the agency from providing a type of intervention, such as homemaker service, that some of the agency staff may feel is essential to service effectiveness. In this more complex and potentially troublesome situation, the information, perspectives, and preferences of staff would be essential throughout the change process, but especially in the early stages.

EXPECTATIONS AND CAPACITY OF STAFF. Administrative subordinates will vary in the degree to which they expect and desire to be involved in deciding upon whether change is necessary and how it is to be implemented. Alluto and Belasco (1972) for example, have found that some staff desire more involvement and influence in decision-making, others less, and still others are satisfied with their level of involvement. For staff who feel overinvolved ("saturated" in Alluto and Belasco's terms), a participatory or delegative leadership strategy may be contraindicated not only because the quality of subsequent involvement may be poor, but also because additional responsibility may contribute to a sense of staff burnout or alienation.

Subordinates' expectations regarding involvement in the change process may also be influenced by their past experiences. For example, in agencies that have undergone frequent change, particularly of the kind that has been unilaterally imposed by superiors or external agencies, one often finds a guardedness and even cynicism. Repeated good faith efforts to plan and implement changes in policy or procedures, only to have these efforts aborted by new mandates, quite naturally makes some employees hesitant to invest in yet another round of change. The manager who seeks to employ a participative or delegative strategy in a change situation should be sensitive to the potential effects of history on staff motivation. In short, staff may simply be unwilling to expend energy in a change project which, based on past experience, is likely to be short-circuited.

Another dimension of staff involvement concerns what Hershey and Blanchard (1977) refer to as task maturity or the extent to which staff have task relevant skill, information, and experience. Where staff are high in task maturity, where for example, they have experience and expertise with regard to the organizational problem in question, or a record of successfully planning and implementing previous change projects, a delegative leadership style may be appropriate. Where staff lack the experience or expertise necessary to address a problem, on the other hand, the manager should probably play a more central role in the change process. One caution must be noted here. If the manager deems the staff incapable of constructively participating in the change process and assumes a directive posture, he or she may be setting in motion a negative circular process such that a lack of staff expertise leads to directive leadership, which in turn leads to a lack of experience in effecting agency change, which then promotes the need for directive leadership in subsequent change situations. The point is that the manager's perception of staff task maturity may carry different implications depending on the manager's long-term goals for staff development.

## The Organization's Receptivity to Change

A second major area of concern in deciding upon a leadership approach are those factors that are likely to impede or facilitate the adoption of a change and its implementation by subordinates (Johns, 1973). A useful approach for systematically assessing receptivity and resistance in change situations is the force field analysis (FFA). The FFA takes as its point of departure the discrepancy between a current condition and a desired condition in an organization. This, it will be recalled, was our definition of a problem. This mode of analysis is based on the assumption that most problems in organizations represent a state of equilibrium maintained by roughly equal vectors of driving forces (those that push for change in the desired direction) and restraining forces (those that resist or hinder change). The interplay of driving and restraining forces is, ultimately, peculiar to each organization, but certain categories in each do occur commonly in change situations.

RESTRAINING FORCES. Forces that commonly act as restraints to change are:

1. Sunk costs, or the investments of time, energy, and personal commitment made by organizational members to develop and sustain the current condition or arrangement. For example, staff are often reluctant to forego a service technology in which they have become well-trained and proficient.
2. Social relationships. Employees perform their jobs in the context of social relationships which provide status, identity, and emo-

tional support. These relationships between colleagues are often so interwoven with work performance that alterations in group composition can have an effect on morale and efficiency. Changes which threaten to disrupt social relationships are often resisted for this reason.

3. The distribution of power and resources. Interest groups in organizations tend to protect the resources, status, and power that they possess. Organizational change which has the effect of reducing the power of an interest group will tend to be resisted.

4. Opportunity costs. Some changes, desirable on their face, may be resisted because they detract from, or make impossible, the pursuit of other activities or objectives that are considered even more important. A decision to serve older, hard-to-place children in an adoption program, for example, however desirable in its own right, implies, assuming constant resources, that fewer healthy infants will be served.

5. Lack of knowledge or skill. To the extent that change requires new work behaviors or the abandonment of old behaviors with which employees have felt comfortable, it may be seen as undesirable and therefore resisted.

DRIVING FORCES. Some of the restraining forces mentioned may, in certain situations, serve to facilitate rather than impede change. For example, organizational change which requires alterations in interpersonal patterns may be considered desirable by employees if existing social relationships are conflict-ridden or otherwise stressful. Similarly, changes that increase the power and status of certain groups in an organization may be warmly embraced by those groups even while they are resisted by others who stand to lose as a result of the change. In addition, however, there are several other forces which frequently serve as catalysts or facilitators of change. They are:

1. Dissatisfaction with program performance. In those instances where data regarding program impact are relatively clear, negative feedback may prompt a reassessment of organizational policy and/or service delivery arrangements.

2. Funding cutbacks often require service or program reduction, but they may also stimulate a rethinking of objectives, service priorities, and target populations to be served.

3. Threats to organizational domain in the form of competition from other agencies, a declining demand for services, or changing ideology, may force an agency to examine itself or risk losing its rationale for existence.

4. Opportunities and inducements such as new grants or contract

funds, or the prospect of extending services to a new catchment area are often catalysts for organizational change.

Let us illustrate briefly how an FFA might look in a concrete case. Assume that the manager of a foster care program believes the children are remaining too long in foster homes (current condition) and that significantly more could be returned to their natural parents (desired condition). The manager might propose to increase the number of children returned to their homes by instituting a mandatory periodic case review procedure to facilitate the early identification of and planning for such children. Restraining forces in such a situation might be:

—workers' comfort with a familiar method of operation
—workers' desire to maintain autonomy in placement decisions
—workers' fear regarding reoccurrence of neglect and abuse if children are returned to their natural parents prematurely
—lack of skills on workers' part to strengthen natural families
—excessive existing workloads

Driving forces in such a situation might be:

—the high cost of foster care
—the successful adoption of case review mechanisms in other foster care programs, with evidence that length of placement can be significantly reduced when case review is instituted
—the difficulty in recruiting and retaining good foster homes
—the belief by some workers that impermanent living arrangements are harmful to children
—pressure from the manager to increase the cost effectiveness of the foster care program

These forces are illustrated in Figure 12–1.

IMPLICATIONS FOR LEADERSHIP STYLE. If the driving forces in a situation are more powerful than the restraining ones, and especially if these forces emanate from both within and without the program, any of the three leadership approaches may be effective. In this situation, the equilibrium that has maintained the existing condition has begun to break down, thus creating a favorable opportunity for organizational change. The question for the manager under these circumstances is how much control he or she wishes to exert on the timing and nature of the change. If there is little time to effect the change, the problem is clear and easily analyzed, and the manager is strongly committed to a specific objective,

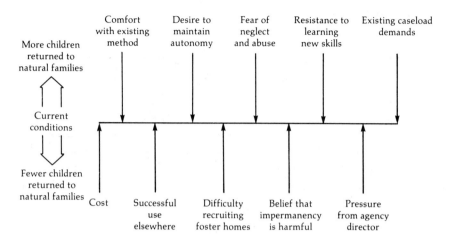

**Figure 12–1** Force Field Analysis

a directive style would be indicated, especially in the early stages of the change process. In this approach, the manager would channel the energy of the driving forces toward a particular outcome. If on the other hand, no immediate urgency prevails to achieve change, the problem is unclear and any one of several change objectives appear possible and feasible, then either a participative or delegative approach may be indicated. The choice between these two styles should depend largely on the experience and capacity of subordinates (see earlier discussion).

In a situation where driving and restraining forces are nearly equal or where the latter outweigh the former, and where such forces are largely internal, then a manager will usually find a participatory leadership style more effective in inducing change. This approach enables the manager to promote an awareness of the problem confronting the organization, to understand fully any resistance to change that may appear, and to negotiate compromises that are sensitive to staff concerns. The participatory style, in other words, is directed at reducing the strength of the restraining forces and thereby altering the equilibrium that maintains the existing condition in the organization. Neither the directive nor delegative style is likely to be an effective approach in this situation. The directive style often has the effect of engendering or consolidating resistance; the delegative style runs the risk that given a choice, staff will decide to take no action whatever. If this is not an acceptable outcome to the manager, then he or she should not delegate responsibility to staff.

*Impact of Leadership Style on Staff*

A third set of factors to consider in choosing a leadership style concerns the impact that one or another style is likely to have on the staff.

RELIANCE ON STAFF FOR IMPLEMENTATION. There is little question that most administrators hope to obtain the commitment of subordinates to changes introduced in an agency. Agreement with the change objective and a willingness to carry out the means necessary to achieving this objective are desirable outcomes of the change process. In some situations, however, employee commitment to change is not only desirable, but essential as well. In those situations, for example, where the manager cannot feasibly monitor and control employee behavior, where compliance is largely discretionary, effective implementation of a change rests squarely in the hands of subordinates. One need only be reminded of how many apparently good innovations are never carried off because agency employees, notwithstanding the encouragement and even threats from superiors, are opposed to their adoption. Management information systems, new practice technologies or procedures, and interdepartmental coordination mechanisms are a few examples of organizational changes whose success is heavily dependent on subordinate cooperation.

In situations like these where voluntary compliance is necessary to effective implementation, considerable evidence suggests that a participative or delegative approach to leadership should be utilized as early in the change process as possible (Vroom, 1977). This is not to suggest that employee cooperation cannot be obtained when a directive style is employed because clearly that is not the case. Employees sometimes support a change that is being instituted even though they have had little or no part in determining the objectives or planning for implementation. In other cases, a fear of sanctions or simply a desire to please superiors are sufficient to motivate compliance. Neverthless, these exceptions notwithstanding, the probability of obtaining active support and commitment for organizational change from subordinates, especially those changes that require significant behavioral or attitudinal modifications, is greater when employees have had significant and early involvement in the change process.

EMPLOYEE SATISFACTION. Insofar as possible, the leadership style used to initiate organizational change should not generate undesirable secondary effects on staff. Organizational changes of any magnitude are major events in the social psychological life of Child Welfare agencies, since they tend to highlight and intensify such processes as authority relationships, conflict, and communication. It often happens, therefore, that events experienced in change projects have a lasting impact on employee morale and job satisfaction. To initiate a change in an agency only to find that subordinates are disaffected or alienated from their jobs and colleagues is a Pyrrhic victory, indeed.

The implications of this dilemma for leadership are twofold. First, to minimize the negative residual effects of change, managers should, wherever feasible, err on the side of participatory leadership and do so as early in the change process as contextual circumstances permit. This leadership style is found to be related to job satisfaction (Fallon, 1978; Hage and Aiken, 1969). Second, where a directive style is used, as it sometimes must be, it is important for the manager to maintain active communication with subordinates so that he or she has the best possible information on which to base decisions, and to keep subordinates informed of the rationale for the change objectives, the change strategy, and the implementation (Lawrence, 1969). Finally, where a delegative approach is indicated, it is important for the manager to provide staff the support and resources necessary for them to plan effectively and to implement the change project. A failure to do this, whether or not intentional, can have very harmful effects on relationships between colleagues, as well as on the morale of individual workers.

In this chapter we have suggested that managers who seek to initiate change in Child Welfare organizations should make a deliberate choice of leadership style based on their assessment of contextual and intraorganizational contingencies. There is no formula which permits precise calculation in this regard. The weight an administrator attaches to the factors discussed will no doubt vary with his or her philosophy of management, long-term goals, and personal characteristics, as well as the organization's relationship with its task environment. In other words, two managers looking at the same set of contingencies may well assign different priorities to these variables and thus arrive at different conclusions regarding the leadership style called for in a given instance. One manager may conclude that the most important contingency is the need to initiate change in a short period of time and thus adopt a directive style of leadership even though other factors may contraindicate it. Another manager faced with a similarly short time frame to accomplish change, may decide that employee commitment and cooperation in implementation is so important that a participatory approach is called for, even though using this style may cause delays. All this is to say, simply, that an analysis of the contingencies in a change situation does not inexorably lead to a choice of one or another style of leadership. A manager must ultimately make a judgment based on personal, political, and value preferences. The kind of assessment suggested here can assist the manager to make this choice more deliberately.

# CHAPTER 13

# Administration in Child Welfare

Henry L. Gunn III

This chapter examines issues related to practice and challenges central to Child Welfare administration. These issues and challenges are presented to the reader as if the reader were a recently hired Child Welfare administrator faced with the need to understand the agency, his or her role as an administrator, the roles of agency staff and consumer and advocacy groups, the political and economic philosophies governing the agency, and the nuts and bolts of agency operation. The content of this chapter is based principally on the author's own practice-related experience in several administrative positions, including one as director of social services for a state department of welfare.

## Becoming an Administrator

*Why You?* Child Welfare administrators are not born into their positions. What then is the process through which these persons assume the title of Director of Child Welfare? Behind this question are even more basic and profound personal questions which, when explored, should give

I would like to acknowledge Jan McCarthy and George Haskett for their contributions to this manuscript.

the prospective Child Welfare administrator clues to the role he or she can play in the Child Welfare system.

How do people obtain positions as administrators in Child Welfare? Some are political appointees who sometimes have little or no Child Welfare background or experience. Some come from the military, private, or business sectors. Some are veteran Child Welfare staff who have come up through the ranks into positions of power. Then there are those who have been fortunate enough to appear at the right place, at the right time, with the appropriate credentials.

Prior to accepting employment, the prospective administrator in Child Welfare should ask four basic questions: (1) What do I want to do? (2) What do I like to do? (3) What can I do best? and (4) What do I want to do least? It is critical for the prospective administrator to asnwer these questions frankly, as the role of the Child Welfare administrator is largely defined and influenced by complex technological, legal, political, economic, demographic, and cultural factors. Prospective Child Welfare administrators must be clear about what they want to and can do within the framework of a Child Welfare agency. As social workers and Child Welfare administrators, we often ask clients to develop a strengths–needs list to use as guides in setting goals. This same process can be applied to our own goals before major decisions regarding employment are made, which in turn dictate the role we perform daily.

## What Are Your Options?

The person seeking employment in Child Welfare administration has three basic agency settings from which to choose, the public, the private, and the voluntary sector. It is important to understand the basic characteristics of these three types of agencies as the specific role of the administrator will be influenced by differences in agency philosophy and practice. The public Child Welfare administrator is first of all a public servant who implements a complex set of federal, state, and local mandates established by Congress, state legislatures, and local governing bodies. This administrator's major source of funding is public and he or she is accountable to the public for the expenditure of these monies. Therefore, the constituent group is all of the public and the administrator cannot elect to work with a small select group with special needs. The private Child Welfare administrator is an employee of a privately administered agency, responsible mostly to a governing board which operates under a charter or set of by-laws. These limit and clearly define both services and target population. Thus, the parameters of administrative authority are clearly outlined and less subject to outside pressure. The voluntary Child Welfare administrator also operates within a clearly defined charter or set of by-laws and delivers specialized services to a defined target population. The administrator in this setting is also less subject to outside pressure and can have more of an impact on the design of services and those populations to be served. However, both the private and voluntary Child Welfare administrator must be sensitive to their agency's public images as both look to the community for much of their financial support. Positive image building and public relations are essential functions of these two administrators as they are for the public Child Welfare administrator.

## The Role of the Administrator in the Public Sector

Public Child Welfare administration is a complex institution that operates within an already complex government. The Child Welfare administrator operates within a social and political system that expresses its will through laws; these laws are implemented through bureaucratic systems which may be a part of federal, state, or local government. The following discussion will examine both the common and the differing roles Child Welfare administrators perform within these three similar, yet different, systems.

### Interpreting and Implementing the Public Will

It is the responsibility of the public Child Welfare administrator and staff to interpret governmental and legal rulings and to design policies and programs to implement these rulings. Very often, however, laws are not drafted clearly or their purposes are not well-defined. Agency administrators and staff must seek clarity to insure that the intent of the governing body is carried out. Therefore, at all three governmental levels, the Child Welfare executive has through legislative mandate been delegated the authority to develop Child Welfare goals and objectives, as well as the responsibility to insure that these goals and objectives reflect the will of the people.

Prior to the issuance of policy and regulations, the administrator may pursue several options in an effort to interpret the intent of the lawmaking body correctly. He or she may meet with the committee and subcommittee members of the body that drafted the law, review the minutes of the working session during which the law was drafted, request both legal and programmatic interpretation of the regulations or guidelines that may accompany the law, or draw up proposed policies and procedures for review and comment by the public and staff involved in drafting the law.

The administrator in Child Welfare is the chief agent responsible for insuring that implementation of the public mandate is carried out properly. To perform this role the administrator directs staff to develop and issue regulations which support the spirit and intent of the lawmaking body. In most cases the administrator will be required to issue proposed regulations in a draft form for public review and comment, and must be knowledgeable of the state, federal, or local requirements and process used for the issuance of policies and regulations. To complete the cycle of implementation the administrator is responsible for seeing that subordinate agencies begin to implement the regulations and policies, that regulations are issued in a timely manner, and that the agency develops the necessary reporting requirements to enable staff to monitor the status of implementation either on site or through other accountability systems.

## Beyond Implementation

In many instances, public governing bodies have passed mandates that the administrator has not lobbied for or supported but nevertheless must implement. This means adopting a reactive role in carrying out measures that are already in effect. Short is the career of a public Child Welfare administrator who fails to fully recognize and accept this responsibility.

On the other hand, the administrator also has personal commitment and professional responsibility to the beliefs, philosophy, and standards of Child Welfare practice. Therefore, it is essential also to assume a proactive advocate role and to provide leadership and direction in the drafting and sponsoring of sound family and children's legislation, policies, and procedures. To accomplish this, the administrator must get out of the office and into the field—be in contact with direct service agencies and observe how the implementation of the laws and policies is affecting those whom the program is intended to serve. The proactive advocate role extends to participation in professional organizations, such as the American Public Welfare Association, Child Welfare League of America, American Humane Association, National Urban League, National Alliance of Black Social Workers and other minority organizations, Council on Social Work Education, Children's Defense Fund, and others. Later in this chapter we discuss the administrator's role in working with citizen and client consumer groups. The administrator must not only stay in step with the trend in Child Welfare services but also provide leadership in setting such trends.

*Technical Assistance*

The capable administrator not only implements laws and regulations, but also facilitates this implementation through technical assistance to agency staff. This role requires a knowledge of current trends, creativity, and an awareness of the impact these laws and regulations will have on staff at all levels, particularly on the service delivery level. The administrator must understand what technological knowledge and skills workers will need to carry out new regulations. He or she may be helped to develop plans by involving supervisory, fiscal, mid-management, staff development, and line worker personnel in the process of reviewing new laws and regulations and developing an impact analysis that indicates their strengths and needs regarding implementation. Such an analysis forms the basis for a plan to support staff in the areas of identified needs. The administrator may consider options to:

1. develop and implement a program of staff development with the objectives of providing skills training to meet new skill needs
2. waive specific agency policies to allow service delivery agencies the autonomy to experiment with new approaches to providing services
3. secure and allocate monies for pilot demonstration projects
4. employ consultants and/or trainers to design and assist staff in implementing new and current technologies which have proved beneficial in other agencies around the country
5. remove program barriers that staff have identified as detrimental to implementation of these new laws or policies

*Financier*

The public Child Welfare administrator at the federal, state, and local levels is responsible for securing adequate funding for the agency's operations. At the federal level, this can involve lobbying Congress and the Office of Management and Budget for adequate funding. The state level administrator must be persuasive with the state's legislature and budget office, while the local administrator must be capable of selling the Child Welfare agency's position to the local governing body.

The following strategies may enhance this process:

1. *Be truthful:* Never present false or misleading information. A loss of credibility undermines the possibility of success in the role of financier.

2. *Be factual and concise:* Have facts well organized and well documented with supportive data. If a voluminous document must
   be submitted to the governing body, it should be accompanied
   by an executive summary of the most relevant information.
3. *Be visible:* Assume responsibility to present the agency's case.
   Occasionally technical and fiscal staff may accompany an administrator, but staff should not be sent to do the job. Too many
   spokespeople for the agency will tend to give the appearance of a
   lack of clear leadership.
4. *Follow-up:* Should any matter arise for which there is not an immediate answer, the administrator should follow up promptly
   with accurate data to support the cause.
5. *Avoid social work jargon:* Although governing bodies are concerned about the welfare of their citizenry, they do not appropriate monies based on feelings. Statements like "I feel society owes
   its children adequate care" will mean little unless supported by
   facts, a need assessment, and a fiscal statement.

In order to be effective in the role of financier, the administrator
must be thoroughly familiar with his or her own operations, and the
financing presentation should be supported by documentation of figures and facts presented by staff. The governing body reviewing this
request for financial support will require both the facts and appropriate
justification for those requests.

## Counselor

The public Child Welfare administrator must be aware of the staff's
professional and personal needs. In a large agency the administrator will
need to depend on mid-management and supervisors to keep informed.
Sometimes employees will find themselves writing policy statements
when they really want to work directly with clients. Other staff may be
handling purchase of service procedures when they would rather be
writing program content. The results of these kinds of mismatches are
poor work and low morale. Even the most responsible employee finds it
difficult to do something in which he or she has no interest. A sensitive
administrator can identify these problems quickly and strive, through
in-house transfer or other means, to find the positions where staff members can function most effectively.

## Integration

The public Child Welfare administrator is confronted with the complex
task of integrating the agency's efforts with other public human service

agencies. This is particularly crucial in times when resources are short and governing bodies demand less duplication of services. The role of the administrator is to pull things together, to take charge and direct. This role demands a variety of talents and capabilities, such as

—being able to read and analyze complex federal, state, and local laws and mandates

—understanding the legal charge to the agency as well as those to other human social service agencies with which he or she must work

—being skilled in communicating with and directing staff to communicate with staff members of other agencies

The last skill mentioned is particularly valuable when a number of agencies try to design and implement programs so that they do not duplicate services, present redundant or conflicting eligibility requirements, or set up bureaucratic barriers to clients. For example, in planning for the delivery of adoption services for children with handicaps or other special needs, the administrator should coordinate the planning and delivery of not only the social service but also any health services that may be needed. The administrator may also participate in interstate activities and contracts which facilitate the placement of children from one state to another, coordinating the delivery of and the payment for needed social services.

## Unique Roles of Federal, State, and Local Administrators

Having identified several roles common to all Child Welfare administrators in the public sector, the roles unique to federal, state, and local administrators will be discussed.

FEDERAL. The Child Welfare administrator at the federal level assumes a decision-making role which will have an impact on national policy by supporting laws passed by Congress. The federal administrator will be responsible to report to Congress, the federal administration, and the Office of Management and Budget on the status and impact of the implementation of these laws. In performing this role it is important to be in touch with state Child Welfare administrators, advocacy, and consumer groups.

The federal administrator is also a national trend setter. By developing criteria that must be met by states in order to receive federal funds, the federal administrator creates incentives for states to follow the intent of federal law. For example, states may opt not to become involved in subsidized adoption for children with special needs. However, when federal funds are made available to those states that have a subsidized adoption program, the trend toward subsidized adoption widens. Trends may also be set through the creation and funding of demonstration projects (e.g., the Oregon Permanency Planning Project) which, when successful, lead toward the implementation of such projects throughout the country. Further, in the area of training and staff development, the federal government may stimulate the creation, publication, and dissemination of materials that can be used by state and local agencies to train and support Child Welfare staff.

STATE. The administrator at the state level will be responsible for implementing laws passed by both Congress and the state legislature. Child welfare programs in some states are directly administered on the state level while others are locally administered with state supervision. The type of organization the state has will make a difference in the role of the Child Welfare administrator.

The administrator within the state supervised system can determine policy and procedure to be implemented statewide; however, he or she only has responsibility and authority to supervise the implementation through locally employed staff governed by local boards. The administrator's major role in this organizational structures is to develop state guidelines, monitor, evaluate, and provide technical assistance to the implementation process. On the other hand, the administrator within the centralized state system has direct line authority over local administrators and can bring about dismissal of a local administrator should good cause be shown. This single authority provides the state administrator significantly more leverage in implementing state and federal mandates. Also, the administrator in this type of system has one board governing the administration of services. Unlike state supervised systems, where each political subdivision has its own board, the state administrator is free from the potential pressure of these local welfare boards.

LOCAL. The role of the local administrator differs greatly from the state or federal administrator, the major difference being direct involvement with clients. All administrators must be sensitive to the impact of state and federal policies on the client, but the local administrator sees the impact firsthand and must, therefore, assume the advocate role for clients in relation to state policies, which can cause major personal and professional conflicts. While the administrator may experience organizational pressure to implement the law as designed, he also has the responsibility to demonstrate the possible negative effect of poor policy on the community and client. The situation can also work in reverse. For example, a local administrator may disagree politically and philosophically with awarding food stamps to strikers. However, he is charged with the responsibility to uphold, in this case, the federal law.

In order to be responsive and effective, the local administrator must be visible within the community. This role in support of the agency demands much time attending civic functions, participating in fund-raising activities, and developing connections with the local power structure. It is essential to be visible and accessible and not become isolated from community and constituent groups.

## The Role of the Administrator in the Private and Voluntary Sector

For this brief discussion we will group together the major roles of the Child Welfare administrator in private profit, not-for-profit, and voluntary organizations. These include fund raiser, visible and accountable leader, service provider, and advocate for public services.

*Fund Raiser.* The Child Welfare administrator of the private profit, not-for-profit, or voluntary agency depends on donations or grants as well as fees charged clients to continue or expand services. This is especially true of those without large, long-standing endowment funding. Therefore, the administrator must be able to package and market attractively and convincingly in order to secure community, state, federal or private sector donations.

To be successful the administrator, the agency's services, and the agency must be visible to community and funding sources. Brochures, literature, and speaking engagements are always essential. Quality service and reasonable rates that are competitive with other agencies are also a must. In some cases professional fund raisers are employed; however, the most successful approach is to offer quality service at a reasonable rate or no rate at all. If rates for services are not charged, then a positive public image is critical to the funding issue.

*Visible and Accountable Leader.* The administrator must be visible not only within the community, but also to the governing board, and must keep board members informed of agency activities as well as its needs, by updating the board through oral and visual presentations. He or she may also invite board members to attend special activities sponsored by the agency. Should the private or voluntary administrator elect to recruit public funding, he or she must first share ideas with the board, as some board members may elect not to accept public monies because of differences in philosophy or a reluctance to give up some of the agency's autonomy.

This administrator must be accountable, demonstrating to the governing body how the funds are being used and outcomes of expenditures. Should the administrator be using public funds, he or she must also report in the same manner to the public agency. High quality, effective reporting will assist in efforts to receive public funding.

*Service Provider.* The private or voluntary agency is the service provider, and must be sensitive to service needs in the community. An attempt to provide adoption services in a community that has no children to adopt or parents wishing to adopt will prove disastrous. It is essential the agency keep in tune with changing trends in the demand for services. For example, an adoption agency must realize that fewer and fewer babies are available for adoption and that the agency must focus on placing older and handicapped children.

Should the agency elect to use public funds, it is the responsibility of the administrator to insure that the agency meets all state and federal licensing requirements. Failure to do so may result in the loss of much needed support. Also, even if public monies are not used, private and voluntary agencies must meet licensing standards if they provide services regulated by state government, for example, in foster care or adoption services.

*Advocate For Public Services.* As is the case with the administrator in the public sector, the private and voluntary Child Welfare administrator can perform a vital role as an advocate for public service priorities and strategies. In fact, the private administrator, from an outside position, experiences fewer constraints and more flexibility in working for change. He or she must assume a proactive role in approaching public agencies as they are complex in structure and often slow to reach out to the private sector. In this proactive role administrators in the private sector

> must accept the fact that many public officials may not be interested in discussing the fine points of social work practice. Their concerns for accountability, eligibility, and the elements of licensing are direct functions of their institutional base. To wish they were more sophisticated or helpful regarding the issues of service delivery, or to fault their lack of theory, is counterproductive. Similarly, for the public official to wish the private agency provider were as concerned with questions of management information systems or unit costs as he is with the impact of separation of a child from his family, is equally counter-productive.(Levine 1978: 105)

For example, the public administrator must understand that complex licensing and purchase-of-service policies can easily drive up unit costs for services, virtually eliminating small service agencies. Therefore, both the private and public Child Welfare administrator must be aware and sensitive to the mandates, roles, and responsibilities of the other. Each must be able to communicate those concerns, barriers, and qualities of his or her system effectively and to work collaboratively to develop service delivery systems that take into account the necessary operations of each agency.

## The Role of Citizen, Advocacy, and Consumer Groups

Today, perhaps more than ever, citizens, advocacy organizations, and consumer groups are participating in the decision-making process with Child Welfare administrators. This shift is particularly visible within the public sector. Title XX of the Social Security Act, which funds the majority of states' Child Welfare services, requires extensive public involvement in the planning process. Beyond planning, the general public is given a forty-five day period to review and comment on the States' Draft Social Services plan before it is rewritten in final form.

The state of Virginia used a process not unlike that used in many other states to develop its 1980–1981 Social Services Plan. Local welfare directors were instructed to obtain input from local public officials, clients, service vendors, donors and other interested citizens. Communication was assisted through the use of an advisory committee consisting of state, local and private agency representation, and through use of an information bulletin directed to some 3500 organizations and individuals within the state (Virginia Comprehensive Plan of Social Services under Title XX of The Social Security Act, 1980).

The Adoption Assistance and Child Welfare Act of 1980, Public Law 96–272, calls for the establishment of a statewide advisory committee on all phases of Child Welfare service programs and committees in administrative jurisdictions where programs are locally administered and even suggests that states may involve citizens in reviewing foster care cases. Some states such as South Carolina currently utilize Citizen Review Boards to assist the agency in reviewing its foster care cases. Advocacy organizations exist in each state with the purpose of upgrading the Child Welfare delivery system in that state. In fact the Children's Bureau of the Department of Health and Human Services distributes a directory of child advocacy programs found within each state. This directory lists the purpose of these organizations and their current advocacy activities within the states.

Advisory committees made up of consumer groups play a major role in assisting agencies in designing and implementing needed service programs. Groups which have significantly assisted agencies to improve their Child Welfare programs include: national and state foster parent associations, local child protective service multidiscipline teams, national, state, and local adoptive parent groups and advocacy organizations, and state and local client involvement committees that advise the agency on a range of service activities. Groups of consumers and advocates may prove essential to agency administration by assisting in the design of more effective grievance and appeals systems which facilitate the grievance procedure and reduce costly court appearances. They may also participate in the development of agency policy and in program operation, increasing agency awareness of the impact of its programs, as well as the public's understanding and support of those programs.

Child Welfare administrators must be able to listen to and learn from advocacy groups. Defensive responses will cut off communication and lead to misunderstandings. Both the advocacy group and the agency administrator need to have a clear understanding of each other's purpose and intent, an understanding that can only be achieved by listening closely to each other.

## Involvement of Volunteers and Paraprofessionals

Child Welfare administrators should assume a proactive role in recruiting and involving volunteers and paraprofessional staff from all income and cultural levels within the community. While paraprofessionals are generally paid, agency policy should also allow for reimbursement of volunteer expenses such as transportation, child care, and other necessary incidentals. These staff can be most effective in serving as parent aides, homemakers, and chore service providers. They may also have special skills, such as conducting surveys or program evaluations. The important thing for the administrator to remember is that volunteers and paraprofessionals may in many cases perform functions similar to those performed by paid staff. Therefore, the administrator must widen his or her vision when designing a volunteer or paraprofessional program.

Support of the agency professional staff is essential to effective implementation of a volunteer program or a new program involving the use of paraprofessionals. If the professional staff does not desire or request the services of the volunteers, then no volunteer program exists. Planning for the use of volunteers must be done by representatives of both the professional staff and the administrative staff and agency workers must be trained in the appropriate use of volunteers and paraprofessionals. Once a volunteer program has begun, the volunteers must be included in staff meetings to facilitate communication between professional staff and volunteers, and to provide a vehicle for both groups to air concerns.

It is also critical that the plan for a volunteer program include: a recruitment program with all agency service areas in mind; a program to orient the volunteer staff to agency policies and practices; provision of adequate office space and equipment; reimbursement of costs; supervision and guidance by agency staff. If possible, the agency should design a career ladder through which volunteers may increase their skills and services to the agency. Without a plan such as this one, volunteer staff may quickly become discouraged and leave agency service with a negative impression. The administrator should be aware of organizations within the state or community that may assist in these efforts. Many states have a state office on volunteerism that may be of help in recruiting and training volunteers for agency service. Also, the administrator should be aware of any state or local laws or ordinances governing the involvement of agency volunteers.

## Politics, Philosophy, and Economics

The Child Welfare administrator at all levels should be aware of the political, philosophical, and economic factors which govern the agency in which he is employed. He or she should be familiar with state statutes which govern the administration of the organization, including the specific statutes relating to funding programs, use of boards, involvement of consumer groups in planning, and mandated services. In studying the code governing Child Welfare services, the administrator should note sections which are unclear, as these often provide an area for administrative flexibility in drafting federal, state, and/or local guidelines. In this effort the administrator should study all Child Welfare program policies and guidelines and the state plan of services. Public Child Welfare agencies are governed primarily by two major pieces of federal legislation, Titles XX and IV-B of the Social Security Act. The administrator must become acquainted with the state's plan and policies governing its implementation. It is an error for public administrators to depend on veteran employees for interpretation of law and policy. Veteran employees can contribute to an understanding of such complex laws; however, the administrator who fails to do his own research will fail in efforts to approach service delivery with creative and innovative ideas.

### Discovering and Altering Agency Philosophy

The administrator must continually evaluate whether the agency's philosophy is consistent with its funding and service plan. Do the agency's program priorities actually reflect stated purposes and goals? For example, the state or agency may verbally communicate a philosophy of services to families and children. It may advocate a strong network of preplacement services to prevent the separation of children from their parents. To test this, however, the administrator need only refer to the agency's plan of services. In doing this, it may be discovered that state funds for homemaker services are limited to recipients of supplemental security income unless the locality can allocate all the match money to draw down the federal funds. In many cases there may be only a small amount of money allocated to fund services to the family prior to separation. It is the administrator's responsibility to call attention to such contradictions.

An effective administrator can set direction, sponsor effective Child Welfare legislation, and issue sound and practical regulations. He or she can align fiscal resources to support stated agency objectives and philosophies. An administrator, of course, must listen to what supervisors, board members and subordinates have to say regarding agency direction. An attempt to re-establish direction will, in many cases, be met with resistance. The most effective way to handle resistance is to have facts available to document a position. In doing this, it must be recognized that an array of professionals with different interests will be involved. For example, an administrator must be prepared to defend his or her position to fiscal staff, whose primary concern is money. Documentation of current underutilization of resources is important. An administrator can demonstrate how preventive placement services preserve the family and reduce public expenditure or that cash outlay to purchase services from the private sector to place a handicapped minority child for adoption is cheaper than maintaining that child in foster care. In presenting a position, the administrator must be as knowledgeable of the fiscal picture as the person being dealt with, and must stick to the facts. The key to success in an administrator's efforts to effect political and economic change lies in planning and implementation. If time allows, representatives of all groups affected should be involved in the planning, and policy committees should be staffed with consumers, fiscal people, reporting line workers, and program staff. Within the overall structure of Child Welfare legislation, there is considerable room for innovation, change in implementation, and in planning service strategies. A little more time allocated to planning with proper involvement will provide amazing results in accomplishing change.

## Organization and Staffing

### Organizational Structure

Most public, private, and voluntary Child Welfare organizations provide all or a variety of services to families and children, including adoption, day care, foster care, child protection services, and services to prevent separation of children from their parent(s). Agencies will organize differently to provide these services, and the administrator must assume responsibility for analyzing the agency's structure and staffing pattern.

An effective way for making such an assessment is functional analysis, a process through which the administrator reviews the mandate of the agency and examines its staffing and organization to determine whether the staff is appropriately allocated to carry out this mandate. There are many administrative options open in determining what changes are needed in an agency. The new administrator may choose to go outside the organization and contract with consultants to complete an organizational analysis and recommendations for change. In many cases this approach may be the best because the contractor can be more objective. However, this service is expensive and the administrator may find that real needs were not met.

One often overlooked method of organizational review is the internal review, completed with the help of existing staff. Administrators may be quick to discard this option for fear that it will ignite internal power struggles, that concerned staff will not be open and candid in their observations, or that they will be overly subjective. Although these concerns are sometimes valid, this author believes internal review holds promises and that administrators can underestimate staff willingness to be honest and objective. The main objective of functional analysis is not to determine how well individual staff perform their day-to-day tasks, but how well the organization performs its mission. The process itself is useful since it is often discovered by participating staff that the organization's mission is unclear or is not well understood.

The overall objectives of the functional analysis are: (1) to examine and identify the mandate the agency has to provide Child Welfare services, (2) to examine the agency's organization and staffing pattern to determine whether or not the agency can meet the mandate within the existing framework, and (3) to make recommendations to the administrator which will enhance the agency's ability to carry out its charge. The process is intended to explore and identify the federal and state mandates for each Child Welfare program, and to clarify what specific and generic functions staff are performing. On the basis of this information, several questions may be raised: Do staff functions and responsibilities overlap and create duplicity? Are program goals and objectives clear? Do the program units interface and support each other? Are there imbalances between staffing and program responsibilities? Is supervisory support lacking or overlapping? Obviously the administrator can develop the interview schedule to address additional concerns. However, the main objective is to give the administrator a picture of how well the organization performs its mission.

To implement the functional analysis, a committee or several committees with well-defined objectives may be appointed, and target dates set up for completing their work. While maintaining leadership in this effort, the administrator should also appoint a project coordinator from the staff. Other committee members may come from fiscal operations, the reporting section, local agencies, satellite or regional offices, and other Child Welfare organizations within the community. Also, Child Welfare experts in nearby universities can be sought out to provide feedback on committee recommendations. This approach offers the administrator some distinct advantages. The administrator remains in control and has not delegated authority to an outside agent. Staff members are involved in a proactive role as opposed to a reactive role, which tends to heighten morale and lower anxiety levels as they participate in designing change for their organization. Through the process itself, the staff broaden their understanding of the complexity of the organization and become more knowledgeable about how various Child Welfare programs interface. Finally, an important advantage is that the cost to the agency is considerably reduced.

During the self study the administrator must support staff, assisting them in prioritizing their time and protecting time for them to carry out this additional assigment. He or she must also be undefensive when hearing or reading statements which may appear to be personal attacks. The administrator must keep these statements in perspective and keep the objectives of the analysis in mind.

Even with the disadvantages to this approach, it will yield ample data through which an administrator can make decisions regarding changes in staffing patterns and organizational structure. Also, the administrator is much more likely to find that the staff is ready to support change.

## Change

Once the administrator has presented recommendations for change, regardless of the process used, he or she should involve management and supervisory staff in the review of the recommendations. When final decisions are made, they should be shared with the entire staff and the process by which the decisions were made and the plan through which implementation will occur should be spelled out in detail. Further, all agency staff members should have an understanding of the specific impact the change will have on them and their jobs.

## Budgets

Budgeting in public Child Welfare agencies underwent two significant changes in the 1970s. The first change occurred when Title XX of the Social Security Act required the development of comprehensive annual service plans, changing public Child Welfare budgets from line item budgets to program budgets specifying services to be provided, individuals to be served, and implying unit costs. Since Title XX is the major funding source for public Child Welfare services, most Child Welfare services are presented in program budgets.

Although Title IV-B of the Social Security Act is the official funding source for Child Welfare services, Title XX is the most substantial source, providing the major funds. Through the 1970s, the annual federal allocation under IV-B was only $50 million, compared with the nearly $4 billion in federal, state, and local expenditures annually under Title XX. In most Child Welfare agencies, budgeting is only a peripheral responsibility for most staff. An agency comptroller or fiscal officer usually handles the majority of the budgeting and fiscal management responsibilities, drawing on agency staff to supply information necessary to the budgeting process. The lack of involvement by program staff is troublesome in that no matter what the stated agency goals are, the budget is the blueprint for agency activity.

In many Child Welfare agencies, the principal budgeting problem is resource allocation. When the resources for Child Welfare services are insufficient, how does the administrator establish priorities for allocation. For example, how much money should go to foster care services and how much for services to children in their own homes, which might prevent the need for foster care? Once this decision is reached, which individuals should have priority for receiving the limited services? There are no easy answers. Budgeting involves accountability and evaluation: The basic tasks of the administrator are to determine what does the most good, that is, to discover whether a certain amount of money invested in preventive services will accomplish more than if the same amount were invested elsewhere, and to determine the optimal amount to be allocated to a given service.

## Accountability

The passage of Title XX was in part a reaction against the increased expenditures for social services in the early 1970s. A $2.5 billion federal ceiling, which had been placed prior to Title XX, was retained and only modest increases were permitted through the late 1970s. While social services expenditures increased, consensus satisfaction over the return on this investment failed to materialize, and, in fact, concern over accountability lingered.

No simple accountability system is appropriate for Child Welfare agencies, but Drucker (1973) has suggested that any control system must be economical, meaningful, appropriate, congruent, timely, simple, and operational. Accountability is best facilitated by planning for it in advance. For example, development of a management by objectives system establishes the basis for accountability. Concrete action plans provide a blueprint for agency action and an output plan against which to monitor results.

One should recognize at the outset that there may be numerous reasons for monitoring performances. If the monitoring is to be most successful, it should start from the assumption that persons involved in a program will likely be interested in good performance and would prefer to be brought into the planning and development of monitoring procedures. Many organizational constraints will be lessened by this simple, but basic, strategy of inviting staff participation in designing a monitoring system that will provide feedback on results and strategies for improvement. Staff participation also takes advantage of the likely situation that those who are directly involved in delivering a service will know most about it—good or bad. For example, it is more valuable to know the number of children successfully reunited with their families than the number of hours of casework services given in the average case. Therefore it makes sense to try to develop accountability systems that focus on outcomes more than inputs or processes, that is, on what is actually produced by the agency.

## Issues in Purchase of Services

The purchase of services between public agencies was authorized in the 1962 amendments to the Social Security Act and the 1967 amendments broadened the authorization by permitting contracting with private proprietary and nonprofit organizations. "Purchase activity grew during the 1970's and by 1978, states were spending more than fifty percent of their Title XX funds through purchase" (Weidel, Katz, and Weick, 1979: 2). Utilization of purchase varies by state, but "only a few states expend less than ten percent or more than ninety percent of their service funds by contract" (ibid.).

### Procedures

One can hardly do justice to purchase-of-service contracting in a few short pages, but there are a few fundamentals that must be understood by all public agency administrators. First, it is necessary to know the particulars of the system in which one operates, as purchase-of-service policies and procedures vary from state to state and sometimes within states. Some systems use firm fixed-price contracts in which a unit price is negotiated. Other systems use reasonable cost reimbursement contracts in which exact costs are not specified beforehand. In some systems, blocks of service slots are purchased; in others, terms and conditions contracts are negotiated by fiscal and administrative staff and individual purchases under the terms of the contract are ordered by agency line workers.

Second, administrators may play a variety of roles in purchasing services. For example, contract negotiation frequently is handled at one level in government while purchasing often takes place at another level. Furthermore, administrative staff are frequently involved in contract negotiation while casework staff actually write purchase orders, handle vendor invoices, and have the most frequent contact with the vendor and the recipient of the service. Thus, while most agency staff will not be involved in the contract negotiation, they may have crucial information which can help in that process. Given this separation of responsibilities, coordination of efforts and sharing of information becomes important and there must be some method of assuring that the valuable information of the casework staff is communicated to administrative staff.

Finally, the role of public agency workers also will vary with the type of vendor one is purchasing from. Many services are purchased from individuals who provide homemaker, chore, foster care, and day-care services. Other services are purchased from private proprietary and nonprofit organizations that range from small group homes to large complex childrens' residential facilities and "conglomerates" that administer a number of service delivery agencies. Obviously, the job of the purchaser will vary.

The literature on purchase has grown as purchase activity has increased. Administrators will find the range of literature helpful, but should not expect to find specifics for dealing with day-to-day problems surrounding purchase. Weidel, Katz, and Weick (1979) have included a comprehensive bibliography in their recent work, providing one of the better guides to purchase literature.

Most important, in monitoring purchase-of-service contracting agency administrators should be mindful of two fundamental purposes: that the client receives a satisfactory service and all of the services the agency has paid for, and that the agency has paid a reasonable and fair price.

## Private Agency Concerns

The public Child Welfare administrator must be aware of the concerns of private providers of service. In establishing rates, the private administrator will look for equity and flexibility, and will want quality as one criterion for setting rates. In the free enterprise system the private administrator will not tolerate a rate structure that rewards poor providers of service and penalizes quality providers, but will want to have a voice in the rate-setting process and to understand the procedure the agency uses to hear provider grievances.

The private provider will also be concerned regarding the amount and frequency of paperwork required by the public agency, since every demand for accountability, reporting, unit costing, and so on drains valuable resources that could be used to deliver services. The public administrator must be aware of the economy of scale as it relates to meeting the public requirements and that smaller agencies may be driven away from providing services to the public sector because of onerous administrative requirements.

Finally, the private administrator will want some assurances that public agency service priorities will not shift from month to month or year to year. The private sector can and will gear up to deliver needed services but not if funding is insecure or if the public agency is known to make frequent and unplanned program changes. To deal with these and other private agency concerns, a standing committee comprised of public staff and representatives of both the small and large providers of services can enhance communication and facilitate planning.

## Trends for the Future

The decade of the 80s is witnessing a major decline in national leadership in the area of social service planning. This shift away from federalism to more state autonomy is having significant impact on the design and implementation of Child Welfare services. The following is a brief discussion of some of the issues.

### Public Funding

With a shift toward more state autonomy comes block grant funding, in which states receive a block of money earmarked for social services with few federal requirements for spending. The federal government is, thus, less involved in establishing program priorities. Although the state Child Welfare administrator has always dealt in politics, this funding shift requires even greater political sensitivity. An administrator must develop practical and easy methods to implement needs assessment processes, must be able to communicate well with powerful self-interest groups, and have a thorough understanding of the balance between service demand and resource allocation. The administrator also must be extremely articulate with the governor's office and the state legislature in order to successfully defend agency priorities in the face of shrinking dollars and various political pressures. The implications of block grants for service delivery are discussed at length in the exemplar following this chapter.

## Purchase versus Direct Services

With more state and local autonomy private agency service providers will be more vulnerable to shifting service demands. This is especially true for those agencies utilizing large sums of public money. The public administrator must be aware that the private sector is vital to bridging the gap between service need and delivery, keeping aware that constant state shifts in priorities will create confusion and frustration in the marketplace of private providers. Not only will these rapid shifts discourage good private agencies, but they will all but eliminate an administrator's private base of support in requesting needed funds. In facing shrinking budgets and demands for less government, the administrator will need to become more sophisticated in planning a service delivery system. He or she must deal with the issue of whether or not it is cheaper to provide services directly or purchase them from the private sector. Furthermore, any shift away from providing services to purchasing services requires a re-examination of the function of the agency.

## Direction

As a result of the shrinking of our social programs, it is likely we will again witness a surge of welfare client advocacy groups. At the forefront among these should be Child Welfare advocates. There is no doubt that without federal incentives, knowledge, and the benefit of the collective experience, services to families and children are being set back a decade. The examples of the past are all too clear: Only when the federal administration stepped forward with incentives and technical assistance did *most* states begin to design and implement quality, comprehensive Child Welfare programs in adoption, foster care, day care, and child protective services. The model Adoption Assistance and Child Welfare Act of 1980 and special assistance from federally supported regional adoption resource centers have done much to assist states in finding homes for hard-to-place children. Without the incentives and technical assistance provided under the Federal Child Abuse Prevention and Treatment Act of 1974 (extended 1978) most states would have been slow to respond to the problem in their states. Without national leadership in 1976 in the area of permanency planning, most states would have failed to address the problem of foster care drift. What the decade of the 80s appears to be bringing is the old cycle of service neglect and consumer advocacy, which may lead to a later resurgence of national leadership.

# EXEMPLAR III–A

# The Shift from Categorical Programs to Block Grants
## Implications for Child Welfare Services

MILAN J. DLUHY

In the summer of 1981, President Reagan, speaking before the National Conference of State Legislatures, sketched many of his ideas about the future of federalism in America.[1] In this speech, he called for another "great revolution and experiment to return federal authority to state governments systematically." At the center of Reagan's approach to "New Federalism" was the use of block grants as the major mechanism for delivering federal aid to states and localities. The culprit over the years, according to this approach, has been the proliferation of categorical grant programs and their concomitant problems. The argument is that these categoricals have been basically obtrusive, duplicative, and inefficient. It is further argued that in the long run they are unnecessary since the states should properly have both the responsibility for these programs as well as the tax resources to pay for them. If there are to be major changes, they should be in the direction of the devolution of authority and responsibility from Washington to the various states and localities.

The debate about the desirability of using block grants instead of categorical programs when giving federal aid to states and localities is not a new one. Former Presidents Nixon and Ford made block grants a key part of their approaches to federalism (Advisory Commission on Intergovernmental Relations, 1977; Anton, 1982). Even President Carter showed considerable interest in grant reform and more specifically in how block grants could be used to simplify and streamline the system of delivering federal aid. Given all of the rhetoric about block grants over the last fifteen years, it is significant to point out that only four block grants were adopted between 1965 and 1981 (Conlan, 1981).

Against this background, President Reagan's proposals for block grants appear to be consistent with the intentions of previous Presidents rather than any radical departure. However, a closer examination of his 1981 proposals incorporated into law in the Omnibus Budget Reconciliation Act of 1981 and his fiscal year 1983 Budget proposals released in February of 1982 demonstrate that Reagan's use of block grants is far more extensive and comprehensive than in the past. When these program consolidations in the form of block grants were tied to substantial funding reductions in fiscal years 1981, 1982, and 1983 the Reagan administration clearly was doing more than paying "lip service" to "New Federalism." It was attempting in a short period of time to alter significantly the nature of federalism in this country for years to come. Regardless of this, skeptics continue to say that the likelihood of drastic changes or system-wide grant reform is still not very great. Yet it should be clear that President Reagan has already instituted more changes in the grant-in-aid system in just the first two years of his presidency than his last three predecessors were able to accomplish during fifteen years.

It is particularly important to focus on the potential consequences of using block grants as the major mechanism for assisting states and localities in the Child Welfare area, since historically federal involvement in Child Welfare has been largely through a myriad of categorical programs which have targeted assistance to either very narrow problems like nutrition, adoption assistance, and day care or target groups like disabled children, crippled children, and poor children. A rapid, dramatic shift from categorical grants to block grants should concern Child Welfare advocates because the rules of the "new game" are still, for the most part, unknown. Ironically, the last major effort by the Child Welfare community to influence the service system culminated in the passage of another categorical piece of legislation, the Adoption Assistance and Child Welfare Act of 1980 (Public Law 96–272), which has been continuously under threat of being folded into a Child Welfare block grant and has also been consistently underfunded. The history of Child Welfare services in this country has been one of selective programs aimed at the highly selective needs of different populations of children and their families.[2] If future federal involvement in Child Welfare changes substantially from a selective or categorical emphasis to a block grant or more general and less focused emphasis, the Child Welfare community will need to examine very carefully the potential consequences of this change so that they can determine whether to oppose it, modify it, or accommodate to it.

## The Development of Block Grants

Over the years, categorical grant programs have been criticized for such things as being duplicative, having onerous reporting and other administrative requirements, not being sufficiently responsive to local needs within each state, and inhibiting program coordination between state and local governments and the federal government.[3] The standard solution suggested to alleviate these problems has been the use of the block grant as a substitute for categorical programs since, at a minimum, the block grant is supposed to consolidate various existing categorical programs. It is differentiated from other mechanisms used to give federal assistance to state and local governments in five ways:

1. Federal aid is authorized for a wide range of activities within a broadly defined functional area.
2. Recipients have substantial discretion in identifying problems, designing programs to deal with them, and allocating resources.
3. Administrative, fiscal reporting, planning, and other federally imposed requirements are kept to a minimum.
4. Most of the federal aid is distributed on the basis of statutory formulas which adds a sense of fiscal certainty to recipients.
5. Eligibility provisions are statutorily and usually narrowly specified, favoring general purpose governmental units as recipients and elected officials and administrative generalists as decision-makers. (See Conlan, 1981, for a more complete discussion.)

During the early years of the Reagan administration, many categorical programs were consolidated, and funding for these programs shifted to block grants. No attempt will be made here to present the details of this complex and shifting picture, but certain trends in the new methods of financing social programs have become apparent, trends that have important implications. First, the states are clearly in charge. They are left almost completely free to determine which branch of government will have actual administrative control over the block grants and what procedures and processes they will establish and use to make resource allocation decisions. The block grant legislation has instituted few requirements for the states' handling of the funds, and monitoring by the federal government is cursory. States have considerable flexibility in determining who gets what, when, and how, within a broad functional area.

Secondly, just as major responsibility for social programs has been shifted to the states, they have had reduced financial resources. Block grants have been funded below the level of the categorical programs they replace, funding for some programs has been eliminated entirely, and funds continue to be cut each year.

Any slight hope that states could pick up the slack on reduced budgets or finance eliminated programs out of state funds was destroyed by the impact of the recession on state resources.

In sum, promises of giving more control over services to the states in a variety of functional areas are being made, but correspondingly reduced resources have been available to the states to pay for these services. One result has been that the states have to shoulder more of the criticism and handle more of the potential pressure for budget cuts as they take the major responsibility for setting priorities in each of these functional areas.

## Implications for the Future

If economic conditions had been more normal and the social philosophy of the federal administration been different, it might have been possible to decentralize program responsibility to the states and localities while at the same time increasing funding for each of the functional areas covered by the block grants. State and local administrators would then have been able to maintain existing service levels while also being able to respond to new priorities and needs. However, without this constant funding, state and local administrators will have little relief from denying and cutting back services as overall funding in the human services is reduced. Sharp reductions in federal funding will highlight the shift from categoricals to block grants more dramatically and stimulate the Child Welfare community to keep abreast of every procedural change associated with this shift. Block grants are deceptively simple in concept and very appealing when they are coupled with increased or at least constant funding, but when the budget is cut so drastically, people involved in the delivery of Child Welfare services will become protective of their particular services or programs. Among other things, some very significant fiscal, organizational, and political implications at the state and local level will need to be considered as we shift from categorical programs to block grants. The more important implications are identified here so that the Child Welfare community can formulate a reasonable response to them.

With perhaps a few exceptions, the prospects are very poor that the states will be able to allocate their own fiscal resources for programs included in the block grants cut hard by federal reductions (see Page, 1981). It is more realistic to expect diminished financial support for human services at both the federal and state level in the near future. Under these conditions, a significant fiscal implication is that any service inequities between states and within individual states that currently exist will more than likely be exacerbated by block grant funding. For example, a recent study of Child Welfare services in the states documents the tremendous variation in spending for Child Welfare services (Kirst, et al., 1979). While there has been a conscious attempt over the last twenty years to decrease inequities in spending for education across the country, a similar attempt has not been made to correct the inequities in the Child Welfare field. Federal or state guaranteed minimum foundations virtually do not exist for the provision of social services to children and their families (ibid.). Currently no state financial guarantee exists for a basic level of service available on an equal basis to all children throughout the state. This is a traditional equity concern, and one that becomes more critical with funding cutbacks. Underserved parts of a particular state, states which have not traditionally spent very much on Child Welfare, and target populations of children who have not benefited from programs in the past will do worse under the block grant programs because they will be fighting for limited resources with already established services. Without new state or federal funds to reduce service inequities, currently underserved geographic areas and unserved or underserved populations will suffer even more in the future. This point is further illustrated by the fact that the funding formulas for the block grants passed in 1981 distribute funds with the exception of the social services block, principally based on the proportionate shares received by states in fiscal year 1981 for the programs consolidated (U.S. DHHS, 1981). Thus, any inequities between states prior to 1981 become more permanent inequities unless Congress deals with them in the future. Substate allocations are also unlikely to change since each service will attempt to at least maintain their current funding level.

States that have had a tradition for low levels of interest in and commitment to Child Welfare services are unlikely to change very much. In this respect, the more stimulative categorical grants at least provide some incentives to states to improve their Child Welfare services.[4] With block grant funding the states will receive that proportion of the resources available nationally, based on their earlier commitments. From a fiscal standpoint, it is also feared that many states may attempt to pass the costs of service programs on to local governments because of the recent state spending limitations (propositions) passed or other economic problems (Page, 1981). Many local governments are in worse shape than the states, so that any attempts to shift the burden for funding of service programs to them will increase the likelihood of more severe service cutbacks. In short, the shift to block grants coupled with budget cuts will reinforce rather than rectify the current inequities existing in Child Welfare services between states and within individual states.

The shift to block grants also raises the question of how ready and capable state governments are to perform the various planning, analytical, data collection, and managerial tasks associated with responsibility for block grants. A number of organizational implications need to be considered. First, it is not clear whether a single state agency, several agencies, offices of management and budget, the governor's cabinet, or some other designated group will be charged with responsibility for overseeing block grant funds. It is also unclear what role state legislatures will want to play in monitoring block grant funds. While some state legislatures have already taken some steps to be more actively involved in block grants, a consistent pattern is not yet clear (see Yondorf and Benker, 1982). There is likely to be considerable conflict within each state over the tasks associated with managing block grants. The only experience most states have had with block grants has been with the administration of the social services block grant, Title XX (Suzuki, 1980; Zinn, 1981). This experience amplifies the concern over which organizational units will perform which functions. Moving from one block grant to, possibly, sixteen may mean organizational chaos for most states over the next few years. No single model of state administration stands out, and the near future is likely to bring confusion, conflict, and continuous experimentation. For the Child Welfare community, this shift means trying to have input into whatever planning, resource allocation, and administrative process is designed in the states. For the next few years, it will be a challenge just to obtain an accurate "score card" detailing the processes being used and the key actors involved.

The issue of organizational capability at the state level is also of concern to many.[5] Much of this concern involves whether the states have the capacity to conduct research and development activities, analytical and planning tasks associated with resource allocation, and data collection activities connected to auditing and evaluation. Here, the record is likely to be mixed since only a small number of states have demonstrated these capabilities in the past. Again, Child Welfare services will suffer until states are able to develop these organizational capabilities. Without additional federal funds for this purpose being made available to states and without any other incentives, prospects for the efficient management and overseeing of block grant funds are poor in the short run. If individual states have not done well with the existing block grant, it is questionable whether they will do any better with as many as fifteen block grants.

The final issue to be raised is basically a political one. With very little specification as to how the money will be spent within each block, the states will have the major responsibility for prioritizing the service needs. The direct implication of this responsibility, in light of the budget cuts discussed earlier, is that conflict over needs will become paramount. Client bumping will most certainly take place. More troublesome clients, unpopular services and programs, and client needs that have little political support in the state will not do well in a resource allocation process with substantially less money available for distribution. The risk is that the Child Welfare community will fight with other groups, such as the aging community, youth, health professions, and public welfare groups for diminished resources. Without broad-based coalitions, the general human service community will become more segmented, factionalized, and self-serving—perhaps the cruelest implication. For years, organizations at the national level have worked hard to establish their service needs in the form of categorical programs. The shift to block grants means that these same organizations will now have to work within each state to establish the priority of their client group or service. Under these circumstances, the best organized, but not necessarily the most in need, will be successful within each state. In fact, there is some speculation based on previous Congressional behavior that if certain client groups or services are ignored under these block grants, Congress will attempt to "recategorize" the block grants by earmarking funds for certain purposes (see Conlan, 1981). If this happens, the nature and intent of block grants as an instrument would be seriously in doubt.

Categorical grants are very economically efficient because they call for the use of one delivery mechanism for each separate goal sought.[6] However, block grants are wrought with conflict because they seek to achieve many different goals for each instrument used, and thus political feasibility, not economic efficiency, becomes the dominant criterion emphasized. Politically, the block grant in conjunction with funding cuts can only mean more conflict over service needs, more client bumping, a redirection of advocacy organizations to state-level lobbying, and in the long run inadequate or minimal services being available for unorganized but needy clients.

Block grants coupled with budget cuts will definitely make the job of Child Welfare advocates more difficult. Less popular services and less visible client groups will need all the help they can get in an era of diminished resources for human services, and neither the rhetoric nor the reality of block grants will make this job any easier.

# EXEMPLAR III–B

# Civil Rights and Child Welfare

Mary E. Davidson

Title VI of the Civil Rights Act of 1964 has important implications for the delivery of Child Welfare services to minority children. The Civil Rights Act was passed by a Congress aware of America's historical indifference and injustice to its racial minorities. Title VI of that act contains the prohibition that no person in the United States by virtue of race, color, or national origin shall be excluded from participation in, be denied the benefits of, or be otherwise subjected to discrimination under, any program or activity receiving federal financial assistance. Under Title VI, programs, financial aid, and benefits are defined as any action provided in or through facilities supported by federal financial assistance. The Department of Justice is responsible for coordinating the enforcement of Title VI in all federal agencies that provide financial assistance. In the Department of Health and Human Services (DHHS), the Office of Civil Rights (OCR) is responsible for carrying out this function (General Accounting Office, 1980).

Title VI requires written assurances from all applicants for federal financial assistance that the requirements of this regulation will be met.

This article was presented at The National Symposium of The National Association Social Workers, Washington, D.C., Sunday, November 20, 1983. Research for this was supported by the U.S. Department of Health and Human Services, Office Rights. Portions here appeared in "Achieving Simple Justice: Identifying Discrimination the Delivery of Social Services," *Journal of Intergroup Relations*, 12, Autumn

318

by the agency or program. In discussing the application of Title VI, the regulations explain that "in Federally assisted programs for the provision of health and welfare services, discrimination in the selection or eligibility of individuals to receive the services, and segregation or other discriminatory practices in the manner of providing them are prohibited" (Code of Federal Regulations, 1979). This prohibition applies to political subdivisions of the state, if the state is the grantee, to all facilities and services provided by the grantee, and to third party services purchased by the grantee. However, the implications of this prohibition for Child Welfare and other social services have not been generally understood; indeed, the application of Title VI to social service delivery and to social work practice has been little explored.

This paper presents an approach for uncovering Title VI violations in the decision-making activities of policy-making and planning, and in implementation, that is, in the day-to-day decision-making of supervisory and line staff service providers. The following discussion raises a series of questions to alert policy-makers, administrators, and practitioners in Child Welfare and other social service agencies to the need to review our own practice for compliance with Title VI.

## Policy and Planning

Policy and planning decisions are broad guides for future action. They are often set forth as standards for action, goals to be achieved, or priorities for what will be done. Uncovering discrimination in policy-making and planning can be considered from two perspectives: (1) the composition of the policy-making or planning structure, and (2) the content of decision-making. Policy-making and planning usually take place in organizational entities variously referred to as boards of directors, councils, planning committees, or task forces. The first step in carrying out a review for Title VI compliance is the identification of all policy-planning or advisory structures involved in the program, agency, or service delivery system under scrutiny. For example, if a state Child Welfare system is the focus of investigation, the state recipient agency, as well as all private subrecipients, should be scrutinized for compliance with Title VI.

In evaluating compliance a central question revolves around board composition: To what extent are those protected by Title VI represented and given a chance to participate in decision-making? In other words, are minorities serving on the policy-planning body? If not, to what extent are minority members given the opportunity to serve on boards or other policy-planning structures? Questions should be asked about the criteria and process of member selection. The Board must not have policies which implicitly or explicitly exclude minorities. Is there, for example, a nominating committee which submits names for memberships? Does this group search for minority persons to be considered? Are there financial requirements that may discourage if not prevent minority participation? Are there other criteria for membership that may be disincentives, such as meetings held during working hours or in socially intimidating settings? Disadvantaged minorities may be invited to participate but effectively denied an opportunity to do so because the meeting place is distant or inaccessible by public transportation.

In some parts of this country, the absence of minority membership on policy-planning boards may indicate language barriers, as in many areas of the Southwest. In such situations, some provision can be made by policy-planning boards and similar bodies to provide for bilingual participation, just as program implementation requires bilingual service provision.

When minorities do serve on boards it is important to ask to whom they are accountable. How were they chosen—by appointment, through an election, or by self-selection? Minority board members may not necessarily represent the interests of minority persons in the target or beneficiary population of an agency; they may be no more sensitive to the plight of poor and disadvantaged minorities than are their nonminority counterparts. Sometimes they may simply not understand how to decide substantive decisions in the best interests of the minority disadvantaged community because they have never been a part of the disadvantaged sector of their own groups. Also, the presence of minority individuals on boards raises the following question: Are they represented in executive positions and on crucial committees? If not, the selection processes should be analyzed to determine whether they intentionally or unintentionally discriminate against minority board members.

In many instances, minorities may have full access to participation but lack the technical, educational, or experiential qualifications to participate fully as equals with nonminorities. Participation by minorities who lack the knowledge required to make thoughtful choices takes away from the minority community the representation it needs. Under such circumstances provisions should be made to assure "informed" participation. Minority board members need the opportunity to consult with experts from their own groups, as well as from the nonminority community, so that they can contribute not just their presence but influence the nature and quality of decision-making.

## Content of Decision-Making

Another object of scrutiny for possible discrimination is the actual content of policy and planning decisions. What is the substantive content of the decision? Is it in compliance with Title VI? If not an important issue becomes whether the board knew that when the policy was approved. Policies and plans that discriminate on the basis of race, color, or national origin are in violation of Title VI.

Budgets and other planning documents approved by boards and agency staff should be carefully examined. Such documents put into action service priorities and represent consensus on the type and mix of services to be delivered. When examining such documents, consider the following: Which geographic areas are scheduled to receive services? Do they include needy minorities? What services are to be provided? Do they include the priority service needs of the minority communities? Who is to deliver services in each area? Does the plan include providers who are geographically accessible to minority members of the target population? Does it include minority service providers? Are the providers sensitive to the special needs of the range of minorities in the service delivery system? Too often we forget the special needs of Asians, American Indians, South Sea Islanders, and other less prevalent minorities. Too often agencies fail to promote aggressively their services in non-English speaking communities. Therefore, it is essential to determine the extent to which agency promotions, literature, and staff reflect an awareness of and commitment to serving the non-English speaking and those with limited proficiency in English.

## Implementation

Implementation is the everyday execution of policy, carrying out the intention after the boards and executive staff of social agencies and organizations have made their decisions. Implementation is the provision of the care, the service, or other product to the individual or group with a need.

The differences in service delivery systems—at the point of contact between the person with a need and the service provider—make the task of uncovering incidents and patterns of unequal treatment in social agencies very complex. Consideration will be given to two avenues by which Title VI can be violated in implementation: denial of access and provision of inappropriate services.

Access issues center on the differential application of eligibility criteria for needed services, geographic inaccessibility of primary and third party service providers, and on racial steering, the selective referral of minority applicants. The central issue is whether minorities and non-minorities have comparable access to services. For example, agency policy will often state clearly *who* is to be served. But it is always necessary to review and, to the extent possible, determine the population actually *being* served by an agency in all of its general and specialized programs.

We must be especially alert to possible disparities in the receipt of personalized service. Usually such services—homemaker, chore services, or supportive counseling—are purchased from the private sector. Are they available in minority neighborhoods? With regard to any supportive personalized service provided to poor and disadvantaged clients in their own homes, we must be alert to the possibility that black and minority poor may be disproportionately underserved, based on the actual levels of their need.

Given the proportion of minorities in the target population, there may be discrepancies between those eligible for and in need of general or specialized services and those actually receiving those services. If so, what effort is the agency making to remedy the situation?

To determine the extent to which the eligibility practices of an agency, organization, or other provider are in keeping with Title VI, the Child Welfare advocate, administrator, or practitioner should ask: What are the agency's policies for accepting clients for services? Do these criteria vary from one to another of the services offered by the agency? The eligibility policies for some programs may be more rigid than for others. It is not unusual for some agencies, if resources are scarce, to tighten eligibility requirements, thus reducing the pool of eligible clients. If such action is taken with respect to those programs that have a disproportionately large minority beneficiary population, compared with other programs where their proportions are small, the agency may be violating Title VI. The service needs of minorities and nonminorities should be compared with agency eligibility criteria and their application in different agency service programs. Even when both minorities and nonminorities have comparable need for services, differential application of eligibility criteria can result in minority applicants being disproportionately underserved relative to their level of need and to their number in the target population. A common example of this latter situation is the alleged lack of evenhandedness sometimes seen in the certification of mothers for Title XX day care. It has frequently been more difficult for minority mothers to obtain such services.

Similarly, the way in which agencies recruit and approve adoptive foster homes, and child and adult day-care homes should also be examined. Even when the eligibility criteria of an agency are in conformity with Title VI and are applied equitably, they may, nevertheless, create undue hardships for minorities and unintentionally may have the effect of denying them access. For example, in adoption, foster care, and home day-care programs, families must be recruited, studied by a social worker, and certified as eligible for placement. Staff may apply unwittingly restrictive agency policies about finances, educational accomplishment, or resources for leisure time activities in such a way as to discourage minorities.

The location of services can interfere with, if not prevent, service utilization by minorities. For example, agency service facilities may not be equally available in districts where there is a large minority presence. It is common practice for state recipient agencies to purchase services from the private sector. Frequently those private agencies have their service facilities located in mostly nonminority neighborhoods, in suburban areas, or in other places inaccessible or unfriendly to minorities. To the extent that private agency offices and foster homes are located out of the minority child's neighborhood (or city or state), the child's family is hampered in its use of the agency services. Such a situation can defeat an agency's own program objective of "family reunification in most cases." It denies access to full service benefits and, if disproportionately burdensome on minority families, is a violation of Title VI.

For example, in *Gary W v. Louisiana,* private segregated Child Welfare institutions refused to accept black children, which resulted in black children being sent to institutions in Texas. Focusing on "right-to-treatment" issues in out-of-state placements, the plaintiff alleged racial discrimination because a disproportionate number of black children were sent to Texas institutions. The court found this not to be conscious discrimination but rather the result of a segregationist policy, that is the refusal of Louisiana private Child Welfare institutions to accept black children. The court concluded that the State of Louisiana must formulate standards to insure that contracts awarded to private (vendor) Child Welfare agencies protect against racial discrimination.

Related to, but different from, the problem of geographic location of service delivery facility is the practice of licensing foster homes in neighborhoods that do not welcome persons of different race, color, and national origin backgrounds. Agencies may deny minorities access to services by licensing foster homes or day-care homes that discourage minority participation. A violation of Title VI may occur when a social agency licenses foster homes in neighborhoods where foster families refuse to accept children of a different race. Violations should also be suspected if resources for preventive and supportive problem-reducing services are underallocated to neighborhoods with high proportions of minority residents.

The way in which agencies fail to refer or "steer" minorities to needed services may also reveal a pattern of Title VI violations. For example, an agency may tend to place black children in need of treatment in foster homes or custodial institutions, reserving its expensive therapeutic institution placements for white children. Some agencies may use one set of private sector providers for minorities and another for whites.

In the course of investigating an adoptions complaint, the Office for Civil Rights discovered an example of intraprogram disparity in violation of Title VI. After being told by a caseworker that they could not be considered for an adoptive placement of a white child, a Hispanic family alleged that the state vendor and a private Child Welfare agency were making adoptive placements solely on the basis of race and national origin, and filed a class action complaint with the Office for Civil Rights. Upon investigation, a second Title VI issue was identified: the steering of state-referred black and white children to two different racially segregated programs administered by a private Child Welfare agency. The Office for Civil Rights did not find a class violation but did find that the complainant Hispanic family's rights had been violated by the caseworker's arbitrary decision to deny adoptive placement of a white child. This is a very complex issue as there has been strong concern expressed in minority communities about the placement of minority children in nonminority families; good practice dictates that every effort be made to place children with families of their own race. The Office of Civil Rights also found racial steering and ordered the racially-segregated agency programs to be integrated. In such situations, both the referring (state recipient) agency and the direct service providers (the third party vendors) are in violation.

## Quality and Appropriateness of Services

The quality and appropriateness of services offered to minorities should be comparable to those provided nonminorities. "Appropriateness" may be defined as the extent to which the services offered are fitting and pertinent to the clients' needs. Agency methods of administration should encourage the provision of appropriate services to minorities. A Child Welfare agency, for example, may provide families with day care, parent aid services, family counseling, child therapy, pre- or postadoptive services, and home management services. To be nondiscriminatory, the service mix provided to minorities should be the same as or similar to that provided to nonminorities when there are similar presenting problems and agency diagnostic profiles.

In social agencies a wide range of service may be available. But some agencies may offer more quality services than others. Part of the rationale for a long-standing court case is just this concern. In *Wilder v. Sugarman*, now referred to as Wilder 1, the religious matching provisions of the state statutes governing Child Welfare services in New York City were challenged. The court dismissed Wilder 1 on the grounds that the laws were *prima facie* constitutional. The children's rights project of the New York Civil Liberties Union refiled Wilder 1 as *Wilder v. Bernstein*, known as Wilder 2. Wilder 2 alleged violation of Title VI because placements in New York City were being made on the basis of religion and because the majority of black clients were served by Protestant or non-sectarian Child Welfare agencies which were alleged to provide services inferior to those provided by the city's Jewish and Catholic agencies. Denial of access was also an issue because it was alleged that more appropriate services were offered by agencies that were less likely to serve black children. The defendants, the New York City Department of Human Resources et. al., moved to dismiss the case, but the court found the allegations of religious and racial discrimination sufficiently specific to certify class action on behalf of black Protestant (i.e., non-Catholic and non-Jewish) children. Wilder 2 remains in the courts. The court's findings in Wilder 2, once settled, will provide additional clarification of the applicability of Title VI and related laws to the provision of foster care services.

Title VI also may be violated if practice interferes with the agency's own program objectives for quality service provision. A delivery system that, albeit inadvertently, allows administrative practices to "distance" families, rather than reunite them, violates Title VI when those families are in a protected class. The way in which this type of violation occurs has been seen most clearly in terms of Title VI complaints on behalf of Hispanics and Native Americans.

Based on a complaint filed with the Office for Civil Rights and in the courts, a state Child Welfare agency was required to offer bilingual foster care service. The court consent decree responded to a class action suit alleging Hispanic families were denied bilingual foster home services, thus interfering with the state agency's own program goal of family reunification. The Office for Civil Rights concurred with the court's consent decree, which bound the agency and their subrecipients to assure Hispanic families the right to choose a bilingual foster home placement. The nonavailability of bilingual homes means that Hispanic children lose their proficiency in Spanish and their ability to communicate with their non-English speaking biological parents.

Responding to another complaint, the Office for Civil Rights, using case records as evidence, found a state Child Welfare agency in violation of Title VI for failing to provide for the special needs of American Indian children. Social workers had identified the need for special and culturally sensitive services for American Indian children in foster care, but there was no pattern of follow-up on social worker recommendations. The Office for Civil Rights found that the agency failed to use its own administrative and staff mechanisms to fulfill its stated program objectives with respect to such children, particularly in terms of reuniting families. They found that the American Indian advocates within the state agency were either not utilized or underutilized and many times not even informed of tribal claims that needed to be filed on behalf of American Indian children.

Suspected Title VI violations, and complaints alleging violation, frequently are not settled straightforwardly. Agencies, supervisors, and line staff often make decisions to further legitimate and non-discriminatory agency objectives that when implemented create a pattern of disparity. In settling such suspected Title VI violations the Office for Civil Rights has employed an "adverse effects" test. In applying this test the burden is on OCR to establish that the adverse effects place disproportionate burden on minorities. The recipient organization or agency must demonstrate that a legitimate objective will be furthered and that no alternative course of action can be adopted that will further that same objective with a less disproportionate adverse effect on Title VI protected classes. Testing for adverse effects involves a consideration of the following:

1. Will the action have a disproportionate adverse effect on persons of a particular race, color, or national origin? If the action will not have a disproportionate adverse effect, it will not violate Title VI.
2. If the action will have a disproportionate adverse effect, and it is not necessary to further a legitimate objective of the organization, it will violate Title VI.
3. If the action will further a legitimate objective, are there alternatives available that would further that same objective with a lesser disproportionate adverse effect? If such alternatives are available the action will violate Title VI.[1]

Application of this three-step principle usually involves consideration of the percentage of minority persons to be adversely affected, compared with nonminorities. If, for example, a social agency must retrench and close one of two district offices, disproportionate adverse effect is more likely to be established if the agency closes an office in a neighborhood serving a majority of the agency's black foster home population, leaving few of its white clients affected.

The validity of an "effects test" in Title VI was upheld in a recent interpretation handed down by Supreme Court in the case of *Guardians Assn., et al., v. Civil Service Commission of New York, et al.*, decided July 1, 1983. The court found that where a plaintiff sought retroactive relief for some harm done, the burden was on plaintiff to prove purposeful "intent" to discriminate. Importantly, however, the court found that when plaintiff sought only an injuction of a change in future policy or practice, then it was necessary to prove only "adverse impact," or more specifically that the policy or practice falls more heavily on blacks or other minorities than on whites.

Let us consider the consequences and application of "adverse impact" theory on our day-to-day practice. When we do uncover allegedly intentional or unintentional examples of the violation of Title VI, we should consider turning to the Office for Civil Rights, the federal agency responsible for monitoring and enforcing Title VI in Child Welfare and health and human service programs. It is remarkable, however, that since passage of the Civil Rights Act in 1964, only nine complaints had been filed alleging Title VI discrimination in the provision of Child Welfare adoption and foster care services through December, 1981—nine complaints in all ten federal regions since 1964 (Davidson, n.d.). Most were brought by attorneys and children's advocacy organizations. Only one was filed by a social worker on behalf of aggrieved clients.

Uncovering racial discrimination in the provision of Child Welfare and social service programs will not be easy.[2] The process continues to be clouded by a context of societal discrimination based not on race, color or national origin but on social and economic class distinctions that contribute to discrimination against all the needy. Further, because the system remains less than perfect for all recipients—regardless of race, color, or national origin—it is important to remember that poor or inadequate services do not necessarily mean "discriminatory" services. Nevertheless, as policy-makers, administrators, and practitioners committed to the values and ethics of the social work profession we will be remiss if we do not look inward and examine our own decisions and day-to-day practices for compliance with Title VI of the Civil Rights Act of 1964.

# PART IV

# Keeping Families Together
## Work with Families and Children in Their Own Homes

In Part IV we explore what is perhaps coming to be the heart of Child Welfare practice: the provision of preventive, protective, supportive, and rehabilitative services to families at risk. Until recently, although the maintenance of the family was a stated value of the Child Welfare system, only a small proportion of expenditures and services has been devoted to the prevention of placement or the rehabilitation and re-unification of families. On the contrary, Child Welfare has primarily been an institutionalized arrangement for the provision of substitute care.

In fact, services provided to families to prevent placement have even been discouraged by fiscal policies. For example, until recently, most purchase-of-service contracts between voluntary agencies and the public sector reimbursed agencies on the basis of "days in care" while services to a family when the children were at home were nonreimbursable. Foster care, generally conceived of as a temporary solution to family difficulty, a stop on a circular path to the reunion and rehabilitation of the biological family, more often than not became a one-way street toward permanent out-of-home care. Further, while some children found stable, loving environments, many others were subjected to a dismal succession of emotionally damaging separations and placements in foster homes and institutions. In some cases the State proved a less reliable parent than the original, neglecting and even abusing children entrusted to its care.

A slowly developing ideological shift toward permanency for children culminated in the passage, in 1980, of Public Law 96–272—legislation that has stimulated federal and state initiatives focusing on the prevention of placement, the maintenance of families, and the provision of permanent families when the biological family cannot be a resource. At least in principle, most Child Welfare professionals now agree with and are willing to act on, the first tenet of the permanency movement: If at all possible, children should remain with their parents.

Despite this philosophical and policy shift, work with families continues to falter, preventable placements occur all too frequently, and reunification services are often inadequate. What is the source of this seeming reluctance to focus major efforts with the biological family? There are undoubtedly many factors that should be considered. One is certainly a national, historic tradition of "leaving families alone," a tradition contradicted by the doctrine of *parens patriae*, under which the State, here as represented by the Child Welfare system, takes over for parents.

It is possible, however, that some of the reluctance is based on failed past efforts, on feelings of hopelessness in terms of helping stressed, overwhelmed, and disorganized families. Line staff and supervisors are often put to the task of preventing placement and rehabilitating families without access to either the skills or the resources required to do the job. This double-binding situation is currently being dramatically demonstrated. At the same time that prevention of placement and support of the family is established as a major goal and priority, required social services and economic supports are cut, social worker positions are declassified, and training departments in agencies sharply reduced or terminated.

How can we help oppressed and troubled families at risk? How can we engage them, understand them, and act with them to master a crisis or enable them to take some steps which can make a lasting difference in their lives? This section focuses on these questions, describing programmatic and practice responses to families as they come into contact with the Child Welfare system.

Each of the four chapters in this section focuses on working with biological families in such a way that, if possible, the family may be maintained and at the same time children protected and nurtured. The chapters are followed by several exemplars in which specific practice responses to or programs for families and children at risk are explored. Central themes or principles recur throughout the work of the different authors and emerge as the core of serving families in the Child Welfare system.

First, families can be helped within the context of a strong working alliance between the worker, as a person and as a representative of an agency that has specific responsibilities, and the family. The barriers to the development of such an alliance must be identified and overcome if families are to be engaged and services made available. Some of these barriers are organizational and structural and have been described elsewhere in this volume. On the level of direct practice, these barriers are often a function of the social distance between the worker and the family, distance that is an expression of differences in race, class, culture, status, and role.

In his chapter on beginnings, Seabury describes how barriers to engagement can be overcome through demonstrated attitudes of respect and empathy, as well as through a careful and open mutual clarification of roles, purposes, and procedures. Leigh, in his exemplar on the ethnically competent social worker, emphasizes the importance of understanding and dealing openly with cultural and racial differences between worker and client so that barriers to trust can be overcome.

A second theme concerns the centrality of the assessment process in all practice. Emphasized throughout is the importance of the worker's gaining a holistic, systemic understanding of the family's situation, an understanding based on a careful assessment of the complex ecological system in which the family is embedded. Seabury demonstrates initial assessment techniques through the use of the eco-map, an assessment tool that helps the worker and family focus, not on deficits within the family, but on the family's relationship with its world, on the resources needed, and on stresses and deprivations experienced. Such a focus enhances relationship building, since families at risk, frequently trapped in an uncaring, depriving, and even hostile environment, experience themselves as being understood by the worker.

Laird expands the assessment process to look back over time and inside the family. Building on an ecological perspective, she demonstrates how the structure and process of the family as a system may be understood. She also adds the historical dimension to family assessment through her discussion of the importance of intergenerational themes and prescriptions for the functioning of the family unit.

The contemporary Child Welfare worker must be able to assess the family-in-environment and the family as a system, as well as the quality of particular family relationships and of individual development and adaptation. Shapiro focuses on one crucial aspect of this complex ecological system, the mother–infant relationship. Applying the findings of recent clinical research on infant mental health, she describes in practical and concrete ways how, through careful observation, a worker may discover the quality of the interactions between mother and child, assess the infant's development, and identify children potentially at risk.

Assessment is particularly crucial when the safety of the child is at stake. Ceravolo, in her discussion of service opportunities available through a crisis nursery, describes the advantages of being able to complete a careful assessment and develop a plan with a family in a situation where the safety of the child can be assured without removal, thus reducing tension for both family and worker and freeing energy for planned change.

In recent years, the problem of sexual abuse of children has generated increasing concern and attracted considerable attention in the professional literature. The issue here is usually not so much a matter of immediate physical danger or neglect but the longer range destruction of the psychological well-being of a child. Careful assessment and sensitive, nonreactive intervention, as demonstrated in the Stovall exemplar, is particularly important. Families in which sexual boundaries are being violated may be helped to restructure and to reorganize in ways that better respect children's autonomy and establish more appropriate generational and other family relationships.

Finally, many of the authors emphasize the importance of the family's participation and sharing in the assessment process. Such participation is the first step in helping the family gain control over their situation through enhanced cognitive mastery, planning, and problem solving.

Yet another theme surfaces throughout the authors' discussions of work with families: empowerment. Not only must families be empowered through greater access to services, material supports, opportunity, and the acquisition of skills, but help must be given in such a way that enhances client competency, autonomy, and self-esteem.

The provision of concrete resources or counseling may help clients through an emergency or relieve immediate stress, but a family may not necessarily achieve a new sense of mastery, or develop new and ongoing coping skills; the family may not be empowered. In fact, being the passive recipient of help from a person in authority may further diminish self-esteem and stimulate feelings of helplessness, giving the person or family little opportunity to enhance competence.

A belief in empowerment on the part of the worker shapes approaches to engagement and assessment. Seabury describes how, as social distance is bridged and worker authority is diminished or limited through open sharing of information and through a careful, mutual contracting process, respect for the family's knowledge, values, and beliefs is enhanced.

In discussing intervention, Laird emphasizes the importance of enabling families to gain access to needed resources and opportunities, of advocating with them for their rights and entitlements, and of helping them to understand the powerful forces and patterns in their own families and environments which militate against change. Olson, in her discussion of the use of groups for mothers in the Child Welfare system, emphasizes the importance of people with shared concerns and experiences joining together to maximize their power to help themselves. She describes how hopeless and defeated women met together and, by their association, were eventually strengthened to the point that they were able to take action on their own behalf, bringing about change in the Child Welfare system. Not only was a desirable change achieved, but the women learned advocacy skills and experienced themselves as "causes," as they were able to make changes in what originally seemed to them an overwhelming and intractable system.

Autonomy and empowerment issues are also crucial in the delivery of supplemental care through the use of day-care and homemaker services. These services must be used in such a way that parents' skills are enhanced and their own ways of doing things respected. The successful day-care center, for example, plans for active parent participation on a level that preserves parental authority, gives parents new opportunities to enhance their effectiveness with their children, and encourages network building with other parents. Homemaker services must be delivered with great sensitivity so that the homemaker may model and share skills without usurping the parents' roles or demeaning their competence or lifestyles.

Issues of empowerment in the giving and receiving of help are highly sensitive and complex. The lessons of the 1960s brought home to social workers the subtle presence and the dangers of noblesse oblige and colonialism in our albeit well-intentioned efforts. In work with families at risk, these lessons continue to have particular relevance.

Finally, throughout this section on work with families the authors repeatedly emphasize that families cannot be expected to "go it alone." The task of rearing children without support, without respite, and without concrete resources is overwhelming. Middle-class families, if they don't have extended family or a friendship network available, have the financial resources to buy help to supplement their parenting.

Other families, although poor in material resources, have supporting extended kin networks they may call upon, or they may be helped to tap into kin-like mutual aid systems that make possible the informal exchange of help and concrete resources. Families that come to the attention of the Child Welfare system are often socially isolated and have been struggling to "go it alone." For these families, the Child Welfare system must supply what a viable kin network would supply, or what families with means are able to purchase: a range of supplemental caring services that can support families and obviate placement of children. These services, described by Robinson, Ziefert, and Ceravolo, may range from an hour or two of respite care to full-time homemaker service or a brief stay at a crisis nursery. Such services must be provided, not in ways that take over from or compete with families, but rather in ways that complement and strengthen the family's existing competence.

# CHAPTER 14

# The Beginning Phase
## Engagement, Initial Assessment, and Contracting

BRETT A. SEABURY

This chapter describes the initial phase of work with families who enter the Child Welfare system, and is organized around three basic concepts—engagement, assessment, and contracting. In addition to presenting the ways in which these particular concepts apply to Child Welfare practice, this chapter also focuses on some of the basic problems and dilemmas that face social workers in the beginning phase.

## Engagement

The basic task of the social worker in engaging a family is to develop a working relationship with the family. In Child Welfare services a working relationship cannot be taken for granted; the social worker must make conscious, persistent, and skillful intervention in order to facilitate relationship development. If a working relationship cannot be developed, then it is unlikely that worker and family will agree on a service contract; therefore, it is unlikely that plans will be successfully achieved.

### "Working Relationship" Defined

The social work literature suggests that the ideal conditions of a good, collaborative, working relationship are trust, mutuality, acceptance, positive sentiments, caring, and respect (Biestek, 1957; Leonard, 1972; Perlman, 1979). In such an ideal relationship the social worker is expected to be empathic, sensitive, and understanding and, in return, the client is expected to feel secure in the encounter and be willing to share very personal thoughts and feelings. This description of the ideal relationship is very different from what usually happens in the initial encounters between a social worker and parents who have been referred for neglect or abuse of their children or whose child has been placed in foster care. Especially in protective services, this initial relationship will be characterized by guardedness or reluctance to share information, avoidance and a desire to leave the relationship, and strong negative feelings, such as anxiety, anger, suspicion, guilt, or despair.

The relationship that develops between the social worker and family in Child Welfare services should not be conceptualized as the idealized relationship of a voluntary therapeutic encounter (Perlman, 1979). In Child Welfare services, it is unlikely and not expected that worker and parents will be attracted to each other. Nor is it likely or expected that worker and parents will achieve a high degree of mutuality and positive feeling for each other. Though these are desirable qualities and may in fact emerge in some situations, it is unrealistic to expect that this degree of positive relationship develop between worker and parents. Instead it is more realistic to expect that the essential characteristics of the working relationship should be honesty (Chaiklin, 1974; Halleck, 1963) and clarity.

The social worker and parents are expected to develop a capacity to communicate openly and honestly their various perspectives about themselves and their situation (Goldberg, 1975). It is common for workers and parents to have many differences of opinion and disagreements in their perspectives, and these differences are to be courageously pursued and explored. Conflict and disagreement are not viewed as something to be avoided, but as realities that must be explicated and understood. Bringing these discrepancies to the surface helps to clarify confusion, to remove tensions that may overwhelm parents as service progresses, and to prevent hidden agenda from dominating later agreements.

Honesty and clarity are the best policy, but by no means are they easily achieved. The next section focuses on five practice realities that social workers must address in order to engage families in Child Welfare services: common negative feelings, clarification of purpose, potential role problems, authority issues, and demographic barriers.

## Common Negative Feelings

Both parents and worker may enter their relationship with a variety of negative feelings, some of which are the consequences of giving or receiving help in our culture, and some related to the special circumstances of Child Welfare. In the United States, a marked disparity exists between the attitudes and feelings of those who give help and those who receive it. Helpers often have a very positive feeling about their side of the helping transaction; they are often glad to be able to help, and the helping process leads to their feeling responsible, respected, valued, and even powerful. Understandably, helpers desire appreciation for their efforts.

On the other side, the individual who asks for or receives help often feels negative or uncomfortable about it. This person may feel helpless, guilty, dependent, unworthy, or scared. In our culture it is "more blessed to give than to receive." Our values do not condone dependency. We ignore, stigmatize, and even persecute those individuals who cannot live up to our ideals as "rugged, independent individuals." Any welfare recipient, aged institutionalized person, or terminally ill patient can testify to this point.

Another major source of negative feelings is the special situation facing parents involved with the Child Welfare system. For example, the fact that the child has been placed out of the home may generate feelings of loss, failure, and guilt. Parents may feel inadequate and ashamed that they cannot care for their child as other parents do. If the child was removed by court order, then parents may not only feel guilt, but also anger and rage. These are very real and expected feelings for parents in this situation, and the worker can expect to receive the brunt of these reactions in the initial encounter.

This situation may be compounded if the worker has initial negative feelings for the parents. To the worker, the parents may seem "sick," destructive, or just another "sad case." Until a working relationship is established, workers may not see the parents as complicated human beings with complex difficulties. Sometimes, if the workers have dealt with many similar situations, their actions may become mechanical or bureaucratic—a response to another difficult case in an already overburdened caseload. When a worker is punitive rather than understanding, parents will not be helped to improve their circumstances or to come to terms with any guilt or shame they may already feel.

How then can worker and parents establish a working relationship when there is such great chance for conflict and so many negative feelings that characterize the initial phases of building a relationship? The worker can begin by assuming the responsibility for recognizing and dealing with these feelings as they emerge. Two skills are central to success in handling negative feelings. The first is empathy: the ability to recognize subtle expression of feelings and to help the parents express these feelings. The worker is also expected to have a fairly "thick skin:" a capacity to take the brunt of negative feelings as they emerge.

A worker may find it helpful to be prepared for the intensity or the multiplicity of negative feelings that may occur in the first encounter with the parents. The worker must try not to become defensive or to counterattack when the parents express their own bad feelings. It is necessary to recognize these feelings as they emerge and accept them as reasonable and realistic for a family in this circumstance—as in the situation of threatened or actual removal of their children. It is appropriate that parents are reactive and it is the worker's task to facilitate ventilation of feelings as they begin to emerge. Once the worker has helped the parents express these feelings, he or she can demonstrate that they are understood and accepted. In this phase, it is vital that the worker can communicate directly and explicitly to the parents that he or she still wants to work with them to help solve their problems.

## Clarification of Purpose

Purpose is an important issue that needs to be discussed and clarified in the early contacts between worker and family (Schmidt, 1969). Purpose involves the question "why." Why are Child Welfare services being requested, offered, or imposed on this family? Purpose refers to both the rationale and the overall mission that Child Welfare services are designed to achieve. While they are not always the same in each case, four general purposes usually apply to work with families: permanence, protection, problem solving, and prevention.

A primary purpose of Child Welfare services is to insure *permanence*, to see that children have a permanent family context in which to grow (Mott, 1975). Ideally, this context will be the biological family, but in situations where return of children is not possible, then it is a substitute family. This purpose means that Child Welfare services are *not* designed to break up families but instead are intended to strengthen and reconstitute them so that most children can be raised by their biological parents.

Some Child Welfare services have focused narrowly on *protection* as their primary mission. Protection is an important mission and children do need to be protected from circumstances that are harmful or dangerous, but protection is a temporary purpose and must be accompanied by a plan to assure permanence. In situations of neglect and abuse, protection may require the temporary removal of children from their biological parents, yet concurrent with protective action there should also be *problem-solving* interventions. These problem-solving interventions are aimed at present and ongoing troubles that may have created the circumstances which necessitated removal of the child. The worker may help the family problem solve through a variety of interventions, such as helping the family to identify problem areas, to improve and maintain positive connections to its environment, to discover new resources, and to work on improving its own internal relationships. An ulterior purpose of problem-solving interventions is to strengthen the family unit so that future changes, events, or stresses can be successfully managed. *Prevention* does not guarantee that future problems will not arise, but instead that the family avoids more severe social dysfunction and develops new competencies and coping skills.

Sometimes purpose is not clarified or discussed with families because it may seem so obvious to the worker that it hardly seems worth mentioning. The family, however, is not always clear about the purpose of the worker's involvement with them, and families that are new to the Child Welfare system may be very confused and naive about the purpose of Child Welfare services. Many families may not realize that permanence, problem solving, and prevention are as important in Child Welfare services as protection. To clarify the situation, the worker may state the purposes of Child Welfare services explicitly in the initial contact. This can be an honest statement, and it is best if stated positively— especially in a protective service situation. The following statement exemplifies how a newly assigned foster care worker might greet the biological family for the first time.

> I am here to help you deal with the circumstances in the family that led to the removal of your child. I want to help you change these circumstances so that your child can be returned. I would like to help you identify problems you may be experiencing and to help you locate new resources or strengthen those that you now have that would help with these problems.

The worker may then try to discover how much of this statement of purpose has been received or believed by the family and what their reactions are. By allowing the family to react or state its view of the purpose, some of the misconceptions, suspicions, or fears may be clarified. For example, some families may believe the worker is involved with them in order to build a case to take their children away permanently or to collect evidence that the family might be cheating on its grant. At first, some families—especially in protective service situations—will not believe that the worker's purpose is benign and designed to help them. It may take several contacts and a considerable amount of relationship building before the family begins to see the worker's purpose in a positive light, and then only after the worker actively demonstrates efforts to help.

## Potential Role Problems

In addition to the negative feelings associated with beginnings and misunderstanding of the purpose of service, another major source of confusion and conflict for workers and parents are potential role problems. Two major types of role problems can emerge in the initial encounter between worker and the parents. The parents may be very unsure about what is expected of them, what is expected of the worker, and what is expected of others, such as a homemaker, day-care mother, or foster parent. In addition, some of the expectations that do exist may be very unrealistic.

Even when these ambiguous or unrealistic expectations are clarified at the beginning of service, difficulties can arise because the parents may not accept these role expectations when they are clarified. Parents may disagree violently with the worker's view of their (the parents') role responsibility, the worker's own role responsibility, or a foster parent's role responsibility. This type of conflict must be addressed or it will become impossible for worker, parents, and others involved to establish effective working relationships or work together toward service goals. Research demonstrates that workers and clients are often far apart in their role expectations of each other, and when these expectations are not expressed, clarified, and some agreement reached, clients terminate service early because of the confusion, anxiety, and dissatisfaction they feel in the service process (Levinger, 1960; Mayer and Timms, 1969; Perlman, 1960; Silverman, 1970).

These role problems are not just a product of the parent's attitudes and experience upon entering service; they may be exacerbated by a worker's attitudes. It is possible for a worker, who is familiar with the various roles, to overlook the fact that these roles may be confusing to the parents. These problems can be remedied and premature termination avoided when worker and parents engage in a role clarification procedure early in the service process. Research has demonstrated that a role clarification procedure can effectively reduce the percentage of clients who discontinue service and enhance the service outcome (Perlman, 1968; Hoehn et al., 1964).

What is role clarification and how can a worker use it with parents? When worker and parents make their initial contact, there are two basic roles—client and worker—that need to be clarified from two different perspectives. Each party has expectations about the responsibilities involved in each of these roles. Therefore, four sets of expectations must be articulated in a role clarification procedure. See Table 14–1.

Quadrant 1 of the table represents the parents' expectations of themselves in the service process. These expectations are often difficult to specify because the parents, upon entering service, are the most unsure of what to expect of themselves and of the service process—especially if this is their first contact with the Child Welfare system.

Often parents simply deny they have any responsibilities and try to place it all on the child, the worker, the agency, or some other system.

**TABLE 14–1   Role Expectation and Clarification Matrix**

|  | EXPECTATIONS FOR CLIENT ROLE | EXPECTATIONS FOR WORKER ROLE |
|---|---|---|
| **PARENTS** | *Quadrant 1*<br>—Don't know what we are supposed to do—after all we didn't ask for help!<br>—"Be good" so child can be returned.<br>—We'll wait for you to tell us what to do!<br>—Make an effort to do everything the court says we are to do.<br>—Don't ask any questions or cause any more trouble, just do as we are told. | *Quadrant 2*<br>—Snoop into family business for the court, possibly to remove other children from the home.<br>—Get parents to confess that they are bad parents so that a negative report can be sent to the court.<br>—Solve all of our problems immediately so that the children can come home now!<br>—Hassle us like other workers by pointing out what's wrong with us. |
| **WORKER** | *Quadrant 3*<br>—Share information about the family that will help to resolve family problems.<br>—Be actively involved in service process—not passive recipients.<br>—Maintain contact with children through visitations if placement is necessary.<br>—Follow through on plans and referrals to other resources. | *Quadrant 4*<br>—Work with family to improve their problem solving capacities.<br>—Help family to identify and remove barriers that keep them from using resources.<br>—Connect family to appropriate services and resources.<br>—Monitor progress of family.<br>—Report back to court when necessary. |

This attitude is reflected in statements such as "I tell him to go to school but he won't listen," or "it was not our idea that our child should be removed so it's up to you to decide when to return him." Because of previous experiences with other social agencies or the intransigence of their problems, some parents may be apathetic and passive or they may feel victimized and angry about their hopelessness and impotence. Quadrant 1 is often the most difficult quadrant to explore because parents simply do not know what to expect or have many negative expectations about their role.

The second quadrant represents what the parents expect of the social worker when entering service, including many fears the parents have of the worker and the agency. They may believe that the worker has the power to remove the child at any time or is trying to find difficulties within the family so that their parental rights will be terminated. Some families may expect workers to solve all their problems or miraculously change a problematic child, while others may see the worker as a "court clerk" who is little more than a paper pusher.

Quadrant 3 represents those expectations that the worker has of the role responsibilities of the family in the service process. Specifically these worker expectations should include what the worker expects of the parents' performance in the service process, such as sharing their concerns and feelings, becoming actively involved in solving family problems, and maintaining contact with their children through visitation if placement is necessary.

Quadrant 4 of the matrix represents the worker's personal expectations of his or her role. These expectations must include what specifically is expected of the worker in the service process, such as connecting the family to services, monitoring progress, reporting to court if necessary, and helping to facilitate problem solving.

The role clarification process involves three steps: explicating various expectations, comparing and identifying discrepancies in expectations, and negotiating, compromising, and reaching agreement on expectations.

1. *Explicating expectations.* In this step the parents are asked to state or write specifically what they expect or want of the worker (Quadrant 2) and what they expect their own responsibilities to be in the service process (Quadrant 1). When these two sets of expectations are fairly complete, the worker states or writes what he or she considers to be worker role responsibilities (Quadrant 4) and the role responsibilities of the parents (Quadrant 3). It is important that the parents share their expectations *first* so that the worker's expectations neither contaminate nor shape their initial expectations.

2. *Comparing and identifying discrepancies.* In this step, Quadrants 1 and 3 are compared and Quadrants 2 and 4 are compared. This will display any conflicts or confusion that exist between the worker's and parents' views of their roles. For example in Table 14–1, the parents' expectations of their role are much more passive and reactive than the worker's expectations of the parents' role in service, while the parents' expectations of the worker's role are much more punitive and controlling than the worker's view of his or her role as a "helper."

All discrepancies should be identified, and both worker and parents should acknowledge their existence. When both acknowledge these discrepancies, it is then possible to move to the final, critical phase of role clarification.

3. *Negotiation, compromise, and agreement.* In this final step, worker and parents come to terms with the discrepant and conflicting perspectives. Some parents tend to accept the worker's perspective of service

roles and to deny their own perspective. In order to prevent premature closure of the discrepancies and to keep parents from "selling out" in the face of authority, workers should legitimize both the parents and their own perspectives and then attempt to reach a mutual agreement or compromise in conflict areas. By taking into account the parents' perspective, the worker is assuring some motivation from the parents when later carrying out their role responsibilities.

In situations where the parents have few expectations of themselves or the worker, the clarification procedure may become one of "induction" in which the worker educates and socializes the parents concerning what to expect (Lennard and Bernstein, 1960; Siporin, 1975). Even if this final step does become more *induction* than *mutual agreement*, the consequence can still be positive because ambiguities and potential confusions are clarified. If clients are to be as self-determining as possible, however, workers should make every effort to achieve mutual agreement, rather than demanding that parents "take or leave" the worker's proposed set of responsibilities.

Only with administrative or court-ordered procedures can there be no compromises, but these expectations can still be clarified and conflict avoided by letting parents know what they are and that they are nonnegotiable.

This role clarification procedure can be employed by repeating it with each individual parent, or it can be accomplished by allowing both parents to discuss these areas and reach a common understanding. In either case, the discrepancies about role expectations between parents will have to be recognized and resolved, as will those discrepancies that arise between the worker and the parents. This procedure may be used to clarify any set of complementary roles such as husband–wife or worker–supervisor, or any single role, by simply substituting other categories or positions at the top of the matrix and asking each party to state, compare, and agree on their role expectations. For example, the matrix could add another column and clarify all three major roles in foster care (See Table 14–2).

In such a matrix, worker and parents would then not only be clarifying their own roles, but also their perspectives on another significant position, in this case that of the foster parent. Clarifying this role early in the service process may help reduce some later confusion and conflict when parents and foster family interact around visitation or other issues affecting the child's welfare.

*Authority Issues*

In Child Welfare the authority issue[1] may impede the development of a relationship between the service worker and the parents. Parents who

**TABLE 14–2  Clarification of Foster Parent Role**

| | Expectations for Foster Parent Role |
|---|---|
| Parents | —They may be trying to win our kids away from us for adoption.<br>—Someone to compete with—good parent versus bad parent.<br>—They will be telling and showing us how to parent.<br>—They will be snooping into our family business.<br>—They won't know our child the way we do and can't possibly do a good job!<br>—Because they have all the advantages (money, etc.), they won't really know what it is like to raise our child. |
| Worker | —Provide a comfortable home that meets the child's basic needs.<br>—Help child adjust to the temporary separation from the natural parents.<br>—Cooperate with the natural parents around visitations.<br>—Have no expectations about "adopting" children placed in foster care.<br>—Cooperate with worker on service plans.<br>—Participate in planning when it is appropriate. |

have experienced court-ordered removal of a child, for example, may suspect and distrust their worker. They often view the worker as the agent who removed their child and are not at all clear about the differences in the worker's authority and the authority of the court.

To a parent, both the worker and the court are blended together in a powerful conspiracy that has embarrassed and harassed them and finally removed their child. This situation is exacerbated because some parents who have children in care have a history of dismal relationships with other agencies. They do not view social services as resources or opportunities but instead as systems of social control, harassment, and interference in their way of life (Brager and Barr, 1967). Such previous experiences with other services cannot be ignored or denied because they are a part of the reality that parents bring to a Child Welfare situation.

How then does a worker cope with the issues and consequences of these authority problems? First, it is unrealistic to expect that the parents have the major responsibility for coming to terms with the authority issue. Some parents have severe problems in any authority situation— even the most benign and least threatening—so it is not realistic to simply ignore these issues as if "it's the parents' problem; let them come to terms with it." The worker has a responsibility to help the parents cope with the reality of these issues.

The worker must be comfortable with authority to be able to explore this issue with the family. Authority is not an easy issue to handle for anyone—client, worker, citizen—and worker responses to authority issues may not be helpful to clients.

Some workers mishandle authority by denying that they have any at all. When pushed they try to project the notion that they are totally supportive of the parent; any unpleasant decision will be made by someone else. Some workers may even try to deny their relationship with the court or their own agency. Clients see a worker who professes "no authority" as someone to distrust or manipulate.

Some workers overreact to their own authority by blaming, ordering, and chastising the parents. Such workers perceive authority as an absolute that must be demonstrated and enforced. Actually, clients find this kind of response easier to handle because the worker is clear and this position on the authority issue very predictable.

Neither of these extreme stances helps the parents come to terms with authority in the social work relationship. Whether the issue arises or not, the worker should initiate a discussion of the authority issue by spelling out clearly for the parents his or her connection to the court. The parents should understand the court's authority in the case and how the worker's authority may differ from the court's. In some protective, foster, or institutional care arrangements, the worker is a direct agent of the court; in others, the worker is detached from court decisions. In any case the worker should spell out what the parents' rights are in relationship to the court's authority and that of the worker.

The worker can also use court-ordered decisions as limits or boundaries for the work to be accomplished. Within these boundaries the parents may understand that they have the authority to make decisions and choices. For example, the court's authority may only specify that the child is to remain in care until greater family stability is achieved. This allows the worker and the parents a great deal of latitude in deciding which problems to work on in the family and how these difficulties should be tackled.

A final authority issue that needs clarification is the right of the family to control information collected about them. A great deal of information is collected about families who enter the Child Welfare system, and families should understand that social agencies have certain responsibilities in using this information. Information about the family is not to be shared with other organizations unless the family gives written consent to its release. This release of information is not a "blank check" that the family signs at intake, but instead the family should be given an opportunity to share and review the content of any verbal or written exchange of information. Before consent is obtained, the family should understand what information is being shared, for what purposes, and to whom the information is being given (Schrier, 1980).

But the family's authority over information collected is not supreme, and social workers cannot promise that *all* information will be held in strict confidence. Confidentiality as an ethical issue may be absolute, but in practice, situations arise in which social workers are forced by legal sanctions to disclose information without a family's consent. Even in states which grant, as part of licensure, social workers some form of privileged communication, certain limits to the privilege are specified, and social workers are usually not granted privilege in criminal affairs (Promislo, 1979). For example, social workers are required by law to report instances of suspected abuse to protective services whether the family consents or not. These limits to privilege and confidentiality must be discussed with families and clarified so that the family will know what protections they have when disclosing information to the worker.

## Demographic Barriers

Certain barriers to relationship development can arise that are beyond the control of both the worker and the parents. Social work literature emphasizes relationship problems that may develop when there are demographic differences between clients and workers (Devore and Schlesinger, 1981; Goodman, 1974; Mizio, 1972; Sue, 1981). Especially in the beginning of a relationship, differences in sex, race, age, ethnicity, or social position may create greater social distance between the parties. The consequence may be much greater strain in establishing rapport.

The reason these basic demographic differences are so critical in the beginning of a relationship is that they are the initial data one stranger uses in sizing up another. Even before two strangers speak, they respond to the many available visual cues, such as sex, race, clothing, or mannerisms. These visual cues generate many stereotypes that may be inaccurate and, therefore, detrimental to relationship building.

For example, in a culture that discriminates on the basis of race, sex and age it is to be expected that a black parent may be particularly suspicious of a white worker. In turn, the white worker might be nervous or patronizing in providing service to the family. If workers do not purposely make an effort to understand and modify their own stereotypes, as well as those of their clients, then it will take a considerable amount of interaction before these initial impressions are replaced by a more realistic view.

Several possible strategies for dealing with demographic barriers are suggested in the social work literature. One strategy is an organizational tactic called "matching" and refers to "the exclusive or preferential assignment of certain types of clients to specific types of treatment personnel" (Palmer, 1973:95). Thus, demographic barriers may be reduced by having a staff population that is similar to the agency's client population on major variables such as sex, race, and the like. Still, matching is not an ideal strategy. Organizationally, it is unrealistic to assume that agencies can hire enough different staff to match all clients. It may even be unproductive in some situations to have too much symmetry between client and worker because there would be too much similarity in perspective and little new information added to the client's view of the world! Therefore it is important for workers to have knowledge, skill, and sensitivity about others who are different from them so that they may transcend demographic barriers. The following process can help to address tensions caused by demographic barriers.

• *Assessing differences.* The worker should make a quick assessment of the major demographic differences that may exist between himself or herself and the parents. The following variables should be considered in Child Welfare because they all have potential negative consequences on relationship development:

Race—white, black, Asian-American, American Indian, Hispanic
Sex—male, female
Age—major developmental grouping (such as adolescent, aged)
Family position—spouse (husband, wife), parent (mother, father)
Ethnicity—Italian-American, WASP

For example, a 25-year-old, single, white female social worker without children and a black, middle-aged couple whose children have been removed for neglect have fundamental differences on the first four variables.

• *Selecting critical differences.* Next the worker decides what barriers may be generating negative stereotypes and thus need to be confronted. There are several ways the worker may decide which variables are critical. The most responsive way is to be alert to parental reactions and respond immediately to any cue parents give that indicates some concern about demographic barriers. For example, a parent might say, "I thought I was going to see a black worker" (racial barrier). Or "are you married? Do you have children?" (family positions barrier). Or "I didn't expect to see someone so young, dearie" (age barrier). These leads should be pursued. On the other hand, if parents do not offer any cues, the worker can take the initiative and choose at least one demographic difference and raise a question about it. A worker might say, for example: "Sometimes things about us get in the way of working together, and I wanted you to know that if you have any concerns about me, I would be glad to discuss them. For instance, you may have been surprised to be assigned to a black worker." Even if the parents do not follow the lead, the door is open for future discussion of these issues.

• *Modifying stereotypes.* Once demographic barriers have been selected, both worker and parents can engage in a discussion of their feelings, attitudes, reactions, and concerns in this area. The worker tries to discover what kinds of stereotypic impressions are operating. He or she then supplies information to the parents that might help them alter their impressions. Sharing one's own feelings may be useful, as well as encouraging the parents to explore theirs. If differences surface early and cannot be resolved by discussion or demonstration, it may become necessary to better "match" family and worker, avoiding a struggle that may never be resolved and may continually interfere with the service process.

## Assessment

In this chapter, the process of assessment is introduced and the eco-map, a tool useful in assessing family-environment relationships, is described. The assessment process will be elaborated in subsequent chapters.

Assessment is an ongoing process which involves both worker and family. This process is designed to help both parties identify and understand the various problems and circumstances that have resulted in the need for Child Welfare services. Assessment also identifies the strengths and resources within the family and its environment that can be mobilized to help solve those problems. Assessment is not conceptualized as an exclusive responsibility of the worker, or making a "professional judgment" (Hollis, 1964),[2] but instead it is a shared understanding that involves both worker and family. A "good" assessment is *not* one that focuses narrowly on problems and troubles or distills all information into a specific diagnostic category. A "good" assessment identifies instead the salient issues and difficulties facing the family which all concerned agree need to be addressed (Germain, 1968), as well as identifying the major strengths and resources the family can bring to bear on those issues (Maluccio, 1981a).

There are many reasons why families seek help from or come to the attention of Child Welfare services. Besides neglect and abuse, parents may need help in caring for their children; perhaps they are unable to control or set limits on a child's behavior, they have a child who needs special services, a parent may require hospitalization for physical or mental disorder, or a parent may be facing prison incarceration. Regardless of the initial reason for the contact, many families bring numerous environmental, interpersonal, and personal problems. Poverty, social isolation, poor housing, marital conflict, poor parenting skills, substance abuse, emotional and mental disturbances, and learning disabilities are examples of the kinds of difficulties that families bring with them into Child Welfare services (Cohn, 1979). Often the worker and family are faced with a confusing array of variables and stresses to understand and master. The eco-map (Hartman, 1978) is an assessment tool that was developed to help families make sense out of their relationships with their environments, and to identify their stresses and strengths.

The eco-map is a diagram which the worker completes with the family. This assessment procedure captures in a drawing the various stresses and supports in the family's life space. The eco-map has been used successfully by workers in Child Welfare services to help families identify various ecological stresses and supports, and it is especially useful with resistant families who are reluctant to disclose much information about themselves.[3]

## How to Make an Eco-Map

Ideal materials for this project include a large newsprint pad and some felt tipped pens, but regular paper and pencils will do. The large paper allows the family plenty of space to fill in the map with the various elements in their life space. In the center of the paper a circle is drawn which represents the family boundary. Inside this circle smaller circles are drawn to represent females and small squares to represent males. The names and ages of family members are written within these smaller circles and squares. Solid lines are used to connect these family members to designate procreation.

Drawn around the family circle on the rest of the paper, are other large circles representing the various actors and organizations in the family's environment. These other circles may represent such connections as extended family, friends, neighbors, health care, utilities, police, employment, church, welfare, recreation, education, child care, and transportation. No list could be exhaustive and each family will identify those elements that are important to their particular situation. As each of these environmental systems is identified, the worker and family should discuss what kind of relationship the family has with each unit. Lines should then be drawn between the family or members of the family and each environmental unit. A solid line may be used to represent a continuous, positive relationship; a dotted line may be used to represent a tenuous, fleeting relationship; and a cross-hatched line may be used to represent a stressful, conflictual relationship. Family and worker may want to develop their own codes too for various relationships, and this kind of improvisation is to be encouraged because it will involve the family further in the assessment procedure. For example, in practice some eco-maps represent ambivalent relationships by a wavy line.

It is also vital to take account of those environmental connections which are necessary or life-enhancing but are *not* present. This can be done by drawing in and naming other circles on the basis of some conception of common human needs, but demonstrating the lack of connectedness by drawing no lines to these systems. Relationships among systems outside the family boundaries often directly affect and sometimes harm the family. These, too, may be characterized.

These are the basic principles of making an eco-map.[4] In order to exemplify how a family may identify stresses and supports through the construction of an eco-map, a sample is presented in Figure 14–1. This eco-map describes a single-parent family whose two children have been placed in foster care as the result of a neglect petition.

This family eco-map displays a great deal of information about the family in its environment. The 22-year-old mother has two daughters, aged 3 and 1. The 3-year-old daughter is the product of the mother's previous marriage with her 25-year-old, ex-husband; her 1-year-old daughter is the product of her union with her 29-year-old boyfriend. Both children have been placed in a foster family with middle-aged foster parents. The mother feels very negatively toward the foster parents, the court, the city hospital, the protective service worker, and the foster care worker for their part in the placement of her children.

The mother lacks support or good relations with her parents but makes up for this loss by having positive relationships with her boyfriend, other friends, her church, and her tenants' organization. The mother is in arrears with her utility bill, and the power and light company is threatening to cut off her gas and electricity. This mother is also engaged in a contentious relationship with her landlord and is working with several local housing agencies to force the landlord to make necessary repairs on her apartment. She has been trying but has been unable to locate an adequate job, a training program, or day-care services for her children. The eco-map captures on paper and summarizes the complexity of this family's connections to its environment.

The value of the eco-map is that it is a simple, graphic procedure that actively draws the family into their own self-assessment as a unit. The eco-map is an excellent ice-breaker in beginning assessment because it is nonthreatening and focuses on environmental stresses and resources, which most families find easier to discuss than personal problems. What parent in an early contact is comfortable with a worker discussing alcoholism, impulse control, or incest? Furthermore, many families are surprised and relieved when they sum up and can visually comprehend the difficult circumstances with which they have been

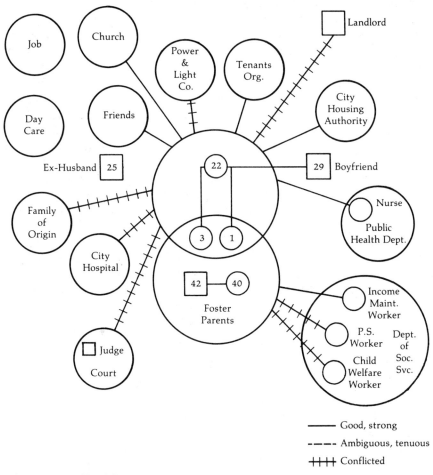

**Figure 14–1**  Eco-Map

struggling; their own feelings of helplessness and guilt become more understandable to them.

By starting with environmental strengths and stresses it may seem that personal or interpersonal problems are being avoided. On the contrary, mapping out the environment diffuses and broadens the context, helps build trust and makes it safer for the worker to approach or raise difficult issues and for the family to share its concerns and experiences. From a successful experience with the eco-map, families may begin to look at other personal problems they are experiencing that may be connected to those identified in the eco-map. For example, the family may recognize that it has few supportive connections with its environment; this realization in turn may enable a parent to disclose feelings of loneliness and isolation. The parent might then share feelings of low self-esteem and frustration at being so isolated and unable to cope with small children, leading to a discussion of how the parent does try to cope with the children, that is, what works and what does not in his or her child-care routine.

Not only is the eco-map useful in exploring the family situation, but it also can be useful in planning what strategies the worker and family might take in improving the family's situation. An examination of the eco-map will identify those connections that exist but need strengthening, those in conflict that need resolving, or those which don't exist or are in short supply and need developing. For example, from the eco-map in Figure 14–1 there are some brokerage options: connecting mother to job opportunities or a training program and locating day-care services for her children. There are some mediating options: improving her relationship with her parents, city hospital, court, and DSS. There are also some potential advocacy options: preventing the power company from shutting off her utilities and helping her to find other ways to pressure her landlord into making needed repairs. The worker may even add resources to her environment by connecting this mother to a parenting class or parent group for families whose children are in foster care or setting up homemaker services to help her organize her living environment.

## The Contract

The contract has been extensively discussed in the social work literature (Estes and Henry, 1976; Maluccio and Marlow, 1974; Rhodes, 1977; Seabury, 1976) and also specifically in the Child Welfare literature (Stein, Gambrill, and Wiltse, 1974). Child Welfare workers have been trained in the use of contracts (Harris, 1978; Hosch, 1973), and contract approaches in Child Welfare practice have been researched (Hosch, 1973; Knapp, 1980; Stein and Gambrill, 1977; Stein, Gambrill, and Wiltse, 1977). The contract approach has produced positive results in significantly reducing foster care drift (Stein and Gambrill, 1977). From all of this literature, the contract has emerged as an important concept for practice and a promising approach in the delivery of Child Welfare services.

In both literature and practice, "contract" has been put into operation in two ways. Contract may be conceptualized as an event (i.e., the service contract) which is a written or verbal agreement between worker and client. This agreement is usually negotiated in early sessions and spells out the major aspects of service. Contract may also be viewed as an ongoing process (i.e., contracting) which consists of a series of shared decisions about service that worker and client are continuously negotiating.

A variety of terms may be negotiated in a social work contract, such as fees, meeting place, or length of service. However, the most essential terms in Child Welfare services are:

1. *Target problems*—family troubles the service is designed to resolve
2. *Goals and Objectives*—what the service intends specifically to accomplish for the family
3. *Plan of action*—particular actions or tasks the family, worker, and other service providers are responsible for carrying out
4. *Time limits*—within what frame of time objectives are expected to be met.

## Characteristics of a Service Contract

Four basic characteristics make up a social work contract: explicitness, mutuality, flexibility, and realism. Though a written service contract between worker and family may resemble a legal contract, there are significant differences. A service contract is *explicit* and clear so that both family and worker understand all terms and nothing is taken for granted. Professional jargon and legalese are avoided; the family's own words are preferred. For an example of a written service contract (Harris, 1978) see Figure 14–2.

In practice, written contracts have been employed to assure that agreements are explicit, and usually copies are furnished to all parties. Written contracts can also be used as a predictive measure. Parents who agree to sign a restoration contract are much more likely to have their children returned than those who refuse (Stein, Gambrill, and Wiltse, 1977). Parents who agree to sign may be demonstrating a stronger commitment to work toward the return of their children, and this underlying commitment may account for restoration success. Unfortunately these results can also be explained by the negative side of these data. The large restoration failure of parents who refuse to sign may reflect the power of Child Welfare agencies to punish "uncooperative clients" by denying the return of their children.

Other research results have challenged whether *written* contracts are superior to *verbal* contracts (Sykes, 1978). In some case situations written contracts simply cannot be used practically (Knapp, 1980). Illiteracy, psychoses, severe mental retardation, deceased parents are contingencies that make written contracts unrealistic. With other families

HAMPTON DEPARTMENT OF SOCIAL SERVICES
HAMPTON, VIRGINIA

AGREEMENT WITH NATURAL PARENTS OR GUARDIANS

THIS AGREEMENT is a contract between *Nancy Dunham*, Social Worker, Hampton Department of Social Services, and *Robert and Sally Smith*, parent(s) of *Alvin and George Smith*.

The purpose of this Agreement is to make permanent plans for *Alvin and George Smith*, whose custody is with the Hampton Department of Social Services. It is the wish of the parent(s) to have the child(ren) *returned to their custody*.

In order to accomplish the above goal the following conditions must be met:

1. *Improvement of parenting skills and proper supervision of young children.*
2. *Reduce alcohol consumption and attend AA.*
3. *Household bills paid up to date.*
4. *Household furniture must meet children's needs.*
5.

The parent(s) and the social worker will be responsible for doing the following things during this part of the Agreement:

| *Parent(s)* | *Social Worker* |
|---|---|
| 1. *Buy baby crib by 1/27/78* | 1. *Register Mrs Smith for parenting class by 1/24/78* |
| 2. *Mrs Smith will attend weekly parenting classes through 3/14/78* | 2. *Arrange weekend visits between parents and children every other weekend from 1/20/78 to 3/21/78* |
| 3. *Mr Smith will attend AA twice a week.* | 3. *Make home visit every other Friday until 3/14/78* |
| 4. *Household bills (rent & utilities) will be paid on time through 3/21/78* | |

This Agreement shall be reviewed on *3/14/78* in order to plan the next steps in the completion of the goal. The total period of time for the accomplishment of the goal of *return of custody* is from *1/17/78* to *3/21/78*.

*Robert Smith*

*Sally Smith*
*1-7-78*

*Nancy Dunham*
Social Worker

**Figure 14–2** Sample Contract

354

who are so distrustful of public agencies, the prospect of signing a written agreement is threatening. When the worker raises the issue of a written agreement, any chance of service may be immediately negated. With this kind of family, a written contract actually deters service delivery that might have been possible with a less formal agreement.

Another issue with written contracts is the resistance this procedure generates in workers who are being trained in its use (Knapp, 1980; Special Family Services Project, 1981). Written contracts can be time consuming and add to a worker's "paperwork." Written contracts seem to pose a threat of accountability that is not true of other service procedures—what are the implications for a worker when tasks are not completed nor objectives achieved? Whether contracts are written down and signed or simply verbalized, the important issue is that agreements be clearly understood by all parties.

Ideally a service contract is mutually established between worker and family. Both parties participate in deciding terms, and the family is encouraged to take part in these decisions. The family's opinions and perspectives are seriously considered, and the worker does not bully the family into accepting the "worker's wisdom."

*Mutuality*, however, is a service ideal and cannot always be realized in Child Welfare practice. Some families may tend to defer to the worker's authority. In order to be "good clients," these families will try to second guess what they think the worker expects of them. In this situation their own aspirations may be overlooked and never seriously considered until they fail to follow through on the worker's ideas. On the other hand, in some protective service situations in which there are court mandates, mutuality is problematic because the family may disagree with the court mandates. Court-mandated terms are not negotiable with the worker and can only be changed through a legal proceeding. But even court mandates may give the family some discretionary power about how mandates may be put into operation in a service contract. For example, a court may demand improvements in a family's child-care arrangements but not specify exactly what and how these improvements are to be accomplished. Within this mandate the worker and family may have a range of alternatives which they can discuss and pursue to accomplish the court mandate.

A service contract is *flexible* so that decisions may be renegotiated as service progresses. Unlike a legal contract which is strictly binding once parties sign, a social work contract is more tentative and represents a dynamic, flexible plan rather than a set of strict rules. When contract terms are not achieved, worker and family may evaluate the impasse and plan alternative actions. In some situations even service goals may have to be revised after a trial period. Flexibility applies to the service contract,*not* court-ordered mandates. The service agreements between the family and the worker (and other service providers) are open to change, while court-ordered actions are much more inflexible and can only be changed by court action. In protective service situations, clarifying the nature of this dual contract situation is essential (Fusco, 1977; Seabury, 1979).

Finally, a service contract is *realistic*. The terms that are agreed on are within the capacity of both worker and family. Workers should not make promises (no matter how desirable) that are beyond their own expertise and agency resources. And the family should not be pushed into accepting terms that demand more than their skills and resources can deliver in the time specified.

Unfortunately in some agencies this principle is being violated and corrupt contracts are being negotiated between worker and family.[5] A worker may deliberately encourage parents whose children have been removed to agree to tackle unrealistic goals or tasks. When parents are not able to accomplish these objectives or complete their plan, the contract failure is then used as a document against parents in termination of rights proceedings.

This situation documents one of the values of a service contract: This service contract can be used as evidence in court proceedings (Knapp, 1980). In a positive vein, the contract can be used to demonstrate the progress that a family has achieved and may help build a case for restoration. Using the service contract as evidence against parents in a termination of rights hearing is not corrupt in itself. What is corrupt is the practice of workers knowingly and deliberately encouraging parents to agree to terms that they cannot possibly accomplish. Instead of using a service contract to help parents make changes in their lives, the service contract is being used as a trap so that parental rights can be terminated. This practice may be one of the unfortunate, unintended consequences of the shift in Child Welfare policy to permanency planning.

## Primary and Secondary Contracts

In Child Welfare practice, two kinds of service contracts are used—primary and secondary. The primary contract represents the service agreement between the family and the Child Welfare worker, which must be supplemented by other service arrangements. Other resources may have to be contacted and the family linked to them. The worker and family then establish service agreements or sometimes less formal arrangements with these other resources, such as with other helping professionals, training programs, or support groups. These supporting arrangements are sanctioned by secondary contracts, again verbal or written, which are designed to support the primary contract.

Secondary does not mean that these agreements are of lesser value than the primary contract. In practice, a secondary contract may be more important to the outcomes of a case than the primary contract. For example, a worker may be helping a family to connect with a day-care program, parenting classes, and homemaker services. Not only can the worker help the family make these arrangements, but in some districts the worker may also be responsible for arranging the payments of these services through a third party contract and monitoring these services as they are delivered. In practice more of a worker's day may be spent working on these secondary contracts—for example, locating resources, planning and conducting case conferences, monitoring other service providers, or working with foster parents—than with direct family contact. This kind of "boundary work" does not mean that the family is ignored (Hearn, 1974). On the contrary the family should be involved in secondary contracts with other services, and the worker should be in contact with the family as each of these arrangements is planned and carried out.

The amount of boundary work required of Child Welfare workers reflects the reality seen in the eco-map presented earlier. (See Figure 14–1). The Child Welfare worker has many tasks to attend to in a given case. Simply "counseling" parents is rarely enough to produce significant outcomes for the family. Workers should maintain good working relationships with foster parents, placement institutions, and all other supportive services and resources that are being mobilized to help the family.

## Benefits of the Contract

Child Welfare services that have employed a contract approach have noted several benefits to this approach. Rather than directing worker and family to dwell on elaborate, metaphorical explanations of the causation of family problems, contracts encourage worker and family to be goal-oriented, specific, pragmatic,and conscious of time restrictions (Knapp, 1980). Because contracts help organize service toward explicit, time-limited outcomes, contracting significantly reduces foster care drift (Stein and Gambrill, 1977). Children entering the Child Welfare system under a contract approach are more assured of time-limited planning and monitoring, and temporary foster care does not drag out into *de facto* permanent care.

Contracts encourage greater parity between worker and family, that is, both have responsibility for decision-making, which requires workers to involve parents in decisions about service. Parents are not allowed to become passive recipients of service, but instead are actively engaged in the major decisions that affect themselves and their children. Workers who use contracts feel that the experience strengthens the worker–client relationship, and helps workers to be more sensitive to clients' needs and aspirations and to develop more receptive and supportive plans (Knapp, 1980).

## Future of the Contract

Little doubt prevails that contract approaches to service will continue to spread in Child Welfare practice. The benefits contracts have for service delivery are promising, yet our understanding of contracting needs to be more developed. Contracts should not be prescribed indiscriminately. Written contracts (no matter how desirable) cannot be expected with all families in all circumstances. More knowledge needs to be developed about what types of written contracts or formats work best with what kinds of families in what kinds of circumstances. Agencies need to be clearer when contracts are not feasible or simply cannot be negotiated, or are contraindicated and might actually hamper service delivery (Seabury, 1979). In these situations workers should not be expected or forced to contract with families. In other situations in which contracting is difficult or problematic, innovations in negotiations need to be developed. For example in the Hampton Project (Knapp, 1980), some families in the demonstration sample did not sign written agreements; however, workers did employ alternative strategies similar to contracts by developing task lists or calendar check-off schemes with their families.

Both the Hampton (Knapp, 1980) and Alameda (Stein and Gambrill, 1977) projects suggest that contracts may be easier to negotiate with families whose children have been removed, than those families in which prevention is the primary purpose. By modifying contract approaches with prevention services, contracting may be made more operational and effective. For example, in a prevention project in Michigan (Special Family Services Project, 1981), the timing of contract negotiation was modified. Rather than negotiating and signing contracts early in the service process, workers engaged families first to establish a working relationship and to help families understand the obstacles that had prevented them from using services and resources in the past. After these obstacles and resources had been identified, the workers were able to negotiate formal contracts with their families. These kinds of innovations, which have been pioneered in demonstration projects, are helping to develop the necessary, practical knowledge to differentiate when and how contracts are viable in the delivery of Child Welfare services.

This chapter has presented three important processes in which Child Welfare workers and families participate in the beginning phases of contact. *Engagement* is not automatic for the worker and family, and many barriers to the development of an effective helping relationship may exist in the beginning. Families may bring negative feelings to the service process, as well as be confused about what is expected of them and the worker. Authority issues and basic demographic differences may strain the fragile developing relationship. With all of these barriers, a worker must struggle to be honest and to clarify the issues facing the family. Honesty may generate conflict, yet it will clear up misconceptions and misunderstandings.

*Assessment* begins even before the worker contacts the family and will continue throughout the entire service process. Not only do workers have the responsibility to understand what is going on, but workers will also help the family to communicate what is important about their situation. Worker and family together will try to understand the special circumstances that created the need for Child Welfare services. Problems, strengths, and resources need to be assessed. The eco-map is an effective assessment tool for engaging families in this assessment process.

The *contract* approach is a significant way of organizing the business aspects of service. Contracts are valuable because they increase clarity and motivation, and they generate pragmatic, time-limited objectives that service can achieve. Whether contracts are written, signed, or only verbalized, they are an important dimension to service and provide the family with greater involvement in the service process.

This chapter has artificially divided the beginning phase of service into three areas. This tripartite division is purely heuristic and represents one way of organizing the complexity of practice. In the real world the Child Welfare worker embarks upon all of these processes at once, and relationship issues, assessment tasks, and contract responsibilities may all be demanding attention simultaneously. With some families the pressures and barriers that a worker faces may seem overwhelming. The resistance that families present, the painful task of, at times, removing children from their families, the complexity of family problems, the pressures of working under court mandates, the reporting and paper work requirements of agency procedures, and the demands of growing caseloads mean that the role of the Child Welfare worker remains one of challenge and frustration.

# CHAPTER 15

# Working with the Family in Child Welfare

JOAN LAIRD

A society that does not tend to the welfare of its children, its future generations, hastens its own demise. The welfare of children can only be enhanced when our society is ready to take the needs of families seriously. This principle has found expression in an ideological shift occurring in Child Welfare, one that recognizes that the welfare of children is inexorably linked to the welfare of their families. It has also found expression throughout this volume as authors have repeatedly emphasized the importance of maintaining the family and enhancing family functioning. Chapter authors have explored the economic, political, cultural, institutional, and professional forces that support, nurture, and empower families and those that generate obstacles to family functioning. However, despite shifts in ideology and in policy, work with families continues to be halting, preventable placements occur, and reunification services are inadequate. Workers themselves are often reluctant to focus their major efforts on biological families.

Some of the reluctance may be a holdover from the historic belief in the privacy of the family—a belief that demands that the State stay out of the lives of families and, when protective action is needed, encourages the care of children out of their homes. Child Welfare workers, located in underfunded and ambivalently sanctioned agencies, have found themselves in conflicting and even antagonistic relationships with the very families they hope to help. Employed in institutions that have monitored, controlled, and taken over child-rearing responsibilities from families who are seen as defective, these professionals have been trapped in, at best, professionally distant and superior relationships with parents and, at worst, adversarial ones.

Furthermore, until recently, the Child Welfare worker's helping role has been conceptualized primarily as investigative, and an interventive role with families has been limited to assessing the extent of abuse or neglect of children and recommending placement or treatment. A pattern has been routinely to refer troubled families to community mental health or purchase-of-service, private counseling agencies for psychotherapy. However, like some of the unsatisfactory solutions that families themselves create to resolve their stresses, this professional solution is inadequate and often perpetuates and even increases family stress.

Referred families often feel coerced into a treatment plan that seems to have little meaning or relevance for their lives, as the mental health center represents yet another authoritarian bureaucracy, a foreign place that threatens their rights and their privacy. Some families are frightened and defensive because, in their world, treatment means they must be "crazy." Furthermore, "working through" or "gaining insight" in a therapeutic relationship is incongruent with their accustomed modes of coping and enhances their feelings of powerlessness in a world that is largely concerned with meeting daily survival needs.

When parents warily and wearily withdraw after one or two visits, the case is often closed with the notation that the client is "unmotivated" or "uncooperative." In some cases, the placement of children may be recommended or reunification postponed since the clients have not followed through with the well-meaning but ill-conceived treatment plan. The inappropriate mental health referral generates its own set of problems in the sense that it helps perpetuate the myth that problems of abuse and neglect are results of individual dysfunction and breakdown and the illusion that these families and children are being helped. As Pelton points out: "Adherence to the myth diverts attention from the nature of the problems and diverts resources from their solution" (1978: 616).

## Who Is to Do the Job?

Increasingly, as Child Welfare is defined as a service primarily geared to the enhancement of the welfare of children within their own homes or to the prompt reunification of families when temporary placement is required, the question is raised, "But who is to do the job?" The widespread use of referral and purchase-of-service resources is beginning to be questioned and there is a growing conviction that Child Welfare agencies themselves, primarily those in the public sector, will have to provide preventive and rehabilitative services to families. Agencies are moving in this direction, are developing preventive units, and are offering services to families to avoid placement.

This emphasis, however, has increased the stress on workers, supervisors, and local administrators, exacerbating their feelings of powerlessness. Line staff are increasingly expected to maintain families intact or to bring about prompt reunification when, in a period of sharp curtailment of social programs and public assistance cutbacks, the network of resources and supports that must be mobilized on behalf of families is not available.

Furthermore, line workers and supervisors often do not have the knowledge or the skills required for rehabilitative work with families. A recent extensive national survey of education and training for Child Welfare revealed an agreement among Child Welfare practitioners at all levels of the system that the greatest training need for Child Welfare staff is knowledge and skill in working with families (National Child Welfare Training Center, 1981; 1983). It has also been the case that until recently most of the training available has drawn upon individually oriented psychological theory, which offers little help in understanding the complexities of family relationships or the relationship between the family and environment.

This situation is beginning to change. In the last twenty to thirty years, with the introduction of ideas and concepts from general systems, communication, cybernetic, ecological, and family systems theories into the helping professions, a rich body of theory and knowledge for Child Welfare thinkers to draw on has developed. These new approaches influence practice and provide a foundation on which to base new training programs. Such new approaches make available to Child Welfare line staff the knowledge and skill needed in their work with families.

## Family-Centered Practice in Child Welfare

In the pages that follow, a model of family-centered practice that can be used in working with families in the Child Welfare system is presented.[1] In this ecologically oriented family systems approach to work with families, it is assumed that society's (and the practitioner's) first priority lies in promoting an adaptive, need-fulfilling balance between the family and the surrounding community. Family-centered practice begins with the conviction that the family in its larger environment should be attended to and nurtured, and that the greatest portion of time, energy, and financial resources of the Child Welfare system must be devoted to preserving families. The goals of family maintenance and the welfare of children are emptied of meaning if workers are unable to help families gather the basic resources needed for survival and for the promotion of competent exchange with the world around them.

Family-centered practice locates the family at the center of the unit of attention or field of action. Family-centered practice is grounded in the assumption that human beings can be understood and helped only in the context of the intimate and powerful human systems of which they are a part. This family-centered view of the unit of attention is pictured in Figure 15–1.

The worker at one or another time may focus attention on the nuclear family or household pictured in the inner circle, on the extended family or particular relationships in that network, on the connections or lack of connections between the family and those other systems or resources that are needed for survival and enrichment, or on the intergenerational relationships which play such a powerful role in influencing current family style and functioning.

A three-dimensional approach to family-in-environment assessment and intervention, one that encompasses all of the dimensions depicted in Figure 1, is necessary. Each of the dimensions is briefly summarized and tools particularly useful in assessment and intervention are described. In Exhibit 15–1, a comprehensive "Outline for Family Assessment," divided into three sections corresponding to the three dimensions pictured in Figure 15–1, is offered as a guide. It is intended as a "thinking" tool to help the worker and family understand the

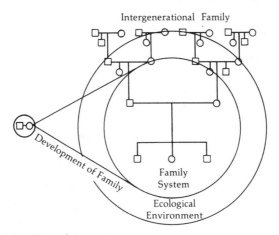

**Figure 15–1**   The Unit of Attention

From Ann Hartman and Joan Laird, *Family-Centered Social Work Practice*. New York: The Free Press, 1983, p. 113. Copyright © 1983 by The Free Press.

*Outline for Family Assessment*

### I. PRESENTING PROBLEM OR NEED

**A.** What needs and/or problems have led to the contact?
**B.** Who recognizes these needs or problems?
**C.** Who initiated contact?
**D.** How do the various members of the family define the problem?
**E.** How do others (school, court, etc.) define the problem?
**F.** What are your initial impressions?

### II. THE FAMILY IN SPACE: ECOLOGICAL ASSESSMENT

Major Data Collection and Assessment Tools: Interviewing, the Eco-Map

**A. BASIC NEEDS**

1. Is their income sufficient to meet basic needs?
2. Does the family have adequate food and shelter?
3. Is their neighborhood safe and a reasonably pleasant place to live?
4. Does the family have access to preventive health care and good medical resources?
5. Can family members get to needed resources, or are they cut off because of location, or lack of public or private transportation or telephone?
6. Does this family have meaningful social connections with neighbors, friends, community organizations? Is it part of an extended kin network?
7. Do family members belong to or participate in any group activities?
8. Does the family have the opportunity to share cultural, ethnic or other kinds of meanings or values with others? Are their values in conflict or congruent with the surrounding environment?
9. Is the educational experience a positive one for the children? Do they and other family members have access to other vocational or cultural enrichment opportunities?
10. Do family members have an opportunity to experience effectance and enhance their competence? Do family members work? Is there any satisfaction or gratification in their work? How long has it been since family members have mastered a new experience, generated something new or different, felt proud of an achievement?

**Exhibit 15–1** Outline for Family Assessment

From Ann Hartman and Joan Laird, *Family-Centered Social Work Practice*. New York: The Free Press, 1983, pp. 345–353. Copyright © 1983 by The Free Press.

B. INDIVIDUAL FAMILY MEMBER'S RELATIONSHIP WITH ENVIRONMENT

1. Is one member more "cut-off" from environmental exchanges?
2. Is one member more involved in stressful connections?
3. Do family members always have "together" transactions with other people or systems or do family members tend to relate to environments separately?
4. Do family members have differential access to and exchange with the world around them?

C. AGENCY–WORKER CONTEXT

1. Are the helping agencies or systems involved with the family pursuing similar or conflicting goals and actions on behalf of the family?
2. Is the family caught between different and confusing sets of expectations?
3. Is the effectiveness of your goal(s) being undermined by conflicting or unclear norms or goals?
4. What is the relationship between your agency and the family? Are the agency's services appropriate and available to meet the needs of the family?
5. Is your agency in conflict with any other important systems in the family's ecological environment?
6. What is the nature of the relationship between you and the family? How do they view you?

D. FAMILY–ENVIRONMENT BOUNDARY

1. Is this family open to new experiences or relationships? Are members free to make individual connections with other people and organizations? Does the family allow others in physically or emotionally?
2. Are the boundaries flexible, i.e., can they expand and contract adaptively in relation to the environment and the changing developmental needs of the family? Does the family protect its members when necessary and allow differentiation when appropriate?

E. OVERALL ASSESSMENT OF THE FAMILY'S RELATIONSHIP WITH ITS ENVIRONMENT

1. Has this family achieved an adaptive balance with its surrounding environment?
2. Is the family in a state of disequilibrium or in danger of being overwhelmed?

*(continued)*

Exhibit 15–1 (*Continued*)

    3. Is most of the energy being drained from the family?

    4. Is the family only "taking in" from outside systems?

    5. Are essential supports or resources to meet basic needs potentially available in the environment or are they lacking? In what particular areas?

    6. Does the family need help or enhanced skills in tapping and making use of these resources?

    7. What sources of strength, support, or resources could be activated or enhanced?

    8. Are there particular sources of stress or conflict?

    9. How would you characterize the most salient aspects of the family-environment relationship? For example, family is deprived, socially isolated, overburdened, etc.

## III. THE FAMILY IN TIME: INTERGENERATIONAL ASSESSMENT

Major Data Collection and Assessment Tools: Interviewing, the Genogram, Documents, Letters, Visits, Photos, etc.

### A. FAMILY PATTERNS

1. What are the most significant family patterns emerging from a study of the genogram?

2. Has the family experienced any major losses through untimely or tragic death, migration, separation?

3. Are there particular themes or events which are "toxic" or around which there is shame, pain, or secrecy?

4. What are the family intergenerational patterns of health?

### B. FAMILY DEFINITIONS: THE FAMILY PARADIGM

1. How does the family define itself? What are the major themes which contribute to its identity, sense of itself, and its particular coherence or construction of reality?

2. What are the major family stories, myths, heroes, and heroines?

3. What family traditions or events evoke pride? How are they marked or celebrated?

4. What rituals and ceremonies are important to the family? What is their meaning?

5. What role does ethnic, racial, cultural, or religious heritage play in the family's identity?

6. How has ethnic or religious intermarriage influenced family relationships and identifications?

## C. INDIVIDUAL IDENTIFICATIONS

1. With whom are current family members associated or identified by the family? In what ways? What are the clues? (Names, occupations, sibling position, etc.)
2. What formal roles do individuals carry and how are they similar to and different from those of past generations?
3. What informal roles do they carry? Who else has carried these in the past?

## D. CURRENT FAMILY RELATIONSHIPS

1. Are there close ties and open communication with extended family? On both or only one side? (Maternal and paternal.)
2. Is there a significant emotional cut-off from either the maternal or paternal side, or among parent-child or sibling relationships?
3. What is the family's explanation for the cut-off? How did it come about? Who is really maintaining it?
4. What effect does the cut-off have on the family or on particular individuals?

## E. SOURCES OF DIFFICULTY

1. Are there serious unresolved intergenerational family issues? How are they being transmitted?
2. Are one or both parents handicapped by too great a degree of fusion with *their* parents?
3. If there is a serious emotional cut-off, what effect does it have on the family or on a particular member?
4. Is much of the family's energy devoted to avoiding intergenerational toxic issues or to maintaining secrets?
5. What dysfunctional roles transmitted from the past are family members carrying?

## IV. INSIDE THE FAMILY: STRUCTURE, ORGANIZATION AND PROCESS

Major Data Collection and Assessment Tools: Observation, interviewing (tracking patterns), family mapping, family sculpture, family drawings, eco-map, observations of families' use of their habitat.

(continued)

Exhibit 15–1 (*Continued*)

### A. FAMILY STRUCTURE

1. *External boundaries (see linkages to ecological assessment)*
    a. Permeability:
        1. Are the boundaries relatively open, for example, clear but permeable?
        2. Are the boundaries relatively closed, for example, opaque, relatively impermeable?
        3. Are the boundaries random, for example, inadequate, little cohesion?
    b. Variation:
        1. Do some members have more or higher quality or less stressed exchanges with the outer world than others? Why?
        2. What effect do these differentiated exchange relationships have on the individual? On the family as a whole?
    c. Membership:
        1. Where are the external boundaries drawn? *Who* is included within the intimate family network?
        2. Is the family isolated from extended family or family of origin?
        3. Does it welcome and embrace new members, for example, through courtship or marriage?
        4. Are outsiders welcome to "share a common table"?
2. *Part-Whole Relationships: Separateness and Connectedness*
    a. Enmeshment or Fusion
        1. Are the parents overinvolved in their children's lives?
        2. Does the family tolerate difference?
        3. Do parents "worry" too much about the children? Each other?
        4. Can members make meaningful connections outside the family system?
        5. Are individuals' efforts to individuate experienced by the family as disloyalty or abandonment?
        6. Are family members able to take "I-positions"?
    b. Disengagement, Emotional Cut-Off
        1. Do the parents fail to attend to important emotional or physical needs of the children?
        2. Do family members seem impervious or insensitive to one another?
        3. Is close emotional or physical contact avoided?

    c. Loving, Caring, and Attachment
      1. How would you characterize this family's affective relationships?
      2. What is the quality of family member's attachments to one another?
      3. Are family members able to be affectionate, nurturing, validating, and appreciative of one another?
      4. How do family members show that they care and care for? How are they unable to show and why?
3. Sociocultural Themes and Values
    a. How is the family's structure influenced by its particular ethnic and religious history? (See linkages here to intergenerational assessment.)
    b. What is valued or not valued?
    c. What are the implications of cultural ethnicity for family-environment boundaries, individual variation in family-environment exchange and in family-membership? (See linkages here to ecological assessment.)
    d. What are the implications for separateness and connectedness? For example, are there cultural norms which influence expectations for family loyalty and the degree and quality of involvement?
    e. Do these norms mesh or conflict with the surrounding cultural milieu? For the whole family? For particular family members? (See linkages here to ecological assessment.)

## B. FAMILY ORGANIZATION

1. *Internal Boundaries*
    a. How is the family system organized?
    b. What are the relationships among subsystems?
    c. Is there a clear boundary between the spouse subsystem and the children subsystem?
    d. Do both adults and children have clearly demarcated time and space for themselves?
    e. Is the parental subsystem marked by clear boundaries in terms of membership, function, consistency of roles, and lines of authority?
    f. Is the parental subsystem accessible to the children?
    g. Do the spouses offer each other mutual aid and support?
    h. Is the sibling subsystem characterized by mutual aid or competitiveness and rivalry?

*(continued)*

Exhibit 15–1 *(Continued)*

2. *Triangles*

   a. What are the central triangles and what purposes are they serving?

   b. What role is triangling playing in the current problematic behavior or issue?

3. *Roles*

   a. Familial Roles

      1. Are family roles clear and consistent?

      2. Are they complementary? Symmetrical?

      3. Do family members possess the skills and competence needed to carry out their familial and social roles?

      4. Is there rigidity or flexibility in assigned roles? Conflict?

      5. How are role assignments influenced by the family's sociocultural heritage?

      6. Is the role structure contributing to the problem or dysfunction?

      7. Is the family's solution to the role problem contributing to new or additional problems?

      8. What is the role of grandparents or other extended family members?

   b. Informal Roles

      1. What are the major informal role assignments, for example, caretaker, scapegoat, distracter, family switchboard?

      2. How are they defined?

      3. Who carries them and how did they get selected?

      4. What are their specific functions and effects in this family?

      5. Who carried these roles in previous generations? What happened to them?

      6. What is the impact on the person carrying this role?

Note: Informal roles may also be assessed in terms of clarity, consistency, conflict, complementarity, etc.

## C. FAMILY PROCESSES

1. *Adaptive and Regulating Forces*

   a. What is the function of the family's or an individual's problem in the maintenance of the family system?

   b. What homeostatic or morphostatic forces are helping to maintain stability?

   c. What morphogenic forces are promoting adaptation
      and change?
   d. What is the family's capacity to receive and exchange
      new inputs and information?
   e. What developmental and/or transitional forces are
      currently operating? How is the family adapting to
      and processing these transitions?
2. *Power and Authority*
   a. What is the hierarchy of and distribution of authority
      and power in the family? Where is the seat of power?
   b. How are family rules enforced?
   c. What happens when a rule is challenged?
   d. What part does power play in the family's game?
   e. What is the role of power in the relationship between
      practitioner and family?
3. *Family Communication Processes*
   a. What is the nature of family communication?
   b. What are the rules that govern communication and
      communication about communication?
   c. What topics can be explored? What subjects are ta-
      boo?
   d. What feelings may be expressed? What emotions or
      thoughts may not be expressed?
   e. Who talks to whom? Where? When? About what?
   f. Are some members left out?
   g. Do some talk for others?
   h. What does the nonverbal communication demon-
      strate?
   i. Is there congruence between verbal and nonverbal
      communication? Between digital and analogic com-
      munication?
   j. Are communications understandable, clear?
   k. Do members validate each other's statements, or even
      their own?
   l. How is communication "punctuated"?
4. *Meta Rules (They are rules about the development, maintenance, and alteration of the family's rule system.)*
   a. Can the family's meta rules be commented upon? Is
      there a process for change?
   b. What are the meanings, values, rituals, ceremonies,
      myths, pattern regulators which maintain the family
      rules?
   c. How are these pervasive themes and behaviors con-

(continued)

Exhibit 15–1 *(Continued)*

> tributing to the family's construction of reality? How are they expressed?
>
> **d.** Is the family immobilized, caught in rigid, repetitive, ritualized behavior?
> **e.** What purpose(s) is this behavior serving?
> **f.** Is the family lacking in ceremonies? Underritualized?
> **g.** What rules are maintaining the family problem or dysfunction?

family-in-environment situation, not as a questionnaire to be used routinely or rigidly.

It should be noted that the distinctions between assessment and intervention, terms that inadequately reflect the dynamic, shared nature of the change process, are largely artificial ones. In practice, assessment and intervention occur simultaneously in a continuous feedback process that begins from the first moment of worker–family contact. As each communication, event, or intervention occurs, so the worker's (and family's) perceptions and understandings are called to question, supported, or altered; each new intervention grows out of an enriched understanding. Similarly, the distinctions among the ecological, intergenerational, and inner family dimensions are contrived, since, as general systems theory informs us, a change in one part of the system will affect the system as a whole and all of the other parts. The family and the worker at any one moment have many choices about where and how to address change, any of which may be helpful.

## Ecological Assessment and Intervention

We turn first to the family–environment relationship as a major focus for assessment and as a target and resource for change. As the unit of attention is thus defined, however, the challenge for practice becomes one of managing a great deal of complicated and often confusing information, information that includes the physical environment, the elaborate social, economic, and political structures influential in a family's life, as well as those personal, familial, or social resources that offer opportunities for self-realization and spiritual well-being, which impart meaning to daily existence. Our knowledge of how to organize and understand such transactional phenomena is limited, although some concepts and principles have been useful in exploring the interface between the family and the environment.[2] Germain (1979) has reviewed the extent of our general knowledge of person–environment transactions, while White (1959; 1976)), Maslow (1954), and several thinkers from the family therapy field, such as Aponte (1976a; 1976b), Auerswald (1968), and Minuchin (1974), have made important contributions to this endeavor.

Adopting the science of ecology as a metaphor for practice suggests a number of principles that may be used as guidelines in assessment and intervention with and in behalf of families in the Child Welfare system. They include the following.

1. The problems of families that come to the attention of the Child Welfare worker are understood as lacks or deficits in the environment. They are also seen as dysfunctional transactions between or among systems, as adaptive strategies or attempts to adapt, or as results of interrupted growth and development, rather than as deficits or disease processes within individuals.

2. Family difficulties are seen as outcomes of the transaction of many complex variables. Thus the effort to locate single causes or solutions is abandoned and a feedback model of change adopted.

3. Families in the Child Welfare system are often overwhelmed with feelings of powerlessness and anomie. Therefore, the empowerment of families should be a major goal, both in the definition of service strategies and the way in which services are provided.

4. Life experience is seen as the model for and primary instrument of change. Therefore interventions with families that make use of natural systems and life experiences that enhance client competence and autonomy are favored over those that rely primarily on therapeutic or professional relationships.

5. Natural means are preferred over artificial means. The effort is to devise strategies that avoid the development of artificial or substitutive helping actions which may have pervasive iatrogenic effects. In the field of Child Welfare, this principle is expressed in the recommendation that the "least restrictive environment" be used for the care of children. This principle also leads to the preference for the maintenance of the biological family as the most "natural" caring system and the least intrusive or restrictive intervention.

6. A change in one part of the system has an impact on the system as a whole and on all of its parts. Seemingly minor interventions, if directed at a key point, can lead to a ripple effect throughout the family–environment complex, thus bringing about considerable change.

7. A single effect can be produced by a variety of means. This is the principle of equifinality, which means that a number of different interventions may, owing to the complexity of systems, produce similar effects or outcomes (Hartman and Laird, 1983: 72–74).

Having suggested principles that guide practice when an ecological perspective is adopted, we now turn to the task of ordering and assessing the complex ecosystem including the family in its environment.

Efforts have been made in several disciplines to develop various tools, such as networking maps or multidimensional visual models and simulations, to help organize and master what is often a confusing and massive amount of information on a single case or family.

One assessment tool adopted widely in the social work field—a tool that was originally developed to help Child Welfare workers understand family-in-environment relationships—is the eco-map, a paper and pencil simulation that maps a person and family in their life space. Instructions for the construction of an eco-map and its application in the engagement and contracting processes are included in Chapter 14.

Several points should be emphasized in the development of an ecological assessment. First, the eco-map, in portraying the nature and quality of family–environment exchanges, highlights particular nurturing and energizing connections between the family and other systems, as well as those that are stressful, in conflict, or are lacking. Those family–environment exchanges needed for physical well-being, as well as those human, personal, social, psychological, and spiritual connections that impart meaning and offer enrichment, all should be identified.

In addition to examining together the nature of each such link, the worker and family should also mentally step back to evaluate the overall picture of the family–environment relationships and the nature of the family–environment boundary. In the case of family boundaries, which consist of an invisible set of loyalties, rules, and emotional connections, it is usually only at the extremes of very closed or open boundaries that dysfunction is likely to occur. In the former case, that of the extremely closed family, the family may be cut off from needed energy exchange, resources, or opportunities for reality testing. When stress or conflict inside the family erupts, the family's own adaptive capacities may become overwhelmed. In the case of a family with randomly open, unclear, or insufficient boundaries, the family itself may lack organization and individual members may be alienated. The family as a unit may not be identifiable enough or cohesive enough to offer its members needed strength when a crisis arises (Kantor and Lehr, 1975).

While assessment of the family ecology will not yield detailed information about family functioning, it will generally surface some data concerning the family's coping style. A shared assessment through the use of an eco-map provides a beginning blueprint for change, since major themes and crucial interfaces will be identified. Section II, items D and E, Exhibit 15–1, "Outline for Family Assessment," to be used in conjunction with the eco-map, suggest the questions that should be asked of the family ecology, in order to guide initial intervention. These questions help reveal those aspects of family-environment relationships that are key, and where change is most needed and will hold the greatest promise for positive contagion throughout the family system. For example, the provision of safe housing in a hospitable neighborhood which is accessible to needed services may alleviate a mother's depression, a troubled son's peer relationships and school performance, and meet the family's needs for such diverse inputs as health services or social connectedness.

It is important to stress that the ecological assessment, facilitated by the eco-map and the outline, is a shared process between professional and family. This open, sharing process, which assumes that family members are experts on their own situation, helps to equalize the worker–family relationship, thereby empowering the client and enhancing self-esteem. The entire family should be encouraged to participate, to identify strengths, stresses, and lacks in their lives, as well as those aspects of their experiences they would like to change. Such a process not only is a respectful one, but also can be a hopeful and empowering experience, as the family is validated by a perspective that communicates that it is not their deficiences but very real environmental stresses and relationships that have contributed to the problems. Further, the process suggests that there may be ways, with the worker's help, that the family can alter an unfavorable and maladaptive ecological balance. Finally, many families known to Child Welfare workers feel disorganized, overwhelmed, and confused, not knowing what to do or where to start to bring about change. Cognitive understanding is the first step in mastery and empowerment and the eco-map helps the family order their situation, sort out and identify both difficulties and resources, and establish priorities.

The way in which problems are identified and understood from an ecological perspective has important implications for what kinds of interventive strategies are chosen. In general, as the principles listed earlier suggest, change efforts are directed not toward characteristics or attributes of individuals but to the relationships between people or between people and other systems or subsystems. A systemic, feedback model of change is adopted, one in which each intervention made is evaluated and tested against the assessment, which is itself continuously modified.

Families, even those considered neglectful or abusive, are viewed as important resources for change. Nevertheless, there is always the danger that, with the growing influence of family-centered practice, we will begin to think in terms of "sick" or deficient families rather than "sick" or deficient individuals, substituting one set of deviant labels for another, one deficit model of understanding human behavior for another. In the approach described here, the emphasis is on building competence and on empowerment, on helping people become effective in managing their lives and in relating to their environments (Pinderhughes, 1983; Solomon, 1976). Strategies may be targeted primarily toward changing the environment, as in discovering or developing a needed resource or stimulating an unresponsive bureaucracy to better meet the needs of its constituents.

As the worker and family join together in brokering and advocacy efforts, family members' skills and confidence in dealing with the environment can be enhanced and their powerlessness diminished. The use of group modalities is particularly efficacious since increasing the size of the client system enlarges the pool of competencies and increases power as families with shared concerns can join forces.

Other particularly useful interventions in increasing parenting and management skills and offering respite to overwhelmed parents may be utilized. These include homemaker services or the community day-care center, both of which can not only offer respite but also often involve parents in ways that enhance their parenting skills and give them the opportunity to enlarge their networks.

The awareness that social isolation has been a major predictor of family dysfunction alerts Child Welfare workers, in their work with family–environment relationships, to help the family seek out and nurture human connections. Environmental manipulation has often been exclusively focused on aspects of the formal service delivery system. Just as important is careful attention to the development and strengthening of natural helping systems and informal networks. Such helping strategies are congruent with the ecological principle that natural means of help and change are preferable to artificial ones.

## Intergenerational Assessment and Intervention

A second dimension of the unit of attention to be assessed is the intergenerational family system. A skilled assessment of powerful intergenerational themes, patterns, and adaptive modes will shed light on the current family's functioning and will surface potential targets and resources for change. Careful intergenerational assessment is based on the conviction that family beliefs and actions and how the family perceives itself and each of its members, emerges to a significant extent from intergenerational family experiences and the ways the family has organized around such experiences (Bowen, 1978). Families are, of course, embedded in and affected by the larger culture as well, but they also develop their own unique styles and cultures and ways of seeing themselves and themselves in relation to the world around them. Reiss (1981) has termed this set of traditions, beliefs, and prescriptions for behavior that develops over the generations and profoundly affects the lives of all family members the "family paradigm." The family's meaning and belief system and prescriptions for behavior, transmitted most powerfully through the family's language, stories, myths, and rituals, guide such life choices as occupations, important identifications, values, choices of mate, and so on.

Intergenerational traditions and earlier events may also underlie destructive behaviors in the current generation. The abuse of a young girl by her mother, for example, may be directly related to the abuse suffered by the mother in her own childhood or to intense unresolved anger in the mother's relationship with one of her siblings which is in turn projected on to a particular child who may be in the same sibling position in this generation, or may remind the mother of the earlier relationship. Possibly, the abuse or neglect of a child may serve as the family's solution to another potentially more dangerous or anxiety-provoking situation, as in the following illustration.

> The custody of Stephanie, age 5, had been awarded to her maternal grandmother Pamela, age 48, a year prior to this incident. Diana, Pamela's daughter and the mother of Stephanie, depressed, unsettled, and involved in drug use, was judged by the court to have given Stephanie improper supervision, on two occasions leaving her in the care of an emotionally disturbed teenage baby-sitter who had molested her. Pamela had not allowed her daughter to see Stephanie for several months, and the conflict among family members was escalating.
>
> A careful assessment of current family relationships, several interviews with the three generations of females (Diana was unmarried and her father, Pamela's husband, had committed suicide many years earlier), supplemented by an intergenerational study of the family, led to a surprising hypothesis. Noting, among other things, the underlying care and concern of Diana for her mother, the worker began to suspect that Diana, although not herself aware of it, had engineered the placement of Stephanie with the grandmother, who had presented repeated suicidal behavior throughout her lifetime, in order to keep her busy and involved with life. The original neglect began to look more like a sacrificial relinquishing of a child to help keep a mother alive.
>
> In this family, in each of the five generations that could be traced, a central family member had committed suicide. Furthermore, there was a multigenerational tradition of grandparents or members of the grandparent generation caring for the grandchildren. Pamela had been cared for during extended periods of time by her own grandmother and a great aunt, and Diana had been cared for by her grandmother.
>
> The process of the intergenerational assessment, the worker's reconnecting of the generations, and the indirect surfacing, through metaphor and paradoxical injunction, of Stephanie's role in keeping Pamela from becoming depressed, led to the return of Stephanie to her mother's care. The worker continued to help the family discover and understand the factors maintaining the depression and the family's repetitive and dysfunctional intergenerational solutions.

An assessment tool useful in gathering this kind of detailed intergenerational data is the genogram, a genealogy or family tree which includes names and important dates, as well as a great deal of personal and social information. The construction and analysis of a genogram has been described in several publications (for example, Hartman, 1978; 1979a; Hartman and Laird, 1983). Familiarity with its use should form a part of every Child Welfare worker's repertoire of tools. With training and experience in the use of this tool, the worker can become skilled at searching for and identifying consistent family themes and patterns, unresolved losses, cut-offs, intergenerational conflicts, invisible loyalties, and unpaid intergenerational debts that may interfere with current family functioning.

A significant loss, unresolved through moves, death, or emotional cut-offs that occurs as the result of old feuds or misunderstandings, for example, may contribute to a mother's sadness and emotional unavailability to an infant. Or the powerful identification of self, spouse, or child with an earlier family figure can play a central role in current family dysfunction as the earlier unresolved feelings are projected on to family members, and old issues or patterns are played out in present relationships. Just as some people, overburdened and guilt-ridden, believe they must make important sacrifices to help pay for a past generation's losses or burdens, so some parents, as children powerless and unable to express their anger at maltreating or unloving parents, may "pay back" or settle unpaid intergenerational debts by projecting the unresolved feelings on to their own child or children. These "invisible loyalties" and unpaid intergenerational debts, as they have been termed by Boszormenyi-Nagy and Spark (1973), may result in the parents' inability to differentiate adequately between their experiences as parents and those as children, reacting inappropriately in current family relationships and even scapegoating or abusing a particular child.

The central goal in multigenerational assessment is to objectify the intergenerational system of family projections, identifications, relationships, experiences, events, and prescriptions for behavior which are influencing family functioning. Most salient are the experiences each parent had in his or her family of origin, the roles occupied, the identifications *their* parents held for them, and how each parent participated in family triangles and conflicts. The genogram helps organize an enormous amount of complex data in a way that makes it possible for important patterns and themes to become visible.

The assessment process, reiterating a point made earlier in relation to ecological assessment, is a shared one between worker and family, since the responsibility for seeking information and for carrying out planned change belongs to family members. The worker in this process is seen as a "coach" or an expert on families. Assessment itself can lead to important change. In the process of gathering information, a parent may be helped to bridge an old and unnecessary cut-off, may learn that a current feeling or behavior is linked to an old and no longer functional family prescription or experience, freeing it from current realities, or may redirect frustration and anger to its original source, opening up new opportunities for resolution. This latter point is illustrated in the following example.

## The Davis Family

The Davis family was referred to Children's Services by the school, because of ten-year-old Robert's angry, hostile, destructive, and bizarre behavior in school. Robert's communications with the teacher were often highly sexualized and seductive, raising concern that the young boy was being inappropriately exposed to sexual activity or might have been sexually abused.

Intergenerational study revealed that Mrs. Davis, the oldest daughter in a family of eight children, had been a parental child, able to gain her mother's love and approval only through her own "mothering" of her younger siblings. An assessment of the current living pattern revealed that she had very little patience with her three children and actually spent as little time as possible with them. Her daily routine consisted of sending the children off to school, cleaning the house briefly, and then heading to her mother's home to visit and help her mother with her chores. She would often remain there until it was time to leave for work at her 4:00 to 12:00 P.M. job, thus seeing her own children only briefly at breakfast.

The worker's hypothesis was that Robert's behavior was directed at attracting his mother's involvement, since she would be called at work and asked to come to the school to collect Robert, who had become unmanageable. The care of the children was left almost entirely to Mr. Hart, Mrs. Davis's live-in partner of many years. Mr. Hart was an unemployed, isolated, dependent, and depressed man who was known to drink heavily but who was considered "sweet" with the children. The children had not been told that this partner was not their biological father, adding to the confusion, secretiveness, and strain in the household. As had been speculated, further assessment revealed that Mr. Hart had indeed involved Robert in sexual activity with him consistently over a period of some three years.

The worker intervened in a number of directions, seeing different subgroups of family members, the living together couple, the entire family, mother and children, and various individuals. She helped Mrs. Davis to reexamine her relationship with her mother, the loss of her own childhood, and her tendency to abrogate her own autonomy in order to gain approval in the relationship with her mother. Initially very angry with her mother, she gradually began to examine her mother's life and to understand how things had happened the way they had, which in turn helped her to begin to differentiate. She began to discover that she had relinquished responsibility for the care of her children, just as had her mother before her.

Mrs. Davis separated from Mr. Hart after reaching the conclusion that she had stayed with him more for convenience than caring. She changed her working hours on the job, and with the worker's help, arranged a combination of parental and supplemental care that better met the children's needs, but also allowed her some respite from the demands of parenting. During the entire time the worker coached and supported her as she struggled to redefine her relationship with her mother, and held several meetings with daughter and mother, as well as two with some of Mrs. Davis's siblings, as this family was restructured and some of the old relationships and expectations altered.

The goal of change, in Bowen's (1978) view, is for each individual to achieve a higher level of differentiation, in negotiating new ways of being with and communicating with each key member of the extended family. Clients are helped to change their *own* behavior with the real life figures; that is, change does not depend on insight developed through the medium of a therapeutic relationship but on altered experiences in real life. The assumption is that as people become more differentiated from their families of origin, they will also become more differentiated and less emotionally reactive in their current love, play, and work relationships.

The worker may call on a range of strategies to help parents deal with unresolved intergenerational issues and to free themselves from dysfunctional prescriptions and patterns. Parents are urged to seek contact through visits, letters, or telephone calls with relatives from whom they have been distant or cut off. Many parents are caught in intense triangles in their families of origin and tend to repeat such triangling in their own families. Parents can be helped to plan detriangulation maneuvers, to alter uncomfortable and dysfunctional roles and behaviors, and to try new ways of communicating in situations which are repeatedly stressful. The worker can also attempt to widen the context for work, as was illustrated in both cases described above. In such efforts the worker needs to be skilled, flexible, and open enough to include all significant family figures in the interview and change process. For example, older generation figures such as grandparents, uncles, or aunts, live-in partners, or other parental figures may be contributing to the difficulties, may be able to add different perceptions, thus enhancing the assessment process, and may themselves be important resources for change. Our experience has been, that as the context is widened and people begin to deal *in vivo* with those events and figures that have influenced current intense feelings and adaptive modes including the abuse of children, the conflict is redirected appropriately and the current danger to children greatly diminished.

## Inside the Family: Assessment and Intervention

The third and final dimension of assessment and intervention is the family itself, a group of individuals that shares a history and is bound together in an intricate system of relationships, rules, and other patterns of behavior. It is a complex system with emergent qualities, that is, it is something greater than the sum of its individual parts. Thus we need tools for assessment and strategies for change that address patterns and relationships rather than individual characteristics.

Five major aspects of the family should be examined in family assessment. They are: (1) *family structure,* including the family's external boundaries and how it deals with issues of separateness and togetherness in individual–family relationships; (2) *family organization,* including the nature of the internal boundaries, the central triangles, and the formal and informal roles various members assume; (3) *family processes,* including the central adaptive and regulating forces, or the family rules which regulate communication modes and processes and the allocation of power and authority. As part of family process, an effort also should be made to discover the family's "meta" rules, that is the rules about the development, maintenance, and alteration of the family's rule system itself; (4) *family sociocultural themes and values;* and (5) the *family's system of meaning* and its construction of reality.

Prevailing theories concerning these dimensions of the family were described in Chapter 7 and thus it is assumed that the reader is familiar with them. Our purpose here is to apply these concepts to practice with families in Child Welfare.

### Tools for Family System Assessment

The best assessment tools for understanding how a family is structured and regulates itself are the worker's own skills at observing and interviewing families in action. Section IV of Exhibit 15–1, "Outline for Family Assessment," can help the worker formulate ideas and questions, and organize the data into working hypotheses.

The worker begins the contact with a tentative hypothesis, based on the information gained about the family from the referral, initial telephone contacts, or any other data that may be available. The beginning hypothesis, which develops out of the available information and the worker's knowledge about family systems, is a flexible working tool to help give direction to the worker's explorations and observations. The hypothesis should be systemic, that is, it should attempt to account for each family member's role in the problem as well as a hunch about the process as a whole, and the worker should be ready to modify it as new data emerges.

The family-centered worker's central task is to help the family redefine or reframe the problem as one that involves and concerns the entire family and one that requires the entire family's help and participation to resolve. This redefinitional and broadening process is often enormously relieving to a family, which has usually defined the problem in individual terms, blaming the troubles on a "bad child", a "sick mother," a "violent father," or a "nosy neighbor." Reframing the problem challenges the family's often dysfunctional perception of events and offers a context for new understanding and altered behavior.

The worker needs to communicate very firmly that all of the involved and responsible adults in the household must participate, challenging any efforts the family may make to leave out an important member such as a live-in partner or a powerful grandmother. Of course the worker needs to be flexible enough in terms of schedule to arrange times for meetings when all household members can be present. While later interviews may be scheduled with various subgroups of the family, in the beginning it is important to gain everyone's participation and every member's view of the problem and of the family.

Family interviewing is quite different from individual interviewing. Most workers have been trained to explore individual feelings and thoughts and to assess individual attributes and behavior. The focus, in family assessment, is on tracking family interactional, communication, and relationship patterns, and in encouraging the emergence of the family's structure, its ways of organizing, and its world view—that is, the ways it understands itself and its relationship with the world around it. Questions are often asked indirectly or metaphorically, in ways that will help the family structure and its system of rules to emerge from the data (Hartman and Laird, 1983; Selvini-Palazzoli, et al., 1980; Papp, 1980).

In addition to tracing interactions, sequences, and patterns, the worker may also learn about the family's world view, its paradigm, by listening to the family's special metaphoric language and observing its use of important symbols or attachment to special objects. The family should be encouraged to share its favorite stories, which can reveal multiple dimensions of family life, including its charters for belief and behavior, as well as any major myths that may be influencing family functioning (Laird and Hartman, 1984). The worker should also carefully explore the family's important daily and special rituals, for it is during these times that the family most vividly exposes its system of beliefs and the rules that regulate interactions and behavior.

Observing nonverbal and paralingual family communication and movement is also an important tool in family assessment (Watzlawick, Beavin, and Jackson, 1967). How the family monitors access to and egress from its territory, how family members use and move in space and in relation to each other, how they attend and respond to each others' communications and movements, are valuable parts of data collection, particularly in helping the worker understand how dysfunctional, rigid behavior is maintained. It is particularly helpful if Child Welfare workers can work in teams, allowing one worker to take major responsibility for interviewing the family, while the other is freer to observe interactions and to look for overarching family patterns.

As part of the assessment process, the worker may also wish to interview other important figures in the family's life space, such as a teacher, neighbor, extended family member, or a court worker. Whenever possible, these people should be interviewed with the family. This kind of openness and sharing not only demonstrates respect for the family, but it also avoids misunderstandings, secretiveness, and conflicting agendas or goals. Also, it mobilizes the help of all concerned in the service of change.

Family mapping, a tool pioneered by Minuchin (1974) and adapted by others (e.g., Hartman and Laird, 1983), is a way of depicting family relationships, coalitions, boundaries, and other patterns. The use of family sculpture or choreography (Duhl, Kantor, and Duhl, 1973; Papp, 1976a; 1976b), either with the family itself or in consultation and supervision with colleagues, can quickly and dramatically reveal the family's structure and its system of emotional relationships. Family mapping and family sculpture are assessment strategies that, like the eco-map and genogram, involve the entire family in a shared assessment process and help them to experience and perceive themselves in new ways. They can highlight, in ways that are nonthreatening, particular patterns or relationships that maintain dysfunctional coping strategies.

The worker, with the help of the assessment tools described, organizes the data in ways that can provide systemic explanations for the family's behavior as a whole and the roles each family member is playing in the maladaptive or dysfunctional processes. It should be pointed out that all of these assessment tools are also intervention tools. For example, as the worker interviews relationally and systematically, the problem automatically becomes reframed or redefined from an individual one. The context is widened and the search for blame and self-blame interrupted, as the family's view of reality is altered. In family sculpting, for example, the family often experiences its own emotional system in a new and very powerful way, thus stimulating and even providing a blueprint for change. In the telling of a family story, a pervasive and dysfunctional family myth may be revealed and thus become available for some kind of modification.

## Families in the Child Welfare System

Families that come to the attention of the Child Welfare system are, for the most part, like all families, except that more of them are poor. They come from a variety of ethnic and socioeconomic backgrounds and present a wide range of needs, problems, and symptomatic behaviors.

It should be strongly emphasized that families also vary widely in terms of their structures and organizations, in their beliefs, in their lifestyles and styles of communicating, and in how they handle issues such as separateness, protection of territory and use of space, and role assignments. None of these dimensions is in itself functional or dysfunctional. Family patterns are strongly influenced by cultural and historical factors so that, for example, what seem like conflicted, chaotic, enmeshed family relationships to a middle-class WASP worker may be quite "normal" in an Italian or Jewish family, while the more isolated nuclearity of the middle-class white family may seem dysfunctional to a black worker from a large, close, extended family. Clearly the worker's own ethnic and socioeconomic background, as well as his or her family experiences and idealized notions of how families ought to be, influence perceptions and assessment. The worker is further influenced by the community's norms as they are expressed in agency and judicial criteria for family functioning. Thus it is crucial that the worker be aware of and take into account these influences in the effort to evaluate the safety and well-being of children in families that may be quite "different."

Many of the families referred for various types of child neglect and abuse are overstressed, overburdened and have become disorganized or what Aponte (1976b) has termed "underorganized." In some cases they are very poor and in some isolated and cut off from their roots as a result of relocation or migration, often located in unfriendly or alienating surroundings. In other cases, anomie has led to apathy, depression, the overuse of alcohol and drugs, or other adaptive responses that result in the neglect of children (Polansky, Borgman, and DeSaix, 1972). The underorganized family lacks coherence as a family unit. The use of time and space may be random, with few of the rituals or rules for behavior that help order daily life and define "familiness." For example, some families may lack consistent rules about times for sleeping or eating, for attending school or doing school work, for completing household tasks, or for managing family–environment connections. Many underorganized families lack clear boundaries among various subsystems, so that, for example, children may assume roles more appropriately performed by adults and be expected to meet the emotional needs of adults, while adults may lack clarity about who is in charge, feeling helpless and out of control.

As Shapiro points out in Exemplar IV–D, underorganization does not necessarily imply lack of caring; a high level of affection may exist in such families. If a child is abused, it is often directly related to stress or frustration, rather than to the family's need to scapegoat a particular child. In some underorganized families, however, individual members may be highly alienated. There may be little response to the emotional or physical needs of family members, and little empathy or meaningful communication. In these families, which Minuchin (1974) has termed "disengaged," all but the most dramatic bids for attention or help may be ignored.

In some families referred for protective services, particularly families in which one child is symptomatic or is being scapegoated and abused, the family may be rigidly organized, with very closed boundaries. In the highly enmeshed family, it may be that the child's disturbance or the abusive behavior is providing a dysfunctional solution to other problems in the family, the recognition and expression of which would be threatening or even terrifying. Often the situation that is most threatening is a deep but unexpressed level of disappointment in the marriage, combined with a fear of marital dissolution. In some cases a wife, for example, may fear separating from an abusive husband, because she has few resources or is afraid to be alone. In some situations, the marriage may protect her from a worse danger, the return to or reliance on a fusing, critical, or abusive parent. The scapegoated or abused child, defined as the family problem, becomes the target of tensions and siphons off the unacknowledged and unresolved conflicts in the marriage, in the family's relationships with the world, or in intergenerational relationships and experiences. The scapegoating or abuse pattern is maintained by an elaborate system of rigidly adhered to rules for behavior—rules which are usually unspoken and cannot be commented on by the child (Bermann, 1973; Spiegel, 1957). Removal of the child usually does not resolve the issue, since the family is likely then to induct another child into the same role.

## The Family Unit as Target and Resource for Change

Before turning to a case illustration that exemplifies family-centered work in the Child Welfare system, a sampling of change strategies that may be used in strengthening or altering aspects of the family structure, or in helping the family begin to change rigid, dysfunctional patterns, will be described.

One assumption that underpins these approaches to change is that life experience is the most powerful instrument of change. The worker's role, in many change efforts, is to provide a context within which the family can have a different experience, and to engage the family, either in the family meetings or through assignments and directives, in experimenting with new ways of doing, being, thinking, and relating to each other. The fact that much of the work with families in the Child Welfare system is done in the family's home enhances the worker's potential for using actual experience for change.

The assessment process provides the worker with a blueprint of what shifts might be helpful in the family. Perhaps the boundaries between the adults and the children need clarifying or strengthening or perhaps the children in a single-parent family have taken control of the household, and the authority and skill of the single parent needs to be enhanced. Perhaps there is growing alienation between a son and his father, resulting in abuse by the father, as a result of the son being pulled into the marital conflict as his mother's confidante and support. Or, perhaps the family is chaotic or underorganized and needs help in ordering its use of time and space and establishing coherence.

The worker may help the family address these issues during the home visit or in an office interview. An atmosphere is provided in which the family can talk together about their concerns and the worker can act as a consultant in problem-solving efforts. Possibly, the worker may direct the family to make a structural alteration during the session in an "enactment" (Minuchin, 1974) which helps them experience themselves as a family in a different way. For example, in an enmeshed family the worker may begin to construct clearer generational boundaries by separating the children and the parents, giving each subsystem a task to work on, and intervening when necessary to block family members' efforts to cross the boundaries. A role play or family sculpture may be used to help the family experience the emotional system differently or to practice a new way of handling a troublesome interaction or situation.

The structured use of space and time is an important aspect of family life, and the worker may help the family examine and alter the ways they deal with these two dimensions. For example, in underorganized families, when a child is hungry, instead of participating in a planned or regular meal, he may go to the cupboard or refrigerator or to the corner store, snacking anytime and anyplace.When he is tired, he may curl up anywhere and sleep, rather than having a consistent time or space for napping and bedtime. Children from such families are often poorly nourished, tired, and inattentive in school. Over a period of time, the worker, through discussion in the session and through the giving of assignments, helps the family begin to bring more order and coherence into their lives.

Although family meetings with the worker may begin a change process, it is essential to follow up these beginnings with assignments and directives that carry the change into the days and weeks between family interviews. Family assignments are not simple "suggestions" or "advice," rather they are behaviorally specific enactments to be carried out at specific times in particular ways. These enactments give the family an opportunity to experience and to practice change.

Directives should be given in a ceremonial manner, with great seriousness and with every detail of the assignment carefully spelled out. They should be appropriate to the lifestyle of the family and should not tax its resources. Every member of the family should be included in an assignment. For example, if the assignment involves the father and mother doing something alone together, the children, the grandmother, or other members of the unit should be given tasks that support the central purpose of the assignment, even if one's job is to "stay out."

Recently, some family therapists have made increased use of rituals in their work with families as there has been a growing awareness of the functions rituals perform in family life. Rituals enact and transmit family values, rules, and structure; they help the family achieve and maintain coherence and synchrony as they provide the template for the patterned ways that family members come together and perform certain tasks. Rituals also enact transitions in family life, helping families to experience and integrate major changes such as marriage, birth, death, or the leaving home of the last child (Laird, 1984).

Underorganized families can also be understood as underritualized families. Family cohesion and coherence are not choreographed sufficiently through ritual, as individual family members "do their own thing," the family's organization is random, and its sense of itself as a unit with pride, tradition, and a clear system of values and meaning, is poorly defined. A powerful and useful strategy for developing order in a chaotic family is to help the members, step by step, begin to build new family rituals. A Sunday dinner or a "going to bed" ritual, for example, can provide a beginning. It is important to reach back with the parents to rituals or components of rituals that had meaning in their own growing-up and to fashion new enactments that are connected in some way to the experiences in the family of origin. This leads to continuity not only within the family week by week, but also across generations.

Rigid, stuck, overritualized families also may come to the attention of the Child Welfare worker. In such families, rituals are utilized to control and to suppress feelings and avoid change. Families organized around destructive ritual enactments—such as ritualized child abuse or substance abuse—may also be seen. Families will generally be unable to give up these destructive rituals because, as oppressive or destructive as they may seem to the outsider, they may be the glue that holds a fragile family together. It is important to help such families replace these destructive rituals with others that can serve some of the same cohesive functions.

Many families seen in the Child Welfare system may be termed "unmotivated" or "resistant." Some of this resistance may be the product of fear and distrust of the system the worker represents. Through slow and careful building of relationships, trust may be enhanced and with it the family's ability to join the worker in seeking change.

However, for other families, it is the prospect of change itself that is frightening. The abberant behavior is integral to the maintenance of the family system and any expectation that the behavior be changed is a threat to the family's coherence and stability. Hoffman (1981) refers to such families not as "resistant" but as "persistent." Hoffman, Selvini-Palazzoli et al. (1978), and other family therapists have taught us that challenging such families frightens them, hardens their position, and drives them away. Throughout contact with the family it is essential to recognize and support the family's efforts to survive, to be on the side of the family's coherence, and to join the resistance—or, more accurately—the persistence.

With these families, it is essential to come to understand how the seemingly problematic behavior is not the problem but the family's solution to another, more threatening, problem. A young mother's helplessness and neglect of her child for example, may be a way of keeping her mother, the grandmother, involved with her. An incestuous relationship between a father and daughter may be sustaining an otherwise untenable marriage. A twelve-year-old boy's delinquency may be keeping his mother, who is becoming restless and spending increasing amounts of time away from home, close to home and distracted from other pursuits.

Intervention is tailored to the function of the problematic behavior and the intensity and rigidity of the family's "persistence." For example, when the problematic behavior is the abuse of one child, in some less rigid situations the family may be led carefully and gently to identify and work on the underlying issues, as the problem is reframed from one that centers around a "bad," "sick," or "out-of-control" child to one that concerns a family trying to maintain itself.

In one situation involving two young girls who were truant and labeled "school phobic," most of the teachers and others who were trying to help the family had been trying to convince the mother to stop holding her daughters so close. The Child Welfare worker, who hypothesized that the children were afraid for their mother's well-being and were staying home to keep her safe, made an immediate relationship with this very resistant family when she joined the family's world view by commenting very positively on what a close and caring family they were. "Going with the persistence," the worker designed a series of interventions and assignments that prescribed closeness and security. She made arrangements with the school that allowed the daughters to call home several times a day and the mother to visit the school each day. As the worker helped mother come to terms with her divorce and with her plans for the future, the daughters' attendance increased remarkably and they soon abandoned the daily calls and visits.

In other more rigid situations, more powerful interventions, such as the use of paradox or of judicial authority, may be needed. In some cases the worker may be able to ready the family for a referral for family therapy and in others, those families most resistant to change, a child may need at least temporary removal for protective purposes while the family's openness to change is tested further. No matter what the intervention, change efforts must be made with the recognition and support of the importance of the family and its effort to survive.

Although three dimensions of work with families have been presented separately, in actual case practice a single family situation may well involve intervention into the family–environment relationship, the intergenerational family system, and the current family unit, as the following case demonstrates.

## The Marino Family

This case illustrates the placement of an abused child with extended kin and work with both nuclear and extended family toward the return home of the child. The worker in this case had no in-service family training, but had attended a family workshop and done some study on her own. She was convinced that even the most difficult families might be helped to stay together. The case is presented here because the circumstances under which the worker tried to help this family are typical of those faced by most Child Welfare workers in public agencies. The case, which had a surprisingly favorable outcome in spite of many obstacles, demonstrates the complexities, but also the advantages, in choosing the rocky road of placing a child in a highly conflicted, but caring, extended family situation.

> The Marino case was opened in Protective Services after Eddie Marino, age 24, called to express his concern about his son Jeffrey, age 5 months, who had been hospitalized the night before with severe burns over the bottom half of his body. Jeffrey had been scalded while being given his bath, but Eddie hastened to assure the worker that he felt certain his wife had not

intentionally hurt the child. He further indicated he had been separated from his wife since before Jeffrey's birth, had another child Allison, age 2½, and was not supporting the family. He said he had just gotten back into town two weeks ago, has a new job, and plans to meet his responsibilities. Eddie volunteered considerable information about his wife and his wife's family's behavior during this initial call, but little about himself or his family. Following this telephone intake, the worker called the hospital, learning that the child might not survive and that the hospital was planning to refer the case as suspected child abuse.

The Protective Services worker was involved with the Marino family for approximately two years. In the initial stages, efforts were concentrated on assessing the family and the context in which the tragic event had occurred, the first concern being the safety of the little girl. Later phases of the case included making a feasible and acceptable plan for substitute care for Jeffrey, continuing work directed toward the return of the child, and after the child's return home, intervention to help monitor and stabilize the reunited family.

## Family Assessment

The abuse of Jeffrey can be understood as the culmination of a number of variables on many levels. The clearest precipitant was Eddie's abandonment of his wife, Julie, one week before Jeffrey's birth. Eddie, who had been involved in an extramarital relationship throughout the pregnancy, left with "the other woman." Julie described her terrible rage, loneliness, and sense of hopelessness as she gave birth to Jeffrey. Her own family, offering little emotional support or concrete help, reinforced the theme: "That S.O.B. left you to take care of his brat. We told you that you were crazy to marry him in the first place. Well, you made your bed, now lie in it!" During the next few months, Eddie occasionally called Julie, stimulating her hopes that he might come back, berating her for what a poor wife she had been, while she in turn would try to convince him she had changed. Eddie finally promised to come see Julie and the children on a Thursday morning three days before the scalding. Julie waited all day and evening, growing more anxious and agitated by the moment, calling everyone she knew to try to locate him. He finally called late Thursday night to say he hadn't been able to come over that day but thought he would come on Sunday. On Sunday the pattern was repeated. Around 6:00 P.M., Julie later indicated, by this time sobbing and desperate, she rushed to answer the telephone, leaving Jeffrey in the bathroom sink where she had been giving him his bath. She said that he managed to turn on the hot water tap, and by the time she got to him he was badly burned. She then sought the help of a neighbor (Julie had no transportation), the neighbor applied ice packs and rushed mother and child to the hospital.

Based on many conversations with Julie, the extensiveness of the injuries, and an inspection of the sink itself, the worker did not think that this explanation could have been totally accurate. The severity of the burns, the unlikelihood the baby could have activated the tap, and Julie's own detachment from any feelings of distress or concern about the child himself during this period, led the worker to believe the incident could not be described as "accidental" and that Jeffrey's life, should he return home, might continue to be in danger. An early decision was made to make the child a temporary ward of the county until a more complete picture could be obtained.

As more information was collected from a variety of sources, both parents, both families of origin, neighbors in Mrs. Marino's building, and from the worker's observations, a number of hypotheses emerged. First, the young couple was quite socially isolated, even before Eddie's departure. They had few friends, few interests, marginal exchanges with neighbors, and limited financial resources, since Eddie's job as a store clerk was low-paying. While Eddie's family was a source of frequent help and Julie had been leaning heavily on her mother-in-law for advice and support, the couple was quite cut off from Julie's parents, whom Eddie defined as "crazy and violent."

After Eddie left town, Julie applied for financial assistance. However, feeling angry and deprived, and with little experience in budgeting, which Eddie had handled, she quickly accumulated a number of bills and spent her first assistance check on new living-room furniture. Without adequate funds to meet her needs, she appealed with little success to her own family and soon discovered that Eddie's family, whom she was pressing for information about Eddie, was avoiding her. The withdrawal of this vital resource, who were themselves caught in a loyalty conflict, and the lack of supportive emotional and financial sources of help in the environment, intensified the steady move toward a total breakdown of this increasingly fragile and vulnerable family unit. (See Figure 15–2.)

The worker learned little about the families of origin themselves or significant intergenerational patterns in part because of the constant daily crises and because of her own lack of family training. It did seem clear, however, that Julie's relationship with her abusive and violent father had been a highly conflicted, ambivalent one, and perhaps an additional source for her anger toward her own male child. Her mother, said to have been hospitalized "for mental problems" on several occasions, was described as passive, withdrawn, and not someone on whom Julie felt she could rely. The worker was unsuccessful in her efforts to encourage Julie's family to participate in the planning and limited herself to coaching Julie to learn how to take a more independent stance in dealing with her father's verbal abuse and in trying new ways of seeking their help and support.

The marriage itself had been a source of constant mutual disappointment and conflict. Eddie described Julie as dependent, clinging, depressed, and

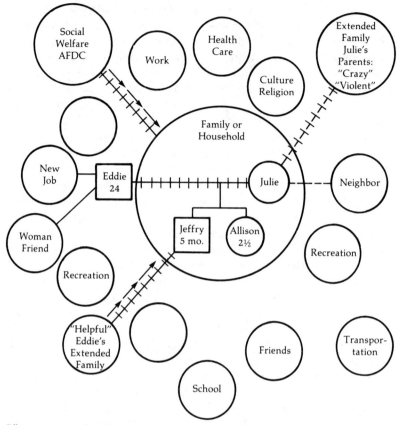

Fill in connections where they exist.
Indicate nature of connections with a descriptive word or by drawing different kinds of lines:
─────── for strong ─────── for tenuous ++++++++++ for stressful.
Draw arrows along lines to signify flow of energy, resources, etc. ─→ ─→ ─→
Identify significant people and fill in empty circles as needed.

**Figure 15–2** Eco-Map of Marino Family at Time of Abuse. This clearly demonstrates the isolation and stress the family was experiencing and points the way to change.

The basic eco-map diagram for this illustration is reproduced by permission of the copyright holder from Ann Hartman's article "Diagrammatic Assessment of Family Relationships" in *Social Casework* (Oct. 1978); copyright © 1978 by the publisher, Family Service America (New York).

often unable to care adequately for the home and children. He said almost all of the responsibility fell on his shoulders and when he would complain, Julie on occasion threatened to kill herself and the children. She, on the other hand, described him as dictatorial, remote, and distancing in the relationship. Both seemed to agree that it was Julie who was the unstable, underfunctioning half of the pair. When he left, Julie felt tremendous panic. During the first interview with the worker, which took place in the hospital, Julie seemed obsessed with how she might get Eddie to come back to her, and alternated between angrily and hostilely attacking the worker and appealing for her help in convincing Eddie to return.

The worker's impressions of the marriage were based on what she could distill from the participants' reactive and biased views, since she never saw the couple together. In observing Julie with the little daughter, the worker concluded that Allison was in no physical danger because she was not the threat of her mother's unresolved and conflicted rage, although it was obvious that parent–child boundaries were extremely unclear. Julie's expectations for the behavior of a 2½ year old were unrealistic, as were her needs for emotional gratification from Allison. For example, Julie interpreted Allison's constant whining, clinging behavior as a demonstration of Allison's love for her, instead of a manifestation of her own failure to attend to the child. (See Figure 15–3.)

## Intervention with the Marino Family System

The worker, confronted with the obvious need for multiple interventions on many levels, nevertheless maintained her conviction that there was a

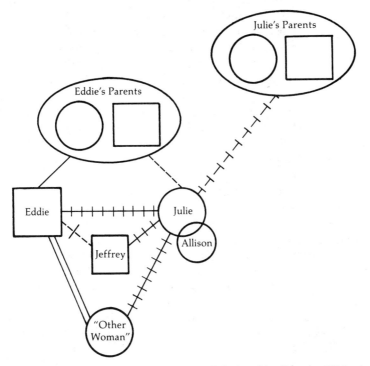

**Figure 15–3** Map of Marino Family as a Relationship System. This demonstrates the major triangles, fusion, and emotional distance in the family.

chance this child might be returned to the young couple, or if not to both, at least to one parent. As it drew close to the time that Jeffrey might be released from the hospital, a decision had to be made concerning his placement. The worker did not believe that the issues which had triggered the abuse in the first place had been sufficiently resolved to risk returning Jeffrey to either parent. Further, Jeffrey would be in need of very special care, requiring visits to the doctor each week, and several "at home" exercising sessions each day. These sessions, extremely painful for the child, were necessary so that the burned tissue could heal and stretch and his legs develop normally. The worker knew that whoever cared for Jeffrey had to be able to devote extraordinary time and emotional energy to him. She had met Eddie's parents on several occasions and, whatever else their conflicts or difficulties, they seemed to be concerned and loving grandparents. They had repeatedly visited the hospital, checked on Jeffrey's progress, and after a time had even somewhat healed the rift with Julie.

Julie, although still hurt by what she experienced as their abandonment of her, was now talking to them and allowing them to take Allison on occasion. Although her supervisor warned her against it, predicting it would create an "unbelievable hassle," the worker decided to explore the possibility of placing Jeffrey temporarily with the paternal grandparents who appeared to be the people in the situation with the most to offer the child. The various alternatives were first discussed with Julie, who agreed that she was not ready to assume care of Jeffrey herself. In suggesting Eddie's parents, the worker encouraged Julie to consider all of the reasons this placement could be extremely problematic and indeed wrenching for her. Her own parents would undoubtedly feel even more angry and competitive, and might conceivably cut her off further. She might feel extremely resentful at having to visit Jeffrey on her in-laws' turf. And she was still angry about the fact they continued to tell her they did not know where Eddie was or give her any information. After several discussions, Julie decided upon and indeed argued for that plan, probably because at least in part this insured her own continued contact with her in-laws who had become so important to her, and through them, some continued hope of contact with Eddie. She also had few illusions about her own ability to take care of Jeffrey during this period and knew her mother-in-law's strengths.

Several interviews were held simultaneously with the older Mr. and Mrs. Marino, going over the same issues. In addition to the potential for conflict, it was also foreseen that they might have difficulty in later relinquishing Jeffrey or concurring with the agency's decision around permanent planning and custody. They too felt ready to take the risk. The worker was unsuccessful at involving either Julie's family or Eddie in the decision-making process, but Julie herself took a stand with her family concerning the proposal, describing her reasons for consenting to the placement.

The supervisor's prediction that the placement with the grandparents would be a "hassle" turned out to be an understatement! Family rivalries and loyalty conflicts activated a series of interlocking and highly stressful triangles. Julie felt caught between her parents and her in-laws. The in-laws were caught between Julie and Eddie. The worker was constantly being called upon to take sides as the various players in the complex family game attempted to triangulate her. However, as she refused to be triangled, maintaining open and direct communication with all those involved, and held several problem-solving sessions including Julie and her in-laws, the tension in the system began to be reduced.

Jeffrey's progress in the grandparents' home surpassed everyone's expectations. It had originally been feared he might not walk, but by his first birthday he was taking a few steps. The placement had unanticipated consequences for Julie's adaptation to the dissolution of the marriage and her own emotional adjustment. Neglected and emotionally deprived in her own disturbed family of origin, her relationship with her in-laws had been extremely important during her marriage, and she saw the elder Mrs. Marino as a positive maternal figure. The abandonment by her husband represented a double loss, as she also felt again betrayed by parental figures.

A key element in the placement was Julie's right to visit, and the understanding that if possible she would resume care of Jeffrey after a period of time. This process was not without its crises and conflicts, but its positive results were significant. Much of Julie's bitterness dissipated as she was able, on somewhat changed terms, to establish a workable relationship with her in-laws, and to take a more adult stance in relation to her own parents who kept threatening her with isolation if she had any contact with the in-laws. She was gradually able to understand her own role in the marital conflict and family triangles. She could even accept Jeffrey's need to have a connection with his father.

Simultaneously with the extensive work in relation to the extended family, many other interventions were made aimed at ameliorating Julie's social isolation and discovering opportunities for Julie to enhance her competence and her self-worth. She obtained a part-time job selling cosmetics door to door which not only earned a little money but offered an opportunity for her to meet other women. She struck up a friendship with another single parent and the two shared an occasional meal and exchanged baby-sitting. This friend's accepting and easy going approach to her four-year-old child helped Julie revise her expectations of Allison.

Tension mounted considerably when plans began to be made for Jeffrey's return to his mother. The elder Marinos, although sad to see him go, were assured by Julie that they would continue to have a major part in his life—and in hers. Jeffrey moved home with ease, partly because he had never really been moved out of the family relationship system.

In conclusion, this chapter has stressed the importance of a family-centered perspective in work with biological families in Child Welfare. Workers need to be given the training and the resources that will help them preserve the vitality, strength, and cohesion of the biological family and to avoid, wherever possible, major cut-offs and disruptions in the family relationship system.

# CHAPTER 16

# Supplemental Services for Families and Children

Nancy Day Robinson

The home and the family are venerated in the United States, but more public funds have always been directed into out of home care than to care to keep families intact in their own homes. The thrust of recent federal legislation and the principles embodied in permanency planning present an attempt to reverse this traditional position. Increasing emphasis has been placed on the maintenance of children in their own homes and on the enhancement of family functioning. This chapter presents an overview of the major kinds of child-care services that supplement and support rather than substitute for the family. Primary emphasis will be placed on the two most extensive programs, homemaker–home health aide services and day care. The chapter will include a discussion of some of the key practice and program issues and dilemmas in this field and will end with a brief discussion of developmental services which may enrich the lives of children while they remain in their own homes.

As will be seen, day care and homemaker–home health aide services have much in common besides their role in maintaining the family intact, since many aspects in the development of the services and in the issues around them are similar. In both services the role of the social worker involves working with professionals who are not social workers, and with paraprofessionals.

## Homemaker–Home Health Aide Services

Homemaker–home health aide services originally were developed to help families cope with problems caused by illness.[1] Such services were designed for children whose mothers could not care for them because of illness or delivery of a new baby, or to care for the children and the mother together. Organized homemaker programs probably date to the 1920's when the Jewish Welfare Society of Philadelphia and later the Jewish Home Finding Society in Chicago set up housekeeper programs to care for children who would otherwise be placed in institutions or foster homes (Morlock, 1964).

However, the service had begun to spring up by the 1890s in the United States and around the same time in several European countries. It is believed that as early as 1892 in New York City the Little Sisters of the Poor went out during the day to clean the house and help out in the homes of children whose mothers were incapacitated. They continue this practice to this day in some cities.[2] In 1903, the Family Service Bureau of the Association for the Improvement of the Condition of the Poor "employed four visiting cleaners who supplemented nurses' services in caring for sick mothers and their children" (*Homemaker Services in the United States*, 1959:1). Nearly a century later, it might be supposed that these happy beginnings of a practical service for which need is great, in a society which has built a great social and health structure, would have developed into a major resource for family and child care. Unfortunately, this is not the case.

A 1978 nationwide survey of public social services to children and their families showed that only 7 percent of the cases reported received homemaker service. Care outside the home, however, was reported used four times as often (Shyne and Schroeder, 1978a:4). In their work, researchers concluded that:

> The infrequent recommendation and use of homemaker service raises the question of whether the service is not available or its potential values are not recognized. Sending a trained homemaker into a household for any length of time may be expensive, but only relatively so as compared with any form of foster care for a sibling group. A good homemaker not only makes it possible to maintain children at home during a period of parental absence, incapacity, or stress, but provides a teacher and role model to family members in managing the household and caring for the children. This is a service that has never had strong support. The systems survey report quotes program staff as expressing "frustration at their inability to demonstrate, in cost-effective terms, the merit of using homemakers for child welfare purposes." (Ibid.: 153–154)

Homemaker–home health aide services have grown enormously in recent years, as indicated by data compiled by the National HomeCaring Council. In 1958 there were only 150 agencies known to have homemaker programs; 77 percent were in voluntary agencies, the remainder in public agencies. However, the provision of home health aide services under Medicare through Title XVIII of the Social Security Act stimulated an immediate and rapid growth of these services. In 1963, before Medicare, 303 units were identified, while in 1966, one year after Medicare, there were 759 units. By 1984 there were an estimated 8,000 units in the United States and Canada. Profit making agencies have mushroomed so rapidly that they may now provide more than half of existing homemaker–home health aide services. Moreover, there is a new kind of organization delivering this service, the private not-for-profit agency, which is not the traditional voluntary, community-organized agency. Again, it is not known how many of these exist. The staff members of such agencies are salaried and no profit is shown so that, although there may be personal gain for trustees and staff above reasonable and usual salaries and fringe benefits, they are categorized as private not-for-profit agencies (Etzioni and Doty, 1976).

The massive growth in homemaker–home health aide services, however, has had little impact on the welfare of children. The National HomeCaring Council estimates that 85 percent of the homemaker–home health aide services provided are to the elderly, while the remaining 15 percent are divided between families with children and disabled adults who are not elderly. For example, federal funding sources for homemaker–home health aide services are less often used for homemaker–home health aide services for children than for older persons. In July through September, 1979 homemaker services provided under social service funds were classified as to primary recipient: 6 percent to children, and 94 percent to adults; 14,915 children and 250,237 adults.[3] The actual percentage and numbers of children receiving service are somewhat higher, because if a sick parent is in the home, she or he might be classified as the "primary recipient;" moreover, some homemaker service to children is classified as protective services to children. Still, using the best data available in the country, we know that very little homemaker–home health aide service is provided to help children remain in their own homes. Only two of the 140 accredited and approved programs of the National HomeCaring Council provide homemaker–home health aide services only to families with children. More often programs provide services to adults only, and an agency providing service to both adults and children is likely to provide 80 percent or more of their services to elderly persons. Also, the imbalance in service appears to be increasing.

When staff members of the National HomeCaring Council were asked "Why is there money for homemaker–home health aide services to elderly people but not for children," a variety of responses were elicited:

"The elderly are the new power group."

"Children do not vote."

"We are in a period of reaction from the effects of the baby boom of the 1950s. Children are devalued because there are so many and they have recently been at the age of causing problems to society. People are almost afraid of them."

"We don't really value children in this society. Especially we haven't valued them in the past eight years."

One of the reasons clearly relates to the fact that money for health services, while inadequate, is more plentiful than money for social services for any age group. However, a great deal of money is poured into foster care, a system of care which is costly and which cannot take the place of a child's own family or own home. Moreover, any form of care in which a child is removed from home tends to become long-term, as a number of studies have shown (Burt and Blair, 1971; Fanshel and Shinn, 1972; 1978; Jenkins and Sauber, 1966). It is indeed puzzling and undoubtedly significant that our society has continued to support such a radical and complex solution as out-of-home care when families are unable to provide adequately for their children rather than the far less expensive and more conservative option of supplemental family services.

## The Uses of Homemaker–Home Health Aide Services for Families with Children

To use the available homemaker–home health aide service to best advantage, one should understand its uses, the role of the social worker in relation to the other persons involved in providing or receiving service, and the issues. One of the joys of using homemaker–home health aide service is that it is much more versatile and flexible than either foster or institutional care. If there is money to pay for it, it can be tailored to the needs of the family situation in complexity, intensity, and duration of service (Robinson et al., 1974:vi).

Complexity refers to the mix of homemaker–home health aide and professional services. In the simplest situations, the homemaker–home health aide may function as the only direct service provider, largely doing housework. In the most complicated situations, the aide may be a teaching homemaker who helps and shows how to manage a family and household while working with any set of direct service providers who may be on the team, such as the caseworker, public health nurse, home economist, nutritionist, visiting teacher (either instructor or social worker), occupational therapist, physical therapist, speech therapist, or physician.

Intensity refers to the number of days in the week and hours in a day that service is provided. Children who have a parent who is out of the home only for certain hours of the day do not need the 24-hour care they receive if placed in foster care. On the other hand, if they need 24-hour-a-day care seven days a week for a while, it can be provided through homemaker–home health care services.

Duration of care is defined as the length of time service is provided to a given family and can be as long or as short as needed, from one visit to months of care. Moving a child from home to another house or to an institution and back again is more cumbersome and complex from every perspective than leaving the child at home and having the homemaker–home health aide move in and out, which allows far more flexibility in terms of intensity and duration of service. Intensity, duration, and complexity can be varied for a family as its needs change, as well as it can be varied among families.

When is homemaker–home health aide service the appropriate care for families with children? The criteria are simple. (1) The children can be cared for safely at home. (2) It is believed that at least one family member will be able to care for them after an interval of homemaker–home health aide service. If these two conditions do not apply, placement outside the home is probably indicated.

In making the decision to utilize homemaker–home health aide services the social worker, who must consider cost as well as what is best for the child, may take into account the following:

—The number of children to be cared for. Homemaker–home health aide service becomes more cost-efficient as the number of children increases.
—The presence of a family member who can care for the children some of the time, usually in non-employment hours.
—The likelihood that the need for care will be of short-term duration. Although some communities are prepared to place a homemaker–home health aide in a home for years, they are few.
—The presence of a convalescent parent or other adult for whom the homemaker–home health aide prevents institutionalization or hospitalization as well as for the children.
—The number of possible disruptions, in addition to loss of the caretaking family and the familiar things and routines of home, to each child's life if placement out of the home occurs. Examples are change of school, change of companions, loss of contact with extended family and neighbors, and loss of contact with pets.

What are some of the situations in which a homemaker–home health aide can help families with children? Often the original stimulus for homemaker–home health aide services is the difficult birth of a new baby, which may keep the mother in bed up to two weeks. The home-maker can take care of the older children, the mother, and the new baby. Even now in some European countries a homemaker works with a new mother, helping her while she regains strength and showing her how to take care of the baby. In Finland, by policy, preventive services includ-ing homemaker–home health aide services are used frequently in mater-nal and infant care especially where there are problems with mother or baby. In this country this practice is infrequent. However, there is a beginning: Blue Cross and Blue Shield in Rochester, New York, to re-duce hospital costs, have set up "a bridge between home delivery and the safety of a hospital delivery." Three days of homemaker service, daily visits by a community health nurse, and laboratory services are provided to mothers who are discharged from the hospital within twen-ty-four hours after a normal delivery (Blue Cross, 1981:1).

The hospitalization of the caretaking parent for physical illness or for mental illness may precipitate homemaker–home health aide ser-vice. Homemaker–home health aide care for pregnant mothers at risk, such as diabetics, who must have bed rest during the last trimester, and for their families, to keep the family together during this time, has been suggested. A demonstration project for this use of the service is needed to document the outcome to the mothers and children. Homemaker–home health aide service may also be available for other incapacitated parents who are at home and who are able to relate to the children but unable to care for them physically. Or the service may be used to over-come "situational neglect" when, for example, the caretaking parent may be so overwhelmed with a large family or with caring for a sick husband that the children are not receiving the care they need.

Neglect because the caretaker is immature or uninformed or disor-ganized may well be remedied by a homemaker–home health aide who teaches and assists at the same time. In some cases of situational neglect the immaturity of the parent is a contributing element. For example, a homemaker–home health aide was assigned to teach and assist a young unmarried woman, 23 years old, in the care of her own three children and two of her own siblings, whose care fell to her because her mother was an alcoholic.

Suspected or known abuse calls for the use of an especially well-trained and competent homemaker–home health aide and close monitoring and support from the social worker responsible for case management. The homemaker–home health aide is in the delicate posi-tion of helping, teaching, observing, and reporting. If the children's safety cannot be insured, they or the endangering parent must be re-moved from the home, such as in the following example in which the homemaker–home health aide had the helping-teaching-observing role:

> A homemaker–home health aide was assigned to teach and assist a 16-year-old unmarried mother in the care of a newborn infant. At first the young mother was enthusiastic about the baby and made progress in learning to care for him. Gradually, however, she became bored and wanted freedom. She became involved with a boyfriend and talked of getting married, but the boyfriend was involved with another woman. The aide was increasingly concerned and kept in close touch with the supervisor, as she began to suspect that the mother was leaving the child unattended at night. One morning when the homemaker arrived she could hear the baby crying, but she was unable to get in for quite a while until the mother came home. The aide found the baby on a plastic mattress—unkempt, wet, soiled, hungry. He had not been fed since the day before. The homemaker began to care for the baby. The young mother suddenly appeared with a gun. The homemaker–home health aide managed to disarm her and telephoned her supervisor who instructed her to bring the baby to the agency. The baby was placed in a foster home.

A child who is retarded or physically disabled, mentally disturbed, or terminally ill, and the child's family may all be helped by a homemaker–home health aide who assists, teaches, and provides emotional support. Some agencies, for example, maintain a list of families who can use respite care on short notice. When a homemaker–home health aide telephones the supervisor to say that a scheduled assignment has been aborted, as when the client is not at home or will not let the homemaker–home health aide in, the supervisor arranges for the homemaker–home health aide to go to the home of a disabled child where the usual caretaker needs respite. An occasional chance to have time away from the demands of a disabled child may relieve the parent from continuous stress. In Sweden the working mother of a child who becomes ill and cannot attend the usual day-care center or school can ask for a home aide to stay with the child so she does not absent herself from employment.

It is clear, then, that homemaker–home health aides can prevent disruption in families experiencing a wide range of difficulties and with varying needs. We have only begun to tap the potential usefulness of this service in supporting family continuity and cohesion.

## The Role of the Social Worker in Homemaker–Home Health Aide Service

The term "paraprofessional" is much misunderstood. The first definition of the prefix "para" in Webster's Dictionary (1983) is "by the side of, beside, alongside of," and that is descriptive of a homemaker–home health aide: a homemaker–home health aide is a paraprofessional in the full meaning of the word, one with responsibilities as great as but not the same as those of the professionals on the service team. The social worker finds that working with the family through the medium of a paraprofessional takes special skills. Too often social workers do not understand the roles of paraprofessionals or their own roles in relation to them. This role interface is rarely explored in social work education and there has not been much research on it. One recent study in family service agencies of homemakers found, not surprisingly, that the home-maker–home health aide tends to resolve role conflicts by meeting the supervisor's expectations rather than the consumer's (Tiagha, 1982).

The central role of the social worker generally is that of supervisor or case manager. The National HomeCaring Council had a great deal of trouble in defining those terms, especially in developing accreditation standards where "good supervision" must be defined for practice. Turning to the results of Shinn's research (1976; 1979) in this area for direction, the Council defined case management functions as those re-lated to a specific case, including intake, assessment, planning, imple-mentation of plan, recording, and supervision of the worker. Service management is defined as including administrative supervision, recruit-ment, training, scheduling, and evaluation of workers, as well as agency and interagency coordination, program quality assurance, and commu-nity relations.

In family cases where the presenting problem is neglect, abuse, or absence of the caretaking parent, and the team members are all em-ployees of the social service agency, service management and case man-agement are both social work responsibilities. Issues in such situations may have to do with what tasks may be conducted by an upgraded homemaker–home health aide. It is generally agreed, however, that while case management and service management tasks may be assigned in such a situation, to a homemaker–home health aide, the professional must have responsibility for in home assessments and plans for care.

Many patterns make up the division of service administration func-tions. In a small agency one social worker may handle all functions. In a large one it is usual for a caseworker in the counseling department to be responsible for case management, while a supervisor in the home-maker–home health aide department is responsible for service manage-ment. A similar pattern is followed when two agencies work together. Often a visiting nurse association handles case management, while the agency employing the homemaker–home health aide is responsible for service management. Working with another professional on the team may take as much skill as working with a paraprofessional. If the nurse or other health professional and the social worker fail to understand and respect each other's role, they can become involved in a turf battle, in which everyone, but particularly the family receiving service, loses.

The social worker on the homemaker–home health team is a catalyst between agencies on the one hand and between client and aide on the other, providing assessment, consultation, and support. As one caseworker reported:

> When Mrs. Thompson was assigned as the homemaker–home health aide in the family I was working with, I was in such awe of her experience as a mother that I didn't help her at first. But I soon found out that her personal experience didn't tell her what to do with these children who were so different from her own. I didn't need to tell her how to take care of them or how to clean the house, but I could help her understand their behavior and give her some support so she could live with it awhile.

Sometimes the social worker is neither case nor service manager but a consultant to a home care team, perhaps to a visiting nurse agency. The National HomeCaring Council standards require every homemaker–home health aide program to have social work and nursing supervision and/or consultation available. If either a social worker or a nurse "is not on staff, the expertise of that professional must be available through a written contract or agreement" (National HomeCaring Council, 1981: viii–5).

## The Issues

A discussion of the issues around homemaker–home health aide services is a discussion of the issues of our time: auspices for the service, allocation of resources, fragmentation in services, standards and regulations, organizational structure and function, deployment of workers, training, personnel practices, the rights of women, of minority groups, and of children. This list is not complete nor is any one issue independent of the others. Even the name of the service is at issue: "homemaker–home health aide;" it is cumbersome and redundant, but a necessary accomodation. The person in this role was at first generally called a housekeeper or cleaner, then a homemaker. The latter was a good job title and is still used by many agencies; however, the regulations for the Medicare Law allowed for the use of "home health aides" and not for "homemakers," although both provide personal care and care for the environment.

What is now the National HomeCaring Council initially was organized to represent the service in both health and social work agencies, which was, in fact, the resolution of one of the first problems in the field.

What were the auspices of a national organization? When national organizations and agencies of the federal government met in 1959 and 1961 to discuss homemaker services, the possibility of placing the representation for them in either the National League for Nursing or the Family Service Association of America was discussed. The consensus of the attendees was that either placement would result in fragmentation of a service which should be unified. A new national organization, therefore, was incorporated as the National Council for Homemaker Services, later Homemaker–Home Health Aide Services, now the National HomeCaring Council. The subscript "Representing the Homemaker–Home Health Aide Field" is often added.

The issue of fragmentation was only partly resolved through using a generic name for the homemaker–home health aide. Funding legislation continues to call the aide by many other names, such as chore worker or personal care aide, and the states use varying job titles with varying definitions. There are still agencies which have homemakers, generally paid for by social service funds, and home health aides, paid for by health funds, sometimes working in the same home. Homemaker–home health aides and funding for them in social programs are so scarce, while eligibility requirements for the funding that does exist are so stringent and limiting, that the social worker must put every effort into making the most efficient use of resources.

As a partial solution to the problem of fragmentation, the National Council advocates that agencies provide basic generic training to their homemaker–home health aides, who keep time logs on the job so that their time can be allocated to the appropriate funding sources, and one homemaker–home health aide can perform both social work and health-related care in the home.

Other issues in the field concern accreditation. The National HomeCaring Council's accreditation program has two major functions: setting standards and monitoring the conformity to the standards by agencies which apply for accreditation of their homemaker–home health aide services. Thus far the standards that have been developed are intended to set the minimum below which a program cannot fall and still provide safe, efficient service. They do not purport to describe the ideal in homemaker–home health aide service. Therefore, the overriding question in both accreditation and monitering is: "What is safe, efficient service?"

For example, how much training does a homemaker–home health aide need to do the job well? The traditional attitude toward women's care of their families and homes has been that they knew what to do without special training. This undervaluation of a complex role has carried over to the homemaker–home health aide, who is expected to function in many kinds of families experiencing varying physical and emotional crises. The current standards specify a basic generic training course, with specified content, and regular follow-up training thereafter. Additional training may be provided to homemaker–home health aides working with specific groups, such as developmentally disabled children or families in which there is mental illness. National organizations, such as the National HomeCaring Council, the American Cancer Society, and the Child Welfare League of America are important sources for consultation and materials like training manuals.

Another unresolved issue related to standards concerns the minimum ratio of supervisors to aides; yet this decision has everything to do with whether good service is given at a price which seems reasonable. In a field where competitive bidding for contracts is the rule, and where most contractors look mainly at the cost per hour of service, the burden is on the agency to prove that professional case management is cost-efficient. This can be done. For example, Medicare program statistics on utilization of home health services have shown, for every year to date that statistics have been published by the Health Care Financing Administration, that cost per case for visiting nurse associations is significantly less than for proprietary agencies.

The field has been unable to agree on a minimum ratio of supervisors to aides because so many variables are involved: the kinds of cases which the homemaker–home health aides are serving, their training and experience, the responsibilities the supervisor carries in addition to supervising the aides, and whether the supervisor is responsible for all the tasks in case and service management. The professional social worker who is working with the paraprofessional has a responsibility beyond ascertaining that the family is competently and safely cared for; that responsibility is to the homemaker–home health aide. The homemaker–home health aide is usually a woman, often a woman who is black or from another minority group, and poor.

Some communities employ paraprofessional aides as individual contractors or providers, more aptly a designation for someone like an attorney, architect, or caseworker in private practice. These individuals may be expected to pay their own Social Security, provide their own insurance, and prepay estimated income tax. The homemaker–home health aide, who is contracted for as an individual, fails to receive fair wages and fringe benefits and may have little or no training or supervisory support. Where agencies are well-supported by their communities and are supportive of their aides, the aides are on annual salary with the same fringe benefits as other employees of the agency. In some large cities such as New York City, San Francisco, and Chicago, the homemaker–home health aides are unionized, and their personnel benefits have improved accordingly.

Some of the most difficult issues in homemaker–home health aide service arise when an aide is placed by the court in a family suspected of child abuse. The goals of service are to strengthen parenting skills, but also to observe the interaction of the family and to facilitate removal of a child in danger. The presence of this aide may initially be a threat to the family given the choice of homemaker–home health aide service or immediate removal of the child. Only the most highly trained and sensitive aides can be used in such a family. A supervisor must always be available for assistance to the aide if there are difficulties. In protective cases, both the homemaker–home health aide and the supervisor should be limited to small caseloads.

In most homemaker–home health aide cases the family and the agency sign a plan of care agreement, but this may not be possible in a court-appointed homemaker–home health aide case. The agency cannot insure confidentiality in a case where it may have to report to the court and may have to testify in court against the parents in order to remove the child from the home. In cases of suspected child abuse and even in less threatening situations, if the family wants to tell the homemaker–home health aide something in confidence, the aide must caution that as a representative of the agency she or he cannot promise to withhold information important to the family and to the agency. Since the agency and the homemaker–home health aide are in the household on behalf of the family, honesty must form the basis of all their communications. The priority in service must be the welfare of the child.

## The Future of Homemaker–Home Health Aide Service

An increase in home care for elderly people came about largely in response to a need to save money on hospital and nursing home care. As the costs of foster care, institutionalization, and hospitalization of children in relation to the costs of homemaker–home health aide and other supports to the family for care in the home are better understood, homemaker–home health aide care for children may be expected to increase. Shyne and Schroeder (1978a), in their national study of social services to children and families, argue strongly for expansion of homemaker services, stating:

> Homemaker service can not only avert placement of children, but teach parents and other family members to manage their household and child-rearing tasks. Again, if prevention of placement, sustaining the family, and improving the child's home environment are of concern, the availability of homemaker service must be greatly expanded (1978a:156).

Given the obvious financial advantages and the possibility of better serving children and their families, research is needed to determine the reasons for the failure of social workers and agencies to use homemaker–home health aide services. Therefore, it behooves social workers who are aware of the value of such services for the maintenance of families to accept the responsibility for advocating for services of good quality and to use the homemaker–home health aide service whenassessment indicates it is appropriate.

## Day Care

On the continuum of care for children, homemaker–home health aide service is probably the one that calls for the fewest adjustments by the child; day care is next. Like homemaker–home health aide service, day care is provided under various auspices, with different mixes of professional and paraprofessional staff. The federal definitions for day-care services discussed in this paper are:

> *Day care services for children*—comprehensive and coordinated sets of activities carried out for purpose of providing direct care and protection of infants and preschool age children during a portion of a 24-hour day, inside or outside of the child's own home.

> *Day care center*—a licensed facility in which care is provided part of the day for a group of 12 or more children.

> *Day care home, family*—a licensed or approved private family home in which children receive care, protection, and guidance during a part of the 24-hour day. A family day care home may serve no more than a total of six children (ages 3 through 14)—no more than five when the age range is infancy through 6—including the family day care mother's own children.

> *Day care home, group*—an extended licensed and approved or modified family residence in which family-like care is provided, usually to school age children. It provides care for up to 12 children.

> (*Annual Report to the Congress on Title XX*, 1980:59–60)

*Day treatment*, another form of day care, might be defined as therapy-intensive. In 1979 day treatment was available under Title XX to children and youth in 30 states. As is true for other services under Title XX, each state defines day treatment differently and targets different groups for the care. Sometimes day treatment is for physically and/or mentally handicapped children, for emotionally disturbed children, or for a specific subgroup such as blind or developmentally disabled children (Kilgore and Salmon, 1979:238–242).

One distinction made between day-care centers and nursery schools is that the former generally have the hours of a working day, five to seven days a week, and the nursery schools have shorter hours. Sometimes nursery schools are in session only two or three days a week.

Further, day-care centers were developed to provide a protective environment to children of working mothers, while nursery schools, designed around theories of child development, tend to be more educationally focused. It is ironic that the day-care center, an all-day, every-day environment that is more apt to care for children of families lower on the socioeconomic scale, is less likely to provide a planned educational experience for children than is the nursery school, which tends to cater to middle-class families. Head Start, and, in a few states, public prekindergarten classes for children three to five years old, are exceptions to this general pattern. Both programs enroll children for educational purposes regardless of the mother's employment status (Kadushin, 1980:267–268).

The history of day care is tied to the employment of mothers outside the home. This has been documented as far back as 1767 in Switzerland when a day nursery was set up for children whose mothers worked in the fields (Kadushin, 1980:269). However, day care's major growth came as urban industrialization took the place of cottage industries and farm work and mothers became employed at a distance from their homes (Kamerman and Kahn, 1979:86). A center for custodial daytime care for the children of working mothers was set up in Paris in 1844 and in New York City in 1854. As the widows of Civil War casualties went to work, the number of day nurseries in the United States increased. By 1898, when the National Federation of Day Nurseries was organized in the United States, there were already 175 known day nurseries. The first organized family day-care program was started in 1928 and, like the first organized homemaker–home health aide program, it was started in Philadelphia. In the 1930s, during the Depression, day nurseries were set up as a means of employment for poor women through the Works Progress Administration. Social workers were employed in some of these programs. During World War II there was another upsurge in day-care centers, as women were needed in industry. After the war many centers were closed (Richman, 1965:243–244), and the service was not revitalized until the 1960s. Day care has been called the first public social service targeted mainly to the working poor (Lewis, 1974:428).

In fiscal year 1979 more federal social services money (Title XX, Social Security Act) went to day care than to any other service; homemaker–home health aide services were second. The difference is that homemaker–home health aide services were provided almost entirely to elderly persons, while only about 2 percent of day care was provided to adults of any age; 98 percent was to children. Day care, in some form, is now provided in all fifty states and the District of Columbia. Three-fourths of the public money is directed to day-care centers, rather than to family day care. Day-care funds under Titles XX and IV of the Social Security Act were used for 526,000 children in the last quarter of fiscal

1979.[4] An additional 400,000 children were enrolled in Head Start, a comprehensive preschool program that includes medical, nutritional and educational components, and social services. It is targeted toward low income children generally from three to five years old. By law, at least 10 percent of the Head Start children must be handicapped (Calhoun, Grotberg, and Rackley, 1980:69–70).

## The Uses of Day Care

Day care is most often a means of having children cared for during the work hours of the caretaking parent, usually the mother. It may also be used to enhance the social and cognitive skills of the child and as a means of providing respite for the caretaking parent of a physically, mentally, or emotionally handicapped child, or assistance to a physically, mentally, or emotionally handicapped parent. Day care may be used in conjunction with homemaker–home health aide service when the caretaking parent is absent or incapacitated. Short-term day care is sometimes provided by religious or recreational facilities, even by shopping centers, to free parents for various activities. Day treatment is more a remedial service than is ordinary day care. Day treatment centers are costly because of the specialized personnel and equipment needed, and they are much less apt to be available in a community than is an ordinary day care center.

## The Role of the Social Worker in Day Care

The social worker may participate on several levels in a day-care program: director, intake worker, counselor, consultant, referral source. He or she may serve on the board of a day-care agency, as a volunteer in a day-care program, or may work in the community as an advocate for initiation, improvement, or expansion of a day-care program. The social worker's ability to work on a team with professionals from other fields, as well as with paraprofessionals, is critical. The liaison role between the center and the family is often occupied by the social worker who may organize other community resources for the child and family, such as transportation, health care, or food stamps. Further, an assessment which assists the day-care center to judge whether the child is to be admitted to the center, and which helps the family determine whether a day-care center is right for the child and for the whole family is often completed by a social worker, who may also assist the child, the family, and the day-care family or center in adapting to each other in the new situation. Finally, the social worker may provide training programs on child development for the staff of the day-care center and for parent groups, as well as assisting the teaching staff to understand and work with individual children.

In most day-care centers there are no social work employees and the other employees of the center or family day-care mothers generally do not have professional qualifications. Ruderman (1968) found that 24 percent of day-care center directors and 71 percent of family day-care mothers have only high school educations. Almost one-third of the family day-care mothers had less than a high school education. Many of the teachers in the centers also did not have advanced degrees: 26 percent had high school or less and 44 percent were college graduates. Only 7 percent of the day-care centers had the regular services of a social worker (ibid.:102–104). The lack of professional workers in day-care centers makes it even more important that the Child Welfare worker know what to expect from day care so that the goals in placement are realistic.

## Issues in Day Care

The issues in day care cluster around its objectives, standards, auspices, effects on children, personnel practices, and training. The lack of clarity in national policy and in indecisiveness on the part of the individual social worker, demonstrated by a dearth of plans for care reflect the widespread ambivalence about these issues. Concerning objectives, writers in the field all seem to agree that a clear national commitment to day care which benefits children is lacking and that day care provided solely to take women off welfare rolls is of questionable value. A Brookings Institution study noted:

> There has simply not been enough thinking about the benefits and costs of a good day care program to merit the faith political leaders now express in day care as a dependency-reducing mechanism. Federal day care program requirements are oriented to the idea of day care as a learning experience. They are, therefore, on a collision course with supporters of mass day care as an aspect of the struggle to reduce welfare costs. (Steiner, 1971:65)

Kahn and Kamerman (1975), for example, doubt the cost benefits of paying to put a child in day care to enable a welfare mother, who may earn close to the minimum wage, to go to work. Obviously, the objectives of day care programs are often unclear or even conflicting.

The strengthening and extension of standards for day-care centers and ongoing monitoring to assure adherence to those standards could clarify the goals of centers and the means for achieving those goals. Standards do exist. At one time or another, singly or jointly, standards have been developed by the National Federation of Day Nurseries, the

Children's Bureau, the Office of Education, the Committee on Infant and Preschool Child of the American Academy of Pediatrics, the Child Welfare League of America, and the Council on Accreditation of Services for Families and Children. In 1980 the Department of Health, Education, and Welfare published day-care regulations for both day-care centers and day-care homes but these were never adopted. First the Child Welfare League and now the Council on Accreditation have accredited day care centers. The National Association for the Education of Young Children has drafted standards and expects to have an accreditation program for day-care centers in place in 1985 or 1986. Only a small percentage of those now in existence are actually accredited.

Most states require licensing of day-care centers, generally giving the state department of social services the licensing function. The social workers who evaluate may also provide consultation but one study has found that licensers tend not to use their supervisory role to force acceptance of consultation recommendations. The researchers believed that licensing and consultation should be separated (Lounsbury and Hall, 1976) and Kadushin observed that the licensing departments in many areas are too understaffed to do more than check out complaints. Adequate penalties for violations of state standards are not imposed (1980:279). The Council on Accreditation now accredits family day-care and group day-care homes; however, licensing and accreditation in this area are very weak.

The greatest controversy in day-care standards has been over a major issue that plagues many accreditation programs, and that is the ratio of personnel to recipients of a service, in this case, of staff to children. The ratio question is especially difficult in regard to care of infants and toddlers. One study (Ruopp et al., 1979) found that for children three, four, and five years old, the most important variable in determining the quality of program was group size. Smaller groups were consistently associated with better care, more socially active children, and higher gains on two developmental tests. The caregiver to child ratio, within a range of 1:5 to 1:10, made a difference, but it made less of a difference than did group size. On the other hand, for children under three, both group size and caregiver to child ratio were strongly associated with the measures of quality. Child-related education and training, but not experience or formal education, were related to better care for children three, four, and five years old, while the formal education of the caregiver was associated with differences in quality of care for children under three.

These findings were used in the development of the 1980 federal day-care regulations, which were not adopted. Standards on size of group and training of caregiving personnel were established. Ratios were set, allowing more children per caretaker than the standards of the

Council on Accreditation of Services for Families and Children. The Child Welfare League of America is now liberalizing its standards on ratio of teachers to infants and the Council is now following suit.

Head Start programs are not under these regulations because they are governed by the now separate Department of Education. However, Head Start personnel are on notice that they must obtain the Child Development Associate credential for their child caretakers (Van Camp, 1981). The Child Development Associate is a term used for both an assessment tool and the credential. It was developed out of Head Start and involves an on-site assessment of day-care personnel, most of whom are paraprofessional.

Another issue in day care concerns its auspice. There is a great deal of controversy, as there is in the homemaker–home health aide field, about offering day care under profit-making auspices, yet a large percentage of day-care centers are profit-making. Shyne and Schroeder (1978) found that proprietary agencies were more frequently the source of both day care and of day treatment in their sample. Keyserling found poor quality care in half the proprietary day-care centers rated in her study and in some cases found it "to be very bad indeed" (1972:3), while Avrin discovered that profit-making day-care centers in the Boston area tended to care for large numbers of children in one location and to have a low ratio of teachers to children. Wages ranged from minimum wage to a salary well below that of public school teachers. Working conditions were poor and teachers tended to work long hours without a break. Parents had no involvement (Avrin, 1974). Ruopp et al. (1979) found that profit-making centers provided fewer supplementary services, such as physical and psychological testing, counseling, and assistance in obtaining other services to parents than did nonprofit centers. They also reported that wages to day-care center caregiver staff were low everywhere, but especially in profit-making centers and that the frequency of parent participation in center activities was much higher in nonprofit centers.

Because profit, advertising, and lobbying are added costs for a proprietary center, various means tend to be used to lower overhead, such as lower wages, fewer fringe benefits, less expensive facilities and equipment, more children in a center—clustered in larger groups— (economies of scale), smaller ratio of adults to children, and less involvement with parents. If there could be assurances concerning the quality of care in all centers, if agencies receiving public funds or contracting service to public agencies were required to meet basic national standards and were monitored consistently, and if public funding or the license were withdrawn for violations of standards, the controversy over auspices would probably diminish.

Providing day care to children under two or three is another issue which has generated considerable controversy. Good care for infants and toddlers is expensive. They need much warm, individualized attention to insure normal development and safety. Contagious diseases and illnesses are hazardous to the health of all children in group settings, but especially to infants and toddlers. Many people believe that all-day, every-day group care for infants and toddlers is poor policy generally and some states prohibit group care of children under three. However, Kamerman and Kahn point out that there is "no certain knowledge as to the effects of varying periods of separation on children of different ages" (1979:82). There are possible alternatives to extensive day care for infants and toddlers. These include homemaker–home health aide service, family day care, flexible work schedules, and providing financial support to enable a parent to stay at home with the children or to take only part-time employment.

Finally, some people in the field believe that day care should be a universal service available to all children, or at least to those three to five years old. Under the current patchwork system, welfare mothers and the poor working family may qualify for public funds, but there are many families who cannot afford day care but also do not qualify for public funds. Families with more discretionary income with one unemployed parent may search out nursery schools where the objective is social and cognitive development of the child. Means-tested day-care programs tend to segregate the children of the poor (Morgan, 1977). An alternative to this two-track system of day care can be found in at least two cities, Orlando, Florida, and Wichita, Kansas, where there is a sliding fee scale and parents can choose from three or more centers, none of which is allowed to receive subsidy for more than 30 percent of its children (ibid.).

## The Future of Day Care

Regardless of whether these issues are resolved, day care is an established and growing institution. Funding will be cut and restored and cut again, but as single-parent families increase and as the employment and education of women increase, ways to care for dependent children must be found. As day care is extended, thought must be given as to the best care for an individual child; otherwise children will be put wherever care is available and affordable. Day care is a service that parents will fight for, but they will not always know the full range of options available to them, nor how to judge the quality of care available. The social worker in social policy, the researcher, and the caseworker doing an assessment and plan of care, all have a responsibility for examining the options and the issues.

## Other Supplementary Services

Other services which supplement parental care and offer developmental opportunities for children should also be considered as part of a potential network of support for families and children. For example, organizations which provide volunteer big brothers and big sisters to children exist in most communities. Big Brothers/Big Sisters of America is a federation of locally funded agencies throughout the United States, which supports the matching of a young person, usually from a single-parent family, with an adult who is to act as friend and role model. A trained social worker provides the match, assesses, and reassesses, involving parents, children, and non-family adult volunteers (Cole, 1980). Social and recreational organizations for school age children also exist in almost every community. Among them are Boy Scouts, Girl Scouts, Boys Clubs of America, Young Men's and Women's Christian and Hebrew Associations, Four-H Clubs, Future Homemakers of America, and various after school programs.

Child Welfare workers, wishing to supplement family and parental care, should think beyond the more extensive interventions, such as homemaker and day-care programs and remember that most communities have a network of services which can enrich the lives of children and young people. Brokering such services to children and families is an important aspect of Child Welfare practice.

One way to conceptualize a continuum of care for children is on a line from least to most adaptation required of the child; another way is from most to least involvement of the parents in the child's well-being. The two lines will probably coincide. However, if we add a third line representing the involvement of the social worker with the parents and children, we may well find that it requires just as much time and skill on the part of the social worker to work with parents whose children live at home, as it does to work with the parents of children who have been placed out of the home. In the long run, however, this investment will pay off in financial, as well as in human, terms. In a sermon on July 29, 1981, the Most Reverend Robert Runcie, the Archbishop of Canterbury, made a statement which could be axiomatic for Child Welfare workers who are working to keep children in their homes:

> If we solved all our economic problems and failed to build loving families, it would profit us nothing, because the family is the place where the future is created good and full of love—or deformed. (*New York Times*, June 30, 1981:A11)

# CHAPTER 17

# Homemaker and Day-Care Services

MARJORIE ZIEFERT

Theorists and practitioners in Child Welfare have, in this decade, reached a consensus that the starting point in the delivery of Child Welfare services is the family. This volume is a testament to that consensus. Despite this agreement we are still a nation with 350,000 children in foster care (Zigler and Hunsinger, 1978). 100,000 children labeled as delinquent, dependent, neglected, or in need of supervision are placed in institutions, 27,000 are psychiatric inpatients and 95,000 are child residents of institutions for the retarded and handicapped (Kamerman and Kahn, 1978). Minimally this means that some 572,000 children in our nation reside outside of their own families in situations which are temporary alternatives. The national cost for this care is enormous, far exceeding the amount spent annually to provide services to children and families to maintain them as family units. Particularly alarming is the disproportionate number of minority children who have been separated from their families and remain in temporary alternatives. Black children, who comprise 13.6 percent of the youth population, account for 36 percent of children in placement. American Indian children are in placement at rates that range from 5 to 1,600 times greater than white children in states with high Indian populations (Bryce and Lloyd, 1980).

The tendency to rely on institutional rather than family-based alternatives has been consistent throughout the evolution of Child Welfare.

Only recently do programs and policies endorse and enable the provision of home-based services. For example, the provisions of the Title XX Amendment to the Social Security Act have promoted home-based services as an alternative to placements, anchored largely on the underlying goal of placement in the "least restrictive environment." Perhaps the most significant commitment in this direction is Public Law 96–272, passed in 1980. Political realities, however, cast doubt on the extent of financial support this legislation will receive.

Although this new thrust towards providing in home supports to families provides sanction and some funding for programmatic alternatives to foster care and institutions, whether these programs will succeed is dependent upon the manner in which services are funded and delivered. Traditionally, much of social work practice has reflected a deficit orientation, defining problems as internal to the individual or family system. This approach fails to take sufficient account of the environmental factors which influence the family. Through a deficit model, services tend to be "plugged in" to families, thereby encouraging passivity and absence of involvement on the part of recipients. The family's lack of involvement is then manifest in their resistance to service or in there being no observable gains when the service is terminated.

The life model of social work practice reframes the entire context within which services are provided to families (Germain and Gitterman, 1980). In this model people and environments are viewed as potential resources for each other, and people are seen as having the inherent capacity to adapt to their environments and environments as having the capacity to respond to human needs. Within this context human service intervention focuses on strengthening the adaptive capacities of individuals and increasing environmental responsiveness to needs.

This chapter will focus specifically on exploring supplemental services needed by families to strengthen their capacities to provide nurturing care to their offspring. Social work intervention concerned with family integrity must emphasize mobilization of community resources to respond preventively to families at risk and to the overwhelming needs of families in crisis. How services are provided must be assessed in relation to the ultimate goal of enhancing the family's adaptive capacities and potential for long-term survival.

Many programs have been successful in preventing child placement in high-risk families. These successful programs appear to share certain common elements of approach or perspective. These include:

Services which grow out of a collaborative effort between the family and the service provider
Services that are delivered in a timely manner
Services that have a long-term commitment to families

Services that are coordinated
Services that are sensitive to culture and community

These common elements reflect the central principles of the life model. According to Germain and Gitterman, the life model of practice is "designed to engage peoples' strengths and the forces pushing towards growth, and to influence organizational structures, other social systems, and physical settings so they will be more responsive to peoples' needs" (1980:2). Two specific services, homemaker and day care, will illustrate how these principles are creatively and effectively used in programs.

## Homemaker Services

Homemaker services have long been a resource to Child Welfare workers. Traditionally they have been used to supplement the maternal role in families where the mother is temporarily incapacitated by illness or other crisis (Kadushin, 1980). The mother may be present or absent from the home at the time the service is provided. Homemakers perform roles beyond that of housekeeper. These roles have been differentiated in two respects:

1. The homemaker goes beyond merely doing the housework and feeding the family. She accepts some responsibility for meeting the emotional needs of the children, minimizing their anxiety and maximizing their feeling of security.
2. The homemaker is, in effect, a member of a team charged with responsibility of implementing a casework plan to help restore and strengthen parental functioning or otherwise assure that the child has the care he needs. As a member of the team, the homemaker is supervised by the social agency, to ensure coordination of her activities with the overall treatment plan (Kadushin, 1980:238).

Homemaker services are resources which historically have been utilized to maintain families as intact units. Their value to "high risk" families has been demonstrated continually from the inception of the service (Burt and Balyeat, 1974; Watkins, 1953). Their use, however, has been fairly narrow in scope and their availability minimal in comparison to the numbers of families who might remain together with the benefit of such service (Kadushin, 1980).

Within the home the responsibilities of the homemaker may be variously defined. He or she may perform all of the traditional homemaking tasks from nurturant child care to cleaning and meal preparation. The homemaker may act as a teacher and role model to a parent who feels too overwhelmed or inadequate to meet these responsibilities. Most frequently the homemaker will perform a combination of these two roles, since the actual function of the homemaker is dependent on the situation at hand. According to Kadushin

Homemaker service is appropriately offered when:
1. The mother is temporarily hospitalized
2. The mother is in the home but is ill or convalescing
3. The mother needs tutorial help in developing homemaker skills
4. The mother needs assistance in caring for a handicapped child
5. The mother has died or deserted and the father needs time to make adequate, more permanent plans for the care of the children (1980:261)

For the most part, the conditions outlined above call for short-term involvement of the homemaker. They are for the most part situational crises which can be overcome with the assistance of this supplemental aid. There has been much demonstrated and written concerning the effectiveness of homemaker service when utilized in these situations. Of particular value has been the use of this service when there is short-term illness or when there is permanent absence of the mother; in these situations continuity of the home is maintained until appropriate long-term plans can be made (Arnold and Goodman, 1966; Goldstein, 1973; Hammell, 1969).

In other family situations where there is a high risk of family disintegration, such as in multiproblem families, in families with developmental disability, or in families where either the child or parent is otherwise handicapped, homemakers have played a particularly central role in multiservice efforts to maintain the family's integrity. Because of poor intervention histories and the continuing presence of severe poverty, unemployment, deviant behavior, or diagnosed mental illness, helping systems have often chosen to dissolve these family units rather than to work further to keep them intact (Shyne, Sherman, and Phillips, 1972). Through the use of comprehensive programs which offer a broad range of resources needed by such families, including homemaker service, helping systems have become significantly more successul in maintaining the integrity of threatened family units. In fact, several program evaluations suggest that the homemaker role has been the most effective component of multiple services interventions (Bush, 1977; Mott and Lunsford, 1979).

In New York City the Lower East Side Family Union is a prototype of such a program. In a community characterized by high unemployment, widespread poverty, and rising crime, the Family Union serves families whose difficulties include a combination of economic disadvantage, poor health, interpersonal conflict, inadequate housing, and substance abuse problems. In response to these conditions the Family Union combines the use of a homemaker with a range of social work services. In these situations, the homemaker relieves the immediate demands on the families by baby-sitting, cooking, performing housekeeping tasks, and accompanying family members to service agencies. They also instruct parents in household skills, managing their money, nutrition, and child-rearing. They are available to spend nights or weekends in clients' homes in emergencies. (Bush, 1977:50)

The results of this intervention are most impressive. Of the 390 families served in 1976, 141 were considered high risk for foster care placement. In a one-year follow-up study only ten of the families involved in the Family Union program had children in placement, and even these were all temporary placements lasting a few months—well below the average length of other placements (ibid.).

The Parents and Children Together (P.A.C.T.) Program in Detroit, Michigan, is another example of a comprehensive and successful alternative to foster care. As summarized in its statement of goals, the program is designed "to help clients in as many ways as reasonable toward creating an organized, sanitary and rewarding home environment; developing skills and techniques in parenting and child care; improving the health and nutritional status of each member, effectively utilizing available community, financial and social resources, ridding themselves of nonfunctional behavior; and building each family member's self esteem" (Mott and Lunsford, 1979:44–45).

The core of the P.A.C.T. program staff is a Home Management Specialist who spends two or more days a week with the family teaching them living and management skills. These include organizing and maintaining a comfortable home environment, developing healthy living and nutritional practices, and increasing the parents' understanding of their own and their children's developmental needs. As with the Lower East Side Family Union, the program primarily serves families experiencing severe environmental deprivation and multiple, related interpersonal problems. Again, the evaluation of this mode of intervention demonstrated that even in this high-risk group, a very small percentage of children entered or remained for long periods of time in out-of-home placement. Some positive change was seen in approximately 62 percent of the project clients (ibid.).

The second high-risk population for whom homemaker services can reduce the chances of placement are families in which either the child or a parent is handicapped. Frequently families must institutionalize a handicapped child simply because of a lack of available resources (Moroney, 1980). Similarly when a parent has a disability that interferes with his or her parenting capacity, the likelihood of placement becomes greater if other high-risk factors also exist. With supplemental services which ". . . mobilize the strengths of the family and build in supports to offset parental weaknesses" families can be helped to provide nurturant and need-fulfilling environments (Hammell, 1969). This requires a long-term commitment to a family so that it can continue to function at an adequate level. With such a commitment, the agency must see itself in the role of extended family and must be involved with the ongoing tasks and conflicts related to the development of all family members (Taylor, 1972). Programs that provide services to families with disabilities have had success in offering very needed practical assistance and in reducing stress sufficiently to allow the family to begin to attend to each other's needs (Arnold and Goodman, 1966).

Programs which succeed in maintaining families intact share a stance which is consistent with the five general principles outlined earlier in this chapter. Operationalizing these principles provides an effective model for practice.

### The Service Plan Should Develop Out of a Collaborative Effort between the Family and the Service Provider

When family members are seen as resources to the homemaker and to each other, they can become more active participants in the helping process. When the family, in order to get the service, must be viewed as having a deficit, acceptance of the homemaker and participation in the change process become doubtful. Involving the family in a mutual assessment is the first step in the change process. For parents to accept the homemaker as a substitute or assistant they must see the value in the service (Einstein, 1960). One program describes their process as follows:

> At intake clients are introduced to the Families Service Team. The team discusses with the family the reasons why they are there, explaining the nature of the services they offer and the necessity for the family's involvement in and commitment to solving its problems. The intake discussions are held in the family's home. (Mott and Lunsford, 1979:33)

Research has indicated that the most successful cases using homemaker services are those in which the family members understand and willingly accept the service (Kadushin, 1980).

Joint assessment is but a first step in the collaborative relationship. Homemaker services must be designed to supplement, not supplant, the family. Experience with services to handicapped children and their families has indicated that professionals tend to take over the care of the children rather than supporting families in their role as caregiver (Moroney, 1980). Whether or not the parent is at home during the provision of the homemaker services, patterns set by the parent can be maintained. If these caretaking styles are problematic, discussion with the parent and possible alternative suggestions communicate respect and the expectation that the parent is a participant in this effort (Einstein, 1960). One study suggests that ". . . the progress made was not so much on the basis of the homemaker's skill and proficiency in homemaking and child care as because of her intuitive ability . . . to give the mothers in these families the kind of acceptance, respect and understanding that in many cases they had not encountered before" (Shames, 1964:18).

Parents' self-blame and passivity can be reinforced when the homemaker's attitude and actions indicate that they must be replaced in order for change to occur. A mother will frequently feel threatened when a substitute can more competently fulfill her role, keeping the home organized and the children well disciplined. In order to prevent feelings of low self-esteem, isolation, and displacement the homemaker must engage the client in a reciprocal relationship with mutual sharing of ideas and suggestions. Only through such involvement can the parents begin to develop competence in managing these tasks on their own. The "supplanting" approach leaves the family without enhanced personal resources to use when the service provider withdraws. Even when the homemaker is providing a needed service by performing a task rather than by teaching, if this is done in a collaborative manner, the family will be left with a sense of accomplishment and perhaps with the ability to ask for help again should it be needed. This ability to reach out for and make use of help is in itself, for many families, a new and very useful skill. For other families the new learning may be their realization that with support their family can remain intact and functioning through difficult times.

## The Service Must Be Delivered in a Timely Manner

Homemaker services, as with any other resources needed by overwhelmed or crisis-ridden families, must be available when the need arises. Services that exist from 9:00 A.M. to 5:00 P.M., five days a week, may not meet the needs of families experiencing stress. Special times of the day such as dinner or bedtime may be particularly stressful (Gil, 1973). Support during these periods can avert crisis and may teach parents new methods of coping. A comprehensive study of services for neglected and abused children in the State of Tennessee, conducted by the Urban Institute, indicated that the lack of 24-hour-a-day emergency services to families sometimes necessitated institutionalizing children on weekends or after 5:00 P.M. weekdays (Burt and Balyeat, 1974). Services created in response to these findings included:

1. Twenty-four hour a day intake for all family cases.
2. Emergency Caretaker Service for temporarily abandoned children or

emergency situations which leave children without parental supervision, and

3. Emergency homemaker service to maintain children in their own homes where parents cannot provide parental care on a temporary basis. (Ibid.:168)

In the first year following initiation of this new system, referrals to the children's residential institution for neglected and dependent children were reduced from 454 to 74. These dramatic results demonstrate that, with appropriate support services, children can be maintained in their own homes rather than being institutionalized.

## Services Must Have a Long-Term Commitment to Families

Not only must services be promptly delivered, but a long-term commitment must also be made to families at risk. Crisis intervention has been tried by agencies time and again, but since many of the families that come to the attention of the Child Welfare system are chronically overwhelmed, it often is unwise to withdraw service when the immediate situation is alleviated (Goldstein, 1973). Ongoing assistance which provides opportunity for learning, for development of personal skills, and for experiences which enhance individual growth and competence are necessary. Homemaker services can serve as an effective and efficient means of achieving these goals.

There are many situations where it must be acknowledged that long-term service is probably required. For example, a family with a handicapped child who needs 24-hour supervision and extensive physical care cannot be expected to provide this care alone. The following is an example of such an ongoing need and a service that made child placement unnecessary.

> Mrs. Paul is a single parent who must work outside of the home to support her three children ages 5, 9, and 14. Steven, her nine-year-old son, is a parapalegic who has cerebral palsy. He is in need of considerable physical care as well as intellectual and physical stimulation. Mrs. Paul struggled to keep him at home until she became overwhelmed with her teenager's acting-out behavior and her five year old's resistance to starting school. She came to the social service agency requesting placement for Steven as she was feeling that she could no longer provide care for him. She was very depressed and seemed desperate. The caseworker learned that Steven was in a special school program but it was after school that all three children's needs converged on the mother and became too much to handle. She felt she could not cope with the situation and considered placement of Steven to be the only solution.

The caseworker helped her to clarify her needs and acknowledged the realistic difficulty of the situation, which immediately helped to reduce Mrs. Paul's guilt. Upon visiting the home the worker observed the evidence of Mrs. Paul's depression and feeling of helplessness. The house was disorganized and filthy although the furnishings revealed that the home had been cared for at one time, before, it was learned, Mr. Paul's desertion of the family.

The worker suggested an option of homemaker services, which he believed would serve two functions. First, the homemaker could help Mrs. Paul restore the house to a livable condition, cleaning and organizing with her. Second, she could come in regularly several days after school and for some time on the weekend to care for Steven and relieve Mrs. Paul of some of her household chores. Mrs. Paul was willing to try this arrangement, hopeful that it would mean that Steven would be able to stay home.

A three month evaluation by Mrs. Paul, the homemaker, and social worker revealed that Mrs. Paul had trained the homemaker in caring for Steven and the homemaker had helped her to organize her house so that things were more orderly and accessible. It was agreed that the homemaker should spend some additional time with the other children in order to reduce Mrs. Paul's sense of isolation in her situation.

The family has remained intact for several years using this service. As the younger child became more independent and the older more self-confident and absorbed outside the home, the homemaker began to reduce her hours. She still remains a resource, coming in for four hours on Saturdays to give Mrs. Paul an opportunity to leave the house to do her errands and to have a little time for herself. The agency is committed to maintaining this service for an indefinite period.

This case illustrates the need for long-term services. Overwhelmed and alone, with no supports, Mrs. Paul would have been forced to place Steven in institutional care. Withdrawing the homemaker assistance at the end of three months or even a year would have quickly moved the family back into crisis. This long-term commitment has been successful in saving both the human and financial resources that institutional placements drain.

The likelihood of a family remaining intact when the parent has one or more major deficits is also small. Providing long-term support to such families can maintain them as intact and adequately functioning units. Some of these families do well with intermittent service at times of crisis or particular vulnerability (Taylor, 1972). They can learn to identify signs of crisis and understand the need to seek additional support at these times. Other families need continued support which can be provided by an agency serving in the role of extended family. The assessment of the stresses at different points in the family life cycle aids in anticipating the particularly vulnerable periods a family may experience. The skills needed to cope with an infant, for example, vary greatly from those needed with an adolescent (Goldstein, 1973). The following case illustrates a situation commonly found in neglecting families when placement becomes the only choice if no support services are available.

> The G family came to the attention of the child welfare agency because of severe neglect of their two children. A neighbor called the police to report that the oldest child, a six-year-old girl, had not been registered for school. It was subsequently learned that both she and her two-year-old brother were malnourished and developmentally delayed. A psychiatric evaluation revealed that both parents were functioning in the low-average range of intelligence. The mother, who had been hospitalized for several years in a state hospital, was on medication which left her lethargic and listless. Observation of the family members together revealed a great deal of warmth and caring. It was recommended that services be provided to see if the parents were capable of learning skills that would insure the normal growth and development of their children. Both parents were very fearful of losing the children and cooperated fully with the homemaker who was assigned to teach them meal preparation, cleaning, and child management skills. Other services, such as day care for the younger child and special education classes for the older one, were also provided. Discussion with the after-care clinic staff led to a reduction in medication and the mother began to feel more energetic. The family made a good deal of progress in learning to get the children to school on time and in preparing more nutritious meals. After six months, homemaker services were reduced to once-a-week visits during which the family's progress was monitored and needed support and encouragement provided.

The ultimate success of the G family case is dependent on the continued availability of services on an as-needed basis. Homemaking services not only played a central role in assisting the G's in attaining an adequate level of functioning, but also offered continued supervision of the situation and ready access to services should the homemaker and family decide they were required.

In this situation, the homemaker served as an observer, providing ongoing assessment and intervention planning. It is critical that this be done from the perspective of the family's strengths. When monitoring takes on the tone of "spying" it is a clear violation of the family's privacy and may undermine the family's self-esteem and developing autonomy.

## Services Must Be Coordinated

The homemaker does not function alone in a care situation; he or she is a member of a team. With the overwhelming situations experienced by high-risk families it is unrealistic to expect that any one service provider can meet all of their needs. Support and assistance from the caseworker and an interdisciplinary team of consultants relieves the pressure and provides needed expertise (National Council for Homemaker–Home Health Aide Services, Inc., 1971).

Other community services are also often used by the family along with homemaker services. As one project evaluation reported:

> Teaching Homemaker Service is not a panacea for the multi-problem family, nor should it be used as a stop-gap service when none other is available. However, its usefulness as an effective instrument in raising the level of family living should not be underestimated. . . . Nevertheless, the ultimate success of Teaching Homemaker Service will usually be in direct relation to the availability of other needed health and social services and their effective coordination. (Ibid.:44)

The client's role in this coordinated service system should not be ignored. The initial meeting of the service team can take place in the client's home, establishing the family as the focus of service, the parents as members of the team and the home as the base of service (Mott and Lunsford, 1979).

The social worker on the team is generally responsible for coordinating the activities of the various service providers engaged with the family. As the team member who generally has the initial contact with the family and the ongoing responsibility for planning, the social worker develops, with the family, an overview of their needs which determines which services are most appropriate. Referral to homemaking services is thus based on a mutual assessment between worker and family. In some communities homemaker services are provided under the auspices of a multifunction social service agency while in others they may be a part of a separate and distinct homemaker service organization. In either situation the social worker can provide help to the family and the homemaker as they work to accomodate each other. The social worker maintains ongoing contact with both the family and the homemaker, evaluating whether agreed upon goals are being met by the service and reevaluating the appropriateness of the goals. The homemaker uses the caseworker for support and consultation. This reduces the likelihood that the homemaker will feel overwhelmed and isolated as she intervenes in what are often highly demanding and painful situations. Furthermore, a natural triangle exists among the three major parties involved in the service, the worker/agency, the homemaker/agency, and the family/children. The worker, in the relationship with both homemaker and family, must avoid triangling or being triangled, and must be prepared to resolve the conflicts which often arise among the parties involved. The worker is engaged in a relationship of mutuality and reciprocity with the homemaker and must demonstrate respect for and acceptance of the homemaker as a full partner in the intervention process.

## Services Must Be Sensitive to Culture and Community

The homemaker's relationship with the family must be predicated on the knowledge and acceptance of their cultural values and lifestyles. So much of what occurs in a household is bound by culture. Whatever new ideas are introduced to the family must be consistent with this reality. The Family Union takes this variable into consideration when engaging families. Bush notes:

> In a Hispanic family, for example, the father feels that providing for his family is his responsibility and he is reluctant to seek help, even to accept such benefits as food stamps and Medicaid. If there's a man in the household, any work you do with his wife could easily be sabotaged by him. We sometimes have to reassure the man that we're not trying to intrude or take over his role, but that we want to help. A lot of times they don't want the help. (1977:85–86)

If the homemaker ignores culturally determined patterns of relationship or insists on changes which are incongruent with the family's values, the homemaker's help will surely be rejected either overtly or passively.

To insure that the assistance provided has some utility to recipients programs must be based in the community. Experience has shown that services which are developed with the participation of community leaders are more likely to be accepted (Kline, 1978). If, however, the values reflected in the program represent the dominant white culture, the resulting value judgments and imposition of middle-class norms will foster mistrust rather than functional survival skills. Homemakers are frequently recruited from the community they serve which allows them to bring to their work "a wide range of knowledge and experiences which reflect the dreams and aspirations of the community, as well as the trials and tribulations" (Mott and Lunsford, 1979:218). The homemaker's knowledge of the community allows her to assist in mobilizing the natural helping networks which may be available. Baby-sitting, transportation to appointments, and food shopping for a homebound mother are examples of services a homemaker can make available through use of her own community network. Teaching families how to use formal resource systems also becomes an easier task when one is intimately familiar with where and how these systems operate.

Homemaker services may provide short- or long-term, partial or full in-home care for children whose parents are unable to provide this care. This supplement to family resources may well obviate the need for the placement of children, preserving families and reducing both human and financial costs. We now turn to a consideration of day care, the other major type of supplemental care for children.

## Day-Care Programs

The varied history of day-care programs for children has shaped both their focus and design. The earliest child-care centers were developed to protect children of poor and immigrant working mothers. As such, they emphasized the custodial care of children who would otherwise be left unsupervised while their mothers worked (Steinfels, 1973). The kindergarten movement, which also emerged in the mid-1800s, was primarily concerned, in contrast, with the education of young children of middle-class families. As these two parallel movements developed over time, they maintained the fundamental distinctions between day care as a Child Welfare service and nursery school as a middle-class educational institution. It was not until the mid-1960s that these two approaches began to converge and that day care began to be recognized as a vital resource for a broad range of families. First, the Economic Opportunity Act of 1964 recognized that day-care services should be broadened to meet needs other than those for custodial care. This Act also emphasized the paramount importance of the parents in the child's development. The design of Head Start reflected this orientation. Similarly, the vast increase in the number of middle-class women in the work force prompted strong advocacy for both quantity and quality in day-care programs (Steinfels, 1973).

As a consequence of these changes, day care has developed into a service that can support families with young children in their role of child-rearing. It has become a central concern of the child-care movement to advocate for such services to be available to all families who desire or need them (Roby, 1975). The rationale for this position is a strong one, since such a service assists parents in meeting economic needs, fulfilling themselves as individuals, and sharing the burdens of child-rearing. At the same time day care allows children to develop their potential in a safe, healthy environment that promotes social, emotional, and cognitive growth.

As with homemaking services, child day care has increasingly been viewed as a resource for the prevention of placement of children from high-risk families (Fanshel and Shinn, 1978). The central element of day care as a supplemental service is a focus on the needs of both the child and the parents, of the total family. Many such family-focused child-care settings have dealt with a variety of at-risk populations. Their successes have strengthened the view that providing appropriate and concrete support to families at-risk is the key to maintaining families as intact units.

A wide variety of day-care services for at-risk families have been utilized. These include drop-in centers, crisis nurseries, and intensive therapeutic settings. Occasionally family services are integrated into existing day-care programs, and many programs will assist families with transportation to enable them to make use of a day-care program. Given the variety of needs that potential consumers of such services might have, a community seriously committed to diverting families from child placement will find ways to provide a spectrum of day-care services.

Drop-in centers provide free or low cost respite services for overburdened parents who have few financial resources and limited social supports. Undemanding and high quality child care which gives parents "time out" brings families to these centers. In such programs, parents may simply "drop off" their children as need dictates, or they may stay and participate in the care of the children. Parents who meet together at the centers often benefit from the friendships, mutual support, and peer education which are nurtured through contact in drop-in programs (Pettiford, Hasenfeld, and Raney, 1976). The following vignette illustrates this latter point.

> Mrs. Sima Evans, a young Iranian woman married to an American, brought her three-year-old daughter Marina to a neighborhood drop-in center at the suggestion of hospital staff, who had noted Mrs. Evans's anxious and sporadic visitation with her husband, who was hospitalized with an acute illness. Mrs. Evans was grateful for the hospital's wish to help, but she was also very worried about leaving her child at the center. She told the staff that Marina had never been left with a baby-sitter in her own home. The drop-in staff listened carefully to her concerns, shared information about their program, and gave both mother and child plenty of time to explore the facility. Mrs. Evans was reassured that Marina would be safe and well cared for in her absence. Upon her return to the center, she was surprised to learn that her daughter had played with the staff and other children, only occasionally asking when her mother would return.
>
> After several days of bringing Marina to the center, Mrs. Evans began to share information about herself, particularly her feelings of fear and loneliness. Her husband's illness, their financial stresses, her own sense of being cut off from family and her isolation from anyone she could turn to for help, and her dependence on her child to provide companionship all were unfolding as the staff went through this crisis with the mother. Slowly she began to talk to other parents at the center, to feel more comfortable about leaving her daughter, and to explore some of the community resources suggested by staff and other parents.
>
> When Mr. Evans left the hospital the family continued to use the center several times a week. Mrs. Evans developed several friendships with other women and began to arrange exchanges of child care with them so that her daughter could play with other children, in the process beginning to overcome her own isolation.

A drop-in center clearly is a very helpful resource for parents who, like Mrs. Evans, are under some particular stress and need relief from child-care responsibilities by dropping a child off to stay with responsible adults in a familiar setting (Broadhurst, Edmunds, and MacDickens, 1979). Such centers may also provide nonstigmatizing, natural environments where entire families may be helped to reverse cycles of dysfunctional interaction or to prevent total breakdown.

The crisis nursery provides an example of short-term service specifically designed for families at risk of dissolution. Usually available twenty-four hours a day, seven days a week, a crisis nursery can give parents prompt relief from their children when they are experiencing overwhelming stress (McQuiston, 1976) and can provide protection and care for children while assisting parents in finding and using the resources that will reduce their stress (Shapiro, 1980). At the Crisis Care Center in New Orleans about 90 percent of the children housed in the Center overnight have been returned home. It is estimated that, if the Center did not exist, about 50 percent of the children cared for would have been placed in foster homes (Shapiro, 1980). Certainly these statistics indicate the crisis center's potential in preventing unnecessary child placement.

While therapeutic day-care programs are varied in their design (Bean, 1975; Gardner, 1975; Mirandy, 1976), they share a common focus on the total family. In this model, the day-care center serves as the focal point for coordination of service delivery to the entire family. The Family Stress Center in Chilla Vista, California typifies this holistic approach. The goals of this program include promoting optimal development in both children and parents and teaching "positive parenting" as a means of dealing with stressful situations. To these ends, the Center provides a myriad of service components which include: positive parenting training program, parent aide program, emergency caretakers, child-care center, individual and family counseling; pre- and postpartum parents groups, mothers' group therapy, baby-sitting, advocacy, transportation, psychological testing, children's group therapy, and Parents Anonymous groups (Virginia Commission for Children and Youth, 1977). Interestingly, the day-care component of this project was not central in its initial conception. Only over time has it become recognized as being essential to the children and the parents. For the children, the center provides a break from the conflicts at home; for the parents it provides time to "effectively integrate and utilize the insights they gain from counseling" (Virginia Commission for Children and Youth, 1977:3.3.10).

Another program exemplifying the productive attributes of this model is PACE (Parent and Child Education) in the Bronx, New York. This program provides parents who have been labeled as mentally ill an opportunity to improve their personl and parental functioning while receiving needed concrete support from the nursery school. The PACE staff might, for example, engage the family by involving fathers in couples therapy, accompany a mother to school to meet with teachers of older children, and include older siblings in their program during holidays or vacations. Follow-up of PACE participants indicated that they "seem better able to use community resources . . . are less isolated, less likely to be on medication and better able to separate their own problems from those of their children" (Knitzer, 1982:36). All of these changes are indicative of these parents' increased adequacy in their parenting role.

Even when a day-care program is not equipped to offer multiple services to the family, it can still provide for the developmental needs of children and give parents needed respite from parenting. Because many needs of families first come to the attention of child-care staff, the day-care program should strive to integrate and coordinate community services for its participating families. To facilitate this mobilization of services, community-based child-care programs should have a social work staff person to work with families and other social agencies. When such a staff member is available, day-care programs become better able to integrate children from high-risk families into their programs with minor adjustments in their regular routines (Mirandy, 1976:233). The Children's Center in Biddeford, Maine, for example, integrates handicapped children into a community-based day-care program. What makes the program particularly helpful is the attitude of staff toward parents, depicted in the following excerpt.

> Potluck dinners, picnics, trips, open houses, the Annual Halloween party, the Wednesday morning coffee hour, are a few of the numerous informal parent activities that revolve around the center. Sheila Cook, the social worker responsible for the Wednesday coffee hour, characterizes it as "a time when parents can make connections with each other. A lot of these mothers really haven't had much of a chance to socialize—they are home with young kids, with not very much money." Conversations at the coffee hours cover many topics. One morning, a mother started to talk about a legal dispute she was involved in. It was striking to watch the way the group worked. Everyone offered suggestions. There was no sense of the staff member's being apart from the parents—except that after the meeting he took responsibility for offering to call the Legal Aid Society. (Galinsky and Hooks, 1977:102)

As can be seen, a variety of possible options exists in supplemental child care for high-risk families. Although each program may be novel in its structure and components, each has several common principles of practice which make it uniquely suited to strengthen families and to prevent child placement. The same five principles applied to homemaker services will be discussed as they are put into action in day-care settings.

*The Services Plan Should Develop Out of a Collaborative Effort between the Family and the Service Provider*

Investigators of "quality" day care largely agree that family involvement is an essential component of child-care programs (Provence, Naylor, and Patterson, 1977). Whether parents use day care so that they can be free to work and to provide income for their families, because they need respite, or because they or their children are committed to enhancing their coping skills, the role of parent must be acknowledged, supported, and strengthened. Recognition of this has led to program designs which incorporate parents and focus on the developmental needs of both parents and children. The collaborative process in day care is therefore twofold. It implies that programs will be implemented so that parents and caregivers comfortably share child-rearing responsibility, and it also involves the parent and staff in planning together for individual needs.

Research from the Yale Child Welfare Research Program strongly supports this notion. These outcomes indicate that "since the young child's development at any point is closely linked with his parent, immediate and short-range goals for enhancing development must be addressed to the parent–child relationship and interaction" (Provence and Naylor, 1983:150). This evidence further reinforces the principle that child care must be supportive of the parental relationship and not attempt to supplant it. Further, "improving the adaptive capacities of the parent, assisting them in their lives as adults as well as parents, exerts, in most instances, a positive influence on their functioning that continues into the future to the child's benefit" (ibid.:150). In practice, maintaining a commitment to a collaborative process between parents and staff dictates individualizing services based on joint assessment of need. The Yale project successfully incorporated this principle by designing a program which communicated to the parents the belief that they were full partners. Goals for children were developed by consensus between parent and staff, and the ongoing operation of the center included parents in all aspects—through frequent communication with staff, regular contact with the center, and modification of the program based on parental concerns. The creation of a bridge between the center and the home, accomplished through such activities as staff visits to the home, parental inclusion in center activities, and the use of telephone calls and photographs of the parents to reduce separation anxiety, was the most significant demonstration of their ongoing centrality in their children's lives.

In providing services to the parents themselves, the Yale project maintained a commitment to this collaborative process through their awareness that "one must distinguish . . . between outreach and intrusiveness, between guiding parents and lecturing them, between providing them with the tangible supports they appear to need and enabling them to get these for themselves, between imposing, even in a benevolent fashion, one's own goals for them and helping them to define and consider their goals for themselves" (ibid.:161). The long lasting success of this project for the families who participated has been attributed to this philosophical stance and the implementation of these goals in practice (Trickett, Apfel, Rosenbaum, and Zigler, 1982).

## The Services Must Be Delivered in a Timely Manner

High-risk families frequently lack a "lifeline"—a network of informal relationships to which they can turn during crisis or when under a great deal of stress (Beezley, Martin, and Alexander, 1976). Programs designed to provide assistance to these families must keep in mind that stress and crisis do not just exist between eight and five on weekdays.

Crisis intervention services, extended hours, weekend programs, and hotlines for this population have all been developed to be responsive to the needs of families in crisis. Fearful that their situations will label them as "bad parents," many high-risk families do not seek help until they are experiencing a crisis. The crisis intervention staff often has the task of engaging parents in their first helping relationship.

At the Crisis Nursery established at the National Center for the Prevention and Treatment of Child Abuse and Neglect in Denver, Colorado, sensitivity to the needs of all family members has shaped a program which meets the immediate need for child care and focuses attention on both children and parents. Recognizing that bringing a child to the nursery may often be a veiled attempt by parents to ask for help for themselves, the staff facilitates that reaching out by minimizing paper work and providing a supportive and welcoming atmosphere (McQuiston, 1976). Establishing this relationship with otherwise reluctant parents can be critical in constructing needed links with community resources and in enabling parents to use helping agencies and share the care of their children for the first time (ibid.).

Many programs which offer ongoing assistance to high risk families recognize their families' needs for crisis services, too. The PACE program, discussed earlier, has a 24-hour hotline to respond to program participants' crises and has staff available to make home visits, if necessary. Waiting lists are also minimized in this program by providing an ongoing entry group for new participants until there is room for full involvement (Knitzer, 1982).

Timely child care services are not just appropriate for crisis situations. Parents may need child care to attend ongoing therapy sessions, go shopping, see a movie, or relax. Recognizing this need, some communities are even providing short-term drop-in care at shopping malls. Other communities are responding to the needs of single-parent families who work afternoon and night shifts with child-care programs open in hours most suited to families' needs. Still other programs illustrate attentiveness to the plight of working parents with ill children by including an infirmary or having staff who can go to the home.

## Services Must Have a Long-Term Commitment to Families

Many programs which are designed to work with high-risk families are treatment oriented and therefore are time-limited. Families' needs for child care and support, however, do not end because the course of treatment is terminated. In fact, the child-care needs of most families at risk are inherently long-term. Running a treatment program conjointly with a day-care setting allows for a smooth transition for both children and parents who may have a difficult time maintaining relationships (McQuiston, 1976). Other programs concerned with this transitional issue for children and parents have considered establishing "follow-through" centers where parents and children can continue to get needed support (Gardner, 1975). The issue of transition is not limited in relevance to high-risk families. Continuity of care is one of the mainstays of quality child care for all populations (Provence, Naylor, and Patterson, 1977).

It is important to remember that child-rearing is an ongoing process of many years duration. A child's needs for nurturing and a parent's need for support continue through all the stages of childhood. Child-care programs have the potential of providing supplemental nurturing and support throughout those years. Interestingly, research has shown that family-oriented social work services greatly increase the length of time a family will use a particular day care center (Heinicke and Strassman, 1977), thus increasing the continuity of care. The implications of this research for the design of child care programs is great. It has been recommended that social work services supportive of parenting roles and of the development of adults and their children should be available as part of all day care services (Heinicke and Strassman, 1977). This type of service would certainly increase the potential for child-care programs to have a long-term positive impact on families. Where such programs exist currently, high-risk families are able to get needed assistance from a program which is available until the preschoolers reach school age. Sadly, in many instances the support that parents and children receive in child-care programs is nonexistent in public schools. Many programs report parents coming back to seek help. Some day-care programs are realizing that if the program "truly offers enrichment rather than merely care and protection, some degree of contact even after the child is in primary school is essential" (Caldwell, 1975). One approach to the notion of long-term commitment is for child-care centers to establish after school programs for their graduates. Parents who work or need the support provided by the child-care program could certainly benefit from such an arrangement.

## Services Must Be Coordinated

The issue of day care for children from high-risk families cannot be addressed without reference to coordination. Quality child care is always an interdisciplinary effort requiring expertise in child development, interpersonal relationships, health, and nutrition. The comprehensive nature of a child's needs requires that multiple services be offered to promote optimal development. We have already discussed the belief that this includes services to total families, since child and family developmental needs are interdependent. Whether the child-care program is comprehensive and has a variety of components (as exemplified by the Family Stress Center and the PACE programs) or it uses community support systems to supplement its own functions, the various service providers must be coordinated in their efforts to support the family in its functioning.

The staff social worker most frequently occupies the role of coordinator. In programs where there is no social worker on staff this role generally falls to the director. Since service coordination is crucial with high-risk families, who are usually involved with a variety of service providers, programs without a staff social worker may not be as effective. The social worker is the center's liaison with families and with the community. Using their knowledge of family and community systems they provide consultation to other staff, work with families to develop service plans, make referrals, collaborate with community resource people and are "casefinders," identifying families with need for support services (Woods, 1973).

The Head Start program is particularly relevant as an example of a community-based service which provides both internal and community coordination as part of its mandate (McLain, 1978). The objective of Head Start in closely coordinating its own and community resources is "on ending the immediate jeopardy, meeting the individualized needs of the child, helping the parent(s) deal with their own needs, and assisting the parent(s) in mobilizing the needed community resources" (McClain, 1978:22). Without coordination to address these concerns and integrate the component services into a well-synchronized whole, the varied systems tend to work at cross purposes or to duplicate services, compounding the family's stress and further reducing their coping ability.

## Services Must Be Sensitive to Culture and Community

Child-care programs serve as vehicles for the socialization of young children and therefore must be sensitive to and consistent with the values and child-rearing philosophies of the families they serve. Providing a variety of options is the only way to insure that parents will have the opportunity to select a program with such sensitivity and consistency. By including parents in the planning, reflecting parental attitudes in the development of program, and responding to parental concerns as well as the needs of the children at every step in the process, child-care programs can increase their sensitivity to and support of parental roles and family cohesiveness.

Evelyn Moore of the National Black Child Development Institute suggests the shape child-care programs might take to meet the specific needs of the black community. To enhance a child's self-esteem, she states, the program "must emphasize the parents' values, and reflect the heritage of the Black Community" (Moore, 1982:419). She goes on to suggest that parent participation be encouraged, that the curriculum be ethnically sensitive, and that social and health services be integrated into a comprehensive child-care services plan to reduce the difficulties families experience in trying to cope with the bureaucratic maze. Project Head Start is seen by Moore as a model for child-care programs. Although grounded in a deficit model which labeled its participants as disadvantaged, "by combining novel elements of community control and parent involvement with quality educational programming and access to social services, it successfully overcame any 'deficit' mentality in its conception" (ibid.:422).

Certainly these same ingredients are relevant to the planning of any child-care program. Child-care programs should be part of the ecological life space of the families they are designed to serve. These programs and the professionals working in them must involve and be responsive to the ideas, lifestyles, and values of families, rather than, as professionals so often seem to do, "take over" from parents the rearing of their own children.

In conclusion, Child Welfare services must support families and children. As Margaret Mead has said: We now expect a family to achieve alone what no other society has ever expected an individual family to accomplish unaided. In effect, we call upon the individual family to do what a whole clan used to do (Margaret Mead, quoted in *Information Canada*, 1974:4).

Historically, Child Welfare services have tended to supplant rather than to supplement parental care. Operating from an "all or nothing" position, the tendency has been either to neglect families totally on the grounds that government should not interfere in family life, or to respond to troubled situations by placing children out of the home, often for long periods of time. In recent years, the principle that care should be given in "the least restrictive environment" has become the touchstone for policy and service development in health, mental health, and social welfare. Translated into Child Welfare, this principle dictates that the maintenance of the biological family is the preferred option in the care and protection of children. Homemaker services and day care are only two of the many supplemental resources needed to help maintain families at risk, to enhance parental care, and to prevent the placement of children.

The essential characteristic these programs have in common, when they appropriately address their goals of supporting and strengthening family life, is the ability to tap family strengths and to help families to develop their own competence as parents and as community members—in other words to perform, in our modern world, the functions of the clan.

# EXEMPLAR IV–A

# Group Work with Mothers of Mistreated Children
## A Method of Empowerment

MIRIAM MELTZER OLSON

There is an abundant literature pointing to the usefulness of groups as a vehicle for service delivery in settings which deal with the problems of child abuse and neglect. Many different kinds of groups, such as those focused on psychotherapy, family life education, parent self-help and structured parent skill training, have been found to contribute to improved parent–child relationships (Collins, 1978; Dinkmeyer and McKay, 1976; McNeil and McBride, 1979). Despite differences in method and goal, a large measure of success in any group is related to the powerful phenomenon of sharing experiences with others in like circumstances. However, all groups are not equally successful, nor are all groups equally attractive to their intended beneficiaries (Mannino and Conant, 1969). In fact, both the literature and the practice experience in many agencies suggest that forming and sustaining groups in protective services can be very difficult (Wayne, Ebling, and Avery, 1976). Of course, developing relationships with parents suspected of or found abusing or neglecting their children is a difficulty in all protective service practice—not just group work.

Yet the purpose for which a group is formed can be a crucial factor in its capacity to engage. The purpose and subsequent design of a service generally emerge from a perceived need. What the perception of a need or the definition of a problem is, then, takes on paramount importance in the creation of any given service. The approach to helping described in this paper emerges from a particular view of the needs of a population of parents who come to the attention of Child Welfare agencies because of mistreatment of their children.

It is most often women, and particularly poor and minority women, whose relationships with their children are likely to come to the attention of Child Welfare agencies. Despite some currently changing views, our society continues to hold men not very accountable in the care of their children. While incidents of child abuse and neglect occur in all segments of society, middle- and upper-class families are often protected from involvement with the public Child Welfare system by influential relatives, family physicians, or referral to mental health centers or private psychotherapists. Among the effects of the inequities in the assignment of responsibility for treatment of parent "offenders" is that the stigma attached to child abuse and neglect is assigned to the protective agencies. That, in turn, further stigmatizes the protective services clientele. Neither the inequities nor the stigma escape the notice of those women who are seen by protective service agencies. In fact, involvement with these agencies is, for many poor and minority women, only another instance of their wide experience with these phenomena. The conditions of their present lives, their own childhoods, and even the routes by which they enter the service system attest to this fact.

Data drawn from work with such stigmatized women in numerous public Child Welfare agencies will be used throughout this paper to illustrate their situations and practice responses to them. In the interest of confidentiality, specific identifying data have been omitted or changed. The following is one example taken from a group formed for mothers of children referred because of neglect and risk of abuse.

> The Greenville agency is set in the small urban center of a largely rural area which lost its main industry twenty-five years ago and has persisted as one of the country's economically most depressed areas for a generation. The overwhelming majority of the population is white and descended from central and southern European ethnic groups. The women comprising the group reflect the ethnic mix of the community, its geographic dispersion, as well as the problems of the community's economy, which include high unemployment, inadequate housing, and lack of public transportation.
>
> The group consisted of five women who at the time they entered the group were 18, 19, 20, 21, and 29 years of age. Three of the women had three children each, two had two and one of these was expecting her third, and one women had one child. The children were all five years of age and under, with siblings very close in age. Two of the women had had three children in less than three years.
>
> Three of the women had been married once and divorced. They did not marry the men they subsequently lived with, nor had the other women

married the men with whom they lived or who were the fathers of their children. With few exceptions, the men involved had limited occupational skills and were sporadically employed.

Although all of the women were of average or above average intelligence, none had completed high school or had held a full-time job. Most had serious limitations in their ability to read and do math. All were receiving public assistance. With the exception of one of the members who had obtained a comfortable apartment through a housing assistance program, all had problematic housing situations, such as substandard living conditions and little safety, and all had moved frequently.

Unemployment, alcoholism, and physical violence were common conditions in the families in which the women had grown up. Three had been known to the agency as mistreated children. Lack of supervision and truancy were chronic complaints of reporting agencies and housing had been a persistent problem for their families. Just as the group members suffered abuse from the men with whom they lived, so had their mothers before them been abused by their husbands. The women's entry into the child protective service system as parents came mostly as a result of application for public assistance and request for housing assistance. Investigators, finding conditions such as instability in living arrangements, volatile family relationships, and inadequacy in children's diets, had made referrals to the Child Welfare agency.

Even in the absence of certain specific data about the unique aspects of each woman's situation and personality, it is apparent that their needs for help could be perceived in many different ways. Two perspectives have dominated in Child Welfare practice. These two perspectives focus, reasonably enough, on the mothers *qua* mothers. That is, in one view, the mothers are seen as having shortcomings in their ability to care for their children, because of emotional immaturity, unmet dependency needs, and other personality defects stemming from their own mothers' failure to care for *them* adequately as children. In the other approach, parental performance is viewed as a learned function and the mothers are seen as deficient in acquired skills necessary for executing their maternal role. Both approaches do recognize that the mothers' social milieus play a part in sustaining or mitigating the problematic interactions between mothers and children and may offer some assistance with problems in the environment.

The approach which is presented here is based on the view that the social milieu is central to the problem of child mistreatment. That is, even if the women were emotionally malnourished themselves and therefore unable to satisfactorily nurture their own children, or if they had inadequate opportunities to observe and learn necessary skills of child care, their experiences as parents are profoundly shaped by their social circumstances. Without money and education, the women occupy a lowly status in the community, and their relationships are marked by a lack of power.

Women like the group members in Greenville, or like parents who grew up in urban ghettos, continue to be subject to a double penalty as women. They have been, on the one hand, offered little or no preparation or encouragement for giving direction to their own lives. On the other hand, because of the poor job opportunities for men with limited skill and education, they have had little chance of realizing whatever benefits accrue to women whose husbands provide their economic and social status. The alternatives available to these women, then, for meeting such basic needs as food, clothing, housing, and medical care, are few and usually require reliance on public institutions. Their vulnerability to the authority of impersonal agencies is thus one of the distinguishing characteristics of these women's relationship to their social environment, including the manner in which the women come into contact with the child protective system.

The women in the group described were referred when they sought financial assistance and assistance in locating housing. In communities with large public housing complexes, reports of suspected child mistreatment often originate with housing managers. In cities where poor families tend to receive their medical care through clinics or hospitals, especially teaching hospitals, mistreatment investigations are frequently undertaken in response to reports made by doctors, often interns or residents, with whom the parents have had little or no prior contact and who may never even discuss their findings, questions or intent to file a report with the parents themselves.

The point in this examination of the route into the Child Welfare system is not to question the alertness of institutional representatives to the susceptibility of children to mistreatment. It is rather to note not only that poor women are more involved with institutional representatives than others, but that their involvement subjects their behavior, their housekeeping habits, and their child-rearing practices to the scrutiny and judgment of those institutional representatives. When there are questions about their families' circumstances, they are referred to other institutional representatives—in this case, Child Welfare workers—for further scrutiny and judgment. These referrals involve no choice for the women and are often made in a highly impersonal manner.

The powerlessness vis-à-vis institutional authority which characterizes the women's social status is associated with the hopelessness the women demonstrate about the circumstances of their lives and in the lack of expectations they hold about possible change or the idea that they can be contributors to change in their lives. In turn, their alienation from social institutions and their hopelessness about change are reflected in the difficulties protective services workers experience in trying to establish helping relationships with these women.

Because women's social situations play a central role not only in parent–child relationships but in determining whether the women come to the attention of the child protective service system at all and the expectations they have of that system, the service design proposed here operates from the position that the needs of the women as mothers cannot be adequately served except by dealing with the needs of the women as women. The aim of the service is to help the women overcome the powerlessness which marks their relationships and their images of themselves.

The choice of a group approach to service follows directly from these considerations. Groups have the potential for offering a multiplicity of helping relationships and diluting the authority of the worker. They can afford members the opportunity to garner strength through numbers and joint efforts and provide for the giving and taking of help as equals. This is not to say that all service groups by virtue of being groups can effect a change in the usual power relationships between clients and workers. Rather, specific measures are required to realize the group's potential for making such a change.

To begin with, rather than being preprogrammed, groups should be, initially and continually, open to input from members about the particulars of group process, including its purpose, norms, priority issues, format, and so on. Such openness recognizes that the women's perceptions of their own needs are valid, are valued in the shaping of the service, and that the "expert" power of the worker has limits. When groups are offered to prospective members with a statement of intent to provide help in dealing with the stresses in their situation, and allow for contract negotiation, the groundwork is laid for greater equity in the service relationship. Since contract negotiation involves the development of a working agreement about not only the aims of the service, but also its methods, the issue of relationship can be directly addressed from the start. That is, the initial deliberations should include discussion of the way members can be of help to each other and the worker a resource to them in their interaction.

Of course, simply discussing an approach to working together is not sufficient for overcoming the social distance between worker and clients, given the depth of experience the population under consideration here has had with social agencies, and given the real and imagined threat of the protective agency's power to remove their children from them or otherwise intrude into their lives. The worker needs to acknowledge that threat and to be continuously vigilant to any expressions—however subtle they may be—of the apprehension and mistrust the women feel. The worker needs to assure members of their freedom to voice their fears and to seek and find validation from each other, as well as being able to accept without defensiveness the feelings the women may express about him or her. The aim of this very careful attention to the relationship between the women and the worker representing the Child Welfare system is not to deny, but to recognize, the power differential and therefore to move past some of its barriers. Also the aim is to provide the women with a model for other relationships in which they might exert greater influence.

To serve the group purpose, the worker needs also to be vigilant to issues that reflect difficulties arising from other relationships the women have with institutional authority. The call for vigilance here stems from the fact that because of their lack of expectations, the women may voice complaints about their children's teachers, clinic personnel, or others in their lives who may have power over them, commiserating with each other but not presenting their concerns as issues to be examined or problems to be solved. The worker therefore needs to engage the members to move beyond ventilation to an examination of the issues. In the process of exploring problems, the worker is likely to find that the members' outlook on difficulties, as in the case of their sense of helplessness and hopelessness, keeps them from solving problems. When this occurs, the worker needs to alert the members to their attitudes and ask them to consider their effects.

The work of helping the women deal with troublesome relationships requires, in addition to exploration of the problem and encouragement of active responses to them, detailed consideration of measures for coping. It cannot be assumed that even as the women come to accept the possibility of taking action in their own behalf that they would be adept at implementing their intentions. Looking at alternatives, rehearsing possible dialogues, and anticipating pitfalls, are examples of important steps in group process that recognize the fact that new ways of relating to old situations are usually very difficult. In groups which followed the process described here, members found, for example, they could initiate conferences with teachers and raise questions about their children's progress, rather than waiting to be "summoned" because of a problem. With preparation and persistence they could get understandable answers to their questions from doctors. Through joint effort they could get the Child Welfare agency itself to consider the feelings of its clients and use unmarked cars for transporting them.

This last situation provides an excellent example of the process described and especially of the conversion of "gripes" into meaningful work. The situation occurred in a group for mistreating parents in Fleetwood, a small suburban community:

During informal conversation, as the members were assembling for their meeting, one woman mentioned the unpleasantness of having to be brought to the agency in the yellow station wagon with its large "Welfare Department" insignia painted on the doors. There were sighs and nods of agreement, and a few women described problems they had with their children when "transportation" took them for a clinic appointment or elsewhere, especially if a car called for them at school. The worker picked up on the subject and acknowledged the discomfort the women felt. Although the women merely shrugged at that point, and appeared ready to "begin" their meeting, the worker asked that they continue to look at the problem. They wondered what good it would do, and the worker pointed out to them that transportation was a service, that they got it because they needed it, and that she didn't think they should have to be humiliated when they used a service to which they were entitled. The women were not quite as incredulous at hearing the worker speak about their rights as they had been the first few times she did it, and talked heatedly about their humiliation and embarrassment in many situations.

Out of this discussion the women recognized a theme that had been emerging over several sessions—frequently they and their children ended up at odds with each other over an outside provocation which actually they shared. As such connections continued to be made over time, and as jokes about the "yellow bus" persisted, the worker asked the women if they thought they ought to do something about it. They disparaged the idea, could think of nothing to do, and complained that it was futile to try to get "the county" to change. The worker pointed out how frequently they were bothered by things they believed they just had to endure, asking them to consider how that attitude had come about. While most of the women were unable to identify any specifics, and maintained the view that it was "just the way things were," they did acknowledge that they had had many disappointments and didn't like to get their hopes up any more, and that they felt worn out and angry that some people got what they wanted and they never did.

After further discussion of the effect their exhaustion and anger had on their day-to-day activities, and particularly on their relationships with their children, the worker again proposed testing the possibility of dealing directly with the source of their frustration. A member who had been helped by the group to seek legal aid to deal with a housing problem supposed that "it would break up the monotony, anyhow," and following her lead, the women agreed. Role playing and other problem-solving measures were then used to chart a course of action and to help the women prepare themselves for it. The women ultimately met with the head of the protection unit, whose help the worker had enlisted, the agency executive, and the regional supervisor for children's services. They presented their position with clarity and forcefulness and were very well-received. The problem for the children made a particularly strong impression. When the women were told that the situation would definitely "be taken under advisement," they were prepared and asked for a date when they could expect to hear what would be done. They were given a date and were actually informed prior to that date that, for the time being, agency staff cars rather than the station wagons would be used for transporting children and that the questions of what to do about the station wagons was being looked into. At the very least, it was expected that when new station wagons were bought they would not be made so conspicuous.

The women were very pleased with themselves and each other over the manner in which they had handled themselves during the meeting and were glad they were getting some action. They remained guarded in their expectation of the future outcome of the situation and suspicious of the motives of the people with whom they had met. As they reviewed their experiences in the situation, they decided that what they had done was to get rid of a problem which often made them act like "bad mothers," yelling at and hitting their children for causing trouble when they had to use "transportation," and that by doing something about the problem for their children, they had acted as "good mothers."

The problems such women have with powerlessness and hopelessness enter into many of their closest relationships as well as their institutional ones. It is in their most intimate relationships that the inability to perceive change is often most deeply embedded. Also, exposing the details of these relationships to the Child Welfare worker often places the women in the greatest jeopardy of being sanctioned by the agency. For these reasons, and because in general the movement in helping situations is from the less to the more intimate, the potential for helping the women reconsider their dealings with parents, spouses, lovers, and others depends on the trust and confidence developed through the work on institutional relationships, including those with the worker.

A telling consequence of the effort to bring about change in the typical worker–client relationship in one group of agencies was that at least one member of every women's group brought to the group a concern which revealed activities and events that were threatening to her child's well-being and could have prompted the kind of worker intervention that the women most guarded against. In one situation, a woman who had not followed through on a plan she had made with the support of the group to move out of her unheated, rented room to her parents' home admitted that she feared her father might sexually molest her daughter as he had molested her as a child. In another group, a member told of her despair over her husband's violence, and of her four-year-old wandering off unnoticed while a fight went on between her husband and his friends at their home. A neighbor returned the child after he had been gone for several hours.

In addition to revealing a new openness to help from the groups and the workers, a part of what makes these illustrations telling is that the group workers had also had prior casework contact with the women and had what appeared to be reasonably positive working relationships. The women dealt with other social workers as well. However, information about the molestation, the violence, and other incidents had been carefully kept from agency scrutiny. Once opened, it was possible for the women to try to help each other find ways to extricate themselves from abusive relationships. It was also possible, in one case, for plans to be made for the temporary placement of a child at risk of abuse while the mother worked out a suitable plan for herself and her family.

In all these situations and others, such as the one involving the transportation difficulty, the women brought to the group problems in relationships which affected them as individuals and affected their interaction with their children. As they also examined and worked on finding more satisfying ways of managing those relationships, they also examined the ways in which they dealt with their children. They gained understanding of their children's needs and increased responsiveness to those needs.

The movement within such groups from work on institutional relationships to work on intimate relationships may not proceed smoothly or directly. As mentioned earlier, the possibility of change in their personal relationships may seem even more remote to the women than change in impersonal relationships. To facilitate the women's consideration of new ways of managing their personal relationships the worker may again need to call the members' attention to their views on change. At this later stage in the group's evolution the worker should also be able to point the women in the direction of their past accomplishments, and help them to draw on their experience in handling relationships differently. Again, acknowledging and helping the members examine the difficulties which attend changing established patterns may be needed. Reflection on the subject of rights in relationships may also again be indicated. In general, then, the work of the group needs to be supportive of the women achieving equity in close relationships as well as others.

Clearly, the proposal presented here for an approach to work with certain mistreating parents has its roots in a concern for the damaging effects that classism, racism, and sexism have on them and their families. The method of working to help them overcome some of those effects does involve consciousness-raising. However, consciousness-raising groups per se are not being proposed. For the most part, organized liberation groups are perceived by these parents to be a part of the social order from which they feel alienated. The consciousness raising, therefore, has to arise from the necessity to deal with specific events, to solve specific problems. For these women there is a necessity to preserve their relationships with their children. If their experience in mutual aid, born of that necessity, helps them to achieve a new effectiveness in situations which had earlier distressed and demoralized them, participation in other change-oriented empowering groups can follow. Tenant action groups, groups for abused spouses, welfare rights organizations, home and school associations, and food cooperatives offer further opportunities for the women to work with others on particular common problems and to advance their interests. Helping the women become connected with such groups, as well as with consciousness-raising groups, needs to be a part of the work with them.

Numerous other necessary components make up the provision of services to families of mistreated children. While they are not the subject of this presentation, two particularly important and related components of this approach should be noted: work with men who biologically or socially are the fathers of the children and work directed toward the political, social, and economic conditions which contribute to the vulnerability of children to mistreatment.

To summarize then, the focus of this discussion is direct group work with parents of mistreated children whose involvement with the Child Welfare system is linked to their low status as poor and minority women. The concern is with helping the women overcome the powerlessness and hopelessness which are functions of their status and which undermine them as parents. The group approach outlined makes full and deliberate use of mutual aid for problem solving and for correcting the power imbalance between clients and the protective service system. It gives attention to helping the women deal with day-to-day stresses and problems which arise from power unbalances in various relationships. Helping the women know and claim their entitlements in their dealings with institutional representatives is seen as necessary both for its own sake in more effective coping and as a step toward managing troublesome intimate relationships more effectively. Helping the women experience themselves as effective, influential participants in relationships is seen as a vital contributor to improved parent–child relations.

# EXEMPLAR IV–B

# The Ethnically Competent Social Worker

JAMES W. LEIGH, JR.

The "melting pot" theory of American culture has, in the last twenty years or so, lost its adherents and its validity. The notion of cultural pluralism, given impetus by the value changes emerging from the civil rights movement and by other social forces as well as by a number of research studies, has taken hold among the public, among social scientists, and in the social work profession. It has become increasingly evident that to be effective in service delivery, the social worker of today, and of the future, must be sensitive to ethnic considerations and competent in dealing with ethnic concerns.

Ethnic competence is defined as the knowledge and skills which result in the worker's ability to understand and utilize ethnic information in daily practice. This information includes the world view, customs, language, common history, family patterns, relationship and parenting styles, values, and other characteristics of various groups linked to ethnicity.

A distinction should be made between the concept of "ethnic" and the concept of "minority." In this exemplar, the focus is on ethnic *minorities*. "Minority," as used here, refers to those ethnics of color in America who have been oppressed throughout history and have suffered various forms of racism. These persons are mainly Asians, blacks, Mexican-Americans, Puerto Ricans and others of Hispanic origin, and American Indians. The term "ethnic" is clearly a much broader one and is variously defined. However, in general, "ethnic" refers to any people with a common culture, history, and identity. Minority is also broadly used in society and in the professional literature to refer to subgroups that experience oppression and discrimination related to such variables as age, gender, sexual preference, handicap, political affiliation, or social deviance, as well as to race or ethnic background.

With these concepts as a foundation, what are the skills, attitudes, and practice concepts needed for effective and ethnically competent service delivery?

## Skills and Attitudes of the Ethnically Competent Social Worker

Our practice skills grow out of and are largely influenced by our personal world views as well as our social and cultural experiences. Social workers, like most people, tend to view more positively and to relate more comfortably to those people who are most like themselves in terms of class, gender, values, and ethnicity. Moreover, although "difference" can become more acceptable when we experience it and understand it, often the "other" or the unknown is abstracted and depersonalized. People who differ from us are not thought of as men, women, or children, but as characteristics or symbols of a particular race, caste, or class. Representatives of "different" groups become dehumanized, and to the more threatened among us, persons whom it is only right to destroy by conscious design or benign neglect.

Persons of an ethnic minority, either individually or in groups, overtly or covertly discriminated against and defined negatively by the majority, often internalize the negative images and thus become handicapped by overwhelming feelings of powerlessness and hopelessness. What often seem like individual or personality problems then may be understood as a combination of social structural deficits and obstacles and individual lack of skill or confidence in negotiating existing resources. The social worker's challenge is to help ethnic minority persons to overcome their sense of powerlessness and to engage their environments more competently, as well as to influence their environments to be more responsive to their needs.

The Child Welfare worker must be able to assume, even in one case situation, a multiplicity of roles including those of social advocate, educator, broker, case manager, counselor, and therapist. Cleckley (1980) indicates these additional skills:

1. Ability to analyze and understand individual and social problems.
2. Capacity to conceptualize the issues and apply theoretical knowledge within the realm of direct services.

3. Ability to consider and examine the prevalence and incidence of social problems, and the effects of discrimination and racism with a view toward increased feeling, understanding, and commitment to change.
4. Ability to assess the strengths of individuals and families.
5. Ability to select the modes and levels of intervention needed to support the problem-solving efforts and outcomes.

Cleckley further delineates the attitudes of the practitioner in the following four areas:

1. Concern and interest in minority individuals and institutions.
2. Commitment to needed change, i.e., to eliminate, modify, and/or prevent such problems as racism, poverty, poor housing, mental illness, and mental retardation among minority populations as best one can.
3. Willingness to alter basic assumptions about the social structure, minority persons, and minority communities.
4. An unpatronizing attitude based on a thorough understanding of the history, culture, and needs of minority groups. (Ibid.:27)

Knowing about the culture of the ethnic minority person is essential, but it is not enough; that knowledge must be translated into practice. It does little to appreciate an ethnic minority culture and not appreciate the people of that culture. In the following pages, three concepts will be advanced that reflect current thinking about practice with ethnic minorities: empowerment, hope, and race.

## Empowerment

Empowerment is a very important concept that primarily through the work of Barbara Solomon has taken hold in the social work practice literature, particularly in relation to ethnic minority persons. Empowerment is a process through which the social worker engages in activities with the person or unit of attention that aim to reduce the powerlessness caused by negative evaluations based on membership in a stigmatized group (Solomon, 1976).

To be powerless is to be unable to manage emotions, skills, knowledge, and material resources in a way that effective performance of valued social roles will lead to personal gratification. These power deficiencies stem from a complex and dynamic relationship between the person and a hostile environment.

The social worker may intellectually learn the concept of empowerment; applying it to the process of helping is a different matter. Along with discussions of empowerment and its meaning, one has to make further differentiations between levels of power. Indirect power blocks occur on three levels:

— At the primary level, negative evaluations or stigmas attached to racial identifications become incorporated into family processes and prevent optimum development of personal resources . . . i.e. positive self concepts, cognitive skills, etc.

— At the secondary level, power blocks occur when personal resources that have been limited by primary blocks in turn act to limit the development of interpersonal and technical skills.

— At the tertiary level, power blocks occur when limited personal resources and interpersonal and technical skills reduce effectiveness in performing valued social roles. (Solomon, 1976:17)

These three levels are incorporated into the developmental experiences of the minority person through relationships with important others. Direct power blocks, on the other hand, are based on negative evaluations that are not incorporated into developmental experiences, but are applied directly by a representative of society's major institutions. These also occur on three levels:

— At the primary level, this may occur when inadequate health services in a community lead to poor health conditions . . . Thus, there is a direct block to the development of good health—a valued personal resource.

— At the secondary level, blacks as individuals may be denied an opportunity to develop interpersonal or technical skills through limitations placed on educational opportunities. . . . The individual has the personal resources required to develop these interpersonal or technical skills but is not permitted to do so.

— At the tertiary level, either the valued social roles themselves are denied or some resource important to the effective performance of the role. (Ibid.:18)

Empowerment as a practice concept has implications for both assessment and intervention. For example, empowerment in process means we, as social workers, actively engage the ethnic minority person in case planning. We begin to share our power with those who feel powerless.


## Hope

The quasi-religious emphasis of certain concepts such as hope, faith, and charity have all but disappeared from social work education. Hope is a necessary attribute of the ethnically competent social worker. An absence of hope stimulates feelings of powerlessness about oneself and the environment. Infusing hope into the relationship can become a communication process among people in a helping situation. It is a truism that hopefulness, both on the part of the client and of the social worker, is a necessary condition for achieving power or becoming empowered.

Hope is defined as a feeling that what is wanted will happen; it is a desire accompanied by expectation. Hope is a subjective term, an expectation that there is an opportunity for achieving a goal. These subjective states are directly related to anxiety because greater expectations imply challenges and obstacles. Thus many of us may, to ward off anxiety or risk, set only limited goals for ourselves.

The social worker can communicate hopeful expectations regarding the client's ability to overcome problems and to achieve goals. The worker's optimism can serve as a catalyst, but in the end the energy and the ability for change must come from the client. If the worker can stimulate hope, which in turn leads the client to hope, to act, and to act more confidently, then the client begins to develop a sense of mastery. These successes, in turn, encourage clients to hope more and to risk more actions for themselves.

While the ability to communicate hope is essential in social work, hope which is inappropriately communicated can be more harmful than helpful. Some workers may communicate hope mechanically, in ways that belie conviction or belief in the client's ability to succeed. Some workers may assume that the communication of hope is enough, underestimating the seriousness of the problems, the damage done by repeated failures of the past, and the desperate need for more active advocacy on their part. Other workers may communicate hope unrealistically in situations where little or no remedy, or at least the remedy hoped for, is likely to occur, thus stimulating avoidable despair.

## Race

The key to successful practice in "racial social work," according to Brown, is "the recognition of the client's racial identity and the strengthening of their racial group identification, by drawing attention to the inherent positives of their race" (1976:24). The assumption that racial similarity or difference between worker and client has a profound effect on the helping process has been widely researched. In fact, it is well known that, in work with the ethnic minority client, racial or ethnic difference may be a barrier to relationship formation and solidification of the therapeutic alliance. Husband (1980) believes that race and ethnic identity are critical elements in determining whether a member of a particular ethnic group will even become a client of a particular social service agency.

Thus the social worker engaged in a working alliance with a minority client has to be able to recognize and deal with the implications of racial difference. Race as an issue must always be listened for and references to racial issues pursued. This is not an easy task. "Some clinicians," according to Alexander and Sillen, "tend to avoid discussions about race, either because they are uncomfortable about the subject, unclear about their own views, or fearful that such discussions will be painful to the patient. This can happen in the treatment of children as well as adults" (1976:143).

Every cultural group has its own modes of and rules for communication. Thus some traditional techniques, such as reflection, reaching for feeling, or asking for insights concerning a thought or feeling, may not work well with some ethnic or racial groups. A particular query may be seen as inappropriate or intrusive, thus failing to elicit a useful response and increasing the minority client's sense of distance and distrust.

The client's communications about race or racial issues may be direct and open, comfortable or angry and hostile, or they may be expressed symbolically or metaphorically. Language can be used to mask real meanings and personal concerns. The social worker must listen very carefully to tease out the meanings behind overt communications, since the client's language idioms, cultural symbols, and attitudes toward authority may affect the nature of expression.

Whether communication about ethnic or racial difference is open or masked, the worker needs to create an atmosphere in which the client feels it is acceptable to discuss or demonstrate these feelings. The following case vignette illustrates how references to racial issues may be made symbolically.

> Dan, a 10-year-old American Indian, was placed in a disrupting white foster home and was being seen by a white female foster care worker to help prepare him for a replacement. Dan was playing with toy men of different colors, red, green, black, white, and yellow. He would pair the toy men off and have one knock the other down. This play went on for some time with no conversation between the worker and the child. The worker noted that the red toy men always seemed to remain standing, victorious in the encounter.
>
> The worker asked what had happened to the fallen men. Dan replied that they were all dead. The worker observed, "All but the red men." The child agreed. He then began lining up the red toy men in a row, placing one of them in front as if to form an army unit with a leader. The worker said nothing. The child and worker gazed at each other. There was a silent period of time, and then Dan placed the red toy man he had designated as leader on a horse and rode him off. Dan then said he was leaving, and walked out of the room.
>
> The worker was very aware that the child expressed through his play his wishes to be more powerful, to join with others of his race, to lead, and to conquer. Underneath, of course, were his feelings of helplessness and

alienation. This ethnically competent worker, however, recognizing the importance of silence and of symbolic and nonverbal expression in the Indian culture, did not attempt to translate into words the powerful interaction between them.

Workers must also be able to understand the implications of racial prejudice and discrimination not only for the client but for themselves. A worker must be able to acknowledge his or her particular difficulties with "difference," to recognize personal blind spots, and to ask for help from the client and other representatives of a particular ethnic group when confused, or in need of more knowledge.

While knowledge about cultural characteristics and experiences is vital for ethnic-competent practice, it must be remembered that each individual in any ethnic group has unique experiences and interpretations of those experiences. The practitioner sensitive to ethnic concerns must walk a fine line between using cultural knowledge for greater understanding or using it in stereotypical ways that block the individualizing of a particular client in a particular environment.

## Assessment and Intervention in Ethnically Competent Practice

Central to professional social work practice is the assessment of the data gathered from observations, interviews, and other sources. Accurate assessment should include a descriptive summary and interpretation of data to guide the planning for change. In relation to ethnic minority clients, as with all clients, a full assessment requires an examination of personal, family, and community strengths, so that such strengths may be mobilized and supported. An accurate assessment also implies a recognition of the interrelationship between conditions of deprivation, social stresses, and behavioral or emotional disturbances.

In the social welfare field, however, assessments of minority clients are often limited because of lack of cultural understanding, and social services to such clients are predicated on incomplete knowledge of the minority client's circumstances, strengths, resources, motivations, and problems. Interventions based on such incomplete assessments are, at best, irrelevant and, at worst, harmful. In many cases, assessment proceeds from a deficit notion of minority functioning and is thus limited to individual family "pathology." Similarly, the target for change is limited to the individual or family rather than to any of the oppressive conditions which continue to breed hopelessness and powerlessness.

The following case, involving a Mexican-American mother and her children, presents an example in Child Welfare of what can be seen as a failure of ethnic sensitivity and competence.

### The Vasquez Case[1]

Mrs. J. Vasquez, age 38, arrived in a Midwestern industrial city from Mexico at the age of 16. She subsequently married and gave birth to six children in as many years. At the age of 23, Mrs. Vasquez was divorced by her husband. Overwhelmed and alone, she abandoned her six children in a public park. Mrs. Vasquez was charged with neglect and abandonment and the children were placed in foster care, where they remained over the years. Mrs. Vasquez herself received no follow-up services.

This young woman, in the following years, gave birth to eight more children. The oldest is now 14, while the youngest, a girl named Marisa, is four. With the exception of one child who lives with relatives, all of the children have been raised by Mrs. Vasquez. In 1977, Mrs. Vasquez was charged with neglect and this second set of children was removed from the home. However, these eight children, as official wards of the court and under the supervision of a caseworker, were returned to her the following year.

Mrs. Vasquez and her children, at the time of this incident, were living on AFDC assistance of $900.00 per month, supplemented by food stamps.

In April of 1980, three years after the return of the children, a relative of Mrs. Vasquez phoned the social agency to report that Marisa, the four-year-old, was being neglected by her mother. A caseworker visited, was refused admission by Mrs. Vasquez, and left, not to return again. In June, 1980, (three months later!) another caseworker visited and entered the home, since she found the front door open and no one at home. She discovered Marisa alone in a back room. Marisa, filthy and unkempt, was huddled in a corner. She weighed, it was learned later, only 14 pounds. The police were summoned and Mrs. Vasquez was arrested. Marisa was taken to a hospital and the other children were placed in emergency foster homes.

After her arrest, Mrs. Vasquez tried to explain that Marisa was epileptic, and that she was ashamed of her. It was learned that Mrs. Vasquez had tried several times to abort the pregnancy but had been unsuccessful. The child was born crippled after a difficult breech birth, and shortly after her birth, began to suffer seizures.

Mrs. Vasquez was ordered to have psychiatric tests. Her court-appointed lawyer stated that Mrs. Vasquez was unable to communicate with him even through a Spanish interpreter nor could she understand the role of the lawyer, the judge, or the prosecutor. However, a psychiatric examination concluded that Mrs. Vasquez was mentally competent. The psychiatrist stated that she was not suffering from any active hallucinations or mental delusions that would challenge her competence to stand trial.

It was learned that Mrs. Vasquez had herself been a victim of child abuse. She pled guilty to the charge of cruelty to a child, her lawyer raising the question of why only one child was singled out for neglect. Mrs. Vasquez was sentenced to two to four years in prison for deliberately starving Marisa.

In discussing the case, an Aid to Families with Dependent Children supervisor felt that there were three reasons why casework services were so lacking in the case.

1. There is no system of routine home visits because the system cannot afford house calls.
2. The quality of life is incidental to welfare services. Only Children's Protective Services becomes involved in such things as the quality of life.
3. The law protects the privacy of individuals. Inspection of homes cannot be done without a court order.

The director of the state Department of Social Services requested an intensive review of Children's Protective Services cases and stated the Vasquez case was a symptom of pervasive problems in the service programs. These problems included: (1) inadequate case reviews; (2) high worker turnover and insufficient staff training; (3) unjustified removals and inadequate screening of parents before children are returned home; (4) weak counseling and homemaker services; and (5) shortage of foster parents.

In the Vasquez situation, it is probably accurate that all these issues related to service effectiveness were factors in the neglect of Marisa and in the tragic outcome of the case—the virtual destruction of a family unit. Issues not raised, however, include the minority status of the family and how this influenced the lack of services, the ethnocentrism of the helping community, and the ethnic competence of the helping professionals involved.

The following question must be raised: Would a Child Welfare worker with the knowledge and practice skills needed to engage Mrs. Vasquez, and to understand and interpret her needs and her actions in the context of her cultural history and ethnic identity, have been able to intervene more helpfully and effectively in this case?

This case, although sensationalized in the media and lacking in detail, may be instructive in stimulating us to think about what ethnic competent practice might imply for work with such a family. We may safely conclude that Mrs. Vasquez was not understood and indeed was neglected by an unresponsive if not discriminatory society. It seems incredible that a woman may give birth to and raise six children, only to have all of these children permanently placed. We can only ask whether this family was identified as "at risk" and helped at any stage. Do we wait until whatever fragile homeostasis that existed has totally broken down?

How is it that this mother, whose first set of children was removed permanently, who presumably had no additional resources or help, was able to raise another set of children and presumably to neglect one or more of them without notice or intervention? And after the second set of children was removed from the home and later returned under court and social services supervision, how could the child Marisa come close to literally starving to death over a long period of time without those workers accountable for help and supervision to this mother and her children noticing? Once again, having failed to prevent or even to monitor the tragic neglect of another set of children, and at the point of another total family breakdown, the courts and the social welfare system seem to have only one solution available—the total dissolution and perhaps permanent destruction of the family as a unit. This case is a shocking illustration of social and professional neglect.

Ethnic competent practice implies, first of all, that it be recognized that Mrs. Vasquez is an overwhelmed single parent, poverty-stricken, and cut off from her roots, in alien surroundings. One can only surmise the growing sense of hopelessness and powerlessness she experienced over the years. Did any of the workers who had contact with Mrs. Vasquez over the years speak or understand Spanish? Did any of them have any understanding or appreciation of her culture or her values? For example, did anyone have any understanding of what it might mean to a Mexican woman—and to her place in the community—to be abandoned by her husband, or how someone of her background might understand and interpret a seizure disorder?

One must ask: Was help extended in a way that she could understand and accept? Was a worker assigned, who even if English speaking, could understand and transcend the communication barriers in helping this mother who was uncomfortable with English and in stressful situations had difficulty communicating in her own language? Was any effort made to transmit hope for change or progress, or to empower such hope? Did anyone ever discover what resources might exist among extended family or friends, and then encourage and support these resources on behalf of the family? Did anyone try to discover the meaning of Marisa's epilepsy or her disability for Mrs. Vasquez? Did anyone try to help her understand the malady and seek and use appropriate medical care?

We don't know the answers to these or many other questions that should be raised. But we do know that 14 children from a single family became disrupted and separated, cut off from family and perhaps from all that was familiar. We know that a hopeless and disenfranchised mother has been defined as a criminal, rather than as someone badly in need of help from a society that turns its back on many of its minority members.

Unless our society can develop a system of resources and services delivered in effective and ethnically competent ways, we may predict a dire future for many ethnic minority children. The future of social work as a profession depends on our commitment to creating a more just society for all of our people. Each individual must be addressed in ethical and ethnically competent ways. "We can be ethical," according to one humanitarian, "only in relation to something we can see, feel, understand, love or otherwise have faith in" (Aldo Leopold, in Gibbons, 1981). The direction is clear as we work with ethnic minority families and children. We must see them, we must feel with them, we must understand them, we must love them, and we must have faith in them.

# A Family Treatment Approach to Sexual Abuse of Children

Bennie M. Stovall

Only recently has sexual abuse of children emerged as a central concern in the field of Child Welfare, in spite of the fact that knowledge of the nature, causes, and treatment of child abuse and neglect has been accumulating for some time. Even in those cases where sexual exploitation of children is blatantly exposed, the remedies are usually fragmented, simplistic, or superficial, and in effect are no remedies at all. To some extent, at least, this situation reflects the tenacity of societal taboos concerning human sexuality and sexual behavior. It also reflects a reluctance to invade family privacy, or to interfere with the sanctity of parental autonomy over children.

## History of the Project

Children's Aid Society of Detroit (CAS) is a private nonprofit Child Welfare agency. Founded in 1862, the agency has provided the traditional services of adoption, foster care, and medical and dental assistance, as well as services to single parents. Over the years, in addition to direct services to children and families, the staff has been actively involved in identifying and seeking ways to meet the changing needs of the community.

In July, 1973 CAS initiated a demonstration project, the purpose of which was to develop a treatment model for sexually abused children. Unique in the state of Michigan, actually the program evolved slowly over several decades and represented a response to a culmination of concerns shared by professionals in the Detroit area. The futility of the various approaches attempted by law enforcement agencies, juvenile and criminal courts, child placement services, and individualized psychotherapy or casework efforts brought professional leaders together to consider alternatives. In a context of increasing public awareness and social change, impetus for the design of a comprehensive treatment approach to sexual abuse of children grew.

With the moral and financial support of an informed and sensitive board of directors, the agency hired two masters' level social workers to provide this special service. The professional community responded very quickly in referring families for service, confirming the hypothesis that there was indeed a significant unmet need. A commitment in the form of a purchase-of-service contract was obtained from the Department of Social Services in 1974 and was renewed annually for several years. The CAS project, entitled "Special Family Problems Services (SFPS)," was funded originally by Title XX through a contractual agreement with the Protective Services Division of the Michigan Department of Social Services.

When beginning to work with these families, we had limited information about how best to provide the service, although we were aware of and excited about new theories and approaches to family assessment and intervention developing in the family therapy field. We believed that sexual abuse of children should be viewed as one aspect in a constellation of family problems and, therefore, that it must be treated within the context of the family.

Sexual abuse of children is defined as "adult exploitation of the normal childhood developmental process through the use of sexual activities, e.g. touching, kissing, fondling, genital manipulations and actual intercourse" (Stovall, 1974). While this is neither a legal nor a social definition, it clearly defines what we have seen to be a consistent relationship between the child and the abuser. Using this definition, we limit our intervention to "in-family" situations, that is, to sexual abuse involving a member of the child's biological family, or situations in which the adult person has an intimate or integral relationship with the child's family such as that of "significant other" or "living-together partner."

During the course of the demonstration project, the two workers were able to provide services to approximately forty families. In the first contract year, the staff expanded to four social workers and a supervisor. Since 1975, the unit has expanded to six workers and a supervisor, and has provided service to an average of about 350 families per year. In the ten years of experience, we have seen more than 2,000 families and have developed expertise in a diagnostic team approach, therapeutic investigation, in individual, family, and group counseling modes, as well as in coordinating community resources and networks on behalf of these families and children.

"Diagnostic team" refers to the use of two practitioners in a team or tandem model, even though the case is assigned to one practitioner. The purpose of the team model is to accelerate and objectify the initial and ongoing assessment processes. It is also used to provide the family with an "informed" resource in the absence of the assigned worker. This approach also reinforces safety factors and can reduce individual burn-out as one shares the responsibility of therapeutic decision-making.

"Therapeutic investigation" is a process in which the first contact is made in a positive or "joining" manner. It is essential in this first contact to convey the agency's wish to help the family rather than an intention simply to confirm abuse, although the agency has a protective responsibility which must be clarified for the family. From the beginning of the first contact, considerable emphasis is placed on identifying the family's strengths.

We define individual, family, and group counseling broadly, and draw upon a wide array of methods and techniques in identifying the patterns of difficulty and in developing resources for change. We do not believe the admission of abuse by the adult individual or other family member is necessary for progress.

The reinforcement of community networks requires the SFPS worker to intervene on behalf of the family to establish constructive links with needed supportive and strengthening resources and less stressful connections with those systems with which the family may be negatively associated, such as the schools, police, Departments of Social Services, or the courts. In assuming these mediating, brokering, and advocacy roles, the worker also may have the opportunity to help educate agencies that may be critical or punitive to better understand the problems and needs of families in which sexual abuse occurs.

## Focus of the Project

In the past, prevailing responses to child sexual abuse have been "offender-focused," geared toward the apprehension, punishment, and sometimes the rehabilitation of the offender. While legal action may be called for in some extreme cases, in the process of seeking a conviction the child's developmental level and ability to understand or participate, his or her attachment to the abuser, or the broader familial and social patterns that contribute to the abuse may all be ignored, exacerbating the emotional trauma to child and family alike. Punishment without family change is rarely a solution to the range of difficulties most of these families encounter. Whether or not the family itself chooses to pursue criminal prosecution, the focus on the offense and offender diverts attention from other underlying family system problems and from the rehabilitative tasks confronting the child and the family. The following case example is representative of referrals received by the unit.

Mary Turner is a thirteen-year-old white female who confided to her maternal grandmother that her stepfather had been sexually molesting her for several years. The grandmother contacted the police who, after investigating, determined that there was insufficient evidence to pursue the case from their perspective. A Protective Service referral was made and subsequently SFPS was assigned the case.

Collateral contact with the police confirmed that Mary had given a statement that her stepfather had been "touching" and "kissing" her (in a sexualized manner) for the last three years. She also added that he had asked her to undress for him, a request that she refused. The last incident was reported to have occurred one week prior to the police report. At that time, her stepfather also allegedly touched her breast. According to the police, the parents have denied all allegations and have stated that Mary has a habit of exaggerating the truth for attention. There are three other minor children in the family.

The initial contact was by telephone with Mrs. Turner, the mother, who was somewhat reluctant to talk about the situation but agreed to set up an appointment after the child protection law was explained. In-person contact was made with Mrs. and Mr. Turner, who vehemently denied Mary's allegations and identified her as the problem. Throughout the visit it was observed that Mrs. Turner orchestrated the conversation while Mr. Turner assumed a more passive role. Efforts were successful during this visit in joining stepfather and acknowledging his difficult position in the family. Mother was also joined around her difficulties in parenting a "defiant" adolescent. The definition of the problem was partially reframed from one of sexual exploitation of a child to the challenges presented by remarriage, stepparenting, and solidifying a new family.

By the end of the session, a preliminary contract was formulated. It was agreed that: (1) Mary would be included in the next interview; (2) the worker could talk with the grandmother, who had made the original referral; (3) the worker would assume a liaison role between the family and the police if any further contact was needed; and (4) the worker would help the family in its communication with Mary's school, which was aware of the allegations.

In the next interview, both parents and Mary were present but Mary was reluctant to speak in the presence of her mother and stepfather. The worker had observed that Mrs. Turner tended to speak for all three of them, while Mary angrily objected and the stepfather made feeble attempts to mediate. The worker's first task was to comment on and alter the communication rules enough for some meaningful dialogue to take place. As Mrs. Turner was gently coached to allow the others to speak, Mary allowed to express her opinions without interruption, and Mr. Turner encouraged to articulate his position in the family, the family's central issues began to be revealed. Mary identified the family's difficulty as her mother's overly restrictive rules which prevented her from meeting and establishing friends of her own, her mother's nagging, and her stepfather's making her anxious and uncomfortable with "always trying to get too close." Mr. Turner said that he had never really felt that he had any "right" to interfere in the parenting of Mary, and that his wife became angry if he tried to develop his own relationship with his stepdaughter. He also complained that his wife's mother had never liked him from the beginning, and that his wife and her mother were "too close," excluding him. Mrs. Turner said that she felt she did not get real support from her husband in understanding the difficulties of raising a teenager, and that he was willing to share the "good times," but never wanted to help set limits or discipline Mary when she ignored her mother's rules.

Subsequent work with this family involved interviews with the parents, various individual members, and with the whole family, including the grandmother. Structural interventions were designed to help realign and strengthen the spouse subsystem, to establish a more solid parental sub-system, and to reinforce more appropriate boundaries between the spouse and child subsystems. For example, as the meaning of Mr. Turner's role as stepfather became more clearly defined by the couple, he was able to better share the authority role in parenting with his wife. As they began to agree on the rules of the household, Mrs. Turner was able to take a less rigid position in relation to Mary. Once her husband was willing to assume some of the disciplinary and rule-setting functions, Mrs. Turner was less threat-ened by the genuine warmth in the relationship between Mr. Turner and Mary, and she herself began to enjoy her "rebellious" adolescent daughter. In the two interviews which included Mrs. Turner's mother, the grand-mother shared her sad feelings about the loss of her first son-in-law, whom she had cared about a great deal, and was able to see that her loyalty to Mary's father had prevented her from giving Mr. Turner a chance to join the family in a fully accepted way. Mrs. Turner was encouraged to share her concerns and worries with her husband rather than with her mother, while the grandmother, as she became more accepting of Mr. Turner, was herself more welcome to spend time with the family.

To summarize, at CAS we believe that incest and sexual abuse are symptoms of dysfunctional family patterns. In the context of a systemic understanding of the issues, the worker may more clearly understand his or her role as one of helping to resolve, rather than confirming and "investigating," a problem of sexual abuse. As the family accepts this helping relationship, it becomes willing to risk sharing more information about family patterns and difficulties and more willing to risk the consequences of change. By remedying dysfunctional aspects in family structure, communication, or other family processes, the family stress level is reduced and thus the possibility that children will be subjected to further abuse. Practitioners can use the crisis state of the family (the public awareness of the abuse) as a mechanism for "unbalancing the dysfunctional homeostasis. The family becomes more accessible for intervention, and therefore services must be available immediately. A sexual abuse program should, then, be capable of immediate or near immediate response.

Finally, any such project should include a community education component. For the project to be successful, the community, including the professional community, needs to know that a service exists that has had success in working with families in which sexual abuse is involved, and the community needs to understand something about the ideology and approach of the program.

# EXEMPLAR IV–D

# Translating Infant Mental Health Research into Child Welfare Practice

Vivian B. Shapiro

In chapter 8, recent research findings in child development studies were eloquently reviewed. Robert and Patricia Pasick suggest that a vast treasure of scientific data awaits translation to policy and practice in fields such as Child Welfare. One area of research that may prove to be particularly applicable to Child Welfare practice is the study of infant development and infant mental health. This research is taking place in the fields of medicine, nursing, developmental and social psychology, psychiatry, and social work.

A theme that emerges from this research is the importance of the infant–parent relationship to the developmental and emotional well-being of the child. It is generally recognized that a stable, predictable, empathic, care-giving environment is the cornerstone of optimal development. Clinicians have begun to include infant–parent observations in the assessment of infants referred because of developmental difficulties, or infants at-risk because of suspected abuse or neglect. It has been found that detailed naturalistic observations of the infant–parent relationships broaden the purely medical or cognitive evaluation, and are an important addition to the evaluation of the mental health status of a baby.

It is the purpose of this exemplar to report on some findings of the Child Development Project in the Department of Psychiatry, University of Michigan, directed by Selma Fraiberg. This clinical research unit served a wide range of infants at risk, many of whom were referred by Child Welfare workers. The findings of this research unit pointed to two important areas that caseworkers need to consider in working with high-risk infants and their families: (1) the development of a working alliance with the family and (2) the inclusion of home visits and naturalistic observations in the assessment process. Findings have already been translated from the university-based research unit to the domain of Child Welfare practice.

## Opening the Door for the Assessment: The Parent–Caseworker Relationship

The Child Development Project (CDP) saw over 400 infants referred by a range of agencies. Many of the families were on AFDC and/or receiving Child Welfare services. When a child was referred to the CDP clinic for assessment, it was often at a time when the family was under extreme stress. Unemployment, physical or emotional illness, maternal depression, divorce, family dysfunction, or crises often precipitated a call for help. Sometimes a referral was made because the parents had been seen as inadequate and questions were raised about the children's safety and emotional well-being—referral factors familiar to practitioners in the Child Welfare field.

One of the most important set of findings of the CDP centered on the need for developing a working alliance with the parents. While the caseworker may have the intention of "assisting the family," frequently the caseworker is not received by parents as a "helping person." The development of a working alliance often tested the caseworker's skill and personal commitment. These were urgent cases, as infants at-risk are very vulnerable and caseworkers felt great responsibility to assess the at-risk status of the child and family. Why is getting started so difficult when the caseworker comes with good intentions and offers help and support?

The CDP study found that for all parents it is difficult emotionally to have concerns raised about their baby or their parenting. Despite often grim circumstances, each new baby had presented a hope for a better future. When things became difficult, it was painful for the parents to face disappointment in their baby, their circumstances, or their parenting. Furthermore, many of these parents had a poor history of object relationships, and had experienced many losses. There was little reason to trust a new and unknown caseworker. Trust and hope were largely absent in the families with a history of emotional deprivation and neglect, and expected disappointment or apathy was transferred to the new "helping person." Negative feelings toward authority figures often surfaced, and the caseworker was seen negatively, as having the authority to make decisions which would affect the family.

The research found that the caseworker had to support actively the development of a positive working alliance. Frequently, this meant addressing such issues as lack of trust, worry, hostility, and fear in the early stages of the assessment process. In addition to addressing the parents' feelings and concerns, the caseworker had to establish a common starting point about the need for the evaluation and what might come of it.

For example, in a case of a baby referred because of failure to thrive, the caseworker acknowledged that taking care of an unhappy and ill baby was difficult for the 17-year-old mother who was depressed. She suggested to the mother that by observing the baby together, talking about what had happened since the baby's birth, and assessing the baby's medical and developmental progress, some ideas might surface about what was the matter and why. The assessment might help reveal to the mother why the baby was having so much trouble: Was it because the baby wasn't able to keep food down, or was she difficult to feed? Rather than approaching mother in a negative way, this approach facilitated a strong working alliance as mother responded with tears acknowledging how difficult parenting was for her. Identifying with the plight of the family *and* that of the baby could pave the way for a working alliance.

Also, working with parents and infants was often a difficult and emotional experience for the caseworker. It is not easy to see a neglected baby and not be upset with the baby's parents. The worker's own strong feelings often made it difficult to be objective in the assessment process. Caseworkers needed the support of their colleagues in working through their own feelings, particularly in cases of abuse and neglect.

In court cases of abuse and neglect, the caseworker also had to address the issues of confidentiality and purpose of the assessment with the parents. It was found that a straightforward but sympathetic statement of the caseworker's legal responsibility, linked to the caseworker's willingness to help the family remain united if at all possible, was helpful in establishing a beginning alliance.

Involving the parents in the assessment process was also found to be important to the diagnostic process. The best picture of the social development of a baby is revealed in seeing the baby with the parent(s) in as natural a setting as possible. Babies feel and behave differently with parents than with strangers; at home rather than in a new or stressful place (like a hospital); when healthy rather than when ill; when relaxed rather than when tense. Therefore a relaxed parent was helpful in obtaining the best picture of the baby.

Furthermore, if a parent could engage in the assessment process with the caseworker and develop a working alliance, this was a positive diagnostic statement about the parent's own mental health status and level of ego strength. As we shall see in Case 2, where the parent was out of touch with the urgency of the baby's needs and the caseworker's concern, the prognosis was quite poor.

## The Assessment

The babies referred to the CDP were often referred because of developmental delays, atypical behavior, failure to thrive, or at-risk factors in the family. It was found that the best assessment of an infant's mental health and developmental status required a series of visits that included at least one home visit, and took place over a period of a few weeks. A thorough assessment required the integration of a medical and developmental history, observations of the baby's social responsiveness, and an assessment of the quality of the infant–parent relationship. An assessment also needed to include clinical interviews with the parent(s) to understand their general psychological health and feelings about the baby. Of course, it was important to understand the socioeconomic family context within which the baby lived, and whatever stresses had precipitated the referral.

Usually the caseworker was trying to assess three areas to judge the at-risk status of the child and the level of intervention needed. These areas are:

1. the stability and safety of the baby's environment (available through clinical history and observations and referral material)
2. the adequacy of the baby's medical, nutritional, and developmental status (available from medical data and developmental tests, such as the Bailey Scale of Infant Development, 1969)
3. the adequacy of the parents' responsiveness to the baby's health and developmental needs (available through clinical interviews and naturalistic observations)

Following are two case studies which illustrate the way in which the assessment process, including home-based observations, is helpful in formulating the treatment needs of families. In each case, the referral raised questions of abuse and neglect but the assessments revealed differences in the degree of risk to each child.

### Case Illustration 1: Delia

Delia was a four-month-old baby living with her unmarried mother and three-year-old sister. The family was impoverished and receiving AFDC aid. Delia's mother, Ms. M, was in her early twenties, obese, slow-moving, depressed, and disorganized. The Child Welfare worker saw the house as unkempt and uncared for, and was worried that Ms. M was unable to care for the baby, as she obviously was unable to care satisfactorily for the house or herself. A referral was made to the CDP for assessment and possible treatment.

Before the referral was mentioned to Ms. M, the Child Welfare worker and the CDP caseworker planned how the assessment would be presented to Ms. M. The assessment would be offered as a service that Child Welfare provided to parents who might need support or help with their children. They would offer concern to Ms. M regarding her feelings of loneliness. A child development specialist would visit and together with mother assess what needs she might have in relation to her parenting. A first visit was arranged at the home, at mother's convenience.

In preparation for the first visit, the CDP caseworker reviewed what a normal four-month-old baby should look like. The caseworker had an idea of motor and hand development, and also the language, social, and emotional development of an infant that age.

What did the caseworker see? Amid a home which was clearly impoverished and disorganized, was a young, heavy, and sad-looking mother whose eyes lit up whenever she looked at the charming active baby on her lap. Delia, the baby, obviously had had a great deal of social attention from her mother. Delia was expressive, responsive, and happy. She had excellent gaze exchange, and sought out mother's eyes as well as the caseworker's. She was more interested in people than in things. She smiled easily and vocalized responsively. When shown a new toy by the caseworker, she turned back to look at her mother and smiled, sharing the event with her. All these observations spoke of normal development.

The baby looked like she had been held a great deal. She was cuddly and relaxed as she nestled in her mother's arms. She had had experience sitting, evident in her motor and trunk development, as well as her hand and eye coordination. She held her head up well and used her hands appropriately for her age, bringing them together, and reaching for the rattle the caseworker had brought. Delia's sister, too, seemed attentive and interested in the toys that were part of the assessment of the baby's sensory–motor development. There was a general feeling of harmony and responsiveness within the family.

While the family was very poor, the baby did not seem to be suffering from malnutrition, nor had there been any serious illnesses. The assessment took place over four visits. Over the weeks, one set of observations was worrisome. Delia was not visually tracking well for her age. During the Bailey Development Test, it was evident Delia could not follow a pencil in an arc, losing track of it at midline. Her sister, too, seemed to have visual problems. It was clear that both children needed eye examinations.

What was the stability and quality of the parenting environment? Ms. M clearly was attached to her children and was empathic and responsive. She showed good judgment, provided accurate descriptions of what the baby could do, knew what the baby liked, and was familiar with the baby's sleeping and eating patterns. She was a good observer and a careful reporter. The greatest concern of the child specialist was Ms. M's depression and loneliness. The specialist acknowledged how difficult it must be for Ms. M to respond to her baby's cries when it seemed she might feel like crying herself.

What did this home-based assessment reveal? Delia was a healthy, expressive, four-month-old baby who showed signs of a very positive attachment to her mother. She had a visual problem which required medical attention. She was adequately cared for in most areas, except cleanliness. She was at some risk in that her overburdened mother was suffering from depression and without help might not be able to continue the good care she was presently providing.

The Child Welfare worker was able to use the assessment in case planning. The mother obviously needed further support for her own emotional needs, as well as guidance in housekeeping and some aspects of health care. The Child Welfare worker, however, could support mother for her good mothering and point to the progress her baby was making. Rather than revealing a situation of neglectful parenting, this evaluation opened the way to appropriate medical planning and supportive treatment plans.

## Case Illustration 2: Sandra

Let us now consider the case of Sandra. Sandra was a four-month-old baby girl referred for evaluation to the CDP by a public health nurse. The nurse's referral notes stated: "Sandra appears neglected. She is left to herself. She is always dirty. There are three other preschool age children at home and no father present. Mother seems unable to show warmth. She has refused help offered by the public health nurse and other agencies. Sandra was premature by one month. Her weight was 5 pounds, 3½ ounces at birth. She has been rehospitalized three times for illness, and her development seems retarded."

This referral indicated a number of at-risk signals. Sandra was a premature, ill baby, and therefore difficult for anyone to care for. Her mother, however, was having considerable difficulty providing basic nurturing care, cleanliness, and emotional responsiveness. In the referral, the baby was noted to be at high risk medically, as indicated by the three hospitalizations. Her development was in question.

A public health nurse encouraged the mother to phone the CDP clinic for an appointment to get help with Sandra. Although uneasy and suspicious, the mother did call and arrangements were made for a home visit where the infant specialist might explain to Mrs. A the services the clinic could offer.

All methodical planning for the visit was futile, however, because of the chaos and disarray the infant specialist encountered on the first home visit. Sandra lived with her three preschool siblings and her 25-year-old mother in a dwelling that showed signs of poverty *and* grave maternal inadequacy, perhaps mental illness. The rooms looked and smelled as though no one had ever cleaned them. The odor of feces was everywhere. There was no lock on the door, and the toddlers climbed on the staircase leading to the street. Mrs. A, haggard and unkempt, could only talk with anger about the two men who had fathered her children and left. Undirected rage and disorganization permeated the small apartment and surrounded the anxious toddlers. It was difficult for Mrs. A to concentrate on her children.

Where was Sandra? Sandra was almost invisible in this chaotic situation. The case report by the infant specialist reads: "On one of the straight-back chairs, there was a tiny infant lying on her back. Near the baby's cheek, but out of her grasp, is a bottle filled with milk. The baby is dressed only in a diaper on this cold day. An old shirt or rag is placed between the baby and the edge of the seat" (Fraiberg, 1980:43).

Since the mother knew the infant specialist was coming on that first visit, and also knew the public health nurse's concern regarding the infant neglect, diagnostically one must ask whether the mother was trying to convey how difficult and desperate her situation was. Perhaps she was telling the infant specialist that she was unable to provide adequate care to her needy baby by herself.

Over the next few weeks the grave status of this family became even more evident. Sandra's mother appeared increasingly depressed and distraught over her personal misfortunes. All her energy was directed to revenging those who had "betrayed her." The home situation became more chaotic as strangers drifted in and out of the house. There was little evidence of stability. Even the CDP infant specialist was treated like a shadowy visitor by the mother. He was allowed in, but Mrs. A could not focus on the concerns he had about the baby's health care needs. If Sandra were to cry, for example, the other children were ordered by her to get Sandra a bottle or to change her. Milk was often sour or unavailable.

What did Sandra look like over the four-week span? Because of the family stress, a Bailey Developmental Test could not be arranged. But, the observations of Sandra followed a consistent pattern. The case report states: "The baby was alone and unattended. The baby cries and no one responds. The baby clad only in a diaper in cold apartment. The baby positioned on chair or playpen so that she has no contact and cannot see others."

From this assessment report one sees impoverishment in the area of human attachments. "In the area of human attachments, there are no observations which show that Sandra recognizes her mother or discriminates her from other persons. There are no smiles for mother or vocalizations, no reaching for mother or anticipatory response to mother. This passive, unresponsive baby's behavior is consistent with others who approach her, like the infant specialist." There was nothing in Sandra's repertoire that spoke of human attachment or social pleasure.

In the cognitive–motor sphere, Sandra was very far behind. She did not meet the developmental milestones expected of a four-month-old baby. She could not track or visually follow an object. She did not attempt to reach for an object. She did not have midline organization, that is, she did not bring her hands together. She had poor trunk and neck control, perhaps because of no holding. Vocalizations were muted and they were not socially reciprocal if they did occur. Developmentally she was at least two months behind, according to the Bailey Scale of Infant Development (1969).

Diagnostically one had to raise questions as to whether the developmental retardation was due to prematurity, illness, organic factors, or the clearly inadequate home environment. The limits of Sandra's potential improvement were unknown, but it was clear that the status quo was inadequate and the medical and developmental risks very high.

Very soon the assessment took a serious turn when Sandra developed a cough and the infant specialist took the mother and the baby to the hospital. Sandra was diagnosed as having pneumonia, and the hospitalization was seen as a turning point wherein an extended reassessment of the family situation had to be arranged.

The observations of the infant specialist in the home visit situation indicated a very grave situation. Mrs. A was unable to provide any stability, health care, or safety for Sandra or the other children. Sandra was developmentally impaired in the emotional and sensory–motor spheres of development, while the other children also had poor language development and seemed pathetically neglected. Mother was emotionally very fragile and depressed, and unable to bring good judgment and even the most meager sensitivity to her child care. She was caught in a vortex of many conflicting emotions. The quality of her object relationships was very poor, both with regard to her children and her own personal relationships. She could not develop a working alliance with the caseworker and was unable to participate as a "partner" in the assessment process. Diagnostically, an important question needed to be asked: Was this mother sufficiently psychologically healthy to use professional and supportive help at this time, so that the development of her children could be protected?

The immediate prognosis did not look good to the infant specialist. The specialist's recommendation to the public health nurse was that this family needed to be referred to Protective Services and Sandra either kept at the hospital or in foster placement until a more comprehensive assessment of mother's mental health could be obtained. Unfortunately no extended family was available to help. This recommendation was made with the goal of protecting the children, rather than punishing the mother. It would be important to assess whether, with an active outreach program and concrete support, such as day care for the children, medical and nutritional supervision, and long-term treatment for herself, Mrs. A could be helped to achieve a higher level of parental functioning. One positive sign did emerge, however. During the hospitalization of Sandra, it became evident that Mrs. A could respond to the baby's medical needs, at least in her understanding of those needs, and she was willing to accept the fact that Sandra might need special attention, at least by others. This could be interpreted as a basis for treatment planning acceptable to mother.

While this case did not have as positive a prognosis as the case of Delia, the assessment process was helpful in articulating the various needs of the family and the urgency of these needs.

In this exemplar we have tried to illustrate how infant assessments and home visit observations may be helpful to Child Welfare workers whose task may be to assess the well-being of young children.

It was found that in order to assess the developmental well-being of children, it is important to establish a working alliance with the parent(s). This working alliance is helpful in completing a good assessment, and also is diagnostically relevant as the strength of the alliance indicates a great deal about the family's capacity to use help. The assessment of a young child needs to include attention to health, cognitive–motor development, social–emotional development, and parenting. Home visits are very helpful as the observations of child–parent relationships in a naturalistic setting strengthen the assessment. Each family situation is different, and the assessment and treatment plans lead to modified and unique directions for each family. The process is often stressful for the caseworker, as the infant at-risk is vulnerable to environmental factors, which adds a sense of urgency to the caseworker's tasks. The caseworkers themselves need collegial support and supervision.

Finally, it has been found through a statewide training program for infant workers that these research findings are translatable to Child Welfare practice in community settings (Shapiro, Adelson, and Tableman, 1982). It has also been found that Child Welfare workers themselves, by their observations and effort, are adding to knowledge in this field.

# EXEMPLAR IV–E

# The Crisis Nursery
## A Metropolitan Island of Safety

FLORENCE M. CERAVOLO

One of the most common characteristics of abusive parents is the absence of family and community lifelines during periods of stress and crisis. Studies indicate that in almost three-quarters of abuse related fatalities, the families had not been known to child protective authorities (New York City Human Resources Administration, 1981). Lack of appropriate resources, apprehension of losing permanent custody of their children, and fear of being stigmatized as abusive parents have often kept parents from seeking help before patterns of escalating violence become so entrenched that severe injury or death are likely to occur.

Recognizing the need for outreach services for potentially abusive families, the New York City Human Resources Administration responded to proposals developed by the Mayor's Task Force on Child Abuse and Neglect by establishing an "Island of Safety" program in New York City. In March 1982, the Crisis Nursery at the New York Foundling Hospital for Parent and Child Development was designed to provide a "cooling off" period for troubled parents and brief residential care for children at risk of potential or suspected maltreatment.

This exemplar will address the purpose, philosophy and day-to-day operation of a metropolitan crisis nursery, and will describe those elements essential in the development and administration of a crisis nursery. The nature of the program's in-service training and ongoing crisis supervision will be reviewed and an outline of the program's public awareness campaign will be included. Several case vignettes will be used to illustrate program function. Statistics, including the results of follow-up studies, will be presented.

The philosophy of the Crisis Nursery is based on a recognition that even "normal" parents may, at times, be overwhelmed by the demands of parenting due to a variety of personal and situational stresses (Dyer, 1965). Statistics indicate that, in the absence of significant family, social, and public support systems, diminished capacity to cope may lead to maltreatment of preschool and early latency age children by their parents and caretakers. In response to these realities, the New York Foundling Hospital Crisis Nursery was established as a nonthreatening resource with a mission to reach out to an isolated and frightened population.

To bring this service to the public's attention, a massive public campaign was undertaken jointly by the Human Resources Administration of New York City and the New York Foundling Hospital. Flyers were mailed to social service agencies, hospitals and schools; posters in English and Spanish were placed in income maintenance centers, unemployment offices, day-care centers, and housing projects. Television and radio spot announcements and interviews furthered public visibility of the program. As the program evolved, parents who had used the services of the nursery volunteered to describe their contact with the program as part of its public awareness campaign.

## Purpose and Description

The Crisis Nursery maintains a 24-hour capacity to respond to the needs of families in crisis to immediately reduce the potential for the maltreatment of their children. The Crisis Nursery has three major objectives: to provide a safe environment for children at risk of abuse; to serve as a nonpunitive resource for their parents; and to connect families in crisis with community-based services to diminish further the possibility of maltreatment. In addition to parents themselves who may call or walk into the Crisis Nursery, referrals are accepted from all public and private agencies. The program serves children and their families from all five boroughs of New York City and there is no fee for service.

Consisting of three major program components, the Crisis Nursery maintains a direct 24-hour Parent Helpline that provides immediate contact with social service staff, a residential facility that provides 24 to 72 hours of care for children at imminent risk of maltreatment, and a counseling service that provides crisis intervention, advocacy, and community referrals for preventive and supportive services to families even if their children do not require admission to the nursery facility itself.

## Services Provided by the Crisis Nursery

### The Parent Helpline

Staffed on a 24-hour basis, the Parent Helpline is the most common introduction to the services of the program. Bypassing clerical personnel, the telephone represents the most immediate link between the program staff and a parent in crisis and a child potentially at risk of abuse. As such, the phone serves a critical diagnostic and evaluative function. It is essential that workers be well-trained to respond with warmth and concern to the caller's needs. Acute sensitivity, in the absence of visual cues (Miller, 1973), is required to judge appropriately the immediacy of risk to the caller's child. A wide range of responses may be necessary depending on the nature of the situation. After careful exploration, some calls may represent straightforward requests for referrals to community resources; others, after establishing an empathic relationship, may require structure and in some cases, financial assistance to facilitate the parent's arrival at the nursery with their child. Still others may constitute a life-threatening emergency that requires immediate contact with the police or the city's Emergency Children's Service.

### The Nursery Facility

The residential facility provides ten beds for preschool and early latency age children. Divided into sleeping, dining, and play areas, the nursery is a cheerful and well-equipped temporary home. All children admitted to the nursery receive a medical examination both to assess the nature of their injuries, if any, as well as to rule out possible contagious illness. For many children who have received inadequate medical care, the examination—in which the parent is generally included—serves an additional purpose in alerting parent and staff to the need for further medical services.

Although most of the families who use the services of the Crisis Nursery are multiproblem, admission to the facility itself must disclose a connection between the presenting problem and the safety of the child to be admitted. For example, having no home is not sufficient to lead to a needless separation of parent and child; however, when the impact of being homeless is such that a child may be endangered, a brief respite is provided to parent and child until other arrangements can be made.

Recognizing the implications for young children of even brief separation from their families and familiar environment (Laird, 1979), casework efforts are directed toward involving the parent in the process of helping their child understand the need for separation (Simmons, Simpert, and Rottman, 1973). When a parent is too stressed, angry, or disorganized to do so, staff is trained to help a child sort out the confusion and fear evoked both by an unfamiliar environment and by whatever events have preceded their admission.

Maltreated children have very particular needs, each child requires specialized attention, and each may respond to admission in many different ways. Some may be extremely angry and act out; some may withdraw into passivity and despair; others may sob endlessly. Children who have been victimized may often view themselves as responsible for those acts of violence committed against them. Skill is required to enable them to understand that they are blameless. The predictability and consistency of the nursery schedule is as essential for confused, frightened, and hurt children in brief placement as it is in extended care.

## Counseling Services

A variety of counseling services are provided to clients of the Crisis Nursery. Counseling is based on a crisis intervention treatment model, focusing on the immediate precipitant and the feelings evoked by the precipitating event (Hoffman, 1975). While pathology can not be negated, a thorough exploration of client resources, strengths, and hopes enhances the ability of client and worker together to find the most appropriate plan for the immediate well-being of the client's child. Inclusion of significant family members may often prove helpful in stabilizing a distraught parent. The fluid nature of a crisis often lends itself to the beginning of a sound therapeutic process that can be continued in preventive community programs.

Advocacy may be required for families discouraged in their attempts to negotiate those bureaucratic structures necessary for their survival. Inadequate income maintenance services or hazardous housing conditions may often be ameliorated by staff persistence, relieving parental stress.

A crisis nursery must develop an extensive resource file and maintain close working relationships with community programs. The nursery may need to facilitate a decompensating parent's admission to a psychiatric facility. Staff may need to expedite foster care or residential placement for children whose parents may be unable or unwilling to resume their care. Caseworkers may need to secure homemaker or day-care service quickly for the immature or overburdened parent.

Thirty-day, three-month, and six-month follow-up studies were built into the program to insure that the client family has received services essential to minimize future potential for maltreatment. Follow-up contact is maintained with the service(s) to which the family has been referred, and should clinical judgment dictate, with the family itself. For those clients who are particularly tenuous, follow-up by nursery staff may continue on a daily basis until a well-established connection has been made with an appropriate resource.

Many clients, whose first contact with a helping agency has been the Crisis Nursery, initiate their own follow-up. Often viewing the Crisis Nursery staff as "family," clients keep workers apprised of their satisfaction with day-care arrangements, their success in finding livable housing, or their progress in vocational training programs.

## Liaison with Child Protective Services

All states, including New York, require a report to be filed when maltreatment has occurred. To insure that the self-reporting clients of the Crisis Nursery are treated with sensitivity and understanding, links were established with designated New York City borough Child Protective Service (CPS) offices, familiarized with the nature of the Crisis Nursery Program. When a report is required, parents must be fully informed prior to its filing. Parents need to be helped to understand that involving CPS does not represent punitive action or an attempt to place their child but rather serves the function of securing appropriate services more rapidly.

## Program Staff

One of the most critical elements in the success of a Crisis Nursery is a well-trained and committed staff. Line staff, consisting of three social workers, two family assistant workers, seven child-care workers, and the program secretary, were carefully selected on the basis of warmth, sensitivity, flexibility, and prior training. As working with abusive and neglectful families is emotionally draining, considerable thought must be given to staff needs to avoid worker burnout (Daley, 1979; Freudenberger, 1977). To insure staff cohesiveness and interdependence in an atmosphere of anticipated continued crisis, all workers were included in an initial in-service staff training program. Training was both didactic and experiential. In addition to program purpose and function, course content focused on those factors indicating various forms of child maltreatment and the particular needs of abused children. Role play was used as a training modality to humanize parents adjudged abusive.

Since the work is crisis-oriented, traditional supervision was often waived in favor of crisis supervision. In a setting in which newly trained workers are called upon to make potentially life-or-death decisions, the availability of immediate consultation minimizes worker anxiety, builds worker confidence and leads to enhanced productivity. Frequent team meetings serve as a forum where generic issues can be addressed, and as a vehicle where staff can air their frustrations and share their ideas for improved program function.


## Case Illustrations

Many parents may seek help for their children indirectly. Presenting requests must be fully explored in a sensitive manner to insure that the needs of the family are understood. When parents are discouraged in their initial attempts to secure service, they may refrain from seeking additional service until their family situation has become so desperate that fear of punitive repercussions are overshadowed by concern for their children's well-being. The following case example was chosen to illustrate this point.

> Betty S, age 26, called the Parent Helpline, stating directly that she had pushed one of her twin boys, age four, down a flight of stairs. Although she believed that her child had not been hurt, she requested help in preventing herself from further harming her children. Relieved by the worker's nonjudgmental approach and supportive description of the services of the nursery, Betty readily agreed to bring her children, Scott eleven months, the twins, and Timothy, six, to the nursery immediately.
>
> A single parent, severely abused herself as a child, Betty had worked until Scott's birth when she was advised to give up her clerical job for medical reasons. Her aunt, who had been a major source of emotional support, had died shortly after Scott was born. Betty had no contact with the children's fathers. Medical examination revealed both old and fresh scars and burn marks on the bodies of the three oldest boys. Scott had not been harmed. The worker learned that Betty had requested temporary foster care from the city's public child welfare agency. Unable to discuss what at that point constituted only mild abuse, she had requested service based on her inability to care for the children on a public assistance budget. Denied foster care, Betty did not follow through on the agency's referral to a community service program. At the Crisis Nursery, Betty openly acknowledged her fears of resuming care of her children. While the children remained in the nursery, the worker filed a maltreatment report, and working with CPS, secured immediate foster care for all four children. Referred for individual and group counseling, Betty continued in treatment while visiting her children regularly. Betty established a close relationship with the children's foster care mother.
>
> Six-month follow-up found Betty preparing her home for a trial discharge

of the twins to her care, to be followed by the return of her youngest and oldest sons. Betty remains in continual contact with the Crisis Nursery, dropping in periodically to report on her progress. The attractive appearance of this formerly dishevelled client reflects the inner peace that Betty now describes.

Betty's situation is not atypical. A number of parents have reported that New York City's Special Services for Children workers refused to place their children because they had not been abused or neglected. This phenomenon may reflect the implementation of the New York State Child Welfare Reform Act (1981) which seeks to keep children from unnecessary placement. However, insufficient exploration by an overburdened staff and lack of built in follow-up may lead to the escalation of a situation in which children may be placed in serious jeopardy. Requests for foster care are generally not made lightly and must be treated with great sensitivity.

The following case illustrates a single parent's increasing difficulties in caring for her own child, a planned change-of-life baby, purposely conceived in an out-of-wedlock relationship with a married man. Many women, confronting their biological time clock, view the birth of a child as a means of completing their lives. Denying the sacrifices implicit in raising a child alone, single mothers are often unprepared for the adjustments required by parenting.

Maria B, age 43, called the Parent Helpline, her voice quivering as she described a severe spanking administered to her active thirty-month-old daughter. After learning of the program's facilities, Maria's terror of separation from her daughter was such that the worker gently suggested that Maria visit the nursery with her daughter before making any decisions. The worker learned that, prior to Erminia's birth, Maria had worked as a receptionist. Unable to find a reliable and affordable baby-sitter, Maria had turned to public assistance for support. Abandoned by her daughter's father during her pregnancy, Maria was forced to move to substandard housing where she had made no friends. Erminia was admitted to the nursery for the evening; there was no indication of maltreatment.

By the following day, Maria had been enrolled in a parent education program. Initial follow-up contacts indicated that Maria had begun to learn more appropriate means of structuring and disciplining her lively and curious daughter. Erminia was subsequently placed in group day care while her mother was referred to a computer training program. Advocacy efforts had proved helpful in ameliorating the most hazardous conditions in their apartment. Maria has been delighted to share her academic achievements with the Crisis Nursery staff and describes with pleasure her daughter's progress in the day-care program in which she remains enrolled.

In this situation, the worker chose to mitigate Maria's anxiety by inviting her to visit the Crisis Nursery without pressing her to make a commitment to admit her child. Rather than exacerbating parents' fears, a warm invitation to chat informally on a face-to-face basis often helps a frightened parent to feel sufficiently supported while exploring the services of a potentially helpful program.

Although most clients who use the services of the Crisis Nursery are mothers raising their children alone, the following case describes a family's situational stress exacerbated by role reversal.

> Dr. N called the Parent Helpline, inquiring about the nature of the program's services. After explaining the program's purpose and function, the worker warmly asked if the program could be of help to the family. With much hesitation, Dr. N revealed that, by profession, he had been a dentist in the Middle East until he and his wife had immigrated to the United States. Dr. N had failed three attempts to pass the qualifying examination that would allow him to practice dentistry in this country. His wife was now working in a clerical position. Dr. N cared for their 14-month-old daughter while preparing for yet another attempt to pass this examination. Empathizing with his obvious distress, the worker gently commented on the difficulty of studying while also caring for the needs of his daughter. With much hesitation, Dr. N revealed his recurrent fantasy of strangling his daughter. Allying herself with Dr. N's concern for his child, the worker helped Dr. N agree to bring his daughter immediately to the nursery.
>
> Alyousha was admitted to the nursery that day. The admitting examination provided no indication of maltreatment. At the worker's urging, Dr. N agreed to ask his wife to join him at the nursery. With the worker's assistance, he was able to share his sense of terrible despair with Mrs. N. After her initial shock and horror, Mrs. N was able to become more supportive of her husband. Working with CPS, family day care was secured for Alyousha following her discharge from the nursery. Dr. and Mrs. N accepted a referral for joint counseling. Thirty-day follow-up revealed that Alyousha remained in day care while her parents continued in treatment. The three-month follow-up found that, in addition to day care and counseling services, Dr. N had secured work as a dental assistant while continuing to prepare for his next examination.

In the N case, sociocultural factors had precluded parental discussion of a potentially life-threatening family crisis. Dr. N had been unable to discuss his feelings of personal failure while his wife had struggled alone with the unfamiliar world of work. The benign atmosphere of the Crisis Nursery facilitated an exchange that led to a beginning improvement in this couple's communication, and the avoidance of possible fatality.

## Statistical Overview

During the first twelve months of the program, the Parent Helpline received 1,997 calls. In that same period, 367 children from 217 families were admitted to the nursery. An additional 78 children from 44 families received in-person services without requiring admission to the nursery. The volume of service activity included: 626 in-person interviews or counseling sessions with parents and other involved relatives; 1,924 telephone discussions with parents and other family members; 1,015 collateral telephone contacts with various agencies and hospitals; and 945 calls to and from components of New York City's Special Services for Children's Child Protective Services.

The age of the mothers known to the Crisis Nursery ranged from 15 to 45 years of age, with an average age of 27.3. Approximately two-thirds of the mothers using the services of the nursery were between 20 and 30 years old. There was no father present in over three-quarters of the families seen. The average number of children per family was 1.9. Almost half of the families had one child only and almost another third had two children. Only 2.4 percent of the families served had six or more children, including one family of nine children.

The majority of families were receiving public assistance. Five percent of the families had been recently cut off from public assistance and 3.9 percent were attempting to receive benefits. Ten percent of families seen were receiving Social Security benefits, disability, or unemployment insurance.

Over 90 percent of the mothers seen at the Crisis Nursery were from minority groups: Blacks represented 57 percent of the population and Hispanics 37 percent. Although child abuse is to be found in all socioeconomic, racial, and religious groups, the above statistics may reflect both the nature and direction of the public awareness campaign as well as the reluctance of middle-class families to use agency services.

Almost one-third of the parents seen at the nursery indicated that they themselves had been abused or neglected as children. Over one-fourth of the families seen related a history of current or past substance abuse.

Most of the parents who came to the Crisis Nursery had more than one presenting problem; however, the consistent presenting concern was parental fear of loss of control or violent impulses toward their children. Slightly more than one-fourth of the parents reported difficulty in coping with their hyperactive and acting-out children. In almost one-fifth of the cases, parents verbalized distress over spanking or hitting their children because such a response was atypical or much stronger than their usual disciplinary measures. In 18 percent of the cases, family violence was a current problem. In 23 percent of the cases, family conflict had not yet reached the level of violence. Other presenting problems that occurred in a significant number of cases included psychiatric problems that required hospitalization, depression, severe health problems, recent desertion or separation of a parent, and disputes over public assistance.

Almost 15 percent of the children admitted to the residential facility were found to have overt signs of abuse or neglect. Thirty-seven percent of children seen were reported to the New York State Central Registry of Child Abuse and Maltreatment. Thirty-three percent of children seen were placed in foster care, including children from 15 percent of mothers who had specifically requested the services of the program in securing temporary foster care.

In addition to foster care placement, the most frequent referrals were: counseling (51 percent), day care (20 percent), rehousing (16 percent), income maintenance (13 percent), parent education programs (14 percent), temporary living arrangements (11 percent), homemaker service (8 percent), and employment or vocational service (4 percent).

## Follow-Up Results

For a population of such high vulnerability, the results of follow-up studies were gratifying. In slightly more than half the cases, the services to which families had been referred had been provided and their children were no longer considered at-risk. In 7 percent of the cases, the family was waiting for service, while 5 percent were partially engaged in referral services. In one-fourth of the cases, families had not followed through on referrals and additional outreach service had been initiated by the Crisis Nursery Staff.

Child abuse is a complex problem for which there are no simple solutions. This presentation focuses on the preventive services of a crisis nursery to illustrate the long-term effectiveness of timely intervention during periods of intense family crisis (Rapoport, 1962). Crisis nurseries, early parent education, and other preventive services can make a considerable dent in the incidence of maltreatment. However, the lack of a comprehensive family policy that would serve the needs of primary prevention, significantly reducing the risk to our nation's children, remains a major issue.

# PART V

# Adolescents as Clients
## Special Issues in Working with Today's Teenagers

It has been said that adolescence and the prolonging of dependence is an invention of modern society, of the ever lengthening preparatory period that is intended to ready young people to take on adult roles. As a liminal or transitional stage, adolescence is a period that is neither adulthood nor childhood, a period that is poorly defined. Adolescents are sometimes thought of as large and therefore potentially dangerous children or as immature and therefore irresponsible and potentially dangerous adults. Parents shake their heads in confusion as they comment, "She's twelve and going on twenty-eight." Yet societal responses tend to be geared, not to the developmental needs of young people in a period of transition and preparation, but to manipulation and social control. We are afraid of our young people. If they appear to be out of control, we lock them up, throw them out, or cut them off.

Obviously, none of these responses helps teenagers with their complex and, in some respects, paradoxical task, namely to prepare for adulthood without assuming the roles, rights, and responsibilities of that status and to differentiate from their families at the same time that they need their families' help in achieving that differentiation. Not only is the adolescent's position paradoxical, but institutional responses to adolescent needs and problems also have been ambivalent and paradoxical, as is well illustrated in the three chapters that comprise this special section on teenagers.

As adolescents are minors and members of families known to the Child Welfare system, the contextual, policy, and practice issues presented throughout this volume have relevance to them. In this section, however, the focus is on the issues and problems that seem especially related to this complex and stressful transitional stage and that also come to the attention of society and its representatives in the Child Welfare system.

In the first chapter, Sarri explores the often contradictory societal responses to young people in trouble, presenting a thoughtful review of the juvenile justice system as it has developed historically and as it functions today. She explores the relationship of that system to Child Welfare and details the problems and discrimination that have resulted from the lack of integration between what are two parallel but often isolated child-caring systems.

Sarri demonstrates how our fear, our ambivalence, and our unclear identification of adolescence as a special status have been expressed in societal responses to young people in trouble. Deprived of the legal protections and due process that are afforded adults, adolescents may be incarcerated for offenses that, if committed by adults, would not be considered misdemeanors. She explodes the rhetoric of the adolescent crime wave, which she believes has been used to create more punitive and retributive correctional programs, with facts from studies that demonstrate that juvenile crime has been slowly but consistently declining.

The chapter ends with a call for reforms that would recognize that delinquency is not a characteristic of young people, called delinquents by agents of social control, but a property of the social system in which young people are enmeshed.

In the next chapter, Loppnow explores other unsatisfactory solutions sometimes adopted by families, the larger society, and adolescents themselves in their efforts to cope with the conflicts and tensions of this demanding transitional phase. Running away, or an abrupt and unplanned effort to escape the family, is one solution chosen by many adolescents. These young people, however, are not all alike and they run for a variety of reasons. Loppnow feels that the major variable in developing a typology of runaways and in devising an intervention plan is the extent of alienation that exists between the parents and the young person. Runaways and their families, by choosing this solution to their difficulties, have preempted the gradual and painful but necessary tasks of the "leaving home" or individuation process. Frequently, intervention entails efforts to help adolescent and family heal the parent–child alienation and work through a more gradual and constructive plan for independent living.

The second group of teenagers who come to the attention of Child Welfare workers are those who have been victims of abuse and neglect. Although many teenagers have suffered long-term abuse and neglect,

Loppnow focuses on situations in which abuse has erupted for the first time during adolescence, either as an expression of the conflict growing out of the young person's struggle for autonomy or of the family system's inability to handle the adolescent's developing sexuality.

Most Child Welfare caseloads include a number of adolescents adrift in the foster care system. In many cases, these children may be considered victims of societal neglect, bereft of familial ties and struggling with diffuse or shattered senses of continuity and identity. Loppnow describes interventions that hold promise for reclaiming such displaced youngsters. The chapter ends with an exploration of one of the most difficult and tragic social problems facing our society today—adolescent suicide, the most irreversible solution to the seemingly unresolvable problem of becoming an adult. Based on an analysis of the situational and personal variables that appear to be linked to these teenage deaths, the author outlines a preventive and interventive program geared to helping youngsters at risk find other solutions.

In the final chapter of this section, Crawford and Furstenberg explore teenage pregnancy and parenthood, the area that perhaps more than any other expresses the paradoxical situation of the adolescent and the ambivalent attitudes of society. Our modern invention of adolescence has created an extended period in the human life cycle when young people are biologically, but usually not economically, socially, or emotionally, ready for sexual activity and for parenthood.

This disjunction and its corresponding societal responses have produced many social problems of concern to Child Welfare. Among these are unwanted pregnancies, unwanted parenthood, and premature parenthood. Crawford and Furstenberg explore the factors contributing to adolescent sexual activity and parenthood and the consequences for both teenage parents and their children. The contribution of societal and parental ambivalence toward adolescents is apparent in the confused and often double-binding stances taken in educational and birth control programs which then fail to help children handle their emerging sexuality responsibly.

Teenage parenthood is of double concern for Child Welfare workers. When children give birth to children, the welfare of both the child parents and the infant may become the concern of the Child Welfare system.

All of the authors, although exploring different issues and making different specific recommendations, join in the concern that the larger society is inhospitable to many young people as they reach toward adulthood. All emphasize the importance of prevention, and the development of economic, social, and educational supports. Finally, all stress the need for jobs, job training, education, and an opening up of the opportunity structure and a removal of the obstacles that block a smooth transition into the adult world.

# CHAPTER 18

# Juvenile Justice as Child Welfare

ROSEMARY C. SARRI

Americans think of themselves as child-oriented, and there is much in the culture to support such a view, particularly in the popular culture and in our views about ourselves as young, resilient, and pragmatic. Moreover, we have created an elaborate system of age-graded social institutions in schools, sports and recreational organizations, in Child Welfare, and in juvenile justice agencies which some assert are ample evidence of our placing a priority on children. Others assert that youth are our most valuable asset and use such statements to justify various sanctions, programs, appropriations, and decisions. Whether or not these assertions were ever true would probably be long debated, but in the 1980s clearly children and youth are no longer considered an important national asset. An examination of indices of poverty, illness, suicide, education, unemployment, and substance abuse among youth would reveal that they are both ignored and undervalued relative to other societal priorities. Sanford Katz (1974) predicted several years ago that children would be a "minority class," and substantial evidence now appears to support such a prediction. Nowhere is this situation more true than in juvenile justice and Child Welfare institutions where so much emphasis is now being placed on incarceration and control of children and adolescents.

Youth do not have the protection afforded to adults in most spheres of their lives. They have no political power and few acknowledged civil rights. For all but a privileged few, our schools are more like warehouses than places for useful learning, and performance continues to deteriorate. The reductions in social welfare programs that have been implemented since 1981 have disproportionately fallen on children and youth, especially those from minority groups. Children have lost cash benefits, child care, health care, school lunches, educational services, and even shelter. Research by the Children's Defense Fund (1983) indicates that several million children and youth have experienced severe losses. More than 21 percent of the nation's children now live below the poverty level—far higher than the percentage of adults in that category (U.S. Commission on Civil Rights, 1983).

This chapter examines the juvenile justice system and the children and youth who are the focus of that system as central elements of the larger Child Welfare system. We will trace the development of the present juvenile justice system as it has evolved during the twentieth century, considering the extent to which societal expectations for this institution have been met. The major issues presently being confronted will be examined along with alternative solutions for resolution of contemporary problems. Our focus will be on children between the ages of twelve and eighteen years, because youth in these years are the primary concern of the juvenile justice system. Although a small number of youth as young as seven years are processed as juvenile delinquents in some states, and in many states children thirteen years or older are processed and treated as adults for selected criminal behavior, the overwhelming majority of delinquent youth in the juvenile justice system are between twelve and eighteen years of age (American Bar Association, 1982; Levin and Sarri, 1974). Because the Child Welfare and juvenile justice systems interact at numerous junctures in the processing of children and youth in our society, it is important to clarify what is distinct to each and where there is overlap. This clarification is essential because in some jurisdictions the systems operate quite separately, whereas in others, sole responsibility for all services resides within single units of state departments of social welfare.

## The Domain of Juvenile Justice and Child Welfare

Much of the contemporary Child Welfare literature appears to address only needs and services for preadolescent dependent children, ignoring those children involved in the juvenile justice system because of delinquency, despite the fact that initial processing for dependent, neglected, delinquent, and abused children begins in the juvenile court. Those who become of concern to society because of their own misbehavior or illegal acts receive little or no attention from many of those who see their primary responsibility in the Child Welfare system. Nonetheless, it is important to note that federal definitions of Child Welfare services have nearly always included this population. The *1962 Amendments to the Social Security Act* is the more recent formal federal definition. It states that Child Welfare services include:

> [S]ocial services which supplement, or substitute for, parental care and supervision for the purpose of 1) preventing or remedying, or assisting in the solution of problems which may result in, the neglect, abuse, exploitation, or delinquency of children; 2) protecting and caring for homeless, dependent, or neglected children; 3) protecting and promoting the welfare of children of working mothers; and 4) otherwise protecting and promoting the welfare of children, including the strengthening of their own homes where possible, or, where needed, the provision of adequate care of children away from their homes in foster family homes or day care or other child care facilities.

Clarification of the parameters of the Child Welfare system is only one part of our task because the juvenile justice system extends into other arenas far beyond Child Welfare, such as adult criminal justice and public education. The juvenile justice system is comprised of those organizations which apprehend, process, adjudicate, and treat youth and their parents for delinquency, dependency, neglect, and abuse—as these behaviors are defined in statutory, case, and administrative law. The key actors comprising the system are: juveniles falling under statutory definitions for delinquency; police and law enforcement officials, prosecutors, judges, defense counsel, probation officers, and administrative personnel, as well as persons who have special responsibilities for youth—parents and guardians *ad litem*, foster parents, teachers, and treatment personnel (Binder, 1979; Empey, 1979; Sarri and Hasenfeld, 1976).

National variation in the definition of juvenile behavior by age, marital or parental status, and living arrangements is significant in determining jurisdiction as are the social limits established for the permissible range of juvenile activities, lifestyles, and liberty. The system is characterized by variability within and between states; moreover, the federal role is of recent origin and is far more limited than in the case of some other Child Welfare programs. Thus, to refer to juvenile justice as a system is undoubtedly an oversimplification because it lacks many of the essential qualities of a social system as Rosenheim (1976) has noted, but we will refer to it as a system in this chapter to simplify our analysis.

It is nearly impossible to arrive at any definitive statement of the size of either or both of these systems in terms of the numbers of juveniles at-risk or receiving services. Kadushin (1978a) estimated approximately 6.4 million children were in serious need of Child Welfare services as defined under the 1962 social security amendments. Although the size of the cohort between infancy and eighteen years has declined in the intervening years, events since 1981 have substantially increased the proportion at risk due to poverty and reductions in major federal social welfare programs (Children's Defense Fund, 1983; Danziger, 1982). Estimates by both Kadushin (1978a) and Kahn (1977) indicate that about 3 million children received some type of child welfare service in a given year in the late 1970s. As of 1979 the National Center for Juvenile Justice reported that 1.4 million juveniles were processed by the juvenile court for delinquency. Thus, it is probable that nearly half of all juveniles receiving child welfare services receive them in the juvenile justice system. Moreover, for adolescents, Child Welfare services are almost exclusively those provided under the aegis of the juvenile justice system. Obviously, therefore, it is important to understand the interaction between these two essential child care systems.

## Historical Development of the United States Juvenile Justice System

The beginning and end of the nineteenth century witnessed the establishment of three social institutions of critical importance in the understanding of Child Welfare and juvenile justice in the United States today: the child-caring institutions which began in 1824; the juvenile court which originated in Illinois and Colorado in 1899; and the public and private Child Welfare organizations which emerged over a period of time during the latter part of the nineteenth and early part of the twentieth centuries. The creators of the Child Welfare and child-care institutions sought to separate children from almshouses and congregate care facilities, but they also sought to develop institutions which would facilitate industrialization of a rapidly growing frontier country during a period of tremendous immigration of persons with vastly different cultures and languages (Platt, 1977; Rothman, 1971; 1979). Zimring states that the new theory of child saving rested on three postulates:

1. childhood is a period of dependency and risk such that supervision is essential;
2. the family has primary supervising responsibility, but the state should play a primary role in education and should intervene if the family "fails";
3. when a child is at risk, the state is the appropriate authority to decide what is in the child's best interest. (1982:31–32)

With such a framework, the basis was set for unbridled intervention into the lives of children and youth, especially for those deemed at risk by powerful forces in society.

The designers and founders of the juvenile justice system sought to create new mechanisms that would reduce the harsh and undifferentiated treatment of juveniles, but would also foster the goals and acculturation noted above. The founders were both idealistic and optimistic about what could be achieved through intervention by the State into the lives of the young. They established new organizational mechanisms whereby the state would intervene for rehabilitative rather than punitive or retributive purposes. But at the same time, they were concerned about social control and the moral development of immigrant working-class children. They believed that the state had the right to intervene benevolently to see that children were "properly" socialized to assume adult roles in an industrial society (Empey, 1979; Krisberg and Austin, 1978; Rothman, 1971; 1980).

The first Juvenile Justice Act passed in Illinois in 1899 specified that the law be "liberally construed to the end . . . that the care, custody, and discipline of a child . . . shall approximate that which would be given its parents" (Revised Statutes of Illinois, 1899, Sec. 21). Empey (1979) observed that with the establishment of the juvenile court, this society not only invented juvenile justice, but it also established an institution to enforce the "modern" concept of childhood, and it established the court as a surrogate for the family and community to prevent delinquency, decriminalize children, and then rehabilitate them. Substitutes were created for the family rather than the provision of resources to strengthen the family and community (Bremner, 1971; Rothman, 1971).

The new social mechanisms that emerged in this period drew support from a combination of optimistic social theorists, sincere social reformers and the elites who felt a need for social control (Gaylin, et al. 1978; Platt, 1977; Schlossman, 1977). Also, concern for moral development of youth was an additional force. Socialization of youth to the prevailing moral standards led to overreach and to high levels of coercion in many instances (Platt, 1977; Schur, 1973; Tannenbaum, 1938). The juvenile court movement spread rapidly throughout the country so that by 1925 these courts were in operation in all but two states. Programs and policies were implemented with the hope that they would be beneficial to both youth and society, but there was almost no evaluation of the outcomes, costs, or benefits of these various approaches during the first half century.

Following World War II and continuing up through the early 1970s much greater skepticism characterized the development of new policies and programs. It became increasingly apparent from evaluative studies and observation that the system was not succeeding as had been expected, and states such as California began to modify their state laws governing delinquency. Fundamental changes did not occur until the late 1960s and early 1970s, but the federal and state changes then were comparable in significance to those which occurred at the beginning of this century. Dissatisfied with the operation of the juvenile courts and correctional facilities, many states sought to develop structural alternatives outside the juvenile court. Most agreed that the original hopes for the juvenile court had not been met. Whether one used court decisions, official statistics about the numbers processed, legislation, or community alternatives, the conclusion was that the original goals had not been achieved (Empey, 1979).

The initial response was one favoring increased use of formal control and due process mechanisms through the juvenile court, thereby de-emphasizing its role as rehabilitation organization. Change in this direction was fostered by decisions of the United States Supreme Court in the Kent (1966), Gault (1967), Winship (1970), McKiever (1971) cases, and in several subsequent related decisions. Although these decisions resulted in statutory change in many states, and required the allocation of vastly increased resources, results were far less than had been expected or were not in the predicted direction (King, 1980). Critics continued to express sentiments similar to those of Wheeler:

> The juvenile justice system is a paradox. In the name of benevolent intervention and rehabilitation, it has operationalized a sentencing and parole procedure that discriminates against the young, the least serious offenders (1980:21).

The impact of statutory change and case law on juvenile court practice was minimal for the majority of youth processed by the court. The vast discretion of the juvenile court in decision-making, the lesser status of youth in society, and the lack of superior court surveillance all appear to have contributed to the maintenance of the status quo (Paulsen, 1979; Sarri and Hasenfeld, 1976; Stapleton and Teitelbaum, 1976).

The impact of statutory change can be illustrated in the state of Washington where major change was implemented in 1977 (Schram and Schneider, 1981). Virtually all sections of the existing code were changed and the following provisions implemented:

1. The extension to juveniles accused of crimes all the rights available to adults with the exception of trial by jury
2. The formalization of court procedures
3. The institutionalization of an accountability-based division system
4. The implementation of proportionate and determinate sentencing standards which greatly reduce judicial sentencing discretion
5. The elimination of status offenses from court jurisdication

Nowhere in the new Washington code is rehabilitation of the offender mentioned as a purpose or goal. Primary emphasis is placed on a "justice" approach and accountability. Schneider and Schramm (1983) have reported that many of the expected outcomes occurred, but the new law was not effective in reducing incarceration, particularly in detention facilities, nor did it result in markedly increased provision of services to diverted youth by the Child Welfare system. It did however change the behavior of law enforcement officials. "Justice" ideology replaced that of rehabilitation, and high levels of conformity with sentencing guidelines were enacted. However, females and minorities continued to be handled differentially, often not in conformity with the statute.

In the 1970s a series of policy alternatives were variously used as social control measures in juvenile justice. Many of these were fostered by federal grants, as we shall note subsequently, to local communities for innovations inside and outside the justice system. Thus *decriminalization, diversion,* and *deinstitutionalization* were perceived as key concepts for action almost simultaneously along with *deterrence, punishment,* and *retribution.* Behavior associated with each of these concepts could be observed throughout the country in programs and policies. The pattern was often haphazard, and the fundamental contradictions implied by these two contrasting paths were largely ignored. Implementation of programs associated with the former strategies resulted in contraction of the juvenile justice system and should have led to greater use of Child Welfare and mental health resources; focus on the latter strategies resulted in an expanded system of juvenile justice (Blomberg, 1983; Cressey and McDermott, 1974; Empey, 1979; Sarri, 1983).

The juvenile justice system was not unaffected by the national movement to deinstitutionalize large closed institutions as Vinter, Downs, and Hall (1976); Miller, Ohlin, and Coates (1978); and Lerman (1982) have noted. Between 1965 and 1975 there was a substantial decline in the nation's reliance on traditional state correctional institutions for juveniles (Krisberg and Schwartz, 1983; Vinter, Downs, and Hall, 1976), but once again results were mixed for many youth who were recycled into the mental health and private care system. Lerman (1982) has noted that one cannot analyze changes over a short period of time only, or just in one part of the "youth in trouble system." His comparative analysis of the "youth in trouble system" in the 1920s and 1970s shows a significant decline in the institutionalization of dependent and neglected children, but a marked increase in juvenile correctional and mental health institutions, especially in short-term and private facilities (Lerman, 1982: 140). Obviously, this was not a case of recycling as occurred in the late 1970s, but it does indicate a societal predilection toward placing large numbers of youth in closed residential programs.

While the United States was embracing increased formalization in juvenile justice in the 1960s and 1970s, changes in many Western European countries and Australia were in the opposite direction. These countries moved from more legalistic approaches toward greater informality and creation of dispute–resolution mechanisms outside the formal justice system, sharply restricting the jurisdiction of the juvenile court. In Sweden, Scotland, and South Australia, the mechanism of juvenile panels was developed and utilized for the majority of juvenile delinquency cases. Only in New Jersey was such a mechanism implemented in the United States and there only on a limited scale (Sarri and Bradley, 1980).

Lastly, during the late 1970s and early 1980s two major trends have dominated formal policy-making in juvenile justice: (1) concern with serious and violent crime as an increasing phenomenon; and (2) development of national standards to guide the behavior of actors and organizations in the system. The first trend will be addressed in our subsequent examination of juvenile crime. Development of national standards and goals in the adult criminal justice field in the early 1970s led to a similar movement in juvenile justice. At least three sets of national standards for juvenile justice have been developed, and all them could potentially have a significant impact on the operation of the system. They include: the American Bar Association Institute of Judicial Administration (1982); the American Correctional Association (1978–1980); and the National Advisory Committee for Juvenile Justice and Delinquency Prevention (NAC, 1980). These standards codify existing practice, establish guidelines for the implementation of legislation, and present principles for the achievement of greater uniformity and fairness in the administration of justice in all jurisdictions. Despite the vast resources that were utilized in the formulation of these standards, there has been little evidence in the 1980s of efforts to implement them, except in one area. Standards advocating determinate sentencing of juveniles in accord with the adult model have been enacted in several states (Schram and Schneider, 1981).

## Federal Legislation and Incentives: The "Carrot" Approach

Passage of the Juvenile Justice and Delinquency Prevention (JJDP) Act in 1974 provided substantial financial incentives to states for deinstitutionalization of certain classes of juvenile offenders, for avoidance of adult jails and secure detention as placement alternatives for most youth, and for development of community-based programs as the preferred model of juvenile corrections. The author of the Act, Senator Birch Bayh, described its purpose as: ". . . designed specifically to prevent young people from entering the failing juvenile justice system and to assist communities in developing more sensible and economic approaches for youth already in the juvenile justice system" (Bayh, 1974).

The original act provided grants to states to remove status and minor offenders from secure institutions and detention facilities. Although implicit, there was no stated requirement that Child Welfare and youth-serving agencies provide services to those who were diverted from juvenile justice. Use of the "carrot" approach worked because more than forty states quickly participated. Incentives for community-based programming were increased in the 1977 Amendments, and in 1980, the act was reauthorized for five years with strong prohibitions against placement of youth in adult jails. Public Law 93–415 contained many laudatory provisions for innovative juvenile justice programs, but the amounts of money available to the states were always small and have declined progressively through the 1980s. Moreover, federal grants under Child Welfare and Title XX provisions made many more dollars available for the placement of children in private and public institutions, thereby defeating the goals that the JJDP act sought to achieve (Lerman, 1982).

In their systematic assessment of the impact of the JJDP act on deinstitutionalization, Krisberg and Schwartz (1983) observed that the results were disappointing except in the reductions that were achieved in the detention of status offenders, especially females. However, increasing percentages of property and person offenders were held and held for longer periods of time, as we shall see subsequently. Krisberg and Schwartz also pointed to the vast differences in processing among the states with some consistently high in deinstitutionalization and others making no progress at all. In their more limited study in one state, Minnesota, they noted the phenomenon of recycling of youth into Child Welfare and youth-serving institutions as well as into residential mental health facilities. There was an overall growth in out-of-home placement of youth with the private sector playing an increasingly larger role.

Since 1891 federal administration priorities have shifted away from minor offenders and community care toward increased concern about serious and violent crime, determinate sentencing, and increasing incarceration. The federal government is no longer providing leadership, either in the Department of Health and Human Services or in the Office of Juvenile Justice, for the goals established in the original JJDP act as passed in 1974.

## The Juvenile Court—Gatekeeper of the Juvenile Justice System

The juvenile court controls entry of juveniles into the justice system because it has been allocated the power and discretion to determine when the State will intervene into the lives of individual youth and their families. However, this power is not discharged uniformly or consistently within or between states. A national survey of juvenile courts revealed that the rate of commitment of youth to correctional facilities varied between one percent and 43 percent of youth referred to the court. The rate of nonjudicial handling varied from one percent to 96 percent (Hasenfeld and Cheung, 1981; Sarri and Hasenfeld, 1976). Similar patterns were observed by Pawlak (1977) and later by Stapleton and Smith (1980).

Due process protection in court processing is especially lacking in decision-making at intake, detention, and disposition—the junctures at which social agencies could be actively involved in the provision of alternate services. Sosin (1977) observed that inconsistency in decision-making was the usual pattern. Youth charged with serious felonies were more likely to have their rights fully protected than were youth charged with minor or status offenses.

The findings about "input" and "output" in the National Assessment of Juvenile Justice (NAJC) National Study were noteworthy. Law enforcement and parents were the principal referral agents with little involvement by youth-serving agencies (Sarri and Hasenfeld, 1976). Non-white youth were three times more likely to be referred than were white youth. Status offenders comprised 40 percent of all referrals, but females constituted the majority of this group. Nearly 70 percent of all cases that entered were handled informally or dismissed. Juvenile court staff tended to see their mandate as social control and deterrence, despite the fact that most cases involved minor behavior and the majority were subsequently dismissed.

Examination of the relationships between the juvenile court and other key organizations led to the conclusion that the courts operated in an isolated manner with little dependence on other organizations—least of all Child Welfare and youth-serving agencies—in their processing of delinquents. They only reacted to the overtures and actions of youth-serving agencies rather than reaching out in a proactive manner. As a result, youth under court jurisdiction were more likely to be thrust into a limited pool of court services and were excluded from many community services that were readily available to nonoffending middle-class youth.

Results from the NAJC research and that of Schneider and Schramm (1983) in Washington point to the inescapable ambiguities and contradictions in the goals, ideology, structure, and operations of juvenile courts, as Table 18-1 indicates. Courts operate under the assumption that they exist to protect the community, yet the bulk of cases referred to them are "juvenile nuisances" (Rosenheim, 1976). They develop complex decision-making structures and elaborate procedures only to send the majority of youth referred to them away with little more than a warning and a negative social label. Most of the rest are placed on probation or in institutions where custody and surveillance receive far greater emphasis than does rehabilitation.

**TABLE 18–1 Dimensions of Control–Rehabilitation–Justice Ideologies**

| DIMENSION | CONTROL | REHABILITATION | JUSTICE |
|---|---|---|---|
| Primary goal | Crime reduction Protection of others | Needs and interests of youth | Youth and societal well-being |
| Ideology | *Parens patriae* Police Power | *Parens patriae* | Equal justice, due process, procedural fairness |
| Perceptions of problem | Youth viewed as endangering peace and stability of community | Youth viewed as handicapped, ill, or disadvantaged, and victim of environment and psychological forces | Focus on behavioral allegations and definition of criminal behavior |
| Courts' roles in processing | General and special deterrence Retributive justice | Treatment, provide resources to protect against and overcome adverse circumstances. Informal | Determine guilt or innocence, process fairly, uniformly, quickly, and formally |
| Organizational outcome | High rates of detention and institutionalization | High rates of detention and all types of postadjudication programs | Low rates of detention, disposition equity |
| Correlation between offense and sanction | Medium | Little or none | High |

A key factor in the contradictions and ambiguities is the inherent incompatibility between control and rehabilitation goals. Table 18-2 contrasts facets of the three key ideologies found in juvenile courts: control, rehabilitation, and justice. Juvenile courts long sought to optimize rehabilitation and control by asserting "what is in the best interests of the child" would also be "in the best interests of the community." Clearly they floundered in the simultaneous pursuit of both. Then, in the 1970s, "justice" ideologies were added and became dominant in some states (Schramm and Schneider, 1981). When juvenile courts attempt to implement all of these goals they generate a system riddled with internal

TABLE 18–2   Rates of Detention in Selected States—1979

*States with Highest Rates of Detention (per 1,000)*

| | |
|---|---|
| Nevada | 5.685 |
| District of Columbia | 4.875 |
| California | 4.393 |
| Washington | 3.420 |
| Arizona | 2.826 |

*States with Lowest Rates of Detention (per 1,000)*

| | |
|---|---|
| South Carolina | .256 |
| Alaska | .350 |
| Wisconsin | .371 |
| Rhode Island | .375 |
| Iowa | .426 |

*Source:* U.S. Bureau of the Census, *Children in Custody: Census of Juvenile Detention and Correctional Facilities, 1971–1979.* Washington, D.C.: U.S. Department of Justice, National Institute of Justice, 1982. (Wyoming, Vermont, and Montana reported no youth in detention, but each used other types of facilities for that purpose.)

inconsistencies and paradoxes. The behavior of judges, probation officers, and others serving youth appears capricious and irrational.

The trend toward emphasis on justice models and determinate sentencing of juveniles corresponded in the 1980s to the concern about serious and violent offenders. There was an explicit shift from diversion, prevention, and early intervention programs toward primary concern with the serious offender. Therefore, one must consider the nature and extent of delinquency in this decade before analyzing the key issues which are of particular concern in Child Welfare.

## The Nature and Extent of Delinquency

Although there is consensus among criminologists and other students of the juvenile justice system that delinquency is a widespread phenomenon, precise definitions of it do not exist (American Bar Association, 1982; King, 1980; Levin and Sarri, 1974). Nearly any misbehavior could be labeled as delinquency in one or more states. As Rosenheim (1976) notes, society faces a dilemma in that so-called "nuisance behavior" is not differentiated from behavior otherwise identified for adults as felonies or misdemeanors.

Examination of arrest records for 1981 indicates that a total of 1.8

million youth were arrested (1.4 million males and .4 million females). The vast majority of arrests were for property and status offenses (FBI, 1982). Less than 5 percent of juvenile arrests were for serious violent crime, contrary to popular public opinion. Juvenile crime and violence have not become increasingly serious in recent years as Laub's recent study (1983) indicates. Using National Crime Survey data to compare patterns from 1973 to 1979 he concluded that the rate of juvenile crime showed a steady or declining pattern—an overall decline of 6 percent. The largest declines occurred for property and status offenses with a very small decline in serious violent crime (Laub, 1983). He also noted that no evidence suggests that weapon use has become more prevalent. A similar comparison by Galvin and Polk (1983) yielded nearly identical results. As of 1981, 4.6 percent of all juvenile arrests were for serious violent crime, 37.8 percent for serious property crime, 38 percent for all nonindex crime; and 20 percent for status offenses.

Galvin and Polk (1983) suggest several reasons for the decline in youth crime: decline in the youth population, success of public policy initiatives, and success due to the innovative practices implemented during the previous decade. Whatever the reason, the fact of the decline remains, but public concern about juvenile crime continues to grow as has the willingness to incarcerate, to process youth as adults, to ignore treatment and rehabilitation as worthwhile objectives, and to rush to restitution, "just desserts," and punishment, almost without regard to the nature and the extent of crime. Undoubtedly the policy recommendations of Wilson (1975, 1983), Van den Haag (1975) and von Hirsch (1976) have been important to legislators and law enforcement officials in their decision-making, because many states have adopted more rigid and punitive juvenile codes.

When one considers the society's response to juvenile delinquency, one sees clearly that the juvenile justice system is being reviewed in the light of conservative trends in social welfare, the economy, politics, and the public mood. Judges and prosecutors have greater power in decision-making today than do social workers and other treatment personnel. Although rehabilitation goals have not been discarded, the principles of "just desserts" and incapacitation have greater support today. One hears calls to "get tough," and policies are proposed to deal with the "juvenile crime wave" despite the fact that juvenile crime has declined.

## Policy Issues Facing Juvenile Justice and Child Welfare

Numerous important policy issues simultaneously confront juvenile justice and Child Welfare as two critical components of the youth care system in the United States. We have chosen three which appear to be of current critical importance: detention, diversion, and the response of Child Welfare to the deinstitutionalization of status offenders. The chapter concludes with recommendations for future directions in meeting the needs of youth who come to the attention of the juvenile justice system.

## Detention

One of the more problematic and change-resistant elements of the juvenile justice system is the detention of youth in juvenile detention facilities and in adult jails. In the juvenile justice system in any given year, 9 out of 10 youth incarcerated will be found in detention or jail (Sarri, 1983). Estimates suggest that nearly one million youth spend one or more days in a lock-up, jail, or detention unit in the United States each year. The monitoring provisions of the Juvenile Justice and Delinquency Prevention Act greatly increased the accumulation of routine information about the detention and jailing of youth (Pappenfort, 1983; Poulin, Leavitt, Young, and Pappenfort, 1980). Pronounced interstate variations exist in code provisions as well as in organizational behavior so that comparisons across states must always be viewed in terms of relative variations.

Detention is defined as the "temporary care of children who require secure custody for their own or the community's protection in physically restricting facilities pending court disposition" (Sheridan, 1967:23). About 20 percent of all court referrals are held in detention and/or jail prior to court adjudication—nearly double the recommended national standard of 10 percent (National Center for Juvenile Justice, 1982). Variability among localities and states is the pattern, not the exception. Poulin et al. (1980) report that the rates of detention varied between 4,734 per 100,000 juveniles in California to 44.7 per 100,000 in North Dakota—a difference of about 100 times.

Information from the Census Bureau annual surveys of children's facilities, *Children in Custody,* provides us with comparable data for comparisons over time and across states (U.S. Bureau of the Census, 1981). Table 18-2 presents the rates of detention in 1979 in the five highest rate and the five lowest rate states. Nearly 60 percent of the admissions occurred in five states where less than 20 percent of the U.S. population resides.

Overall the rate of detention was 1.57 youth per 100 for the population between the ages of twelve and eighteen, the principal years for most detention and juvenile jailing. Youth are also held in private detention units and on a given day in 1979, 273 males and 653 females were held in private units—most of which were in New York, Kentucky, and

Vermont (U.S. Bureau of the Census, 1981). Youth are also detained in state training schools in 13 states, and 9,063 of such admissions took place in 1979, primarily in Maryland, District of Columbia, Alaska, and New Hampshire.

In attempting to ascertain reasons for the variability among the states, many factors have been studied. Urbanization, the availability of bed space, the number of facilities, and the rate of referrals to courts are all positively correlated with detention (Poulin et al., 1980). Offense behavior influences detention practice, but it is less important as an explanatory variable than are race, family characteristics, sex, and having had any type of prior contact with the system.

## Jailing

Placement of juveniles in jails with adults is clearly deplorable; it remains a problem of major concern because there has been only slight reduction in jailing despite considerable national effort, and despite the provisions for the elimination of jailing explicit in the 1980 JJDP Amendments. Approximately 2,500 to 3,500 youth under the age of eighteen will be found in adult jails on any given day, depending upon the season of the year. The national Survey of Jail Inmates in 1978 revealed that 2,944 youth were in jail on a February day when the count is often the lowest. Only Massachusetts, New Jersey, Maryland, and Vermont had no youth in adult jails. At the other end of the continuum ten states accounted for 60 percent of all juvenile jailing: Virginia, California, Tennessee, Texas, Kentucky, Ohio, New York, Mississippi, South Carolina, and Wisconsin.

In contrast to detention, jailing occurs more often in rural areas, and strangely, it is strongly correlated with arrest rates for status offenses. Obviously the latter youth should receive services from the Child Welfare system rather than be placed in adult jails as occurs often today. A national coalition of children's agencies was formed after passage of the 1980 JJDP Amendments, but it remains to be seen whether or not it will be successful in removing all children from adult jails.

In Tables 18–3 to 18–5 we can compare the placement of children and youth in detention with placement in other types of juvenile justice facilities. Moreover, the longitudinal and gender data permit us to make some interesting comparisons over time. Table 18–3 reveals a decline of nearly 12,000 youth in public correctional facilities between 1971 and 1979, but most of this decline occurred in public training schools. Private facilities held 28,707 juveniles in 1979, an increase of more than 7,000 since 1974, the only date for which a comparison could be made. There were 496,526 admissions to detention in 1979 out of a total number of

**TABLE 18–3  Selected Characteristics of Public Juvenile Custody Residents and Facilities, 1971, 1973, 1974, 1975, 1977, and 1979 in the United States**

| CHARACTERISTIC | 1971 | 1973 | 1974 | 1975 | 1977 | 1979 |
|---|---|---|---|---|---|---|
| *Number of residents* | 57,239 | 47,983 | 47,268 | 49,126 | 45,920 | 45,251 |
| Juvenile | 54,729 | 45,694 | 44,922 | 46,980 | 44,096 | 43,089 |
| Male | 41,781 | 35,057 | 34,783 | 37,926 | 36,921 | 37,063 |
| Adult | 2,510 | 2,289 | 2,346 | 2,146 | 1,824 | 2,162 |
| *Average Age (years)*[a] | NA | NA | NA | NA | 15.4 | 15.4 |
| Male | NA | 15.2 | 15.3 | 15.3 | 15.3 | 15.5 |
| Female | NA | 14.9 | 14.9 | 15.0 | 15.1 | 15.1 |
| *Number of admissions*[b] | 616,766 | 600,960 | 647,175 | 641,189 | 614,385 | 564,875 |
| *Number of facilities* | 722 | 794 | 829 | 874 | 992 | 993 |
| Short term | 338 | 355 | 371 | 387 | 448 | 458 |
| Long term | 384 | 439 | 458 | 487 | 544 | 535 |
| *Number of personnel* | 43,372 | 44,845 | 46,276 | 52,534 | 61,060 | 60,889 |
| Full-time | 39,521 | 39,216 | 39,391 | 41,156 | 43,322 | 44,234 |
| Part-time | 3,851 | 5,629 | 6,885 | 11,378 | 17,738 | 16,655 |
| *Juveniles per full-time staff member* | 1.4 | 1.2 | 1.1 | 1.1 | 1.0 | 1.0 |
| *Expenditures (thousands of dollars)* | 456,474 | 483,941 | 508,630 | 5994,146 | 707,732 | 839,895 |
| *Per capita operating cost (dollars)*[c] | 7,002 | 9,577 | 10,354 | 11,469 | 14,123 | 16,512 |

*Note* Data for 1971–1975 are as of June 30 and for 1977 and 1979 as of December 31, except for figures on admissions, expenditures, and operating costs, which are for an annual periood, either calendar or fiscal year.

*NA = Not available

*Source: Children and Custody, Report on the 1979 Census of Public Juvenile Facilities,* U.S. Department of Justice, Office of Juvenile Justice and Delinquency Prevention, October 1980.

[a]Based on juvenile residents only.
[b]Based on all residents (juvenile and adult).
[c]Based on average daily number of residents.

admissions to all types of public facilities of 564,875. Pappenfort's recent replication of the 1966 census of children's institutions reveals that as of 1981 there was a significant decline in facilities for dependent and neglected children, no change in delinquency institutions, and significant increases in mental health and short-term detention placements (Pappenfort, 1983). These findings correspond with those of Lerman (1982) and Krisberg and Schwartz (1983), suggesting that recycling of delinquent youth to mental health institutions has clearly occurred and that detention facilities process more youth than all other residential facilities combined.

Increases in the numbers of facilities, staff, and in fiscal resources occurred throughout the 1970s—suggesting that it is unlikely that the detention of juveniles will decline unless policies and practices are significantly altered. These census data also make it clear that the vast majority of youth held in detention never end up committed to a training school, providing ample reason to question the high rate of use of these facilities.

Comparisons of female–male differences in Table 18–4 and 18–5 indicate that some significant changes occurred during the 1970s, and it is probable that the reductions in female admissions can be attributed to the impact of the JJDP act implementation. It is increasingly clear that males are at far greater risk for incarceration, regardless of whether we examine admissions or daily census counts. Although the youth population, 10–18 years, has declined substantially in this decade, the rate of detention has declined only slightly for females (26.3 per 100,000 to 23.4), while the detention of males has increased from 51.7 per 100,000

**TABLE 18–4  Juvenile Admissions to Public Institutions, 1971, 1974, and 1979**

| ADMISSIONS | 1971 | | 1974 | | 1979 | |
|---|---|---|---|---|---|---|
| | *Number* | *%* | *Number* | *%* | *Number* | *%* |
| *Detention* | | | | | | |
| Females | 147,119 | 30 | 157,850 | 30 | 95,643 | 21 |
| Males | 349,407 | 70 | 371,225 | 70 | 356,167 | 79 |
| Total | 496,526 | | 529,075 | | 451,810 | |
| *Training Schools* | | | | | | |
| Females | 14,686 | 22 | 13,669 | 20 | 8,444 | 13 |
| Males | 53,089 | 78 | 53,737 | 80 | 56,972 | 87 |
| Total | 67,775 | | 67,406 | | 65,416 | |

*Source:* U.S. Bureau of the Census, *Children in Custody:* Census of Juvenile Detention and Correctional Facilities, 1971–1979. Washington, D.C.: U.S. Department of Justice, National Institute of Justice, 1982. Wyoming, Vermont, and Montana reported no youth in detention, but each used other types of facilities for that purpose.

**TABLE 18–5   Census of Juveniles in Public Detention Centers in 1966, 1971, 1974, 1979**[a]

| YEAR | NUMBER OF UNITS | NUMBER OF JUVENILES | | | RATE PER 100,000 POPULATION[d] | | |
|------|-----------------|--------|--------|----------|--------|--------|----------|
|      |                 | Male | Female | % Female | Male | Female | % Female |
| 1966[b] | 242 | 7151 | 3248 | 30 | 51.7 | 26.3 | 35.3 |
| 1971[c] | 305 | 7912 | 3836 | 33 | 50.5 | 25.4 | 38.2 |
| 1974[c] | 331 | 7698 | 3312 | 30 | 50.6 | 22.1 | 37.7 |
| 1979[c] | 438 | 8230 | 3278 | 28 | 56.7 | 23.4 | 40.3 |

Sources: [a]These data reflect the number of youth in detention facilities on a specific date in each of the above years, usually June 30.

[b]D. Pappenfort, D. Kilpatrick, and A. Kuby, *A Survey of Children's Residential Institutions, 1966*, Chicago: University of Chicago School of Social Service Administration, 1970.

[c]U.S. Department of Justice, *Children in Custody Report* for 1971, 1975, 1979, Washington, D.C.: NCJISS, 1980.

[d]Rates were calculated for the youth population 10–18 years old. See *U.S. Census Current Population Reports Series*, P25, 1982.

youth to 56.7. Complete data on length of stay are not available, but existing information suggests that the average length of stay increased from 12 to 15.5 days per admission. Thus there is corroboration for the hypothesis that if facilities are available they will be utilized, regardless of the behavior of youth. Moreover, extensive information is available about the negative effects associated with overuse of detention, but it appears to have little impact on practice.

Alternatives to detention, such as "home detention," are now offered in many jurisdictions, and evaluative results indicate that the outcomes are positive. Incentives for this development came from special grants under the JJDP act, but recently many of these grants have been terminated under the new "get tough" policies which encourage secure detention.

## Diversion

In 1967 a nationwide effort began to divert youth from the justice system into a variety of programs outside the system. It was assumed that reducing penetration into the formal system would lessen the dangers associated with labeling and negative associations within the system. Vast amounts of federal dollars were spent in the design, implementation, and evaluation of diversion programs. Diversion became a national strategy for combating delinquency, and programs were implemented throughout the country, funded by the Juvenile Justice and Delinquency Prevention Act.

Nejelski (1976), Cressey and McDermott (1974), Klein (1979), Blomberg (1983) and Sarri (1983) as well as many others have reviewed the results from the evaluation of diversion programs. They argue that diversion can only be effective as an alternative to traditional processing of minor and first offenders if community resources in the Child Welfare, education, recreation, and employment sectors are readily available to youth who are diverted. The findings from the hundreds of completed evaluation studies suggest that the vast majority of programs were initiated and/or operated under the aegis of law enforcement and judicial agencies. Thus, they have come to have had a "net widening" effect as a social control mechanism because of the coopting of power by the law enforcement agencies and the failure of the Child Welfare and education systems to become involved effectively. The studies of Spergel in Illinois are particularly informative. He observes that Child Welfare agencies responded when resources which they desired became available, but their response was one which reinforced traditional modes of intervention. He concludes:

> The availability of resources and the attempt to deal specifically with certain types of status offenders resulted, generally, in more rather than less penetration of these systems—particularly official agencies—by troublesome youth, mainly youth from low income communities. . . . Based on ISOS experience, social reform is largely an ideological and political process. It is not basically characterized by a planned or unplanned effort. (Spergel, 1982:24)

Despite the pessimistic results in many evaluations of diversion programs, they also suggest that positive results can be and have been achieved, particularly in those programs which operate independently of the justice system (Klein, 1979). They are more benign, humane, and less stigmatizing. Programs also need assurance of continuing financial support because many effective programs have been terminated due to federal policies which limit support to two or three years. Advocacy, family crisis counseling, opportunity enhancement, and skill development all have yielded positive results. Most observers conclude that needed public and private social services have not been readily available to delinquent youth, but that if they were, diversion programs could succeed to a far greater extent.

## Deinstitutionalization of Status Offenders

A third priority goal of the Juvenile Justice and Delinquency Prevention Act was the removal of status offenders from closed institutions. States and localities were offered federal funds if they removed these youth from closed institutions and provided services to them in the community. This policy was in accord with the primary recommendation of the 1967 President's Commission that deinstitutionalization of juvenile offenders be effected expeditiously. However, until the 1974 legislation was passed, results were spotty and limited throughout the country. The legislative mandate stated that juveniles who are charged with or who have committed offenses that would not be criminal if committed by an adult shall not be placed in juvenile detention or correctional facilities, but must be placed in shelter facilities or returned to their homes.

The majority of the states committed substantial resources to reducing the numbers of status offenders in both detention facilities and in institutions holding adjudicated youth. Results for females were particularly noteworthy because the majority of incarcerated females were held for status offenses. The removal of status offenders and nonoffenders from secure institutions was one of the more successful juvenile justice policy thrusts of the 1970s as Krisberg and Schwartz (1983) report in their longitudinal study of youth in correctional facilities. Similarly, the findings of Kobrin and Klein (1982) from their national study of status offender programs indicated that there were significant reductions in status offender admissions to detention centers and training schools. They also report that female admissions, as expected, dropped more significantly than did those of males.

The greatest success in deinstitutionalization was achieved in Massachusetts under the directorship of Jerome Miller, Commissioner, Division of Youth Services. He reorganized and then closed the five public correctional facilities and retained only a small number of secure beds. Another apparent factor in the success of the deinstitutionalization policy was the discretion to purchase services from the private sector with federal funds. Diversification and decentralization grew rapidly in many states, but recently there is evidence that many private vendors "cream off" the more treatable youth and leave the more difficult and minority youth in closed public facilities. Vinter, Downs, and Hall (1976) observed in the early stages of deinstitutionalization that states with high proportions of poor, undereducated, and minority youth had less deinstitutionalization.

Other research by Lerman (1982) and Handler and Zatz (1982) indicates that the picture is much more complex if one assumes that recycling of youth to other types of residential facilities might well take place when local community-based services are not readily available and provided effectively to youth and families in need of such services. Particularly noteworthy were the marked interstate differences in response to the legislative mandate. Lerman (1982) points out that offsetting changes do exist in the use of residential treatment institutions associated with Child Welfare, private facilities, and psychiatric wards of general and state hospitals. Federal Child Welfare funding was available in much larger amounts for reinstitutionalization of youth in the above facilities so it is not surprising that it has occurred. Also, there is growing evidence that four circumvention tactics have been utilized by juvenile court staff: using the "contempt" power to "bootstrap" a status offender into a delinquent; referring or committing a status offender to a mental health facility; developing semisecure facilities; and, alleging juvenile delinquency where the facts only support a status offense.

Information about institutionalization patterns in the 1980s are not readily available because of federal discontinuance of many routine censuses and surveys of these programs. However, given the continuing decline in the juvenile crime rate and the prevalence of processing of juveniles for status offenses by juvenile courts, it appears that the circumvention tactics may be succeeding for those who desire continuance of out-of-home placement of children and youth in institutions. Rates of admission overall have remained constant; length of stay has increased substantially for males and females; bed occupancy has been remarkably constant; and, the incarceration of poor and minority youth appears to have increased substantially (Krisberg and Schwartz, 1983; Lerman, 1982).

## Reform: The Challenge of the Future

The problems in juvenile justice and Child Welfare are deep-seated and will not be quickly resolved in this society where, it appears, there is little sympathy for progressive youth development policies. The recent conservative trends have resulted in a tremendous growth in adult prison populations and in punitive laws. These patterns of justice are now being applied to youth in several states, and the results may well be far more negative for society in the long run, because we have a low birth rate and an increasing aged population. Current juvenile reform legislation now calls for more mandatory sentencing, lowering of the upper age of juvenile jurisdiction, greater ease of waiver to adult court, and greater access to juvenile records. Also, much preoccupation with chronic and violent offenders and about retribution, deterrence, and selective incapacitation continues. These policies are being developed by persons who believe in the traditional system of punishment, but Child Welfare personnel and agencies are doing little to stem the tide. Damaging or wasting "child and youth power," as we have been doing, will yield serious social problems in the twenty-first century when these persons will be needed as capable and responsible adults.

Numerous policy alternatives could be offered and considered to enhance positive interactions between the Child Welfare and juvenile justice systems, so as to enhance the well-being of youth. I would like to offer eight which seem to be particularly pertinent for the 1980s.

1. *National youth policy.* A national youth policy is urgently needed which promotes institutional change to enhance the well-being of children and youth and reduces commitment to policies and programs which focus on control, suppression, and behavior modification. Zimring (1982) has noted that the legal status of adolescents in the United States is most unclear despite the changes that have occurred in the past twenty-five years. He argues for a new distinct legal conception of adolescence as a foundation for more effective social policies that recognize the contemporary status of all youth in this society. Criteria for such a policy would include: youth involvement; integration of programs across sectors; programs directed toward opportunity enhancement and productive participation of all in mainstream society; programs serving positive national goals; policies which break down barriers between education and employment; and, policies which treat youth as a resource, not a collection of problems.

2. *Removal of service barriers.* Barriers to effective service to adolescent youth by the Child Welfare system must be reduced. Among these barriers are the lack of flexibility in the use of available funding resources; lack of comprehensive adolescent service networks; lack of effective assessment capabilities; lack of available creative service options; lack of 24-hour care to meet the needs of youth; lack of adequate staff training for work with adolescents; and, lack of standards for accountability and client tracking. Services can be delivered far more effectively when these barriers have been eliminated.

3. *Increased informal handling of youth.* Formalization of the juvenile justice system must be reduced for minor and status offenders, accompanied by reductions in the numbers of youth processed through that system. Needed are new mechanisms to facilitate dispute resolution in our local communities. The experience of Sweden, Scotland, and South Australia provides evidence that such mechanisms can be effectively developed to serve youth in the local community—either in the professional system or in lay community networks (Sarri and Bradley, 1980). These conflict resolution panels offer flexible mechanisms for responding to delinquency without the formal stigma of a court hearing. Because the focus is toward the future rather than the past, the youth and his or her parents are actively involved in developing solutions.

4. *In-home care.* Research findings from many recent studies indicate that more effort needs to be directed toward services to youth and their families in their own homes. One strategy for such programming is now, strangely enough, referred to as "in-home care." In-home detention has been successfully tested in several metropolitan communities and is now widely accepted, although the extent of the practice is still

relatively minimal. In contrast, in-home care of adjudicated delinquents, even serious offenders, has developed only recently in the United States. It has been extensively tested and evaluated in England, South Australia, and several European countries. The Kent Project, begun by Nancy Hazen, provided one of the most effective models for the placement of serious offenders with foster families for intensive care (Hazen, 1981). This model also incorporated involvement of the natural family, wherever possible, in the treatment program along with youth and foster parents. A similar program for intensive intervention has been developed in South Australia, and there emphasis is placed on three basic elements: self-responsibility and direction by youth and their families; community involvement; and normalization principles in the development of the program. There is also extensive training for all staff who are involved in any aspect of the program, careful program monitoring, 24-hour back-up support services, and respite care for families. Results from the evaluation of both of these programs suggest that they can be successfully implemented and provide far more positive outcomes than traditional foster care services. Moreover, the involvement of natural parents can be accomplished to a far greater extent than many professionals presently assume.

5. *Job creation and youth employment.* The level of youth unemployment in the United States today should be viewed as a serious crisis, but it remains a matter of minimal concern to most adults. Needed today is a long-term proactive strategy with primary initiative from the public sector. It is already quite apparent that the private sector alone will not be able to resolve the problems of youth unemployment and subsequent deviance, and a serious labor shortage can be anticipated for the 1990s. Unless effective programs in employment and career development are implemented now, we will have a cohort of adults who cannot carry out necessary adult responsibilities in the years ahead. The recent proposals for a National Service Corps in which all youth at about age eighteen would spend one year in an organized public service program is a positive social policy toward rectifying the current situation. Our past experience with a variety of service corps provides ample support for the viability of such a program. In addition, more extensive career-oriented apprentice training programs, systems of job sharing, and legislation to insure the right to employment are necessary to meet the particular needs of adolescents and young adults. All youth should have a reasonable expectation that given appropriate behavior on their part, they will be able to participate in the regular labor force of the country. The need for employment is more urgent for the youth and young adult age group than for any other population in our society, despite adult protestations to the contrary.

6. *Right to education.* Although lack of success and involvement in

education is one of the strongest predictors of delinquency, far too little has been done to enhance the educational experience and performance of thousands of our society's youth. Today's secondary school programs must address the needs of working-class and blue-collar youth far more directly than they have been doing in the past. Attention has been directed toward the needs of middle-class and upward-bound students, but far too little toward working-class youth. Alternative school programs provide a variety of models for the development of nontraditional secondary education. Many years ago Robert Havighurst, the noted educational psychologist, recommended that greater attention be focused on achievement of equality of educational outcome for all students rather than focusing our attention only on equal access to education. He further argued that the vast majority of American adolescent youth could successfully complete all of the educational competencies that have been established for secondary school programs. Clearly then the need is to pursue more seriously implementation of the proper types of educational programs.

7. *Income maintenance and well-being.* Finally, and perhaps most important, this society must reverse the policies stringently implemented by the Reagan administration, policies that were initiated in some cases by the Nixon and the Carter administrations. These policies are rapidly increasing the poverty population of the United States. Moreover, that population now is composed primarily of children, youth, and their mothers. As of 1983 one in five children in the United States lived in a family whose income fell below the poverty level, and for minority children that proportion was one in two. Clearly, it is utter folly for a society not to care adequately for its children since the perpetuation of a vital society requires the health and well-being of youth who are its future adults.

The child-support system currently operating in the United States does not furnish a reasonable standard of living for children living with single parents, and it encourages family dissolution. Proposals are now forthcoming to require parental support (primarily by male parents) through the mechanism of enforced automatic deductions through the Internal Revenue Service. Legal enforcement of parental responsibility will fail without strong social norms as back-up support. Few of the advocates for coercive legal enforcement appear to have examined some of the unanticipated negative consequences that occured under previous programs. Obviously, all desire to have both parents assume full responsibility for their children. But if parents do not do so voluntarily, can the State enforce that responsibility without, at the same time, creating situations in which child abuse, domestic violence, and other problems emerge? Given the current rate of adolescent pregnancy, of pregnancy outside marriage, and of unemployment, it is difficult to see how a coercive enforcement of parental financial responsibility could work effectively. Greater effort must be made to implement the perspective that children are the responsibility of everyone in the society. The United States remains the only major industrial country without a national provision of child support for all children.

8. *Enhancing community resources.* The local community is crucial to the development of youth policies and the delivery of effective service; it is central to youth socialization through formal and informal networks and to the prevention and control of crime. More knowledge is needed about the characteristics of a community that will encourage youth, as well as strategies and tactics for creating that type of community infrastructure. The well-publicized fears of crime can be alleviated through the development of dynamic community action programs in which youth are viewed as a constructive force in crime prevention and control. Such action is acutely needed to resolve the serious racial and ethnic conflicts increasingly prevalent in this decade.

Juvenile justice today is an overworked, disjointed, and haphazard system of coercive social control. This system processes far too many youth and families for it to do so effectively. As a result, it does not enhance the well-being of youth, their families, or the society, as its founders intended.

Delinquency is really a property of the social system in which people are enmeshed rather than a characteristic of those persons called delinquents by agents of social control. Today the United States urgently needs to develop constructive community-based social control systems in which families, friends, neighbors, businesses, and schools are engaged cooperatively with youth in the development of policies and programs to enhance youth well-being. In doing so they will improve the society. All of the recommendations proposed here will require very strong support and perseverance as well as organizational advocacy if they are to be accepted and implemented. Obviously, priorities among these recommendations are necessary. These priorities need to be established at federal, state, and local levels, as well as in the public and private sectors. However, the 1980s is an opportune time to begin this effort since there appears to be an emerging concern in many spheres of society about social policies and programs for youth and their families.

# CHAPTER 19

# Adolescents on Their Own

Donald M. Loppnow

Adolescence has been characterized as a time of moving from dependence on the family for physical, emotional, and financial support to interdependence within the adult community. As a stage of development adolescence involves significant physical, social, and psychological changes and adjustments. Although adolescence is frequently refered to as a transition, it is not a passage but rather a time of life that implies particular needs and challenges.

Sometimes viewed as in a liminal phase, betwixt and between childhood and adulthood, adolescents have historically fallen "beween the cracks" in the social welfare and legal service systems. There has been much debate and confusion about whether adolescents, particularly young people on their own or those with various kinds of behavioral problems, should be treated as adults or as children. Youth in trouble have also been handed back and forth between the Child Welfare and legal structures. Currently, the Child Welfare system is assuming increasing responsibility for meeting the needs of this population and thus it is important for administrators and staff to become knowledgeable concerning their special characteristics, problems, and needs.

The issues that bring adolescents into contact with the Child Welfare system are likely to result from a combination of the normal changes occurring during the adolescent stage and of extraordinary family and environmental stresses that impinge on the teenager. Child Welfare practitioners typically work with adolescents and their families on such issues as: sexuality and teenage pregnancy, teenage parenting, school truancy, "incorrigible" behavior, drug use and abuse, physical and/or sexual abuse, neglect, leaving home, running away, delinquency, depression, and suicide.

In this chapter four distinct but interrelated problems which come to the attention of the Child Welfare field will be highlighted: running away, abuse and neglect, adolescents adrift, and depression and suicide. In each of these areas, a brief overview of the extent of the problem, our existing knowledge about it, and implications for program and practice will be presented. An assumption is made that the problems experienced by adolescents should be veiwed ecologically. Adolescents, like all human beings, must achieve some sort of adaptive balance with those systems on which they depend for nurture and stimulation (Germain, 1979; Hartman and Laird, 1983). In Child Welfare practice with adolescents, these environmental systems include families, peers, neighborhoods, communities, organizations, and a range of helping or potentially helping resources.

While it is important that Child Welfare workers have knowledge of adolescent development and are familiar with the needs and challenges of this stage, an ecological perspective implies that the problems encountered by adolescents must be understood in a larger context. Problems are seen as deficits in the environment, as dysfunctional transactions among environmental systems, as a lack of individual or family coping skills or strategies, or as the result of interrupted growth and development. Thus the unit of attention is considered the adolescent-in-environment, and both assessment and intervention focus primarily on the "goodness of fit" (Germain and Gitterman, 1980) between the adolescent (or adolescents) and those other systems with which he or she is in transaction, the most central of which is generally the family.

## The Runaway

Various studies have documented that between 600,000 and one million youth, or approximately 2 to 3 percent of all youth ages ten to seventeen, run away from home each year—at least overnight—without the consent of parents or custodians (Brennen et al., 1975:18). Nearly 3 percent of all families with one or more youth aged ten to seventeen will have at least one runaway per year. Contrary to popular belief, the adolescent who repeatedly runs away is a small minority. The majority of runaways run only once and most runaways return within a week. Runaways are represented in all socioeconomic groups and the majority come from families with both parents in the home. The majority of runaways are male and their average age is fifteen. Generally, the length of time the runaway is gone increases with age. Most runaway episodes are poorly planned and reflect impulsive behavior responses (Walker, 1975).

During the time they are away from home and living on the streets, these adolescents are in a vulnerable position and may be exposed to exploitation and other dangers as they struggle to survive. It is not uncommon for runaways to become involved in panhandling, shoplifting, drug use or prostitution. Many are arrested. And some become victims of physical assault, sexual abuse, or rape.

While the term "runaway" generally refers to the youth who voluntarily leaves home without parental permission, in recent years the terms "pushout" and "throwaway" have been coined to refer to youth who leave home because their parents (or legal custodians) have encouraged them to leave, have abandoned them, or have abused and neglected them. Nearly 25 percent of the youth who are considered runaways are, in fact, "throwaways" (Gullotta, 1979:112).

Until early in the twentieth century running away was considered to be a form of youthful adventure rather than a social problem. From 1930 on, the former relative freedom of adolescents eroded. Most states established compulsory education laws and began enforcing a new type of "crime" called the "status offense." Status offenders are youth whose behavior would not result in a criminal charge if committed by an adult. When the juvenile court system was created, no distinction was made between those children who committed crimes and those who were disobedient to their parents, unruly, truant, or ran away. These "wayward" children were punished in ways similar to adults who violated criminal laws.

The Juvenile Justice and Delinquency Prevention Act of 1974 was, in part, an attempt on the federal level to structure policy toward status offenders. This act provided that, in order to be eligible for federal money, states must provide shelter facilities for status offenders rather than placing them in juvenile detention and other correctional facilities. This piece of legislation also emphasized the need for community-based services and diversionary programs for status offenders. (See Chapter 18 for a more complete discussion of this legislation.)

The concerns raised by the increasing incidence of runaway and throwaway youth resulted in the Runaway Youth Act of 1977. This legislation provided assistance to states to develop programs designed to serve youth while away from home and living on the streets. By 1978, the National Runaway Youth Program had funded 166 runaway programs that were providing services to over 32,000 runaway youth and their families. The National Toll-Free Communications System was also established to serve runaways and other homeless youth and their families. The National Runaway Switchboard serves as a neutral channel of communication between runaway youth and their families. This system serves as a crisis intervention service for runaways and a resource file for agencies which operate programs around the country (Office of Youth Development, DHEW, 1974).

A review of the literature regarding runaways reflects an evolution of understanding about factors which contribute to running away. The majority of articles, especially the earlier ones written a decade or more ago, reflect a traditional psychopathological school of thought in which the reasons for running away are attributed to individual pathology or dysfunction, such as poor impulse control, low frustration tolerance, poor self image, or poor judgment. In more recent years, the literature reflects a shift to an environmental context in which the reasons for running away are more likely to be attributed to situational factors outside the individual adolescent, such as family dysfunction or abuse and neglect. Some experts argue that running away for some youth may be viewed as a positive and adaptive step in the normal growing-up process. Regardless of the theoretical perspective and orientation toward runaways, the features most often associated with running away are inadequate parent–child relationships and stressful home environments.

Although many different causal typologies of the running away phenomenon have been presented in the literature (e.g., Brennan et al., 1975; Dunford and Brennan, 1976; Homer, 1973), only recently has attention been paid to distinguishing the various kinds of "running away" in order to develop appropriate differential plans for intervention. For example, Orten and Soll (1980) focus on the degree of alienation between the adolescent and his or her family, and on how much the adolescent has internalized running away as a response to stressful situations. They posit three degrees of alienation, defined as follows:

> Alienation is determined as a clinical judgment rather than a precise measurement, and is based on such factors as the quality of the emotional exchanges between parents and child, the type and duration of the problems that precipitated the running, the degree to which parents and child are involved in nonproblem activities, and the overall quality of family relationships prior to the running experience. A simple measure of the degree of adolescents' internalization of running is the number of times they have run away. (Ibid.: 253, 255)

Practice guidelines are built on the principle of working with the family and vary based on a continuum of severity of alienation between the parents and adolescent. Orten and Soll present two subtypes of "first degree runaways." The "walkaway" is usually a young person 15 years or older who has run away for the first time. Consistent with the findings of others (Dunford and Brennan, 1976; Howell, Emmons and Frank, 1973), these runaways are stable, "normal" adolescents for whom leaving home is an existential experience.

> The literature suggests that they usually run once, learn from their travels, and return home. They go back with a renewed appreciation for home, and their parents, having learned from their experience, are more responsive to them . . . these youngsters do not feel powerless and are not fleeing intolerable situations. . . . (Orten and Soll, 1980:255)

The "fugitive" is another subtype of first time runaway whose circumstances reflect very different practice insights. These adolescents are younger, leave homes which are troubled, feel rejected by parents, and feel powerless and frightened. More one-parent families and more child abuse occur within this subgroup. These adolescents are psychologically dependent on their families and other significant people in their lives, are vulnerable, and have not been very skillful in managing their own day-to-day lives. Situational factors are highly important in affecting what happens to this group. Running to runaway shelters or responsible friends or relatives enhances the likelihood that they will return home whereas, if they become involved in the street culture, they are likely to become more alienated from home. For both the walkaway and the fugitive, family treatment involving the entire family and aimed at reunion of the adolescent with the family is the preferred treatment strategy.

As we move along the continuum toward a greater degree of alientation and conflict between the adolescent and his or her family, Orten and Soll identify "second degree" runners as adolescents who experience serious alienation from the family. Running away is internalized as the result of a single traumatic crisis between the parent and adolescent such as a strongly disapproved behavior (e.g., drug usage, adolescent pregnancy) or through repeated runaway episodes that add to a sense of hopelessness on the part of other family members.

The social worker's first task is to enable the adolescent and parents to decide whether the adolescent should return home to live. When a decision is made to explore an alternative living arrangement, such as residential group care, foster care, or independent living, the worker should focus on both involving the family and adolescent in the planning and maintaining a connectedness between the adolescent and family.

When a decision is made for the runaway to return to the family, it is important to enhance the reconciliation by developing plans with the adolescent which insure that he or she will not run away again. This may be as informal and straightforward as getting a commitment from the adolescent not to run away or, in instances where delinquent behavior is involved, as formal and structured as probation under the auspices of the juvenile court.

When a decision is made by the adolescent and family that a separate living arrangement for the adolescent is preferred, this decision should be followed by family sessions to help parents, siblings, and the adolescent to sort out feelings about the separation, and to plan for a smooth transition, continued contact, and, hopefully, a reunification.

The greatest alienation between the adolescent and the family is apparent in "third degree" runners.

> This person is typically strongly alienated from family and has little or no contact with them. Usually older than the modal age for runaways, the third-degree runner has typically lived on the streets for a year or more. He or she has acquired the skills in theft, con games, and the other aggressive behaviors that ensure survival on the streets. There is little or no motivation to return home and often none on the part of the family to have the child back. (Orten and Soll, 1980:259)

If this type of adolescent seeks help, it is usually because he or she is required to do so by a correctional agency. Social work intervention is usually focused on life planning and arranging for productive independent living. Whenever possible, parents and other family members ought to be involved in the process to attempt to keep communication channels open and to maintain ties to the relationship.

Family relationships with the runaway adolescent are the key factor for the practitioner to consider when developing an intervention strategy. Runaway behavior should be approached by the practitioner as a family systems problem (Spillane-Grieco, 1984). Communication problems and lack of empathic understanding between runaway adolescents and their parents appear to be common phenomena.

> What is noticeable in families experiencing this situation is the lack of communication between parents and children and the type of communication that occurs when they do communicate. Youngsters perceive parents as not listening and parents perceive children as disobedient, uncaring, and insensitive. Neither side is anxious to risk sharing, for neither side is secure in their role or positions. (Gullotta, 1979:113)

A recent study of parents of runaways found that "parents were truly concerned for their runaway children and hurt by their departure, but they were not able to express their affection to the children and . . . the children could not express their affection to the parents" (Spillane-Grieco, 1984:165). Findings of this study and others suggest that a primary focus for practitioners should be on enhancing effective communication skills with a special emphasis on communicating positive statements between the runaway and his/her family.

As noted, adolescence is not simply a phase in which young people experience particular "turbulence" and rebellious feelings. Young people today cannot be sure that a job will be available, what their roles should be in society, what marriage will hold, or indeed that they can count on a clean, safe world in which to create their own new families. Many, understandably, have not consolidated their own identities sufficiently enough to move ahead with purpose, and our society offers few guidelines or rituals to help young people move from adolescence to adulthood.

In some cases "running away" is the only solution imaginable to the adolescent, to escape from what seems an unmanageable problem, either with parents who may place inappropriate burdens or expectations on the young person, with school and peers, or with others in his or her environment. The Child Welfare worker needs to help the young person and family, and at times other people or systems in the life of the adolescent, and examine alternative ways to resolve the stress.

## Abuse and Neglect

The incidence of abuse and neglect of adolescents is extensive. Studies show that approximately one-third of all of the abuse cases reported to state registries involves adolescent victims. Mouzakitis (1984) indicates that a 1983 American Humane Association report documented 65,350 confirmed cases of abuse of youth between the ages of eleven and seventeen. These data underestimate the actual incidence of adolescent abuse since many cases are not identified as involving abuse if other problems such as running away or delinquent behavior are present (Fisher and Berdie, 1978; Garbarino, 1980; Mouzakitis, 1984; Ziefert, 1981). Frequently adolescents who are labeled as delinquents, status offenders, prostitutes, drug abusers, runaways, suicidal, pregnant teenagers, are actually unidentified abused and neglected youth.

The varying patterns of abuse experienced by adolescents necessitate differential treatment approaches. Generally speaking, abused adolescents can be divided into two groups: chronically abused, those who have been abused and deprived since infancy and early childhood; and nonchronically abused, those whose abuse started with the onset of puberty. "Both groups have certain common characteristics; the most prominent are: . . . they all experience the physiological and emotional upheavals of adolescence; . . . they all have been physically abused or otherwise deprived at the time of the initial contact with the authorities; . . . they all present minor or serious acting-out behavior and/or they are involved in minor or serious delinquent acts" (Mouzakitis, 1984:150).

The literature provides ample references to document that children who are subjected to abuse over long periods of time will experience negative effects on their self-concepts, interpersonal relationships, and general adjustment. Some of these children have great difficulty in peer relationships or in controlling their own aggression. Some become involved in serious crime while the response of others is withdrawal into drug use, depression, and mental illness.

For the nonchronically abused adolescent, maltreatment begins in adolescence and may be triggered by the tension between parental needs for control and the adolescent's striving for independence from parental control, or by the fact that the adolescent occupies an untenable position in the family. The young person may occupy an inappropriate role in the family (for example, the responsibility of meeting mother's emotional needs), in response to which he or she rebels or begins to demonstrate some kind of individual acting-out or other dysfunctional behavior. These children may engage in sporadic delinquent behavior.

Mouzakitis (1984) argues that it is important for the worker to obtain a comprehensive history of the adolescent's abuse and family situation so that a judgment can be made about the chronicity or nonchronicity of the abuse. This judgment will enable the development of a differential treatment plan. Generally, cases involving chronic abuse will require long-term treatment and the usual goal of returning home may be problematic. Since such youngsters may have considerable difficulty establishing relationships with adults as parental figures in the intimacy of a family context, when placement is the plan, a treatment-oriented group or residential care facility may hold more promise for rehabilitation. By contrast, where nonchronically abused adolescents are involved, a short-term crisis-oriented approach may be more appropriate. The treatment approach should include and focus on the entire family with the intended goal to re-establish family equilibrium. If temporary foster care is necessary, it should only be very short term to minimize alienation of the adolescent from the family. Regardless of the approach, involvement of the family is crucial.

Evidence suggests that abuse of adolescents results in a disproportionately high incidence of runaway behavior. In a study of physically abused adolescents who had been arrested by the juvenile authorities, 40 percent of the arrests were for runaway infractions compared to 17 percent among the nonabused juveniles. Similarly in a sample of sexually abused adolescents, 55 percent of their arrests were for runaway offenses (Gutierres and Reich, 1981). These findings demonstrate the interrelatedness of the problems and the necessity for Child Welfare agencies to develop multifaceted services to address these factors.

Nationally there is evidence to suggest that the most successful services for adolescents are offered by "outreach" and "alternative" programs, such as crisis centers, runaway houses, and hotline services. These "specialized" agencies collaborating with more traditional multi-service agencies represent the beginning of a service delivery network with special expertise in serving families with adolescents. Networks of services rather than single purpose agencies appear to be the answer (Garbarino, 1980; Ziefert, 1981). Self-help groups for victims of abuse, volunteer adolescents trained as peer counselors, educational programs aimed at increasing the awareness of adolescents about the problem, and peer networks have become an important adjunct to more traditional agency services.

A number of exemplary programs which provide services for abused adolescents have been developed in recent years. One such program is a multifaceted agency whose primary purpose is serving adolescents and their families (Hirose, 1979). It provides emergency programs such as a 24-hour telephone hotline and counseling service and a licensed 24-hour housing shelter for adolescents. The program provides information and referral services and ongoing counseling for youth and their families. Adolescent volunteers, trained as peer counselors, meet on a daily basis with abused youth to provide support, share feelings, and explain agency and community resources. Workshops are offered for adolescent clients and the community on topics such as human sexuality, reproduction and venereal disease, incest and molestation. The agency also provides short-term foster homes for adolescents who are awaiting placement, who need longer term crisis resolution services, and who are preparing for leaving home, but who have not fully developed skills for independent living. Agency staff are active on a multidisciplinary team composed of professionals from a variety of community agencies who are providing protective services for abused and neglected youth. A philosophy appears to be present which includes a respect for and incorporation of the ideas and self-help abilities of adolescents.

Another agency promoted a peer helping network which grew out of the void in services available to counter the social isolation associated with abuse and neglect. "Social isolation of the victim-perpetrator dyad is seen as a major block to effective intervention" (Garbarino and Jacobson, 1978:506). The program takes an ecological perspective in trying to bridge the social isolation of maltreated youths. An adolescent-oriented program was developed to include several components: a youth staffed hotline, a self-help group for abused adolescents, and a public awareness campaign aimed at youth. A service bureau staffed by youth trains teenage volunteers who want to become peer helpers. Some of the peer helpers are assigned to work in other agencies in the community which serve maltreated youth. This network of adolescent volunteers in the agencies can add to, in the eyes of youth, the credibility and effectiveness of the services offered by the agencies.

The self-help groups offered by the agency are intended:

to provide a supportive setting in which youthful victims can talk about maltreatment; to provide a context in which youths can discuss strategies for coping, including foster care, court appearances and child protective services; to provide a support system for youthful victims who need encouragement to seek adult intervention in abusive or neglectful family situations, by defining the kind of treatment and care they have a right to expect; and to teach skills that will make it less likely that members will become mistreating parents in the future. (Ibid.:508)

This agency also developed a manual to assist other agencies in creating self-help groups for abused adolescents.

The public awareness component of the program involved developing and widely distributing a pamphlet prepared by youth for youth which defines maltreatment, explains the conditions for initiating action, and suggests ways to get help. In addition, essay contests and workshops regarding abuse and neglect of adolescents were presented in secondary schools by peer helpers and staff. The entire peer helping program builds on the informal peer networks common among adolescents, but which may be closed to adults without the direct involvement of adolescents themselves.

A program which recognizes the high incidence of runaway behavior among abused adolescents incorporates services for runaways with comprehensive crisis services for neglected and abused adolescents and their families (Lourie, Campiglia, James, and Dewitt, 1979). The agency offers temporary emergency shelter, a 24-hour crisis telephone line, and a special recruitment program for foster homes for abused and neglected adolescents. The agency has also organized a community forum composed of representatives from agencies and other community service organizations that is intended to confront the service needs of abused and neglected adolescents. Since youth typically find runaway services and related community-based alternative services more accessible and easier to use than traditional protective services, offering services to treat adolescent abuse and neglect within runaway youth programs enhances the accessibility of counseling services to adolescents and their families.

## Adolescents Adrift

A third group of adolescents well known to Child Welfare workers includes those "displaced" young people—victims of foster care drift, who, over time, have been cut off from family but have not had the opportunity to establish permanent roots in a new family. It is difficult to know how many such young people continue adrift in the Child Welfare system. Fanshel and Shinn (1978) are among those whose research drew attention to these children in limbo, contributing to the development of the permanency movement which has reduced, and hopefully will continue to reduce, their numbers.

However, Child Welfare workers continue to find these alienated teenagers on their caseloads. Many have been in multiple placements and their sense of continuity and of identity has been severely damaged. Drawing upon a model of family of origin work developed in the family therapy movement (Bowen, 1978; Hartman and Laird, 1983), combined with the use of the "life book," these young people can be helped to heal their ruptured continuity and establish a firmer sense of self. Moreover, frequently careful exploration of agency records and other "detective" work may reveal resources in the extended kin network that might become available to the young person, as was the case in the following situation.

> Martha, a 17-year-old girl living in a group home, had been adrift in the child welfare system since her birth in a state hospital to a chronically mentally ill mother. She was placed in foster care since, before the days of permanency planning, she was considered a serious risk for adoption because of her mother's illness and the fact that paternity was unknown.
>
> By the time she was seventeen, Martha had been in eleven different foster homes. Early placements had been disrupted by the illness of one foster mother and a move to another state by another. As each move exacted its toll, Martha had increasing difficulty accepting or attaching to any adults. She became an angry, distant, and often destructive young girl, thus precipitating new disruptions.
>
> At seventeen, she had little memory of most of her previous homes, was confused about when she had been where, and showed no interest in clarifying that confusion or in talking about the past. In time, with much patience and persistence, the worker was able to engage her in a reconstruction of her life. They developed a "life book" together, identifying each of the places she had lived, the people in the different homes, some of the experiences she had had, the schools she had attended, and even the parade of social workers she had known. In time, old neighborhoods were visited, landmarks remembered, and reunions arranged with three of the foster families.
>
> In searching the agency records, a partial family genogram was constructed. In the early years, a younger sister of her mother had visited her a few times. After considerable searching, this aunt was located. Martha learned that her mother had died in the hospital but, as she moved toward independent living, she found herself with a family which, although unable to offer much in the way of concrete assistance, was interested in and concerned about her.

In an early Michigan demonstration project aimed at permanency planning for children in foster care, a pilot group of foster care workers received intensive training and follow-up in a family-centered foster care model. The following letter from a worker to the supervisor of the Temporary Foster Care Project speaks eloquently of the success of this project.[*]

September 14, 1977

Dear Gloria:

John's mother died shortly before his third birthday and his father abandoned him shortly thereafter. He was raised by his paternal grandparents. His grandmother died when he was eleven years old and he was made a temporary ward of Probate Court . . . when his grandfather could no longer care for him. His grandfather died [a year later].

[Early this year] John shared with me a very prized possession of his, a baby book, kept by his mother who died shortly before John's third birthday.

The book was obviously the reflection of a very loving, caring mother who adored her first born son. Every shower, every shot, every sickness was entered in detail and I have never seen a more comprehensive history.

John has no idea of how his mother died or what her middle initial "J" stood for. He had only seen a picture of her once and even then it was only part of her face and taken from quite a distance.

True to every baby book written, this one contained a family tree and a wealth of information. The author had done such a complete job that every baby gift and its giver's name was entered. Addresses were there as well as newspaper clippings.

John knew none of the people mentioned. He said he'd never thought about contacting them but maybe some day he would.

Our recent training session emphasized the significance of the treasure I had in my hands and I found it difficult to put it out of my mind.

I already knew I was going to the Boston Marathon in April and well . . . if you're in Boston, Maine is right in the neighborhood.

The problem was that all of the names and addresses were almost twenty years old. I won't detail all of my investigation but sum it by saying I found George and Alice Taylor, maternal grandparents, in Maine.

I called ahead of time and arranged an appointment to meet. I felt much apprehension as I approached the house. Did they want to see me? Would they care about John? What dark family secret would explain his circumstances? How did his mother die at 21-years-old?

They were anxious to meet me and I was warmly welcomed in. There, on a large oval coffee table in the center of the room were literally hundreds of pictures of John and his mother, up until the time John turned three years

*Letter from Sue LaFramboise, Foster Care Worker, St. Clair County, to Gloria Thomas, Director, Michigan Temporary Foster Care Project, September 14, 1977.

old. Every letter John's mother had ever written was there. They had been looking for John for fifteen years.

As John has already said before me, "It's difficult to put feelings into words," and I cannot describe the atmosphere in the living room that evening. We spent most of the time in the past and the anger and hurt surrounding their daughter's death was still very real. But their concern for their grandson was just as obvious. He is their only grandson; they have three granddaughters.

We mapped a genogram for me to take back to John and they gave me several pictures of John's mother and her obituary card. I exchanged them for the high school picture John had given me last fall. His resemblance to his mother was striking. There were tears in all of their eyes when I left.

Again, it's so hard to describe John's reaction when I told him the Taylors were more than just names in a book, they were real, live, wonderful people, who wanted to know everything about him. Then I gave him the picture of his mother and the obituary card and after a while, the genogram—he was fascinated with it.

In July of this year, John's foster parents . . . took him to Maine. What was it like? In John's words, "It was the greatest thing that could ever happen to me. I felt so good knowing that I had them, along with an aunt, uncles, and cousins. . . . A really great thing about it was that after just being there one day, I had felt as though I had always been there." When John returned, he said to me, "In foster care, everybody is nice to you but even though nobody will admit it, you know you don't belong there. I never felt as though I belonged anywhere and now I feel like I belong. I am somebody, and that is the best feeling anyone could have."

John was astonished by the similarities he found between himself and his family—the food they like, the way they talk, and the fact that they are all very emotional people. He seems to have internalized his identity as a Taylor and now projects a sense of confidence about who he is and where he is going. Confidence and goals were never characteristics of John's personality. They came after he "knew he was somebody."

Sincerely,
*Sue*

All too often Child Welfare workers, perhaps overly identified with the isolated teenager or feeling hopeless about the families they assume don't care, fail to explore adequately the potential of the past and of the extended kin network in helping an adrift young person come to terms with self. The solution is often to discuss hurt feelings rather than to pursue potential permanent family connections on behalf of the young person.

These examples illustrate how a family-centered worker, confronted with the teenager adift in the Child Welfare system, may help the young person make identity building connections with the real figures in his or her past.

## Depression and Suicide

Adolescents must master the life task of changing from control by others to self-control, a process that brings considerable challenge. Stresses in the environment combined with the relatively unstable mood swings experienced by some adolescents can create a potentially volatile situation. Child Welfare practitioners often come in contact with adolescents who may be depressed and who are at risk of suicide.

Generally speaking, adolescent crises are family crises. Adolescents face crises which can be grouped into three types: problems in coping with a developmental task (e.g., peer relationships, sexual problems, independent living); inability to adjust to the norms and expectations of an important social institution (e.g., the law, school); and problems caused by family relationships in which the adolescent handles the problem in a way that threatens family functioning or the family relates to the adolescent in a way that threatens his or her well being (e.g., running away, abuse of drugs, suicide attempt, physical and sexual abuse) (Dixon, 1979).

When people experience stress, they may draw on a range of coping strategies to avoid becoming overwhelmed. When these coping strategies are unsuccessful, Highland (1979) believes that a four-stage process wherein people may go from denial to anxiety, to anger, and finally to depression typically occurs. He suggests that people are subject to depression if they are faced with enough stress and their individual capacities and environmental resources are insufficient to alleviate the tension and anxiety. Child Welfare practitioners encounter adolescents who are experiencing highly stressful situations—deprivation, physical abuse, substance abuse, unwanted pregnancy, running away, and removal from home and placement under the custody of the court. It is imperative for the worker to be alert to the possibility that the adolescent client may be vulnerable to withdrawal, depression, and even suicide. Two of these at-risk situations are discussed below: the adolescent preparing to leave home, and the adolescent victim of family abuse.

Teenagers who are experiencing separation, loss, rejection, or simply the prospect of emancipation as they face a transition from home to foster care, institution, or other forms of substitute care, or from one substitute care setting to another, or are ready to "graduate" to independence and self-sufficiency, commonly experience reactive depression (Anderson and Simonitch, 1981). In varying degrees, reactive depression occurs as a response to loss or disappointment. Adolescents who have experienced deprivation and misfortune, and are struggling with the losses that may be involved in working toward emancipation may experience reactive depression even when facing ordinary losses and disappointments.

Anderson and Simonitch (1981) describe several practice guidelines to follow when working with an adolescent during the emancipation process. They describe four stages which are common during the adolescent's adjustment to emancipation. During the first stage in the process, the adolescent experiences the loss of significant adults who have been primary caretakers and displays anxiety and low frustration tolerance even at minor setbacks. The practitioner must be supportive and work toward building trust in the working relationship. Frequent telephone contacts, informal contacts, and ready availability will help to establish this trust.

In the next stage, immediately after the move to independent living, adolescents tend to be elated, to feel that they have "arrived." However, shortly thereafter, the realities of the relatively mundane day-to-day responsibilities of caring for oneself lead to an emotional letdown. The initial elation may be followed by shock, disbelief, and feelings of helplessness and disappointment, especially if they are isolated or experience serious economic and social obstacles. The worker should be available to help the adolescent plan, to connect with needed resources such as employment or housing, as well as simply to listen and to understand.

The third stage is characterized by fear and loneliness. The adolescent at first may recognize neither the variety of tasks and problems which must be handled when living independently nor his or her own limitations and lack of resources. Young people may experience loss of self-esteem as they discover that they are not as competent at managing a serious situation as they had thought. The social worker should be in close contact to provide encouragement and may assume a coordinating and instructional role by, for example, providing or personally teaching money management; offering tips for shopping, housekeeping, and cooking; connecting the young person with medical care or job leads; and so on. Anderson and Simonitch note that the depression which adolescents experience at this stage is often masked by anger. The social worker may be the target for these feelings and needs to be prepared to accept the hostility without personalizing it. The worker must also be alert and sensitive to a young person's growing disillusionment and potential depression. The worker can play a crucial role in helping the adolescent to express and deal with feelings as well as to remain connected with immediate or extended family, friends, school, and work associates who may also provide encouragement and support.

Anderson and Simonitch advise the worker as follows:

Avoid setting up dare situations, stay out of power struggles, don't give adolescents all of the answers; respect their right and need to find out most things for themselves, avoid lecturing, negotiate with and contract with the youngster to work on realistic and achievable goals; overlook and ignore little things, don't get upset when the adolescent demands the last say, ask questions when you are after answers; turn negatives into positives when you are dealing with pessimism and defeatism, provide social prompting, and give heavy doses of positive social reinforcement (1981:388).

If the adolescent masters the first three stages successfully, the last stage will bring a sense of confidence that he or she can cope and succeed independently. Now, the young person should be developing new and lasting relationships. In most cases the reactive depression should be resolved in a period of six months to a year after the emanciaption process begins.

The adolescent who has been deprived or abused is also at risk of becoming depressed or even suicidal. Similarly, parents who deprive and abuse their children are themselves often depressed; thus an intergenerational cycle of dysfunction is perpetuated. Kinard (1982) suggests that the feelings of loss associated with abuse may be more difficult to cope with than those feelings associated with the death of a parent.

Abused adolescents, especially those who have been chronically abused, have experienced both the stress and deprivation that makes them vulnerable to episodes of depression. Child Welfare practitioners should pay special attention to the careful assessment of potential depression and, when appropriate, plan interventions that include both treatment of the depression and amelioration of the noxious environmental conditions that may be hindering the young person's functioning. As Kinard points out: "Both child abuse and depression commonly occur in environments characterized by poverty, isolation, and stress. These contributing factors must be considered in any efforts to plan effective intervention strategies" (1982:410). In effect, one cannot view adolescent depression as a purely psychological phenomenon. It is a social phenomenon as well and thus the ecologically minded Child Welfare worker must view the adolescent-in-environment as the unit of attention. Interventions will range from counseling or arranging treatment for the adolescent, alleviating tension between the young person and other individuals or systems on which he or she depends, and locating or developing new resources.

There is a close relationship between depression and suicide among adolescents. It has been estimated that 80 percent of all suicides were experiencing acute or chronic depression (Den Houter, 1981). Of special concern to Child Welfare practitioners is the fact that the incidence of adolescent suicide has increased sharply in recent years and, in fact, has become the second leading cause of death in persons from ten to twenty years old. Nationally the highest suicide rate has shifted from the elderly to the adolescent years. The rate of adolescent suicide doubled between 1950 and 1973 (ibid.). Data on suicide rates among adolescents are underestimated because many families understandably are reluctant to acknowledge publicly that their child has committed suicide, and because numerous automobile or other fatalities, which are officially recorded as accidental, may actually be suicides. Experts estimate that 14 to 15 percent—one in seven—of all fatal automobile accidents are suicides (ibid.).

In addition to the rise in incidence, research on adolescent suicide shows wide distribution by economic, educational, and geographic factors. Not surprisingly, the incidence of adolescent suicide is also highly associated with unstable family circumstances (ibid.). Suicide is frequently associated with the separation or loss of a significant relationship and with especially stressful events or series of stressful experiences. The suicidal behavior may be a communication from the adolescent that he or she is unable to cope with a problem and feels hopeless about solving it. Suicidal behavior "can further be understood in terms of its effect on those receiving the communication. A suicidal attempt may arouse feelings of sympathy, anxiety, anger, or hostility on the part of the individual's family or friends and therefore serve to manipulate relationships" (Aguilera and Messick, 1982:115). The young person may even, consciously or unconsciously, believe that his or her death is the only solution for a troubling individual or family problem. Thus, in some incidences it may be viewed as a sacrifice.

A crucial factor in the successful treatment of the suicidal person is the inclusion of family members in the treatment since the family may unwittingly organize around the suicidal behavior in such a way as to encourage or perpetuate it. Innovative programs for treating adolescents who are suffering from depression and/or suicidal tendencies often include hotlines, intensive and immediate crisis counseling, peer support groups, and the involvement of family members and other significant people in the adolescent's network.

Adolescents frequently believe that they are isolated and on their own in dealing with life circumstances. In many instances this perception has grown out of a history of deprivation, abuse, and stressful family circumstances. The young person's response is often to cut off from family, which leaves him or her isolated, alienated, and more at risk of being unable to resolve old misunderstandings, hurts, and grievances. A prevalent theme in the literature regarding adolescent runaways, abuse of adolescents, and stress, depression, and suicide among adolescents is the importance of the family and young person together as the focus of and vehicle for intervention. In the past, workers often believed young people needed help in separating from and "giving up" their neglectful or troubled families. Current knowledge suggests rather that young people need help differentiating from the troubling aspects of their heritages but remaining connected in whatever ways possible to those biological figures central to their identity and experience.

An ecological perspective for practice with adolescents takes into account the interrelatedness of the many factors which combine to create stress for adolescents. A review of a sample of successful service programs for adolescents reveals that a common feature of all of these programs is a well-trained staff committed to working with adolescents and their families together.

# CHAPTER 20

# Teenage Sexuality, Pregnancy, and Childbearing

ALBERT G. CRAWFORD
FRANK F. FURSTENBERG, JR.

One of the most troublesome social problems facing our society today is the marked increase over time in the number of adolescents who have become parents but are insufficiently mature, unable, or unwilling to provide the adequate care, protection, and nurture a child needs.

These parents, who are little more than children themselves, and their infants and young children, frequently come to the attention of the Child Welfare system, either through complaints to protective services or when the overwhelmed parents, who initially choose to keep and raise the child, begin to discover what is actually involved in the demands and responsibilities of parenting.

This chapter explores the many issues involved in the phenomenon of childbirth among teenagers, primarily from the perspective of prevention. It reviews behavioral trends in our sexual practices, describes some of the costs created by the absence of a workable system of sexual education and pregnancy prevention, and addresses some of the problems of designing new policies for managing sexual behavior among adolescents in order to minimize the social and psychological costs of early and unwanted sex, pregnancy, and childbearing.

Knowledgeable observers agree that significant and substantial changes have occurred in the sexual practices of the young during the past twenty years. As we shall detail here, rates of sexual activity among teenagers have soared, and out-of-wedlock childbearing has become more prevalent and conspicuous despite the greater availability and use of contraception and abortion. It is important, however, to put these trends into historical perspective and not to lose sight of the fact that the problems created by premarital sexual behavior are not novel. In many respects we have finally been compelled to face a long-standing contradiction in the management of nomarital sexuality in our society.

The recent sexual revolution, which Shorter (1977) dates in the 1960s, has probably been more evolutionary than is immediately apparent. Virginity was still highly prized in the 1950s, but rates of premarital pregnancy at that time suggest that virginity was often more publically valued than privately observed. In the 1960s premarital sexuality was treated more openly, and hence it appeared as though practices were suddenly changing. Though, undoubtedly, the incidence of intercourse increased dramatically, especially among the very young, it is equally true that "pluralistic ignorance" declined; that is, teenagers no longer felt as obliged to conceal their sexual conduct from others. As the change in sexual standards became more visible, it served to erode the existing social deterrents to premarital sex, thus accelerating the pace of change in the 1970s.

The recent changes in sexual standards should not be viewed in isolation from a more general revision that has been occurring in courtship, marriage, and family formation. Age at marriage has been rising to almost unprecedented levels in response to the growing premium put on education, the precarious economic position of young people, the changing social roles of women, the rapidly increased practice of cohabitation, and the elevated risk of divorce. All of these factors have played some part in changing the meaning of marriage. At one time, in the not so distant past, marriage was part of a tightly ordered transition to adulthood. When individuals married, they typically also initiated their sexual career, established their own household, and rapidly moved on to childbearing. While these events did not always occur strictly in order, the ideal sequence was widely accepted. Increasingly since then, however, the transition to marriage has become a more autonomous event, independent of the passage from virginity to sexuality, the establishment of a new household, or the initiation of childbearing. Accordingly, the significance of sexuality is undergoing change. Adolescents are not prepared to delay intercourse until marriage because they cannot foresee so easily a definite time when marriage will occur. The delay of marriage and the possibility of cohabitation have the consequence of blurring the boundaries of sexual behavior. Since marriage is no longer the appropriate occasion to begin to have sex, it is difficult to establish a normative schedule that regulates the timing of the onset of sexuality. The result is a cultural dilemma: One system has broken down, but a new one has not yet been established to take its place.

## Current Levels and Trends of Teenage Sexuality, Pregnancy, and Childbearing

Teenage childbearing must be viewed as the outcome of a long, elaborate social process. Clearly, sexual relations are a necessary but not sufficient condition for pregnancy, and pregnancy is a necessary but not sufficient condition for childbirth. Specifically, contraception and subfecundity (a reduced biological potential for reproduction) intervene in the first part of the process, and outcomes such as spontaneous, as well as induced, abortions and also stillbirths intervene in the second part. In addition, out-of-wedlock childbirths can be avoided by marriage prior to the birth; and, complications for the mother, father, and infant can be reduced, in varying degrees, by marrying following the birth or by putting the baby up for adoption. The following discussion, both of the incidence of sex, pregnancy, and births among teenagers and of the factors which influence these phenomena, will deal with this complex social process.

As discussed, a rapid increase in the level of teenage sexual activity has taken place in the United States during the last two decades. For example, premarital sexual activity among women aged fifteen to nineteen living in metropolitan areas increased by some two-thirds from 1971 to 1979. At present, roughly 80 percent of young men and 70 percent of young women have sexual intercourse by age nineteen (Zelnik and Kantner, 1980).

As noted by Paulker (1969), the most parsimonious explanation of teenage pregnancy treats it as the outcome of sexual activity and accident, rather than employing any more complex variables and hypotheses. Accordingly, teenage pregnancy rates, particularly for younger teenagers, have risen steadily since 1960 (Baldwin, 1976). The high rate of increase among younger teenagers in particular parallels their high rate of increase in sexual activity.

Nevertheless, several contingencies intervene between sexual activity and childbirth, namely contraception and subfecundity. Contraceptive use reduced the number of teenage pregnancies in 1976 by an estimated figure of 689,000—from a hypothetical figure of more than 1.5 million to an actual figure of around 780,000 (Zelnik and Kantner, 1978). From 1973 to 1978, the proportion of teenagers who became pregnant rose from 10 percent to 11 percent, but the proportion that became pregnant among those who were sexually active fell from 27 percent to 23 percent. A major reason why the overall rate of teenage pregnancy has risen more slowly than the total level of teenage sexual activity is increased and more consistent contraceptive use (Alan Guttmacher Institute, 1981). The level and regularity of such contraceptive use generally increased throughout the 1970s. However, while the proportion using the most effective methods—the pill and the IUD—almost doubled between 1971 and 1976, this proportion declined by 8 percent between 1976 and 1979. There is now a larger pool of sexually active teenagers, though an increase in the number using the most effective methods has been outweighed by an even larger rise in the number using ineffective methods, particularly withdrawal (Zelnik and Kantner, 1980).

Zelnik and Kantner (1978) find that while teenagers are now generally better prepared to use contraception, their rate of pregnancies has not declined, in part because the rise in sexual activity among the youngest teenagers has not been paralleled by as great an increase in their practice of contraception.

Another source of higher rates of teenage pregnancy may be a biological one: a decline in subfecundity. The age of maturation has been falling throughout the twentieth century, as a result of improved nutrition and medical care (Stickle and Stickle, 1975). With a mean age at menarche at present of 12.5 and a range of 8.5 to 16.5 and an historically typical pattern in which first ovulation occurs two years after menarche, the minimum age for a first pregnancy is 10.5 or even younger. Moreover, postmenarche sexual development has accelerated, so that the age of fecundity has dropped even further (Rauh, 1973).

When an out-of-wedlock teenage pregnancy occurs, it may be resolved in a variety of ways: The woman may let the pregnancy proceed to term and give birth, or she may obtain an abortion; and, if she gives birth, she may marry in order to legitimate the birth, or she may put the child up for adoption, or she may do neither.

A recent analysis estimates that among girls who were fourteen in 1978, around 40 percent will experience a teenage pregnancy, 20 percent will give birth, and 15 percent will have an abortion by age nineteen (Tietze, 1978). The 1973 Supreme Court decision and the subsequent legalization of abortion throughout the United States generated a rapid rise in the number of abortions performed on teenagers. For example, between 1972 and 1976 there was a 60 percent increase for all teenagers, and a 120 percent rise for those under age fifteen.

Of roughly 1,142,000 teenage pregnancies in 1978, 38 percent terminated in abortions, 13 percent in miscarriages, 22 percent in out-of-wedlock births, 10 percent in legitimate but premaritally conceived births, and 17 percent in legitimate births conceived within marriage (Alan Guttmacher Institute, 1981). Almost two-fifths of those fifteen to nineteen years old currently end their pregnancies with abortions, and more than half of all pregnant girls under age fifteen have abortions (Henshaw, Forrest, Sullivan, and Tietze, 1981). The availability and use of abortion is the major reason why there has been no increase in the teenage birth rate in the last decade. Moreover, the increased availability of abortion produced a leveling out of the trend in the illegitimacy rate in the mid-1970s, although the rate began to increase again in the late 1970s as fewer teenagers married to make their child's birth legitimate (Alan Guttmacher Institute, 1981).

Although there has been a leveling off the teenage birth rate is still reason for concern in the United States at present, since it is among the highest in the world and considerably higher than in most western European societies. The decline in both the rate and number of teenage births is restricted to those who are married; the rate of out-of-wedlock childbearing is rising for both older and younger teenagers. While, at present, most teenagers who give birth are married, if present trends were to continue, that would not be the case for long. In fact, already a majority of births to females under age eighteen occurs out-of-wedlock (see Table 20–1).

A major factor which accounts for the increased rate of out-of-wedlock childbearing is the smaller likelihood of marriage, especially among blacks, as a way of legitimating the birth. During the 1970s, rates of teenage marriage declined by 4 percent among whites and by 45 percent among blacks (Alan Guttmacher Institute, 1981). More specifically, the proportion of premarital teenage pregnancies which are legitimated by marriage prior to the birth has steadily declined in recent decades (see Table 20–1).

Finally, the probability that a teenager will bring her pregnancy to term and then give the baby up for adoption has diminished markedly during the last decade. The major factor is the greater availability of abortion as a way of resolving the dilemma. Currently, in cases where a child is born alive, 87 percent of the mothers keep the child; 5 percent give the child to others (usually relatives) in an informal adoption; and 8 percent give the child up for a formal adoption (Zelnik and Kantner, 1978).

## Causes of Teenage Sexual Activity, Pregnancy, and Childbearing

*Overview*

Theories about the etiology of early childbearing have often failed to take into account the fact that parenthood is the result of a social process. A major tendency has been to search for psychological factors

**TABLE 20–1  Selected Natality Indicators for Women Under 20, United States, 1950–1979**

| AGE | 1950 | 1955 | 1960 | 1965 | 1970 | 1975 | 1977 | 1978 | 1979 |
|---|---|---|---|---|---|---|---|---|---|
| **Number of births (in 1,000s)** | | | | | | | | | |
| 15–19 | ... | 484 | 587 | 591 | 645 | 582 | 559 | 543 | 549 |
| 18–19 | ... | 334 | 405 | 402 | 421 | 355 | 345 | 341 | 349 |
| 15–17 | ... | 150 | 182 | 189 | 224 | 227 | 214 | 203 | 200 |
| <15 | ... | 5 | 7 | 8 | 12 | 13 | 11 | 10 | 11 |
| **Birthrates (per 1,000 women)** | | | | | | | | | |
| 15–19 | 81.6 | 90.3 | 89.1 | 70.4 | 68.3 | 56.3 | 53.7 | 52.4 | 53.4 |
| 18–19 | ... | ... | ... | ... | 114.7 | 85.7 | 81.9 | 81.0 | 82.4 |
| 15–17 | ... | ... | ... | ... | 38.8 | 36.6 | 34.5 | 32.9 | 33.1 |
| <15 | 1.0 | 0.9 | 0.8 | 0.8 | 1.2 | 1.3 | 1.2 | 1.2 | 1.2 |
| **Out-of-wedlock birth rates (per 1,000 unmarried women)** | | | | | | | | | |
| 15–19 | 12.6 | 15.1 | 15.3 | 16.7 | 22.4 | 24.2 | 25.5 | 25.4 | 26.9 |
| 18–19 | ... | ... | ... | ... | 32.9 | 32.8 | 35.0 | 35.7 | 37.8 |
| 15–17 | ... | ... | ... | ... | 17.1 | 19.5 | 20.7 | 19.5 | 20.4 |
| <15 | | | | | | | | | |
| **Ratios of out-of-wedlock births (per 1,000 births)** | | | | | | | | | |
| 15–19 | ... | 142 | 148 | 208 | 295 | 382 | 429 | 441 | 461 |
| 18–19 | ... | 102 | 107 | 152 | 224 | 298 | 344 | 367 | 386 |
| 15–17 | ... | 232 | 240 | 327 | 430 | 514 | 566 | 587 | 612 |
| <15 | ... | 663 | 679 | 785 | 808 | 870 | 882 | 873 | 888 |

*Sources:*

National Center for Health Statistics, 1978. Final Natality Statistics, 1976. *Monthly Vital Statistics Report*, 26(12). Washington, D.C.: National Center for Health Statistics, U.S. Department of Health and Human Services.

National Center for Health Statistics, 1980. Final Natality Statistics, 1980. *Monthly Vital Statistics Report*, 29(1). Washington, D.C.: National Center for Health Statistics, U.S. Department of Health and Human Services.

which motivate adolescents to enter parenthood prematurely, such as the need for affection, the quest for adult status, the resolution of the Oedipal conflict, the desire to escape parental control, or the inability to foresee a more gratifying future. No doubt some of these reasons apply in some instances. Most studies, however, show that only a small minority of teenagers become parents because they consciously want to have a child (at least at the time of conception). Most become pregnant unwillingly and unwittingly, though to be sure many are reluctant to terminate the pregnancy by abortion once conception occurs. Teenagers typically formulate reasons why they want a child once they have become pregnant, but these reasons do not necessarily explain why the pregnancy initially occurred.

Before embarking on a discussion of the determinants of pregnancy and childbearing, it is important to note that the principal reason teenagers become pregnant is that a large number are sexually active and do not use contraception effectively enough to avoid pregnancy. Teenagers often take risks, engage in wishful thinking, and are careless about preventing pregnancy. In these respects they are not fundamentally different from adults, even those who are married, though teenagers are probably less prepared to take precautions, for a variety of reasons, than their adult counterparts. Later in this chapter, the problem of practicing contraception successfully will be discussed.

Often, teenage women undertake sex as a result of direct pressure from their partners, who may have little or no stake in preventing a pregnancy. Little is known about the interpersonal dynamics of sexual encounters among the very young, but there is reason to suspect that the boundary between enticement and rape is often not very distinct. Research on gender aggression suggests that the introduction to early sexual activity is, for females, frequently involuntary. Early sexual behavior frequently takes the form of a contest in which males attempt to "score" while females put up mild, and sometimes uncertain, resistance. This is not to say that females are not complicitious, but the complicity should be seen as part of a bargain which exchanges status in the peer group for sexual acquiescence.

We do not know very much about the transition to nonvirginity among young adolescents. What we do know suggests that relatively few become sexually active *in order* to become pregnant. While pregnancy may fulfill certain of the teenager's needs, it is often, to use Merton's term, "the unanticipated consequence of purposive social action" (1968). Teenagers have sex to remain popular and frequently become pregnant as a result of unplanned or poorly regulated sexual encounters. Nonetheless, pregnancy may not be an entirely random process, given varying rates of sexual behavior. Some teenagers manage to use contraception successfully, and it may be useful to explore some of the reasons why certain teenagers are more prone to becoming pregnant than others.

## Psychological Factors

Daniels (1969) finds a source of teenage pregnancy in a "dependency–deprivation syndrome," comprised of family instability, competition for attention between the adolescent and her siblings, physical punishment, and an emotionally unrewarding relationship between the teenager and her mother. Friedman (1971) holds that female delinquents who "act out" sexually are characterized by emotionally deprived family backgrounds, unfulfilled needs for closeness and tenderness, rejection by parents, failure in the area of parental control, inappropriate sexual identities among the parents and thus among the adolescents, and sexual threats by one parent or the other. J. D. Paulker (1969) sees teenage sexual intercourse as motivated by an unconscious need for love, perhaps rooted in a lack of love in early childhood. Alternatively, Rainwater (1965) views lower class sexual behavior, pregnancy, and childbearing as ways of legitimating one's manhood or womanhood, which can be scarce commodities, given deprivation and exclusion by the wider society and a resulting loss of self-esteem. In all of these theories, sex, pregnancy, and childbearing fill a gap in the teenager's own life and often in that of her family of origin as well. Nevertheless, it is important to keep in mind that these descriptions of the functions of childbearing may involve post hoc rationalizations and should not necessarily be taken as explanations of the onset of sexual activity or pregnancy per se.

The foregoing ideas about psychological factors have found their most elaborate formulation to date in Bolton's (1980) review of literature and theoretical statement about the associations between teenage pregnancy and child abuse and neglect. The dynamic factors related to both parental abuse and neglect of children and the children's own pregnancy and childbearing as teenagers include, among the parents, unrealistic expectations of their children and a distorted view of their needs, lack of knowledge about child development and child care, unresolved dependency needs which create a role reversal between parents and children, rejection of the children early in their childhood, and poor relations between the parents themselves. Among the children, as consequences of parental attitudes, the dynamics are low self-esteem, fear of rejection, a low tolerance for frustration, and feelings of isolation.

Irrational and punitive parental behavior, including inconsistent affection and discipline as well as physical and emotional violence, retards the child's development. Such parental behavior produces in the growing child an inability to trust others and a poor self-image, combined with intense dependency needs. (See also Helfer, 1975, on the World of Abnormal Rearing Cycle.) These dependency needs cannot be consciously acknowledged, but they may eventually be fulfilled when the girl, now a teenager, gets pregnant and feels that she can now have "someone of my own to belong to" (Daniels, 1969). (This theory, thus, may better serve to explain the teenage mother's adaptation to the pregnancy than to account for the occurrence of the pregnancy itself.) The teenage mother is often emotionally, if not residentially, isolated from her parents, from the father of the child, and from her friends. And, even in the event of a marriage, the partners' relations are often inadequate. To complicate the problems produced by the teenage mother's isolation, she may be too immature and resentful to appreciate the infant's needs and may blame the child for her own problems. Her expectations are often too high and her level of knowledge too low. Finally, various health problems, particularly those resulting from poor prenatal care, may exacerbate the teenage mother's childrearing difficulties and heighten her frustration, leading to the possibility of abuse and neglect of her child.

Bolton's theory clearly describes a cyclical process. As the individual reared in a dysfunctional family situation seeks to compensate for the emotional deprivations in his or her own background, he or she sets up precisely the same potential need for compensation in his or her own offspring. These processes involve a direct or indirect transmission of dysfunctional child-rearing values or practices from one generation to the next. However, in this case, as in other cases of an intergenerational vicious cycle of family problems, recurring institutional problems, such as high unemployment among the poor and among minorities, contribute at least as much to the problem. For example, Polansky, Hally, and Polansky (1974) note that maltreatment is a product of both inadequate standards of child care and problems of poverty and family instability. And, Gelles (1979) emphasizes the roots of child abuse both in our society's high levels of unemployment and poverty, which inevitably generate parental frustration, and in our acceptance of violence as a means of child discipline.

We have included Bolton's rather speculative formulation because of its relevance both to the welfare of teenagers in their own childhood and adolescence and to the welfare of their own children. Nevertheless, it must be noted that virtually no research evidence exists to support these ideas.

*Economic Factors*

Another theory, labeled the "brood sow" theory by Placek and Hendershot (1974), is that poor teenagers have children in order to collect welfare benefits and to become independent of their parents. A variety of sources of evidence contradict this thesis. Furstenberg (1976) finds that few of the teenage mothers in his Baltimore sample wanted to get pregnant. More specifically, the vast majority were shocked and distressed when they learned that they were pregnant, as were their parents. These reactions provide particularly useful data insofar as they tap initial emotional reactions rather than rationalizations after the fact. Also, the welfare mothers in Furstenberg's sample were not significantly more likely to get pregnant again after they went on relief than the young mothers who were not receiving public assistance. This finding suggests that there is no reason to single out the welfare mothers as unwilling or unable to regulate their childbearing. Moreover, most of the teenage mothers in Baltimore studied by Furstenberg and Crawford (1978) stayed close to home, especially during the early years of the study; rather than seeking independence and rejecting parental aid, most of them availed themselves of such support. Similarly, Presser (1974) finds no differences in variables which might indicate motivation or intention to get pregnant between those teenagers who actually became pregnant and those who did not. Finally, an analysis of national sample survey data by state of residence indicates that "the level of AFDC benefits and the AFDC acceptance rate do not seem to serve as incentives to childbearing outside of marriage for either blacks or whites" (Moore and Caldwell, 1977).

While there is little, if any, evidence for the "brood sow" theory, this conclusion should not imply that economic circumstances play no role in the processes which lead to teenage pregnancy and childbearing. Considerable evidence indicates that the teenage father's occupational and economic prospects are a major determinant of the teenage mother's decision to marry him in order to legitimate an out-of-wedlock conception (Bowerman, Irish, and Pope, 1963–1966; Coombs and Friedman, 1970; Furstenberg, 1970, 1976; Rains, 1971; Rainwater, 1965). However, a finding by Rapoport (1964) suggests not only this possibility but also another one: Delay of marriage is associated not only with cases where the man's income is inadequate to support a family, but also with those where lengthy specialized training is necessary for his career. The man's interest in promoting his career development may be contrary to the woman's interest in attaining some measure of financial security through his support. In many cases, the premature assumption of family responsibilities limits a man's ability to promote his career, although such responsibilities may also spur achievement. In this regard, research indicates that the teenage father's economic status and prospects may influence his choice of sexual partners and his contraceptive practice, as well as his willingness to marry the mother in the event of an untimely pregnancy (Rainwater, 1965; Whyte, 1943). Still another possibility is that the couple may feel, perhaps with good reason, that their economic prospects will not improve with time; therefore, they may ask, "why should we wait?". The fact that such early and inauspicious marriages are highly likely to break down may not deter the couple, even if they can foresee such a likelihood.

Various other noneconomic factors, including the lower age at which girls begin to have sexual intercourse and to become pregnant, may contribute to the declining rates of marriage as a way of dealing with the problems of teenage pregnancy. Changing sex roles may play a part in accounting for such lower marriage rates, along with general apprehension about the chances of marital stability, and interest in the option of cohabitation, which allows adolescents to hedge their bets. Pregnant teenagers, even those who opt to give birth, may now be less committed to the idea of marriage, particularly if they perceive the difficulties they would face in an ill-timed marriage.

One of the most significant factors accounting for the diminishing likelihood of marriage following pregnancy, however, *is* an economic one: rising rates of youth unemployment. Such rates, as is well known, exceed 50 percent in many communities. In such a hopeless environment, prospects of economic and, in turn, marital success, are bleak.

## Intrafamily Communication about Sex

In contrast to the theories described earlier which argue that teenagers are motivated, at some level, to become parents, it is more likely that pregnancy and parenthood are consequences of the inability or unwillingness not only of teenagers, but also of society in general and parents in particular to confront the issue of teenage sexuality. Specifically, parents, despite their hopes, do not play a major role as sexual socializers of their children, except in the negative sense of implying, through their silence, that they disapprove of their children's sexual activity. For example, one survey showed that 73 percent of teenage women had received information about sex from their friends, while only 5 percent had received it from their parents (Connell and Jacobson, 1971). And, Tryer, Mazlen, and Bradshaw (1978) argue that the parents' fears heighten the teenage woman's anxiety about deciding to take responsibility for sexual activity and contraception and thus make her more embarrassed to seek information from either her parents themselves or from other knowledgeable sources such as physicians.

The key family relationship bearing on the teenage woman's orientation toward sex and contraception is her relationship with her mother. Various problems in mother–daughter relations have been thought to be associated with the daughter's pregnancy: generally poor quality relations (Cheetham, 1977); the daughter's dislike of her mother or evaluation of her as an inadequate role model (Abernathy, 1974); or an emotionally disturbed, ambivalent, or unrewarding relationship between the two (Daniels, 1969; Friedman, 1971; Kane, 1973). While there is some evidence, albeit of a tentative nature, that poor quality relations in the family are associated with early sexuality and pregnancy, the link between these factors has not been well explored. One plausible reason, as suggested above, has to do with resulting problems in communication that accompany strain in parent–child relations. Yet communication about sex is *generally* inadequate between parents and children, regardless of the overall quality of family interaction.

In this regard, some social class variations in intrafamily sexual communication are worth noting. The conventional view is that lower- and working-class parents are more permissive than middle-class parents regarding their daughters' sexuality. Recent reports, however, strongly suggest that, rather than being more tolerant, such lower status parents are actually more restrictive. The reluctance of lower-class mothers to talk with their daughters may be a product of their lack of knowledge and vocabulary about sexuality and contraception, as well as their anxiety about such communication being misconstrued as an endorsement. The result is a mutual denial on the part of both mother and daughter, which has the unintended consequence of increasing the likelihood of pregnancy, especially insofar as it decreases the likelihood of contraceptive use.

## Factors Affecting Contraceptive Use

Individuals who receive family planning information and instruction are, of course, less likely to experience an unplanned pregnancy. Several studies suggest, however, that even among those teenagers equipped with the means of contraception, many have difficulty using them faithfully over a sustained period of time (Ricketts, 1973). While psychological factors undoubtedly play an important part in the rate of contraceptive use among teenagers, we should recognize from the outset that contraception is not easy to use over a lengthy period of time, even for adults.

What accounts for teenagers' failure to use contraception or to do so consistently? An important factor is the guilt which teenagers feel about the sexual activity. Consistent contraceptive practice requires an acknowledgement that sexual relations can be planned and controlled rather than remaining purely spontaneous and uncontrollable. Most teenagers who plan to have sex and to use contraception have accepted their sexuality and come to terms with the guilt often associated with implicit or explicit parental disapproval. But, among those who have not made such an accomodation, contraceptive use may exacerbate feelings of immorality or even promiscuity; in such cases, denial of sex as an act for which one is responsible often reduces these feelings but simultaneously increases the risk of pregnancy.

Research shows that the likelihood of contraceptive use rises with the frequency of intercourse, the development of a relationship characterized by exclusivity and commitment (rather than a merely casual sexual encounter), and the event of marriage itself. Rains (1971) proposes a model of the stages in the teenage female's neutralization of guilt about her sexuality and contraceptive practice. Basically, according to this model, she does not practice contraception until she feels that she is in love and is in a relationship characterized by commitment (see also Kantner and Zelnik, 1972). In such a stable relationship, sex becomes more predictable; the male is more reliable; there is more at stake for both the male and the female, should a pregnancy occur; and the female has more power in the relationship, as a result of the male's commitment.

Another complication for teenagers lies in the biological fact that there is an interval between the age of menarche and the age of first ovulation, usually lasting around two years, during which conception is impossible. As more and more teenagers become sexually active during this "safe" period, an increasing number develop the mistaken impression that pregnancy cannot occur thereafter. As a result, they deny the risk of pregnancy. Further complicating this process is the egocentrism of adolescents, noted by Cvetkovich et al. (1975) and Elkind (1967), which promotes the development of a "personal fable" of invulnerability to harm, including pregnancy.

Another hazardous way in which teenage girls cope with guilt is to abdicate responsibility for sex and contraception to their boyfriends. For example, among the sporadic contraceptive users in Furstenberg's (1976) sample, 54 percent said that the responsibility for birth control was their partner's rather than their own. This abdication is problematic for at least two reasons. First, as we noted earlier, males may have very different interests and goals from those of females; for instance, they may seek sexual conquests as means of enhancing their status in their peer group. Second, even when males have less exploitative motivations, they know less about sex and contraception than females (and neither males nor females are very well-informed to begin with).

One finding which highlights just how great the risk of pregnancy is for younger adolescents is that the younger the age at first sexual intercourse, the greater the risk of pregnancy during the first months of exposure: specifically, half of all premarital teenage pregnancies occur during the first six months of sexual activity (Zabin, Kantner, and Zelnik, 1979). The less frequent use of contraceptives by such inexperienced teenagers outweighs any biological advantage resulting from their subfecundity. Moreover, for a variety of reasons, unmarried teenagers who become pregnant during the first few months of sexual experience, and especially those who subsequently give birth, are more likely to become pregnant again during their teens (Trussel and Menken, 1978). Viewed from the other side, the older the age at first coitus, the greater the probability of using a medical, that is, effective, means of contraception. Additional factors which have been found to predict contraceptive use include age, education, frequency (and, presumably, acceptance) of sexual intercourse, specific attitudes about sexuality, and the existence of a stable heterosexual relationship (Kantner and Zelnik, 1972). Contraceptive regularity may also be a function of one's fear of pregnancy, which, in turn, may result from having been pregnant in the past, having a friend who was or is in that position, or being close to the attainment of a goal such as completing high school.

Finally, a common problem among adolescents generally, and among those who are poor and/or members of minority groups in particular, is a sense of powerlessness to affect their fate; such fatalism clearly undermines efforts to control one's fertility (Fox, 1975; Chilman, 1979; McDonald, 1970). Among the psychological correlates of this orientation are low self-esteem, low ego strength, and a low sense of competence (Rosen, Hudson, and Martindale, 1976). Among the sociological correlates are reduced aspirations, which, in fact, are often a realistic adaptation to the lack of opportunities available to the poor, as well as to blacks and other minority group members.

## The Consequences of Teenage Childbearing

Unlike the investigations of the cause of early childbearing, the studies of the consequences have produced remarkably consistent and compelling results. Some observers have intimated that because the issue of teenage childbearing is not really a new one, its social significance has been exaggerated. However, in the face of the evidence on the serious deleterious effects of premature parenthood on mother, child, and family, the charge that the problem is overblown seems unjustified and even cynical. In the following discussion it will become apparent that the medical, psychological, and social risks associated with early childbearing are considerable.

### Health

A large body of research findings details the effects of teenage childbearing on the health of both mother and child. Despite the gravity and range of the implications which we shall document, however, few, if any, of these studies employ careful statistical controls for race, socioeconomic status, or other relevant social or demographic factors whose effects may be confounded with those of early childbearing. Thus, conclusions beyond those stated at the end of this section must await further research. For example, the relationship between the mother's age and prematurity or low birth weight almost disappears when family income is controlled (Kovar, 1968). Similarly, birth weight has been found to be a function less of age or parity than of the trimester in which prenatal care was first provided, which, in turn, is a function of socioeconomic status (Wiener and Milton, 1970). Early pregnancy, as a separate condition, may not always be hazardous in and of itself; it often becomes hazardous because it places already vulnerable individuals at even greater risk.

With the cautions stated above about the lack of statistical controls in mind, we can review the findings in the literature. Nationally, the death rate for infants born to teenagers is 2.4 times that for infants born to older mothers, and the maternal death rate is 1.6 times as great for teenagers as for others (Thornburg, 1979). Moreover, the maternal death risk of those under fifteen is 2½ times that of those aged twenty to twenty-four (18.0 versus 7.1 deaths per 100,000 live births).

Not surprisingly, non-fatal medical complications are also more common among teenage mothers. Anemia is 92 percent more likely among teenage mothers than among those twenty to twenty-four; toxemia is 15 percent more common; and complications resulting from a premature birth are 23 percent more likely (Alan Guttmacher Institute, 1981). Mothers under age sixteen are twice as likely as those aged twenty to twenty-four to have premature or low birth weight babies (those under 5.5 pounds) (National Center for Health Statistics, 1980). Low birth weight, in turn, is a major cause of infant death, asphyxia, and a variety of birth injuries and handicaps (Menken, 1972; Newcombe and Tarendale, 1964; Pasamanick and Lilienfeld, 1956).

All of these pregnancy complications are more likely to occur when the mother fails to get proper prenatal care. A greater likelihood of such a lack of care exists when the mother is poor, non-white, and/or unmarried (Herzog and Bernstein, 1964; Jones and Placek, 1981). Such a lack of prenatal care has serious consequences: the infant death rate is 116.6 per 100,000 live births for those who do not receive such care, but only 32.2 for infants who do receive it (Pakter, O'Hare, Nelson, and Sorgar, 1973). Various factors account for the fact that many teenagers do not obtain adequate services during the course of their pregnancy. Problems in the health care delivery system may present insurmountable barriers to some disadvantaged pregnant teenagers. Moreover, their own problems may complicate the situation—for example, they may be seeking to conceal the pregnancy. In addition, they may not realize the value of obtaining preventive services rather than just responding to emergencies or other acute illnesses (a propensity which is often reinforced by the current organization of the health care delivery system) and they may be indifferent to medical symptoms which are significant, but not painful or otherwise problematic. And, finally, even when teenagers realize the importance of such services, they often cannot afford them. For all of these reasons, many pregnant teenagers wait until the second or even the third trimester to seek vital prenatal services.

In summary, research has regularly shown that very young mothers and their children are subject to increased health risks during pregnancy, around the time of birth, and during the first year of the infant's life. To our knowledge, no studies have attempted to document longer-term effects. Higher rates of fetal mortality are found for women under age twenty. Also, infants of teenage mothers have higher mortality rates both in the first month of life, when mortality results primarily from problems existing at birth, and in the remainder of the first year, when environmental conditions play a greater role (National Academy of Sciences, 1975).

## Education

Researchers have consistently found that teenage mothers are more likely to drop out of school than women who delay their first childbirth until they are in their twenties (Bacon, 1974; Chilman, 1979; Moore et al., 1978). Moreover, women who have their first child out of wedlock have considerably less chance of completing their schooling than those who delay motherhood until after marriage (Card and Wise, 1978; Cutright, 1973). Significantly, these differences are not merely a product of the woman's background. In fact, the detrimental effect on educational attainment of an early or out-of-wedlock first childbirth is even greater than the detrimental effect of minority status, poor socioeconomic background, or a low level of academic aptitude. For this reason, it is fair to conclude that early or out-of-wedlock parenthood is a major *cause* of low educational attainment. Much further evidence documents that teenage parenthood is a causal factor—between one-half and two-thirds of all female high school dropouts cite pregnancy and/or marriage as their principal reason for leaving school (Coombs and Cooley, 1968; Furstenberg, 1976; Huber, 1970; Moore et al., 1978; Mott and Shaw, 1978; Presser, 1976; Trussel, 1976).

While most studies have focused on failure to complete high school, one must ask whether the long-term sequelae are as adverse as the short-term effects. Research that follows the teenage mothers' careers over a span of a decade or more has the disadvantage of informing us about consequences for previous rather than current cohorts of young mothers, but it is still valuable for providing a long-term view. The results of such studies are consistent: The earlier the age at first birth, the fewer the years of schooling the mother ever completes (Bacon, 1974; Moore and Hofferth, 1978; Trussel, 1976; Waite and Moore, 1978).

Undoubtedly, an important reason why teenage mothers fail to complete their education lies in the enormous difficulties of simultaneously meeting the demands of school, marriage, and child-rearing. In this regard, some recent evidence shows that marriage may actually be the principal complicating factor. Women whose teenage childbearing leads to an early marriage are twice as likely to drop out of high school as teenage parents who remain unmarried (Moore et al., 1978). One possible implication of this link between early marriage and lower educational attainment is that, as fewer teenagers marry, even when confronted by the possibility of an out-of-wedlock birth, their likelihood of completing their schooling will increase.

In spite of the fact that many teenage mothers choose a full-time homemaker role rather than preparing themselves for employment, strong evidence suggests that a teenager pregnancy is not merely a convenient excuse to drop out of school. A majority of teenage mothers resume school after delivery (Furstenberg, 1976; Moore et al., 1978). Moreover, an early birth is not an insurmountable barrier to graduation from high school, as shown by the fact that a majority of the young mothers in Furstenberg's Baltimore study managed to complete this level of schooling. Nevertheless, finishing high school is obviously not just a matter of choosing to do so. As one might expect, teenage mothers from advantageous socioeconomic and family backgrounds are more likely to recoup their losses by completing high school than those with poorer backgrounds.

## Occupational and Economic Achievement

Not surprisingly, teenage childbearing also seriously injures a woman's occupational and economic prospects. As was true for the effects on schooling, these consequences are both independent of and even more severe than the disadvantages resulting from minority status or poor socioeconomic background or a low level of academic aptitude (Card and Wise, 1978).

The material detriments of early parenthood can be traced to a variety of sources. Typically, teenage mothers have lower levels of education and experience difficulty in obtaining employment. They are less likely to have enduring marriages and, therefore, cannot count on the economic support of a spouse. They have higher levels and more rapid rates of childbearing and thus are unable to find employment without child-care assistance. For all of these reasons, teenage childbearers are more likely to become dependent on public assistance (Moore and Hofferth, 1978). Even if her family lends a hand, as they often do, a teenage mother's family rarely can shoulder the entire burden of support.

Thus, the consequences of early childbearing for economic independence depend primarily on the woman's marital career. In this regard, it should be noted that the ultimate economic position of women who marry and whose marriages subsequently break up is worse than that of women who never marry (Furstenberg, 1976). For all teenage parents— single, married, or formerly married—child care is essential to their efforts to find stable employment. Thus, a supportive kinship network that can provide child care is a critical condition determining whether young mothers can work or must rely on welfare (Furstenberg and Crawford, 1978).

Another key factor in the socioeconomic career of the young mother is her fertility pattern following the birth of her first child. Those women who avoid further childbearing are much more likely to be steadily employed than multiparous women. In fact, marital status is largely irrelevant to work patterns when the number of children is held constant. A large family further complicates the already difficult problem of arranging for child care. As noted, the presence of a young child presents an especially severe barrier to employment.

## Subsequent Fertility

Research has shown that the younger a woman's age at first childbirth, the greater the level and pace of her fertility (up to fifteen years later) and the greater the proportion of illegitimate and unwanted births (Bonham and Placek, 1975; Bumpass et al., 1978; Menken, 1972; Trussel and Menken, 1978). However, women with an illegitimate first birth do not subsequently bear more children than women whose first birth was within wedlock. In addition, the consequences of early childbearing vary little by race or level of educational attainment. In fact age at first birth accounts for around half of all racial and educational differences in completed fertility. These results suggest a need for family planning services among all groups of adolescents, younger and older, single and married.

The second child typically represents a major setback to the future plans of the younger mother, proving especially damaging to her prospects of economic self-sufficiency. Existing evidence indicates that a pregnancy in early adolescence signals the beginning of a rapid succession of unwanted births. Although estimates vary, depending on the experiences of the women following the first birth, most studies show that at least one-half of all teenage mothers experience a second pregnancy within thirty-six months of the first delivery (Ricketts, 1973).

## Consequences for the Children of Early Childbearers

Among the few studies addressing this topic is Card and Wise's (1978) reanalysis of the Project TALENT data. They find that the children of teenage mothers, while in high school, have lower cognitive test scores, lower grades, and lower educational expectations than their classmates whose parents were at least in their twenties when they were born. As these children grow older (toward age 30), they have lower levels of education, earlier first marriages, and higher rates of marital dissolution. Nevertheless, most of the observed cognitive differences are the result of disadvantages in socioeconomic and family background, particularly higher rates of family instability. Card and Wise propose a recurrent pattern of disadvantage: Early childbearing results in marital dissolution, which in turn leads to cognitive impairment to the child and subsequent educational deficits. And, this educational disadvantage helps to perpetuate, among the offspring of early childbearers, the same cycle of early marriage and childbearing and high fertility which their parents first experienced.

Several explanations might account for the differences in cognitive achievement. They could be traced to physiological conditions such as prematurity, low birth weight, and complications at delivery. An alternative explanation might be that early childbearers are themselves less intellectually endowed, and the differences observed among the children could be linked to genetic factors or to the parent's capacity to provide early infant stimulation. Finally, possibly the young age of the mother may make her a less capable child rearer, which would, in turn, be reflected in the child's slower rate of development of cognitive skills.

Some evidence with which to evaluate these competing interpretations has been marshalled in a recent review by Baldwin and Cain (1980). Their review indicates that the effects of young maternal age on low birth weight and perinatal infant mortality are highly dependent on the quality of prenatal care available to the mother. However, regarding observed deficits in the children's cognitive development, much of the problem lies in the social and economic consequences of early parenthood. In one sense, then, early childbearing contributes to an intergenerational perpetuation of poverty and disadvantage. On the other hand, it should be noted that no vicious cycle, this one included, can persist without society's continued indifference to the problem of economic inequality.

*Teenage Childbearing and Family Support*

In her extensive review of the literature on the social aspects of adolescent childbearing, Chilman (1979) discusses the need for research on the financial aid, child care, and social and psychological support that grandparents can provide to teenage parents, and on the effects of the provision of such support on the relationships between the generations and on the lives of the grandparents. Two recent analyses conducted by the authors bear on these questions.

The Baltimore study data contain a record of the composition of the teenage mother's household at each of four points during the first five years after delivery. When inspected longitudinally, these data on residential situations show that mothers were much more likely to receive substantial amounts of familial financial assistance and child-care support when they remained with relatives (cf. Cantor, Rosenthal, and Wilke, 1975). Moving out of the parental household, whether to marry or to establish an independent residence, not only reduced the subsidies provided by the family in the form of room and board, but also lessened the chances that a relative would be available to provide day care.

Not surprisingly, then, most mothers stayed close to home, especially during the early years of the study. At pregnancy, when most of the women were in their early or middle teens, nearly 90 percent lived with a parent or another close relative. Separation from the family of origin became more common in the ensuing years, but even five years after the birth of their child, nearly half (46%) remained with their parents or other kin. One popular stereotype of the teenage mother portrays her as a social isolate, removed from parental or conjugal support, but our data belie this image: Only 26 percent of the young mothers were living alone at the time of the five-year follow-up.

The teenager's family shouldered much more responsibility when she remained single than when she married. Especially in the early years of the study, most of the women moved away from their families only after they had married. From responses to unstructured questions, we learned that a major deterrent to marriage was that it might require forfeiting family support. The decision to remain in the home after marriage may, of course, be dictated by economic considerations, but we suspect that it also reflects ambivalence about substituting a tenuous conjugal bond for a functioning family network.

Given the inclination of all but a few parents to lend assistance, the family's ability to aid their daughter became a major factor shaping the young mothers' residential careers. Tenagers were much more likely to remain in couple-headed households than in female-headed households, and those in couple-headed households were also more likely to return to and remain in school. Evidently, either the greater economic resources of the couple-headed families were used to purchase child-care services, or, more likely, the grandmother remained at home to care for the child while the young mother resumed her education. Moreover, space was more abundant in two-parent households, providing less pressure on the young mother to leave the parental home. Young mothers were more likely to move out of their parents' household when a second pregnancy occurred, and such a repeat pregnancy occurred more frequently in female-headed families, which were already pressed for space and generally strained for resources.

Teenagers who remained with their parents were more likely to advance educationally and economically, compared to their peers who left home before or immediately after their child was born. Also, most participants in the Baltimore study stayed home, at least in part, because they were being provided with child-care assistance by a parent, a sibling, or another relative. The last two interviews, three and five years after the first birth, revealed that the young mothers who lived at home received more help from family members than those who were not residing with relatives. Losing these advantages often forced them to terminate their education, or, in the event they were working, to quit their jobs.

How did these collaborative child-care arrangements affect the well-being of the mother and her offspring? The information obtained directly from the children themselves indicates the benefits of collaborative care. On a test of cognitive performance, the Pre-School Inventory, children of unmarried mothers achieved significantly higher scores when their parents were not their full-time caretakers. Perhaps children receive more stimulation when they have multiple caretakers, or perhaps the quality of care is higher when the mother receives supervision from an experienced relative or when she is simply relieved of full-time responsibility for child care.

## Summary of Consequences

Taken as a whole, the research literature lends firm support to the proposition that early childbearing creates high social and economic costs for both teenage parents and society as a whole. One of the repeated findings concerns the role of education. Card and Wise (1978) found that even when race, socioeconomic background, academic aptitude and achievement, and educational expectations are held constant, the young parents are more likely to curtail education than those whose initial childbearing is postponed. Taken together with other studies of the economic consequences of teenage childbearing (indicating lack of education as the primary cause of low occupational status and income), the results concerning educational effects lead inevitably to the conclusion that programs geared toward helping young parents further their studies may help alleviate the deleterious consequences of early childbearing.

Regarding the children of teenage parents, Baldwin and Cain (1980), in their review of a broad spectrum of studies, find few consequences for the child that are directly related to parental youth. Indeed, even the well-documented increased risk of perinatal morbidity and mortality of infants born to teenage mothers may be eliminated with excellent prenatal care. It is true that increased health risks continue during the first year of life, especially if there is no adult other than the teenage mother to care for the child. Still, low socioeconomic status is the villain in most cases. Since young parents are disproportionately poorer and less well-educated, and since early childbearing often leaves the parents poor and poorly educated, their children are really the victims of these circumstances rather than of young parental age per se.

What can be done to aid parents and children? The importance of family support networks is emphasized in the research conducted by Furstenberg and Crawford (1978) and in the studies reviewed by Baldwin and Cain (1980). These investigations do not suggest that special programs should be designed for the children of teenage parents. Indeed, such categorical programs would be inappropriate and could be damaging insofar as they would stigmatize the children. Rather, the findings strongly suggest that the appropriate focus of program intervention is on the young parents—starting before the birth and extending well beyond it—to prevent the health, educational, and economic hardships that are transmitted to the children through the handicaps imposed on the young parents.

## Implications for Social Programs

What can be done to lift or lighten the burdens imposed by premature parenthood? Much of the social welfare literature on teenage parenthood concentrates on constructing ameliorative social programs for young parents. However, we feel that prevention strategies would be far less expensive and much more effective.

### Prevention Programs

Professionals working with teenagers are constantly amazed at how little they know about sexual functioning and contraception. It is widely assumed that in the present era of sexual enlightment, young people have become reasonably sophisticated in their knowledge and attitudes. However, much of the information which young people receive, including that from the mass media, is inaccurate. Most teenagers are ill-informed when they begin to have sexual relations, and most do not become much more knowledgeable thereafter.

Programs of sexual education tend to provide too little information too late. Although there is widespread public support for such instructional programs, many communities only institute sex education in senior high school, if at all. Nine out of ten parents of teenagers support sex education, and 8 out of 10 favor programs in the public schools. Moreover, most of the public (7 out of 10) advocate including material about birth control. Still, despite this public endorsement of sex education, only ten states and the District of Columbia require or even encourage it in the curriculum. Not surprisingly, then, only a minority of teenagers report having had a sex education course in school, and less than one-third report having received information about contraception (Alan Guttmacher Institute, 1981).

As things stand, teenagers are often kept ignorant until they become pregnant. Although there is no evidence to support the belief that sex education programs increase the likelihood of sexual experience during the teenage years, the fear of "promoting promiscuity" still deters the development of preventive programs. Unfortunately, as a result, most teenagers only visit a clinic after a conception or a pregnancy scare (Presser, 1974).

Clearly, we must rethink the relatively passive approach we have taken in preparing young people for the responsibilities of sexual activity. As noted by Furstenberg, Lincoln, and Menken:

> Our best strategy is to prevent as many unwanted pregnancies as possible in the first place. To do this, society will have to make the difficult decision to transmit the knowledge and the means of pregnancy prevention to *all* teenagers—not just those known to be sexually active. There is the chance that some, thereby, may be encouraged to experiment with sex somewhat earlier than they would have done otherwise, although there is no evidence that provision of information about sexual decision-making or contraception encourages teenagers to initiate sexual intercourse earlier than they might have done without such information. (1981:15)

DESCRIPTION OF EXISTING PROGRAMS.   A survey of 125 cities with populations of at least 100,000 showed that most (107) had some special programs for pregnant teenagers, but few (31) of these programs served 1,000 or more clients per year, and fewer still were comprehensive programs. The emphasis is typically only on education rather than on additional services to prevent pregnancy (Alan Guttmacher Institute, 1981). The network of contraceptive services available to teenagers has expanded enormously. These services, virtually nonexistent in the mid-1960s, have been extended to well over one million teenagers in recent years. Specifically, the number of teenagers who visited family planning clinics rose from 214,000 in 1969 to 1.5 million in 1978. Most of the increase is accounted for by larger numbers of younger clients, and, nearly as many teenagers see private physicians as attend clinics. The influence of clinics on contraceptive use has prevented some 689,000 unwanted births and probably an even larger number of abortions (assuming that the majority of adolescents who use contraceptives would prefer having an abortion to bearing a child). That is the bright side of the picture.

In a less optimistic vein, Dryfoos and Heisler (1978) also report that a majority of teenagers at risk of pregnancy still do *not* receive family planning services from public or private agencies or private physicians. Contraceptive services are still unavailable to one-half of all sexually active female teenagers and to a far higher proportion of males. The unavailability of services for females is clearly problematic; and insofar as we cannot identify high-risk cases well enough to target services to them, it would be wiser simply to make such services available to all. The irony in not extending preventive efforts to males is that while male contraceptives are technically inferior, male teenagers themselves are more influential than their partners in making decisions regarding sex and contraception.

RECOMMENDATIONS FOR THE IMPROVEMENT OF PREVENTION PROGRAMS.
More clinics are needed to serve the expanding population of sexually experienced teenagers. Moreover, clinics must deliver their services differently if they are to attract and hold a teenage clientele (Edwards, Steinman, Arnold, and Hakanson, 1980). Programs designed for the convenience of the health provider may not suit teenagers. Evening and weekend hours, outreach programs with neighborhood follow-up efforts, and allowances for unscheduled visits may be inconvenient to service deliverers, but they will better serve the special needs of teenage clients.

Program designers must also tailor services to the needs of very different groups of teenagers. Because of their similarity in age, there is some tendency to regard teenagers as homogeneous. However, teenage populations are quite diverse, because of differences in sexual experience, psychological development, social background, and fertility goals. The challenge for program planners is to provide a variety of alternative approaches suited to the various causes of teenage pregnancy and to the divergent demands of young people in need of services (Osofsky and Osofsky, 1978). Furthermore, there is a general need for coordination of the entire human service delivery system and a specific need for new organizations to enhance coordination in the area of pregnancy prevention, particularly through monitoring and evaluating the services provided to teenagers.

## Teenage Males and Fathers

The teenage male is often the key decision-maker regarding contraception, particularly when the female abdicates responsibility. At the same time, the male and the female may have very different interests and goals, especially where the teenage male subculture places a premium on sexual conquests. Clearly, more attention needs to be paid to the education and sensitization of teenage males to issues of both sex and contraception.

Turning to the males who father children, the consequences for their socioeconomic careers are typically not as severe as those for females, given that males do not experience pregnancy and typically are not required to assume responsibility for early child care. Nevertheless, males still experience educational deficits and subsequent occupational and economic career costs. Moreover, in the case of married couples who experience a premarital pregnancy, the male's ultimate levels of education, income, and assets are lower than in the case of couples whose first child is conceived within marriage (Coombs and Freedman, 1970; Freedman and Coombs, 1966). The focus of efforts to aid young fathers must be on their socioeconomic career development, insofar as the subsequent welfare of father, mother, and children hinges on their economic position.

## Promoting Family Involvement

The family, including parents, siblings, and extended kin, are implicated in the entire process of unplanned parenthood. The degree of involvement by family members has an important bearing on when and how the teenager becomes sexually active and on her efforts to avert a conception (Fox, 1981). Moreover, families play a central role in assisting the pregnant teenager (Furstenberg and Crawford, 1978). The family undoubtedly provides more services, economic and child-care services in particular, than all outside sources combined. Yet, it has been virtually untapped by programs to assist the teenager. To the contrary, programs have often designed services that either do not take account of the family assistance to teenagers, or, worse still, undermine the network of familial support.

In hindsight, it seems very plain that many of the early programs for teenagers were designed to minimize family involvement. Some programs did so deliberately, out of an ideological commitment to the teenager's right to privacy. Other programs were pervaded by an ethos of individualism, that is, services were directed to individuals with little regard for the social context in which those individuals lived. These family planners may have assumed too quickly that teenagers were simply another population of neglected consumers, who only required, with some minor modifications, the same kind of services available to mature adults. In making this assumption, the family planners did not take account of the vulnerable situation of the teenage client and, in particular, the delicate issue of sometimes providing services to her without her family's knowledge and support. In any event, regardless of whether the practice was intentional or not, the family was often not so much excluded as ignored in these two types of initial efforts to reach adolescent clients. Finally, a third group of family planners viewed parents as culturally backward and, in their counseling efforts, either covertly or overtly attempted to bypass the family, directing services exclusively to the teenagers. We believe that all of these policies have been unwise and unwarranted. It is true that parents are often confused about how to train their children to become sexually responsible, and it is probably also the case that most parents look to other agencies for support in this task. However, parents do not necessarily wish to abdicate their role, and many would probably welcome the opportunity to collaborate with family planning agencies.

Recent evidence suggests that more and more family planning programs have been reaching out to the family. One survey shows that a substantial proportion of family planning programs have designed services for parents or are attempting to involve the family in services provided to their teenage clients (National Family Planning and Reproduction Health Association, 1982).

One example is provided by the efforts of the Family Planning Council of Southeastern Pennsylvania, which recently undertook an experimental project to promote family involvement with teenagers seeking contraceptive services (see Furstenberg, Herceg-Baron, and Jemail, 1981). Its aim is to build family support for using birth control by fostering more open communication about sexuality between the teenager and a designated family member. With the teenager's full knowledge and consent, family planning counselors attempt to approach the family, usually through the teenager herself, and to discuss ways of assisting her to prevent an unwanted pregnancy.

The initial problem faced in implementing the project was not resistance on the part of the teenager, or her family, but resistance from family planning counselors who lacked the skills and the conceptual approach that would equip them to involve family members in preventive services. Some viewed their role as primarily educational and could not accept the idea that they should broaden their function to intervene more actively in the family system. Others accepted the wisdom of the approach, but found it difficult to implement in clinic settings which were geared for highly concentrated, short-term services.

In addition, of course, some teenagers themselves resist the idea of involving family members. Nevertheless, only a small proportion (16 percent) of teenagers who were randomly assigned to the family support treatment group were unwilling to avail themselves of the family support services after they were briefed on the program. Thus, few teenagers are categorically opposed to having family planning clinics make contact with their families, so long as they have some role in deciding who is contacted and what method of contact is used.

The experimental efforts of the Pennsylvania program have shown that some teenagers welcome a greater measure of family support when they seek contraceptive assistance. However, parents or even siblings are not always regarded as reliable confidants. More importantly, family members are sometimes unwilling to play more than a passive role in the sexual socialization and support of the teenagers.

An ominous development that may obscure the potentially supportive roles families can play is the political drive for parental notification. At present, sentiment is mounting among a small minority for mandating parental notification when adolescents seek contraception. No evidence supports the belief that parental notification will improve family communication, reduce teenage sexual activity, or increase contraceptive vigilance. More likely, notification requirements will encourage teenagers to stay away from family planning programs, to rely on nonmedical methods of birth control, or to falsify the information that they provide to contraceptive clinics.

Our knowledge is lacking in how to foster greater responsibility among the young regarding decisions about whether or not to become sexually active or to take measures to prevent unwanted pregnancies. Still, it is easy to forget that, until two decades ago, there were virtually no programs providing sex education in the schools or providing contraceptive services to teenagers. The laissez-faire approach taken toward teenage sexuality and pregnancy in the past did not succeed either in controlling premarital sexual activity or in preventing unwanted and untimely pregnancies. But we must also realize that there are no quick or simple ways of dealing with the problems of unwanted teenage sexual activity, pregnancy, and childbearing. However, remarkable changes have occurred in the last twenty years, and the impatience of planners and policy makers with finding "solutions" must be seen in this perspective.

# PART VI

# Temporary and Permanent Child Placement Services

The provision of substitute care for dependent, neglected, or abused children has long been the primary and indeed, until recently, almost the exclusive function of the Child Welfare system. Although attention and resources are now shifting to the maintenance of children in their own homes, placement services continue to be an important part of the Child Welfare system. Placement, however, and the values and views about children and families that shape programs and direct decisions, have undergone major change since the early 1970s.

In the following chapters, the current programmatic and practice approaches to children in need of out-of-home care are presented. In reviewing these chapters, certain themes emerge as they are expressed in major shifts in program, policy, and practice.

Influenced by both the "rights" revolution of the 60s and the child advocacy movement, a pervasive theme has emerged that affirms the rights of all children to the kind of care that will best provide them with the opportunity to develop their potential, no matter how extensive or how limited that potential may be. For the first time, child placement has become truly child-centered in the sense that the rights of the child are of central concern. This concern has been translated into the permanency movement and is expressed in the fundamental notion that currently guides Child Welfare practice: Every child has a right to a permanent home with his or her own family or, if that is impossible, in an adoptive home.

The centrality of the rights of children is demonstrated, for example, in the changes in adoption practice. Twenty years ago, adoption was primarily a program which provided childless couples with infants. Most children in the Child Welfare system, even if legally free, were considered "unadoptable" by reason of their age or some physical, emotional, or mental characteristic. Sometimes children were even considered unadoptable if minimal information about them was available. Today, as Cole tells us in her overview of adoption, no child is unadoptable. Adoption has been redefined as a service to find permanent families for children—for all children who cannot be with their biological families. The permanency movement and the focus on the permanent placement of older children and children with special needs have altered the face of adoption, as described by Cole, and have had major implications for practice.

For example, as Hartman describes, a wide variety of families is now recruited as potential adoptive resources for children, and the process of family assessment and placement has been redefined as a shared decision-making process between family and agency. Moreover, the complexity and demands of special needs adoption require the development of a range of supportive programs for adoptive parents who take on these challenges. Further, adoptive agencies have become increasingly aware of the need for placement services throughout the adoptive family's life cycle.

Child Welfare has become child-centered, but at the same time it has become family-centered. Thus the first choice for all children is permanency with their biological families. This view has caused a redefinition of foster care. Foster care, which was in many cases long-term but impermanent care substituting for parental care, is now widely redefined, according to Wiltse and McFadden, as a temporary service to parents and children. Wiltse reports on research that has revealed that many children who were thought to be in "permanent" out-of-home care can be and have been, with intensive services, reunited with their families.

With these changes, the role of foster parents is reconceptualized from one in which they replace the parents to one in which they are a part of a team to help the parents toward reunification. McFadden outlines the kind of training and ongoing opportunities for support and development that must be available to foster parents as they assume more varied and more specialized new tasks.

The emphasis on the family and the importance of family life for all children has joined with a larger national movement toward deinstitutionalization and toward the use of what in federal legislation has been termed the "least restrictive environment," dramatically decreasing the number of children living in institutions. Where once an institution with a strong educational and "habit training" approach was considered the best out-of-home care for a child and reformers dreamed of an orphanage in every county, those child-caring institutions that remain tend to be used highly selectively, primarily for children that require a therapeutic milieu and around-the-clock treatment or protection. The most recent development in family-centered deinstitutionalization is seen in programs, described by the Roses, that are moving developmentally disabled children, even the severely disabled, into foster and adoptive homes.

A third theme, which also grew out of the child advocacy movement and is shaping current Child Welfare practice, is one of distrust of the Child Welfare bureaucracy and distrust of professionals. This distrust has led to an emphasis on accountability and on citizen participation in determining the directions and in monitoring the progress of Child Welfare services. Cole and Wiltse describe the citizen and court review and tracking systems in adoption and foster care which have developed in response to the pressure for increased accountability.

Questions about whether professionals and formal systems should be the only sources of help has led to widespread use of self-help and other alternative interventive strategies. This phenomenon has had an important impact on child placement; foster and adoptive parents have become a part of agency recruitment and assessment programs, as experienced families mentor families assuming care of their first foster or adoptive child, and foster and adoptive family networks have developed to exchange supportive and concrete help. Partridge exemplifies the power of such helping systems in her discussion of the adoptee self-help movement.

A final thread which appears throughout the chapters on out-of-home care is the theme of continuity. Current Child Welfare practice is being shaped by a growing awareness of the importance of continuity in the development of human beings through the life cycle. The importance of parental visiting in the maintenance of family ties and in predicting eventual return home is stressed by both Wiltse and McFadden, and practice tools such as the "life book," tools that are designed to help prevent and to heal the potential damage of ruptures in continuity, are described. Waldinger's discussion of subsidized adoption demonstrates how such a program can help foster parents who have been providing long-term care for a child make that child a permanent part of their family through adoption.

The potential of "open" adoption for providing permanency for children without the total severing of the biological tie is explored by Hartman. Partridge stresses the importance of the search movement in

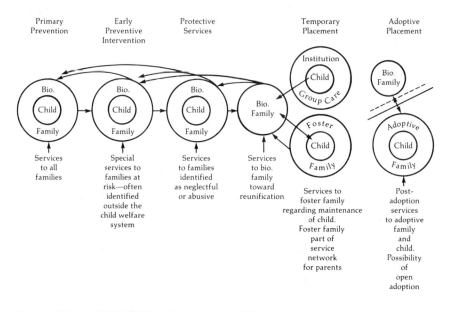

**Figure VI-1** Child Welfare Continuum of Services

helping adult adoptees reconnect with their birth parents so that they may better complete the process of identity consolidation, while coming to terms with the original rupture in continuity that occurred when they were placed.

Just as continuity is important for the individual child in the Child Welfare system, so must continuity be built into the service delivery system itself. Taken together, the chapters in this section present a picture of child placement today but they also conjure up a vision of a Child Welfare system in which placement services are offered as part of a well-integrated continuum of child-centered and family-centered services, pictured in the figure. As can be seen, the series of services or environments moves from that which is least intrusive and restrictive to that which is most. A decision to move a family and child from a less to a more radical mode of service must be justified through careful assessment. With the exception of adoption, as shown by the returning arrows in the figure, the effort is to return to the less intrusive helping system as soon as possible.

Integration and the maintenance of continuity among the various systems in the Child Welfare service delivery network is essential on both the individual and programmatic levels. Fragmented and poorly integrated services increase the potential for damaging separations and loss of continuity in the lives of families and children.

# CHAPTER 21

# Foster Care
## An Overview

KERMIT T. WILTSE

Every society can be said to have some system of substitute care. Children are born to biological parents who rear them in a continuing arrangement of interaction and interdependence called a family. When parents fail or are unable for any reason—to meet their children's essential needs, a substitute may become necessary.

We tend to define a family by its child-rearing function. A broader conception of a family includes any continuing relationship of interaction and interdependence between two or more people who care about each other and think of themselves as a family. Nearly always this includes joint residence, the "household" idea. This broader definition includes elderly couples, gay couples, small communal groups—in other words a great variety of arrangements distinguished essentially by intent, continuity and frequency of interaction, and freely assumed obligations toward each other.

In a book about Child Welfare, the parent–child relationship is the defining criterion of a family. Child Welfare is concerned with assuring to each child a growth-enhancing parent–child relationship. Foster care, as the term implies, means sharing nourishment, nurture, and sustenance, and has come increasingly to mean foster family care although other types of out-of-home care, especially care in group homes and small residential institutions is often included under the same rubric. In this chapter, the focus will be upon foster family care.

The manifest preference for family care over group care, especially for young and preadolescent children, is evidence of a widespread recognition of the importance given to parent–child relationships as the preferred medium in which to nourish the child's developing personality. In this sense there is no substitute, and foster family care is an effort to replace that which the birth-parent is unable or unwilling to provide. The insistence upon permanency planning to achieve continuity of care as the antidote to the condition of children who have been spending extended periods of their young lives in foster homes underscores a prevalent belief that a firm parent–child relationship is the best medium for a child's growth and development. A group caring environment is an inadequate substitute, never a replacement, for the parent–child relationship lost through the biological parents' inability to perform an essential nurturing function.

A great amount of research and an extensive literature documents the importance of the infant's attachment to a parenting person, which usually means the child's mother. Deprived of the opportunity to bond with a mothering person, the infant fails to thrive and to develop physically, and its ability to engage in social interaction with adults and even other children is impaired. Rarely, however, is modern day foster care concerned with infants. Most foster children today are older children for whom the time for infant–mother bonding has passed. With respect to older children, those past the infant–toddler stage, it is less clear they must have the opportunity for permanent attachments to parenting persons. Yet insofar as there is a "theory" of foster family care it is grounded on this issue.

In an exhaustive and generally critical examination of recent research on foster care, Kadushin (1978b:141) concludes with the comment:

> We still lack a clearly defined theory of substitute care which might result in an orchestration of programmatic research. We still depend heavily on intuition, common sense, and practice wisdom for the work that we must do.

It is the purpose of this chapter to examine the question: Is there a theory of substitute care? Since my focus is foster family care, it is against that background that substitute care is examined. We will begin with a brief look at the history of substitute care in this country to establish a screen against which to project the national ferment about foster care that arose in the 70s, a ferment resulting in important programmatic and legislative changes which point a new direction for the next decade.

## Historical Background

An historical background on foster care in America usually begins with colonial times. A comprehensive examination would look backward to the European, especially English, roots of foster care, but quite unlikely would even note that America was occupied before the colonists arrived by a great number of different Indian tribes, each with its own unique history and culture including methods of substitute care. I call attention to these groups to note the fact that Indian tribes were generally confederations of extended families occupying a given geographical area. At this tribal level of organization, children were part of constellations of persons of all ages and varying degrees of blood relationships. The tribe, not alone the biological parents, was the child-rearing system, and as part of this larger group the individual child could scarcely ever become dependent or neglected in a sense comparable to a child of a modern nuclear family. Nurtured and protected by the larger system, a child always had substitute care at hand.

At a broadly conceptual level, Child Welfare services to neglected and dependent children, in an industrialized society such as our own, can be viewed as efforts to reproduce the safety net under each child that the extended families or tribal groups at one time supplied. The Indian Child Welfare Act of 1977 is based on the principle that Indian children who must have substitute care are not to be disconnected from their own tribe and its distinct cultural heritage except under unusual conditions. The consequences of this legislation for many dependent Indian children will be to reconnect them with their tribal group on the premise that maintenance of their ethnic identity is critically important. Should maintenance of cultural identity be considered an important aspect of the "theory" of substitute care? Certainly for most adults an emotional connection with cultural identity is a fact of existence. When asserted as important for dependent children, maintenance of cultural identity can be considered a dimension of the theory of how substitute care should be provided.

Foster family care in early colonial America was influenced by the English origins of most of the colonists; hence the child indenture system grounded in English Poor Law is cited as the basis of American practice. The Poor Laws provided for the apprenticing of dependent and destitute children until their twenty-first birthday. Life in colonial America was difficult and dangerous for children and adults alike, and the problem of abandoned or orphaned children was a recurrent theme of colonial government. Indenture, by which a child was apprenticed to a master who would provide life's necessities and the rudiments of a trade (in the case of male children; females became housemaids) in return for the child's labor was a ready and obvious recourse. It is equally obvious that indenture permitted all sorts of abuses and exploitation and assured the child practically nothing short of minimal sustenance. No doubt most indentured children received about as much as other children of poor families of the time, except a sense of identity grounded in each child's feeling valued for his or her own sake. This is an important exception which will be discussed later in the context of permanency planning for children in foster care.

Vestiges of indenture continued into the early twentieth century despite the fact that it had been largely replaced by ostensibly more enlightened methods of substitute care. Indenture of dependent and destitute children was grounded in English law and tradition, and as a system of substitute care enjoyed a roughly similar tenure in England. We must not forget, however, that America received and was formed by extensive waves of immigrants from diverse cultures. Therefore, in addition to the shrinking native Indian population—a population rapidly being decimated by war and disease—these immigrants were bringing traditions of child care often very different from English or northern European concepts. Also, a substantial black population, legally emancipated after the Civil War, maintained child care traditions and practices different from whites. In short, the history of child care in America is not circumscribed by those aspects which stem from English tradition.

Indenture was an expedient and effective method of handling a persistent and expensive social problem. It could scarcely be described as motivated solely by concern for children's welfare. It did, however, provide many children a semblance of family life in addition to a minimum level of physical care.

Charles Loring Brace is credited with originating modern foster family care. His avowed motive was to rescue children from the exigencies of destitution and vagrancy. The street vagrants and the children's institutions of New York City were his first and primary sources of destitute and dependent children. Brace became secretary of the New York Children's Aid Society in 1853. His training as a minister pointed him toward the conviction that Christian charity could be stimulated among people in a position to provide homes for dependent children, especially people living in idealized environments of farm and small town life. As head of his Society he set out to transfer thousands of children from New York City to the presumably wholesome environment of rural life. Brace made an effort to prepare the people in the areas which became destinations for his children's trains, destinations as far west as Oklahoma and as far south as Florida. Committees of local citizens prepared the way with appeals to Christian charity spiced with an appeal to people's self-interest in that the farmers and tradesmen who took a destitute child would obtain free labor for farm or shop. In substance, appeals by present day foster home recruiters are much the same except that the appeal to charity is more subtle and the appeal to self-interest expressed in cash rather than in kind—that is, board payments rather than free labor.

Although the Society retained control of the child's custody and could remove him at any time, follow-up was limited and replacements rare. In practical terms placements were permanent and final. About 100,000 children were placed in this manner over the 75-year history of this practice (Langsam, 1964:27). Was the program as Thurston (1930:136) says, merely, "the wolf of the old indenture philosophy of child labor in the sheepskin disguise of a so-called good Christian home?" Or might we see in Brace's commitment to the idea of permanent family homes for these children a clouded vision of permanency planning for children in foster care that was to re-emerge, though differently articulated, more than a century later?

Judging both by what he said and did, it seems fair to say Brace grasped the importance to children of being a part of a continuing and permanent family. He had a theory of foster family care and acted upon it, though his methods were often arbitrary, uncautious, and disrupted whatever family and cultural ties remained for the children swept up in his operation. The temptation to judge him and his methods harshly must be tempered by a recognition that society's continuing effort to serve the needs of children, particularly the record of foster family care as a Child Welfare service, has fallen short of the hopes and expectations of even its most determined advocates. At least his methods must be considered in terms of the conditions of his times and the alternatives available for destitute and dependent children.

Rescuing children from unsavory environments, even when the child's own home was disrupted in the process, accorded with an increasing emphasis by nineteenth-century social scientists on the importance of environment over heredity in shaping a child's character. "Child saving" was the central thrust of Child Welfare activities in the second half of the nineteenth century, and the "good Christian family" perceived as the ideal haven for rescued children.

## The Modern Era of Foster Care

Charles Birtwell, as director of the Boston Children's Aid Society between 1886 and 1911, is credited with moving foster family care theory into the modern era. Birtwell saw "what does the child need?" rather than "where shall we put the child?" as the appropriate question to be addressed whenever placement of a child in foster care was under consideration. His approach not only required viewing each child as an individual in terms of problems and needs, but also careful consideration of each alternative available, not ruling out the possibility that no substitute would be more likely to meet the child's needs than an effort to sustain or repair the child's own home (Thurston, 1930). Birtwell set the stage for foster family care to be viewed as a temporary and treatment-oriented service to families and children. The first White House Conference on Children called by President Theodore Roosevelt came out strongly in support of public aid to mothers of children dependent by reason of death or disability of the family breadwinner. Participants at that first White House Conference believed a national system of aid to mothers would avoid resorting to foster care by reason of dependency alone. They expressed a clear preference for foster family care over institutional care for normal children in need of placement with these words: "the carefully selected foster home is, for the normal child, the best substitute for the natural home" (White House Conference Report, 1909). Nearly a half century later Charnley restates this preference in terms of the accepted practice wisdom:

> There appears to be complete accord among social workers and psychiatrists who write on the subject that all children under six need foster home care. The only exceptions are those few unusual children who have been so severely damaged that around age four, five or six they need brief stays in institutions for intensive treatment so that they may be made ready to accept what they so desperately need—parent substitutes. (1955:86)

By implication, institutions are suitable placements only when they are used for a definite treatment purpose. All other children who need placement, most especially the younger ones, belong in a foster family home.

By the second half of this century certain premises, loosely defined but evidenced in practice, had developed in the field of substitute care in this country. Foster family care was the appropriate resource for normal children; for troubled or seriously disturbed children the emergent residential treatment setting was an appropriate placement. The old style congregate care institution for dependent children was no longer acceptable as a child-rearing environment if indeed it ever had been. Most institutions of this type were passing or had already passed from the scene. Conceptually, all foster care was "treatment" in the sense that it was seen as a temporary substitute to remedy or replace a specific deficiency in parenting.

In an influential text on casework services in Child Welfare, Gordon stated this conception of the purpose of foster care succinctly: "Foster care may be for a short period, to meet an emergency, or for months or years, to help parents and children overcome some distressing problem" (1956:34). The fallacy in this image of foster care as limited to either meeting a temporary emergency or overcoming a distressing problem in the lives of parents and children should have been dispelled forever with the publication in 1959 of Maas and Engler's classic study, *Children in Need of Parents*. This study revealed that more than half the foster children they studied in nine sample communities across the nation would be likely to remain to their maturity in foster care. Only a few would be adopted, and only a fraction could expect to ever return home. It is true they excluded from their study children who had been in care less than three months, thus enhancing the appearance of foster care systems in these representative communities as having become "holding tanks" for large numbers of children with little movement toward either restoration to their biological parents or adoption by new ones.

This image of foster care is in sharp contrast to the promise of substitute care as a temporary, treatment-oriented service to children for a planned period of time. In defense of foster care it should be said that an unknown but substantial proportion of children who entered foster care remained only briefly. Receiving homes, short-term and emergency foster homes, and various types of diagnostic homes and facilities were being used for dependent children among the many different juvenile court and public welfare jurisdictions across the nation. A lack of consistent definition of the different types and of reliable statistics on their use has obscured understanding of the total spectrum of foster care.

The findings of Maas and Engler made clear to everyone that something was seriously remiss in the way the foster care system was working. No longer tenable was a conception of foster care as a temporary service while the biological family was rehabilitated, or where that was not possible, adoption into a new family was arranged. Most of those children who remained more than a few months in foster care were destined to grow up there; only a fraction would ever return home and a similar fraction ever moved into adoptive homes (Wiltse and Gambrill, 1974). The then prevalent conception, of placement in foster care as a "tool in treatment" (Charnley, 1955: xiii), could be met only with the question "treatment of what or of whom?" If the goal of treatment were the rehabilitation of the biological parents' home and the child's eventual return, Maas and Engler's research demonstrated that this was little more than a pious hope. They found that more than 70 percent of the parents of the children they studied had either no relationship or a negative relationship with the agencies responsible for their children (1959:391). If treatment was in the sense of helping the child, it seems almost ludicrous from the vantage point of the 1980s that Child Welfare professionals could ever have believed, or at least acted as if they believed, that placement of large numbers of normal children in foster family homes in which they would likely spend most of their childhood years could ever have been considered for the good of the children.

## Foster Care since 1959

In 1957 there were 254,000 dependent (excluding delinquent) children in all types of foster care in the continental United States and its territories (Department of Health, Education and Welfare, 1959). The ratio of children in foster family homes compared to institutional placement was then approximately three to one. By 1970 there were 263,000 children in foster family homes and 93,500 in institutions (National Center for Social Statistics, 1972). Thus the approximate three to one ratio of family to institutional care continued, and there was no evident reduction, taking the national increase in child population into account, in the rate of retention of children in foster care as a consequence of the Maas–Engler findings. If anything there was an increase. A lack of reliable state and national statistics on substitute care of children is a problem which the 96th Congress sought to remedy as part of the Adoptive Assistance and Child Welfare Act of 1980. However, the figure of 500,000 dependent children in all types of foster care had become an accepted estimate by the middle of the decade. Concern about statistical accuracy however becomes rather specious in the face of the obvious evidence no matter what the exact figures are, that foster care has functioned as a retention rather than a decision-making system.

The decade of the 60s can be characterized in two ways with regard to foster care. On one hand there were stirrings of concern that the system was serving children badly, following the Maas–Engler findings, and that change was necessary; on the other hand there was a flurry of descriptive studies of children in care, the net result of which was to fill in the essential "holding tank" image of the system that the Maas–Engler findings first projected. Tentative or partial alternatives to the impermanence of foster care were held out by various authors, such as more aggressive efforts to press toward termination of parental ties to achieve adoption (Malone, 1960; Pennypacker, 1961); or long-term foster care and quasi-adoption by design (Andrews, 1968; Lawder, 1966; Madison and Shapiro, 1970; Taylor, 1966; Weaver, 1968). Research focused upon the characteristics of children entering foster care (Jenkins and Sauber, 1966) or of those remaining in care (Fanshel, 1971; Jenkins, 1967) contributed to the general realization that neither client characteristics nor predictions based upon diagnostic judgments had much to do with what happened to children in foster care. Emlen summarizes the situation at the end of the decade with these words:

> The sixties came to an end still preoccupied with description of what was and with prediction of outcomes in the then existing systems. It was a decade of concern about the impermanent character of foster care, but not a decade of resolve to change it in fundamental ways. The concept of permanency simply meant stable and continuous relationships and the belief was

that foster care would be stabilized or made permanent in this sense. The Child Welfare League published a national reassessment of foster care by 21 experts . . . in which the papers revealed little of the attention to permanency that was to take center stage a few years later. (Emlen in Downs, 1981:4)

The 70s was a decade of change in foster care. The accumulating concern about the impermanence and "drift" which characterized the condition of nearly a half million foster children coalesced into a realization that the system was serving these children badly. It was not easy to determine just how or why this state of affairs came about. Crucial information was not available at state or national levels: information as basic as exactly how many children were in foster care, how long they had been there, what relationship, if any, they retained with their parents, and what the obstacles were which stood in the way of their being adopted if parental rights were terminated. This lack of information in itself pinpointed the system's fundamental deficiencies; case planning and case management were clearly absent, or else this kind of information would have been routinely available as the essential baseline of planning.

An upsurge of activity concerning foster care during the 1970s took many different forms. A limited number of research and demonstration projects made major contibutions, not only toward identifying the deficiencies in the way specific foster care systems were serving children, but also contributing significantly to new technologies for addressing these deficiencies. At the top of this list is what came to be known as the Oregon Project, specifically the original Project to Free Children for Permanent Placement, and the subsequent Dissemination and Utilization of Permanent Strategies for Children in Long-Term Foster Care. Moving from an initial identification of obstacles to permanency planning, the Oregon Proiect went on to develop technologies for reducing agency, court, and community obstacles, and eventually to disseminating these techniques to nearly every state (Downs, 1981; Downs and Taylor, 1980; Emlen, L'Ahti, and Downs, 1978; Pike, 1977). In Alameda County, California, Stein and his colleagues tested the application of specific assessment and intervention techniques to a sample of foster care cases, and demonstrated their effectiveness in achieving permanency for children (Stein, Gambrill, and Wiltse, 1978). Two influential studies by national advocacy organizations, the Washington, D.C. based Children's Defense Fund (*Children Without Homes,* 1978) and the New York based National Commission on Children in Need of Parents (*Who Knows? Who Cares? Forgotten Children in Foster Care,* 1979), each detailed the nationwide failures of the foster care system to accomplish its avowed goal of serving the best interests of children and made sweeping recommendations for legislative reform.

The 1970s was characterized by an outpouring of documentation of the need for advocacy on behalf of foster children, for improved management information and administrative processes for better case planning and case management techniques, for streamlining the legal processes, and of the need for legislative reform. It was a decade of unprecedented activity in every aspect of Child Welfare, but with respect to foster care the attention focused on permanency planning. The United States Children's Bureau was at the center of much of this activity, and before the end of the decade had formulated its goals for Child Welfare training in no uncertain terms as preparing social workers to accomplish permanency for each child (Children's Bureau, 1979).

The national climate of ferment for change coalesced in legislation aimed at reforming foster care and adoption services. After four years of effort, the Adoption Assistance and Child Welfare Act (Public Law 96–272) was signed into law by President Carter in June, 1980. This act incorporates the essential elements of permanency planning for children in foster care. A Children's Bureau brochure describes this new legislation as aimed at 503,000 children living in foster care, and pinpoints the aim of the Act as redirecting the nation's efforts towards strengthening families so that placing a child in foster care can be avoided, and if that is not possible, reuniting children who are in foster care with their families as soon as possible, or if that is not possible, placing children in loving adoptive homes or in appropriate permanent placements. This Act of the 96th Congress puts the capstone to a process begun with the Maas–Engler studies in 1959; it is a process to which many contributed—social workers, lawyers, researchers, advocates, journalists, legislators, and many concerned citizens.

## The Concept of Permanence

At the conclusion of their exhaustive longitudinal study which followed a cohort of children in foster family care in New York City for a period of five years, Fanshel and Shinn state:

> It is no longer considered sufficient that a child be afforded a placement situation in which his basic needs are being cared for in terms of shelter, food and clothing and a benign environment in which positive emotional growth can be enhanced. A newly emphasized criterion is being used to assess the adequacy of an agency's performance, namely, whether a child can be assured *permanency* in his living arrangements and *continuity* of relationship. It is not enough that he be placed in a foster family home that offers him family-like care. If he cannot regard the people he is living with as his family on a permanent basis, his situation is increasingly regarded as reflecting something less than an adequate resolution of his life situation. (1978:477)

With the basic notion that family-like care is the only appropriate substitute when biological parents are unable to supply it, a new and critical dimension was clarified: *permanency* in living arrangements and *continuity* of relationship. This concept is the first essentially new one enlarging the fundamental theory base of foster family care since Charles Birtwell promulgated the principle of fitting the home to the needs of the child.

Some might argue the concept of permanency may be considered comparable to a child's inalienable right to have his or her fundamental needs considered, a right Birtwell asserted eighty years ago. The fundamental purpose of service, the *why* of foster care in this instance, frames each of the different identifiable clusters of techniques—initial assessment, homefinding, placement, termination, adoption—in other words, the entire continuum of foster family care is cast within the planning-for-permanency framework. With respect to each aspect of the continuum, for example, that of developing a written contract with biological parents toward the goal of restoration, there has been a development within the last ten years of specific techniques for its accomplishment (Stein, Gambrill, Wiltse, 1978). In this instance theory is a seamless web of purpose, principle, and technique. Technique is inseparable from purpose in the sense of each being elements of a body of theory explaining why and how foster care of children is to be provided.

Early in the 70s Kline and Overstreet (1972) published an influential book setting forth the principles of social work in foster care entitled *Foster Care of Children: Nurture and Treatment*. These words, "nurture and treatment" capture the older image of the task of the foster care agency that has given way to a very different one: the foster care agency engaged in decision-making rather than treatment. The emerging view is of the foster care agency planning and making decisions toward permanency for each child encountering the foster care system. The crescendo of criticism of foster care that had been building during the 60s finally overwhelmed the "treatment" conception. The "stability and continuity," which Kline and Overstreet saw as deriving from the foster care agency's role in relation to each child came to be seen as the essence of the problem. That agencies had provided stability and continuity of a sort could scarcely be argued in view of the fact that most foster children spent many years in care. However, from the viewpoint of the child experiencing foster care, stability and continuity were inherently limited. The child remained a foster child, not like "normal" children who were reared by their own parents, and unlike those who were securely grafted into a new family by adoption.

The infamous "limbo" condition of the child in foster care which came in for so much critical attention is largely inferred from the statements of children actually living the experience or those who have lived through it. The feelings of abandonment and anger directed toward their own parents, and ambivalence and guilt over feelings of attachment to their foster parents are documented by numerous anecdotal reports. How typical of all foster children are these feelings lacks firm empirical verification. It came to be widely believed that the indeterminancy and uncertainty of the foster condition inhibits development in foster children of self-confidence, a firm sense of identity, and an ability to risk close personal relationships. Though there was general acceptance of this belief that the impermanency of foster care is bad for children, it is difficult to support this conviction with empirical evidence. Fanshel and Shinn, at the end of their exhaustive longitudinal study that follows 624 foster children over a five year period and uses nearly every conceivable measurement of social and psychological adjustment, conclude that children who are not living with their own families and are not adopted may come to think of themselves as unwanted human beings (1978:479). They reach this conclusion despite the fact that their extensive empirical data fail to show the specific damaging effects of foster care.

Instability of placement, the fact that a child rarely remains in a single foster home during the entire foster care career, is usually cited as an obstacle to the child's achieving a sense of permanency and stability in his or her psychological life (Mnookin, 1973). In the extreme instances of many replacements, the repetitive shifts are arguably both a cause and effect of the child's evident emotional troubles. This lack of permanence is widely discussed in the literature. Ambinder (1965) found that on the average a 13-year-old foster child had experienced four to five placements. On the other hand, a national study pointed out that half the children in foster care had been in only one foster home, although obviously the other half had experienced two or more moves, and about 37,000 in this study had experienced four or more different placements (Shyne and Shroeder, 1978a). Placement stability can be argued either way. For example, Kadushin, who cites a series of studies done since 1970 to show that most children experience two or fewer placements, concludes from these data that the criticism of foster care on the grounds of its instability is exaggerated (1978:101).

It seems fair to conclude that in fact, a high degree of stability does exist for children in foster care if the proportion who experience frequent replacements is taken as the indicator. Averages are deceptive, since only a few children, usually those with severe emotional or physical problems, experience many replacements, thereby raising the average, whereas for most children their foster care career is relatively stable with at most one or two replacements. I suggest the whole issue has received more attention than it deserves because even those who remain in the same foster home for many years still know very well they are foster children, and that their lives and relationships are not like children in their own homes. The possibility of being returned to the agency for replacement remains a present reality to any child in foster care whether or not he or she is ever actually moved. Any belief that the social agency will supply the one stable reality in the foster child's life is illusory in view of the excessive worker turnover characteristic of Child Welfare agencies. One study (Moynihan, 1963) found that children who have lived in the same foster home eight years from date of placement had a different worker every year. The national study done by Shyne and Shroeder (1978a) found that 48 percent of those in foster care two years or longer had had at least four caseworkers. These and numerous other studies documenting excessive social worker turnover would suggest that to the child in foster care the agency scarcely can feel a stable and unwavering reality in an otherwise uncertain existence.

The Maas and Engler study was a benchmark in the realization that the system of foster care was serving children badly. A great many studies and reports during the subsequent decade contributed to the recognition that more than technical improvements or methodological adjustments were necessary in the way foster care services were delivered; a more fundamental change in the purpose and goals of foster care was required. The Oregon Permanent Planning Project described earlier focused the attention of the Child Welfare field on permanency planning as the basic antidote for the acknowledged drift of children through interminable years in foster care. Permanence came to mean assurance to each child who encounters the Child Welfare system permanence in his living arrangements and continuity of relationship to parenting adults. Permanence describes intent. A permanent home is not one that is guaranteed to last forever, but one intended to exist indefinitely (Pike et al., 1977:1). The idea of intent is critical, because it is this intent communicated to the child in placement which counters the child's feeling of uncertainty and indefiniteness about his future, the infamous limbo of being a foster child.

Planning for permanency is an attitude or stance on the part of the Child Welfare agency which results in a continuum of specific acts. At every stage of this continuum of service delivery, from assessing the problems of a disordered or abusive family to final disposition of those children for whom a period of foster care is necessary, the goal of permanency and continuity of care focuses the decision-making process.

Acceptance of the goal of permanency for each child who encounters the foster care system alters every aspect of service delivery. This shift requires that all levels of personnel, social workers, supervisors, and managers understand what permanency planning means. It also means adopting the specific attitudes and acquiring knowledge of the new techniques which are necessary if the change is really to be implemented.

Earlier chapters of this book which describe social work practice to keep children in their own homes, and subsequent chapters which will describe practice in foster care and adoption present an image of practice in all these essential aspects of Child Welfare that is quite different from that presented in texts on Child Welfare practice written before 1970. A very different model of practice is presented in a recent text in the field (Stein, 1981). It is a case management and decision-making model which contrasts markedly with the individual treatment model that pervaded practice in Child Welfare prior to the emergence of the concept of planning for permanency.

## The Research Basis for Change

The 70s witnessed a shift in thinking about foster care (Wiltse, 1979), stimulated and accompanied by a deluge of books, pamphlets, reports, and articles written for both professional and popular consumption. The two particularly influential publications with a strong advocacy orientation pinpointed the problems of the foster care system and recommended comprehensive measures for their correction (Children's Defense Fund, 1978; National Commission on Children in Need of Parents, 1979). Every aspect of child welfare was receiving attention. Social work with families to prevent placement, adoption, homefinding, foster parent training, working with minority families, and the critical area of family support services, such as emergency homemaker services and respite day care, experienced a renaissance of new ideas.

Two studies are selected for mention because each went beyond identifying the problems of foster care systems to actually designing and testing specific methods of intervention and measuring the results. These were the Oregon Project in Permanency Planning and the Alameda County, California Project conducted by Stein and his colleagues (Stein, Gambrill, and Wiltse, 1978).

The Oregon project was a special three-year project conducted within that state's Children's Services Division. Between 1973 and 1976, the Division worked intensively toward the goal of obtaining a permanent home for each of 509 children. These children were chosen according to four criteria: (1) considered by the caseworkers as unlikely ever to return to his or her own home, (2) under 12 years of age, (3) considered adoptable (4) and had been in foster care at least a year. Most had been in care a great deal longer. The purpose of the project was to demonstrate ways of moving children out of foster care who otherwise seemed destined to remain there indefinitely. Caseworkers were selected and trained to work aggressively toward achieving, first, the return home of the child, or if that was not possible, to work toward freeing the child for adoption.

The results achieved were gratifying, even startling. Though their caseworkers had considered all 509 unlikely ever to return home, as of November, 1976, 26 percent of the children had been restored to their own parents. More than a third of the original 509 children, 36 percent, had been adopted by their foster parents or new parents, 3 percent had gone to relatives, 10 percent were in long-term foster care under specific contractual arrangements, in 18 percent of the cases the implementation plan was still in progress, and in the final 10 percent the original plan had not been successful and was under revision. Hence permanency already had been achieved for nearly three-fourths of the initial sample, demonstrating conclusively that assertive, goal-oriented casework, focused around precise carefully drawn plans for achieving permanency, and buttressed by a determination to overcome all bureaucratic and legal obstacles, can accomplish permanency for most children drifting in foster care.

The Alameda project began a year later and covered nearly the same time span. A sample of 227 experimental and 201 control cases were selected from the Foster Care Division of the Alameda County Welfare Department by three principal criteria (1) at least one biological parent present in the county, (2) one or more foster children in the family under 16 years of age, (3) child in foster family home: Institutional placements were excluded. The three project workers and project director all held M.S.W. degrees and the project workers were given special training in behavioral methods for assessing cases and designing interventions to achieve decisions within a limited time frame, generally six months. The results of the focused decision-making efforts of the project workers demonstrated that permanence and continuity could be achieved by these methods as compared to the usual methods used by the regular foster care workers employed by the county. Of the total 428 children involved in the Alameda project, 82 experimental unit cases and 53 control cases were closed for miscellaneous reasons unrelated to casework decision-making, leaving 145 experimental and 148 control cases as the basis for comparison of results.

The striking difference between the two groups is the proportion of children either out of placement or headed out of placement—79 percent of the experimental group as compared to 40 percent of the experimental group. Almost half of the children in the experimental group were either restored or in the process of being restored to their parents, and 30 percent were in adoptive or legal guardianship arrangements. Sixty percent of the control group children remained in long-term foster care as against 21 percent of the children in the experimental group. The experimental staff directed service primarily to the biological parents, whereas service in the agency foster care units was directed mostly to foster parents. In general, variables describing the client did not predict outcomes. Time in care was predictive for children in the experimental group, that is, children were more likely to be restored to biological parents during their first year. No such relationship was found for control group children.

Focusing service upon the biological parent was in accordance with the decision-making framework of this project. How else is either restoration to be achieved or a determination made that this parent is unwilling or unable to be a parent, and termination the logical alternative? Yet numerous studies have documented that of the parent, child, and foster parent triad, biological parents receive the least attention from social workers (Brieland, Watson, Hovda, Fanshel, and Carey, 1968; Gruber, 1973; Jeter, 1963; Maas and Engler, 1959). The Alameda project demonstrated a decision-making methodology in foster care service delivery based on behavioral assessment and contracting with biological parents and children followed by intervention directed to removing or reducing the problems in parent–child relationships which necessitated placement.

In sum, these two projects have demonstrated that continuity and permanency can be achieved for children in foster care. In the two decades since Maas and Engler's *Children in Need of Parents* (1959) describing the "drift" of children in foster care, studies such as the Oregon and Alameda projects have demonstrated that change is possible. How much change there has been across the nation among the thousands of local Child Welfare systems during the 70s, or how much there will be in the next decade, is difficult to predict. Goal change is the necessary first step, and a new technology of service delivery is in the process of creation and dissemination. Schools of social work are of critical importance to making this technology work, and they, like bureaucratic delivery systems, are entrenched in a social work treatment ideology resistant to the incorporation of the decision-making ideology and methods of permanency planning. Finally, the vagaries of national and state politics do not augur well for a consistent implementation of permanency planning in foster care. The impetus of the Adoption Assistance and Child Welfare Act of 1980 may be eroded by budget restrictions and the block grant approach to financing social services. Many of us who hailed this new initiative in national leadership may feel we are again at the beginning.

## The Legal Base of State Intervention

A critically important shift is occurring in the legal basis of state intervention into parent–child relationships, a change bearing directly upon both entry into and exit from foster care. Removal of children from neglectful or abusive parents or freeing them for adoption when in foster care depend on proving their parents are incapable of providing a minimum level of care. Initial removal or eventual termination are both on sounder bases when grounded in statutes which require a clear demonstration that either the child's remaining with or being returned to the biological parent risks continued specific harm to the child.

The substance of this argument is made very effectively by Wald (1976). He proposes standards for removal or termination that compel the foster care or court worker to document specific harms to the child rather than socially reprehensible parental behavior or unsatisfactory home conditions. Parental substance abuse or deviant sexual behavior, and low housekeeping standards or home sanitary conditions, are each examples of a socially disvalued behavior or condition, but none automatically translates into specific and demonstrable harm to children. The distinction is fundamentally a moral versus a scientific basis for decision-making with reference to when the State intervenes into family relationships.

Statutes governing state intervention have not always held to this distinction (Katz, 1975), with resultant confusion about what might or might not need to be changed in order for parents to keep the children or have them restored subsequent to removal. This greater specificity is reflected in model legislation proposed for possible adoption by state legislatures (Katz, 1978) and in new standards for decision-making by the courts in child abuse and neglect cases (American Bar Association, 1977). Stein and Rzepnicki state the case for precise standards in the following quote:

> An acceptable alternate decision making standard must lend itself to the development of operational criteria that can be reliably applied on a case by case basis to determine whether child care meets minimally acceptable standards and it must lend itself to setting attainable goals. It should also respect the ethnic and cultural diversity of American society by being specific to limit the use of individual discretion by the court and child welfare workers. This is best accomplished *if intervention decisions require evidence that a child has been harmed or is at risk of harm in the near future.* This evidentiary requirement serves a dual purpose: first, it recognizes that efforts to make long-term predictions are not fruitful. Second, it represents an effort to reduce the chances that intervention will occur for moral reasons alone. (1983:273)

Precisely drawn standards (Gilman, 1980), meaning statements which call on the social worker to document the case for intervention into a parent–child relationship with behaviorally based observations, increase the probability that judgment will be made upon a scientific rather than moral basis. The search for standards which call forth evidence of specific harm to a child before removal or termination is recommended has been an important aspect of the permanency planning thrust of the past decade (Hardin, in Downs, 1981:2.41). Improved legal standards and legal practices, plus dissemination of revised standards and legal practice manuals among attorneys, judges, court workers, and social workers have been important facets of an emerging body of new theory of foster care.

## Ethnicity, Race, and Permanency Planning

A stress on achieving a permanent home for each child in foster care adds a sharper edge to a continuing concern that ethnicity and race considerations be adhered to in placing children for adoption. Black children especially tended to illustrate the "holding tank" nature of foster care systems heretofore untouched by the stress on planning for permanency. For example, in Alameda County, approximately 20 percent of the population of the county is black, yet about 50 percent of the children in foster care are black children. Black children enter the foster care system in disproportionately higher numbers because the stresses of poverty and racism produce higher incidence of family breakdown. For the system to process black and white children toward permanency with equal efficiency, there must be effective recruitment of black homes. A lack of effective adoption homefinding programs for black children as in the instance of Alameda County and for American Indian children in localities and states where they are a substantial segment of the foster care caseload has led to rationalizing interracial adoption as the only viable alternative.[1]

Black and American Indian populations have objected strenuously to this practice. With reference to foster care, it is necessary to emphasize that as permanency planning is accomplished in any given Child Welfare agency which has a substantial minority group in its population, the argument over interracial placement for adoption inevitably will intensify. The Indian Child Welfare Act of 1978 requires that the Tribal Government of the group with which an Indian child in foster care has an identity must have dispositional authority over any permanent plan for that child. There is no comparable statutory expression with reference to black or other ethnic or racial minority, but emerging ethnic consciousness is characteristic of all ethnic groups, and Child Welfare agencies must include an awareness of this consciousness in their planning with respect to children in foster care.

## External Review of Foster Care

National concern about children remaining too long in foster care has led to an emerging demand for external review. Generally this means some type of review and monitoring of case planning for individual foster children by someone outside the system itself. External review has taken a number of forms in different states and localities. Its essential feature is that a group other than the professionals directly involved in designing and implementing individual case plans monitors the progress of their implementation. Proponents of external review argue that it is necessary to open up the foster care system to external scrutiny to bring about change (Chappell, 1975). An additional consequence is that citizen involvement produces a knowledgeable group of new advocates for better child services (Chappell and Hevener, 1977).

Administrators and managers are generally wary of external review on two grounds, (1) any system of external review means another layer of bureaucracy upon an already overloaded system, and (2) it is demeaning to have nonprofessionals, especially people external to the system's actual operations, "looking over the shoulder" of those actually responsible for day-to-day operations.

The different forms which external review have taken are described in a report by the National Institute for Advanced Studies (1979). Each form has strengths and weaknesses in terms of accomplishing the goal, namely improving decision-making for permanency for children in foster care, and early evidence suggests each has had the desired effect. In no instance has there been sufficient experience with a given form of external review for a comprehensive and definitive evaluation of its effectiveness. The proponents of each form of review claim evidence of furthering the goal of permanency for foster children in its geographical area of application.

External review of individual foster care case planning is a new development in public administration that goes beyond the accepted policy forming role of citizen boards to an actual monitoring of agency performance on specific cases, especially where this review is done by boards or committees of lay citizens. The demand for external review represents a response to serious concern about the drift of children in foster care. Whether the review systems which have developed represent a transitory or a permanent feature of the Child Welfare field remains to be seen.

This overview of foster care of children in the United States began with a quote from Kadushin, one of the nation's most prolific scholars of Child Welfare, which said that we still lack a clearly defined theory of substitute care. The focus of this examination of substitute care of children in America has been foster family care. We have highlighted the belief of the early critics of institutional forms of substitute care of children—a belief held throughout the history of Child Welfare—that family life is the only appropriate arena for rearing children. Hence foster family care has been viewed as the nearest and best substitute when the child's own family is unable or unwilling to care for him or her.

The evolution of foster family care as a treatment service for disordered families and dependent children was traced briefly. For complex and perhaps obscure reasons, Child Welfare systems staffed by people with profound concern for children and unwavering commitment to their welfare were not providing permanent homes for children. By 1959 a benchmark study showed that foster care systems had become like holding tanks for the many thousands of children adrift within them. A crescendo of study, criticism, and clamor for change ensued. The decade of the 1970s was one of exceptional research and demonstration activity, out of which emerged a new direction for foster family care: planning for permanency for each child in foster care in terms of living arrangements and continuity of relationship to parenting persons. Two prominent scholars of foster care, Fanshel and Shinn, suggest this new thrust signals a revolution in Child Welfare analogous to that of the closing down of mass congregate institutions in favor of family care as the appropriate choice for children, a revolution that dominated thinking in the Child Welfare field for a century prior to the Great Depression of the 1930s.

In the sense that a new direction in foster care has emerged in the press toward permanency planning, evidenced in new statutes and new directions in state and national leadership, we can say we have a new theory of foster care. It is an image of the foster care agency as a decision-making system rather than a treatment service to families and children. It is an image which will revolutionize social work practice in foster care in the ensuing decades. Stein and Rzepnicki (1983) detail this new image of the Child Welfare agency as a decision-making system.

With the passage of the Adoption Assistance and Child Welfare Act of 1980 (Public Law 96–272) by the 96th Congress, some Child Welfare people saw it as the dawn of a new era. Others, more cautious in their appraisal of the rapidity with which change can occur in the systems of Child Welfare bureaucracies across the nation, saw it as the beginning of a slow and painful process of attitudinal change and social work methodological retooling.

# CHAPTER 22

# Practice in Foster Care

EMILY JEAN MCFADDEN

Foster care is often described as a triangle consisting of the family, foster family, and worker linked together in common concern for the child. As in most relationships of a triangular nature, potential exists for difficulty and conflict. Maintenance of the precarious balance among the interested participants requires continuous adaptation and feedback. If stress increases or boundaries are not kept open, one segment of the triangle may be excluded or extruded. In other situations, conflict may be avoided and coalitions and subsystem alliances may form. The child of course is caught in an awkward and vulnerable position, as the adults responsible for his or her well-being struggle to maintain and define their roles. An example of the difficulties inherent in this configuration follows:

> The Stanley foster family grounded 11-year-old Jimmy for the weekend because he had skipped school. Jimmy's mother complained to the social worker that the punishment was too severe, and that it would interfere with her scheduled visit. The social worker visited Jimmy at school to discuss it with him. The foster parents wondered what had been discussed with Jimmy, and if the worker was displeased with their actions. They felt uncomfortable with the social worker's power to move Jimmy from their home if all was not well. Jimmy's mother called the Stanleys before the

social worker got back to them. They told her they didn't know what to do about the visit, but that they felt they must discipline Jimmy for skipping. Tempers flared, with the mother stating, "You have no right to treat me or my son that way" and the Stanleys responding, "Well, Lady, maybe you lost some rights when you neglected your child and he had to come here." Jimmy stared at the TV and thought about running away.

Several less than positive resolutions of the triangulated configuration are possible: Jimmy could run away; his mother could disengage; the foster parents could threaten to have Jimmy removed if they can't discipline him without interference; the worker could move Jimmy; or the system could remain in uneasy equilibrium with periodic bursts of conflict among all parties. To avoid these effects of the foster care triangle, it becomes necessary to clarify roles, boundaries, and communication and to facilitate a situation in which all subsystems are able to function with minimum triangulation.

*The family system as unit of attention.* Traditionally in the Child Welfare field, the child has been viewed as the client. The hapless victim of a "bad" or "pathological" family was rescued from circumstances which hampered healthy development or had caused actual physical harm. Foster care placement provided the child protection from his or her family and a healing setting in which to flourish and grow.

Viewed in a family-centered ecological perspective, the foster child cannot be understood as an isolated fragment split off from the family of origin. The child is seen rather as part of a sustaining fabric of kinfolk, memory and tradition, carrying the genetic gifts and bearing the name of his people. Laird states the case clearly:

> Kin ties are powerful and compelling and the individual's sense of identity and continuity is formed not only by the significant attachments in his intimate environment but is also deeply rooted in the biological family—in the genetic link that reaches back into the past and ahead into the future. . . . Ecologically oriented child welfare practice attends to, nurtures and supports the biological family. Further, when it is necessary to substitute for the biological family, such practice dictates that every effort be made to preserve and protect important kinship ties. (1979:177)

Although Child Welfare League of America standards for foster care emphasize the objectives of "healthy personality development of the child and amelioration of problems that are personally or socially destructive," the importance of the family is explicit—workers are to "maintain and enhance parental functioning to the fullest extent" and "bring about the child's ultimate return to his natural family whenever desirable and feasible."

As the biological family system and child are conceptualized as the focus of attention, practice inevitably shifts to those approaches which will best support the entire family and strengthen the parent–child bond during the vicissitudes of separation. Maluccio and Sinanoglu (1981) provide an urgently needed fresh perspective: the families may be clients, involuntary clients often, yet they are partners—helpers as well as helped—resources as well as those in need of resources.

*The worker as decision-maker and enabler for permanence.* If foster care is to serve its purpose as time-limited temporary placement within a plan for permanence, the worker must be actively committed to decision-making, contracting, and review, so the child will move quickly through the system and not languish to endure the iatrogenic effects of repeated separations and multiple placements (Stein and Gambrill, 1976; Gambrill and Stein, 1981). An earlier emphasis on treatment of the child may have resulted in prolonging the time spent in placement. It is often a less demanding task for the worker to focus on the child's developmental needs than it is to engage in aggressive outreach to the child's family to remedy persistent and long-standing family problems.

When the service is conceptualized as rehabilitation and reunification of the family, the worker will utilize a myriad of helping persons and systems, such as vocational training, legal systems, health services, parent education, substance abuse rehabilitation, homemakers, parent aides, and mental health professionals. According to Pike and colleagues, the social worker "has the central and indispensable role of coordinating these people and service agencies. It is safe to say that without the interest and expertise of a knowledgeable caseworker, a child adrift in foster care will simply continue to drift" (Pike et al., 1977:6).

Thus the role and task of the worker in the initial case example would shift dramatically. Rather than talking to the child who has skipped school (a traditional "treatment approach" which perpetuated the triangulation between parent and foster parent) the worker would communicate directly with the parent and foster parents, hopefully in a joint meeting, to help them to resolve the questions of handling Jimmy's "skipping" behavior while insuring that visits would be maintained.

*The foster parent as part of the professional team.* Earlier literature depicts the foster parents in a variety of positions, ranging from that of a quasi-client whose need for a child must be met by the agency with skilled casework support to that of an independent service provider whose volunteer status must be acknowledged (Lawder, 1964; Reistroffer, 1972). Within the past decade, paralleling the development of the National Foster Parent Association and numerous foster parent training programs, foster parents have redefined their roles as trained professional members of the helping team (Rodriquez, 1982). The responsibilities of foster parents include coordination of a variety of services for the child and working supportively with the biological families toward the goal of reunification (Ryan, McFadden, and Warren, 1979).

Although the foster parents in the earlier case example might have experienced feelings of antagonism towards Jimmy's mother, had they conceptualized their role as a professional one committed to the importance of visitation, they would not have entertained the possibility of denying visitation between parent and child; in all probability they would have directly involved Jimmy's mother in solving the problem about Jimmy's school attendance.

*A team approach to foster care.* The nature of the foster care configuration is triangular, yet can also be viewed as a series of subsystems operating within a larger systemic context. (See Figure 22–1.) The worker and foster parent are a team, with the foster parent taking primary responsibility for delivery of services to the child and the worker focusing on providing services to the parents (Ryan, 1979). As a team, they are part of a larger helping system consisting of the variety of resources brought into play through the worker's brokering and coordination activities. Although the foster child may be physically residing within the foster family system, he or she remains unequivocally a part of his or her own family system. A foster parent–biological parent subsystem works together with the child on the issues of visitation, health care, school

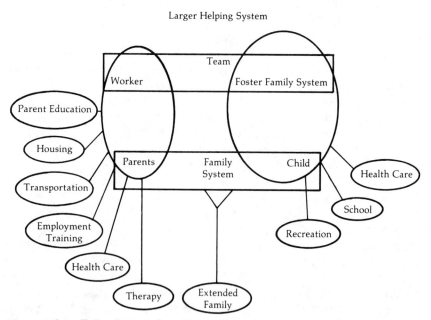

**Figure 22–1** Team Approach to Foster Care

activities, and recreational events. The extended family is viewed as a potential resource to the entire family system, and may be used as a support for the parents, and/or a visitation or placement resource for the child.

In summary, this chapter assumes a flexible team approach, clear delineation of roles and boundaries, and the importance of maximum involvement of the biological parents for the goal of preservation of family integrity, identity, and continuity within the broader context of permanency planning.

## Placement of Children

Children come into placement under widely differing circumstances, for a multitude of reasons, and through processes which may vary from agency to agency, county to county and state to state. Shapiro's (1976) research lists the reasons for placement as (1) unwillingness or inability of the parent to continue care, (2) neglect or abuse of the child, (3) mental illness of the parent, (4) unwillingness or inability to assume care (in the case of a newborn), (5) child's behavioral or personality problems, (6) illness within the family, (7) incarceration of the parent, (8) conflict within the family, (9) drug addiction of the parent(s), and (10) alcohol-related problems. While other studies cite the reasons for placement in slightly different ways or order of importance (Ferleger and Cotter, 1976; Jenkins and Sauber, 1966; Shyne and Schroeder, 1978a), a configuration of factors common in many placement situations includes poverty and/or lack of resources, breakdown of family system functioning, and insufficient informal support networks to tide the family over through a crisis situation or provide respite in a situation of chronic difficulty.

The process of placement may occur through parents seeking temporary help on a voluntary basis; through court ordered removal for reasons of neglect, abandonment, abuse, or delinquency after prior interventions have failed to correct the malfunction of the family system; or through legal action involving children with emotional, intellectual, or physical handicaps who require out-of-home specialized care. The placement may be handled by a protective service worker or police if an emergency exists, by a foster care intake worker, or in some instances by a desperate parent who abandons the child on the doorstep of the emergency shelter. Children may go directly into the foster home in which they will remain, they may spend several weeks in a shelter, receiving facility, or emergency foster home or they may be moved planfully from a hospital or institution into a preselected home.

*Basic Practice Tasks*

Despite the plethora of reasons for and processes of placement there are several basic practice tasks which should be accomplished regardless of the setting or situation. They are: assessment of the need for placement; coordination of systems; selection of the most appropriate available foster home; provision of adequate information to the foster family; recognition of the impact of separation on both child and family, and handling the child in a way which minimizes confusion and trauma. Even under the most extreme of emergency placements, these minimal steps should be attended to, as outlined in the following example:

| | |
|---|---|
| *Assessment of need* | A newborn infant was found in a Goodwill drop box, and was taken by the police to a nearby hospital. |
| *Coordination* | While unsuccessful attempts were being made to locate the parents, and the protective services worker was filing the petition, hospital staff were evaluating the child's condition. Worker and medical personnel agreed that the child should be moved into a family setting as soon as possible. Experienced foster parents who had cared for other infants were selected. |
| *Provision of information* | They went immediately to the hospital to discuss the medical assessment with the nurses and doctor, and to establish contact with the infant during the critical period for bonding. The foster parents visited daily. Several days later when the child was released, the foster parents had written instructions regarding the formula and follow-up medical evaluation appointments. |
| *Handling to minimize trauma* | The foster parents had spent adequate time observing and handling the child in the hospital so that they knew his interactional cues, and the transition was a smooth one. |

*Additional Recommended Practice Tasks to Insure Parental Involvement*

In most cases, parents have at least some awareness of the need for placement but are often excluded from full participation in the placement process because of agency practices, or the worker's uncertainty as to how parental involvement could be accomplished. The following practice tasks assume the potential for parental involvement, although they may not be applicable in situations where parents are missing at the time of placement, or are so distraught, immobilized, or angry that it is difficult to effect maximum involvement. Those tasks which facilitate parental involvement and insure a transition that will be least damaging to the child and the integrity of the family system are: engagement of the family; data collection and problem identification; establishing a preliminary contract; joint planning of the placement process; insuring continuity of family ties; and recognition of the impact of separation on the family.

## Engagement of the Family System in the Placement Process

In many instances the family system will be involuntary clients with considerable degrees of hostility, resistance, self blame, and dysfunction. The inexperienced worker, ambivalent about the placement process, may find it difficult to reach out to the family for fear of encountering negative reactions. Yet the step of enlisting parents as partners in the process is a most crucial one, and predictive of eventual reunification.

An approach that focuses on the needs of the child and investigation concerning the inadequacy of parental care risks alienation of the parents, while empathy and concern for the needs of the parents provides a climate in which the partnership can emerge. It is important to remember that families are usually ambivalent about placement, and often encounter pressure from other family members and members of their support networks. The thought of "losing" a child can trigger memories of all unresolved earlier losses and flood the parents with overwhelming thoughts of inadequacy and self blame. If the worker is able to express genuine concern for the parents, a conviction that parents want to do the best they can for their children, and to offer support, the parents may be able to take a first step toward developing a relationship. The parents are facing a significant loss, and may display various grief reactions such as denial, anger, protest, despair. Simultaneously, they may be experiencing relief.

The role of the worker, as in any crisis intervention situation, is to help the parents express their feelings, to convey a sense of hope, reinforce parental competence and to join the parents in active problem-solving. Even though parents may appear hostile or resistant during initial contacts, the worker should not assume that there is little possibility for a working relationship. Rather, the worker should understand that parental behavior may be a defense against real pain and feelings of vulnerability.

## Data Collection and Problem Identification

The family may identify intervention by protective services or the court as "the problem," or state that the reporting system (the school or the doctor) is "out to get them." They often convey the idea that if only the intervening systems would get out of their lives and leave them alone things would be fine. Confrontation or active refutation of the parental stance at this point proves fruitless and alienates the family. The worker acknowledges the parental feelings, restates concern, and moves on to exploring the needs of the family. How can the agency be of service? Would help with housing or employment be beneficial? Is the parent feeling lonely and frustrated with the responsibility of the child? Are relatives supportive? Is there a financial need? Is there anything about the child that makes him or her a difficult child to parent?

## Assessment of the Need for Placement

To the extent that is possible within a given case situation, the family should be involved in assessment of the need for placement. Have all supportive and supplementary services been tried? Would day care or homemaker services be useful? Are there relatives, friends, or god-parents who could provide respite or serve as foster homes? What would the parental reaction be to using relatives as a placement? Would it create more stress because the relatives are critical of the parents? How great is the degree of risk to the child and family? Is the need for placement immediate, or is there some flexibility to allow time for planning the placement? What will be the benefits to the parents if placement occurs?

## Coordination of Systems

If the worker discovers that placement indeed seems necessary, the focus shifts momentarily to the need for coordination. Coordination is an ongoing responsibility, but repeatedly becomes a focal point as decisions are made. At this point a case conference or consultation proves useful. Review of the mass of information gathered, from parents, referral sources, schools, health care systems, and other sources helps to clarify the placement picture and provide support to the worker. A court petition must be filed or a voluntary service agreement developed. Unfortunately case transfer from one unit to another may occur at this point, after disrupting case management and continuity of care. Permission for emergency medical care is needed. Information must be compiled and exchanged between workers and units, or between the agency and the court. The importance of coordination cannot be over-emphasized. Inadequate transfer of information from worker to worker, failure to obtain necessary medical permissions, or conflict in approaches between one helping system and another have all too often seriously jeopardized service delivery and the well-being of children and families.

## Preliminary Contracting

When it becomes clear that placement is necessary, the worker informs the parents of the reality and begins the preliminary contracting about the placement process. A summary of the need for placement is given; it states not only the child's need, but also the needs of the parents. Although the parents may be protesting or denying the need for placement, the positive side of their ambivalence can surface if the worker can focus with some empathy on the parents' need. One approach might be as follows:

> I can tell this is very hard for you. But I know it would be even harder for you if your child were reinjured. You've told me how frustrating it is for you to make Johnny mind, and how bad you feel about his broken arm. You told me how desperately you have needed to get away from the hassle of the police and the hospital and your mother-in-law putting you down. It would be hard on you to go through this again, especially if Johnny were hurt worse the next time.

As the parents accept the reality of the placement and the concern of the worker, the goals of permanency planning should be reaffirmed simply: that children are best served within their own families; that foster care is designed to be temporary; that a service contract will be developed; and that the child will not be allowed to remain indefinitely in foster care. Within the parameters of the reality of placement, the parents have an option to be involved actively in helping the worker with the placement. Specific tasks of the parent are outlined, providing information to help in the selection of a foster home, communicating information to the foster parents, preparing the child for placement. The worker expresses the understanding that placement is a difficult time for the parents and will make supportive services available to them. Provision of a parents' handbook, such as the one developed for Child Welfare League of America, can help provide role clarification and underscore the worker's statements of concern (Rutter, 1978).

*Selection of the Most Appropriate Foster Home*

The biological family represents a valuable source of information regarding the child. The process of obtaining information from the family reinforces their parental status and importance to the child. Foster parents will need as much concrete information as possible to help ease the child's transition into care. Often the parents are the only source of the needed information: What are the child's favorite foods? Are there any known allergies? What are the health problems? Who are the medical personnel who have treated the child? Are immunizations up to date, and where are the records? What are the child's favorite belongings (blanket, teddy bear, etc.) which can be transitional security objects for the child? Are there behavioral problems (fire setting, aggression toward younger children) the foster parents should know about? If the child is young, what are his or her words for the bathroom? Does the child have a bedtime ritual, or fears of the dark? What do the parents perceive as the child's most important emotional or developmental needs, and what sort of foster home would best serve those needs?

Selection of the most appropriate available foster home involves variables, such as location, ethnic and cultural similarity, availability of community resources for the child, and self-assessment by the foster parents of their ability to meet the needs of the child, sibling group, or parents.

As the emphasis is on reunification of the family, accessibility of the foster home is crucial. A parent without transportation will have great difficulty in maintaining ties through visitation if the foster home is at the other end of the county. On the other hand, sometimes compromises must be made. If the agency or foster parents are able to provide transportation, and the only black home is distant, which variable— proximity or ethnic similarity—is more important to the family, the child's identity or the reunification plan?

Does the placement involve a sibling group? It is sound practice to place siblings together unless compelling evidence dictates otherwise. When facing separation from parents, brothers and sisters should be spared the additional separation from each other. Often they have depended greatly on each other for companionship and sustenance and placing siblings together can reduce separation trauma (Aldridge and Cautley, 1976). In the case of a large sibling group which cannot be accommodated by a single foster family, it is important to find two foster families in close proximity who will work together to maintain children's contact with each other as well as with their parents. If this is the case, parental input will be sought as to which children should be placed together.

If the child has intellectual, physical, or emotional disabilities, the foster family and worker must assess the availability of resources to serve the needs of the child such as special education, health care or treatment facilities in proximity to the foster home. If handicapping conditions of the child require a restructuring of the foster family's home environment (wheelchair ramp or locking away all potential hazards), the foster parents need to make an informed assessment of the capacity of their family to adapt.

If the child has known behavioral problems the foster family and worker must decide if the foster family has the resources, experience, and confidence to take on a challenging child. The selection process requires maximum input from both foster family and biological family. As the worker narrows the range of possibilities and decides on the best setting to insure the principles of continuity and the importance of the family to the child, the decision should be based on assessment with both families.

## Preplacement Visit

When possible, at least one preplacement visit in which parents and children both have an opportunity to meet with the foster parents is useful. Some foster parents prefer to have this initial meeting in the neutral territory of the agency office. On the other hand, many parents and children are curious about the home setting of the foster family. Office visits, home visits, or a combination thereof can be structured by the worker to minimize the inevitable feelings of discomfort and awkwardness by all parties.

At this initial contact, the parent has an opportunity to communicate information about the child to the foster parent, who should record relevant details. If an initial preplacement visit is not possible, it is extremely important for the worker to have all information about the child in written form to pass on to the foster parents. If the parent is incarcerated, confined to a treatment setting, or otherwise unavailable, a telephone contact with the foster parents prior to placement may be used successfully.

## Insuring of Continuity of Family Ties

Access to the resources of the extended family, particularly when the parents are unavailable, helps to assure continuity and identity for the child. When possible, it is important to gather information about the extended family prior to placement. Names, addresses, and relationship to the child should be documented. What resources can the extended family members provide to a placed child? Are there important family events forthcoming such as family reunions or weddings in which the child should be included? The genogram, discussed in Chapter 15, is an excellent tool for recording relationships and family history, helping to enhance the child's sense of continuity while in placement, or in the event that the child ultimately moves on to adoption. Family photographs, special toys or gifts from family members, and even in some instances a pet should also be obtained to accompany the child into placement.

Whenever possible, visitation arrangements and agreements should be developed prior to placement. It provides hope and comfort to child and parents to know when, where, and how contact will be maintained. If one or both parents will be unavailable after placement, relatives, godparents or close family friends may be available to provide support for the child.

## Recognition of the Impact of Separation

Although there is extensive literature of the impact of separation on the child (Charnley, 1955; Littner, 1950), with several notable exceptions (Jenkins, 1967; Jenkins and Norman, 1972), less attention has been paid to the impact of separation on the family. As stated earlier, placement is a crisis for the entire family system. Handling of the actual separation may have an important influence on the parents' ability to remain invested in or available to the child. In the words of a parent whose children were placed:

> I had already lost my husband. Now I was losing everything, my self respect, my children. I was losing myself. I felt like a piece of shit. My father had told me that I'd get no help from my family because I had disgraced them. I knew that I'd lose my financial assistance (AFDC). Something was dying in me. I wanted to kill myself. I couldn't think clearly about anything. I thought that maybe other people wanted me to kill myself. Thank God my Parents Anonymous sponsor came down to the hospital emergency room while my children were being examined and taken away. She told me I shouldn't kill myself because if I killed myself then I couldn't get my kids back. I think I probably would have done myself in if she hadn't been there to help me at a time when I lost everything.

Whenever possible the parents should be prepared for separation with anticipatory guidance. The worker can be supportive to the family by acknowledging that separation is difficult and can explore with the parents the potentially supportive people in their environment (a friend, a relative, a minister, or a PA sponsor), someone who can be with them in the difficult hours surrounding the separation. A restatement of visitation plans, and an agreed upon plan for achieving the changes needed to accomplish reunification, may provide a needed element of hope. The opportunity for the parent to provide a verbal or written message to the child about the parent's feelings and hopes about the placement may be useful to both parents and children. As the parents are assured of the agency's help in resolving the difficult situation which led to placement, so they in turn may be enabled to help their own child master the separation. The child needs to know that he is not to blame for the placement, that there is a plan for reunion, that visitation is already planned, and that he may take important reminders of home, such as a photograph or treasured object. If a preplacement contact with foster parents has occurred, some positive aspects of the placement can be pointed out by the parents in concrete detail, such as a lovable pet in the foster family or that the foster mother knows that the child's favorite food is fried chicken.

## Handling the Child and Minimizing Confusion and Trauma

A former foster child recalls:

> I was so scared when the court took me away from my family. I remember sitting in the hall of this big building, and my Grandma was crying and I didn't know what was going on. I thought I must have done something terrible in talking to that social worker and it was my fault my family was so upset. I tried to ask questions and nobody paid any attention to me. Finally somebody took me to some kind of emergency shelter. I didn't understand what it was, but I saw bars on the window and thought I was in jail for being bad. I don't know how long I was there, but it seems like years. I think maybe it was a day or two while they were finding me a foster home. But I had lost all idea of time, since I didn't know what was happening. It seemed like forever, sitting there crying and blaming myself.

If placement must occur, it should be planned carefully, and the trauma of separation minimized for both child and parent. In reality, however, abandoned children are found and wait in police stations while social workers are called; abused children are taken to hospital emergency rooms for diagnosis; children are placed in a temporary shelter facility pending location of a foster home, or children sit in the waiting room of a public welfare agency while the worker frantically makes telephone calls. In these most difficult of situations, it is imperative to remember the loneliness, confusion, self-blame, fear, or anger the children face, and to provide whatever human supports are available. The presence of a supportive adult can make a crucial impact on a child's adaptation to separation.[1]

Skilled foster parents with sensitivity to the child's needs are invaluable to the placement process. If foster parents are available to accompany the worker to the police station or hospital to pick the child up, the process of providing reassurance is accelerated and enhanced.

### Summary of Placement Practice Tasks and Principles

Inevitably some placements will be made under crisis conditions, will be hasty, and will not necessarily allow for maximum parental and foster parent self assessment and involvement. Inherent difficulties occur at every step of the process, and in many instances some tasks will not be accomplished prior to placement. Yet the assumptions and principles on which the tasks are grounded have value in directing the social worker's activity. Essentially, placement of a child is a crisis for the family system. The use of techniques of crisis intervention can mobilize the family system's adaptive capacities and promote engagement in the placement process. The placement decision is an awesome one which requires cooperation and coordination of many systems. Maximum involvement and planning by the parents enables an appropriate placement selection and reduces the trauma to the family system. Self-assessment by potential foster parents, based on provision of adequate information, and when possible personal exchange of information with the parents, facilitates the selection and placement process. A recognition of the impact of separation requires the presence of supportive persons for both child and parents. The goal of permanence should be articulated throughout the process.

## Integration of the Child in Placement

Like other families, the foster family is a boundary-maintaining system, with rules, roles, and patterned transactions. Eastman (1979) suggests that the successful foster family must both be an open system with flexible boundaries, and have sufficient role clarity to maintain the family identity and handle the separation anxiety inherent in temporary placement. Issues of inclusion and exclusion emerge within the foster family system. Is the foster child a part of the family? The statement made by more traditional foster parents, "I love all my kids [foster and biological] the same, and treat them all the same" is a denial of the differential status of the foster child. The position of the foster child is unique. The foster child brings to placement the genetic and psychological inheritance as well as the socialization of his own family, life experience different from the foster family system, and a legal status which is temporary.

Similarly, the relationship of foster parents to the foster child is different than the parenting relationship they have with their own children. They lack the years of bonding and attachment they have to their own children. While it is true that foster parents may have deep caring and commitment for the foster child, it takes time and a greater degree of permanence for attachment to develop with the foster child. Yet at the same time foster parents acknowledge the differential status and unique qualities of their relationship to the foster child, they are expected to perform all the essential nurturant roles of a parent. While they have limited responsibility for the foster child in some areas (financial support, providing consent for nonemergency medical care) foster parents have additional tasks and responsibilities in other areas (facilitating parental visitation, keeping records of the child's progress, communicating information to the agency) which exceed the tasks performed for their own children.

The relationship of the foster parents' children to the foster child is complicated, in that each time a new foster child enters the family system, the entire family's relationships, roles, and positions are realigned. The four-year-old, who may have been "the baby" of the family, is suddenly displaced by the arrival of a two-year-old foster child. A previously "uninvolved" father may develop a strong attachment to a foster child. The ten-year-old daughter who has never had to share a bedroom finds herself with a seven-year-old roommate who breaks her favorite toy. The differential application of family rules may be necessary, but is often problematic for both children and foster parents. The integration of the foster child into the family system requires a high degree of adaptation by all members of the family, especially the children.

In addition to the adaptations within the family, the relationships with community systems often change with the arrival of the foster child. The foster family may be highly active within their own church, but the foster child may be of different faith, which may mean that the foster family has to connect with a different church to arrange attendance of the foster child for religious observances. The foster parents may never have had more than routine contacts with the school their own children attend, but the arrival of the foster child necessitates a number of school conferences, planning sessions, and trouble-shooting attempts. Neighbors who have formerly been friendly and tolerant of occasional misbehavior by the foster parents' own children may react with hostility or suspicion to the escapades of the foster children. A foster child who is of a different ethnic group or social class may trigger anxiety on the part of the neighbors, while the physically or mentally handicapped foster child may elicit other concerns. The feedback received by foster parents from their immediate environment—"You must be saints, but is it true that some people are in it for the money?"—creates an uneasy double bind for the family.

Traditionally, it has been considered the role of the social worker to help the foster family through the period of adjustment and integration of the child into the family and community. However, the worker's role in a team approach to foster care is one of monitoring the placement, clarifying role expectations, and facilitating the foster family's use of more natural support networks. Foster parents have defined three such supports needed; foster parent training, foster parent associations, and a system of having experienced foster parent "buddies" or "master foster parents" who help guide them through the early apprenticeship periods of learning a new family identity and role (National Congress on Foster Family Care, Position Paper on Education and Training, 1978).

Adequate preservice foster parent training and preplacement information sharing enhance the foster family's ability to integrate the child into their home. Yet in addition to the worker's support and reassurance there is need for planning and negotiations of roles: Who will provide transportation to medical care, the agency or foster parent? Does the child's behavior indicate a need for psychological assessment? If so, will the worker or the foster parent make these arrangements? Is this child afraid of men? Then what is the most effective approach for the foster father to use? Are there no doctors in the immediate area who accept Medicaid cards? Will the worker recommend different medical personnel, or will worker and foster parent advocate jointly with local practitioners? Thus while the use of foster parent training and other foster parent support networks is promoted, it remains the worker's responsibility to clarify and negotiate tasks and responsibilities on a case-by-case basis. In this conceptualization, foster parents are viewed as direct service providers responsible for managing the period of adaptation to the new foster children with the support of the agency and other foster parents, but without quasi-therapeutic intrusion by the agency.

## Tasks of the Integration Period

ENTRY.  However well the placement process is handled, the foster child enters the foster home in a state of confusion and uncertainty, needing time and help to assimilate the change in circumstances. Sensitive foster parents contribute greatly to the child's well-being by the ways in which they handle the entry period. Rather than immediately scrubbing a dirty child and discarding his or her clothes—an important link to home—they wait until the child is comfortable before suggesting that a bath might feel good. They do not overwhelm the child with rules of the house; instead they point out a few important features such as the bathroom and refrigerator. They encourage the child to display photographs of the parents, and comment sincerely that "Mommy has pretty brown eyes like yours." They enlist the aid of their children in showing the newcomer the house and toys (Felker, 1974). They prepare a simple meal of the child's favorite food, but understand if the child does not feel like eating. At bedtime, they ask if the child would like a night light and mention that often kids wet the bed when they are first away from home, and not to worry if it happens. With a young child, they may rock the child to sleep, while with an older child they state that if the child can't sleep he may read, or wake one of the family members if she feels lonely.

INITIAL TASKS. During the first week, the foster family assesses the initial adjustment, and begins contacts and appointments with community services. An important topic to be discussed with the child is what he or she will call the foster parents. Many children are uncomfortable with calling foster parents "mom and dad" yet feel that "Mr. and Mrs. Jones" is too formal. The foster parents may suggest some options (Auntie, Mama Jones, Grandpa Charley) and help the child decide which form of address will be most comfortable at that time. Before the child encounters neighbors and enters school, it is important to help decide how to explain his status ("I'm staying with the Joneses while my mom is in the hospital," not "My mom went crazy and the police came to get me and now I'm a foster child"). The foster parents should accompany the child to initial contacts with the doctor and the school, as they, not the worker, are the current source of security for the child. In enrolling the child in school, foster parents need to be aware that educational placement testing done early in the period of separation may not be a good indicator of the child's potential performance. The foster parent needs clear guidance concerning what information should or should not be conveyed to school personnel. Similarly they must have absolute clarity from the school and agency as to which school-related parental permission forms they may sign, and which must be reserved for the signature of the biological parent.

As the foster parents observe the child during the period of adjustment, they may note behavior which conflicts with their values or rules. With the support of training and other foster parents they can understand that Johnny's hoarding of food and midnight raids on the refrigerator may represent a survival skill which was adaptive in his former environment, and does not need to be dealt with as "stealing." Their role is one of education and clarification for the child: "Johnny, in our house there is always enough to eat. You may get a snack when you need one from the bottom shelf of the refrigerator, but stay out of the other shelves. We expect you to eat at mealtime with us." Puzzling behaviors should be noted for future references, to be clarified with the help of the social worker and parents.

Arrangements should be made for the first parental visit as soon as possible; timing should vary with the needs and time sense of the child. An older child may mark the days off on a calendar, while the younger child may only realize the time has arrived when he sees his parents coming up the walk. The responsibility for scheduling and handling the first visit rests on the social worker, who should be present and make all efforts possible to insure the parents attend. Whether the initial visit is to be held at the foster home or the agency is a decision based on input from both sets of parents as to which option appears more comfortable. Whatever the setting, the foster parents and/or worker should attempt to help clarify the child's role, and the purpose of the visit. "You can serve cookies to your folks and take them to see your room. I'm sure you'll want to spend some time alone with your parents, and you should feel free to take them out in the yard. We'll need to spend some time talking with your parents too." The initial parental visit occurs before the child has learned what is expected of him by the foster parents. The child may experience confusion as to who is in charge, and which set of norms and rules to obey. It is helpful to the child if parent and foster parent explain that while the visit is in the foster home the foster parents' rules are to be obeyed, but that when he or she goes for a walk with the parents, they are in charge.

Visitation by the biological parents before the integration of the child into the foster home may escalate anxiety on the part of the foster parents. They may interpret the child's tantrum as a rejection, or as evidence of mistreatment by the parents during the visit. They may view the quiet awkwardness or belligerent questions of the parents as a personal attack on their family. If the parents fail to keep the first scheduled visit, the foster parents may overidentify with the hurt and disappointment of the child, failing to understand how difficult it is for parents to see their child under someone else's care. The worker's role is of crucial importance in facilitating the first few visits, and in providing adequate preparation of the foster parents through anticipatory guidance and training. Failure to facilitate initial visitations may result in disruption of the child's integration into the foster family, and a breakdown in the potential for foster parents and parents to work together for the child.

Long-term Tasks.    The foster parents, with the support of the worker and agency, perform roles of mediator, broker, facilitator, and advocate in behalf of the child in the community. If the child has difficulties in school, the foster parent requests tutoring. If the agency cannot pay for

Sandy's gymnastic lessons at the YWCA, the foster parents seek scholarship funds. Recognizing the child's need for peer group acceptance, the foster parent may convince the Boy Scout troop to accept its first handicapped member, or become active in Little League to insure the foster child's participation. Through participation in local foster parent association potlucks and picnics, the entire family gains new friendships. Such activities may create stress in the family as greater demands are made on resources of time and energy, but also may provide new opportunities, excitement, and an enhanced family identity.

The foster family also introduces the foster child into their own family networks, and mediates between the child and an extended circle of foster relatives. Sensitive issues must be negotiated with the extended family. If all the grandchildren get lavish Christmas presents, are the grandparents also willing to include Johnny in the gift-giving? How do the foster parents protect their biracial foster child from the well known racism of Uncle Harry? When Cousin Sally says that she wants to adopt Jimmy, what is the tactful way to explain that Jimmy already has parents? At a time when the foster family network is accessible to the foster child, and may be offering more resources to the child than he or she had at home, it becomes imperative to promote the foster child's own unique identity. The foster child may be *in* the foster family, but is not *of* it.

### Continuity of Identity

Although many workers view themselves as the guardians of the child's identity, it is actually the foster parents who deal with this critical issue on a day-to-day basis. The worker is not present when Sally cries at bedtime and says, "Why doesn't my mom want me?" or at breakfast when Jimmy states, "I have nappy hair and I don't like the way I look." The worker can prepare the foster parents to deal with such questions and can emphasize that by pointing out strengths in the biological family, the foster family can strengthen the child's self-esteem.

Ideally, foster children should be placed in a home which is ethnically like their own. If this is not feasible, the foster family can promote positive ethnic identification by serving ethnic foods, utilizing the library as a resource for ethnic literature, and pointing out role models on TV or in other media. Their efforts to keep the child involved with his or her own family or other important network figures is the clearest reinforcer of ethnic identity.

Many foster parents keep scrapbooks for the child which serve as a record of their identity and accomplishment while in care. If the child ultimately moves on to another placement or to adoption, the book becomes a transitional object which links past, present, and future (McFadden, 1975).

The genogram is also a valuable tool for enhancing the child's identity, as the worker or foster parent makes connections for the child. "You are good with your hands, just like your grandfather who was a carpenter and your dad who was a mechanic." The living relatives identified on the genogram can be encouraged to keep contact with the child through letters, cards, and gifts. When the school wants baby pictures for a special page in the yearbook, an uncle or grandparent may be able to supply the photograph. I recall the joy experienced by adolescent foster children who received family heirlooms, a handmade quilt and an old fiddle from an aging great aunt who lived half a continent away.

Completing a "Children's Eco-Map" (see Figure 22–2) enhances the child's sense of self and understanding of the current foster care situation.[2] In working with the child, the worker carefully explains that together they can make a picture of what the child's life is like now, and offers a box of crayons. The child picks a favorite color and a least favorite color. They discuss the pictures on the eco-map, and if any other pictures need to be added. As the child colors in his connections to the two homes, the courthouse, and the school, many feelings and perceptions emerge (Fahlberg, 1979). The worker's understanding of the child's perception of this situation leads to an action plan involving worker, parents, and foster parents. If the child is blaming himself for the separation, both sets of parents can provide reassurance. If the child is having difficulty in making friends or feeling uneasy with school, the support of a sympathetic teacher can be enlisted. If the child reveals that the foster family's large and energetic dog is one of the "things that bug me," steps can be taken to give the child some mastery over the dog's behavior. Just as a family eco-map can be used to assess and evaluate progress over time, the child's eco-map can reflect a changing situation. It can be constructed shortly after placement to enable adaptation to separation; a second picture can be drawn during placement to clarify the child's perceptions and needs and to assess change; and it can be used in preparation and planning for a move home to the biological family or to a permanent placement.

However, the key to the foster child's identity is the commitment to permanency by the worker. The skill with which permanency planning is implemented will determine whether the child becomes another rootless "orphan of the living" moving from placement to placement, or lives in a permanent setting where a coherent identity can flower.

## Working with the Family

Work with the family after placement includes continued assessment of the family's potential and needs, contracting within the framework of

By _____
Today _____

I am _____ years old.

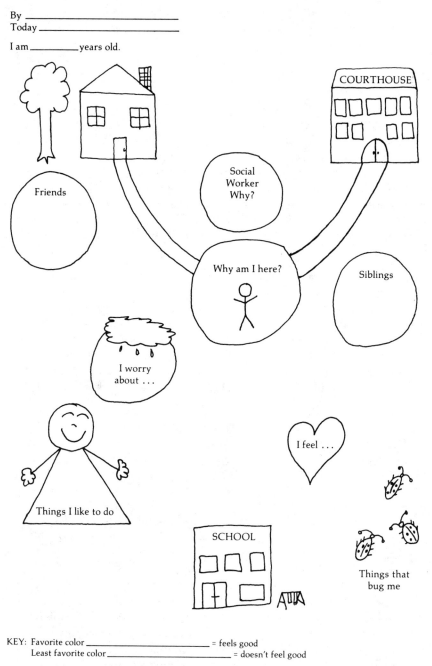

KEY:  Favorite color _____ = feels good
       Least favorite color _____ = doesn't feel good

**Figure 22–2**   Children's Eco-Map

permanency planning, assuring prompt implementation of regular parental visitation, and case management involving brokering of needed services or advocacy for the family to obtain services needed.

## Dilemmas of the Worker

The foster care worker works with a wide variety of systems, and is accountable to the agency and Permanency Planning Review system. Workers are also accountable to their own consciences and to social work ethics. The worker deals with the disintegration of other peoples' lives, the perpetual themes of separation and loss, and the urgency of children's need for permanence. Case management is a chronic juggling routine of balancing the needs of children, parents and foster families against the exigencies of recording, reporting, and coordinating services with other agencies and the chronic lack of resources. As a concerned worker stated:

> How can I contract with the father to work on employment when I know there are no jobs? How can I fully commit myself to this family when I know that within a year if things don't work I'll have to move toward termination of parental rights? Even though I believe in my head that the child should be with her family, my guts and personal values tell me that this child would have a better chance in life if she was adopted by her foster parents. My temptation is to avoid the pain and just go through the motions of working with the family. But my professional values won't allow it.

All too often the foster care worker finds that personal issues are triggered by the dynamics of certain cases. Working with the alcoholic stepfather of a foster child brings painfully vivid recollections of the worker's own alcoholic stepfather. The cheerful righteousness of a foster parent may trigger memories of the worker's own mother and the struggle of individuation from the family of origin. If the worker has handled a previous family reunification which resulted in reinjury or further neglect of the child, the worker may be immobilized when thinking of risk. The birth of a first child in the worker's family, or the transition of the worker's child to adolescence may prompt new identification or empathy with the biological or foster parents.

Faced with such professional and personal value dilemmas, the worker needs supports within the agency. Supervision must accommodate the worker's struggles with cases as well as provide administrative review of permanency plans. The agency must provide clear and explicit guidelines of policy and procedures for planning. Training should focus on needed skills and provide opportunity to integrate the assumptions of permanence within the worker's personal and professional value system. Consultation or shared decision-making must be available to help the worker at the major choice points in case management. The transition from active work with families to stagnation or termination occurs when the worker begins to feel depleted, overwhelmed, or the dilemmas become too great to handle. The success of the Alameda and Oregon permanency planning projects were based in great part on relevant worker training and coherent agency support.

## Assessment of the Family and Their Environment

If preplacement planning and involvement of the family has been carefully attended to, the task of postplacement assessment will be simplified. Just as preplacement assessment focuses on the need for placement, postplacement assessment focuses on supports and changes needed for the return of the child. The family may experience additional stresses as a result of placement: criticism by grandparents and other relatives, manifestations of the impact of filial deprivation such as conflict between parents or the temporary exit of one parent from the system, or loss of resources such as the termination of ADFC payments.

Within an ecological perspective, assessment includes identification of environmental supports and stresses, and clarification of needs, strengths, and competences of the client system. At a time when the family has experienced the crisis of dismemberment, and may have been through a court process which labeled them "unfit" or neglectful, an approach of promoting and identifying competence rather than dwelling on pathology is crucial.

The use of an eco-map promotes active parental involvement in the assessment, helps parents understand the relation of environmental stresses to their current situation, and provides a clear visualization of the need to use environmental supports. Similarly parent–worker collaboration on development of a genogram may highlight relevant family issues such as a history of family dismemberment through placement, or family strengths on which the parents can draw (Hartman, 1978; Hartman and Laird, 1983). However, within the larger ecological perspective of assessment, it is necessary to focus on specific topics of immediate relevance to family reunification and the establishment of specific goals which will facilitate the return of the child.

## Contracting for Family Reunification and Permanence

The permanency planning contract reflects the allegations in the court petition that have been adjudicated as the reasons for placement or, if the placement is voluntary, reflects mutually agreed upon concerns which led to placement. Steps in the contracting process include identification of parental objectives for a child's future, forming a problem profile, problem selection, initial specification of objectives, and the specification of mutual expectations and responsibilities between worker and client. If using a behavioral approach, additional steps, such as gathering baseline information will be employed (Gambrill and Stein, 1981). (Contracting has been elaborated upon in Chapter 14 of this volume.)

The contract clearly defines objectives, time frames, and outcomes which can be evaluated. At a minimum, it should include parental intent to work toward reunification, to maintain regular contact with the child through scheduled visits, to utilize specified services, to provide financial support of the child if indicated, and an indication of understanding that failure to meet the objectives could result in termination of parental rights. The contract also includes agency and worker activities and obligations. These may include keeping the parents informed of the child's progress, insuring regular visits, providing direct services or linking the family with other helping agencies, and meeting regularly with the parents to help in the family's rehabilitative efforts and to evaluate progress. It is signed and dated by both worker and parents.

Contracts are reviewed, renegotiated, and amended as needed. They are mutually agreed upon by clients and workers, and while not legally binding, will document the success or failure of the parent in working toward change. The contract thus provides a focus for intervention efforts and a framework for evaluation of progress.

## Parental Visitation

Visits with their children is a right retained by parents, unless the court has ordered that, for compelling reasons, there will be none. Visits are not a reward to be given for good behavior but a fundamental right of the child and parent to continue their relationship. The importance of visitation to implementation of a plan for reunification has been documented (Fanshel, 1975). The role of the worker is not one of merely allowing or arranging visits; rather it becomes one of aggressively promoting regular parent child contact. For example, following one visit

> the parents stated that they had found it so painful that they could not face the next visit. The children were looking so good, and the foster home was so much nicer than their home that they started thinking the children were better off without them. When it was time to leave the boys had tantrums. The parents tried to intervene, but the foster mother asked them to leave

quickly so she could get the children quieted down. They felt that the children were angry with them, and that visits only upset the children. The worker was able to reframe the situation for the parents, that the behavior of the boys indicated attachment to the parents and a need for continued contact. The worker arranged to accompany the parents to the next visit, and for them to discuss with the foster mother how to best handle the children's reaction to separation as the parents exited the foster home

Parental visitation may well be a barometer of progress or lack of progress in other parts of the parent's lives. The first missed visit should signal to the worker that it is time to re-explore the parent's situation and reactions to placement, and provide whatever services are needed to insure that the next visit occurs successfully. Rather than placing the burden on the parents "motivation" the worker must acknowledge the impact of filial deprivation and assess whether the parent is in an immobilized stage of the grief process or is in need of other resources, such as transportation or child care.

## Facilitating the Foster Parent–Parent Relationship

Foster parents are the best judges of whether or not they can work with families, and how much support they can provide. The foster family must maintain the boundaries of their family, integrate the child into their family system, and provide a number of direct services for the child. The task of working with the child's parents increases the demand on the system's resources. If role clarity is provided by the agency, and such supports as training are available, foster parents can do a great deal to help the family beyond the basic task of visitation. In many instances, once foster parents are acquainted with the parents they become more willing to work with the family. One of the worker's tasks is to facilitate the ongoing self-assessment of the foster parents, helping them to avoid overload or to encourage a new step with the foster child's parents.

As direct service provider to the child, the foster parents coordinate the use of resources for the child. When they involve the parents in school conferences, trips to the pediatrician or the Cub Scout picnic, they not only respect the parental status, they may also be modeling skills of interacting with community systems to a parent who has been isolated and been unable to reach out for services and planning on behalf of the child. If circumstances prevent the physical involvement of the parents in such activities, the foster parent can still reinforce the parental status through joint decision-making on purchases of clothes or asking the parent to sign the child's report card. When the reason for placement includes behavior management difficulties, the foster parent can model appropriate skills, demonstrate techniques, and provide a safe atmosphere in which the parent can practice parenting skills.

If the foster parents have sufficiently open boundaries to involve the parents in their family life, their nurturance creates a surrogate extended family support system, and eases the transition for the child when return is imminent. Inclusion of the parents in the child's birthday, graduation, or school concert enhances the child's identity and supports the importance of the parent to the child. If the foster parents have seen the parents grow in their parenting ability, and resolve the difficulties of their life situation, the foster parents will have greater confidence in the successful outcome of the reunification, and will support rather than sabotage the plan.

### Planning for Return Home

At some point during the time frame of permanency planning, the worker becomes aware that the service goals are nearly accomplished, that new support systems are in place for the family, and that the conditions of neglect specified in the court order have been eliminated or no longer present a threat to the child. Parental visitation has been held in the child's own home with a consistency and frequency indicating the parents can cope, and the children have had sufficient contact with the family to demonstrate that they can adapt to a move. Although the worker perceives that the family's situation may still be far from ideal, there has been sufficient progress to assure that the environment is a "good enough" one for the child to be without significant hazard and one where basic needs are met.

Paradoxically, once the worker is convinced that the time for return is at hand, the most difficult task may be convincing the parents that they are ready. Review and summary of progress with the parents are indicated. The use of an eco-map is helpful, particularly when the parent can compare a current eco-map with the one done at placement. This picture of the family's life situation and support systems provides a concrete way of seeing and acknowledging progress.

If the parents have had a working relationship with the foster family, they may be reluctant to give up its security, or they may feel guilty about depriving the foster family of their child. Strong support by the foster family of the plan, reassurance that the child belongs with the parents, and statements of their availability by telephone for personal contact, or as a resource for baby-sitting or brief respite will alleviate parental concern.

Similarly, the worker reassures the parent that services will continue after the child's return and that the social work relationship does not end at the time of the child's re-entry to the parental home. If such services are not available, many of the gains made through the placement and work with the family may be lost. The move back to the parental home should be facilitated with participation by foster parents and biological parents and should be handled with as much attention and sensitivity as required in any placement.

## Termination of Parental Rights

In a permanency planning model, children are not allowed to drift through years of foster care, and the preferred alternative, if return to the parents or placement within the extended family network is unworkable, is adoptive placement. Accomplishment of termination of parental rights involves a complex set of factors including statutes, legal precedent, biases or idiosyncracy of certain judges, commitment by agencies and courts to principles of permanency planning, and the skills of the social worker augmented by legal training and counsel.

### Assessment of the Need for Termination of Parental Rights

The reality that termination may be necessary is always present in the context of the worker's activities with the parents toward the goal of reunification. The existence of the option lends urgency to the massive efforts to help the parents within the first year the child is in care. However, when these efforts do not bear fruit, there are three primary sources of information in assessing whether termination of parental rights should be considered. These aspects of assessment are: parental input or behavior; reports or evaluations from other agencies; and the time frame established by the case review system.

### Parental Input or Behavior

The contract becomes the framework in which to evaluate parental behavior toward accomplishment of specific goals. The worker ascertains that specified services were provided: referral to therapy, transportation for regularly scheduled visits to the child, assistance in obtaining housing, a homemaker or classes to provide home and child management skills, and so on. Despite the services of the agency and community, and the best efforts of the worker in aggressive outreach to promote utilization of supports, the parents may have failed to utilize these services, and lack of progress becomes compellingly evident.

Through verbal statements or nonverbal behavior the parent may communicate inability to perform the tasks of parenting or unwillingness to assume the responsibility of the child. Or, when confronted with the lack of progress, parents may verbalize a desire for reunion and then disappear for a lengthy period, fail to keep appointments, withdraw from therapy, or get evicted from housing the agency had helped to obtain.

Assuming that the contract is simple, clear, and realistic, and has been reviewed periodically with the parents, the parents know what they must do to achieve reunion. Their inability to take any steps toward reunification communicates a powerful message, one that they may find difficult to verbalize.

### Reports or Evaluations from Other Helping Systems

Reports from other systems that the parent has a chronic substance abuse problem and has refused treatment or will require years of hospitalization for psychiatric treatment help tip the balance toward termination of parental rights, if a clear connection can be made between the problem and an ability to parent the child or between the problem and the neglect. Issues of mental or intellectual disability of the parent require skilled legal interpretation. Organizations such as Parents Anonymous or Alcoholics Anonymous may supply confirmation that the client attended their meetings but are reluctant to report on progress. Sometimes courts or workers hope that psychological testing or psychiatric evaluation will provide a predictive basis for decisions. However, serious question remains as to whether such evaluations can provide more than assessment of current functioning, and a treatment recommendation.

### Case Review Time Frames

Whether case review is an internal administrative function, a citizen review committee function, a full court hearing, or some combination of the three, it delineates the time parameters and is central to the permanency planning process. Although some workers may feel defensive about intrusion into case management, to others it can be a welcome support. Awareness that a review is forthcoming mobilizes the worker to seek agency supports, analyze the information gathered, and make a decision on case direction. If there is still some progress with the parents, and a reasonable prospect of reunification within the near future, the worker is not compelled to press for termination of parental rights, but must justify the delay. However, if no progress has been made, and reports from other agencies do not support a plan of return, the balance shifts to planning for termination of parental rights.

### Planning for Termination of Parental Rights

The worker needs training and legal consultation regarding the state statute under which termination of parental rights is effected. Documentation of the grounds of the petition must be amassed, witnesses must be secured, and articulation of the association between the foster care and adoption units must be facilitated. Many judges and workers are reluctant to consider termination of parental rights unless the resource of a permanent adoptive placement is available.

Furthermore, plans must be made concerning the relationship between the biological kin and the child after termination. Although traditionally termination has signalled a complete cut-off between the child and the biological family, some agencies are experimenting—particularly in the case of older children—with the selective maintenance of contact after termination and with open or semi-open adoption. Whether parental rights are terminated through an adversarial legal process or through a voluntary release, it is important to remember the needs of the parents and to insure that supports will be available at this difficult time. If parents are cooperative, they can help the child's understanding of the situation, provide for a transfer of family memorabilia, and give the child permission to attach to a new family.

The child's understanding of the termination of parental rights will depend on the situation and on information provided by the worker, foster parent and (hopefully) parent, as well as on his or her level of cognitive understanding. The child needs specific clarification that the parents are unable to provide care, that the child will not be returning home, that the good things gained from the parents will remain a part of the child, and that a permanent home will be sought.

## Other Options in Planning and Placement

In addition to the options of family reunification and adoption, less favored statuses or plans exist for foster children: planned long-term foster family care, or, for the older child, independent living. The only options for *permanence* are return to the family or adoption. The other plans involve placement within a temporary legal status that does not provide a permanent family.

Long-term foster family care is used when the child is integrated into the foster home, is not free for adoption, or does not wish to be adopted. It is often effected through contracting between the foster family, the parents (if still involved), the child, and the agency. The contracts signify the intent of all concerned to maintain the child in the foster home until the attainment of majority, and may contain specific clarification of services to be provided. Such a contract is a service agreement, and is not legally binding to parties concerned.

Foster parents may obtain guardianship of the child in a long-term care situation which enables them to sign certain additional consents for the child and may normalize the situation of the child vis à vis the community and reduce the degree of agency intrusion into the family system. Considerable controversy revolves around the use of guardianship, and, since the nature of guardianship varies from state to state, competent legal advice should be sought.

The goal of independent living for an older foster child is similar to the goal of independent living that all or most parents have for their children. The difference in independent living for foster children, and the attainment of independent living by other young adults is that it occurs somewhat earlier with foster teens than is common within broad societal norms, and that the teen on independent living status is funded by the agency and may lack the support system of a family to assist him or her in the process of becoming an independent adult.

Independent living plans are implemented after assessment of the teen's survival skills (financial management, food preparation, etc.) and environmental supports (extended family, school and employment, friends, etc.). It represents a short-term plan within the long-term goal of attainment of independent adult status. It is appropriate when used as a planful step toward maturation, and inappropriate when used as a stopgap when family or small group resources are not available.

## Foster Parent Development

A team approach to foster care practice hinges on the effective development and utilization of foster parents as a resource. The past decade has witnessed the growth of a National Foster Parent Association with regional, state and local units, numerous foster parent education or training programs, and a growing body of literature on the practice of foster parenting. As their professional capabilities increase, foster parents become specialists—for children with special types of needs or with specific age groups—as well as advocates and interpreters of the foster system. A review of innovative practice within the last decade indicates the scarcely tapped potential for agency–foster parent partnership in promoting permanence for children.

## Recruitment of Foster Homes

In recent years, several projects have used foster parents in recruiting other foster parents (Pasztor and Burgess, 1982; Pedosuk and Ratcliffe, 1979).

Not only the agents of but also the themes of recruitment are changing. "Families Helping Families" and "Help Return a Child Home" are two new slogans which reflect the goal of permanence and the redefined role of the foster parent. Agencies that place children with special needs take out classified advertisements requesting professional caregivers who will be trained and salaried. Media accounts of the problems in foster care have been balanced by articles such as "A House Full of Children is a House Full of Love" (*Family Circle*, December 1979) which portrays foster family life, the temporary nature of fostering, and the availability of training. There is no doubt that the most eloquent and realistic recruiters are foster parents who interpret their roles to the community in every facet of their day to day lives. The role of the agency recruiter is then increasingly one of identifying key foster parents who can be supported by the agency to carry their message to community and the media.

The important recruitment of minority foster homes has been furthered by the use of minority workers and foster parents in outreach. Delgado discusses the need for use of Spanish language and personal contact when working with Hispanic populations (Delgado, 1978:428).

## Education and Training of Foster Parents

The proliferation of training programs and state regulations mandating training supports the ongoing professionalization of foster parenting. Content of training generally falls within three broad classifications: role responsibilities, child development, and the care of children with special needs. Training in role responsibilities may include courses or in-service groups focused on such issues as agency policy, the team approach, communicating with other professionals, legal aspects of fostering, working with natural families, confidentiality, or planning for the child. Content on child development includes age-specific grouping and appropriate behavior management, emotional development, moral development, separation and attachment, and ethnic identity. Special needs courses may focus on broad areas—the battered and abused child, the emotionally impaired child—or on narrow issues—the drug addicted infant, nutrition for the hyperkinetic child.

Training is offered through large university-based training programs, by inclusion of foster parents in agency in-service training, and through the vehicle of local, state, regional, or national Foster Parent Association Conference workshops.

A small but significant literature on fostering has been written by foster parents for foster parents (Dickerson, 1978; Felker, 1974). Selected training materials are available in Spanish and French (Ryan, 1979). Foster parent classes have been taught in Spanish (Delgado, 1978). Literature on foster parent education stresses the importance of foster parent input (Noble and Euster, 1981); skills enrichment and empowerment (Jacobs, 1980); training in parental acceptance and child management (Guerney and Wolfgang, 1981); preventive interventions (Runyan and Fullerton, 1981) and the use of principles of adult education.

Foster care has undergone major changes in recent years. Under sharp criticism as an often unplanned service which kept children in limbo, drifting in insecure and shifting situations, foster care has been redefined as a temporary service to parents and children, a service which is integrated into an overall permanency planning initiative.

The changes in the goals and purpose of foster care have altered the roles of foster parents and workers and have pointed to creative ways in which they, along with biological parents, can work together to better serve children.

# CHAPTER 23

# Group and Institutional Care
## An Overview

James K. Whittaker

Child-caring institutions have long been and continue to be an integral part of the Child Welfare continuum of services. The structures of these residential programs vary widely, from small group homes and short-term respite care or shelter facilities to large institutions that provide long-term treatment or custodial care. They all share one feature, however—the provision of care for children with special needs on a 24-hour per day basis. This chapter will provide an overview of group child care and identify some of the most salient policy and practice issues in this area of service.

## Definition and Scope of Group Care Services

The Child Welfare League of America (1981) recognizes at least six different types of group care settings for children who are dependent and/or have behavioral or emotional difficulties. In actual practice, these services may take many forms, including: residential treatment centers, group homes, crisis and shelter care facilities, children's psychiatric facilities and respite care facilities. In many states and jurisdictions, important "child welfare" institutional services are provided under mental health, juvenile correction, and developmental disabilities auspices.

Population estimates of children in residential institutions suffer from many of the same flaws that plague Child Welfare census figures generally—the flaws that caused one expert to observe during recent congressional hearings: "We have a better count of benches in our federal parks, than we do of children in the foster care system!" Kadushin (1980) reports that in 1976 there were some 152,000 children in noncorrectional institutions, including institutions for the dependent and neglected, physically handicapped, mentally handicapped and emotionally and psychiatrically impaired. Another national study of social services to children and their families (Shyne and Shroeder, 1978a) estimated that in 1977 approximately 28 percent of the 1.8 million children receiving public Child Welfare services were in foster family or residential care placements and that, of these, nearly 79 percent were in foster family placements and the remaining 21 percent in residential institutions. This study yields a figure for child caring institutions that is apparently less than the previous two.

The incompleteness of and discrepancies in census figures for public wards in substitute child care was one of the major stimulants to the inclusion of a comprehensive inventory of children in care as one of the requirements of Public Law 96–272, discussed earlier in this volume. One can hope that as this legislation is translated into program, a truly accurate nationwide census of all children in the different kinds of public care will become available. Further, it can be expected that secondary analysis of the 1980 census data may yield an accurate count of the number of children in out-of-home care.

Not only is there uncertainty concerning the number of children in care but also, as the following definitions from the Child Welfare League of America suggest, there is considerable overlap between the various types of group care, as well as a certain lack of precision in terms of their defining characteristics and functions:

Institutional Care for Children (IC)

> To provide care and treatment for children who have behavior or emotional problems and/or parents unable to care for them adequately, and who require separation from their own homes and a group living experience. Service elements include: 1) exploration to determine appropriate service, development of a plan for service, and preparation for placement; 2) work in behalf of or directly with children and youth during placement (including provision of group living facilities and the essentials of daily living, such as meals, clothing, arrangements for education, recreation, religion, medical–dental care; child care supervision); 3) direct provision of or referral for social work, psychiatry, psychology, special education for some of the children on a selective basis, as needed; 4) work with parents while child is in placement; 5) postplacement activities during readjustment period.

(*Note:* This category includes at least two different services: "Institutional Care for Children" and "Institutional Care for Children—Treatment Oriented." The activities in behalf of or directly with children and youth during placement are essential to all services. The treatment-oriented institution can be identified by provision of all the other service elements at levels adequate to meet the needs of children with behavior or emotional problems.)

## Institutional Care for Children—Residential Treatment (RT)

To provide treatment in a group care therapeutic environment that integrates daily group living, remedial education and treatment services on the basis of an individualized plan for each child, exclusively for children with severe emotional disturbances, whose parents cannot cope with them and who cannot be effectively treated in their own homes, in another family, or in other less intensive treatment-oriented child care facilities. Service elements include: 1) study and diagnosis to determine appropriate service and to develop a treatment plan for each child; 2) work in behalf of or directly with children and youth in a therapeutic milieu during placement (including provision of group living facilities and the essentials of daily living, such as dental care, and child care supervision; 3) provision of treatment services as needed by each child (social work, psychiatry, psychology, remedial education); 4) work with parents while child is in placement; 5) postplacement activities during readjustment period.

## Group Home Service (GH)

To provide care and treatment in an agency-owned or operated facility that assures continuity of care and opportunity for community experiences, in combination with a planned group living program and specialized services, for small groups of children and youth whose parents cannot care for them adequately and who, because of their age, problems, or stage of treatment, can benefit by such a program. Service elements include: 1) exploration to determine appropriate service, development of a plan for services, and preparation for placement; 2) work in behalf of or directly with children and youth during placement (including provision of facilities and the essentials of daily living, such as meals, clothing, arrangements for education, recreation, religion, medical–dental care; child care supervision; social work, psychiatry, psychology; special education, vocational and employment counseling; 3) work with parents while child is in placement; 4) postplacement activities during readjustment period. (Child Welfare League of America, 1981: xx–xxi)

Even the implied progression of serving the most severely disturbed child in more sophisticated and restricted residential treatment centers does not properly acknowledge the reality of present practice where severely disturbed children are being treated in less restrictive, more family-oriented settings (Cherry, 1976; Dimock, 1977; Rubenstein, Armentrout, Levin, and Herald, 1978). Moreover, placing a child in residential treatment involves complex considerations of the specific case. There are no universal criteria or guidelines and, due to the diversity among institutions and their populations, the development of such universals seems unlikely (Maluccio and Marlow, 1972).

In sum, we must be wary of attempts to explain "group and institutional care" as a single entity. It is not. This segment of the Child Welfare system contains a range of different kinds of residential placements which overlap considerably in terms of definition, purpose and, quite often even the populations served.

Current practice wisdom based on clinical impressions of children coming into group care suggests more severe presenting problems than was heretofore the case. There does appear to be some empirical justification for this impression. For example, Kadushin (1980) notes that while 75 percent of children in "children's homes" were full orphans in 1923, only 8 percent fit that category in 1957. The proportion of full orphans has probably continued to shrink. The steadily declining mortality rate as well as the use of other service options such as foster placement and adoption have dramatically reduced the need for group care placements simply on the basis of the child's dependency. At the same time, the population of children referred for residential placements presents a range of complex and difficult behavioral/psychological problems. For example, Weintrob (1974) documents the shift over a brief four-year period in an adolescent treatment center to a more troubled population, to youngsters with more complex psychopathology and greater incidence of prior hospitalization. A more comprehensive study by the California Association of Services to Children of over fifty of its member agencies (Ford and Youkstetter, 1981) yields a composite picture of a child coming into care with multiple problems and, very often, a history of prior placements.

Many children entering residential placement and, in particular, those entering residential treatment, present a multiplicity of problems—interpersonal, familial, emotional, and educational. Some commonly observed problems are described below (Whittaker, 1979):

> *Poorly developed impulse control.* Numerous clinicians have noted the low tolerance for frustration and the limited ability to postpone gratification that are characteristic of many of the children who come into residential or day treatment. Disruptive outbursts at home and in school are often part of the initial reason that the child was referred for treatment. . . . Lashing out at other persons, at objects, or at themselves becomes the characteristic way for the children to deal with frustration, strain, or anxiety. In purely behavioral terms, the "aggressive child" of Fritz Redl and David Wineman possesses only a limited repertoire of responses for dealing with frustration or provocation (1957). Related to this is the apparent inability of many of these children to screen out peripheral stimuli; they are especially prone to group excitement, and the misbehavior of other children is quickly contagious.

*Low self-image.* "Bad," "evil," "stupid," "troublemaker" are all examples of the ways in which the referred child is likely to see himself. A fatalistic view of the potential for change ("It's always been this way") is supported by a string of unsuccessful experiences in school, at home, and with friends.

*Poorly developed modulation of emotion.* Many children entering institutions also lack skills for dealing appropriately and effectively with such normal emotions as anger, fear, elation, and sadness. In addition to the problem of expressing emotion congruently, they are emotionally labile and have difficulty sorting out mixed emotions, particularly anger and sadness.

*Deficiencies in forming relationships.* In the children's interpersonal relationships, the clinician sees an entire range—from the isolated autistic child who avoids even eye contact to the clinging, overpowering child who seems ready to submerge (or be submerged in) another. Some children are fearful of closeness and leery of adult relationships, whereas others regard male or female figures of authority as stereotypes. Because of their unpredictability, their proclivity to "con" and manipulate, or their tendency to overload an individual relationship with too many demands, these children frequently have few friends. In addition, they may have difficulty in joining and leaving peer groups and have trouble handling specific as opposed to diffuse relationships, as, for example, with a teacher. And, some children simply lack such social skills as small talk, which can be used to facilitate new relationships, and turn instead to disruptive, silly, or bizarre behavior as a means of handling their discomfort. For these and other reasons, such children, if they can relate to adults at all, do so in stereotyped ways. . . .

*Special learning disabilities.* As a group, most children coming into residential or day treatment present some combination of learning difficulties, the etiology of which is often unclear. For many, public school has been an essentially negative experience. In addition to their specific learning difficulties, many children lack the interpersonal skills necessary to negotiate the bureaucracy of the public school. They are thus deprived not only of the possibility of acquiring the necessary competence, but also of the positive social sanction that accompanies success in school.

Unfortunately, the educational component of residential treatment has not always kept pace with the treatment programs. Perhaps because of a presumed dichotomy between emotional problems and learning problems—which stressed a resolution of the former before addressing the latter—the educational component of many residential and day programs for troubled children has, until recently, been an underdeveloped area. Often the clinical aura extended to the classroom reaches the point of seeing personal psychoanalysis as an important part of teacher training. Supporting this line of thought is the view that most learning problems are more psychogenic than physiological in origin.

*Limited play skills.* Play is assumed by many to have an important role in social and cognitive development, and deficiencies in this area are often obvious (Whittaker, 1979, pp. 30–32). Many children have a limited repertoire of skills for playing and tend to overload one or two activities in the same way that relationships get overloaded. Some children not only have difficulty in joining and participating in group activities, they are also unable to play alone. Others have such behavioral problems as a short attention span or low tolerance for frustration that impede any sustained enjoyment of activities. Often a child's bedroom—devoid of colorful decoration, artifacts, and projects in progress—gives a clue to the deficiencies in this area.

Here, then, is a general picture of a child who, in Robert White's conceptual scheme, lacks competence and confidence in a wide variety of spheres (1960). Among the difficulties that are manifested are intrapersonal—with poor control of impulses, poorly developed modulation of emotion, incomplete personality integration, and a low self-image; interpersonal relationships with peers and adults; and environmental problems in school, play, and activities, and in manual and vocational skills.

As permanency planning efforts continue to reach children whose primary "problem" is that they are dependent, we may expect an ever increasingly difficult residual population of children and adolescents referred for group care placement—in particular, residential treatment. Such impressions are quickly confirmed by anyone presently involved in residential treatment, as well as by child welfare staff attempting to secure residential placement for some of their most difficult cases.

## A Historical Overview of Group and Institutional Care

Group child care, almost from its inception, has engendered controversy, criticism and countercriticism—much of it finding its most articulate and passionate expression in leaders of the institutional field itself. The "century-old debate" between group care and foster family care detailed by Wolins and Piliavin (1964) in the early 1960s continues today. If, as Martin Wolins (1978) suggests, attitudes toward what is the best way to care for children who must be placed away from their families predictably swing like a "pendulum" then we are, at present, on the downside regarding assessment of group child care. The milestones in the historical development of the child-caring institution are well documented: The meaning and significance of these are presently in dispute. Among the more important developments were the following:

- The Ursuline nuns establish an orphanage in New Orleans (1729) to care for children orphaned by an Indian massacre at Natchez—the first children's institution in the present boundaries of the United States (Bremner, 1970:60–61).
- House of Refuge, first institution for juvenile delinquents, is founded in New York. Similar institutions are founded in Boston (1826) and Philadelphia (1828) (Bremner, 1970:820).

- The Lyman School, first state reform school for boys is founded in Westborough, Massachusetts (1847) on the model of the German agricultural reformatory. It is not without irony that the Lyman School was also the first state training school to close in the now famous "Massachusetts experiment" in deinstitutionalization in the early 1970s (Bremner, 1970:697–711; 1974: 1084–1086, 1099).
- New York Children's Aid Society sends its first band of children to the West in 1855. What Charles Loring Brace and others saw as saving children from the evil influences of the city and congregate institutions, others—notably, the Irish Catholic community in New York, where children were most affected—saw it as a nativist plot to separate their children from their culture, family, and religion. One direct outgrowth of the placing out movement was the growth of Catholic and other denominational institutions to care for destitute, dependent, and neglected children (Bremner, 1970:669–670, 747–750).
- In the late nineteenth century the move from congregate to cottage-style institutions attempts to achieve a more "family like" atmosphere (Rothman, 1980:265–283).
- The inception and growth of the mental hygiene movement, beginning with the work of Healy in Chicago, emphasizes classification of childhood disorders, differential diagnosis, and treatment (Bremner, 1970:536–538; Whittaker, 1971b).
- Many children's institutions make a slow transition in the 1930s, 1940s, and 1950s from "care" of, essentially, "dependent children" to "residential treatment" of "emotionally disturbed" children (Bettelheim and Sylvester, 1949; Bremner, 1974:637–643; Mayer and Blum, 1971; Redl and Wineman, 1957).
- Recent "discoveries" of abuse and neglect in residential institutions for disturbed and delinquent youth are, in part, responsible for efforts to "deinstitutionalize" service programs in mental health, juvenile correction, child welfare, and mental retardation (National Commission on Children in Need of Parents, 1979; Wolfensberger, 1972; Wooden, 1976).

In a thoughtful and scholarly followup to his minor classic, *The Discovery of the Asylum* (1971), social historian David Rothman examines the institution and its alternatives during the period of progressive reforms in the late nineteenth and early twentieth centuries. He finds, essentially, an enormous gap between the rhetoric and promise of institutions and their actual practices. He concludes that their overriding purpose was (and remains) "social control" and that this fact alone, irrespective of the myriad other problems that plague institutions, precludes effective treatment or humane care. He suggests plainly that those within "the system"—juvenile judges, agency heads, Child Welfare reformers—were unwilling to subject the fruits of their reform efforts in the late nineteenth century to careful scrutiny:

> The judges were full content with their directionary authority. They could give probation to whomever they wished and they really had no quarrel with incarceration, since they could reserve it for the hardcore care. The superintendents, for their part, were not likely to lead a crusade against their own institutions. They had, perhaps, the best of both possible worlds, the justification that a treatment rhetoric provided and innumerable excuses for not delivering it.
>
> The child care agencies, too, were well contented. The public training schools took over the very cases that they wished to avoid; the institutions were their backup sanction and protection as well. (Rothman, 1980:284)

Whether one agrees or disagrees with the validity of Rothman's argument or those of other historians (see, for example, Platt, 1969), we must reluctantly conclude that it is precisely in the area of institutional care that the most egregious discrepancy is evident between the promise of the asylum to care and to treat the dependent, disturbed, or delinquent child and its actual ability to do so.

## An Overview of Outcome Research in Group and Institutional Care

The research on residential child care suffers from many of the same problems that generally plague studies in Child Welfare. A few areas are taken as examples.

> *Absence of Controls.* For ethical and practical reasons, many studies omit the use of control groups required in the classic experimental design. Although this omission leaves the interpretation of results open to question—particularly with respect to "success"—one cannot, for the sake of establishing a control group, deprive troubled children of needed care and treatment. Hence, many outcome studies have tended toward a comparison group design—testing differential approaches to residential and nonresidential treatment on a similar population of referrals.
>
> *Poorly Defined Service Units.* In such an all-encompassing service strategy as milieu treatment, it is often difficult to specify exactly what a service unit consists of and also to identify which interventions are most potent in changing behavior. While such questions are not of paramount interest to the clinician concerned primarily with positive movement in an individual case, they are of concern to executives and planners charged with the responsibility for program expansion. An often-heard refrain in the field is: "We know we are doing some things right, but we are not sure which ones."

*Improper Selection of Outcome Criteria.* All too often, residential programs have allowed themselves to be evaluated on a narrow range of criteria—grades in school, recidivism, absence of police contact—which either are not directly related to services offered or which occur in community environments where the residential program has little involvement, much less control. Such outcome studies typically show discouraging results and lead to the nihilistic conclusion that "nothing works" with these kids. The opposite problem is reflected in some outcome studies where extremely diffuse and poorly defined measures of community and personal adjustment have been used. These ratings often are based on the clinical judgment of the therapists who provided the services and are open to questions about reliability and validity.

*Sample Selection.* Troubled children and youth are seldom randomly assigned to different residential programs; instead, placement depends on such factors as severity of problem, prognosis for positive change, and available bed space. These factors may definitely bias sample selection in a number of ways. For example, some programs may engage in a "creaming-off" operation—accepting only the best-risk children—in order to positively dispose toward program successes. This problem of nonrandom assignment, particularly when coupled with the absence of a control group, can confound the interpretation of results from a program, particularly a demonstration project seeking funds for expansion on the basis of a high degree of success in the pilot phase.

*Lack of Utility.* Because many of the studies of residential child care are outcome studies, often conducted by outside researchers, many child-care practitioners doubt the value of the research enterprise and feel that its findings are of little use in shaping day-to-day practice. Almost by definition, outcome research cannot be directly useful, since it does not focus on the treatment process as it is occurring but on a "payoff" that occurs, if at all, long after children have left care. Moreover, its results are cast in terms of group data—30 percent adjusted "well," 30 percent adjusted "poorly"—and offer little to the practitioner who is looking for help and direction with an individual case. (Whittaker, 1979:187–188)

To control for some of their methodological problems, Durkin and Durkin (1975) propose a multilevel approach to evaluation in residential child care including the use of descriptive care studies, outcome and follow-up studies, process evaluation, and system analyses. Some group care models, such as the Teaching Family Model, have incorporated evaluation directly into their training procedures and operational policies so that program staff and supervisors receive continuous feedback on treatment effectiveness (Fixsen, Phillips, and Wolf, 1978). Other promising developments include the use of single case evaluation procedures (Jayaratne and Levy, 1979) and goal attainment procedures (Johnson et al., 1976). Many residential programs are now actively soliciting consumer feedback from the children, their families, referring agencies, and collateral helpers on treatment effectiveness. For example, the "Who Cares" project of the British National Children's Bureau regularly brings together children and youth in substitute care settings to elicit their views on a wide range of questions, including: which staff are most helpful to them and their degree of "connectedness" to the broader community (Page and Clark, 1977).

The following selective review of some of the major outcome studies is limited to residential treatment institutions.* Other reviews of the institutional research literature are provided by Dinnage, Pringle, and Kellmer (1967), Shyne (1973), Prosser (1976), Kadushin (1980), and, for an historical perspective, Gershenson (1956).

An early study of the effects of residential treatment took place at the Ryther Child Center in Seattle, Washington (Johnson and Reid, 1947). This study, while a classic, contains the previously mentioned weaknesses of outcome research: lack of a control group, poorly defined service units, and ambigious criteria for successful adjustment. The focus and scope of the Ryther study is clearly stated by the authors: "No effort has been made to attempt a classification of either symptomatology or etiology, but rather, to concentrate on the best question as to whether or not the children were helped" (Johnson and Reid, 1947:4). Data-gathering methods consisted of a case record analysis and follow-up reports of 339 children treated from 1936 to 1945.

Successful treatment was measured according to a child's ability to return to his or her biological or foster home with "sufficiently good adjustment," "get along" in public schools or in employment, and accept the "codes and mores of the community." In other words, children were successful if they made enough progress to be accepted in what is regarded as "normal community life in our culture as it exists today" (Johnson and Reid, 1947:8). The measure of success was divided into three categories. The measure of failure was divided into two: those who came with deep personality difficulties and made little progress in therapy and subsequently got into serious trouble, and those who made some gains in therapy while in residence but the gains were insufficient to keep them steady after discharge.

In 74.1 percent of the cases, treatment was termed "successful." There was also a significant increase (from 68.9 percent to 80.6 percent) of "success" cases during 1941–1945 versus 1936–1940. The authors state that this increase is in part due to an increased staff awareness of and ability to avoid cases likely to be "untreatable" within center functioning and facilities—in short, "selective admission."

---

*The following subsection is adapted from *Outcome Evaluation in Residential Care: A Selective North American Review* by James K. Whittaker and Peter J. Pecora (London: Community Care Publications, in press).

Only one factor, disturbances in family relationships, was correlated with child maladjustment. The authors discredit the notion that a "broken home" was a cause (85 percent of children came from broken homes). Analysis of the cases revealed a pattern of emotional disturbances prior to the actual break-up of the home and, thus, severe emotional instability was cited as the major related factor.

Unfortunately, Johnson and Reid confuse correlation with causation in their conclusion that ". . . causation of the emotional instability of the children who came to the atttention of the center lay in disturbances of the interpersonal relationship within the family group" (1947:19). Further analysis of the methodological aspects of this study is difficult due to the lack of details about measures and data collection procedures.

A second study with historical and methodological significance is the Bellefaire follow-up study (Allerhand, Weber, and Haug, 1966). A sample of fifty largely middle-class Jewish boys discharged from Bellefaire, a residential treatment center in Cleveland, Ohio, between January 1958 and June 1961 was studied in order to assess:

—postdischarge status and functioning and, in particular, *adaptation*
—whether verbal accessibility, in the researcher's opinion, a good indicator of accessibility to treatment, predicted a more successful outcome

Three concepts were central to the study:

*Adaptability*—Defined as a "state of readiness to meet demands on a selective basis."
*Adaptation*—Degree to which ". . . the individual masters external reality while achieving a sense of inner unity and continuity with society" i.e., how an individual uses his or her capacity.
*Influences on the Child*—Primarily the child's situational supports and stresses. These were judged constant at Bellefaire, but their postdischarge levels were rated.

These three concepts or measures were studied at four points in time: at 3 months and 15 months after admission, at discharge, and at 1 to 2 years after discharge.

Six major types of data were collected, connecting the three factors with the four follow-up points. These types are:

*Factual Information*—Age of child at admission and follow-up, length of institutional stay, continuation of treatment after discharge, and observable behavior in the community.
*Child Adaptability (potential for adjustment to the surrounding world)*—
At admission, this inner strength or weakness was tapped by an

"Adaptability Index," which used measures of casework accessibility, IQ and other psychometric scores. At follow-up, Adaptability was measured by an "Intrapsychic Balance Index," which used measures of self-attitudes, self-control, psychic energy, growth potential, and identity.

*Casework Variables*—Casework aims, child responses, congruence between worker and child, as well as child's accessibility to treatment.

*Situational Variables*—Predominance of stress or support in the interpersonal situation (relationships with family, other adults and peers), in the living situation (home arrangements and responsibilities) and in the cultural situation (school, work, leisure).

*Staff Evaluations*—Child's problems and progress during course of treatment (e.g., treatment plans and ratings at admission and discharge).

*Child Role Fulfillment*—Sources of this data were observed child behavior and role fulfillment as they related to familial relationships, school work, economics of living, and use of leisure.

In contrast to the Johnson and Reid research, the Bellefaire study used a large number of intricately intertwined variables and measures. One of the major findings concerned the influence of environment to which a child returned after treatment. Although the authors may downplay the dominance of postdischarge environment, degree of stress or support was a major factor affecting client adjustment and future success. Postdischarge environment interacted with Adaptability (Intrapsychic Balance Index), Adaptation (Role Fulfillment Index), Interpersonal Role Fulfillment, and Cultural Role Fulfillment.

In general, Adaptation (overall role fulfillment) improved with boys judged minimally adequate, increasing from 56 percent to 73 percent. This study provides a good illustration of one of the primary deficits of group design (masking of individual experimental effects), as there was much individual variability over time with some children improving greatly while others were deteriorating. More specifically, while children under thirteen years of age improved more, they started at lower levels of functioning and never caught up with the older children.

Adaptability measures after admission and some initial staff evaluations were related to improved adaptation at discharge. "If improved functioning at Bellefaire was the criterion, one might say the institution was having some success and that certain measures earlier in the treatment had some predictive value for who would do well" (Durkin and Durkin, 1975:287). But, as mentioned earlier, the main focus of the research and central criterion was postdischarge community adjustment. The best comment regarding this criterion is provided by the researchers themselves:

Perhaps the most striking finding of the study is that none of the measurements of within-Bellefaire performance at discharge, either in casework or in cottage and school roles, were useful in themselves in predicting postdischarge adaptability and adaptation. Only when the situation to which the child returned was taken into account were performances at Bellefaire related to postdischarge adequacies. In a stressful community situation, strengths nurtured within the institution tended to break down, whereas in a supportive situation, these strengths tended to be reinforced. (Allerhand et al., 1966:140)

In fact, Durkin and Durkin (1975) comment on how the current situation of the child does indeed relate more strongly to the dependent measures than do the Bellefaire measures discussed above. On 12 out of 15 comparisons, children who were judged "adequate at Bellefaire but stressful situation now" do more poorly than "inadequate at Bellefaire but supportive situation." Thus, apart from those cases where children were rated high on adaptability at admission, the postdischarge environment does have an important impact on their successful adjustment.

Also, Durkin and Durkin advise that one be cautious in interpreting the results of this study. Since there was no control group and none of the measures was applied before and after treatment, the study does not evaluate the impact of the Bellefaire experience. However, for all its weaknesses, the Bellefaire study yields several important findings.

1. It more firmly establishes the practice concept that programs which expose residents to more community demands (halfway experiences such as off-grounds schools or work) tend to produce children with higher levels of postdischarge adjustment.
2. "No particular impact on casework fulfillment variables was noted when a change in caseworker occurred" (Allerhand et al., 1966:140). However, what this finding may imply about *casework impact* (or lack thereof) is not clear, that is, caseworker change has no effect because casework itself is not a powerful influence.
3. Casework evaluation and prediction of later adjustment showed a more highly significant relationship with the child's level of success than did objective measuring instruments used in the study (Kadushin, 1971:59)).

Mora, Talmadge, Bryant, and Hayden (1969) conducted an evaluation of a residential center staffed in part by Catholic sisters. The average age of admission of the 126 children studied ranged from 6 to 11 years, with length of treatment averaging 30 months. Children were assigned to groups, each group under the supervision of a nun. Their treatment plan integrated a "small group approach with individual psychotherapy and specialized education" (Mora et al., 1969:586). A sample of children were independently rated on a seven-point scale by two of the center staff using information obtained directly from children, parents, and other agencies. More than half the youngsters were rated as making a good adjustment, and less than 20 percent as making a poor adjustment. The youngest group (those under 13) had the highest adjustment rating.

Analysis of an unspecified portion of the sample revealed that "the most difficult period began two years after discharge . . . and the situation did not improve until the sixth and seventh year after discharge. These years coincide with the onset and duration of adolescence" (Mora et al., 1969:587). For those boys who returned to their own homes, one hazard to good adjustment was parental pathology as measured by the Block–Behrens Scale. There was a high correlation between poor adjustment and seriously disturbed parent–child relationship.

Because more information was not given regarding rating criteria, as well as specific sampling methods, Mora's findings must be interpreted with caution. But the research spurred the institution to move to a more community-oriented model with intensive aftercare services to the children's families, more recruitment of local foster homes, and a group home program.

Taylor and Alpert (1973) were concerned with the role of environmental supports and continuity of experience and relationships as they impact children in residential care. They tested four hypotheses.

1. The greater the degree of *continuity* in the postdischarge environment, the greater the degree of the child's adaptation to the environment.
2. The greater the degree of *support* in the postdischarge environment, the greater the degree of the child's adaptation to the environment.
3. The greater the degree of *preadmission adaptation*, the greater the degree of postdischarge adaptation.
4. The greater the degree of *adaptation* gained in the institution, the greater the degree of postdischarge adaptation.

Although the Taylor and Alpert study did not have outcome evaluation as one of its major objectives, it represents a good case study on measuring the effects of residential care. The study is distinguished by a carefully chosen sample, analysis of nonrespondent characteristics, detailed specification of study objectives, and thoroughly defined measures.

Client responses to the Community Adaptation Schedule (CAS) at follow-up indicated good social adaptation in relationships to friends, work relations, peers at work and recreation, and relationships with the opposite sex. Two-thirds of the respondents fell between 4.04 and 5.06 on a 6-point scale with 6 being the highest rating. However, ratings by professionals in the child's community (in particular, social workers) reveal relatively poor adaptation (mean = 3.57). Of interest was comparison of sample CAS scores with scores of 256 "normal" young adult citizens, 66 posthospitalization psychiatric patients involved in an aftercare clinic, 54 social service professionals, 58 social service clients, and 79 "typical" acute psychiatric patients.

These results indicate that compared to "normals," discharged children were not significantly different in relation to work, social adaptation, professional community adaptation, or feelings and perceptions. However, these children were significantly *less* well adapted than "normals" in relation to behavior, family adaptation, and the larger community.

In relation to the four hypotheses stated earlier, the most conclusive result was *that family support is the single most important factor determining a child's adaptation after discharge,* which supports the researchers' second hypothesis. Moreover, continuity is not independent of family support. When children had both continuity and support, they were more likely to have a positive adaptation after residential treatment, a finding which partially supports the first hypothesis.

The third hypothesis was not supported in that preadmission characteristics (adaptation) were not significantly associated with postdischarge adaptation. The findings parallel those of the Bellefaire study, which also indicated that it "is not possible to predict a child's postdischarge adaptation on the basis of a given set of preadmission characteristics" (Taylor and Alpert, 1973:35). Of interest is that:

> [w]hether or not a family was intact at time of admission did not matter in terms of how the youngster adapted in the postdischarge environment. However . . . stability within the family provided a positive relationship with outcome. . . . This is interpreted to mean that when the child is clear regarding what is happening with his parents he has a better chance of working through his feelings regarding the separation. (Taylor and Alpert, 1973:36–37)

In relation to the fourth hypothesis (positive relationship between intrainstitutional adaptation change and degree of postdischarge adaptation), 23 of the 75 children (31%) were judged to have achieved significant change in both self-esteem and behavioral functioning. Thirty-five (47%) were rated as improved while 17 (22%) made no change or regressed. No association existed between degree of change (improvement) while in residential care and postdischarge functioning. However, attendance at an on-grounds school, parent–child contacts, and parent–staff contacts during placement were related to postdischarge adaptation.

Overall, these results provide further evidence that "social and behavioral adaptation is in large part a function of environmental situation and is *not* transferred from one dissimilar situation to another" (Taylor and Alpert, 1973:45–46). Importance of continuous family involvement prior to, during, and after treatment was also shown.

Herrera et al. (1974) conducted a long-term follow-up study of adolescents treated in an in-patient psychiatric unit. The methodology of the study was rigorous. For example:

—A uniform 10-year interval elapsed between discharge and follow-up.

—Subjects consisted of 55 adolescents admitted consecutively over a specified period of time, regardless of length of stay.

—Firsthand observations by parents, multidisciplinary staff, and relatives were acquired during all phases of treatment.

—The study was one of a series of four posthospital evaluations following the same protocol, using the same population as did follow-up studies at six months, one year, and five years.

—None of the interviewers were therapeutically involved with subjects.

Unfortunately, sample generalizability is limited because patients admitted to the unit tended to be "good teaching cases," selected for intelligence, verbal ability, and acuteness of symptoms; as opposed to chronic, deteriorated patients with evidence of organicity, retardation, or severe acting-out behavior. All but three patients were admitted directly from two-parent homes, albeit with reported intense incompatibility or reversal of "traditional" sex roles. There were also no formal after-care or rehabilitation services available to adolescents.

Ten years after discharge (subjects were 25–29), 42 percent of the cohort showed good or fair adjustment, 23 percent low-fair, and 35 percent poor adjustment. School and work were the areas of greatest improvement and strength while social relationship was consistently the area of greatest failure for the cohort.

Preadmission variables most predictive of good long-range outcome were leadership and "chumship" experiences before hospitalization, both key indicators of the ability to form relationships, and healthy parental attitudes. Degree of illness was the only therapeutic variable related to long-range outcome. Practice recommendations arising from the study data focused on the need for extensive posthospital vocational counseling/training programs and family therapy.

Another type of study, a series of follow-ups, conducted by Davids, Ryan, and Salvatore (1968) and Davids and Salvatore (1967), found that children diagnosed as "childhood schizophrenia" or "passive-aggressive personality" revealed several significant differences in presenting symptoms but very few differences on variables present during treatment or on measures of adjustment following treatment. The studies contradicted each other with the later (and larger sample) study indicating that type of child symptoms at admission was *not* a good predictor of successful long-range outcome. Success rates for both samples were near 50 percent.

The major finding of these studies is that "treatment variables, especially conventional psychotherapy, seem to bear little relationship to subsequent adjustment" (Davids, Ryan, and Salvatore, 1968:474).

The last two studies reviewed are unique in that they both use a form of single-case design (time-series) with individual children serving as their own "controls." Weininger and Brown (1972) evaluated the progress of children prior to, during, and following a child's placement. Children were randomly selected and more detailed behavioral measures were used as criteria for successful adjustment.

Length of treatment averaged 33 months and most of the sample was interviewed by their social worker two years after discharge. Findings included: (1) In the areas of work, family, social, and personal, over 80 percent of the children were making *at least* a fair adjustment, with 59 percent making an adequate adjustment; and (2) School adjustments over time (and treatment) improved. Children rated adequate to very good rose from 7 percent prior, to 71 percent during, to 70 percent two years after treatment. Weininger and Brown conclude that a child's improvement "does not appear to be due to the kind, nature and degree of psychotherapeutic involvement and treatment, as well as to the extent of prenatural family planning and interaction and 'sorting out' that takes place prior to child's return home. Perhaps these factors are more important and of greater clinical significance than the factor of symptom severity" (Weininger and Brown, 1972:14).

Nelson, Singer, and Johnson (1973; 1978) advocate use of a transactional systems model for outcome evaluation in residential child care. Their model uses a four-step method of data collection which incorporates some process evaluation components. They state: "Evaluation concerning effectiveness of treatment at every level must focus upon and show an appreciation of the network of systems from which the individual developed his particular style of life and behavior patterns" (ibid., 1978:167). The four steps and their significance for treatment evaluation are summarized below:

> *Community Baseline*—A child usually enters residential treatment from a family residence and is most often returned to the family at discharge. "Thus it is important that the child's behaviors be identified specifically in the home context, so that the residential treatment staff will have a knowledge of desired behavioral goals for the child." A school baseline is important as ". . . accurate specification of 'deviant' behaviors in relation to specific situa-

tions with significant others, including accurate specification of the current school norms and routines, would be mandatory if the child is to be reintegrated into a public school system at a later date" (ibid., 1973:951).

*Residential Baseline*—Because of the assumption that behavior is largely situationally determined, it is important to determine whether "deviant" behaviors observed in the community can be elicited in the residential setting. "If they do not occur when the child is removed from the community setting, they are inaccessible to modification outside of that setting (at least to those relying on behavioral methods of treatment)" (ibid.). A residential baseline is used to detect these discrepancies and aid in appropriate goal formulation.

*Behavior at Time of Discharge*—Child progress while in treatment should be assessed at discharge. Residential baseline, subsequent in-residence behaviors, and child behavior during the period immediately preceding discharge are compared. The purpose is to learn how many and which goals were reached by discharge and what staff inputs were necessary to do so.

*Community Follow-up*—The critical issue at this point relates to how well the child has been reintegrated into the community situation. This was measured by determining the number of goals maintained at follow-up.

The authors believe that a simple goal attainment model is not sufficient:

> One must learn more about a child's style of interacting within each setting, with any alteration in the pattern being a measurable outcome of the intervention. . . . Clearly, goals are important in measuring treatment progress; but a series of goals, interrelated and accounting for the total target system, is necessary to generalize the treatment gains beyond a residential or treatment center. (Ibid., 1978:166)

Results indicated that the cottage treatment program was successful in achieving 83 percent (97 out of 116) of prestated goals (frequently goal areas included: peer relations, school performance, compliance, and behavioral aggression).

Of interest are the differences between those children who had a support system (home, school, or other environmental structure which assists the child in maintaining community-defined acceptable behaviors) with those who did not. Although the sample size is exceedingly small (22), it is noteworthy that children who were part of some supportive system maintained 71 percent of their goals after discharge compared to the nonsupport group's 50 percent maintenance rate.

In summary, outcome studies of the effects of residential treatment on children's later adjustment tend to be equivocal since the situations are so complex and the interacting variables so numerous. However, a review of such studies does reveal some significant trends.

The most powerful determining factor of the child's postdischarge adjustment is the nature of the postdischarge environment. Central in this environment is, most generally, the family. Thus the extent of family support and the nature of familial relationships are crucial variables.

Further, in light of this powerful factor, other factors such as preadmission characteristics, characteristics measured while in residence, and specific treatment interventions are not strongly associated with postdischarge adjustment. These findings point to the importance of planning residential care within a continuum of services to families and children.

## Group Child Care as Part of the Service Continuum

If residential child care is not a panacea for the problems of troubled and troublesome children, it is clear that we have, and will continue to have, a need for some services away from the child's family of origin. However, residential institutions must not be considered an "end of the line" alternative, but a viable part of the overall service continuum in Child Welfare.

Foster family care, home-based intervention, adoption, and other child services or service strategies, have their limitations as well. Our present task is to work toward a time when group care services will be seen as part of an integrated continuum of care beginning with preclusive prevention, extending through a whole range of family-centered, home-based options and ending with secure treatment institutions for those few children who need them. It has been suggested elsewhere that what we need in Child Welfare is a continuum of care that "softens" the distinction between residential and nonresidential options (Small and Whittaker, 1979). Most certainly, such a continuum would include foster care, respite care, shelter care, day treatment and crisis services along with a variety of residential options integrated within the community. The key objective in developing a service plan for any particular child would not center on whether he or she remained at home or was placed, but instead would focus on how the elements in the total environment could be mobilized into a powerful force for change.

## Ecological Factors and Group Child Care

As the outcome research so clearly indicates "success" in residential care, however defined, is largely a function of the supports available in the posttreatment community environment and has much less to do with either presenting problem or type of treatment offered. Consequently, what has come to be known as the "ecological perspective" has profound implications for residential children's services. It encourages us to view the residential environment as the complex interplay of many different elements both within and outside of the formal service context. Notable here is the quality of the links between the residential program and the family, the neighborhood, the peer group, the world of work, and other potential sources of support in the community environment. The previously mentioned "Massachusetts experiment" in deinstitutionalization highlighted the importance of these community links which interact with the formal service program (Coates, Ohlin, and Miller, 1978). For social workers one potential implication of this trend in residential care is that they will be spending less time in direct treatment of children and more time working with and through the environment particularly in creating and maintaining social support networks for the children and their families (Whittaker, 1979; Whittaker and Garbarino, 1984).

## Parents as Partners in Residential Care

If the residential center is to be seen as a temporary support for families in crises, rather than as a substitute for families who have failed, it must engage families as full and equal partners in the helping process. Traditionally, for a variety of reasons, parents have been kept at arm's length from the process of treatment in institutional settings. In their *Challenge of Partnership*, Maluccio and Sinanoglu (1981) document ways in which parents of children in foster and residential care can assume a meaningful role in helping. These include: parenting education, family support groups, family participation in the life space of the residential institution, and family therapy. As in adoption and foster family care, the enormous helping potential of parents has only barely been tapped.

## Cost of Residential Care

Though accurate comparative data are not easily obtained, many residential treatment centers cost in excess of $25,000–$50,000 per child per year (Wolins, 1978). Though heavily subsidized from public funds, many private residential care facilities operate at a deficit. Therapeutic group home services are typically less expensive than residential treatment centers and both pale before residential "training" schools for juvenile offenders which, along with children's psychiatric inpatient units, average the highest costs of care. For example, while Wolin's summary of cost in residential care shows wide variation, the most expensive facility by far was a "secure detention" institution averaging nearly $3,500 per month per child (1975 figures) (Wolins, 1978:101). Some states and local communities struggling with shrinking service budgets are attempting to put a cap on the number of beds available for residential placement and to strictly monitor their use.

In conclusion, group child care has always been and continues to be an important Child Welfare service. However, a reformulation of the basic tenets of Child Welfare practice is leading to a reconceptualization of group care for children. Primarily, such care is incrasingly being seen in a variety of forms and as a part of an integrated continuum of services available to families and children: services focused on the support and maintenance of the family, on the temporary placement of children in times of crisis or breakdown, and in the long run on the support and enhancement of the family's ability to provide care.

# CHAPTER 24

# Adoption
## History, Policy, and Program

ELIZABETH S. COLE

Adoption is a process that allows for the transfer of the legal rights, responsibilities, and privileges of parenting from legal parents to new legal parents. Most often adoption is from the biological parents to someone new. The practice of adoption has changed profoundly over the last twenty years and more alterations are coming. Understanding what has happened and predicting what may occur in the future requires that we step back and look at adoption in an historical context. Like all social institutions it reflects the predominant needs, values, and conflicts of the times. Moral views have influenced it more than any pragmatic considerations (Benet, 1976:13).

## The History of Adoption

Perhaps the oldest of Child Welfare services, adoptions are recorded in the Bible.[1] Moses was adopted by Pharaoh's daughter. Later the Greeks and Romans adopted to provide heirs and to secure alliances with more powerful families. Many Chinese and Hindus adopted for religious reasons: having a male heir to pray for you insured the benefits of heaven (Hastings, 1908). In agricultural societies and newly industrial countries, adults often adopted children to secure more hands for work. A common thread running through the practice of adoption was that its prime purpose was to serve adults; children were to become the central consideration only after the industrial revolution (Presser, 1972:448).

Adoption is not mentioned in English Common Law, on which American legal systems are based. The English resisted the notion that one could leave property to anyone other than a blood heir. Adoption was repugnant to the English concept of inheritance. It was not until 1929 that their first adoption law was passed, and 1950 that adoptees were allowed to inherit from their adoptive parents (Witmer, 1963).

In England and America, dependent and neglected children were cared for in almshouses. Later they were apprenticed or indentured. These child care alternatives were used here until the mid-nineteenth century when immigration swelled our child population and other solutions were sought. Social workers in our eastern cities believed that children could be saved from the perils of street life and profligate parents by placing them in foster or adoptive homes in the Midwest and West (Brace, 1859).

Aside from apprenticeship and indenture, people commonly obtained custody of children related and not related to them by informal verbal or written agreements. New parents wishing to insure that these children would be their heirs and could not be reclaimed by their birth parents were not satisfied with the lack of safeguards. Indenture of their new children was a fiction. Private bills were introduced into state legislatures calling for recognition of particular adoptions.[2] The evolution of adoption laws would seem to be a natural outgrowth of the former unsatisfactory methods of handling child custody cases (Whitmore, 1876). Because there was no tradition to look to in English Common Law, each state needed to pass an adoption statute: Massachusetts passed the first law in 1851; the last was passed in 1929.

The content of state laws varied. The Massachusetts statute was comprehensive, requiring assurances that the rights and needs of biological parents, children, and adoptive parents would be met. Some states merely reworded deeds for the transfer of property to allow for the transfer of children. Others simply required that the adoption be recorded. The later laws and the case opinions interpreting them expressed the idea that the child's welfare was to be the primary consideration in adoption (Klibanoff and Klibanoff, 1973). The courts were to determine if biological parents made free consent to the adoption and whether prospective adoptive parents were suitable. Over time, the courts delegated more and more of their investigative and evaluative functions to state welfare departments and also accepted the reports of licensed child-placing agencies which may have arranged the adoption.

Adoptions can be accomplished legally in two ways: private agreements sanctioned by the court, or those arranged by licensed child-placing agencies. Today, 45 states allow for both kinds of adoption. Five states—Delaware, Connecticut, Michigan, Minnesota, and Massachusetts—allow the courts to legalize only those adoptions arranged or approved by licensed child-placing agencies. Whether this method should be a model for all states is a hotly contested issue which will be discussed later.

American adoption was not created to solve the stigma and burden of an out-of-wedlock pregnancy. Nor was it intended to ease the pain of infertility by providing children for infertile couples.[3] That adoption practices did both was merely a fortuitous side effect of the primary purpose of adoption: to provide children with nurturant environments in the care of legally recognized parents whose custody, control, responsibilities, and rights were assured.

Early adoption laws were steps in the evolution of the doctrine of *parens patriae*—that the state is the parent of all children and has a right to intervene in matters concerning them. Now a fairly commonly accepted principle, it is a radical departure from previously held beliefs that children were the property of their parents, to be disposed of as they wished.

While the state's intervention into family functions is now generally accepted, little else about this concept is agreed upon. What circumstances should trigger the state's entry into the family? How must they intervene? What are the limits of intervention? These are disputed questions, central to many modern day adoption issues. We will see these issues emerge in discussions of independent versus agency adoptions, birth parents' and adoptive parents' rights, and adult adoptee access to sealed adoption records.

In contrast, there is wide agreement on a logical set of values and principles which underpin the state's interest in adoption. As a society we believe that our future is inextricably linked to the well-being of our children. One way to produce adequate adults is to provide for their good development as children. This can be accomplished if children receive nurturance in a stable family environment, one which provides continuity of care. While the family into which a child is born is usually the best to perform this function, not all parents are willing or able to perform their functions and responsibilities. At the same time, other adults are willing to take and rear children not born to them. Adoption, therefore, became the legally sanctioned transaction for transferring parenting rights and responsibilities.

It is interesting to note how closely the modern Child Welfare League of America's adoption standards parallel these values:

1. All children regardless of their age, sex, race, physical, intellectual or emotional status are entitled to a continuous nurturant environment.

2. For most children, the biological family, in its broadest definition, provides the best environment for this nurturance.
3. When a child's birth family is not willing or able to nurture him or her, the child is entitled to timely placement with a family who will.
4. For most children, adoption provides this family better than any other type of substitute parenting.
5. Adoption is a means of finding families for children, not finding children for families. The emphasis is on the child's needs. (CWLA Standards for Adoption Service, 1978)

The first hundred years of modern adoption policy and practice show that these principles have often been ignored.

## Modern Adoption—A Radically Changed and Changing Service

Recent writings on social services to families urge that professionals take an "ecological view of families" (Laird, 1979). In this view, families are seen as moving in a larger environment which affects how they function. It is important to be able to look at all of Child Welfare services in the same way. The remarkable alterations in adoption services are due to the massive political, social, and moral changes which occurred in the late 1960s and 1970s. These changes gave way to the following trends which have had the most significant effect on adoption policy and practice.

*The "Rights Movements."* Efforts were made by groups to define and obtain civil, political, and legal rights they believed they had been denied them. Most notable of the groups seeking rights were blacks, Hispanics, American Indians, women, and children. The elderly sought to have their rights and entitlements defined and expanded. Attention was given to patients in mental hospitals and residents in institutions for the mentally retarded to insure that their rights were explained and protected.

*Consumerism.* The demand on the part of the consumer of goods and services for quality products, safety of products, and truth in the description of products extended also to the social services arena. The requirement that the purveyors of goods and services in our society be more attentive to the needs, wants, demands, and complaints of consumers was a significant accomplishment of the 1960s and 1970s, and consumers also requested and obtained permission to serve on the governing bodies of social institutions.

*Restrictions on State Intervention.* Concern was focused over seemingly unwarranted interference of the state, county, and local governments and their agents into the lives of individuals and families. The doctrine of minimal interference was articulated. Applied to the family, the doctrine of minimal State interference says: (1) families are entitled to raise children as they think best, free from State interference; (2) the State or its agencies may interfere in the life of families only with serious justification; and (3) the State's intervention must be minimal and restricted to only that amount needed to redress the reasons for the intervention.

*Freedom of Information.* The legacy of Watergate, Vietnam, and a series of assorted exposés about government cover-ups resulted in citizens demanding openness, honesty, and truth. These qualities, desired in personal relationships, were demanded in relationships with institutions and organizations which governed and/or served citizens. During this period the presumption was that organizations could not be trusted to tell the truth. It was also felt these institutions possessed a great deal of information about individuals which the individual had a right to know. The result of these concerns was an emphasis in practice, in law, and in regulation placed on rights of individuals to know what information an organization had about them, to establish under freedom of information acts the right to obtain this information. But in the larger sense, the overall requirement was renewed expectation that the essential quality of the dealings between individuals and organizations would be of a high standard of integrity, honesty, and openness.

*Changes in Family Structure.* In no other period of time in American history has the family undergone such radical changes. The dramatic increase in divorce and remarriage has led to more stepparent relationships and a corresponding increase in the number of single-parent households. Unrelated single parents are pooling households to increase the efficiency and effectiveness of raising children and to reduce the overhead costs. Also, currently the age of couples seeking to marry and to bear children is on the rise. Demographers predict an increase in all these trends.[4]

*Women in the Work Force.* More and more women are working outside the home which is resulting in less time for parenting and delegation of some of the parenting functions to child care, day-care centers, or other arrangements.

*Changes in Sexual Mores.* Americans have reduced or in some instances eliminated the stigma attached to out-of-wedlock sexual activity and pregnancy.

*Increased Emphasis on Fathers.* As a result of the prevalance of women in the work force, the increase in divorce, and changing ideas of men's and women's roles in parenting, there is an upswing in the number of single male–headed families and in the involvement of the father in nurturing and parenting tasks traditionally assigned to the mother.

How these trends have affected adoption services becomes apparent as we look at the roles of the key actors in the adoption process—the children, the parents (biological and adoptive), the intermediaries (agency and independent), and the State (legislature and courts).

## The Children

Complete or up-to-date statistical information on the children who have been placed for adoption in the United States are not available. What facts and figures are we using in the meantime? With all their statistical limitations, the current reports seem to support conventional practice wisdom.

The most recent figures gathered from 42 states and jurisdictions are reported in DHEW's *Adoption in 1975*. Alaska, Arizona, Colorado, Guam, Idaho, Illinois, Mississippi, Montana, North Carolina, Oregon, Rhode Island, and the Virgin Islands did not report. Figures for Nebraska and South Carolina were incomplete and considered not usable. With these limitations, the report goes on to show:

- In 1975, adoption petitions were granted for 104,188 children;
- 62 percent (or 64,000) of the children were related to the petitioner (stepparent adoptions therefore account for the largest single group of adoptions in the U.S.);
- 36 percent (or 37,000) of the children were unrelated to their adopters;
- In 2 percent of the cases the relationship was unknown;
- 77 percent of all non-relative adoptions were arranged by agencies. (This contradicts the notion that the majority of non-related adoptions are arranged by private intermediaries.);
- 63 percent of all non-relative adoptions involved children under one year old, 25 percent of the youngsters were between one and six; 10 percent between six and twelve; 2 percent were twelve and over (adoption still is a service for babies and very young children);
- 72 percent of all non-relative adoptions involved white children, 11 percent were of black children, 17 percent of other races;
- Only 563 handicapped children are reported to have been placed in non-relative adoptions.

Although we know a good deal about the children who *were* placed in 1975, there is no usable information about the larger population of children for whom families were needed at the time. Such information *does* exist for 1978, enabling a better assessment of the current situation. Meezan comments:

> Projections from the *National Survey of Public Social Services for Children and Their Families* estimate that there are currently 102,000 children legally free for adoption services. Of the 97,000 on whom data is available, 62% are

white, 28% are black, 3% are Hispanic and 7% belong to other ethnic groups including Native American and Asian. The median age of these children is over 7 years. Nine percent are under 1 year old, while 31% are between 1 and 6 years old. Fully 40% are over the age of 11. (1980:5)

Both reports point to the kind of children who need to be placed: 28 percent of all children needing adoptive families are black. In 1975, only 11 percent of the children placed by agencies were black or other minorities (Meezan, 1980:4). Strides may have been made in the intervening three years but the gap between what minority children need and what they receive is still large. Over 40 percent of all children needing families are over age eleven. Only 2 percent of all children placed in 1975 in unrelated families were over twelve. Special efforts must be undertaken to find families for this group of youngsters.

One can see from the statistical picture drawn of adoption practice that infants and preschool age children are readily placed by most adoption agencies, including children of all races. Practice experience shows that at least ten to fifteen couples are waiting to adopt for every available baby. The average waiting period is from two to five years.

That all children who need adoptive homes are not in them represents an inability to implement one or more of the steps in the adoption process fully.

### Steps in the Adoption Process

At each one of these steps clusters of policy, practice, and legal issues need to be resolved, and none of these tasks is performed as it was ten to fifteen years ago.

1. Identification of suitable children
2. Freeing for placement
3. Preparation for adoption
4. Selection of adoptive parents
5. Placement with adoptive family
6. Postplacement services
7. Legal finalization of the adoption
8. Postadoption services to the adoptee

IDENTIFICATION. The first step in the process is to insure that every child who needs an adoptive family is identified. One's idea of who is or is not adoptable determines which children are selected or eliminated from consideration. On what basis is this critical decision made? Few children other than problem-free white infants or toddlers were classified as adoptable until the 1960s.

Public attitudes toward adoption have never been entirely positive

(Kirk, 1964). Illegitimacy and a fear of bringing "bad blood" into the family caused doubt about the benefits of adoption. Early findings from psychological testing fed into the belief that defective parents breed defective children. Agencies developed a "blue ribbon" certification of the adoptable child in order to sell adoption.

> Agencies were convinced and attempted to convince the public that they could gurantee them a perfect child; that by coming to an agency, adoptive parents could be sure that the child was without physical, emotional or mental defect; that his heredity was sound and that adopting a child was a far less risky procedure than having one normally. (Reid, 1963:30)

The adoptive parent and children's rights advocacy movement of the late 1960s and 1970s began to challenge agencies. They contended that no child was unadoptable, eventually changing the professional norm to consider older children as adoptable. But this norm, while clearly articulated, is not accepted and practiced everywhere. Identifying worker attitudes about which children are or are not adoptable and correcting them through training and supervision is a significant practice issue. Meanwhile, advocates have encouraged several strategies to press agencies to consider all children. The most significant include:

1. internal case audits and reviews by third parties to examine individual case goals
2. publication of a comparison of agency performance in the adoptive placement of children by the children's characteristics, such as age, race, or handicap
3. witholding funding of foster care programs unless the agency has a pro-active adoption program for all children or links with a pro-active program
4. tightening of licensing requirements for agencies insuring that all types of children are served
5. legal suits against agencies for failure to place all kinds of children in adoptive families

All these activities add up to an affirmation of the principle that adoption is a service for all children, a positive outcome of the last decade's changes. The challenge of the coming years is to keep the focus on this group of children with special needs for attention and action. Communities wanting adequate adoption services need to provide resources equally to those groups serving children with special needs and those serving infants.

FREEING CHILDREN FOR PLACEMENT. Freeing children for placement has two significant aspects: helping children separate from former parents or parent figures, and to attach to new parents; legally terminating parental rights so that they can be vested in another parent or parents.

Separate representation for children in termination cases is a very important concept, which has developed over the past twenty years. In the past, the child's parents and any agency subsequently caring for the child were presumed always to speak in the child's interest. We now believe that this may not necessarily be so. Children appearing in court actions involving themselves or their interests may now have their own counsel and/or separate guardian *ad-litem*. This change is a major one for society's belief that both the parent and the agency will always act in the child's best interest. The principle of separate and equal representation by counsel for children seems firmly fixed. That the child has his own voice in matters affecting him is a newly developed principle which will continue to shape termination and adoption proceedings. How this should be done and who will pay for it are questions which each jurisdiction will face (English, 1981).

Significant issues for children regarding preparation, selection of parents, placement, postplacement, and legal finalization are practice issues and center around how children are involved in each step. A central legal and policy issue is whether or not children should consent to their own adoption, and if so at what age? Should their views be binding on the court, or merely advisory? State practice varies. Some statutes are silent on the issue. Some mark the age at which consent is required at ten, others at twelve or fourteen. Keeping the child's consent nonbinding on the court seems to be the wisest choice. Children are often ambivalent and anxious about important decisions. It should be necessary to solicit their opinions in every case, but the court then needs to weigh the child's wishes with all the other facts and recommendations in making its decision.

Whether or not the state makes an adoption subsidy available to all of its children who need it is another major issue for a very important reason. Adoption subsidy is a resource for children, not for adoptive parents. A subsidy is any financial assistance which goes beyond the legal finalization of adoption. It is designed to be an incentive to the adoption of special needs children, including those who are older, handicapped, or minority. While all states except Hawaii have some form of financial assistance available, most programs are flawed in some aspect. The following is a brief checklist of common problems.

1. Not all children who need subsidy are eligible.
2. The amount of subsidy is less than the foster family board payment.
3. Financial means tests are imposed against adoptive parents.
4. The subsidy is not transferrable should the adoptive parents die.
5. The subsidy cannot be continued if child and family move to another state.

6. Foster parents who are prospective adopters do not know about subsidy or how to obtain it.
7. The administrative process is often cumbersome and takes too much time.

Yet for all the flaws, there is convincing evidence that adoption subsidies are extraordinarily helpful in the placement of special needs children. They are also cost effective. The cost savings among state programs ranged from a low of 19 percent to a high of 60 percent with an average of some 37 percent (Cole, 1981). It is clear that each state should have the most effective and comprehensive program it can.

## Disruption

Many older, handicapped, or emotionally bruised children, as well as others with no ostensible problems, will be placed for adoption but not legally finalized with their first adoptive family. In the past, this process was referred to as adoption failure. Today, the word "disruption" is more commonly used. The change in terms reflects a deliberate removal of the notion of blame or stigma from any one of the parties. It is also meant to reflect the principle that multiple placements before legal finalization may be the norm for some children rather than the exception (Donley, 1975).

Learning how deal with disruption is a significant practice issue. The policy implications include: the need for the agency to reduce their expectation that the first will be the lasting placement; the elimination of the assignment of blame; the need to produce more support resources to child and family; and the need to help staff shoulder the risk involved in these placements.

## Postadoption Services

*Adoptive families need to be free of the agency as soon as possible so that they can function as independently as any other family.* This was a common goal of adoption agencies until well into the 1960s. Recognition that many children being placed will need continued professional help has changed this belief. Some families will need only an occasional educative session, others need more traditional ongoing therapy. In still other families, the child may need a brief or extended stay in a residential treatment setting. Children and their families often need help with information about the child's background or with becoming comfortable with the whole notion of adoption. Adoption services no longer stop on the steps of the court house, but extend on a continuum as long as they are needed. This extension has led to the single most controversial adoption issue today: What should be the nature of service to adult adoptees?

## Adult Adoptees

The central question regarding services to adult adoptees is whether or under what circumstances to allow them information about the identities of their biological families. Adoption in Western society has taken on secrecy as one of its aspects. An English jurist said that the legal process draws "a veil between the past and present lives of adopted persons and makes it as opaque and impenetrable as possible; like the veil which God has placed between the living and the dead" (*Lawson v. Registrar General*, 106 L.J. 204, 1956). This practice is unlike Asian and Polynesian traditions where people more openly arranged transfer of parenting. It is clearly not true in the case of the adoption of older children, who often know names, addresses, and telephone numbers of biological parents and relatives. In the case of foster parent adoption, biological parents may have visited the home, and contact has been known to continue after the adoption.

Secrecy has been the rule in most of the infant adoptions arranged by agencies over the past several decades. It has been the practice of agencies and courts to give adult adoptees varying amounts of nonidentifying background information.

Several trends of the 1960s have joined to create a climate where the challenge to the secrecy structure is now possible. First, the stigma against out-of-wedlock pregnancy has relaxed. Second, there is a general societal move to see openness as better than secrecy. "Sunshine" and "open records" laws have increased a citizen's access to all kinds of records kept about him or her by organizations. Third, the rise of consumerism has fostered adult adoptee organizations which articulate their point of view as recipients of service. Fourth, there is skepticism about the appropriateness for the State to intervene in private issues regarding adults.

Courts and agencies are being asked to decide whether adults adopted as infants have the right to identifying information on their biological parents contained in the original birth certificate, sealed court records, or agency adoption records. The issue is complex. Most statutes give the court the power to open these records for "good cause"— generally interpreted to be a reason connected with a serious threat to physical or emotional well-being of the adoptee. The following are some of the stated justifications for keeping records sealed.

- Sealed records protect adopted children from the stigma of their adopted status; they also protect adopted children who were born to unmarried parents from the stigma of illegitimacy.
- Sealed records protect the adoptive family from future intrusion into their lives by the birth parents; they help insulate the adoptive parents from fears that the child they have raised as their own might transfer his affections and loyalty to his birth parents at a later date.
- Sealed records protect the birth parents from future intrusion into their lives by the adopted child. Many children adopted years ago were children of unwed teenage mothers who later married without telling their husbands of their secret past. Since these women relied on the promises of sealed records, to be suddenly confronted with the appearance of an adopted child would be severely disruptive.
- If birth parents know that the records will not be confidential, they will be discouraged from placing a child for adoption that they would otherwise do with the assurance that records will be sealed forever. (American Civil Liberties Union, 1979:5)

Recently each one of these assumptions has come under attack by birth parents and adult adoptees. They hold that while these assumptions have merit, they can no longer be held to be universally true. Israel and Great Britain have laws which *do* give adult adoptees access to their original birth certificate as do the states of Kansas, Alabama, and Pennsylvania. Their experience shows that the dire consequences predicted as a result of giving information has not occurred.[5]

Adult adoptees acknowledge that their request for identifying information poses a conflict of rights with the biological parents who may explicitly or implicitly have been offered confidentiality from agencies and courts. They believe that their right to the information is paramount for the following reasons:

1. Adoption laws have traditionally held that where there are issues of conflicting rights in adoption they should be settled based on what is in the child's best interests. This principle establishes the adopted person's rights as superior, and carries into the adopted person's adulthood.
2. Every human being has the moral right to know his or her genetic relatives. While circumstances may conspire to prevent many nonadopted people from having this information, it does not abrogate their right to seek and find what exists, should they choose to. Adoptees, by extension, should have the same right.
3. Depriving adult adoptees of birth records and information which other adult citizens may have as a matter of right raises a serious equal protection of the law issue (ACLU, 1979).

Other arguments are also advanced. The continuation of sealed records perpetuates the stigma associated with adoption. Some groups contend that closing records connotes something sordid to be hidden and breeds distrust. Can one violate the birth parents' right to privacy? Is the adoptees' wish for information superior, equal, or inferior to the birth parents' right to privacy? While the issue can be seen as a struggle for rights and human needs, it is also one of shifting or at least equalizing power. In the past, almost all court conflicts over information have been settled in favor of the adoptive or birth parents (Harrington, 1980:29).

Having a registry where birth parents can signify consent to the information has been seen as an attempt to put parents and adoptees at parity. Some insist that adoptive parents must also consent, regardless of the adoptee's age. But all adoptees do not agree and see this as acknowledgement of the superiority of birth and adoptive parents' rights because they are given veto power. They argue that if the adopted child's best interests are paramount during childhood, why are they not paramount when he or she is an adult?

How we choose to answer these questions will fundamentally alter the way adoption will be practiced in the coming years.

## The Biological Parents

Who are the parents of children placed for adoption? Biological parents of children placed for adoption may be categorized into two groups: those who freely consent to the placement, and those who did not wish to consent but were overruled by a court of law. Until recently, most attention has been given to the first group of parents.

### Parents Who Voluntarily Place

Until the 1960s adoption was represented by society as the ideal solution for an illegitimate pregnancy, when the option of marriage of the parents was not possible. Even the term "illegitimate" is value-laden; it means unlawful, both in the moral and legal sense. Children were considered "bastards," a word of unquestionable opprobrium (Dewar, 1969). In many jurisdictions their birth certificates were a different color and their mothers were considered sexually promiscuous—tainted. Their future career and marriage prospects were dim if the fact of the birth were to be made public. Abortion was a legally limited option and had minimal public acceptance. Paradoxically, although all these factors were present in our society, the majority of single parents *never* placed their children for adoption: It has *never* been the parents' preferred option (Kadushin, 1980:441).

Since 1959, the shifts in sexual mores, women's rights, and consumerism have further affected the choice of adoption. Access to contraceptives and abortion has come with expanding women's rights, as have mobility and access to the job market. It is now easier for a young woman to leave home and find a job, while the availability of welfare benefits gives today's mother more options. The stigma of being an unmarried parent has lessened as more and more children are being raised by divorced parents. The single unmarried parent does not stand out in today's community as he or she once did.

While it is easy to recognize that there have always been pressures for unmarried parents to place their children, there are corresponding values which mitigate it. Our society holds that mothers who carry and bear children must want to raise them. A "mystical" bond exists between mother and child. While we recognize the major sacrifice made by many mothers who place their children, it is still seen as an act which goes against nature. What this construct fails to recognize is that there are parents who choose to give birth to a child rather than abort, but do not wish to parent. In the past they could mask this decision with the more unselfish, socially acceptable motive of providing the child with a better family. This may no longer be true.

At a recent conference of pregnancy counselors a great deal of discussion occurred concerning the fact that many current teenagers receive pressure from their peers not to give up their child, as the giving up is "unnatural." It was felt that this was particularly true in those cultural groups where there is a tradition of kinship networks helping raise and support the nuclear family (blacks, Indians, some Hispanics). This trend will increase as minority groups continue to reaffirm their cultural values. It places today's teenage parent in the maelstrom of this cross-current of values and is a perplexing problem as the evidence supports the fact that the teenage mother and her child will, in all likelihood, be at high risk of being medically, educationally, and emotionally disadvantaged (Moore, Hofferth, and Worthheimer, 1979).

## Unmarried Fathers

If it is unnatural for an unmarried mother to want to give up her child, our society apparently still believes it is more unnatural for an unmarried father to want to parent it. In an era of rising entitlements and equal rights the putative father's situation remains an anachronism. Recent American court decisions have held that under certain circumstances putative fathers have some right to be notified of an adoption plan. However, which putative fathers, and under what circumstances, remains unclear and muddled.[6]

Courts and agencies have viewed putative fathers as peripheral; until 1972, it was generally believed that they had no rights at all. Attempts to accord putative fathers with rights have been met by a variety of responses. Some feel we should not reward the unmarried father with rights—he is not worthy. Others feel it is the due acknowledgement of his civil rights and a way to make him responsible for his sexual activity.

Professional social workers express some of the strongest negative opinions about putative fathers. One of the most unpopular provisions of a model adoption law attempted by the Department of Health and Human Services was one that would have reinforced putative fathers' rights to custody. Many agency respondents objected to this move and described putative fathers as unworthy of consideration as parents, characterizing them as "rapists," involved in incestuous relationships," "being rewarded for one-night flings," "callous and uncaring."

Available research on the unmarried father is summarized by Kadushin (1980a) and indicates that these negative attitudes are not borne out by the facts. Most pregnancies are not the result of rape or incest. Researchers have found that the father is not unlike the mother in age and socioeconomic background, and the relationship has generally been of some duration preceeding the pregnancy. Those few agencies serving fathers have described them as concerned and wanting to be of help.

Other factors do come into play. The inconvenience of finding the father and the inconvenience he may bring to the decision-making process also add to the list of agency reasons for avoiding him (Barber, 1975). Whether the policy to avoid dealing with fathers stems from negative attitudes toward them or the purest desire to expedite the adoptive placement of a child, the result may deprive fathers of their legal rights and allow them to escape their moral responsibility for sexual activity.

All of these questions appear to rise out of the equal rights movements and the evolution of an enhanced fathering role for men. Has the responsibility fallen unfairly to the woman in the past? Is it possible for a man who has fathered a child in the most casual of sexual encounters to want to take and raise that child if the mother does not wish to? Is it unnatural for a single male to want to nurture a child? Should the presumption in law and in fact be that he is unfit until he proves otherwise, or that he is fit until proven otherwise? Are there two classes of putative fathers; those deserving consideration as fathers and those who do not? If so, how do they differ? The law does not judge the fitness of the mother by the circumstances of the conception but rather by her capacity to parent. Should the standard be the same for men?

Essentially, these questions acknowledge that our values about the responsibility for sexual activity and the role of fathers, especially single fathers, are changing, and clearly the direction of the expansion is toward according the fathers rights and recognizing their responsibilities. It also seems that because of the sharp difference of opinions more legal clashes between unmarried parents, as well as between agencies and fathers, are inevitable.

## Parents Who Do Not Consent to Their Children's Adoption

As the supply of readily adoptable infants decreased, attention turned to other children in foster care to determine whether adoption would be the best plan although most of these children had not come into care for adoption purposes. In their study, Jenkins and Norman (1972) characterized the biological parents of children in care as having the problem leading to the child's being placed; in few cases did the child's behavior precipitate the move. They point out that the parents tend to be single women—a high proportion from minority groups—with a problem (mental illness, alcoholism, drug abuse, lack of employment) and without a strong support group of extended family or friends. Also, these mothers are generally poor.

The issue with parents of children in foster care is that they have not resumed parenting and have left their children too long in care, raising the need for a planned, permanent family through adoption. The consumer and civil rights movement of the 60s led to more and better legal representation for biological parents, and courts now agree that parents have a right to treatment for their socioeconomic and individual problems. Furthermore, Child Welfare agencies have been criticized because they represent themselves as offering services to parents, holding forth to the community that foster care is only temporary while the biological family is being rebuilt. When no service is given to the parents, agencies are guilty of misrepresentation at the very least.

The political question raised regarding the parents of children in care is whether they are being treated fairly. Should they, the holders of the presenting problem, receive a degree of help at least equal to that given the child and the child's foster parents? Should they be able to receive the same financial and medical benefits received by the foster parents for the child's upkeep? Are they being discriminated against becuase they are women and of minority race? Parents' advocates argue that society does not value these parents as much as the middle class adopters and foster parents (deLone, 1978; Glasser, 1978).

The direction for the future seems to be that more time, energy, and attention will be focused on the parents, with an aim toward preventing the family crises which create the initial separation, or in supporting the family in crisis.

## Termination of Parental Rights

Voluntary termination of parental rights, once viewed as a relatively simple process, is now a thicket of issues and problems. Courts now require evidence that parents know what they are doing and give informed consent, free of fraud or duress. Written records detailing what is said are more important and need to be drawn carefully. There is some support for having all consents or surrenders of custody either taken in court or having a court subsequently approve them. The debate centers on whether the surrender or release for adoption should be irrevocable once signed or if there should be a period where a parent may change his or her mind. If there is a grace period, how long should it be in order to be consistent with parents' rights and yet allow early and secure placement of the child?

As we have discussed, the question of which putative fathers have what rights adds to the muddle. In general, agencies feel that the putative father must be notified of the adoption plan. Then he may either acknowledge or deny paternity. If he acknowledges, he may consent to the adoption or bring forward his own plan, which must be considered.

Here there is a head-on collision between conflicting values of two professions, law and social work, since these notification procedures take a great deal of time. Social workers believe it is in a baby's or toddler's best interest to effect a speedy adoption placement and to spare the child as many moves as possible. Courts believe a person is entitled to due process regardless of how much time it takes to satisfy it.

The resolution of this conflict appears to be emerging in favor of speedier due process. In recommending that courts consider termination proceedings like other emergency cases, Goldstein, Freud, and Solnit (1973) say that procedural and substantive decisions should never exceed the time the child to be placed can endure loss and uncertainty.

## Involuntary Termination of Parental Rights

Involuntary termination of parental rights cases may be divided into two types—contested and uncontested. Uncontested cases are those in which an agency or individual brings a termination or guardianship transfer action where parents have consented, or are incapable of consent (those who are grossly retarded, psychotic, or in a comatose state). The latter cases generally hinge on a determination of parental fitness based on expert witness testimony. Parents are not always represented by counsel or a guardian *ad litem*, who would protect their interests.

There is growing concern about this lack of counsel, with the idea of the routine appointment of a guardian *ad litem* gaining support. Over the next several years this practice should become common.

Most termination cases are contested and commonly involve charges against the parent of abuse or neglect, desertion or abandonment, or a combination of these. Although actions may be brought against parents whose children are residing with them, they are more frequently brought by agencies on behalf of children in foster care.

## Issues in Contested Cases

Several key issues will have to be resolved over the next decade. The first legal question deals with the right to counsel. Parents have been and are being brought to court without legal representation, which is then sometimes ordered by the judge. Not infrequently parents represent themselves and are disadvantaged from the outset. Agencies should urge the courts to see that all parents are adequately represented, both on principle and to protect against later reversal of rulings.

The second major legal issue has to do with the vagueness of the termination statutes. Questions have been raised about their unconstitutionality. Specific problems have to do with the definition of such conditions as "neglect" or "deprivation," which are often the basis of charges brought against parents. If definitions are too vague, the charges are subjectively assessed and difficult to prove.

A parent's right to treatment will become a sharper issue over the next several years. Judges are reluctant to terminate parental rights in cases where the parents have sought but not received help from an agency. They are deferring decisions and ordering agencies to provide the needed help for a stated time to see if this assistance makes a difference. What becomes clear is that, although the relationship between biological parents and the agency is really a contract, the terms are not defined so that each party fully understands and agrees to them. In the absence of a written and understood contract, both parties may misunderstand the other's role. It also becomes impossible for third parties (in these cases, the courts) to sort out who promised to do what, to or for whom, and if there was a breach of the treatment agreement. In a growing number of cases, foster care agencies cannot demonstrate to the court's satisfaction that enough time and effort are spent working with the biological parents of the children in care. Judges characterize workers' contact with parents as sporadic, superficial, and lacking in direction.

## The Role of the Biological Parents after Termination of Rights

It has been customary for the biological parents to have little or no contact with the agency and child after legal rights have been terminated, either voluntarily or involuntarily. This is no longer always true; we should expect a different and continuing role for parents.

First, more adopted children are seeking their biological parents who are unknown to them, signaling that biological parents should know that this is a possibility at the time they surrender the child. Second, more older children, being placed for adoption with foster parents or others, know who and where their biological parents are. In many cases the parents continue contact with the child.

Third, the concept of more openness in adoption is being explored. Biological parents may select adoptive parents from agency studies. They may sometimes meet (with true identities hidden or, in some cases, revealed). They may agree to exchange information either through the agency or directly. At the very least, there is an acceptance of the need for biological parents to keep the agency informed of medical conditions which may affect the child.

Fourth, agencies may be asked to recontact biological parents to determine if they are willing to take back their child after a reasonable time, if the agency has been unable to find an adoptive family. This provision was recently made law in Great Britain. Also, since parents will grieve and mourn the loss of their children, even infants they have barely known, some will need our professional help with this for some time after termination.

## The Adopters

The modern view of adoption as a service to children has farreaching consequences. This child-centered definition rightfully places adopters in the role of resources—much valued, but nevertheless, resources. As a consequence, no person has the *right* to adopt. They have the right to apply, to be fairly considered, but in the end the choice of who will parent must be based on the needs of the children who need placement. As one colleague put it, "adoption workers are in distribution, not manufacturing."

### The Infertile Adopter

A surplus of prospective adoptive parents exists for healthy infants and preschool children. Some agencies estimate having or being able to obtain fifteen to twenty families for each white infant available. This surplus results in: (1) a delay in the time it takes between application and placement (two to five years), (2) a dim chance that a second or third child will be placed with the same family, and (3) the prospect for some couples that a child will never be placed.

The parent surplus accutely affects middle-class couples who have taken on new work and marriage patterns. Changing sexual mores result in young people deferring marriage until an older age. More wives work, pregnancies are deferred, and couples may be in their late twenties or early thirties before an infertility problem is detected.[7] More and more couples may be coming to adoption agencies dangerously close to the age limit (35 to 40) set by agencies for infant adopters.

This parent surplus affects infant placing agencies in other critical ways. The climate of demand makes it easy to identify with the distraught prospective adoptive parents: Agencies soon come to see their major function as finding babies for childless couples. In the popular press and recent Congressional testimony agency executives describe their inability to meet the demand for children by prospective adoptive parents as "the major crisis in adoption today."[8] If one sees finding families for children as the main goal then there is no crisis in infant adoption. Pressure to find children for parents can dangerously skew the way we perceive and offer help to unmarried parents in reaching the important decisions surrounding an out-of-wedlock pregnancy.

Agencies find themselves having to choose from among a number of applicants one family who will get the baby. When the selector has established that all of the applicants are believed to be able to meet the child's basic needs, what criteria are used to decide who will parent? Certainly some personality, temperament, and genetic factors are considered that might rule out certain applicants in making a selection. But even when this has been done, how then are the choices made? Enough practice wisdom and research suggests that a subjective model of "goodness" is employed, one that reflects ourselves or those we aspire to be most like or wish we had as parents (Bradly, 1966). In choosing adoptive parents for a healthy baby with average to above average intellectual potential, how many would opt for the doctor, lawyer, or teacher over the common laborer? Does providing for "the child's best interest" mean placing him in the highest social class? Does it mean seeing that once the parents have established their maturity and emotional eligibility, and can provide economically, that class should not be an important factor?

Some research points out that class expectation factors work to insure that those couples considered "marginal" in education, employment, and personal strengths are often only considered for "marginal" children (those who are disabled or deficient in some way)

(Kadushin, 1962). Current data suggests that this may be due to agency selections rather than the couples' choice. In a study of the adoption of developmentally disabled children, Coyne (1981) noted that in agencies which selected the parents for these children there tended to be a high proportion of blue-collar or working-class parents. In contrast, those agencies which had a high degree of parent participation in the selection had a broader cross section of all classes choosing to adopt disabled children.[9] Should the selection of parents for children be more egalitarian? These value issues need clarification.

## Intercountry Adoptions

Middle-class adopters have other options. They can adopt children from other countries. The expense of these adoptions is high because of the cost of transportation and the fees of the several organizations which may be involved.

The concept of intercountry adoptions is controversial. It illustrates how the same action can be characterized as laudable or deplorable. Adopters may choose this route because they want to parent and there are not enough very young children available for adoption. Many are motivated by the knowledge that not only do other countries have children who need families but that the lives of these children are in jeopardy because of war and poverty; placement is needed to save the child's life. Asian children fathered by Western servicemen often suffer discrimination. Intercountry adoption is seen as a way to rescue these children from that jeopardy.

Not everyone shares these values. Some see what may essentially be a humanitarian effort as class, race, and national exploitation. The countries supplying the children are often wartorn and poor. Most are Third World countries. As Benet says: "But all the expertise and good will of the intercountry adopter will go for naught if their efforts are taken to be yet another form of imperialism, which is increasingly how they are seen by many of the countries whose children have been adopted abroad" (1976: 135). In some instances, attempts have been made by international agencies to solve such political issues by helping to build up a nation's own social service system so that children may find parents in their own country.

Intercountry adoptions increased from slightly over 1,000 in 1964 to 5,000 in 1978,[10] resulting in strained resources for administrators already hard pressed to deliver Child Welfare services in their own states and counties. It is on the administrative level that the real battle will be enjoined. As administrators have less staff and resources, they must find ways to deal with increased demand from adoptive parents for costly intercountry services. Charging a fee for the service might make providing it financially possible. Also, public agencies might consider using part-time employees to provide studies and supervision.

## Interracial Adoptions

Interracial adoption reflects the same tension between humanitarian and exploitative motives. The positions on both sides of this issue are much the same as they are in intercountry adoptions which include many interracial placements, although current research efforts do not support this conclusion (Fanshel, 1972; Grow and Shapiro, 1977). Opponents of interracial placements believe that white parents cannot properly prepare their minority children to cope with an essentially racist society. Furthermore, there is no need to place children across racial lines since there are a sufficient number of minority homes if agencies would look for and recruit them in an appropriate manner (Jones, 1972).

The growth of the civil rights movement has strengthened minority organizations and created an advocacy network. Increased pride in one's race and roots is also contributing to strong efforts to keep children within their racial and ethnic communities. As a result it is likely that the number of transracial placements will decrease.

## The Foster Parent as Adopter

Keeping children with people who are their psychological parents is a cardinal Child Welfare principle often applied to protective service cases. However, it may be ignored when foster parents seek to adopt. Conflicting policies and practices around foster parent adoptions have been brought to light by the focus on placement of older children. Adoption subsidy legislation now encourages foster parents, who in the past could not afford it, to pursue adoption. The conflict generally centers on five major issues:

1. *Foster parents aren't as "good" prospective parents as many waiting applicants.* Foster parents tend to be older and less affluent or less educated than waiting adoptive applicants. Their weaknesses are well known to the agency. Agencies believe that they must select the "best" possible family and this obligates them to select a "better" one if they have it. While the premise may be correct, the conclusion is wrong. If the child has strong ties to a family, the criterion for removal must never be "Is there a better family?" but rather "Will the child be harmed by remaining here?" The same criteria used to justify removal in a biolog-

ical family situation must be applied to foster homes. Foster parents are also entitled to help and support services.

2. *If we allow foster parent to adopt we will lose them as foster parents.* This notion speaks to the policy some agencies have of removing all other foster children from the home when a child is adopted. In contrast, some agencies have never removed the other children and believe this is the less troublesome solution in the long run.

3. *The foster family cannot function without our help and support.* Many foster families rely on the lifeline which they have to the agency. Their need for help is real. But in many cases we overfunction for foster parents and imagine that they need that much help, and/or that we in fact actually do supply it, even when caseworker visits are infrequent. Adequate postadoption services open to all adoptive families may make it possible for foster parents who adopt to get the help they need.

4. *It costs local government more to allow foster parents to adopt with subsidy than to allow them to retain a child in foster care.* The federal government pays one-half the cost of the Aid to Dependent Children Foster Care program with the state and local government providing the other half. When the child is adopted with a subsidy, the state and local governments pick up 100 percent of the cost. The lack of federal financial participation serves as a deterrent to foster parent adoption as local departments may leave these children where they are and use limited subsidy money for those children who need to be moved.[11]

5. *A liberal foster parent adoption program will encourage eager adoptive applicants to become foster parents and seek back-door adoption.* This problem is very real. The solution begins with the identification of those parents who really want to adopt. My own review of 600 cases where foster parent applicants desired adoption revealed that most of these would have been identifiable; for example, they were childless, or they had children of one sex and were specifically requesting a child of the other sex. When such families are identified and their wishes openly discussed, agencies can help them pursue adoptive possibilities, using them for older children (teenagers), who will never be free for adoption, or placing with them a child who does or may shortly need an adoptive placement, such as a youngster who has been in an institution. Agencies then can help create a planned foster parent adoption.

There are practice problems with foster parent adoptions. First, workers need help in exploring the foster parents as potential adopters. It is not helpful to ingore them, or on the other extreme, to coerce them to adopt. Second, foster families need help with the transition from fostering to adoption. They must deal with many of the same issues as all adopters. The family's receipt of an adoption subsidy may compound the need for the child to be sure he knows what this change in status means. Agencies are best served by a policy which: (1) allows and encourages foster parents to adopt, (2) provides an orientation and training program for foster parents which equals that of adoptive parents, and (3) capitalizes on the potential adopter within each foster parent by using him or her as a placement for special needs children.

## The Fertile Adopter

The belief that adoption is for the childless has changed over the past twenty years. In the 1960s, prompted by a concern for population growth, a desire for large families, a social consciousness, and a conscience about children who needed parents, fertile adopters came forward. They expressed interest in parenting older, minority, or handicapped children.

Social workers find, prepare, and serve adoptive parents for special needs children much differently from the way they work with infant adopters. Recruitment is assertive and is often focused on specific children rather than groups of children. The current assessment process puts worker and parent on more equal footing rather than the superior–subordinate relationship characterizing traditional practice. Further, seeing adoptive parents as capable of making major decisions for themselves has also led workers to involve them more in the selection of the child and in the recruitment and preparation of other parents and their support after placement.

While making adoptive parents agency partners is a sound concept, it is not yet practiced everywhere. A number of serious administrative barriers, which agencies identify, prevent us from utilizing the potential adoptive parents in our communities.

- A lack of adoption services. Some counties have no adoption services at all. Others restrict home studies only for their county's own children and will not do one for a family interested in a child from another county or state.
- Fee charging. Some agencies still charge fees even to parents interested in special needs children.
- Postadoptive services. These services are often nonexistent or do not meet the particular needs of the adoptive parents.
- Respite care. Care is not always available as are other supportive services for families.
- Subsidies. Subsidy assistance is not guaranteed for the child's minority as funds must be appropriated each year.
- Travel money. Monies are not readily available if potential parents must go a distance to meet with the agency or visit with a child.
- Services to minority adoptive parents. These services are lacking or faulty. Agencies do not have sufficient minority staff or staff

knowledgeable about cultural differences. Minority parents are not recruited or are not retained.

Difficult economic times discourage people from adopting. They worry about taking on more responsibility. Adoptive parent resources for children with special needs will become scarce in the future. Professionals will need to be as creative and perceptive as possible to identify all possible deterrents to adoption and ways to remove them.

## Single-Parent Adoptions

Adoption substitutes a new family for the one the child was born into. In arriving at a model of which families to use, individual workers and agencies generally use as a norm the two-parent family. Single parents tend to be considered only for those children for whom a two-parent family is not available. Yet, it seems unlikely that adoption agencies will choose single applicants for readily placeable infants and toddlers, although many children placed with couples will be raised by single parents as a result of divorce.

Agencies are becoming more accepting of using singles for children with special needs. The agency with the longest experience and largest number of single adoptive parents is the Los Angeles County Department of Adoptions. They believe that a single parent may be the best choice for certain children whose problems and needs preclude a two-parent family. This move signals the movement of single-parent adoption from last choice resource to a preferred status for some children. Also, in their study, Shireman and Johnson (1976) found single adopters to be faring well with their children.

As single parenthood becomes more accepted in American society so will single-parent adoptions. At present singles are still underutilized by agencies, who continue to be overly suspicious of the pathological aspects of their motivation and overly cautious about their ability to parent. This appears to be another area in which professional practice needs to keep pace with changing community lifestyles.

## Independent Adoptions

Independent adoptions are those in which adoption is planned and implemented without participation of an organized social agency. There are four types of independent adoption: relative adoptions; direct placements; intermediary—not for profit; intermediary—for profit.

The largest single category of adoption in America is *relative adoption*. Most frequently these involve a stepparent who adopts a spouse's child. The continued increase in divorce and remarriage can only result in an increase in stepparent adoptions, and in turn, this practice should have serious implications for new directions in service and policy. These new families can use help in dealing with problems of blending children, grandparents and ex-spouses. The second category of independent adoptions is that of *direct placement* made by the legal parent(s) to someone known to them.

The third category of independent adoption is *intermediary—not for profit*. This may or may not involve payment of the mother's expenses. In such placements, the biological parent and the prospective adoptive parents are usually strangers. Dealings between them are handled by the intermediary. Such placements are different from direct placements in that biological and prospective parents are not known to each other. The fourth category of independent adoption is *intermediary—for profit*. Here, the intermediary usually charges what the traffic will bear.

Relative adoptions are legal in all states. Direct and intermediary— not for profit—placements are permitted in forty-six states and the District of Columbia. In Connecticut, Massachusetts, Minnesota, Delaware, and Michigan, only licensed agencies may place or approve adoption placements. Intermediary—for profit—adoptions are illegal in every jurisdiction. While there is general agreement that such adoptions are wrong, there is no such accord on how to deal with them. Some professionals in this field advocate outlawing all independent adoptions, arguing that no adoption should be a private matter. Others disagree. They believe illegal adoption will not be eliminated but driven farther underground. They point out that research into independent adoption does not reveal problems serious enough to outlaw it (Meezan et al., 1978; Whitmer, 1968). Their case rests primarily on the principle that outlawing private choice of prospective parents is a drastic remedy—a notion that is not supported by the evidence.

It would appear that one might provide the necessary regulation and preserve free choice. The major problem with current investigations of independent adoptions is that they happen after the child is placed— often too late to undo a poor situation. What is needed is a procedure that allows biological parents wishing to do so to choose the prospective adoptive parent. As soon as the decision is made, the court is notified. This would happen before the birth of the child. The court orders a licensed adoption agency to see the biological parents and determine if they have made free and informed consent and have been counseled on their alternatives, and to see the prospective adoptive parents to determine their fitness as parents. The child may be placed only after the court is satisfied on these questions. Under this procedure the child would become a ward of the court. Parental rights would be terminated. The court would order a period of supervision by a licensed agency and issue a final adoption decree when satisfied as to the suitability of the placement. This procedure would in fact insure that every placement would be agency approved, yet maintain the parents' right to choose in those cases where they wish to exercise this right.

The problem of adoptions arranged by a profit-making intermediary might be reduced if the following occurred.

1. Courts required a detailed statement of all monies which changed hands relating to the adoption.
2. Violators were vigorously prosecuted.
3. Sanctions were severe (fines, imprisonment, loss of professional licensure).
4. The community gave enough money to adoption agencies so they could provide biological parents the same level of medical care and maintenance which baby brokers can offer them.

## The Adoption Agency

In the 1970s birth parents, adoptees, and adoptive parents had their rights clarified and gained power in decision-making. As clients' power increased, the agency's necessarily diminished. Parents and children share in case decisions and participate in making policy and evaluating procedures. Prospective adoptive parents share with the worker the responsibility for assessing their own parenting potential and selecting the child suitable for them. Adoptees challenge the agency's right to conceal and control information.

This sharing of power is hailed by some agencies and feared by others. Those who embrace it see it as an expression of our belief that the dignity and well-being of the clients dictates that they make decisions about themselves. Others see it as a shameful capitulation to attacks on the rightful professional authority of agencies.

### Agency Practice and Policy

The current practice of adoption requires a different kind of staff, deployed and supported in nontraditional ways. Workers need knowledge and skill in dealing with minority, older, seriously disturbed, developmentally delayed children. Some staff, specializing in infant adoption, may never have done work with older children. They will need training and experience or will need to be assisted by others who do have needed knowledge and skills. Minority staff needs to be increased. All staff need better knowledge of the differences between cultural and ethnic groups if they are to serve them effectively.

Grouping workers into teams helps to reduce the stress and strain of difficult cases and increase knowledge and skills needed to help a particular family. Another plus would be flexible hours and work weeks permitting families to receive service when they need it and not only at times convenient to the agency. Specialized adoption caseloads are often preferred over generic ones, since they provide workers with an opportunity for in-depth knowledge and experience while at the same time protecting them from being diverted to other crisis cases.

Also, interagency cooperation is increasingly important as we share families and children. Shared decision-making creates conditions when conflict will be inevitable even where the best of working relationships exist. Therefore, formalized interagency arbitration procedures will need to be created.

Agencies need to have a clearer adoption mission statement enumerating the principles quoted from the Child Welfare League Standards. They need clear statements of position on at least these topics: which children are adoptable, which parents are eligible, the process by which parents and children come together and are served after adoption, access to information in agency records, formal and fiscal relationships to other agencies within and without the state and country, and the appeal process for clients and other agencies. Often it is not a clearly spelled out "no" in agency policy which inhibits workers from pro-actively engaging in adoption practice, but rather the absence of a "yes."

## Agency Funding

Both public and private agencies alike will have less money to serve more people. Cost efficiency will be necessary for survival, and adoption is the most cost effective of all Child Welfare services. Public agencies have become more sophisticated in using this knowledge in pleading for a larger appropriation.

Voluntary agencies also have critical funding problems. Most of their revenue comes from donations, United Way or Community Chest funds, fees for service, and purchase-of-service fees from governmental agencies. Donations fall off as the economy worsens and the United Way has steadily been cutting back their support of Child Welfare services in general and adoption services in particular. While fee charging has enabled agencies over the years to fund a large part of the cost of their adoption services, this practice has created a dilemma. Community funding sources see adoption as a service to adoptive parents and expect them to pay for it. As costs increase and available children become fewer or more difficult to place, fees cannot begin to cover the costs. If, as current philosophy espouses, adoption is a service to the child like any other Child Welfare service, why should we charge parents a fee? In return for getting the community to pay a higher portion of the service cost, agencies may need to abandon fee charging.

Whenever a voluntary agency performs a service for the public agency they should be reimbursed the full cost of the service. The absence of purchase-of-service procedures stands as one of the major obstacles to greater interagency cooperation and results in the needless expenditure of tax dollars for the foster care placement of children who might otherwise be placed in adoptive families.

Balancing the contending needs and rights of the parties in the adoption equation is difficult. Social workers in the coming years must exercise leadership in this delicate political process and reweave connections between warring groups. We will need to replace malfunctioning processes with new and better systems. Conceptual leadership will be required to do this. Today's and tomorrow's leaders must have the intellectual clarity and courage to look at changing values and square them with professional beliefs.

Our society does value being raised by the family of birth. In their study on foster care, Fanshel and Shinn compare not having a family to other evils which can befall a child—poverty and racism. They conclude:

> But the crowning insult . . . one that goes beyond all of these in its power to debase the human spirit—is for a child to be born without parents who are willing to take care of him. Being cared for in one's own family by one's own parent is a fundamental and almost universal fact of life in almost all societies. It is taken for granted by most Americans. For a child to find himself bereft of parental care is a condition so different from the nearly universal status of other children as to mark those so afflicted as abnormal in a most profound way. (1978:2–3)

The primacy of the biological family casts a shadow on all those forms of care which would substitute for it. While adoption most resembles the family of origin even it is not totally accepted (Kirk, 1964). However, accepting that varying degrees of stigma are attached to the child raised by other than his or her family does not constitute a case to discontinue these other forms of care. It is necessary to have a full continuum of services to meet the varied needs of children. Accepting the principle that systems of care should, as closely as possible, resemble the biological family does provide a rationale for why some forms of substitute care are valued over others. It points to how important it is to answer the central practice question: How does one choose the most appropriate alternative for each child?

# CHAPTER 25

# Practice in Adoption

ANN HARTMAN

The field of Child Welfare has undergone enormous change in the past decade, but perhaps no area has been more radically altered than adoption. Adoption has been transformed from a program to find parents for healthy infants and infants for childless couples to one that seeks permanent homes for every child. As part of the permanency movement, which was sparked by many converging influences, the position was taken that *every* child is entitled to a permanent home. The first choice is with biological parents or other kin and the second, if placement with family is impossible, is adoption. Such a goal has changed the face of adoption and altered practice at every step of the process.

Traditional adoption has been shaped by the conviction that adoption should, in every way possible, be modeled after biological parenting. This position has been embraced by adoptive workers and adoptive parents alike, and buttressed by the law, which has sealed birth certificates and adoption records, cutting off the child's past as if he or she were born the day of the adoptive placement. The impact of this conception of adoption on practice has been farreaching. First, until the 1970's, only young, healthy children were considered "adoptable." In fact, the process of delaying adoption while children remained in "infant study homes" until they were old enough to be judged free of any mental or physical defect meant that adoption did not even hold the risks of biological parenting.

Second, just as adoptable children have conformed to a norm, so have adoptive parents, and until the last ten years or so, home studies have been, for the most part, careful investigations which measured families against subjective, culturally biased norms. These norms changed over the years, reflecting the changing value systems of the larger culture. In general, however, couples have been required to be young, physically healthy, white, middle-class, infertile, childless, active in church, financially stable, and in their first marriages. Psychological evaluation of husband and wife and an assessment of the quality of the marriage has also been an important part of the home study. Some agencies went so far as to utilize projective psychological testing in their evaluations. Many adoptive families who have experienced this kind of home study process remember it with considerable pain and anxiety. The power differential between the couple and the agency has been enormous and the stakes for both high.

The attempt to submerge the differences between adoption and birthing also led to careful matching of the child to the parents in terms of physical, intellectual, and even some social characteristics. Further, in wanting to simulate birth, the agency has removed itself from the life of the family as soon as possible, as its presence would always be a reminder of how the baby had arrived. Postadoption services generally have not been provided. If adoption is exactly like birthing a child, there is no special reason for help following placement. Also, if the new parents were having trouble, the evaluative and judgmental stance of the home study has precluded their turning to the agency for such help.

In general, the failure to recognize the differences between building a family through adoption and building it biologically, as with any denial or distortion of reality, left those involved in the situation with considerable burden. Unmarried mothers have reported that they were reassured by their workers that they would "forget"; in fact, of course, they did not. When adult adoptees expressed interest in or curiosity about their roots to adoption agencies, it was often treated as a sign of unhappiness or pathology. They were denied information and often "counselled" about their feelings. When the adoptive parents experienced some difficulties in dealing with the special status of adoption, or stress and pain over their genuine differences from families built biologically, they felt, or were led to believe, that something was wrong with them.

Kirk (1964) discovered that the single variable that most predicted a successful placement was that the adoptive family could accept the difference between adoption and biological parenting. Slowly, the traditional guiding principle of practice, that of making adoption as much as possible like building a family biologically, has been eroding. The search movement and the testimony of adult adoptees have helped to alter this notion. The increased adoption rates of special needs and of older children have undermined the use of birth as a model for adoption, for in the situation of an older child it is more difficult to deny the differences between adoption and biological parenting. The child is clearly not a newborn baby. He or she has memory and a past, although these facts are often still insufficiently recognized in practice.

In this chapter we will look at adoption practice as it responds to changes in the philosophy and goals of adoption programs. Adoption practice is in transition. It is varied and often inconsistent, and may be seen as an amalgam of traditional adoptive practices and innovative approaches. We will also find that the knowledge and skills demanded of the adoptive worker in this new world of adoption are extremely broad and varied, covering the range of social work practice modalities and methods. The adoptive worker moving through the range of direct services on the adoptive continuum, from recruitment of adoptive homes to work with adult adoptees, needs skills in working with communities, organizations, groups, families, and children.

## Recruitment of Adoptive Homes

A new area of adoptive practice, one that has developed with the permanency movement, has been the recruitment of potential adoptive homes. Adoption workers of the past were generally faced with the problem of selecting families for the few babies available from among the oversupply of childless couples who wanted them. Now that the goal of adoption is to find a permanent home for all children who are unable to be with their biological families, this task has changed. Some Child Welfare workers have become skillful in organizing community resources, in addressing community groups, and in making use of the media to attract potential homes for special children. Television, radio, and newspapers have all been utilized with some effect. One of the most important areas of recruitment has been to find minority homes for minority children.

Until a decade ago, many of the minority children who were adopted went into white homes. Rarely did minority families approach adoption agencies, and when they did they were often found ineligible on the basis of white, middle-class, ethnocentric standards. The lack of black and other minority adoptive homes was rationalized on the basis that "minority families don't adopt." This was a very inaccurate perception, particularly since informal adoption, or the inclusion of non-biologically related children into the family, was, for example, more a part of the black culture than the white (Hill, 1972). Through the action of the minority communities and minority professional organizations, interracial adoption was sharply curtailed and the emphasis turned to the search for minority homes (Chestang, 1972; Chimezie, 1975).

It became clear that the procedures through which adoptive families became eligible to adopt and the social distance between the agency and the minority communities and potential minority adopting families had alienated applicants. It was evident that agencies must alter their practices, reaching out rather than screening out, examining and altering the ethnocentric biases in their home studies, increasing minority staff, and building bridges to the minority communities. The community organization skills of workers were tested as agencies attempted to move into minority communities, creating networks, identifying sympathetic leaders and gaining their support and help (Day, 1979; National Urban League, 1981). Innovative, community-based recruitment programs such as Chicago's "One Church, One Child" (Veronico, 1983) and the New York Council of Adoptable Children's Hispanic Adoption Program (Valiente-Barksdale, 1983) expanded resources for waiting minority children. Exemplary agencies, such as Homes for Black Children in Detroit, demonstrated outreach approaches to black adoptive families and offered technical assistance to other agencies to help strengthen their minority adoption programs.

Community organization and administrative skills were also required in the development of national and regional adoption exchanges and other programs constructed to facilitate the transfer of information throughout the adoption network in order to find homes for particular children or sibling groups.

## The Selection of Adoptive Homes

The process through which applicants become eligible to be adoptive parents is undergoing rapid change and the variety in these activities is so great it is impossible to explore all directions taken. In general, however, the selection process may be primarily evaluative or educational; it may be done in groups or in individual interviews with couples or single applicants; it may be participatory, or it may be authoritarian, in the sense that the agency makes the final decisions. The selection process may rely heavily on verbal reports gained through interviews with the applicants or on a variety of tools and simulations which capture and organize information in alternate ways.

The Child Welfare League of America's current *Standards for Adoption Service* (1978) describes a process that is primarily evaluative with some educational component, based on verbal communication between the worker and the applicants. It is a process in which the decision-making responsibility rests squarely with the agency. The standards state:

> It should be the aim of the agency to select from among applicants who hope to become parents through adoption those who are capable of developing into parents who can meet the needs of an adopted child, and who can provide the conditions and opportunities favorable to healthy personality growth and development of individual potentialities. (Child Welfare League of America, 1978:59)

The standards go on to state that selection should be made on the basis of the following criteria: total personality of the applicant; emotional maturity; quality of marital relationship; feeling about children; feeling about childlessness and readiness to adopt; and motivation. Further, the "study should consist of a series of interviews in which the adoptive applicants (separately and together, or as a family) and the social worker exchange factual information, discuss emotional factors involved in adoption, and come to recognize feelings and attitudes toward infertility, children born out of wedlock, unmarried parents, and explaining adoption to a child and others" (ibid.:63). Clearly this model, with its assumption that applicants are infertile marital pairs, is still largely influenced by traditional infant adoption practice.

A very different process is described by Barbara Tremitiere of Tressler–Lutheran Service Associates, an agency which places special needs children from agencies throughout the nation. The Tremitiere model is based on the assumptions that

> the applicants are, in almost all cases, dedicated individuals who know their own strengths and limitations and will, with support from the agency and other adoptive parents, be able to parent successfully children with special needs; that they should select the children that they believe will fit best into their homes; and that the social worker's responsibilities are to help educate the family in what to expect and what skills can be used to meet the needs of children, and then to enable them to get together with their adopted children. (Tremitiere, 1979:682)

The actual process in the Tremitiere model consists, first, of a series of nine educational and preparatory group sessions. Generally five to seven couples or single applicants meet together. The first session is devoted to orientation and to informing the applicants about the process. In the next two sessions, the applicants learn about the challenge involved in adopting a child with special needs from panels of adoptive parents who share their experiences. After these sessions, through a self-selective process, some of the applicants are likely to drop out. The next six sessions are devoted to clarification of individual and family values, positive personal interaction in the framework of transactional analysis, and parent effectiveness training with particular emphasis on communication.

Following this course, each family visits a family that has adopted a child similar to the kind of child they are thinking about adopting. The applicants also do much of the written work for the study themselves, including writing autobiographies, preparing health information, and completing questionnaires about attitudes and feelings. The staff workers visit the homes and summarize their impressions, but the main part of the study is written by the applicants. Throughout the process, the families have many opportunities to hear about waiting children and to go through adoption exchange books so that they become more knowledgeable about the children available.

This approach, as described by Tremitiere, is based on the principle of self-determination and the applicants play a major role in evaluating their own families as adoptive resources and in the decision-making process. The professional's role is minimized; he or she is seen as a facilitator, and the question of the agency role in refusing a family is not discussed.

A model of family assessment in adoption practice developed by the author (Hartman, 1979) falls somewhere between these two very different approaches. Applying ecological and family systems concepts to the understanding of applicant families and their wish to adopt a child, this approach shares the decision-making between the worker and the family, although the position is taken that in the last analysis, if consensus cannot be reached, the agency has the responsibility to make the final decision. The study relies on assessment tools and simulations as well as family systems interviewing processes to enhance the worker's and the family's understanding. Some of the assessment process may take place in group sessions and can be used in conjunction with the educational and developmental groups as described. My view is that parent effectiveness and other kinds of educational interventions are more useful when the child is in the home and when the parent is dealing with the real life situation. These, however, are some of the many issues in child welfare practice in need of research.

The ecological family assessment model begins with the use of an eco-map which can be done with a whole family, a couple, or individual applicant, or in a group. In this volume, Seabury, in Chapter 14, describes its application in family assessment, and it is further applied in Chapters 15 and 22. Information about the family's resources, the nature of their social network, and the extent to which their needs are met in their relationships with environmental resources can be portrayed on the eco-map. The extent to which the family experiences cut-offs or conflict in relationships with their world will also surface. The assumption is made that taking a child into a home is a demand and a challenge.

The eco-map helps the family and worker look together at the extent to which the family is supported, stressed, overburdened, or has sufficient resources available to assume an additional demand.

Further, in considering the placement of a special needs child, the kinds of educational and health care resources that might be needed can be identified, as well as can their availability to the family. The map is an assessment tool, but even more important, it can provide a blueprint in helping the family prepare for the placement of a child, since resources needed can be located and mobilized, and obstacles identified and cleared away.

The eco-map also displays certain characteristics of the family. Most importantly, it describes the nature of the boundary between the family and the external world and the ease with which people and resources move across that boundary. The nature of the potential adoptive family's external boundary determines whether a family is able to admit an outsider, such as the child, and also whether the family is free to accept help to meet the needs of a special child. Further, it is possible that families with relatively closed external boundaries may find it more difficult to accept the fact that a placed child has a past and other important connections outside of the new family.

The map also can provide some information about the internal structure of the family system. For example, it soon becomes clear whether this is a family that does everything together or one that allows and encourages individuals to pursue their own activities. It may become apparent that one child in the family is lacking in connections, leading one to hypothesize that one of the motivations for adoption may be to supply an isolated child with a companion. As we know, this motivation often backfires as waiting children are generally not ready to meet another child's needs. Information about the nature of the marital relationship also emerges. To what extent does the marital pair share interest, friends, and activities? Is the father busy and involved out of the home while the mother seems lonely and isolated? How do they talk about their differences—with humor and mutual acceptance or with criticism and bitterness?

The eco-map is rarely a neat and tidy drawing, since most families' connections with their environment are highly complex. However, the simulation provides a springboard for discussion and interaction among the family members that not only helps the family share their lives but also gives the worker an excellent picture of the family in action.

The second dimension of assessment is of the family system itself. Until recently, family assessments were arrived at largely by adding together the individual assessments of each family member. Such an additive approach overwhelms the worker with an enormous amount of information but does not produce a coherent picture of the family. A family systems approach to assessment looks at the family as a whole and identifies certain characteristics for study. For example, one of the most important aspects of the family system is the nature of its external boundaries. Is the family extremely close and cohesive or is it scattered and alienated?

Obviously, families exist along a continuum between these two extremes, and our goal in understanding families and in thinking about adoption is not necessarily to determine what kind of family boundaries are "good" but, rather, what kind of child would fit into what kind of family. For example, a child close to adolescence and a very cohesive family might be a poor match, as would a seriously handicapped child in need of a great deal of personal care and a family of very independent members busy with careers, school, and multiple activities.

The nature of the boundaries between family members should also be assessed. Some families have such open boundaries between family members that there is little privacy or respect for individual difference. In these families, adults may talk for children, intrude into their activities and possessions, and open their mail. In families where the boundaries between the members are opaque, family members may lack mutual empathy and understanding and may be unable to relate to what another is experiencing.

Most families operate within a broad range between these two extremes where there is sensitivity, caring, and concern but also respect for the individual's need to be alone, to be different, and to have some possessions, thoughts, and relationships that are not shared with the family.

Other aspects of the family system to be examined and understood include the nature of the family's communication system and its style of communicating, as well as its rules, role assignments, culture, and values. The nature of the family paradigm or its system of meanings and beliefs and its modes of interpreting itself and the world around it should also be considered.

Assessment tools, techniques, and strategies for gaining an understanding of the family system are many. First, in group educational and discussion sessions, a great deal can be observed about the family's interactive style and relationship system, as well as about their way of perceiving and relating to the outside world. Do people speak for one another? Are differences respected and negotiated? Are humor and warmth present in family interchanges? Are family members, in time, able to relate to the groups and to share or do they maintain a distant and guarded stance? Do they reach out to help others in the group or express concern or sympathy? Are they critical and judgmental of other families? Do they attempt to control the process and refuse to listen? Are they able to take in and consider new information or do they have to see themselves as "right," the experts? Group process reveals a great deal about people's interpersonal styles and relationships.

Visits to the home will contribute additional important information. A family's home and the way the family chooses to organize, decorate, and allocate its space may serve as a visual metaphor that portrays the family's style, interests, and priorities. The worker should be open to the messages communicated by the atmosphere and arrangements of the home, and to discuss with the family how and where they see a child fitting into this space.

Forsythe and Marshall (1984) report that they ask parents to make a scrapbook about the family that will later be used in preparing a child to enter their home. The scrapbook, a family version of the life book so widely used with children in placement, introduces family members and reflects the family's lifestyle, values, and interests. Such information can be very helpful in selecting a child for a specific home.

A family does not just exist in its present space; it also exists in time. Just as the child who will be adopted has an important heritage, so the adopting family has an intergenerational history that has had considerable influence in shaping its style, values, and other important characteristics. The exploration of intergenerational family history leads to an enhanced understanding of the current family and may help to clarify the meaning of the wish to adopt. It may lead to an understanding of why the applicants feel their family is incomplete or why adoption is sought as a way to build a family. It also may be used to reveal expectations for the child and the anticipated role assignments for any child in a particular spot on the family tree.

The genogram, a family tree that includes a considerable amount of social and demographic data, is a widely used tool in the assessment of intergenerational family history (Bowen, 1978; Hartman, 1979; Hartman and Laird, 1983). A careful genogram will reveal family events and realtionships that may play a significant role in the family's decision to adopt. For example, in completing and discussing the genogram, it may become clear to both worker and family that an important and unresolved loss has created a lingering sense of emptiness in the family. Is this child to be a replacement for an important lost person? Will the family be disappointed if the new member fails to occupy that space comfortably? Furthermore the genogram quickly reveals information about the nature of the applicant's relationship with the family of origin. It provides a very natural mode for discovering how various members of the family of origin view the applicant's wish to adopt. In some research, the willingness of the extended family to support the adoption has been a factor in the ultimate outcome (Fiegelman and Silverman, 1977).

Genogram interviews with the family tend to lead to reminiscence and storytelling. Through this kind of exchange, one may begin to learn more about the culture, values, and perceptions of the family and what it means to be member of this unit. Such information is not necessarily used to evaluate the family, but can help them reflect on their own system and consider what kind of child would be more likely to fit into their family. Even more importantly, helping the family to become more aware of its culture can prepare it to help a child—coming to them from a different family with different values and ways—to become acculturated to the new situation. The genogram can become a part of the family scrapbook and can be used in helping the child come to know his or her new family.

## The Evaluative Aspects of the Home Study Process

In sum, there are many ways of obtaining information about families, but how is this information to be evaluated? On what scale and according to what norms? Various students of the field have attempted to construct some picture of the kinds of family rules and characteristics that seem to predict success in adoption and particularly in the adoption of special needs children. Jewett (1978), for example, discusses some of the expectations professionals have of potential adoptive couples. These include personal self-esteem, the ability to handle conflict, optimistic but realistic expectations for the adopted child, demonstrated capacity to overcome problems and handle frustration, the ability to take responsibility for their own feelings, actions, and ideas, and an ability to accept dependency in the child while also being able to help him develop tools for growing up. Tremitiere (1979), who emphasizes adoptive parent self-determination in the decision-making process does, however, suggest that workers check references and summarize their impressions, but does not indicate any standard or norm. Forsythe and Marshall (1984), while primarily relying on group process, take the position that the focus is both educational and evaluative although the specific evaluative norms are not described.

It may well be that all studies are a combination of education and evaluation, with some models emphasizing one more than the other. For example, even in the Tremitiere model, if through the checking of references it is discovered that the applicant has been arrested and convicted for the sexual abuse of children, the agency's and the worker's evaluative role would obviously come into play.

Perhaps one of the most important practice principles in the home study process is that there should be openness and honesty about the evaluative aspects of the process. It would be most destructive to the applicants and their relationship with the agency if the evaluative role of the preparation process is denied. This double-bind communication is not unlike a process which has, at times, taken place in protective services when the worker gains the confidence of the family as a helper, without clearly identifying the child protective role, and later uses information gained against the family in a court action.

It is important to make clear the evaluative aspects of the preparation process and also to make evaluative norms as explicit as possible. The clear recognition of whatever norms are being used keeps the process from being directed by individual worker bias.

## Unresolved Practice Issues in Finding Homes

Adoption practice is thus in transition and as rapid changes take place, several unresolved issues remain. First, as the shift is made from a primarily evaluative to a primarily educational and self-determining homefinding process, the evaluative aspects of the process need to be specified and clarified. Although there are widespread convictions about the qualities that lead to successful adoptive parenting, they tend to be expressions of "practice wisdom," backed by little or no substantiating research.

Second, as adoption practice focuses increasingly on special needs, older, and minority children, a two-track adoption study process seems to have developed. Traditional studies tend to be used to evaluate homes for infants and the newer participatory self-evaluations for special needs adoption. Many of the general requirements for infant adoptions are not a part of special needs adoption eligibility, such as marriage, age limit, infertility, special economic level, or childlessness. Some of these requirements, which may in fact be questionable for infant adoption, are clearly inappropriate for special needs adoption. However, some professionals have expressed concern that families who are somehow less eligible for infant adoption are being accepted for special needs children. Of particular concern is the fact that, in some cases, families with fewer resources are adopting children whose severe problems and needs make great demands on the adoptive family (Fiegelman and Silverman, 1977). These issues concerning a "two-track" adoption system remain unresolved.

A third major transformation in adoption practice has been the growing trend for foster parents to adopt children placed with them. This trend has been accelerated by the foster parent movement, by the growing concern about the damaging effects of moving children attached to foster families, and by the expansion of subsidized adoption. It is directly contrary to traditional practice in which foster parents, from the beginning, were made to understand that under no circumstances would they be allowed to adopt their foster children. In fact, as late as 1974, almost two-thirds of the states had cautionary notes or actual prohibition of adoption in their placement agreements with foster parents (Festinger, 1974). Foster parents are now gaining permanent custody of their foster children on the basis of the child's attachment, sometimes with and sometimes without the blessing of the agency that originally placed the child.

Practitioners have raised many questions concerning the transfer of foster home to adoptive home status, including concern that the original home studies were not exacting enough, or that agencies would lose their good foster homes to adoption, or that the adoption of one foster child in a home would cause hardship for other children in the home who will not be adopted by the foster parents. Others have been concerned that the traditional practice of confidentiality cannot be maintained, since contact with biological family members may be continued.

Despite these objections and concerns, the practice of adoption of available children by foster parents is widespread and encouraged. In fact, in many states, foster parents are now given preference as an adoptive family for children in their care and some adoption subsidy programs have been specifically designed for and even limited to foster parents.

Although most would agree that foster parent adoptions are highly appropriate for older children and for children who have been in a foster home for a number of years, the preference policy has had some unanticipated consequences. For example, a foster home specifically used as a temporary placement for an infant while the mother decides whether or not to relinquish the child for adoption may lay special claim to that child. This home may or may not be the best resource for that child. Although the placement may have been thoughtfully or carefully made, it is just as likely that the worker simply found a good foster mother who had room for a baby, without careful consideration for the future. Further, in this time of shortage of available babies, people who want to adopt are learning that one way to move through the Child Welfare system and to become eligible to adopt is to serve as foster parents.

One solution to this dilemma has been the development of the "three option" or "legal risk" foster home. This home serves as the child's initial placement and, should the child not be returned to the biological family, such parents would assume legal custody. Eventually if the child is freed for adoption, they would adopt the child. However, this blurring of the distinctions between foster and adoptive homes creates particular problems in some of the newer models of foster parenting in which the role of the foster parent is to become part of a team which works to help toward family reunification. (See Chapter 22 for a full discussion of this conception of the foster parent role.) Certainly, foster parents who want to adopt and are developing a strong attachment to the child will find it very difficult to invest wholeheartedly in efforts to return the child to the biological parents (Gill and Amadio, 1983; Lee and Hull, 1983). Underneath this confusion is the implicit notion that different kinds of foster homes are needed, those utilized in the rehabilitation and reunification of the biological family and those that are in reality potential adoptive homes in which the foster parents are ready to assume a "legal risk" status.

But how can decisions be made as to which kind of home is appropriate in a specific situation? Proch (1981) suggests that agencies develop special diagnostic homes in which children remain for up to sixty days while planning is done about which kind of home should be utilized. Such a plan, however, presents two obvious and very troublesome difficulties. First, a temporary placement in a "diagnostic home," entails an additional move for the child, Moreover, such a plan suggests that the worker can make a determination in the space of sixty days or less concerning whether the goal is adoption or return home. However, some believe that such a prejudgment, early in a situation and before a legal determination is made, may have the effect of a self-fulfilling prophecy (Lee and Hull, 1983).

These dilemmas have no easy answers. They are the new practice challenges that have arisen in this time of rapid change. Greater certainty about the solutions to these problems awaits accumulated practice experience and research.

## Preparation of Families for Adoption

The more knowledge applicants can have about adoption and about the children available for adoption, and the more direct experience they can have with the actual process, the better they will be prepared for what is to come. Much of the homfinding process is actually an educational experience. On the basis of exposure to the realities of adoption, the family can make an informed decision concerning whether or not to proceed. It is essential not to gloss over the difficulties in adoption; it is a disservice to a waiting child and to the adoptive parents to present an incomplete or inaccurate picture of the challenges they will face.

Probably the best way to prepare parents for adoption is by facilitating their meeting and working with others who have been through the experience. The North American Council on Adoptable Children, funded by a grant from the Children's Bureau, has developed and disseminated a team model through which experienced adoptive parents take an active part in preparing applicants for adoption (Flynn and Hamm, 1983). The relationships built through the preparation process are often extended into the post-adoption period, as experienced and new adoptive parents form a mutual aid support network available during difficult periods.

Preparation for a specific child can also be enhanced by the use of a total family meeting, either with the worker alone or with other families preparing for adoption. In this meeting, family sculpture may be used to create a living tableau of the family and then, by asking someone to represent the child entering the family, all members can begin to experience and to prepare for the changes that will take place with the addition of a new member. This exercise is particularly useful for the other children in the family who, perhaps, want a new brother or sister but have not fully recognized that they will have to share their parents and their family space with a stranger.

## The Assessment and Preparation of the Child

An essential part of the adoption process is the assessment of the child, that is, an understanding of the child's strengths, needs, potential, and limitations. First, although this is not always feasible, as much information as possible should be gathered about biological kin. Some agencies have begun to gather such information through the use of a genogram when a child first comes into care. This knowledge is then always available to the child and to the adoptive parents and serves to help the child maintain a sense of identity and continuity. The child's placement history should also be carefully investigated and the facts of his or her early life reconstructed. Information should be available about where and with whom the child has lived and what those experiences were like, when and why moves occurred and how they were dealt with by the child and others, and who the major figures have been in each part of his or her life. Such information can be gathered through studying records, interviewing caretakers, talking with the child, teachers, former social workers, or anyone else who has known the child over the years.

This information should be organized in an orderly fashion and made available to the adoptive family both to help them understand and know the child and to assist them in helping the child to remember and to reminisce. The lack of such connections and shared memories can disrupt the child's sense of continuity. The "life book," a scrapbook that contains information about the child's past, has been used with children for this purpose and is also helpful to adoptive parents (Aust, 1981; Beste and Richardson, 1981; Wheeler, 1978).

Other information about the child includes sleeping patterns, bedtime and other rituals, particular habits or troublesome behaviors, food preferences, interests, styles of interacting with adults and other children—in short, any information that can help the adoptive family know and understand the new member of their family. In a recent study of adoptive families' responses to adoption it was discovered that their greatest complaint was that they did not learn enough about the child from the agency. Some adoptive parents have found it useful to contact former foster parents to learn more about the child (Nelson, 1983).

In preparing a child to move into a permanent placement, several steps must be accomplished. First, the child must deal with the knowledge that he or she will never be returning to his or her parents. No matter how long a child may have been in foster care, that child may still harbor the fantasy of one day returning home. The child must be helped to know that this is not the case. The fantasy of returning home will not be given up easily and the child may well deny this loss. Once the child understands that he or she is not going to return to the family, he or she may very well go through a period of mourning. Throughout this process, the child will need help in expressing anger and pain in reminiscing about the past, both the happy and painful events, and in understanding why he or she cannot go home. Although explanations given the child will differ according to age and hence what a child is able to take in and understand, it is important to be absolutely honest. Although adults may try to protect children from painful realities, children who have been neglected and abused have memories and questions about the meaning of their experiences as well as fantasies about the causes of the mistreatment. Open and truthful discussion of these realities is less troubling than denial and secrecy and will, in the long run, be supportive of the child.

A second major part of preparation is the process of helping a child, insofar as possible, attain a greater self-knowledge and awareness of personal history. This may be accomplished through the use of the life book, which combines documents, stories, pictures, time lines, maps, or any other concrete images and information that may help consolidate and render the past meaningful. Children maintain a sense of continuity not simply through their own memories but through hearing stories from their parents and other adults, watching home movies, looking at family photographs, and sharing a continuous life span with others. Children who are separated from their families may lose this sense of continuity. The adoption worker can help a child consolidate his or her identity through gathering information and organizing it into a scrapbook to take to the new home. Relinquishing fantasies about parents and clarifying a child's sense of self as a human being with continuity and connectedness help to prepare the child for the move to an adoptive home.

## The Placement Process

The actual process of placement will, of course, vary with the age of the child and other special circumstances surrounding the adoption. In general, however, the same steps must be taken in any adoptive placement (Donley, 1981). First, the decision is made to consider a particular child for a particular family. This decision may be made by the agency, by the adoptive family, or in a joint decision-making process between agency and parents. Traditionally, as still usually occurs in the case of infant adoption, the agency makes this decision. In the adoption of older and special needs children, however, the situation has changed. It has been discovered that parents may be motivated to adopt a special child through seeing a picture or hearing about that child, thus "choosing" a specific child. Active participation in the selection process by parents has been found to work out quite well as the child has been found appealing by the parents and the parents have responded by "claiming" the child.

Most agencies are finding that an intermediate position is useful, one in which the parents learn about the available children and participate with the agency in identifying a particular child for their home. In the second step, the potential adoptive parents are informed about the child. There has been discussion about how much to tell parents about the child they want to adopt, but increasingly professionals are becoming convinced both that parents should be given all the available information and that the agency should make every effort to learn as much as possible about the child, the biological family, and the child's personal history.

The third step is "showing," which is an important step in any adoption but is of special importance in the adoption of older or special needs children. There are many ways "showing" can take place. Usually the worker takes the child to a public place, such as a playground or a shopping mall, and the adoptive family "happens by," visiting briefly with the worker and child. Some workers object to this procedure because the adults in the situation are not being honest with the child, and they are concerned about beginning such an important relationship with a manipulation. However, it is very stressful for a child to be knowingly put in the position of being "looked over." One woman who was finally adopted at the age of ten from an orphanage over fifty years ago still remembers being lined up with other children to be "shown" to adoptive applicants only to be passed over time after time. Some agencies are handling this dilemma through the use of video or one-way mirrors for observation.

Introducing the family and the child to each other is the next step in the placement process. Some feel that this should not be done in the office but in a more relaxed and informal place. Others feel that it is appropriate for introductions to take place in the agency and that an informal setting within the agency can be used. More important for the success of the first meeting is the worker's ability to let go, to facilitate the connection between the family and the child and then to leave so that the family can be alone with the child and begin to get acquainted.

A series of visits to the adoptive home is an important part of the placement process, as long as such visits are consciously used to facilitate placement and there is disucssion and feedback after each visit from both parents and child. The number of visits, of course, varies with the age of the child: Older children tend to need a longer transitional period and more visits. Although one of the major reasons for visits is to help the child with the separation and the change, visits also help both parents and child test out each other, discover more about each other before the final commitment is made, and experiment with being together. It is important for the discoveries made by parents and child to be processed with the worker.

The final step in the placement process is, of course, the move to the new home. This is a very important day and should not take place until the participants are ready. Understandably there is considerable tension and excitement, and thus plans for the day should be kept simple and as free of stress as possible. This probably is not the best time for a large, welcoming party or other celebration. However, a simple ritual around the dinner table or at bedtime can mark the day and enact the transition taking place. Similarly, anniversaries of the placement day are often celebrated in some way. The use of a more elaborate adoption ritual a few weeks or months after the placement will be discussed later.

The visits and the early weeks after the placement will not necessarily go smoothly and, in fact, are likely to include tantrums, tears, nightmares, fights, or other signs of stress. Fahlberg (1980) has pointed out that such periods of high tension and anxiety can be used in the bonding process. Taking the bonding of the newborn and mother as a model, Fahlberg states that bonding is strengthened when the baby goes through a period of heightened emotion and tension with the mother, is satisfied, and then relaxes in the mother's arms. Fahlberg feels that if adoptive parents can stay with a child through the pain and fear and anger, holding and comforting even if resisted, bonding will begin to take place. Too often, when a child is upset in the placement process, the worker moves in to deal with the child with the result that the bond to the worker, rather than to the adoptive parents, strengthens. It is the worker's task to help the adoptive parents take over, to help them gain the confidence to stay with the child through the storms. This experience of mutual resolution of stress, at any stage of life, is an important facilitator of bonding.

## Opening Up Adoption

With the exception of those adoptions arranged directly between biological and adoptive parents, adoption in this country has been closed. Not only are all legal ties totally severed, but the expectation has been that all contact shall cease between the biological kin and the child. Adoption records are sealed and often minimal information is given either the biological parents or the adoptive parents about each other. This model of closed adoption has been a further expression of the conviction that adoption should be as much as possible like biological parenting.

The past ten years has witnessed a growing questioning of the total cut-off between the child and his or her biological roots. Associations of adoptees have communicated their need to cross over these cut-offs and to search out and know their biological roots. Birth parents also have organized to press for a reconsideration of adoption practices. Family therapists and others who are exploring the importance of the intergenerational family in identity formation and the power of secrets and of mysterious figures in affecting people's lives have expressed concern about the impact of the losses, secrets, and shadowy figures on an adopted person's life (Colón, 1978). Finally, the adoption of older children has forced a rethinking of all of the issues around closed and open adoption (Borgman, 1982). Older children have memories, connections, important relationships; they have a past. Utilizing the principles and methods of infant adoption in this very different situation has been increasingly questioned.

Most of the literature on separation and attachment issues in regard to the placement of older children has been based on the crucial assumption that a child cannot become attached to the new family unless he or she has mourned and relinquished the old family. This assumption needs careful examination and testing.

Today, in the life experience of children in blended families we have evidence of children's ability to accept parenting from several adults. If there is not conflict and competition among the adults in the situation, we find that children can have warm and loving attachments, for example, to both a biological father and a stepfather. In Child Welfare practice, in the case of foster care, we hope that children will become attached to their foster parents at the same time we encourage visiting and the maintenance of the tie with the biological family. It is possible that underneath the assumption about the necessary exclusiveness of filial attachment is the culturally determined view of the exclusive and closed nuclear family so common in this country. Many cultures are less exclusive in filial attachments and a mother, an aunt, and a grandmother may all occupy maternal roles with a child, where mother is "Mommy" and grandmother is "Mama." In other words, there is growing conviction by many that there "is no sound reason to continue the belief that biological parents be banished, or that a child's emotional connections with biological parents preclude the creation of healthy and stable placements" (Derdeyn, Rogoff, and Williams, 1978).

As Colón writes, "I am leery . . . of any practice that attempts to make the child forget his tie to his biological family or foster family. Indeed, the older the late-adoptee child, the bigger the eraser would have to be and the larger the piece of reality the child would have to erase. This approach cannot be constructive because reality cannot be erased." (1978:306)

What are the practice implications of opening up the adoption of older children? The major implications are that, instead of making a case plan according to a general principle such as "all adoptions are closed," the arrangements in each adoption would vary in relation to the particular situation. Case planning concerning the nature of the postadoption connection between child and biological kin (as well as former foster homes, friends, teachers, and others significant in a child's life) involves a careful assessment of the nature of these relationships and the resources available to the child in this network. The life book has been a very useful tool in helping a child monitor her sense of identity and continuity. How much more helpful might be continued contact with the real figures involved?

This is not, perhaps, such a revolutionary view. In his study of 150 older child adoptions, Kadushin (1970) found that 28 percent of the adoptive parents had encouraged or permitted the child's continued involvement with preadoptive relationships and, in a very early article on older child adoptions, Bell reported: "Our agency found great value in . . . the preservation of the child's relationships with certain selected members of his natural family. His keeping in touch with his relatives often strengthed adoptive relationships; the child knows his adoptive parents not only accept him, but that which belongs to him" (1959:333).

Agency open adoptions of infants and very young children are far less common and, perhaps, more controversial, although some agencies are innovating in this area. Perhaps the most useful way to conceptualize open adoption is to think of it as a continuum from fully "closed" at one end to fully "open" at the other. Based on the needs and wishes of all concerned in any particular adoptive situation, the agency should consider where on the continuum the adoption should be placed.

A beginning step in opening up adoption implies part or full sharing of family history and current family information with both the adoptive parents and the birth parents. That is, although identifying information is not shared, both sets of parents have detailed information about each other. Further opening up may involve the exchange of information about and pictures of the child over a specified period of time. In such an exchange, the agency usually acts as mediator. The period of time during which information about the child's development is exchanged may vary from a few months to several years, depending on the wishes of those involved (Sorich and Siebert, 1982).

Another step in the opening up of infant adoption involves a meeting between the adoptive parents and birth parents. The two sets of parents exchange information in person, although identifying information is not usually exchanged. In a yet more open situation, birth parents, relatives, foster parents, or other significant figures in a child's life maintain contact after the adoption, visiting the child on a regularly specified basis. Such visits are planned through a contractual arrangement with the understanding that if it does not work out satisfactorily, the contract may be renegotiated with the help of the agency. Finally, some agencies are experimenting with beginning contact between biological and adoptive parents before the birth of the child, to the point where the adoptive parents come to the hospital when the baby is born and even may serve as coaches during the delivery. This, of course, involves legal risk for the adoptive parents as the child has not been relinquished. It is understood that the mother may change her mind and that she should experience no pressure to relinquish her parental rights. Such pressure is not only a violation of the mother's rights but it also may constitute evidence of undue pressure that later could be used in efforts to overturn the adoption. It is essential, of course, in open adoption, that the legal rights of the adoptive parents also not be compromised or jeopardized.

Some agencies have implemented innovative open adoption services, even in the adoption of infants and small children, and are beginning to report satisfaction with the process. One such agency is Community Family and Children's Services of Traverse City, Michigan.[1] This agency has utilized the concept of a continuum of openness in infant adoption. The agency helps birth parents and adoptive parents to explore how open they wish the adoption to be, ranging from an exchange of information to a fully open ongoing relationship among all of the parties. The birth parents, in fact, may select the adoptive family from among appropriate waiting couples. They may have contact throughout the term of pregnancy and delivery. The infant may be placed immediately upon release from the hospital with the adoptive parents, who must be licensed foster parents to take in the infant. Over the past four years, 90 percent of the agency's adoptions have been open to some degree. Some 10 percent of birth parents who elected open adoption have reversed their decision about adoption and the infants have been returned to them. However, in each one of these situations, despite the painful loss, the adoptive parents have again chosen the open adoption process.

Of particular significance to the welfare of children in considering establishing open adoption services is the experience reported by some experts that young mothers, unable to provide adequate care for their children and yet reluctant to give them up, have been more ready to do so if they do not have to face a total cut-off. Baran, Pannor, and Sorosky (1976:99) report that, when they have raised the idea of open adoption with young unwed mothers, many of the women have indicated that "they could face and even welcome adoption for their children if they could meet the adoptive parents, help in the separation and move to the new home, and then maintain some contact with the children." There is mounting concern about the many children at risk with very young mothers unable to meet their needs adequately. Open adoption may offer a plan which is in the best interests of the young mother, the child, and the family seeking adoption.

## Postplacement Services

In traditional adoption practice, postplacement services have been minimal. Generally, a few home visits are made during the period before finalization of the adoption, with the primary purpose one of determining whether the adoption is taking hold. Once the adoption was finalized, contacts between the agency and the families were likely to end unless, many years in the future, the adoptees returned to gain more information about their biological families.

The adoption of older and special needs children has given impetus to the notion that adoptive parents may well need help after placement, that the adoption of an older or special needs child may present challenges and require skills that are themselves special, out of the average person's experience. A recent study on special needs adoption revealed that adoptive parents felt the need for help in many areas but also felt that they were left to fend for themselves (Nelson, 1983). Further, even in the case of infant adoption, adoptive parents and adult adoptees have indicated that help at various times throughout the life cycle of the adoptive family would have been very useful.

## Postplacement Services during the First Year

Families who adopt an older child or a child with special needs may need help in two particular areas. First, they may need help in understanding and helping their child. Many children placed for adoption today have been through several placements, some have suffered severe abuse and neglect, and most come into adoption fearful, angry, and anticipating one more rejection (Braden, 1981; Ward, 1981). Although the first weeks may go smoothly, this period of superficial tranquility occurs in part because the child is not yet attached to the new family. The child precipitates an end of the "honeymoon" when he or she begins to feel stirrings of caring and longing. These feelings in turn stimulate earlier unresolved pain and loss experienced in relation to adults and to rejection. The child's response to these stirrings is often to fight the new attachment, to show hostility and negativity, and to begin a long period of testing to demonstrate that this family, like other families, will be rejecting. If children anticipate rejection and loss, they are likely to attempt to precipitate the inevitable in order to deal with the anxiety and feelings of helplessness.

The adoptive parents, no matter how well they have been prepared, also often bring the honeymoon to an end, as they begin to experience the differences between their fantasies and the realities of the situation. A relatively minor negative interaction can escalate as the child's acting out triggers the parents' disappointment which in turn stimulates the child's fear that he or she will be sent away. This feeling of course stimulates the child to act even more provocatively, thus amplifying the negative interaction. The adoptive family often needs help and support during this period. They need to know that this behavior is probably a sign that the child is beginning to feel attached to them and they need support to tolerate the testing and to learn to handle it. The parents need to be able to interpret the child's communication, and to learn how to communicate concern and caring while setting appropriate limits. They need to learn to resist demonstrating the very rejecting behavior that the child is trying to provoke.

The family also needs help in terms of the impact of the placement of the child on their entire lives and on the organization and functioning of their family. They may not recognize that some of the new tensions and strains they are experiencing in family relationships and in the family–environment relationships may be attributed to the changes the arrival of the child has set in motion. The family may also require assistance in seeking out and making use of the special health or educational services their child may need.

The particular method of delivering post-adoption services will vary, just as do preparation processes. However, such services should be based on the adoption study and preparation period. If the home study and preparation period are shared and invite the active participation of the adoptive applicants, postadoption services will tend to follow the same model. In programs where groups are used for preparation, these groups may continue, providing ongoing support and sharing for the new adoptive parents. Group members cannot only help each other in mutual aid relationships in the group meetings but, if they wish, outside of the group. They may well call each other in an emergency, asking for advice or even concrete help. Because they are having similar experiences, comparing notes, sharing problem-solving strategies, and even providing respite for one another can be invaluable.

In programs where recruitment and preparation is performed by a team consisting of a social worker and an experienced adoptive parent, the team often continues to provide service (Flynn and Hamm, 1983). In agencies where much of the preparation is done by the social worker, he or she should be available to continue with the family to offer counsel, support, and access to needed resources.

No matter what the particular format for the delivery of services, several areas of focus can be assumed to demand attention. First, the placement of a child in the home may alter the family's relationship with its world. If an eco-map was completed during the home study, a new one can be done, thus helping the family to see the changes brought about by the placement. Even if the map wasn't done before, it is still a useful tool for examining the changes in their lives and the adaptations they have made or need to make. For example, perhaps the adoptive mother has given up several important outside acitivites and is beginning to feel isolated. Perhaps the adoptive brother has had trouble with the neighborhood children because they have been unwilling to accept the new member of the family. Perhaps additional trips to special educational or health services have stressed the family; thought must be given to how these tasks can be better distributed or whether an extended family friend can help. The eco-map not only pictures the family's relationship with its environment but points the way to problem-solving strategies.

The family system itself has also undergone change as a new member has been added. Although children looked forward to the arrival of a new brother or sister, they probably had not fully understood what sharing their space and their parents might mean. Perhaps the demands of the new child have stimulated rivalry and feelings of being displaced, and tension and conflict is escalating. Or, in a family with two other children, perhaps the addition of a third child has created a triangle in which there are two insiders and one on the outside. Or, perhaps the marital pair has not taken time to be together and their relationship is experiencing some strain.

A variety of helping strategies can be called upon during these stressful months. A family sculpture or careful interviewing can surface the shifts in the family structure and the location of tension. Interventions can be made in direct work with the family and assignments can be given to alter the structure and to resolve the tensions, helping the family find a new adaptive balance. Such assignments are often given in the form of specific instructions to the family, directing them to enact or practice a structural change. For example, if a son has felt somewhat abandoned by his father since the arrival of the adopted child, perhaps an assignment would be given to them to spend some special time together. The same kind of assignment might be made in the situation where the parents have neglected their relationship due to new tasks and stresses.

Communication may be enhanced in the family both through meeting with the total group and helping them talk things over but also through encouraging the members of the family and the adopted child to share. The child often must be encouraged to talk about his or her past and to reminisce. This is essential, both for the maintenance of continuity and also for the family to know the child better and to share past experiences through this reminiscence. The life book as well as visits with former foster parents, friends, or relatives can facilitate the sharing process. In the same way, the adoptive family needs to teach the child about his or her new family, for an adopted child will have at least two family histories. The use of photo albums or movies, or drawing a family genogram with a child can enhance his or her knowledge of the new family. Some agencies ask the adoptive family to create a family history book during the preparation period, a book that can later be used to help socialize the child into the new family.

An important way of communicating and celebrating the adopted child's becoming a member of the family is through the use of a ritual. Rituals are a powerful and universal way of enacting, experiencing, and integrating change (Laird, 1984). Many adoptive families have recognized the need for some kind of ritual that enacts the adoption of the child by the family and have expressed disappointment when the final court hearing was hurried and without ceremony.

Entitlement, support, and the social sanctioning of the adoption can be strengthened and enhanced through the use of an adoption ritual which announces the child's membership in the family and celebrates this important event. The adoption ceremony or claiming ritual will vary from family to family, depending on style and preference, but it should be ceremonial, serious, and publicly witnessed. Hopefully, it should be followed by some sort of party or reception. As a part of postadoptive services, the agency, in work with groups or individuals, can help adoptive families consider and design such a ritual.

## Disruption of Adoptions

As older children and children with special needs have been adopted, the number of disrupted placements has increased. The additional demands placed on all of the actors in the adoptive situation are great and no matter how careful the preparation of both child and family, the placement may fail. Negative interactions may escalate in the family to the point that no amount of intervention may stop them. Dysfunctional patterns in the family that were not apparent during the study and preparation period may emerge, and the family with serious troubles may begin to place the child in the role of scapegoat. As a result, the child would be put in great jeopardy of physical or emotional abuse. Adoptive families require the same kind of careful evaluation and extensive supportive and therapeutic services as do biological families where there exist abuse and neglect. (These services have been described in Chapters 15 and 22.) Perhaps the most problematic and intractable situation exists when the family projects all of the difficulties onto the child and refuses to reflect on the possibility that it might be contributing to the problem or to accept help. There will be times when failure needs to be acknowledged.

Disruption is painful for all those who experience it, the child, the family, and the worker. No matter how carefully all of the issues in placement are considered, the risk of disruption does exist and cannot always be avoided. The only way to completely avoid that risk is to retreat from the goal of finding permanent homes for all children.

## Long-Term Postadoption Services

As indicated earlier, agencies have rarely offered services to families after the finalization of adoption. Families have either gone without help or have sought counsel from professionals who often lack expertise in the special aspects of adoption (Nelson, 1983). At predictable points throughout the adoptive family's life cycle, help could and should be made available through agencies that have experience and expertise in the area of adoption. In fact, it has been suggested that adoption counseling should be developed as a specialty (Katz, 1980). It seems particularly important to offer ongoing preventive, supportive, and educational services to adoptive families at certain times.

In the case of infant and toddler adoption, families may well need help in how to talk about adoption to their child. Adoptive families have complained that they never received any assistance with this. Such help could be offered through group services, automatically made available to all adoptive parents when their children are from four to six years of age, the age at which first questions typically are asked. Ten- to twelve-year-old children have other questions and an opportunity to talk with a professional and with other adoptive families may be welcomed by the adoptive parents, and the children well may appreciate the opportunity to meet and talk with other adopted children. The identity issues of adoptees begin to emerge with particular force in adolescence and groups for adoptees as well as for their parents may help all concerned cope with this complex and often stressful time.

Finally, agencies also have a role in helping adopted adults who return seeking information about their biological origins. Although the current legal situation limits agencies' activities and the laws are different from state to state, even during this uncertain transitional period, agencies have service to offer. First, agencies should be sensitive and available to adult adoptees who request information, and although the agency may not be able to comply with the request, the adult adoptee's interest should be considered a healthy wish to gain more self-knowledge and to consolidate identity. It is not a sign that the adoptee is troubled or that the adoption was not successful. Referral to an adoption self-help group is often a useful strategy.

In situations where original birth certificates are available to adopted adults and where an active search and reconnecting with the birth parents is possible, workers should follow the adoptee's lead in their efforts to help. Some professionals have felt that the agencies should act as intermediaries between the adoptee and the birth parents. In Minnesota, for example, where birth certificates may be unsealed with the birth parents' permission, the search and the mediating role has been mandated to agencies by law (Weidell, 1980). This is often not what the adoptee wishes. Many want to keep control of the search process, to do it for themselves. They object to once again being in the passive role while the agency acts for them, controlling their relationship with the birth parents; it seems to them almost a repeat of the original adoption scenario. Consequently, adoptee self-help groups have been advocating for their rights to information about and direct access to their biological families.

Adoption is in a process of radical change and with the change has come an alteration and an expansion of adoption practice. The roles of the practitioner in adoption run the gamut from community organizer and public relations specialist to family therapist. The frontiers of adoption have been moved forward to include older children, minority children, and children with special needs. Programs have also expanded to include a range of preventive and interventive services which may be available throughout the life cycle of the adoptive family.

Many of the cherished principles which long guided adoption practice have toppled and others are being questioned. Innovative agencies and practitioners are exploring new models of adoptive practice in order to give better service to more children, models that are congruent with the growing readiness of the larger society to accept varied family forms. Probably no time has existed when adoption practice has offered more challenge and more opportunities for creative and innovative service to children and families.

# Adoption, Foster Care, and Group Homes for Handicapped Children

THOMAS ROSE
DOROTHEA WEND ROSE

In this exemplar we explore a continuum of alternative programs and services for handicapped children who are *not* now living with their biological families. More than 500,000 children do not live with their families, and are part of the public child care/mental retardation/mental health systems (Children's Defense Fund, 1978).

The stance taken in this paper is that handicapped children should be kept out of institutions, social workers should advocate for deinstitutionalization for those already placed in institutions, and other residential options should be developed in each community. Large, congregate, custodial children's institutions, wards, facilities, cottages, schools, and centers, should be abolished. According to the Department of Health and Human Services:

> the great majority of persons with developmental disabilities are more likely to achieve their maximum potential residing in small facilities which provide them with the opportunity to participate more fully in the normal life of the community rather than in institutions. However, it is also recognized that this will occur only if these individuals are provided with services that are sufficient in amount, appropriate in type, available when needed, and coordinated so that they supplement and reinforce each other. (DHHS, 1983:48383)

The Children's Defense Fund (1978) argues forcefully that ". . . evidence shows intensive nonresidential services in the community benefit

693

children without isolating them and are cost effective." Thus states should stimulate new providers in local communities to provide residential and other services for developmentally disabled children.

The concept of permanency planning in the least restrictive environment applies to all children in the Child Welfare system, including those who are handicapped. Some children will need a more supervised placement, but will develop and move into a more normalized environment. Some will remain in their biological familes. The focus is on a continuum of developmental care and services from infancy to adulthood. Our focus is on diverse types of family-centered residential services rich in educational, developmental, and where needed, treatment resources.

In this exemplar, the terms "developmentally disabled" and "handicapped" are used synonomously, although these terms and labels have practical and legal differences. According to the 1978 Developmental Disabilities Amendments (Public Law 96–602) developmental disabilities are defined as severe, chronic disabilities attributable to mental or physical impairment which are manifested before age 22, result in substantial limitations in three areas of major life activity and require the need for services over an extended period. The limitations are in several areas: self-care, receptive and expressive language, learning, mobility, self-direction, capacity for independent living, and economic self-sufficiency.

The 1975 Education of all Handicapped Children Act (Public Law 94–142) defines handicapped children in *categorical* terms: as being mentally retarded, hard of hearing, deaf, speech impaired, visually handicapped, seriously emotionally disturbed, orthopedically impaired, other health impaired, deaf–blind, multihandicapped, or having specific learning disabilities.

While a range of disabilities will be discussed, the emphasis here is on more severely disabled and multihandicapped children. Improved medical technology, leading to increased rate of survival of handicapped infants, as well as more sophisticated reporting and analysis, implies we should anticipate the need to provide services to larger numbers of very young, often multiply handicapped, children.

## Community Continuum of Programs and Services

Placing a child in a family atmosphere is the preferred living arrangement, even if this means long-term group and foster homes. All children need to feel part of some kind of unit, they need to feel loved by parenting adults, and they need stability, caring and *kinship*. Thus opportunities for social, educational and human development should be available in a family or family-like environment at an early age, during infancy if necessary.

Deinstitutionalization can only occur when a continuum of family-like opportunities are available to handicapped children in local communities. Group homes, foster care, adoption and other community living alternatives should be understood as an array of interconnected comprehensive and integrated long-term programs and services that support a family-like atmosphere. Developmentally disabled children will need some form of family support services to insure long-term family relationships.

The program and service needs of developmentally disabled children and their families require a variety of patterns and designs adapted to particular circumstances, and will require a great deal of interagency support and coordination. *Family support services* (Wisconsin Council on Developmental Disabilities, 1983) should be understood as packages or clusters that may need to include, depending on the particular complexities, the following:

1. Service coordination, case management, resource linkage, and advocacy
2. Central point of entry and tracking system
3. Early screening and medical and developmental diagnosis
4. Medical needs and specialized therapies
5. Educational and developmental services for the child
6. Mental health support services for the child and family
7. Respite care, substitute care, and day care by trained paraprofessionals
8. Education and in-home training for parents and parent substitutes
9. Physical adaptation to the home
10. Direct cash subsidies
11. Quality of care

## Biological Families

The programs and services discussed here are as necessary for the biological family with a developmentally disabled child as they are for a substitute provider. In fact, often, if the biological family had access to these services, the handicapped child would never need the group home, foster care, or adoption. Little is done to help strengthen and develop a family with a multihandicapped child (Featherstone, 1980) or to strengthen the connections between the child in placement and the family.

Sometimes children have complicated multiple handicaps and/or severe and chronic illnesses. Sometimes problems arise because an infant has birth-related difficulties that place too many demands on parents. Sometimes handicapped infants are born into families that already have serious problems, such as lack of income, substance abuse, or limited parenting capacity. Studies suggest that hospital and institutional placements are often inappropriate, yet children in many states are still institutionalized, sometimes far away from their families, and too often even in distant states (Knitzer, 1982).

The point of entry into the service system determines, usually more than just initially, if the child will be returned to his or her biological family, go into a group home, foster care, or be placed for adoption. If the child was initially institutionalized there will be even more confusion as to which system he or she is placed into. In most states there is little coordination among multiple points of entry. Even worse, as Leviton and Shuger write:

> Maryland's current system of delivering services to handicapped children often requires parents to give up custody to obtain services, primarily because Social Services and Juvenile Services provide residential programs only for children who are committed by the Court to agency custody. The policies of the Maryland Department of Education also sometimes work against the state's goal of keeping families intact . . . if a child has a home circumstances problem that necessitates residential placement, the parent must give up custody of the child to get the Department of Education funds for the educational component of the child's program. (1983:1031–33)

## Group Homes

Group homes—small community-based group residences—are one viable form of alternative living arrangements for developmentally disabled children. Small group homes for children may sometimes be referred to as group foster care homes. It is important that the number of children and counselors in the group home be related to family size in the local neighborhood and to the principle of normalization, although the child's real needs are more important than the theory of normalization. Group homes or group residences with from seven to twenty-five children are mini-institutions: in such settings it is impossible to approximate family life, although some exceptions do work, especially in rural areas. Although small group homes can provide excellent service alternatives for children who are developmentally disabled, they have not been sufficiently developed in the United States. In Maryland, for example, there are only three such homes in the entire state.

The typical group home for children is located in a residential neighborhood, is staffed by salaried live-in professional or paraprofessional houseparents, one of whom is the primary caregiver and the other who may work outside the home during the day. The houseparents are responsible for household management and resident supervision, training, and care. Other paraprofessionals fill in during their days off and provide extra support when all of the children are home. This system insures at least two adults for the care of four children. Excellent ongoing training for group home staff is an essential ingredient for success (Montgomery County, Maryland, Association for Retarded Citizens, 1983).

Case management or service coordination is the heart of such projects for each individual child and for the children as part of a family. Programs and services are individualized for each child and conducted to enhance developmental learning. Project programs and services are planned to maximize utilization of public facilities and generic community resources. The legal and human rights of the children and their biological families or guardians are especially important. Frequent visits and participation by biological parents may help them to understand the needs of their handicapped children, and can help reunite children with them.

In Michigan and Nebraska institutionalized children are moved into group homes to await specialized foster care or adoption, making the group homes one station in a continuum. In the Nebraska model medically fragile children live in the group home until their conditions are stabilized and then are returned to their biological families or placed in specialized foster care. Training in the group homes is designed to develop family skills so that children can function more independently. In Michigan, group homes are part of the overall community based service system which includes community training homes providing specialized foster care, alternative family residences which provide more intensive foster care for up to four persons, a biological parent cash subsidy program, and other temporary more restrictive options (Gardner, 1982).

## Individual Foster Care

Child Welfare agencies traditionally have not been willing to provide foster care to developmentally disabled children, and have instead suggested institutionalization. Developmentally disabled children require specialized foster care, coordinated support services, higher reimbursement rates, specialized education, and most important, ongoing training, supervision, and support for the foster parents. Specialized foster parents, like biological parents, need to have relief or respite care and access to emergency services. Many programs consider the foster parents to be counselors for the children and are part of the treatment teams (Knitzer, 1983).

Permanent foster care with continuing case management and supporting services may be a good alternative for some handicapped children. An increasing number of foster families want to adopt handicapped or developmentally disabled children who have been part of their families. Adoption subsidies and other programs can provide an incentive. Several states have passed legislation creating permanent foster care, a form of legal guardianship which transfers the agency's guardianship rights and responsibilities to the foster parents. While this is an important option in a continuum of services, there is some concern that it might be utilized even when adoption is a feasible alternative (Coyne, 1983).

One study noted that few states "gave priority to foster parents for adoption of children they had cared for for long periods of time" (Children's Defense Fund, 1978). Foster care may be the only alternative when children are not yet legally free for adoption, but these handicapped children could be placed with foster families who are committed to adoption but are willing to accept the risk that the children may not become legally free, thus eliminating interim foster placements.

Many families have gained tremendous satisfaction in fostering handicapped children, as related in the Dickerson family's moving account in *Our Four Boys*. This family, over a period of several years, became foster parents to four moderately to severely retarded male teenagers. One of the unique features of this family was that the foster father, a retired businessman, was the primary parent, while Martha Dickerson was employed outside of the home as a social worker.

The Dickersons saw their role as helping the boys to adjust to life outside of an institution and to encourage as independent a style of self-care and responsibility as possible. The Dickersons were aware that after the age of 18, the boys would most likely move into alternative community settings such as group homes. As parenting people working on developing certain skills, the Dickersons found that they "spent an hour to an hour and a half each day in the boy's bedrooms . . . teaching them step-by-step until the learning had all taken place."

They worked in detail giving as many verbal cues as possible such as to turn a sock around or to put the shoe on the other foot. This family certainly found that providing a structured consistent learning environment takes a great deal of time and energy (Dickerson, 1978). Programs that facilitate successful fostering of developmentally disabled or handicapped children take many forms. A few are described in the following examples.

THE CHIMES PROGRAM. In 1982, the Individualized Residential Family Services Program was developed by a private nonprofit developmental disabilities agency in Baltimore. The Chimes program was developed to place institutionalized children with families in the local community, and was staffed by licensed social workers. This project demonstrated that agencies and advocacy organizations serving handicapped children can successfully work cooperatively with the Child Welfare system. Potential foster parents attended an orientation session, and more typically, a home study was then implemented. The foster parent training was contracted to another community developmental disabilities agency, and an ongoing training program is still in progress, including a two-part seminar on sexuality. Future parent training will continue to provide information on topics of interest, as well as support the continuation of the informal support network that has spontaneously developed among the parents (The Chimes, 1982).

THE YPSILANTI PROGRAM. In 1965 at Ypsilanti State Hospital in Michigan a special after care foster home program for children being released from a psychiatric hospital was developed. A team approach was used including intensive social casework supplemented by consultation and direct service from medical, psychiatric, nursing, and education professionals.

Foster families and children were matched on an individual basis. Children were selected for the program because of their perceived ability to function in and benefit from community living. Foster parents who were active in their communities were helpful in encouraging local acceptance of the children. The foster parents were viewed as part of a treatment team capable of carrying out specific treatment plans. Biological parents also received casework services (Bryant, 1982).

THE FAMILY CARE PROGRAM. In 1968, the Family Care Program of California's Community Service Division developed a program to integrate previously institutionalized retarded children at Somona State Hospital back into community living. The children were placed in special foster care homes where the foster parents participated with the hospital in developing individual treatment plans. These plans were written in concrete terms dealing with specific items of toileting and self-care.

It was found that 25 percent of the children placed in regular foster homes were returned to institutional care, whereas only 7 percent of the children in special foster care were returned to the hospital. Once again the value of working with foster parents as part of the treatment team greatly contributed to the success of these foster home placements.

THE ALASKA PROGRAM. In 1977 the Alaska Vision and Hearing Impaired Program, in coordination with the Alaska Developmental Disabilities and the Northwest Regional Center for Deaf–Blind Children began a foster program for institutionalized multihandicapped children.

Foster care represented a more normalized environment. This program has a number of innovative features. In order to recruit foster parents with the necessary expertise a monthly payment of $1000 was budgeted for each placement. The project provided both pre- and in-service training for foster families, and the foster homes were families where trust and interdependence were encouraged. "The youth, rather than working for nutrients or token reinforcers, are learning those behaviors modeled and encouraged by people with whom they have found positive personal relationships" (Farrington, 1981:239). This model encouraged accelerated individual progress, provided much more adequately for individual needs, and significantly reduced the cost of programs and services.

## Adoption

One hundred thousand or more American children are awaiting adoption. About 90 percent of them are older, minorities, handicapped, hard-to-place, or some combination of these characteristics. "Those families who are willing or able to accept the additional responsibilities involved in parenting children with handicaps are not waiting on the doorsteps of adoption agencies. Nor are all social workers prepared to handle the multiple demands involved in special families, in helping them to assess their interest and in becoming parents to these children, and in preparing them to become part of their new families" (Ryan and Warren, 1974:i). Yet, research by Coyne and Brown (1983) indicates that a large number of children of all ages and disabilities have been placed for adoption with few disruptions. It was discovered that (1) agencies in smaller cities are more successful in placing developmentally disabled children for adoption. (2) Adoptions occur at all ages, but agencies tend to delay placement of handicapped infants. (3) The majority of children placed were mentally retarded or cerebral palsied. (4) The presence of highly sophisticated medical service is not a necessary condition for placement, but easily obtained special education services are more important. (5) Half the children in this study were adopted without a subsidy. (6) The lack of an available subsidy should not be seen as an insurmountable barrier. (7) Private insurance, Medicaid, and/or SSI may provide support for these children and should be explored.

Over the past few years more agencies and potential adoptive parents including foster parents, have become interested in adopting handicapped children. This is related in part to the permanency movement, to deinstitutionalization, and to the support available through subsidized adoption. Perhaps even more important in the increase of adoption of handicapped children is that fewer young children without any handicapping conditions are available to the many families who wish to adopt. A greater understanding of handicapping conditions and a great deal more publicity about developmentally disabled children has added to a growing interest, and has led some of these families to consider a handicapped child. At the same time there continue to be structural barriers, bias and misunderstanding, and lack of cooperation, among the Child Welfare, mental retardation, and mental health systems which undermine adoptive programs for handicapped children. Adoptive parent organizations and other advocacy groups like the North American Council on Adoptable Children and Family Builder agencies have taken leadership roles in this area.

Our research and experience indicates, at least for the short-term, that many more developmentally disabled children will be adopted if: we rely on specialized agencies that have a track record; we emphasize local, state, and regional adoption exchanges; and require specialized training for adoption workers, who work with handicapped children and potential adoptive families.

Family Builder agencies provide the largest coordinated effort. In 1982 these agencies placed almost 300 children, 70 percent of whom were disabled. A high proportion were multihandicapped, were older, and had complicated emotional problems. Family Builder agencies:

- charge no fees of adoptive parents;
- seek reimbursement of full placement cost from state and private referring agencies;
- collaborate with other agencies through accepting referrals on children needing families and sharing placement practice experience;
- provide training and consultation;
- provide postadoption services.

Evidence is mounting that local, state, and regional adoption exchanges are effective. An adoption exchange is a mechanism through which children who are available for adoption are brought to the attention of families who are interested in adopting them. Adoption exchanges provide photolisting in small pamphlets and in large resource books at adoption and social service agencies. In some areas they have initiated significant media coverage including regular press and television coverage (National Adoption Exchange, n.d.).

Adoption workers should be aware studies have indicated that "interaction with workers in other counties leads to making placements and more placements, whereas interaction with workers in one's own agency and with workers in other agencies in the same county is negatively related to the number of placements" (CWLA, 1981). Agencies whose staff have attended permanency planning training or other training have placed many more developmentally disabled children in adoption than agencies where workers have not been trained.

A number of training models have been developed, and through federal grants, a significant number of people have been trained in the field of special needs adoption. These include a module on "Children in Need of Special Services" developed by Creative Associates (1983), the TEAM training package developed by the North American Council on Adoptable Children, a training package developed by the University of Georgia (DHHS, 1982), and Project CRAFT developed at the University of Michigan. All of these are available at reasonable cost.

In many, if not most, cases adoption subsidies are needed to help adoptive families bear the increased costs of raising a handicapped child. "For the child, adoption assistance means *permanence* and a clear legal status. For the parents it is the opportunity to assume full parental responsibilities. For agencies, adoption with subsidy means fewer children wait and more foster family spots are available with fewer agency resources expended. And for a tougher population of children without permanent homes, it means hope" (North American Council on Adoptable Children, 1983). The story of Tanya illustrates this point.

Tanya was a bright and active six-year-old, born with multiple skeletal and muscular anomalies, when Kathryn and Norty Wheeler first read about her in the *Chicago Sun Times'* column entitled "Sunday's Child." Each week, a different child was featured. The children were all available for adoption, but were considered hard-to-place because they were older or had physical, mental, or emotional handicaps. Tanya had lived through a series of foster homes, hospitals, doctors, surgical operations, broken bones and braces prior to her appearance in the paper. At one point, a psychologist had recommended that she be placed in an institution because of her physical and intellectual limitations. He felt "that she needed a highly structured environment and that raising Tanya in a home would interfere with the optimal psychosocial development of normal siblings." Fortunately a committed social worker intervened and took into account Tanya's strengths and potential adoptability.

The Wheelers were confronted with the difficult task of dealing with multiple medical doctors, disagnostic procedures, and school personnel. Many parents of severely handicapped children face similar problems with conflicting diagnoses and recommendations. The Wheelers were successful in having Tanya placed in her local public school. The importance of support and assistance in negotiating and advocating for a handicapped child are emphasized. Mrs. Wheeler says that "if you do not have good friends and resources in the community, it will be impossible."

Now, the Wheelers cannot imagine life without Tanya and many of her socially unacceptable behaviors have been greatly modified. She has developed friendships with children in the neighborhood and school.

They feel that their biological son, who is two years younger than Tanya, has greatly benefited from the experience of growing and interacting with Tanya. She has truly become a part of the Wheeler family (Wheeler, 1979). The following profile highlights one of the many programs that have worked successfully in the adoption of developmentally disabled children.

Spaulding for Children, founded in a little farmhouse in Chelsea, Michigan, took early and creative leadership in the adoption of older and handicapped children. There are now several Spaulding for Children agencies throughout the country. One such agency is the New Jersey Spaulding for Children, a free, private adoption agency that works solely for older and handicapped children. These are children who have no permanent families of their own and who are in ongoing public care unless adopted.

John Boyne, Director of Spaulding for New Jersey points out the importance of looking at the whole child and not just seeing the child in terms of a disability. He stresses the importance of expanding labels into descriptions and going into the details of the impact of particular disabilities on day-to-day life. All of this information needs to be shared with prospective adoptive parents. Boyne finds that those who adopt special needs children tend to be quite ordinary people who happen to have a special openness to one or another sort of child and tend to focus spontaneously on what the child can do more than on what he or she cannot do. In the past ten years Spaulding of New Jersey has successfully placed more than 500 children in adoptive homes. 90 percent of those children have reached court finalized adoptions that have endured to date (Boyne, 1979; De Leon and Westerberg, 1980).

## Public Policy and Public Support

Children's services are fragmented in most states. Most of us have a great deal of difficulty understanding which state agencies have the responsibility for which handicapped children. Children with similar needs are often served by different systems. Programs often work at cross purposes; various service systems are segregated from each other; experts in one area of serving handicapped children have little contact within and between agencies. Little substantive training bridges the abyss: Professional practice differences abound. As children get older and are no longer eligible for education and children's services, little transition is provided into services for developmentally disabled adults. It is perhaps simpler, politically, to plan for services that substitute for the family rather than support it. It is often easier to place a child than to offer services to him or her and the family while the child remains at home. Relatives are often prevented from taking care of children. Traditionally Medicaid funds have kept handicapped children in hospitals, nursing homes, and institutions, when living with their biological parents, or in foster care, group homes, or adoptive homes was much more appropriate and cost effective. Some shifts are occurring in this policy and a child living out of an institution may be eligible for Medicaid, provided that: (1) the child requires the level of care which would be provided in an institution; (2) it is appropriate to provide such care outside of an institution; and (3) the estimated cost of providing such care is no more expensive than the estimated cost of institutional care. Some states have developed a creative combination of using SSI and Medicaid to deinstitutionalize children (United Cerebral Palsy Association, 1983). The Adoption Assistance and Child Welfare Act of 1980 supports the move toward the adoption of handicapped children through making possible federal reimbursement for adoption subsidy and for medical coverage for children with special needs.

Despite these beginning changes, progress toward family and family-like care for developmentally disabled and handicapped children is slow. In Maryland, for example, 500 children under 21 are in state mental retardation institutions; 374 children have been placed in out-of-state institutions; another 300 are in state institutions for children who are blind, deaf, and/or multihandicapped; 300 children are placed in state mental health institutions, and Maryland places another 200 in out-of-state mental health institutions. If children with other disabilities are included, the number increases sharply to more than 2,000. Most of these children are placed in institutions for other than educational reasons. In many cases, the biological family cannot care for the child because support services or other community living arrangements are not available (Maryland Developmental Disabilities Council, 1979–1983).

In Maryland the Governor has responded to these problems by establishing the State Coordinating Council on Services to Handicapped Children. The executive director of this office, Philip C. Holmes, believes that interagency cooperation and partnership can be accomplished politically and practically by the executive department of state government. It is Holmes's job in Maryland to coordinate funding, programs, and services to out-of-home, often out-of-state children. The State Coordinating Council is made up of the Secretaries of Human Resources (Social Services), Education, and Mental Hygiene/Mental Retardation, and Holmes is setting up local coordinating councils in each county (Holmes, 1983). The State Coordinating Council has the unique opportunity to coordinate the delivery of services to handicapped children in a state "that is riddled with problems including inappropriate or inadequate services, delays in service delivery, and sometimes a denial of all services" (Leviton and Shuger, 1983).

The goals of permanency planning, deinstitutionalization, and family-based care are yet to be fully realized for developmentally disabled or handicapped children. Clearly a continuum of alternative programs and services is needed, beginning with supportive services, so that biological families can meet the needs of their handicapped children at home. In cases where maintaining the child with his or her biological family is not possible, a substitute family or family-like care should be provided.

# EXEMPLAR VI–B

# Subsidized Adoption
## Explication of a Social Policy Issue

GLORIA WALDINGER

Subsidized adoption is widely regarded as an innovative technology for enabling specific categories of children in out-of-home care, who cannot return to their birth families, to establish new permanent ties, either with the foster families with whom they have been living or with other adoptive parents. In this discussion, the practice of subsidized adoption will be set in its historical and ideological context and related to other forms of substitute care. The current status and use of subsidized adoption will be reviewed, and research findings concerning how it is viewed by participants in it will be presented. Implications for practice will be drawn.

Because it has been demonstrated to be a useful means both for achieving permanent homes for children as well as for saving tax dollars, subsidized adoption has been lauded by both Child Welfare professionals and legislators. The adoption subsidy provisions of the Adoption Assistance and Child Welfare Act of 1980 (Public Law 96–272) appear to have played a significant role in saving that bill from recision in the summer of 1981 when other social programs were incorporated into block grants.

Yet despite the strong political backing and formal support by Child Welfare professionals of subsidy programs as a standard for adoption practice (Child Welfare League of America, 1968; Model State Subsidized Adoption Act & Regulations, 1976), policy analysts representing a range of constituencies persistently voice a measure of ambivalence with respect to subsidizing adoptive placements. Those unsure of this practice include social work practitioners, agency administratiors, educators, and even some adoptive parents (Andrews, 1971; Goldberg, 1977; Joe, 1979; Waldinger, 1979; Watson, 1972).

Arguments against adoption subsidies fall into two broad categories. The first focuses on deficiencies or flaws in the structure and administration of current state programs, only some of which are remedied in Public Law 96–272 (Cole, 1981; Seelig, 1976–1977). The second category of concerns which view the subsidy as incompatible with the ideals of the adoptive relationships is of greater relevance to this discussion. Critics suggest that adoption should be based on affective rather than financial motivations—that adoptees placed with subsidized families could feel stigmatized and resentful because they were "paid for" rather than "chosen." Detractors also feel that the subsidy program might be viewed as the preferred option for all children placed for adoption, rather than just for those whose "special needs" create financial hardships for adoptive families of average means.

In light of the acknowledged positive benefits of adoption subsidies, such reservations seem surprising at first. However, on further reflection those concerns can be understood as illustrating the contradictory strains inherent in this country's unwillingness, since colonial times, to share with families both financial support and authority for the care of their children. The traditional societal response to situations in which parents were unable to provide adequately for their children has been to place them in substitute care until their parents could resume full responsibility. Rarely has it been acknowledged that it invariably costs more to support a child out of the home than to supplement the birth family's income.

## Public Support to Families

The notion of shared responsibility, through which the public sector would assist parents in caring for their children, has never been given serious consideration in this nation's social welfare policy. Similarly, public payment to extended family members to reduce the financial burden of taking in the children of relatives unable to care for them has not been willingly provided. Consistent with that attitude, payment to non-relative substitute parents initially was not provided at all.

In colonial times younger children in need of care and supervision were auctioned or "farmed out" to families who received no monetary payment, agreeing to provide care until the children were self-supporting (Thurston, 1930). Older children were "bound out," expected to exchange their services for board and care. The mid-nineteenth century practice of placing unattached and unsupervised children of immigrant parents from Eastern cities with Midwestern farm families was a more organized version of the same theme. All of these arrangements relied heavily on the notion that large families—extra hands to work—were an economic advantage. However, by the late nineteenth century a number of factors operated as deterrents to the continued use of free foster homes. Among these were: the lack of regulation or supervision of these placements; the failure to match the religion of the children with their new families; and the concern that large numbers were ending up, as young adults, in jails and institutions (Hart, 1924; Thurston, 1930). In addition, the backlog of children who, because of age, behavior, or disability, proved to be "too great a tax" on the average free foster homes increased (Thurston, 1930:137). It is interesting to note that the population of children who meet the current eligibility criteria for the federally funded adoption subsidy program bear a striking resemblance to the children described by Thurston as "too great a tax" on the average free foster home.

## Payment to Substitute Parents

The first law to provide payment to meet the cost of maintaining children in foster family homes was passed in Massachusetts in 1860. Providing financial remuneration rather than expecting child labor to compensate for care was consistent with the humanitarian sentiments of the antislavery movement of that period. It also coincided with an increased awareness of the damaging effect on children of being reared in institutions that housed a broad range of residents, including the sick, insane, and impoverished.

Preference for placing children in family settings rather than institutions became the dominant mode of Child Welfare practice in the 1920s. At about the same time, the use of paid foster homes took precedence over free foster homes. Initially, payments to foster parents were available only through private sources. However, legislation providing for public monies for this service soon was enacted by a number of states, although federal participation in foster family care programs was not authorized until 1962.

For the most part, monies paid to foster parents have been based on costs of maintaining the child and have not included payment for child-care services. Nonetheless, the reluctance to pay persons to parent is firmly established in this country's ideologies; society even views payments to substitute parents with ambivalence. Writing in 1922, when paying foster parents was beginning to be used more widely as a Child Welfare practice, the director of the Child Welfare League of America notes: "No home should be used that does not give the boarded child much more than is being paid for by the board money. This provides against commercialization of the work" (Hart, 1924:12).

Even today, foster parents are suspect simply because they are paid, thereby compromising the altruism of the role (Benet, 1976:71). Moreover, the fact that foster parents have traditionally been recruited from among lower-middle-class families has strengthened foster care's association with financial need. Boarding unrelated children served as one way for women to earn "pin money" without subjecting their families to the major reorganization of roles likely to occur when they sought employment outside the home. At the same time, the perception of foster parenting as a blue-collar enterprise undoubtedly played a part in keeping more affluent families from participating in the program. ("What would the neighbors think?")

Further cause for ambivalence toward foster parenting is the consequence of the high value placed by society on blood ties, and the tendency to view the child's placement in a substitute family as an inferior alternative (Maluccio, 1973:12). Until very recently, foster care has been regarded as a temporary expedient whose goal was the return of children to their birth families. However, because of our reluctance to provide payments to parents who are unable to care adequately for their children, public policy has, until passage of the 1980 Adoption Assistance and Child Welfare Act, favored investing resources primarily in providing substitute care for children away from home. For that reason, funds to strengthen the biological family to remedy the problem that precipitated the child's removal have been sorely lacking. As a result, the temporary nature of foster care has too often been a myth.

Only recently has adoption by foster parents of the children they boarded become an acceptable choice. It was, in fact, standard practice for child placement agencies to require foster parents to sign agreements specifically disavowing interest in adopting children placed in their homes on a foster care basis. A number of reasons for such policies existed, though most were related to the presumed temporary nature of foster care. Prospective adoption applicants had to meet much more stringent criteria than foster parents. It was, therefore, assumed that foster parents were not equally qualified to establish lifelong bonds with these children, or parent them successfully, without the support of agency supervision.

A further consideration is that conversion from foster to adoptive status disturbs the supply of foster homes at a time when such resources are diminishing. Fewer women than in the past are choosing foster parenting for a variety of reasons, among them: increased financial demands on families that place pressure on women to secure jobs that augment family income more substantially; greater societal acceptance of the two working parents family model; and the growing devaluation of the housewife role. In addition, some evidence suggests that the majority of foster families that adopt subsequently withdraw from the foster care program (Proch, 1980). For those who continue as foster parents, little is known about the effect of the adoption of one foster child in a home in which there are other foster children. Clearly this question warrants further study.

## Payment to Adoptive Parents

Until the late 1960s, the notion of linking financial support with adoption would have been regarded as a contradiction. Modern adoption practice which primarily involved placement of healthy, white infants, was essentially a resource to remedy infertility problems of white, middle-class families, while at the same time providing a cost efficient permanent plan for infants born out-of-wedlock and in need of care. For the most part these adoptive parents neither needed financial assistance nor desired ongoing contact with the agency that facilitated the placement. All parties mutually understood that these "socially engineered" families would quickly become indistinguishable from the general population.

Toward the end of the 1960s, because of such factors as more permissive social attitudes toward single parenthood and the legalization of abortion, the number of healthy infants available for adoption declined sharply. At about the same time it became public knowledge that increasing numbers of children were growing up in foster care who, because of age, race, ethnicity, physical, mental or emotional disability, or sibling status had not previously been regarded as adoptable. The search for permanent plans for these children stimulated the development of innovative strategies. One of the most viable options has been the plan to establish adoptive ties between those children in long-term care and their foster families. The passage of adoption subsidy legislation in most states eliminated the financial barrier preventing some foster families from making the legal commitment to children who had already become emotionally integrated into their families. To what extent has this resource been utilized since 1968 when the first enabling statute was passed?

Comprehensive national statistics on adoption activity are unavailable; there are even less complete figures for families involved in subsidized adoption programs. A 1977 report, prepared for a Senate Committee hearing testimony on proposed federally subsidized adoption legislation, summarized the three-year experience of eighteen states. In

1974, 1975, and 1976, there were, respectively, 1,400, 2,400, and 2,700 subsidized placements. Of these, approximately 90 percent of the adoptive parents had served as foster parents for the children involved (U.S. Congress, Senate, 1977:100). Another study, conducted by Shaffer (1977), of a random sample of more than 1,600 subsidized adoptions completed in Illinois between 1969 and 1976, revealed that more than 80 percent of the children had been placed first on a foster care basis. In over 60 percent of these cases, the child lived in the home in a foster care status for more than four years before the status was converted to adoption. A later study (Proch, 1980:12–14) indicated that considerable variation existed across states with regard to adoption by foster parents. Twenty-two states and the District of Columbia responded to a brief questionnaire, reporting that in 1978 adoption by foster parents represented between 12 percent to 60 percent of all public agency placements.

Proch speculates that the variation could be attributed to a number of factors including: availability of other adoptive resources; effectiveness of permanency planning efforts; Child Welfare practitioners' attitudes; and lack of knowledge about adoption on the part of foster parents. A high rate of adoption by foster parents is consistent with the philosophy and intent of most state-subsidized adoption programs, the Model Subsidized Adoption Act, and the new federal Adoption Assistance and Child Welfare Act of 1980 (Public Law 96–272), which give first preference to the adoption of legally free children by their foster parents, provided significant emotional ties have developed (Proch, 1980:13).

## Research Findings

A small number of research studies have attempted to examine foster parent adoptions in greater depth. In 1979, Proch interviewed a randomly selected sample of adoptive foster parents and children residing in the Chicago area. The study was designed to explore such questions as why foster parents adopt, the nature of their relationship with the child placing agency, and the significance of converting the child's status from foster care to adoption. References to subsidy payment related primarily to identifying who initiated discussions about the program and whether the family would have adopted if the funds had not been available. Subsidies were granted to 87 percent of the study families; 77 percent said they definitely would have adopted even if the funds had not been available (Proch, 1980:96).

In a follow-up study of the Oregon Permanency Planning Project, Lahti and her associates (1978) reported that of the 40 percent of project children who were adopted, half were adopted by their foster parents. The focus of this study was on the child's adjustment; they did not address the question of the utilization or impact of subsidy payments. Both Proch and Lahti judged these foster home adoptions to be successful by all measures employed.

The only study that attempted to examine how adoptive families perceive the subsidy payments was conducted by the author (Waldinger, 1979). Fifty foster families that adopted children who had first been placed on a foster-care basis were interviewed. All of the families received a monthly grant under California's adoption program.

Until the state law was changed to comply with federal funding requirements, California's subsidy program differed on two major points from Public Law 96–272 and from subsidy legislation in most other states: eligibility of adoptive parents and duration. Almost half of all state laws included the provision that adoptive parents receiving subsidies only demonstrate that their income was being fully utilized to maintain their family standard of living. The inclusion of an adopted child would, therefore, result in a lowered standard for all members. California's law was more restrictive in that only parents from lower economic and disadvantaged groups could qualify for adoption subsidies. California was also one of the few states that limited the duration of the grant to a specific time (i.e., three years, with the possibility of a two-year extension if need could be demonstrated). In 1975, an amendment was passed authorizing the extension of the subsidy when there was continued financial need related to the chronic health condition that initially necessitated the subsidy.

One of the questions the California study sought to explore was whether these adoptive parents shared the widely held prejudice against paying people to parent and, therefore, felt stigmatized because of their participation in the subsidy program. They were asked to indicate which, on a list of six other transfer programs designed to support or supplement family incomes, the adoption subsidy program was most like. The six programs differ not only in the extent to which they provide support, but also in terms of whether recipients are viewed, by themselves and others, as entitled to that support. Fifty-six percent of those interviewed said they saw the subsidy as most like the negatively regarded public assistance program, Aid to Families with Dependent Children (AFDC). The more socially accepted social programs were selected with less frequency. Sixteen percent considered the adoption subsidy as much like Social Security; 14 percent as similar to child support; 8 percent likened it to an educational scholarship; 2 percent to Army Dependents Benefits; and 2 percent were unable to say.

Subjects had considerable difficulty responding to this question. When this area was probed further, it appeared that association of the subsidy with AFDC stemmed from a number of sources: the respondents' feelings about receiving unearned public funds; the negative views of the larger society toward such assistance; and aspects of the administration of the subsidy program that were experienced as being similar to public welfare. These findings suggest that these subsidized adoptive parents did not see themselves as participating in an entitlement program. The ambivalence they reported reflects this country's traditional reluctance to share with families both funding and authority for the care of their children.

Subsidized adoption cannot be regarded in isolation from other public policies dealing with support to children and their families. There is, however, little likelihood that a coherent national family policy will be forthcoming in the near future. The federal leadership inherent in the new Adoption Assistance and Child Welfare Act of 1980 might have served as an opportunity to establish adoption subsidy as one component of a comprehensive strategy for providing services to children and families at risk. However under the Reagan administration such an outcome is unlikely.

## Implications for Practice

At this point in time, adoption subsidies can best be viewed as a single element of an expanded practice technology that must include preventive services to maintain the integrity of biological families, early reunification services when the child's removal cannot be avoided, and timely permanency planning when children cannot be returned home. Subsidized adoptions belong within that last category of options. The population for whom such a strategy is appropriate differs significantly from traditional adoptive families in terms of the rewards and challenges associated with parenting these "special needs" children. The concept of shared responsibility over an extended period of time is particularly appropriate in achieving the individual plans most likely to enhance the maximum potential of these children.

Finally, it is important to recognize that although Child Welfare professionals have traditionally considered adoption as the preferred or most "tidy" plan for children who cannot be reared by their birth parents (Bush and Gordon, 1982), under some circumstances other permanent plans, such as guardianship or long-term foster care, may be more suitable. When extensive ongoing contact between the child and members of his or her biological family is likely, adoption may present unnecessary stresses. Some foster parents are advanced in age and have limited resources, or possibly the child is unlikely to achieve full social or economic independence; these situations may call for permanent plans, but not necessarily adoption. Further, where there are several foster children in the home, the foster parents may be reluctant to single out one to adopt.

Also, some empirical evidence indicates that postadoption adjustment may be more problematic for children whose foster parents would have preferred to retain the foster status, but felt pressured by the agency to adopt (Raynor, 1980:69–70). On the other hand, research findings also indicate that the child's *perception* of permanence rather than the legal status of the placement is most closely associated with long-term positive outcome (Lahti, 1978:26). Clearly, further studies involving larger samples need to be undertaken. Until then one should view subsidized adoption as an effective tool among a range of possible options for children unable to be reunited with their birth families.

# EXEMPLAR VI–C

# Self-Help Groups in Adoption
## The Search Movement

Penny Callan Partridge

The Indian writer Nagarjuna asks: "If the fear comes from the protector, who is there to protect you from this fear?" Adult adoptees, who have organized over the past decade into an extensive self-help and advocacy network, answer: Our peers. Together we can move beyond the fears of our protectors.

As an adoptee, my experience with the adoptee self-help network has been direct and personal. As a social worker, I believe that all helping professionals can learn much from self-help groups. Furthermore, I believe that people in the Child Welfare field can gain valuable insights from the experiences of adoptees. This discussion will share some of these insights. It will describe what needs we have had for association with each other, what we have learned about ourselves as a group, and what we are trying to change about adoption.

Adoptees who are now adults were born and adopted before the civil rights advances, the increased openness about sex, the emphasis on sharing one's feelings, and other cultural changes of the late 1960s. We were born at a time when our very existence—because, typically, our parents were not married—defied social mores and provoked crises of sometimes tragic proportions in our first families. Our second families often suffered monumental crises too. Our adoptive parents often found themselves unable to produce biological offspring and so had to face the loss of whatever the anticipation of having their own children had meant to them, both as a couple and as members of their extended families.

The adoptee's earliest life history took place within a context of personal upheaval for both his or her birth relatives and adoptive relatives. Indeed, the adoptee's moving from one family to another constituted a partial solution to the problems of both families, but it also partially masked the deeper aspects of those problems, which remained unresolved for both families. No one, however, seemed to anticipate that there would be fallout for the adoptee or that the adoptee's situation in and of itself might be problematic. This denial was shared by all the adults in the situation: by the birth parents who suffered shame and loss, by the adoptive parents who faced infertility and a sense of failure as well as loss, and by the professionals who offered adoption as a solution. In fact, everyone concerned seems to have projected their hopes for adoption itself on to adoptees: It should be a complete and happy solution for all parties concerned. Birth parents and other birth relatives would proceed as if a birth had never taken place and no child had been removed forever from their care and from their world. Adoptive parents would feel completely compensated for their lack of biological children; they could raise their adopted children exactly as they would have raised biological offspring. Finally, it was assumed that growing up in an adoptive rather than biological family made no emotional difference to that person. If adoptees indicated otherwise, this could be explained in terms of individual inadequacy rather than a result of being adopted, as illustrated in the following excerpts from the adoption literature.

> The best-adjusted child is the one who almost never thinks about the facts of his natural birth, or, if he is of the sensitive, introspective type . . . who carries way back in his consciousness, no more than a sense of sympathy for an unfortunate but not repugnant or culpable person. (Cady and Cady, 1956:118)

> For an adopted child to dwell on the fact that his original parents did not want him is to be foolish and wasteful of the realities which are his and the blessings that have come his way through adoption. Parents give up their children . . . for numerous reasons but none of them are of any direct importance to the children. (Schachtel, 1978)

> Some adoptees begin or join search organizations to help others search. One can speculate that an unresolved sense of loss and abandonment has become a dominant force in their lives. (Andrews, 1979:21)

Adoptees, most of whom did not know or had never spoken with another adoptee, assumed that their experience as adoptees was unique to them as individuals. They accepted their protectors' (adoptive parents' and adoption and mental health professionals') views that any discontent or concern over adoption-related issues constituted personal failure to make a healthy adjustment.

In 1973, a book was published which raised the consciousness of thousands and became the catalyst that gave adoptees access to each other and to many of their heretofore unexpressed feelings about being adopted. In *The Search for Anna Fisher*, Florence Fisher told the story of her own immense struggle to learn her origins. She also included communication from other adoptees, for example, from one who wrote poignantly about raising dogs—their ancestry was known while hers was not.

Now over 200 groups are in motion in North America in which adoptees meet together, sometimes joined by birth parents of adoptees and to a lesser extent adoptive parents, to explore the facts and feelings surrounding their adoptions. Turning to each other seems to be the only way we can genuinely sort out what are common adoption experiences and what, on the other hand, are experiences unique to us as individuals. Also it is the only way in which we can do our exploring with others who have a high stake in discovering the truth as opposed to those who cling to the concept of adoption as a "happy ending–no complications" story.

As adoptees have met together and shared, we have learned a great deal about the experiences and responses that seem to be common among us. The following is not a comprehensive profile of adoptees and the adoption experience, but describes some of the major themes that repeatedly emerge when adoptees exchange their thoughts and feelings.

Almost all of us have experienced our adoptive parents as being threatened, at least to some degree, by our interest in our origins. Their discomfort has ranged from honest and open sharing of information, albeit with quavering voice, to not telling the adoptee he or she is adopted (ever, until an enormous family argument, or until a deathbed scene). Some adoptive parents provide inconsistent information about birth relatives or can have coughing fits or even loss of consciousness when the subject of adoption is brought up. Some parents have told the adoptee not to bring up the subject to the other adoptive parent because he or she would be too hurt.

Most of us have attempted to protect our adoptive parents from knowing the extent of our interest in our birth backgrounds. Both as children and later, this has often meant not voicing our questions and concerns. In adolescence and young adulthood, many of us have demonstrated an unusually fierce loyalty to our adoptive parents; and while this no doubt helped to reassure them (and ourselves) that we are really theirs, it also impeded our separating from them and becoming independent adults. Then, in spite of the guilt that "doing something behind their backs" may bring, some adoptees choose not to tell their adoptive parents that they are attempting to find, or have met, their birth parents. Some adoptees have not felt themselves able even to contact a support group until their adoptive parents were dead.

Most of us have felt keenly the absence of biological connectedness to anyone around us. We have a wistful fascination with the physical resemblances in biological families. We often rush toward having children ourselves to provide us with a "flesh and blood" connection. A young adopted man, newly a father, said: "It is just something that makes your whole body feel so good, knowing that there is somebody with your own blood out there in this world." Some adoptees are aware of having acted out some scrap of information they have known about a birth relative in order to better feel a relationship with that person. If, for instance, an Irish background is known, the adoptee might study Irish culture.

Most of us have been aware of the effects of our genetic difference from our adoptive relatives. A friend of mine was the one adopted child in a large family that was very musical. She was also the one child in the family who couldn't play at least one musical instrument very well. Although this could have happened to a child who was biologically related, she had a strong sense, because of this difference, of not belonging to the same extent that the other children did. In a newspaper interview, the writer Harold Brodkey recounted, "I was adopted when I was two. When I was five, the school I went to decided I was a genius—not just a high IQ kid but Newton: my adoptive parents, both of whom had flunked out of college, couldn't bear it; the stink was enormous" (Wolff, 1975:53). Brodkey has written: "Mama said to me, 'It will never be me who will get the credit for anything you do.' She said, 'Make it easy for the rest of us—be ordinary,'" (Brodkey, 1976:90). In addition to not having our genetic inheritances reinforced by having people around us with the same endowments (looks, temperament, talents, etc.), it may be that while our peers in biological families were developing ways to differentiate themselves from their families (becoming distinct individuals in the process), we adoptees were trying to be more *like* our families, to secure our sense of belonging.

A trait adoptees have come to laugh about as we see it in ourselves and others is a kind of indefiniteness. This indefiniteness can take the form of a vagueness in appearance, passivity, a need to please others, or fear of going against them. It may be understood as a result of the feeling that if we differentiate ourselves too much, we may lose our adoptive family as well as our biological connections. It may also be related to the fact that each of us has a large unknown part of ourselves, a part that most people take for granted, which are our origins and what the people we have come from are like. To quote Brodkey again, "My inner sense of everything remained tentative, shadowy, elusory of course, patient—everything in me was placed like a thing I'd found and brought home and that had childishly perceived attributes, glimpsed or stared at, attached to it . . . incomplete; each tag said: incomplete: in time you'll know. Maybe" (ibid.:66).

For so many of us in the last few years, the antidote, after realizing we were emotionally "on hold," has been the decision that our origins are an important part of us, that we are entitled to them, and that we will do what we can to find them. Many fears are associated with this decision, but not the fear that is projected onto us so much by others— the fear of "what we will find." It seems to me that real knowledge is so attractive to us that by the time we pull ourselves together to search for it, we fear less *what* we will find than we fear hurting our adoptive parents or not being able to find much, no matter how hard we try. For example, we fear finding significant birth relatives dead or not wanting to communicate with us, but not what they might have to tell us. The amazing thing about making this decision to search is that even before any step is taken as a result of it, adoptees often experience a significant increase in self-esteem, they no longer feel "on hold," they seem to switch from a passive to an active stance in life.

The process of undertaking a search for origins in and of itself, apart from the decision to undertake it and apart from the information uncovered or the people found, often serves as an extensive personalized course in assertiveness training. The following accounts illustrate this idea. The first comes from Florence Fisher, who has remained a tireless champion of adoptees' right to know their origins. The next comes from the friend of an adoptee, who wrote to share with an organization of adoptees how moved she was by the search her friend made when she was in her late forties.

> Each search has a life of its own. Something happens to the searcher himself. You will change. With each bit of information, each small success, you will become more self-assured, more analytical, more unafraid. Whatever the outcome, whatever you find, you will find . . . yourself. The search will make you strong. (Fisher, 1979:1)

> After some months of tracing her adoptive parents' lines, she rather tentatively began the arduous task of trying to trace her birth parents, particularly her mother. There were days, weeks, even months when she would be discouraged, seeming to find closed doors at every turn. Then there was the ever present doubt, "Should I leave it all alone?," compounded by the many who voiced those actual words. She, however, was most fortunate in the constant support of her husband and children. There then were the days when another bit of information would be added to the growing collection and she would be exultant and sure she was doing the right

thing. Until knowing her, I had not been aware of the adoptee's seemingly universal feeling of incompleteness, and yes, in many cases, inferiority and rejection. Her search has brought her fortitude, determination, insights, and strengths she had never known she possessed to such depths. (Pierce, 1982)

After making a significant discovery about our backgrounds, whether this includes a warm reception from birth relatives or not, adoptees typically use the word "peace" to describe how we feel. There may also be a letting down period—as happens after most major accomplishments—a need to go back into oneself and rest. There is also, eventually if not immediately, considerable energy, which had gone into the search, freed, energy that can be rechanneled into relationships that may have been somewhat neglected, including those with adoptive parents. The adoptive parents themselves, if they have been aware of the search, may be tremendously relieved at this point to discover that their "worst fears" have not been realized, that they will not lose the adoptee to his or her birth family.

Adoptees also sometimes talk about the increased sexual energy they feel after contact with birth relatives. This may be a result of actually feeling "more physical," more in touch with our own "flesh and blood" selves after being *with* "flesh and blood" relatives. It could also be mere exhilaration or a fascination with the new people who may be in our lives. (Many adoptees talk about sexual attraction to birth siblings. Two I know of have acted on it, briefly, probably in part because the attraction had been completely unexpected and because they had not experienced the strong sibling incest taboo reinforced in the biological family. The need to raise the possibility of such unanticipated feelings with adoptees who are searching should be considered.)

Any relationship that develops between adoptees and birth relatives seems to depend very much on the individuals involved—their respective life circumstances and emotional needs, their degree of interests in common, and their feelings about the adoption experience. Just like other potential relationships between adults meeting for the first time, expectations may be compatible or conflicting. Typical patterns in adoptee–birth relative relationships have not emerged.

What do adoptees want? Based on our experience as described above, we adoptees want legal acknowledgement of the right we are claiming for ourselves, the right to know our origins. In most states however, we do not have legal access to the names of our birth parents. State adoption regulations are based on the philosophy that birth parents want and should to able to prevent their relinquished offspring from knowing their identities. State legislators also sympathize with the sentiments of the adoptive parents who express a variety of fears about open records. However, these parents do not state what may be their strongest objection to open records, namely the belief that they, the adoptive parents, are the only parents the adoptee *should* ever acknowledge as parents.

Besides direct legal access to our birth parents' identities, we also want adoptive parents to be sensitized to adoptees' needs to acknowledge four "real" parents, to be set free from the often wrenching loyalty bind in which we have been placed. At least two studies of adult adoptees (Loper, 1976; Reynolds, Levey, and Eisnitz, 1977) revealed findings that adoptees demonstate a striking degree of anxiety. Although several possible reasons could be posited, we believe we should be given the opportunity to resolve some of it, even if this move takes away some presumed rights of both sets of parents.

Surely the institution of adoption can shift toward encouraging both the birth parents and the adoptive parents to honor the deep needs for identity completion experienced by their sons and daughters. Child Welfare professionals can help both sets of parents conquer their fears, while acknowledging the parenting value each set offers in its different way. Child Welfare professionals can also champion adoptees' rights and their need to come to terms with their double heritages. The Child Welfare system can help adoptees do this in a dignified and adult way, not dependent, for example, on professional help for their contact with the birth family. What we want most of all is the freedom to claim our origins on our own terms, in our own ways, with the responsibility for our choices that freedom entails.

# PART VII

# Child Welfare as a Career

The many facets of Child Welfare have now been examined—from context to knowledge and, finally, to practice on all of its many levels and in its varied forms. But practice requires a practitioner, an actor, someone who translates social objectives concerning the welfare of families and children into specific actions. In this final section we turn to the workers and the world of work, both to their public images and to their self-constructions, as they assume identities fraught with stress and contradictions.

In the first chapter, Esposito and Fine explore the paradoxes surrounding the practitioner, and in the second Maluccio draws together the central issues in education and training for practice in this field. A research exemplar by Jayaratne and Chess, examining the factors associated with job satisfaction and turnover, brings this volume to a close.

This volume was conceived some four years ago, during a time of ferment and hopefulness. The Indian Child Welfare Act, the passage of Public Law 96–272, the Oregon Project and the permanency planning movement, renewed federal interest in funding national research and education and training grants, a growing commitment to preventive work with families, and a number of other indicators were attracting renewed energy to Child Welfare. If in the past the placement of children garnered more prestige, resources, and professional expertise than any other function in Child Welfare, the field itself did not rank high among career possibilities for the professional social worker. With a few notable exceptions, schools of social work tended to give it short shrift in terms of specialization or research emphasis. Many of us who took our first professional steps in Child Welfare sighed with relief when we were able to move on to less taxing, less contradictory, and more rewarding practice environments. But as the 1980s began, there was still some hope that fundamental change was occurring and that public and professional support were on the rise. As we go to press, our efforts are directed toward trying to contain the increasing erosion of hard-won ground.

In their pessimistic, but refreshing, exploration of the paradoxical environment of the Child Welfare worker, Esposito and Fine ignore all sacred cows. Over and over as they talk directly to workers, they reveal the series of double-binds that continuously create paralyzing, no-win situations for Child Welfare workers. Workers respond to these double-binds much as any disadvataged or oppressed population caught in an anomic situation would: with ritualistic and unquestioning conformity to established but ineffective ways of doing things, by retreating and abandoning their original aims, by leaving the field altogether, by rebelling, and, sometimes, by innovating.

Burnout, like anomie, is "not a psychological sickness to be treated, but a response to a sickness, to a lack of integrity in society" (Hartman, 1969:137). Just as clients cannot be "treated" for conditions perpetuated by social structural inequities, Child Welfare workers cannot be cured of "burnout" through individual support and improved training. However, Esposito and Fine, if they do not spare us from any of the harsh realities, do not leave us in despair. Their main point is that the paradoxes themselves need to be confronted, and the structural conditions that promote stress changed. Workers, unlike children raised in paradoxical and double-bind environments, can organize and communicate with each other and with the public, commenting on and exposing the paradoxes.

Maluccio touches on the previous chapter's arguments when he calls attention to the fact that Child Welfare education and training tends to emphasize changing people rather than preparing workers to change systems. Just as worker burnout becomes an explanation for apathy, so is lack of appropriate education and training seen as responsible for the service delivery system's failures. He concludes that, if workers are to achieve competence—a "capacity to think, to function autonomously in the face of uncertainty and rapid change"—the work environment itself must be restructured and enriched, and Child Welfare training revitalized. While the extremely high turnover rates in Child Welfare employment seem understandable given the regressive political conditions, confusion, and constant stress surrounding the worker, the research of

Jayaratne and Chess questions facile explanations. Child Welfare workers, in their sample, despite being relatively satisfied with their work and believing they are doing a good job, are also likely to seek new employment. The authors explore possible reasons for this apparent contradiction, in the process exposing how little we can assume about the high turnover rates.

It is indeed the case that Child Welfare workers, like all who become identified with the downtrodden, are in a sense themselves victimized by a cultural and social discourse concerning families and children that is rife with paradox. This discourse, characterized by a perpetual war over the family, pits professional against parent. As Grubb and Lazerson point out, America breaks its promises to its children because as a nation we repeatedly justify public action on behalf of children only when their parents fail rather than when the political and social ideologies or institutions created and perpetuated by particular interests fail.

> Each time children are found in need, humanitarian and benevolent activists propose government programs to overcome the deficiences of family life. Yet we invest reluctantly in those programs, clinging to a desperate wish that parents would adequately fulfill their private responsibilities and resenting their children for requiring public attention and for making demands on our private incomes. The result is that public programs are the "cheapest possible care," as Grace Abbott complained. We end up with a corrupted notion of public responsibility in which the benevolent assumptions of *parens patriae* are subordinated to private responsibility. (Grubb and Lazerson, 1982:51)

As professionals once we have created these programs and institutions, however cheap, we become involved in a perpetual struggle to defend our questionable expertise over that of the family, to preserve our deficient institutions, and our own jobs. So we too must take responsibility for our share in creating and perpetuating a discourse in which we distance, compete with, and proclaim our superiority over the very people we should be serving. According to Grubb and Lazerson,

> if we are to serve families and children we will have to revise our fondest myths about children and our most deeply-rooted institutions. Until we do so, the political representation of children's interests will remain incomplete and contradictory, subject to the familiar limitations of *parens patriae*, corrupted by self-interest and the compromise of moral principle, and undermined by the structural inequalities that generated so many problems for children in the first place. (1982:126)

The task of the future, in our view, is to expose these paradoxes and to join with families who need our help, in a struggle to right injustice and eradicate inequalities which, in the long run, threaten us all.

# CHAPTER 26

# The Field of Child Welfare as a World of Work

Geraldine Esposito
Michelle Fine*

At no time in the past has the field of Child Welfare, or its workers, been as devalued or defunded as in current times, while perhaps at no time in the past have Child Welfare workers served more important and difficult functions. This fact remains a pervasive if pessimistic theme throughout the literature. The consistently negative tone of this literature prompted the authors to seek further information from Child Welfare workers themselves about their jobs. Approximately thirty caseworkers in public and voluntary Child Welfare agencies were surveyed—from child protective services, preventive services, foster care, and adoption. They answered questions about stresses in their work as well as describing their own coping strategies. Also these workers provided candid assessments of what might be done to improve the field of Child Welfare.

The interviews confirmed the cynicism (Jacobs, 1968) and frustration and role conflict (Wasserman, 1970) portrayed in the literature. This chapter, in many respects, perpetuates the somber tone. Here, however, we endeavor to provide an alternative to cynicism—critical awareness. The chapter does not attempt to demoralize those in the field further but to explicate the contradictory elements within Child Welfare

*Authors are listed alphabetically; both contributed equally in the writing of this chapter.

(Lenrow, 1978). Through a systems analysis we suggest conceptual and practical alternatives to the view that holds workers and/or their clients responsible for fundamental systemic weaknesses in Child Welfare (Fine, 1982; Wills, 1978).

## The Problem of Roles

Child Welfare workers are responsible for delivering services to children, to troubled and troublesome youth, and to families. Alternately considered "victims" and "victimizers", the workers' public, professional, and personal images vary with economic, political and social trends (Edelwich and Brodsky, 1980; Lasch, 1979). Sometimes they are considered victims. They work within bureaucracies often without the authority to fulfill either of their sometimes contradictory goals: to work in the best interests of the child and in the best interests of the family. They are fundamentally powerless to change systems that need to be changed; alienated from coworkers who could offer much needed support; laden with responsibilities for which they carry little or no authority; and generally functioning without necessary resources (Ryan, 1981).

Child Welfare workers complain that as they are held increasingly accountable, their positions are further demeaned and declassified. Decisions they make about children's lives and families are reported to be routinely undermined by the police, the courts, and the schools, and often unsupported by their agencies. Committed to assisting clients to overcome what are frequently impossible social and economic barriers, these workers often complain of "burnout" as a contributing factor to high turnover rates (Chatterjee and Ginter, 1973; Cherniss, 1980). Some workers withdraw, becoming depressed and cynical (Beck, Weissman, Lester, and Trenxler, 1974). Others, sometimes considered victimizers, tend to blame their clients, holding them responsible for their circumstances. Such workers may seek to punish rather than rehabilitate or assist, and may resort to verbal or physical violence (Gaylin, Glasser, Marcus, and Rothman, 1978; Lenrow, 1978; Nettler, 1959).

The often conflicting roles and responsibilities of the Child Welfare worker are stressful. These stresses in turn are exacerbated by the conflicting, paradoxical demands imposed by the public, the political system, agency policies, and the Child Welfare worker himself or herself (Wasserman, 1970). The nature of these paradoxes, and their impact on workers, is the focus of this chapter.

## The Public Paradox: Responsibilities without Authority

Child Welfare workers have long been seen as the safekeepers of America's children. They are expected to compensate for abused and abusive families, for unjust economic distributions that inequitably limit opportunities and resources, for inadequate educational systems that deprive minority and poor youth of solid academic preparation, and for policies and institutions that punish working-class and poor families by withholding resources necessary for subsistence. Forced to negotiate with the courts, the schools, and bureaucratic service systems to improve children's chances for a "good life," Child Welfare workers often lack the structural power, tools, or resources to enforce their decisions. One caseworker in New York City described this situation.

> If I can't service them well, should I continue to be part of a sinking system? Child welfare has low status, low pay, and the client is frequently not truly "voluntary." The bureaucracy and inefficiency makes the work so cumbersome. If you can't find personal successes the work is very draining.

Child Welfare workers may be called on to be judges without the power to enforce; teachers without books; police without arms; parents without legal responsibility; and therapists without the necessary time or training. Sandwiched between unequal social and economic structures, unclear agency policies, an underinformed judicial system, and the client population, they carry the burdens of impossible responsibilities and unrealistic goals. Furthermore, their public image has changed with shifting politics and societal needs. The perception of Child Welfare practitioners as legitimate, respected, uncontested experts has greatly diminished over the past two decades. The field once was viewed as a compassionate, necessary thread in the fabric of a wholesome society. Some twenty-five years ago, the Child Welfare League of America described the worker personality required for Child Welfare practice:

> "the child welfare worker must be a person of warmth, maturity, integrity, insight, imagination, creativity, and flexibility. . . . He (sic) must be able to make sound judgments and to act upon them. He must fundamentally enjoy children and be willing to invest himself in a living experience with them. He has to be a sufficiently mature person to give and sustain help in a range of life situations that are fraught with deep emotional significance. (1959:23)

More recently, ominous signals of a radical decline in public commitment to Child Welfare service have emerged. State block grants, reduced social service budgets, transferred responsibilities to the "private sector" and the new reified federal ideology of "merit" as the basic criterion for receipt of human services combine to defeat humanistic social service policy. The Child Welfare field experiences the most basic consequences of these cutbacks, as emplified by the following information from practitioners:

> A child welfare administrator in a Northeastern county receives an order from his Commissioner to downgrade all senior caseworkers. The admin-

istrator holds little faith in assistance from the civil services employees' union.

A young career minded professional relocates to accept a job as a state coordinator of all linkage programs between foster care and adoption. After two months on the job she learns that her position will be abolished due to budget cutbacks. She has no "fall-back" position in the system.

A state staff development director prepares, under strong suggestion, three "contingency" budgets, ranging from maximum funding to virtually no funding for statewide training.

The signals seem clear and increasingly strident: Working in the field of Child Welfare is a high-risk proposition.

While the government abandons the needs of the working class and the poor (and in the same spirit undermines Child Welfare services), members of these social classes turn to government with ever greater needs for assistance. A recent evaluation of a New York City preventive services project reports on the broad-based needs of clients and their respective expectations of Child Welfare workers. Clients expect workers to "arrange services," "talk about problems," and "give advice." Expected to perform both case management and therapeutic roles, Child Welfare workers stretch their pared down budgets, personnel, and limited resources so they can continue to create service contexts in which clients can feel "free to talk," be "understood", and "liked" (Halper and Jones, 1981).

The necessary shift from a psychotherapeutic orientation toward an ecological systems orientation was not only demanded by the clients' situation, but is consistent with theoretical perspectives advanced in progessive social work (cf. Germain and Gitterman, 1980). However, an undermining ideology has accompanied this shift. The systems orientation, unfortunately, is often misperceived as a less skilled approach than a psychotherapeutic one. Many workers fear that the case manager role is considered a reduction, not an enhancement, of former functions.

## The Systems Paradox

Like the public, policy-makers have reflected ambivalence about the Child Welfare field. Two recent trends—toward declassification and increased accountability—suggest this ambivalence. The term "declassification" in Child Welfare refers to the elimination or reduction of educational requirements for entry-level or promotable public social work positions (Gauthier, 1980). Declassification in Child Welfare derives from a general trend toward standardizing job specifications across human services programs. Social work education and professional standards, legislation, training, career mobility, program planning, and organizational politics affect this trend (Pecora, 1982).

Recent studies and surveys reinforce the myth that predominantly low-level skills are required in human services jobs, with the exception of protective service workers who are perceived as having more specialized skills (Harrison, 1980). Worker roles are perceived by administrators and other professionals as those of "matching and connecting." As brokers of service, workers supposedly "put clients in touch" with formal and informal support systems. The value and increasing predominance of this case manager role for Child Welfare workers is indisputable. That formal service systems exist "out there" to assist clients is, however, fiction. The very same budget-slashing conservatism which affects social service programs devastates mental health, health care, housing, and vocational education programs. Objectives notwithstanding, workers can often provide only minimal reassurance that support and adequate planning will ultimately alleviate client situations.

Nationwide surveys of 1975 and 1980 by the National Association of Social Workers (NASW) reveal a continuing decrease by 25 percent, over the five year period, in the number of states requiring the M.S.W. for entry level positions. Concurrently, there has been a 16 percent increase in the recognition of the undifferentiated baccalaurate degree across all job classifications (NASW, 1980).

Many of the workers we interviewed, illustrated in the comment below, felt that the public was joined by state and local fiscal and personnel managers in devaluing their work. They felt that administrators and legislators viewed their jobs as requiring "common sense," not skills, and that a decidedly antiprofessional attitude characterized local administrators:

> The agency pays lip service to the importance of my role, but won't back it with money or a change in my position to formalize my informal work. I doubt that the community understands what I do. The agency is commited to the status quo.
>
> Family court is also a major frustration. Many judges have no knowledge of what is important to a child's development, and many are disrespectful of D.S.S. [Department of Social Services] So a lot of cases are inappropriately dismissed, or children are removed unnecessarily. (Preventive Services caseworker in a suburban agency)

## What about Skills?

Like employment patterns, trends in training and education reinforce the worker's sense that he or she is not appreciated. Over the past decade state-funded graduate scholarship programs for public human service workers have steadily declined. Many agencies, however, provided specialized in-service training programs as they reduced the number of agency supported scholarships. These same agencies are now phasing out in-service training plans to provide for program priorities under the current federal block grant system. Drastic cuts across the board in federal and state student loan programs seriously compound this situation in social work education.

The projected picture for the first half of this decade suggests an inevitable decline in the commitment to hiring highly skilled professional social workers, particularly in the public sector. The report of the National Child Welfare Training Center's *National Follow-up Study of Child Welfare Trainees* indicates that of the trainees who are now working full- or part-time, 58 percent are in Child Welfare–related positions. Of those individuals, 94 percent are supervised, but only 45 percent of the supervisors possess an M.S.W., while 43 percent possess no degree in social work. The salary before taxes of 60 percent of the surveyed individuals working in Child Welfare was less than $14,000 per year (N.C.W.T.C., 1981). These disincentives occur paradoxically as sophisticated techniques for internal accountability and external review are increasingly demanded.

## Issues of Evaluation

Against a backdrop of dwindling dollars and increasing media scrutiny of public expenditures, pressures to maintain accountability and increase productivity intensify. The pressure points are not new. Old questions persist: What should be measured? Who should measure it? How should it be measured? What perhaps distinguishes today's pressures are federal, state, and local mandates which specify mechanisms for internal and external review. Again a somewhat paradoxical situation is suggested in light of diminished budgets and resources, swelled caseloads, and increasing stresses.

We are in an era when individuals of varied perspectives determine guidelines for defining and measuring "inputs." Advocates for cost containment demand reduction of inputs; advocates for higher quality service seek more, often costlier, inputs. The agency is, of course, expected to do both (Richman, 1980). Accountability mechanisms can, no doubt, enhance service delivery if they are instituted by knowledgeable administrators and guided by sensitive policy. Unfortunately people who envision a single, measureable output of service delivery are often those responsible for developing accountability procedures.

Many of the workers we interviewed saw accountability systems as potential protection for themselves and for their clients. They did not, however, fully endorse the specific mechanisms of accountability, as suggested, for example, in the recent federal legislation, Public Law 96–272, which mandates administrative review. Their reservations were based on suspicions that such mechanisms are "political" ploys which could potentially scapegoat workers while failing to protect client rights. Further, workers were often resentful that their reservations were not actually addressed, but were instead construed as resistance to doing the work or fear of exposure for poor performance. In one instance, workers in New York described a coworker who was cited by administrators as having done an exemplary reporting job on his caseload, and workers noted that the individual had boasted to them of seeing his entire caseload for fifteen-minute visits in order to fill out his report forms.

As in the area of role refinement in Child Welfare, accountability measures, when distorted to mean only redundant, time consuming, report systems, workers felt were designed and implemented without their input, producing cynicism and frustration where partnership and productivity were intended. The situation suggests one obvious remedy—the inclusion of worker input in both the design and operationalizing of reporting systems.

## The Agency Paradox: Negotiating for Justice

Our national policies place families and individuals of certain socioeconomic and racial groups at distinct disadvantage, dumping them into an amalgam of youth and family agencies often ill-equipped to assist. Child Welfare agencies sit at the intersection of economic, legal, and social policy contradictions; their successes are difficult to measure, while their failures are aired on the evening news.

Child Welfare agencies are held responsible for the results of economic inequities which place their clients—families and youth—at severe disadvantage. The services offered, even in the best of times, can never adequately respond to the needs indicated. Likewise these agencies must abide by federal, state, and local mandates which often limit the effectiveness and breadth of services that can be delivered. Legal guidelines rarely direct workers toward established ethical procedures. More frequently workers remark that they spend time "figuring out how to get around the guidelines." In response to economic and legal dilemmas which constrict even the most creative Child Welfare administrators, agency policies often encourage conservative decisions by workers, so that unfavorable attention is not drawn to the agency (Daley, 1979).

While insufficient income, alcoholism, domestic violence, acting-out children, and child abuse are by no means exclusive problems of the working class or poor, these groups tend to be overrepresented among the families ending up in court or at Child Welfare agencies. Workers often decide, for instance, whether or not to remove a child from his or her home, recognizing that neither decision will resolve the economic inequities which put these families and children at risk. Either decision could exacerbate the problems both child and family will encounter in the future (Kermish and Kushin, 1969). Workers who realize that they cannot alleviate the economic ills that contribute to the problems of clients often withdraw, feeling unable to activate social change (Wenocur and Sherman, 1980).

Similarly agencies retreat into passivity or conservative directions when conflicting legal policies and community standards define and simultaneously frustrate Child Welfare responsibilities. While state laws vary, human services professionals often face incompatible goals of "working in the best interests of the child" and "working to strengthen the family": Respect for the family unit cannot override obvious danger to one or more members; irresponsible decisions about taking a child away from a parent cannot be tolerated. Workers, faced with a parent suspected of abuse and a seemingly victimized child, must "choose" between disrupting the family by removing a child or preserving the family, possibly at the expense of the child. These grave decisions are made in continual jeopardy. Workers often feel they lack agency support, coworkers they trust enough to "check with," and "guarantees," since the law does little to provide concrete guidelines.

Three employees of the El Paso, Texas, Department of Human Resources faced charges of criminal negligence in a 1980 child abuse case. Although the indictments were ultimately quashed by a Texas judge, this case reflects the basic conflict between competing agency concerns: the protection of the children from abusive parents, and the respect for family integrity, with removal of children only when unequivocally necessary (NASW News, 1981). How can Child Welfare workers act confidently or assertively without assurance, and with little reason to expect agency support? Similarly, what role can agencies play in this juggling of justice?

The agencies themselves cannot be held fully responsible for creating such dilemmas. Instead agencies need to be viewed dynamically. They often sustain the weight of several conflicting pressures. Most obviously, human services provide "clean up" after the aforementioned economic inequities and legislative mandates have wrought havoc (Gaylin et al., 1978). Child Welfare agencies are often placed in a precarious position as reluctant instruments of social control.

The single mother who cannot find a job, does not qualify for

AFDC, and has a truant daughter may have to give the child over to legal authorities, under the "person in need of supervision" classification, in order to receive needed services. The child may be placed in a community, or even a remote, facility for any number of years. Isolated from community and family roots, the child suffers and the government spends thousands of dollars for residential care. Without responsible and equitable economic transfer systems to allocate resources to the mother, who might have preserved the family and avoided the economic, social, and psychological problems incurred, agencies inherit victims of an unfair, paradoxical welfare system. Agencies responsible for impossible, sometimes unjust tasks beyond their capabilities often "burn out." Agencies concerned about survival are unlikely to criticize unworkable policies openly; workers who are critical may even be stifled (Wilgus and Epstein, 1978). Threatened by limited budgets with survival in jeopardy, these agencies do not often consider whether or not their services are necessary, appropriate, or even effective (Gaylin et al., 1978).

## The Worker's Self-Image: At the Intersection of the Paradoxes

*Police call.* "Two kids, ages approximately two and four, abandoned on the Turnpike," in mid-December. Denise—older, found wearing a cotton dress, no coat. George—pants and shirt, no coat, one shoe, no socks. Cop said he "left them at some lady's house. A lady who takes in kids."

*Placement 1.* Found the house finally. Funny how they didn't react, I kept thinking. But then I had only been a caseworker for 2½ months. I was sure it would work out for them. Denise, the spokesperson, kept asking if I could take them to my house.

*Placement 2.* Next day I was back. "You can't expect me to care for these children. . . look at their heads. . . there under the hair. . . completely infected." The hospital. This time there was an urgency in the voices as we drove, as Denise asked PLEASE couldn't we go to my house now. Then the frightened sobbing as they shaved their heads. Two weeks worth.

*Placement 3.* Back to the foster home, but just for a week. "You can't expect me to care for these children. . . I heard the father is a criminal and a drunk. . . he might find out they're here. . . it's too close. . ."

*Placement 4.* More than an urgency in their voices. "Please don't go away again. Please take us home with you." As we drove. As the little fist that belonged to the frightened voice held onto my skirt. As I felt the gentle weight of the little head nestled into my side. And this time no one sobbed. This time Denise screamed and would not let go of me and I stood there feeling pressure dammed up behind my eyes, fumbling to comfort her. The little one stood stunned and quiet. The foster mother shook her head, embarrassed by her own tears as we tried to gently break the desperate grip of arms and legs around me. After a long time I left, with the sound of the pain echoing after me. I drove one block. . . parked. . . watched my tears flood over my knuckles, clenched on the steering wheel, down my own rigid arms. For the first time in a long time I could not think of anything that was "for sure." (New York caseworker's journal)

We have discussed the missionary zeal brought by workers to a set of impossible tasks—their agencies often squeezed by contradictory mandates and realities, and their positions paradoxically defined. In many Child Welfare agencies, feedback is received only after a failure is publicized or a rule has been violated (cf. Nadler, 1977). A sense of success is rare; failure is experienced individually, not collectively. The question "Who was responsible for the Bailey girl being sent home? She was just killed by her stepfather!" often is the type of direct feedback a caseworker receives (Edelwich and Brodsky, 1980; Harrison, 1980).

Child Welfare workers often experience a lack of agency support: "My supervisor couldn't care less about what I do, as long as the agency doesn't look bad." Also, they lack peer support: "My coworkers mind their own business. Nobody wants to know nothing" (Kaplan, Cassel, and Gore, 1977). However, when an action by one worker jeopardizes the job of another, coworker concern gets voiced. "I once hit a kid, and Joe said to me, 'What did you do that for? Now my job is on the line.' I reminded him that he did the same thing last week, so he should keep his mouth shut." The immorality of slapping the youth gets camouflaged by a "who-done-it" mentality evident in many agencies (Maslach and Pines, 1979).

Workers also speak of feeling disappointment (M. Shinn, 1979). Initially they intended to help youth and families; today they say they intend to do their jobs (Lenrow, 1978). Many recognize that the goals of the agency and their personal goals diverge, that being a good helper sometimes conflicts with being a good worker (Wills, 1978). A number of responses to this dilemma have been delineated. Among them are:

*Capitulate* to the goals of the agency, abandoning their own mission

*Not capitulate* to these goals, retain their own visions, and sustain a "radical" image in the agency, activated by anger and relentless commitment to the needs of [clients]

*"Niche-find"* and thereby circumscribe a set of responsibilities sufficiently narrow to reduce the dissonance between personal and organizational goals

*Withdraw*, frequently referred to as burnout; or *become a victim-martyr*, whose chronic bitching permeates the agency structure
(Wenocur and Sherman, 1980)

If workers perceive a discrepancy between agency and personal goals, they confront their own psychological paradoxes. Assumptions that "the world is fair" (Lerner, 1980), and these kids will, therefore, be helped, are disconfirmed. Some grow bitter with the recognition that children and families will not, under present conditions, receive needed help.

Derogation of clients is perhaps the most devastating effect of the powerlessness felt by workers (Snyder, Shenkel, and Schmidt, 1976). Results of a survey of 170 child-care workers in public and voluntary residential facilities for high-risk youth indicate a strong relationship between counselors' sense of powerlessness in their agencies and their derogation of their clients. The less they felt able to help, the more critical were these workers. To reconcile their wish to help with their recognition that the youth are not being helped, disempowered workers concluded that they could not be helped (Fine, 1979; 1982). They blamed the victims. Many also saw themselves as helpless to effect change (Symonds, 1980).

## Burnout: An Ideology to Resolve the Paradox?

Child Welfare workers are particularly vulnerable to being blamed for inefficiences in the Child Welfare system, because it is perhaps easier to identify and rectify a "problem worker" than a "problem-ridden system." Workers, too, often blame themselves instead of voicing criticism of their agencies, policies, or procedures. To retain their jobs, and/or enhance their self-esteem, some may point to unproductive coworkers; some accuse clients of being "beyond help"; many suppress questions about the effectiveness and ethics of their agencies. Such workers reproduce systemic problems in their interactions with clients.

Others, however, recognize systemic inadequacies. To keep their jobs, and perhaps their sanity, many disengage, turning their feelings inward. Many workers feel they are too vulnerable to express their anger, too visible to verbalize their negative perceptions, or too powerless to matter. A few rebel and try to work for change, by coordinating efforts among coworkers. Nevertheless, those who demonstrate symptoms of withdrawal, low energy, and disassociated affect are often considered "burned out" (Carroll, 1980). The burnout ideology fosters the notion that workers are burned out from clients, too much work, or the stresses of human services, obscuring the contradictory responsibilities of Child Welfare workers, and camouflaging systems problems (Carroll and White, 1981; Edelwich and Brodsky, 1980). Cast as a personal *and* personnel issue, rather than a collective and structural issue, this ideology preserves the illusion that all is well in the agency and in the world around it. Described as an individualistic process of disengagement by which a human service worker grows apathetic and uncommitted, the burnout ideology presumes that the unit of analysis is the individual worker (Thomas, 1980). The conceptual focus advanced in this chapter stands in marked contrast. Although agencies and workers alike may collude in an individualized burnout diagnosis, this shared illusion is costly.

## Why Child Welfare Workers?

Are Child Welfare workers more likely than other human service professionals (e.g., police, teachers, nurses) to become disempowered, to actively blame their clients, to evidence symptoms of burnout, to suffer the kinds of victimization described here? We think not. We make no argument that Child Welfare workers suffer more, only that economic, social, and structural conditions affect their roles and responsibilities paradoxically, and that prevailing ideologies such as burnout obscure these paradoxes. Keeping this in mind, we feel that these workers are employed to manage basic contradictions in our society. The idea that families are sacred and not to be violated contradicts the obvious need for intervention when abuse or neglect occurs. Social and political discomfort with government intervention actively obstructs the work of Child Welfare.

Frequently workers experience little support from their agencies: agencies too are ambivalent about whether "to intervene or not." With few rules to follow (unlike the police), and no particular body of knowledge to impart (unlike teachers) workers are called upon generally to make judgments about the life and future of a child; judgments which their agencies, the courts, and the families involved may decide to support—or not. Another contributor to the particular stress experienced by Child Welfare workers is their perceived lack of peer support. Most often they are not union organized; they work in isolation and are not in positions to assist each other with cases, comfort, or advice. Their jobs may be on the front line; their judgments are always on the line. Unlike police who sometimes justify what they observe by the notion that their "clients" deserve to suffer, Child Welfare workers who deal with society's victims recognize that their clients are likely to suffer but do not deserve it. The activities of Child Welfare workers are very public. Unlike teachers, who can exercise a fair amount of autonomy in the classroom, workers' behaviors are visible and accountable to a variety of people and systems. Also their failures are often rapidly reported and publicized by mass media.

Finally, and perhaps most importantly, many of the workers are from backgrounds similar to their clients. They may have experienced personally or through friends and families comparable economic and social disadvantage. Workers may overidentify with their clients, failing to focus or circumscribe their tasks. Such a commitment, combined with ambiguous job responsibilities, can constrain effective case management and limit the number of clients one worker can handle effectively.

## Strategies for Change: Confronting the Paradoxes

The analysis proposed in this chapter suggests that remedies to Child Welfare paradoxes should be targeted not only at individual workers (e.g., through stress management workshops, time off, reduced case-loads, "special" flexible hours, recreational activities) but also at agency structures and policies and at larger socioeconomic relationships. While the latter cannot be tackled by agencies alone, agencies should collectively advocate for economic and policy reforms that aid rather than further oppress families and children. Current policies, such as reduced minimum wage for adolescents, cutbacks in school lunches, and de-funding of C.E.T.A., exacerbate the problems of youth and of the working poor. Likewise, family welfare policies and tax structures that penalize single parents, the working poor, and AFDC families guarantee to swell the caseloads of these agencies. By taking a more active stand politically, Child Welfare agencies can influence federal, state, and local policy-making, clarify and enhance the public image of Child Welfare, and mitigate further agency *and* client victimization.

On an agency level, workers' stresses need to be addressed through structural changes (Moos and Insel, 1974). Strategies targeted at individual change only perpetuate conditions that promote burnout. Structural change can begin with the systematic disruption of the chain of command in Child Welfare—through "democratic deformation" (Sennett, 1980). Workers can be organized, within their agencies and across agencies, to inform policy-makers and administrators collectively about the contradictions in their work. Workers can provide feedback about the conflictual effects of legislative mandates and agency policies; their need for peer supports; the complicated and demoralizing dynamics of working with clients rejected by other social service agencies; as well as about the pervasive tensions in the Child Welfare field (Golembiewski, Carrigan, Mead, Munzenrider, and Blumberg, 1975). Such communication can enhance the policy–practice match and increase the likelihood that policies will be implemented as conceived. "Worker circles," in which workers themselves discuss current practice and problems and assist in developing policies, could ultimately improve conditions, diminish morale problems, and create a sense of collective responsibility (Ryan, 1981). Concerns of workers can be translated through such mechanisms, and remedied as public issues.

In addition, viable mechanisms for appeal and grievance must be available to workers. Structural means by which workers can influence policy formulation and appeal agency decisions will empower workers and heighten their involvement. An appeal may take the form of a grievance committee, a union with collective bargaining power, or structured "gripe" sessions (Fine, 1982).

In-service training leaders must not only confront practice issues, but initiate diagnoses of the work environment and connect workers' stresses to agency structures. Such training can activate agency self-criticism, worker empowerment, and progressive and creative program development (Melzer and Haugh, 1974).

Finally, on an individual level, the work itself needs to be recognized as extremely stressful. Each worker faces major challenges and often feels personally responsible for outcomes—especially negative ones. As in other human service professions, workers may need accessible mental health services that address the impact of work stresses on mental health and help make these stresses less personal. An employee counseling service can recognize Child Welfare work as a clinical issue, a potential threat to mental health, and a potential exacerbator of mental health problems. Counselors can diagnose and intervene in the agency to encourage *agency-based* change, and can use the work group as a support and reference group.

These strategies for change are based on the premise that Child Welfare agencies are self-critical institutions; that Child Welfare workers, when questioning agency procedures and functioning collectively, will receive positive reinforcement; that agencies are interested in supporting their staff and their staff's decisions; and that agencies want to cultivate coworker support systems. In many agencies, these assumption are unrealistic. However, they need not be.

The recommendations discussed attempt to clarify the contradictions and to use workers themselves to generate creative responses. Nevertheless, no easy solutions are likely to emerge, until, on a macro level, social and economic policies are redesigned to benefit children and families of all social classes and races, and until, on a micro level, Child Welfare agencies are restructured with collective worker input into policy and program formulations. Until these changes come about, the agencies will shoulder the burdens of these paradoxes and operate reactively. However, these costs can no longer be tolerated by clients or workers—present or future.

# CHAPTER 27

# Education and Training for Child Welfare Practice

Anthony N. Maluccio

The decade of the 1980s has emerged as the best and the worst of times for education and training for Child Welfare practice. On the one hand, there are exciting developments such as expansion and refinement of relevant bodies of knowledge and practice theories, resurgence of interest in Child Welfare as a field of practice, a renewed vision for Child Welfare services, and readiness on the part of agencies and schools to collaborate toward shared goals. On the other hand, there are numerous discouraging trends, such as research questioning the effectiveness of Child Welfare services, cutbacks in federal funding, and declassification or "reclassification" of social work positions in public agencies in various states.

Against this backdrop of excitement and discouragement, this chapter presents an overview of the current state of education and training for Child Welfare practice with a focus on major trends and issues. Following a brief review of the context of social work practice and education, the chapter will examine the objectives, content, and structure of education and training for Child Welfare practice and will offer selected guidelines for enhancing the knowledge and skills of Child Welfare practitioners.

"Education" and "training" are used interchangeably, although they often refer to different concepts. In this chapter they are seen as overlapping phenomena with certain distinctive features. *Education* is defined as "learning opportunities offered at an accredited educational institution" (O'Neil, 1980: 17). Such opportunities usually involve formal educational credit acquired over an extended period of time, outside reading and assignments, integration of theory and practice, and transferability of knowledge and skills to diverse situations. *Training* refers to short-term learning opportunities that do not entail formal credit and are of a technical nature. Training provides tools and techniques for immediate application and is offered by social agencies, educational institutions, or other organizations (ibid.).

## Context

Educational and training programs are influenced by the societal as well as professional context within which they occur. Societal issues such as poverty, institutional racism, other forms of discrimination, and family violence will affect the context of Child Welfare education and training. Although discussion of these issues is beyond the scope of this chapter, we should take a brief look at the professional context of social work practice and education.

The social work profession is marked by a continuing struggle to identify its key purposes and boundaries. The old dichotomies between cause and function, social action and treatment, prevention and rehabilitation, and clinical and nonclinical practice continue to plague professional endeavors. Moreover, contemporary social work reflects a range of purposes, theoretical perspectives, practice modalities, and roles. Meyer argues that "social work is in the throes of conceptual confusion and political disarray" noting "the present state of affairs in social work does not add up to accountability, coherence, public understanding, or professional equanimity" (Meyer, 1979: 278).

Fragmentation, lack of coherence, and questionable accountability are also evident in social work education, as exemplified by a number of recurring issues: the nature of generic versus specific knowledge and skills and, in turn, the preparation of generalists versus specialists; confusion about practice specializations; and the need to delineate the educational continuum from pre-B.S.W. programs to the doctorate.

What is happening in social work practice and education may be regarded as either a dynamic process of defining and refining professional purposes and methods or as a discouraging example of the profession's inability to take decisive action and develop a clear direction. We prefer the first explanation, especially in relation to the field of Child Welfare. Despite various negative trends, the context of Child Welfare currently includes a number of exciting features symbolized by passage of the federal Adoption Assistance and Child Welfare Act of 1980 (Public Law 96–272). This act places increasing emphasis on preventive services and supports to families to keep children in their own homes and carries an explicit focus on permanency planning in the delivery of Child Welfare services. At the same time, there is evidence of renewed practitioner and student interest in Child Welfare as a worthwhile field of practice.

The new directions and priorities in Child Welfare require highly skilled and knowledgeable personnel. It has been stressed, therefore, that expanded as well as improved education of workers is necessary as one means of coping with the recurring problems in Child Welfare, thus helping achieve the goals of prevention of inappropriate out-of-home placement and promotion of permanent planning for children and youth.

The provision of additional educational opportunities is regarded as crucial, particularly since it has been found that many Child Welfare workers lack the specialized knowledge and skills necessary to function in complex case situations. In a 1976 nationwide survey of Child Welfare programs in twenty-five states, it was concluded that "only a few states have any specialized child welfare training available to staff" (Kadushin, 1976: 72). Similarly, in the 1977 *National Study of Social Services to Children and Their Families*, Shyne and Schroeder found that "only 25 percent of the children were assigned to case workers with social work degrees, usually bachelor degrees" (1978: 77). Less than one-tenth of the children were assigned to workers with either an M.S.W. degree or a doctorate. In most settings, the limited training available tends to be sporadic, fragmented, crisis-oriented, or focused largely on orientation to agency procedures and routines. Furthermore, the diversity of background, education, and experience of workers complicates any efforts to design adequate training programs.[1]

The need for more comprehensive and coherent education and training in Child Welfare has been strongly supported, at least until recently, by the federal government, as reflected in the 1979 establishment of the national and regional Child Welfare Training Resource Centers through the Children's Bureau. During their three years tenure, the Centers provided leadership in the expansion and enrichment of educational and training programs in schools of social work and public agencies.

In particular, as one of its major activities, the National Child Welfare Training Center, in collaboration with the regional centers, carried out a major national survey of education and training in the area of Child Welfare, with data gathered from numerous sources, including trainees, faculty members, administrators, supervisors, and line staff from public Child Welfare agencies. The survey was designed "to determine the state of the art and to identify needs and resources in education

for child welfare practice in all levels of professional social work education and training" (Hartman, 1983: 19). This study documented the extensive commitment to education and training for Child Welfare evident
in schools and agencies throughout the country, as well as the wide
range of content areas, objectives, methods, and expectations (National
Child Welfare Training Center, 1981–1984; 1981; 1984).[2]

Although the regional centers were prematurely terminated in 1982
at the end of the third of the five years originally planned, the federal
government has continued to support education and training for child
welfare through annual grants from the Department of Health and
Human Services.

While one cannot discount the importance of education and training, it should be noted that a questionable assumption is implicit in the
mandate given to the centers, the continuing federally funded training
activities, and the overall thrust toward improving the quality of practice. This assumption is that Child Welfare personnel should be held in
large part responsible for the actual or alleged failures of the service
delivery system. This idea leads to emphasis on enhancing the performance of line staff through improved or expanded education and
training.

To regard education and training as a panacea diverts attention
from the systemic or structural changes that are also necessary to increase the effectiveness of services. This myopic view is encouraged by a
widespread conception of Child Welfare as a residual or remedial service
delivery system—one that "picks up the pieces." Manifestations of the
residual view include the typical emphasis in training programs on techniques for *changing people* and the lack of attention to preparing workers
for *system change.*

## Objectives

Given the wide range of views on the nature and purposes of social
work in general and Child Welfare in particular, it is not surprising to
find that there is no consensus on the objectives of education and training for Child Welfare. The objectives preferred by different persons
reflect diverse conceptualizations of Child Welfare services and their
functions.

In most educational and training programs, the emphasis is on
preparing practitioners to play a primarily therapeutic role with their
clients, an approach which reflects the predominant residual view of
Child Welfare services. According to this orientation, service delivery
should emphasize individual change or remediation rather than prevention; it should focus on helping children and parents with changing the

dysfunctional aspects of the parent–child role network (cf. Kadushin, 1980).

In contrast, others argue that workers should be capable of effecting system change (cf. Billingsley and Giovannoni, 1972). In this perspective, it is believed that Child Welfare practitioners should reject a residual approach and address societal conditions affecting all children by aggressively playing roles in the areas of advocacy, social reform, and prevention.

These contrasting perspectives mirror the dichotomy of social action versus treatment that has characterized social work since its early years. More recently, the ecosystems or ecological perspective has emerged as an integrative approach (Germain, 1980; Germain and Gitterman, 1980). In this model, the central focus of social work is defined as the transaction between people and their environments; workers need to give attention simultaneously to psychological as well as environmental factors, to the internal as well as the external, to individual change as well as societal change.

It is assumed that, through this dual focus, workers are more likely to achieve the central mission of promoting adaptive transactions between people and their environments (Germain, 1981: 325). Toward this end, "workers in child welfare need a broad base of knowledge and a wide range of skills" enabling them to engage in intervention that is environmentally as well as psychologically oriented (Germain, 1980: 4). The ecological perspective is especially suited to Child Welfare, in view of increasing evidence that the problems of people coming to the attention of Child Welfare agencies are created or perpetuated in large measure by societal conditions, environmental obstacles, and lack of resources or opportunities, rather than by psychological defects.

The confusing picture in regard to the objectives of education and training in Child Welfare is clouded further by a related, controversial issue that once again is raging within the profession: Should social work education prepare generalists or specialists? Although it has not been widely adopted or accepted as yet, a solution frequently suggested is the preparation of "generalists" at the B.S.W. level, thus recognizing this as the basic degree for entry into social work practice, while assigning to M.S.W. programs the task of preparing "specialists."

This alternative has been proposed, among others, by the Commission on Educational Planning of the Council on Social Work Education, which defined generalists and specialists as follows:

> A social work generalist is a human service provider with broad-based skills, generic knowledge of persons and environments, and a commitment to social work values. The generalist is able to demonstrate basic competence in working with a variety of clients and services. (Council on Social Work Education, 1979a: 4)

> In order to be considered a specialist in a practice area, a social worker must have a relevant concentration at the graduate level or a demonstrated equivalent via post-graduate continuing education. Concentration should be complex enough to require a minimum of one year of study at the master's level, including field work or practicum, over and above the basic knowledge required to enter the profession. (Council on Social Work Education, 1979b: 1)

While the issue of generalist versus specialist is being debated, largely in academic circles, practice realities are increasingly demanding preparation of generalists as well as specialists. In some settings (such as rural agencies), social workers are expected to carry a generalist caseload and to carry out a variety of roles such as therapist, broker, advocate, teacher, strategist, social reformer, and case manager. In other settings, workers are expected to be skilled in carrying specialized functions, such as child protection or foster home supervision, either in separate units or as members of a service team.

Thus diverse and conflicting expectations of the roles and functions to be carried by Child Welfare workers persist. However, a recent national survey of Child Welfare curricula in graduate and undergraduate schools of social work suggests that the therapist model is the predominant one in most schools; the primary emphasis is on teaching skills in assessment and diagnosis and treatment with children and parents (Lauderdale, Grinnell, and McMurtry, 1980). Also, in the field as a whole, less attention has been given to education of administrators, supervisors, and planners.

Yet, preparation of students for primarily clinical roles seems to be inconsistent with the aims and needs of Child Welfare agencies. "Historically, many students supported by agency stipends have returned to their agencies lacking either the skill or commitment to do the tasks necessary in the agency. Likewise, when they take jobs, many recent graduates have come to believe they cannot practice social work as presented in schools of social work" (Gullerud and Itzin, 1979: 82).

The discrepancy between preparation in schools and agency needs is a common source of friction between schools of social work and agencies. Partly in response to this problem, some authors argue for a case management approach as the preferred framework for educating Child Welfare workers. For instance, Stein notes that in Child Welfare "it is critical that one person have an overview of each case and that this person should have the skills to negotiate for service delivery with professionals from other disciplines" (1982: 107). Stein asserts that the case management model is valuable in this regard, since it "places emphasis on the worker as a broker, an advocate, and a coordinator of services, with a concomitant deemphasis on the worker as a counselor or provider of direct problem-solving services" (ibid.).

However, Lauderdale, Grinnell, and McMurtry's survey of Child Welfare curricula (1980) found that little attention has been given to the role of case manager in schools of social work. Yet this is a role that makes a great deal of sense for Child Welfare. For example, the field of foster care demonstrates the need for a strong case manager as a means of mobilizing the efforts of the multiple "helpers" usually involved in a case situation, insuring that children and families receive adequate help, and preventing the drifting of children through the system.

## Content

The diversity in educational objectives and conceptualizations of practice leads to a wide range of content areas in educational and training programs for Child Welfare.

First of all, all factors agree that Child Welfare practitioners should have—and build on—the *generic* base of social work values, knowledge, and skills. "Base," as defined by the Council on Social Work Education's Commission on Educational Planning, "refers to the constellation of knowledge, values, and skills required for beginning professional practice or to advanced education or education for specialization" (1979b: 1).

The *specific* content areas regarded as especially crucial for workers engaged in delivering Child Welfare services are numerous, and it is tempting to come up with a "laundry list."[3] The most important areas can be categorized as follows:

- attitudes and values regarding children and their needs and rights
- child and family development
- family styles, structure and dynamics
- the service delivery system in Child Welfare
- practice skills and strategies in work with children and families
- knowledge and skills in collaboration with other professional and paraprofessional staff
- racial and cultural diversity

At any given point various topics become prominent and receive greater attention. Currently, for instance, permanency planning, child abuse and neglect, and the interface between social work and the law are much emphasized. Similarly, there is increasing recognition of the importance of cultural awareness, and therefore of content relating to ethnicity, socio-cultural aspects, and minority groups. Some attention is being given to aspects such as family life education, parenting skills, and self-help groups. Also a growing trend is toward the appreciation of knowledge and skills in working with family systems, although the emphasis in Child Welfare curricula continues to be on material relating to the individual functioning of children and parents and on individually oriented psychotherapeutic approaches (cf. Lauderdale, Grinnell, and McMurtry, 1980).

The range of content areas offered and the overlapping of content among the different levels of the social work education continuum are illustrated by a number of exemplary programs in B.S.W. Child Welfare education (cf. Loppnow and Taggart, 1981); M.S.W. Child Welfare education (cf. Martin, 1982); and agency in-service training programs in Child Welfare (Creative Associates, 1982).* Each of these programs incorporates many of the same content areas, although the degree of emphasis may vary, which is not surprising in view of unclear curriculum objectives and insufficient role or task differentiation. For example both the B.S.W. program at Eastern Michigan University (Loppnow and Taggart, 1981) and the M.S.W. program at the University of Pittsburgh (Martin, 1982) include a family and children's services specialty with similar objectives, courses, and content.

## Structure

A number of issues emerge in respect to the structure of education and training for Child Welfare, especially in the following areas: (1) curriculum organization; (2) the continuum of social work education and training; and (3) the relationship between the educational system and the service delivery system.

### Curriculum Organization

In any curriculum development effort, it is necessary to deal with the issue of where and how a particular content area should be lodged within the curriculum. Various approaches are employed in education for Child Welfare.

Some schools offer one or two elective courses that present an overview of Child Welfare as a field of practice. In this approach there is no pretense that students are prepared to practice as specialists; at best, the chief advantage is that students gain an appreciation of the field and its complexities.

A more typical approach involves integration or diffusion of Child Welfare content throughout the curriculum, particularly within required courses in the areas of social policy and services, human behavior and

---

*These and other exemplary materials are briefly described in an annotated bibliography at the end of this chapter.

the environment, and methods (cf. Briar and Payne, n.d.). In addition, in some schools the field placement is specifically chosen and used to provide further learning opportunities highlighting Child Welfare knowledge and skills. Integration helps to insure that all students acquire some knowledge of Child Welfare. Yet, the inevitable dilution of the material raises question about the effectiveness of this approach in preparing workers skilled in dealing with complex demands in Child Welfare settings.

A third model involves organization of Child Welfare content into a specialized cluster of course offerings available to students on an elective basis. This model is particularly evident at the graduate level and is described in terms such as "specialization", "specialty," "concentration," or "substantive area" (cf. Martin, 1982). Tremendous variability occurs in how schools organize this content (Hartman, 1983). Schools range from those with simple expectations (such as one or two courses) to those with more complex and rigorous requirements combining classroom courses, field practice, and integrating seminars. In some graduate schools, the curriculum is organized entirely around a field of practice or problem area (e.g., mental health or family and children); in others, it is structured along traditional method lines (e.g., casework or group work), and students have the option of enrolling in some form of Child Welfare specialization.

In certain schools this specialization is focused exclusively on the Child Welfare field as traditionally defined; in others it refers to a more comprehensive cluster that is labeled "family and children's services" or "family and child welfare." The latter model has the potential of combining concerns about children and families and counteracting the separation of family agencies and children's services that historically has been a persistent and questionable feature of the service delivery system. Consequently, such a model is more likely to prepare social workers with a family-centered focus and with the ability to understand and work with families as dynamic units interacting with other systems in their ecological context.

At first glance, the specialization model seems to be the most promising one, since it combines the advantages of a broad-based social work curriculum with the benefits of immersion in a particular practice field. However, how "in-depth" is the specialization in most schools of social-work? As already indicated, a few graduate schools offer extensive programs such as a second year largely devoted to the area of family and children's services. But, in most schools, the course requirements are much more limited. In some cases, students get little more than a smattering of content relating to Child Welfare, although they may be formally certified as "specialists" in this area.

In short, there are several approaches to the critical issue of organization of curriculum content pertaining to Child Welfare. Continued experimentation with different approaches is needed, along with evaluation of their effectiveness. Current efforts in the profession to delineate the organization, boundaries, and rationale of different fields of social work practice should lead to further clarity about how Child Welfare content can best be organized in the curriculum. Until more definitive guidelines are identified, it seems prudent to maintain flexibility in curriculum development and to avoid structuring the curriculum into particular specialties that may soon become outmoded.

## Continuum of Social Work Education and Training

The continuum of social work education and training currently embodies various levels: agency-based training or staff development; programs leading to the A.A., B.S.W., M.S.W., D.S.W. or Ph.D degrees; and continuing education. As this continuum becomes increasingly elaborate, clarification of the particular focus or function that should be prominent at each level in respect to Child Welfare practice becomes more urgent. This is not an easy question to resolve, as a result of broader issues such as the generalist–specialist controversy, the lack of differentiation in the primary tasks of B.S.W. and M.S.W. graduates, insufficient clarity as to the distinctive mission and scope of bachelor's and master's programs, and the competition among schools for diminishing financial resources. Consequently, confusion and overlapping among the different levels is beginning to surface. Nevertheless, some trends are becoming evident.

Staff development or on-the-job training is regarded as the most effective vehicle for content such as agency policies, procedures, and programs or content on technical skills pertaining to a specific service or practice issue (O'Neil, 1980: 17). Training is also used for Child Welfare personnel other than social workers, such as foster parents, houseparents, and others (Ainsworth, 1981). At the associate degree level, educational programs in settings such as community colleges are concentrating on preparation of such personnel as child-care workers.

At the B.S.W. level, as noted earlier, it is agreed that the focus should be on preparation of "generalist practitioners with a generic repertoire of skills" (Loppnow and Taggart, 1981: 4), along with introduction to basic issues and principles of practice in Child Welfare. On the other hand, M.S.W. programs are expected to provide opportunities for specialization in Child Welfare or other fields of practice: "Graduate education is seen as the forum for closer and more practice-oriented exploration of specialty areas within the field, of which Child Welfare is an example" (Lauderdale, Grinnell, and McMurtry, 1980: 539).

The extent to which these distinctions in focus between B.S.W. and M.S.W. programs are actually implemented by schools is open to question, especially in light of findings from the national survey of Child Welfare education. Reporting on this survey, Hartman concludes: "In summary, it would appear that, at least in child welfare, BSW programs tend to be more, rather than less specific" (1983: 24). For instance, the survey found that specific content areas such as adoption, foster family care, and services to unmarried parents are emphasized in bachelor's programs more than at the master's level (Hartman, 1983). As a result of these findings, Hartman recommends a shift in thinking about the B.S.W.–M.S.W. continuum:

> It is perfectly reasonable to turn the generalist–specialist continuum around, to define the BSW program as a more specific program where knowledge and skills are made concrete in specific applications, to make competence in action more possible and the BSW more desirable in the labor market. The greater demands of mastering a wider and more varied range of knowledge and skill and a higher level of abstraction could occur at the MSW level. (Hartman, 1983: 25).

Beyond B.S.W. and M.S.W. programs, a few schools offer Ph.D. or D.S.W. instruction. In general, these programs focus on research, teaching, administration, or planning in Child Welfare. Finally, continuing education provides varied opportunities for enrichment, refreshment and updating, postgraduate specialization, exploration of new content areas, or in-depth study of familiar areas.

## Relationship between Educational and Service Delivery Systems

Tension between education and practice seems to be a perennial fact of life in social work, which may well be inevitable, since educators and practitioners bring different perspectives on their ultimate, shared goal of providing effective services. Moreover, the tension is not all negative; a certain amount serves to stimulate growth and change.

In Child Welfare, this tension is manifested particularly in the questions that continue to be raised about the effectiveness and relevance of education for practice. Stein (1982) has indicated, for example, that a discrepancy exists between what schools of social work teach and the realities of practice: schools emphasize psychotherapeutic work with motivated or voluntary clients, whereas most persons coming to the attention of Child Welfare agencies are involuntary and unmotivated. In short, as Wiltse contends: "Social work education is often largely irrelevant to child welfare practice, because the practice model or models in which students are educated do not include the ones that best fit child welfare" (1981: 2). Schools tend to focus on practice approaches that seem to be more appropriate for clients of voluntary agencies than those of public Child Welfare agencies.

These authors reflect those criticisms of social work education which are frequently made by agency representatives. The same writers propose diverse ways to cope with the tension between the educational and service delivery systems and achieve a better fit between education and practice. For instance, Stein (1982) advocates shifting from a therapeutic model to a case management model, while Wiltse urges offering educational programs that "imbue students with enthusiasm for work with the disordered families that produce neglected or abused children" (Wiltse, 1981: 6).

Beyond changing curriculum objectives and content, there are numerous ways to improve the relationship between education and practice, as demonstrated in recent years by the National and Regional Child Welfare Training Resource Centers. These include approaches such as joint workshops of educators and practitioners around issues of common concern; joint agency–school participation in curriculum development; sharing resources, such as having agency personnel assume teaching roles in the schools; and clarifying the skills and competencies of B.S.W. and M.S.W. graduates. Above all, through ongoing collaboration in the activities of the centers, schools and agencies have increasingly recognized their interdependence and found it possible to work together in their shared commitment to quality Child Welfare practice. In addition, as Gullerud and Itzin (1979) indicate, continuing education programs can serve as effective links between schools and the practice community. As educators and practitioners engage in planning and implementing continuing education programs, they can learn to appreciate each other's needs and viewpoints and enhance the collaborative process.

## Evaluation of Effectiveness

As suggested earlier in this chapter, there is no doubt that in recent years schools of social work and agencies have been giving increased attention to education and training of social workers and other personnel for Child Welfare practice. This claim is supported, for instance, by the establishment of the National and Regional Child Welfare Training Resource Centers; the development of numerous curriculum guides, training manuals, and audiovisual materials (cf. Pardeck, et al., 1982); and the proliferation of formal and informal educational programs in schools and agencies throughout the country. Whether or not these activities will continue as funds diminish remains to be seen.

Beyond the issue of funds, there is the question of effectiveness. How useful are education and training programs? Do they actually enhance worker competence? What is their impact on the quality of practice or service delivery? There is much discussion, but very little empirical evidence bearing on these questions; studies evaluating the effectiveness of educational and training programs are limited, although there is wide agreement that evaluation is essential.

The value of education and training for Child Welfare personnel is not universally accepted. In an evaluation of child abuse and neglect programs, state agency administrators indicated that a social work degree was not particularly useful for workers or supervisors. In their view, a bachelor's degree in any discipline, coupled with appropriate experience and attitudes, was more valuable than a B.S.W. or M.S.W. degree (General Accounting Office, April 29, 1980: 25–26, 32, 44).

On the other hand, in a careful study, Baily (1978: 84) found that B.S.W. graduates performed at significantly higher levels than undifferentiated B.A. graduates in a variety of social service positions in agencies that included public Child Welfare. Similarly, Olsen and Holmes (1982: 101), in an analysis of data from the 1977 National Study of Social Services to Children and Their Families (Shyne and Schroeder, 1978), concluded that nonprofessionally trained staff did not perform as effectively as professional staff in such areas as provision of substitute care and supportive services, environmental services, and planning for ongoing contact between children in foster care and their biological families. Others have concluded that training programs are successful in changing attitudes, enhancing skills, or improving work behaviors in the trainees (cf. Appelberg, 1967; Broome and Comer, 1971; Maluccio, 1970; Simon and Simon, 1982). Most of the latter reports, however, are based on informal evaluations or impressionistic data.

While few formal studies of effectiveness have been done, certain educational and training programs may be regarded as exemplary. Through these experiences, various approaches have been found to be especially useful in enhancing worker knowledge and skills. These include:

*Participation of clients in the educational process.* For example, biological parents and foster children are involved as resource persons, guest lecturers, or co-instructors.

*Use of consultants.* Agencies are relying on consultants to provide informal, on-the-job training to staff in relation to specific issues. A common example is that of the legal expert. An innovative example is that of the "ethnic consultant," that is, someone with expertise in relation to a specific ethnic group, who is available to help practitioners become more knowledgeable and sensitive in working with members of that particular cultural or ethnic group.

*Follow-up training or consultation.* In addition, to reinforce the learning that takes place in a given workshop or course, some programs have experimented with the use of ongoing consultation to the participants.

The consultant is available to the workers in their own setting, to discuss case situations or practice issues and the application of concepts, principles, and techniques covered in the workshop. Other agencies provide follow-up mini-training sessions.

*Strengthening the educational role of supervisors.* Particularly in response to the high turnover of line staff, some agencies are redefining the roles of supervisors and providing training to strengthen their educational or training function. This approach is of potentially great value, since, workers, according to adult learning theory, are more likely to acquire and retain material learned on the job, especially material timely and relevant to their felt needs.[4]

*Collaboration of schools and agencies in curriculum development.* For instance, through leadership from the National and Regional Child Welfare Training Centers as well as other federally funded Child Welfare training projects, schools and agency representatives have been coming together to discuss curriculum issues and develop curricula relevant to practice.

## Promoting Worker Competence

Educational and training programs, as well as studies of their effectiveness, tend to focus on skill training and narrowly defined competencies, such as skills in contracting with clients, interviewing parents of sexually abused children, or using permanency planning techniques. This focus, which is especially evident at the B.S.W. level and in in-service training programs, is in some ways understandable: Practitioners do need to learn specific techniques and to acquire discrete skills in order to deal with complex demands in their case situations. On the other hand, such a narrow focus, while adaptive in the short run, ultimately is of limited value, since it does little to enhance the worker's competence, mastery, and adaptation, that is, their capacity to think, to function autonomously in the face of uncertainty and rapid change, and to act in a discriminating manner in response to new or nonroutine demands and challenges in their practice.

To prepare workers more effectively, educational and training programs should follow a broader definition of competence. Competence is generally defined as the person's achieved capacity to interact effectively with the environment (White, 1963). It is not simply a property or trait of the person but the outcome of the transaction between (1) the person's qualities, such as needs, motivation, or coping patterns, and (2) the qualities of the impinging environment, such as environmental resources, supports, demands, and pressures (Maluccio, 1981a). Effective functioning requires a "goodness of fit" between workers' needs and qualities and demands and supports available in their work environment (Germain and Gitterman, 1980).

As with human beings in general, workers need to have an "average expectable environment" (Hartmann, 1958), to carry out their roles, use their strengths, and maximize their potentialities. In particular, to help promote the competence of workers, educational and training programs should be offered in an environment conducive to learning as well as to working.

To what extent does such an environment exist? Given the reality of contemporary practice, it is not an exaggeration to say that most Child Welfare workers work in an environment that does not enhance their growth, satisfaction, or development of competence. Now, as in the past, workers experience many strains and stresses that have typically been attributed to the pressures of working with complex and demanding cases. Increasingly, however, we are appreciating that

> various systemic factors put additional burdens on workers—factors such as limited resources, ambivalent societal opinions of their roles and the functions of child welfare agencies; the political context, with frequent investigations and exposés of public child welfare agencies by governmental and legislative bodies and the media; limited administrative support; insufficient recognition of their efforts; and so on. (Maluccio, 1981b: 148)

It follows that the work environment must be restructured and enriched. The revitalization of Child Welfare training—and ultimately Child Welfare as a field of practice—depends not only on the development and dissemination of curriculum and training materials but also, and perhaps more importantly, on factors such as adequate salary levels, manageable caseloads, mechanisms to support staff decision-making, and career opportunities (Seaberg, 1982). Above all, there must be opportunities for workers to function productively and to grow.

Even in an era of diminishing physical resources, such opportunities can be found—opportunities not only for material resources and supports, but also for recognition and gratification, in areas like the following: participation in policy-making and program planning processes; encouragement for workers to exercise their own decision-making powers; respect on the part of administrators, board members, and the community in general; positive feedback; incentives for promotion and for professional development (Maluccio, 1981b: 148–149).

In short, as suggested by Smith (1968) in his formulation of competence development, the agency environment should provide the prerequisite conditons for competent functioning: opportunity, such as supports and resources; respect from others, which enhances self-respect; and power, which supports professional decision-making. Moreover, a competence-centered perspective on education and training for Child Welfare reminds us that, "although the world's physical resources are limited, human resources are underutilized and can flourish in a nutritive environment" (Maluccio, 1981b: 153). Such a perspective suggests many general principles useful in promoting educational and training programs leading to increased competence in workers. Some of the most prominent principles are outlined here.

Programs can involve prospective trainees in identification and assessment of their training needs (cf. Pecora et al., 1983). These programs should also match educational or training activities with workers' felt needs, concerns, and practice issues. Worker participation should be encouraged in the development of each educational or training program, especially in the formulation of learning objectives, selection of content, and choice of teaching methods.

Providing a variety of learning opportunities and teaching methodologies and recognizing the diversity in cultural values, learning styles, and individual coping patterns are also goals of a good program. Specific goals and objectives, which are mutually agreed upon, should be clear to all participants. Also, workers can take major responsibility for developing individualized educational plans based on their self-assessment. In addition, it is important for programs to obtain, on a regular basis, feedback from workers regarding the effectiveness of educational or training programs, their relevance for practice, and suggestions or recommendations for improvement.

Child Welfare is a vast field involving a wide range of needs, services, and consumers. In turn, staff members in Child Welfare bring a variety of backgrounds, personal characteristics, interests, and educational and work experiences. Ideally, educational and training programs can serve as a bridge between the qualities and resources of available personnel and the needs and styles of diverse client populations; they can enhance the goodness of fit between consumers and practitioners.

To accomplish this goal, education and training must increasingly stress the active involvement of workers in the teaching and learning process, the development of curricula relevant to practice and the creation of a nurturing work environment that promotes the competence of practitioners and supports their effective functioning.

In addition, along with the traditional focus on technology and on building skills, education and training should emphasize teaching how to think and how to learn. They should, in other words, underscore preparation for autonomous practice and professional self-development, so that today's students and trainees might also be ready to function tomorrow.

## Annotated Bibliography of Exemplary Materials

Creative Associates. *Child Welfare In-Service Training Curriculum.* Washington, D.C.: Creative Associates, Inc., 1982.

This is the most comprehensive, up-to-date curriculum for in-service training available in the field of Child Welfare. Overall purpose of curriculum is to enhance the knowledge and skills of workers in supporting families and reducing incidence and duration of substitute care. Each of the thirteen modules, which comprise a 168-hour curriculum, can be used as designed or adapted to individual agency requirements. The modules are:

—Family assessment
—Developing a service plan
—Assessing progress
—Serving families
—Children in need of special services
—Adolescents in need of special services
—Planning for permanency planning
—Preparing for substitute care
—Facilitating placement
—Providing services to children in care
—Reuniting families
—Constitutional and statutory framework of Child Welfare services
—Working with the court

Package also contains a guide on "Training resources with cultural perspectives." Specific module on protective services is not included, but is available in Drews, Salus, and Dodge, 1981.

Drews, Kay, Salus, Marsha K., and Dodge, Diane. *Child Protective Services: In-service Training for Supervisors* Washington, D.C.: National Center on Child Abuse and Neglect, U.S. Department of Health and Human Services, 1981.

This training package is designed for use by supervisors in training of protective service workers in public agencies. Training is provided through dialogue on audio cassettes and through self-instructional modules in each of these areas:

—Roles and tasks involved in supervision in children's protective services
—Intake
—Investigation
—Ongoing services
—Court system
—Cultural responsiveness

Loppnow, Donald M., and Taggart, Sarah R. *Family and Children's Services Specialty—The Development of an Elective Concentration in a Baccalaureate Social Work Program.* Ypsilanti, MI: Social Work Program, College of Human Services, Eastern Michigan University, 1981.

This book provides a thoughtful description and analysis of an exemplary B.S.W. program in the area of Child Welfare. It covers rationale for developing a family and children's services specialty at the B.S.W. level, curriculum objectives and design, pending issues in curriculum design, and outlines of individual courses.

Martin, Judith A. (Ed). *Advanced Graduate Course Content—Children, Youth, and Families—An Instructional Guide.* Pittsburgh, PA: School of Social Work, University of Pittsburgh, 1982.

This instructor's guide describes a series of courses offered in an exemplary M.S.W. program focusing on children, youth, and their families. In addition to brief discussion of the overall curriculum and the children, youth, and families concentration at the University of Pittsburgh School of Social Work, the guide includes detailed course outlines and bibliographies for courses in these areas:

—Parent–child development
—Childhood illness and the family
—Policy and legislation in Child Welfare
—Legal training for the Child Welfare practitioner
—Social work in education
—Family treatment in Child Welfare settings
—Treatment of adolescents
—Enhancing parenting skills

National Institute for Advanced Studies. *Child Welfare Training— Catalogue of Training Materials for Child Welfare Services.* Washington, D.C.: U.S. Department of Health and Human Services, 1980. DHHS Publication No. (OHDS) 80–30277.

As an exhaustive annotated listing of curricula, training materials, and audiovisual resources, this book is particularly useful in training Child Welfare workers and supervisors in public agency settings. It contains 150 entries in subject areas such as foster care, adoption, residential programs, emergency services, adolescent services, and supervision.

Pardeck, John T., Hegar, Rebecca L., Nance, Kathy Newton, and Christy-Baker, Cynthia. *Child Welfare Training and Practice—An Annotated Bibliography.* Westport, CT: Greenwood Press, 1982.

This is a comprehensive annotated bibliography including numerous references on training materials and methods in the following areas:

child abuse and neglect; law and the court; substitute care; home-based services; institutional care; minority clients; and special needs children.

*Permanency Planning: The Black Experience—A Training Curriculum.* Knoxville, TN: Office of Continuing Education, University of Tennessee. School of Social Work, 1982.

These unique trainers' and resource manuals are designed for in-service training for caseworkers and supervisors with basic knowledge and skills in permanency planning. They provide training in such areas as:

—Afro-American history and culture
—Communications between black families and white human service workers
—Agency policies and practices as related to permanency planning work with black families and children

# Factors Associated with Job Satisfaction and Turnover Among Child Welfare Workers

SRINIKA JAYARATNE
WAYNE A. CHESS

Although a rich literature on the dimensions of job satisfaction in the American work force can be found, little of it addresses human service professionals (Caplan et.al., 1975; Quinn and Staines, 1978; Quinn and Sheppard, 1974). The primary target groups in these research efforts have been blue- and white-collar workers and business managers. The research and literature on human service professionals generally emphasizes the phenomenon of "burnout" (Cherniss, 1980; Maslach, 1976; Maslach and Jackson, 1981; Pines and Kafry, 1978). Without addressing the nature of the relationship between burnout and job satisfaction, it is sufficient to say that the vast majority of the burnout literature has been on Child Welfare workers (Barrett and McKelvey, 1980; Daley, 1979; Harrison, 1980; Wasserman, 1970), and by and large, is nonempirical and experiential (Barrett and McKelvey, 1980; Karger, 1981).

The present study was conceptualized within the framework of job satisfaction (rather than burnout) for three reasons. First, there is a paucity of information on social workers' perceptions of their jobs. Given the high turnover recorded among social workers, it would be important to understand the sources of job satisfaction better and its relationship to turnover (Armstrong, 1978; Stamm, 1969). Second, since the majority of current writings on service professionals concern themselves with burnout, we decided to concentrate on job satisfaction, since the literature has argued that the two are of a different order (Harrison, 1980; Maslach and Jackson, 1981). Understanding burnout, therefore, does not necessarily lead to an understanding of the nature and character of job satisfaction. Finally, the notion of job satisfaction has been conceptualized and operationalized somewhat better than has the phenomenon of burnout (Dunnette, Campbell, and Hakel, 1967; Locke, 1969; Nord, 1977). The conceptual model employed here views job satisfaction as a multidimensional construct. In assessing job satisfaction, a worker considers the different facets of the job prior to awarding a global rating. Therefore, it is important to know both the global rating and the relative levels of satisfaction for different facets of the job.

## Study Variables

In the present study, which employs a national sample of social workers, we subscribe to the belief that a person's perceptions of the work situation are more important than the absolute nature of the work content. This approach is similar to Lewin's (1951) concept of the "psychological environment"; it is basically an individual's subjective assessment of the work situation.

The two major dependent variables in this study are (1) global indicators of job satisfaction, and (2) intent to turnover. Job satisfaction is measured by the single item: "All in all, how satisfied would you say you are with your job?" Four response categories were presented ranging from "very satisfied" to "not at all satisfied." Intent to turnover is also measured by a single item: "Taking everything into consideration, how likely is it that you will make a *genuine effort* to find a new job with another employer within the next year?" The response alternatives were "very likely," "somewhat likely," and "not at all likely." Both of these measures were used by Quinn and his colleagues in their national studies of work satisfaction to measure the worker's general affective reactions to the job (Quinn and Sheppard, 1974; Quinn and Staines, 1978).

In selecting various facets or dimensions of the job which could be associated with job satisfaction and intent to turnover, we relied both on prior research and on our interest in bridging the notions of job satisfaction and burnout. We included seven job facets as "predictor variables," all of which have been theoretically and/or empirically tied to job satisfaction, turnover, or burnout.

•*Comfort.* This index consists of seven items and has a score range from 7–28: the lower the score, the greater the comfort. This is a measure of the creature comforts offered by the workplace; an item example: "The physical surroundings are pleasant."

• *Challenge.* This index consists of six items and has a score range from 6–24: the lower the score, the greater the challenge. This is a measure of how stimulating the job is perceived to be by the worker; an item example: "The problems I am expected to solve are hard enough."

• *Financial Rewards.* This index consists of three items and has a score range from 3–12: the lower the score, the better the rewards. This is a measure of pay, security, and fringe benefits; an item example: "The pay is good."

• *Promotions.* This index consists of three items and has a score range from 3–12: the lower the score, the better the perceived opportunities for promotion. This is a measure of the workers' perceptions of promotional chances as well as the fairness in the process; an item example: "Promotions are handled fairly."

• *Role Ambiguity.* This index consists of four items and has a score range from 4–20: the lower the score, the less role ambiguity. This is a measure of the perceptions a worker has about the clarity of the work situation; an item example: "Work objectives are well defined."

• *Role Conflict.* This index consists of four items and has a score range from 4–16: the higher the score, the less the perceived conflict. This is a measure of the conflicting demands that a worker perceives on the job; an item example: "On my job, I can't satisfy everybody at the same time."

• *Workload.* This index consists of four items and has a score range from 4–20: the higher the score, the lower the workload. This is a measure of the workers' perceptions of the amount of work that needs to be done; an item example: "How often does your job require you to work very hard?"

## Sample

The sample of 1,173 social workers was randomly selected from the NASW membership. Eight-hundred fifty three questionnaires were returned, a response rate of 72.7 percent. Because of our interest in Child Welfare workers, we oversampled those individuals who identified themselves as working in Child Welfare settings in the *NASW Membership Register.* Our Child Welfare sample consisted of 200 individuals, and we received 140 completed questionnaires, a 70.0 percent response rate. The current analysis is restricted to those Child Welfare workers who are working full-time (40 hours per week) and are currently in practice. These criteria resulted in an analytic sample of 99 workers, which represents 70.7 percent of the Child Welfare sample.

TABLE VII–A–1   Sample Characteristics*

| Characteristics | Number (N=99) | % |
|---|---|---|
| Degree | | |
| B.A. or B.S.W. | 17 | 17.2 |
| M.S.W. | 82 | 82.8 |
| Degree Year | | |
| ≤1950 | 5 | 5.1 |
| 1951–1960 | 12 | 12.2 |
| 1961–1970 | 22 | 22.4 |
| 1971≥ | 59 | 60.2 |
| Age | | |
| ≤30 | 28 | 28.9 |
| 31–40 | 31 | 32.0 |
| 41–50 | 18 | 18.6 |
| 51≥ | 20 | 20.6 |
| Gender | | |
| Male | 40 | 41.2 |
| Female | 57 | 58.8 |
| Marital status | | |
| Married | 56 | 57.7 |
| Never Married | 29 | 29.9 |
| Other | 12 | 12.4 |
| Income | | |
| ≤15,000 | 26 | 26.8 |
| 15,001≤20,000 | 25 | 25.8 |
| 20,001≤25,000 | 27 | 27.8 |
| 25,001≥ | 19 | 19.6 |
| Time in present position | | |
| 1 year or less | 30 | 30.3 |
| 1<3 | 24 | 24.2 |
| 3<5 | 17 | 17.2 |
| 5<10 | 15 | 15.2 |
| 10 years or more | 13 | 13.1 |

*Differing totals reflect missing data.

Table VII–A–1 presents some selected demographics and work characteristics of the respondents. The sample is mostly female (58.8%) and predominantly white (87.6%). The majority of the respondents received their highest degree in or after 1971 (60.2%), and 82.8 percent of the sample possess a masters degree in social work. Slightly more than half the sample (52.6%) earn $20,000 or less from their social work job. Close to a third of the sample have been in their present position for less than one year, and over 50 percent have been in it for less than three years. In general, these data present an overview of the respondents on whom the present analysis is based.

## Results

Several global findings are worthy of note. Of all respondents 82.8 percent said that they are "very satisfied" or "somewhat satisfied" with their jobs. An equally astounding 92.8 percent stated that they were "very successful" (43.8%) or "somewhat successful" (49%) in their professional work. In effect, this sample of Child Welfare workers reports reasonable job satisfaction and the belief that they are good at what they do. Despite this high degree of job satisfaction and perceived success, some elements of unhappiness with the job do appear as recorded by intentions to leave. In response to the question, "Taking everything into consideration, how likely is it that you will make a *genuine effort* to find a new job with another employer within the next year?", 23.2 percent answered "very likely" and an additional 23.2 percent answered "somewhat likely." That is, close to half the respondents in this sample will be job hunting (or at least hope to do so) within the next year. While these data are in keeping with the experiential information published in the literature, it is still surprising given the high levels of expressed satisfaction and perceived success.

One other global finding that was somewhat of a surprise was the relationship between absolute income and perceptions of satisfaction with income. It was noted earlier that more than half the sample earned less than $20,000. In addition, we asked our respondents the following question: "Considering your education, knowledge, ability, experience, and how hard you work, do you think you are . . . ," with the response categories ranging from "underpaid a great deal" to "overpaid a great deal." A surprising 26.8 percent of the sample said they were "paid about right." As expected, 55.7 percent said they felt they were "underpaid a great deal" or "underpaid somewhat." Thus, while the majority believe they are underpaid, a substantial minority of workers believe their compensation to be fair or adequate.

From the data discussed up to now, perhaps the most curious and disturbing finding is the discrepancy between job satisfaction and intent to turnover. One obvious reason for this discrepancy would be that workers use different frames of reference in assessing job satisfaction and intent to turnover. That is, the criteria employed in evaluating satisfaction with the job may be very different from those employed in the job discontinuance decision. However this reasoning in no way implies that these two are totally independent dimensions. In fact, the zero-order correlation between these two variables is .57: that is, the lower the job satisfaction, the greater the probability of turnover. The moderate strength of this association, however, implies that the two variables overlap and that they are not identical.

In an attempt to better understand the factors associated with job satisfaction and turnover, we conducted multiple regression analyses using the various job facets as predictor variables. These analyses use the seven facets of challenge, conflict, financial rewards, promotions, role ambiguity, role conflict, and workload as the sum total of dimensions in assessing satisfaction and turnover. If this model is relatively complete, a high degree of variance is explained by the analyses. And, if the workers employ similar frames of assessment in job satisfaction and turnover intent, then the same predictors should emerge as significant predictor variables. In addition, if these particular job facets are equally important in the decisions, then an equal amount of variance should be explained by the regressions. The results of these analyses are presented in Table VII–A–2.

As this table shows, there is a substantial difference in explained variance ($R^2$) between job satisfaction and turnover. Whereas 58 percent of the total variance in job satisfaction is explained by the seven facets, only 23 percent of turnover intent is accounted for by the same set of predictors. Clearly, these particular job facets are of greater relevance to the workers in the assessment of job satisfaction, and some "unknown" variables of importance in the decision to turnover have been left out of this analysis. What these variables may be are of course speculative, but they may range from social supports available in the work environment, to employment opportunities available for family members in a given

**TABLE VII–A–2  Multiple Regression Analyses on Job Satisfaction and Turnover**

|  | Beta Weight | t-Stat | Significance |
|---|---|---|---|
| *Job Satisfaction* | | | |
| Comfort | .11 | 0.909 | NS |
| Challenge | .31 | 2.992 | .005 |
| Financial rewards | .22 | 2.153 | .05 |
| Promotions | .28 | 2.630 | .01 |
| Role ambiguity | .16 | 1.504 | NS |
| Role conflict | .16 | 1.599 | NS |
| Workload | −.01 | 0.063 | NS |
| $R = .76 \qquad R^2 = .58$ | | | |
| *Intent to Turnover* | | | |
| Comfort | −.16 | 1.015 | NS |
| Challenge | .04 | 0.285 | NS |
| Financial rewards | −.42 | 3.054 | .005 |
| Promotions | −.01 | 0.043 | NS |
| Role ambiguity | .04 | 0.298 | NS |
| Role conflict | .04 | 0.328 | NS |
| Workload | .01 | 0.039 | NS |
| $R = .48 \qquad R^2 = .22$ | | | |

community, to a variety of other work-related and non-work-related factors.

When one considers the predictors of job satisfaction and turnover, however, some important distinctions emerge. Three job facets—challenge, promotions, and financial rewards—emerge as significant predictors of job satisfaction. Challenge is clearly the most important predictor, with this facet alone accounting for over 30 percent of the total variance. In contrast, the only significant predictor of turnover is financial rewards. Apparently, the facets of challenge and promotions lose their valence in this assessment. Basically, these data suggest that a worker would report satisfaction with the job if it is perceived as challenging, if the opportunities for promotion are viewed as adequate, and if the financial rewards are fair or adequate. On the other hand, if the financial rewards are judged as inadequate, then the probability of seeking new employment increases. In this context, note that the majority of workers (55.7%) reported dissatisfaction with their pay. But curiously, challenge and opportunities for promotion do not seem to enter into the decision process where turnover is concerned.

Two final comments need to be made with respect to these data. First, those factors which have been identified in the literature as "stressors" (role ambiguity, role conflict, and workload), do not emerge as significant correlates either of job satisfaction or job discontinuance. In effect, the relative weight of these job facets compared to the other dimensions seems to be minimal. On the other hand, these same dimensions have emerged as important correlates of burnout (Harrison, 1980). These findings may support tangentially the contention that burnout and job satisfaction are of a different order. The second issue references the nature of job challenge, promotional opportunities, and financial rewards. These attributes are under the control of agency policy and procedure. Conceivably, administrative action in these areas may result in increased job satisfaction and decreased turnover.

In summary, while the Child Welfare workers in the present sample are relatively satisfied with their work and believe they are doing a good job, they are also likely to seek new employment. This apparent contradiction seems to be a function of different evaluative frames that are applied in the assessment of these two related dimensions. Job challenge, opportunities for promotion, and financial rewards emerge as the most important predictors of job satisfaction, while financial rewards appears to be the only factor related to job discontinuance. Agency procedures which address these three job facets, therefore, should help increase job satisfaction and decrease turnover.

# Notes

## Introduction to Part I

1. *Webster's New Twentieth Century Dictionary*, 2d edition, unabridged. New York: The Publishers Guild, Inc., 1960, p. 394.

## Chapter 1

1. Human exploitation and deprivation are prevalent in many contemporary societies with economic, political, and ideological systems different from those of the United States. Such societies, however, are not the focus of the critical analysis in this chapter, and thus shortcomings in their ways of life are not mentioned.

## Chapter 2

1. The material in this chapter has come from research I have carried out in preparing a manuscript entitled *Two Sisters for Social Justice: A Biography of Grace and Edith Abbott*, from an ongoing international comparative study of the early child protection movement, and from my research while preparing the manuscript for *Child Welfare: Policies and Practice* (1970).

2. This testimony was presented by David Fanshel before the Senate Subcommittee on Children and Youth of the Senate Committee on Labor and Public Welfare and the House of Representatives Select Subcommittee on Education. See "Foster Care: Problems and Issues," December 1, 1975.

3. The papers of the Illinois Humane Society, found in the Illinois State Historical Library, had not been separated into separate folders of child protection and animal protection at the time I consulted them. They consisted, in large measure, of daily chronological accounts of the society's dual functions on behalf of animals and children. The day-by-day record of the alternate attention to the problems of cruelly treated children and the rescue of badly treated horses, along with other concerns, such as the risk to song birds by careless hunters, provided me with a startling incongruity of priorities.

4. For an understanding of the contrasting characteristics of coercive and assimilative reform, I relied on Gusfield (1966).

## Chapter 3

1. This directive is known as Public Law 96-272, The Adoption Assistance and Child Welfare Act of 1980. This law mandated the gradual evolution of stronger community and family links in Child Welfare practice. The degree of its eventual implementation is unclear at this writing, particularly because of efforts to divest federal regulatory responsibility in Child Welfare and other areas.

2. This statement, extracted from a larger document, was intended to reflect the basic needs of families requiring continual social provisions.

## Introduction to Part II

1. Less dualistic than many social work theorists. Gordon acknowledges the relationship between observer and observed and uses the term "objective" in "the sense of data least influenced by the observer and most influenced by what is observed" (1965:34).

2. See, for example, Geismar and Wood (1982); Heineman (1981); Hudson (1982); and Ruckdeschel and Farris (1981). Heineman's article stimulated a number of responses and counterresponses in the literature.

## Chapter 7

1. For a more elaborate discussion of conceptions of the nuclear family, see Skolnick (1983).

2. There is a stimulating discussion of the interconnectedness of events and trends that are leading to "the death of industrialization and the rise of a new civilization" in the introduction to Toffler (1981: 1–6).

3. Marianne Walters, who has had extensive experience in work with single-parent families, believes such families have special strengths. See a discussion of her view in Hartman and Laird (1983: 276).

4. Laird and Allen (1983) summarize the views, concepts, and assessment and intervention dimensions of the leading "schools" of family therapy according to that aspect of the family system which is seen as the focus for change, such as communication, structure, or rule patterns.

5. See Bandler and Grinder, 1975, and Grinder and Bandler, 1976, in the Bibliography.

6. For a full discussion of the concept of "the ethnic reality," see Devore and Schlesinger (1981).

## Chapter 11

1. See Allen and Knitzer (1983) for a much fuller discussion of the various components of the policy framework for child welfare services.

2. See Greenberg (1977) for further discussion of this issue.

3. The authors recognize that their comments in this section are very time-bound, clearly reflecting the social climate of the period in which this article was written. However, the trends noted seem too significant to be ignored in any discussion of social policy development. We would be happy to be found out-dated if the policy directions introduced by the Reagan Administration should prove to be merely a temporary aberration from the general thrust of social developments in this country or if our predictions of the dire consequences for child welfare services inherent in these comments should prove to be wrong.

4. New York City has since adopted a more sophisticated management information system for tracking the movement of children in foster care.

5. For fuller discussion of the development and learning experiences of the child advocacy movement, see Kahn, Kamerman, and McGowan (1973); Knitzer (1976); and Costin (1979).

6. See Lee (1937) for further elaboration of the concept of social work as cause and function.

7. Other social work authors have argued that manipulation and the use of covert tactics may be appropriate under certain circumstances. See, for example, Brager and Holloway (1978) and Scurfield (1980).

8. See Knitzer (1976) and Children's Defense Fund (1978a) for further discussion of the principles or steps that should be followed to insure that advocacy efforts are effective.

9. We are indebted to Paulette Geanacopoulos for suggesting this tactic (informal communication).

10. The New York City Chapter of NASW, for example, recently compiled a booklet of case vignettes provided by members from a wide range of settings illustrating the harmful effects of recent budget cuts on clients. These booklets are being distributed to legislators for educational purposes.

11. Representative George Miller, Keynote Speech, Forum on Helping Children and Families Cope, Sponsored by the Human Resource Administration and Department of Social Services Advisory Board, New York City, January 27, 1984.

12. See Kleinkauf (1981) for a fuller discussion of guidelines for presenting legislative testimony.

13. "Circular A–122: Cost Principles for Nonprofit Organizations: Lobbying and Related Activities," Office of Management and Budget, Federal Register, 48:214 (November 3, 1983). As of this writing the comment period for these regulations has just ended. However, organizations vehemently opposed to the initial regulations proposed in January 1983 anticipated that these revised regulations generally would be implemented.

## Exemplar III–A

1. For a more complete discussion of the text of President Reagan's speech, see Cannon (1981).

2. For a good review of child welfare legislation historically, see Steiner (1976) and U.S.D.H.E.W. (1976).

3. For a review of categorical programs and their problems, see Advisory Commission on Intergovernmental Relations (1977a).

4. For a comprehensive review of both the advantages as well as the disadvantages associated with categorical programs, see Advisory Commission on Intergovernmental Relations (1977a).

5. For a statement of the reservations that many scholars and researchers have about the states' capability of administering many federal programs, see Broadnax (1981).

6. For a comprehensive discussion of the advantages and disadvantages of blocks versus categoricals, see Break (1981).

## Exemplar III–B

1. Based upon Office for Civil Rights letter of findings dated April 17, 1981.

2. For a discussion of Title VI in child welfare, see Davidson and Anderson (1981; 1982a; and 1982b). Relevant analyses from the area of health are contained in Wing (1978) and U.S. Commission on Civil Rights (1980).

## Chapter 14

1. There are numerous (though apparently ignored) articles in social work literature concerning authority issues. See Fusco (1977); Yelaja (1971); Studt (1954; 1959).

2. Hollis (1964) is quoted here because her views represent a perspective that occurs in practice, yet she herself has abandoned this one-up position. See Hollis and Wood (1981:363–377).

3. These conclusions come from my experiences as a trainer-consultant to Michigan Department of Social Services, Special Family Services Project—a prevention project aimed at high-risk families.

4. The eco-map has been written about extensively in Hartman (1978; 1980) and in Hartman and Laird (1983). It has also been discussed in a number of other works in child welfare and other fields. Moreover, the eco-map has been adopted widely as an assessment and intervention tool in both public and private child welfare agencies as well as in other fields of practice.

5. This conclusion comes from two separate experiences (one in Wisconsin and one in Michigan) and does not represent a scientific sample of child welfare practice in the United States.

## Chapter 15

1. This model is adapted from the author's work presented more fully in Hartman and Laird (1983).

2. For a discussion of these concepts, see Hartman and Laird (1983:69–72).

## Chapter 16

1. The generic term "homemaker–home health aide service" is used by the National HomeCaring Council and is gradually being adopted in federal and state legislation. The term encompasses "homemaker," "home health aide," "homemaker–home health aide," "home aide," and others. See *Issues* section.

2. Information supplied by Nora Johnson, formerly associate director of the Children's Aid Society in New York City, currently a member of the U.S. Committee for the International Council of Home Help Services.

3. Data obtained by telephone from Alice Alderman, Information Systems Analyst, Program Systems Division, Office of Management Services, Office of Human Development Services, Department of Health and Human Services.

4. Alice Alderman from the federal Office of Management Services provided these data.

## Exemplar IV–B

1. The Vasquez case was reported in the media. The name of the family and certain other identifying information have been disguised in the material given in this exemplar.

## Chapter 21

1. For example, Chimezie (1975) discusses the controversy with respect to black children, and Fanshel (1972) describes the practices and consequences of placing American Indian children in non-Indian homes.

## Chapter 22

1. The Jackson County (Michigan) Department of Social Services has a Children's Corner staffed by trained volunteers, where children can relax in an environment geared to their needs while waiting for the worker to arrange a placement or for the foster parents to come pick them up.

2. The Children's Eco-map is printed with permission of Jean Felton, Sharon Miller and Doris Stagg, Branch County, Michigan Department of Social Services. It is based on the Eco-map which was developed by Ann Hartman and originally field-tested in the Temporary Foster Care Project, Michigan Department of Social Services. Detailed instructions for use of the children's eco-map are found in Fahlberg(1979:30–34).

## Chapter 24

1. See Romans 8:14–7, Galatians 4:5–7, Exodus 3:10, Esther 2:7.

2. See, for example, Illinois Laws 1853, p. 485; Kentucky Acts 1841, p. 163; Pennsylvania Laws 1848, p. 201.

3. The earliest records of adoption agencies indicate that the children were most often born to married parents and placed with families with other children. See the New Jersey Children's Home Society annual reports as well as the New York Children's Aid Society.

4. For more information on trends in family structure, composition and habits, see Masnick and Bane (1980).

5. Correspondence between Albert Burstein, Chairman, Model Adoption Law Panel and Secretary, Patricia Harris, Department of Health and Human Services, Nov. 17, 1980. See also Day and Leeding (1980). In a conversation with Aviva Leon, Secretary General for Adoption Services in Israel, she reported to the author that Israel has both open access to adoption records and abortion. In her twenty years experience she has not noted that biological parents turn to abortion when informed of the open information law.

6. Stanley v. Illinois, 405 U.S. 645, 92 J. Ct. 1208 (1972); Quilloin v. Walcot, 434 U.S. 246, 98 J. Ct. 549 (1978); Caban v. Mohammed, 441 U.S. 380, 99 J. Ct. 2560 (1979).

7. Masnick and Bane, ibid.

8. See TEstimony to the Senate Subcommittee on Aging, Family and Human Services, Hearing on Adoption in the United States, July 23, 1981, by Ruby Lee Piester, Executive Director, Edna Gladney Home, Fort Worth, Texas.

9. In unpublished report prepared by Ann Coyne for the Child Welfare League, Developmental Disabilities Project (1981).

10. See TAble 4, "Aliens admitted by classes under the Immigration Laws," *U.S. Immigration and Naturalization Service Annual Reports* 1968–1970–1974.

11. Public Law 96–272 passed in 1980 made federal participation in adoption subsidies possible. Its funding and implementation would eliminate the problem discussed here.

## Chapter 25

1. This information is based on personal communication from Jim Gritter, Community Family and Children's Services of Traverse City, Michigan, May 1, 1984.

## Chapter 27

1. Rindfleisch, et al. (n.d.) discuss the difficulties, as well as the strategies, involved in assessing training needs in the field of children's services.

2. The findings of this survey are presented in full in a series of reports available without charge from the National Child Welfare Training Center, University of Michigan School of Social Work, 1015 E. Huron, Ann Arbor, MI 48104.

3. Forty-four distinct content areas were identified for purposes of the national survey of child welfare education and training (National Child Welfare Training Center), 1981–1984.

4. See Brannon (1982) for an excellent instructional guide to enhancing the educational role of supervisors.

# Bibliography

ABBOTT, EDITH. "A Study of the Early History of Child Labor in America." *American Journal of Sociology* 14 (Nov. 1908):226–227.

ABBOTT, GRACE. *The Child and the State.* Vols. I and II. Chicago: University of Chicago Press, 1938.

———. Statement before the U.S. 69th Congress, 1st Session, House Committee on Appropriations, 1927: Hearing before Subcommittee, Feb. 3, 1926.

ABERNATHY, V. "Illegitimate Conception Among Teenagers." *American Journal of Public Health* 64 (July 1974):662–665.

*Act Establishing the Children's Bureau.* (37 Stat. 79). Approved April 9, 1912.

AD HOC COMMITTEE ON ADVOCACY. "The Social Worker as Advocate: Champion of Social Victims." *Social Work* 14 (Apr. 1969):16–22.

ADDAMS, JANE. *My Friend, Julia Lathrop.* New York: Macmillan, 1935.

ADVISORY COMMISSION ON INTERGOVERNMENTAL RELATIONS. *Block Grants: A Comparative Analysis.* Washington, D.C.: U.S. Government Printing Office, 1977.

———. *Categorical Grants: Their Role and Design.* Washington, D.C.: U.S. Government Printing Office, 1977.

———. *The Future of Federalism in the 1980s.* Washington, D.C.: U.S. Government Printing Office, 1980.

AGUILERA, DONNA C., and MESSICK, JANICE M. *Crisis Intervention: Theory and Methodology.* St. Louis: Mosby, 1982.

AINSWORTH, FRANK. "The Training of Personnel for Group Care with Children." In *Group Care for Children—Concepts and Issues*, edited by Frank Ainsworth. London and New York: Tavistock Publications, 1981, pp. 225–244.

AINSWORTH, M. "Patterns of Attachment Behavior Shown by the Infant in Interaction with his Mother." *Merrill–Palmer Quarterly* 10 (Jan. 1964):51–58.

AINSWORTH, M.; BLEHAR, M.; WATERS, E.; and WALL, S. *Patterns of Attachment*. Hillsdale, N.J.: Erlbaum, 1978.

ALAN GUTTMACHER INSTITUTE. *Teenage Pregnancy: The Problem That Hasn't Gone Away*. New York: Alan Guttmacher Institute, 1981.

ALDRIDGE, MARTHA, and CAUTLEY, PATRICIA. "Placing Siblings in the Same Foster Home." *Child Welfare* 55 (Jan. 1976):85–93.

ALEXANDER, THOMAS, and SILLEN, SAMUEL. *Racism and Psychiatry*. Secaucus, N.J.: Citadel Press, 1976.

ALLEN, LETITIA A. "Child Abuse: A Critical Review of the Research and Theory." In *Violence and the Family*, edited by J. P. Martin. New York: Wiley, 1978, pp. 43–79.

ALLEN, MARY LEE, and KNITZER, JANE. "Child Welfare: Examining the Policy Framework." In *Child Welfare: Current Dilemmas, Future Directions*, edited by Brenda G. McGowan and William Meezan. Itasca, Ill.: Peacock, 1983, pp. 93–141.

ALLEN, WALTER E. "The Search for Applicable Theories of Black Family Life." *Journal of Marriage and the Family* 40 (Feb. 1978):117–129.

ALLERHAND, M. E.; WEBER, R; and HAUG, M. *Adaptation and Adaptability: The Bellefaire Follow-Up Study*. New York: Child Welfare League of America, 1966.

ALUTTO, J., and BELASCO, J. "A Typology for Participation in Organizational Decision Making." *Administrative Science Quarterly* 17 (Mar. 1972):117–125.

AMBINDER, W. J. "The Extent of Successive Placements Among Boys in Foster Family Homes." *Child Welfare* 44 (July 1965):397–398.

AMERICAN BAR ASSOCIATION. *Standards for Juvenile Justice*. Cambridge, Mass.: Ballinger, 1982.

———. Institute of Judicial Administration. *Standards in Relation to Abuse and Neglect: Tentative Draft*. Cambridge, Mass.: Ballinger, 1977.

AMERICAN CIVIL LIBERTIES UNION. "Sealed Adoption Records v. the Adoptees' Right to Know the Identity of the Birth Parents." *Children's Rights Report*. New York: American Civil Liberties Union, Vol. III (5) Feb. 1979.

AMERICAN CORRECTIONAL ASSOCIATION. *Standards for Juvenile Community Residential Facilities*. College Park, Md.: American Correctional Association, 1978.

———. *Standards for Juvenile Detention Facilities*. College Park, Md.: American Correctional Association, 1979.

———. *Standards for Juvenile Probation and Aftercare Standards for Juvenile Training Schools*. College Park, Md.: American Correctional Association, 1978.

AMERICAN HOME ECONOMICS ASSOCIATION. *A Force for Families*. Washington, D.C.: American Home Economics Association, n. d.

AMERICAN HUMANE ASSOCIATION. *Annual Report.* 1906.

——. *Annual Report.* 1912.

ANDERSON, JAMES L., and SIMONITCH, BRIAN. "Reactive Depression in Youths Experiencing Emancipation." *Child Welfare* 60 (June 1981):383–90.

ANDERSON, LYNETTE. "A Systems Theory Model for Foster Home Studies." *Child Welfare* 61 (Jan. 1982):37–47.

ANDREWS, ROBERTA G. "A Clinical Appraisal of Searching." *Public Welfare* 37 (Summer 1979):15–21.

——. "Permanent Placement of Negro Children Through Quasi-Adoption." *Child Welfare* 47 (Dec. 1968):583–586.

——. "When is Subsidized Adoption Preferable to Long-Term Foster Care?" *Child Welfare* 50 (Apr. 1971):194–200.

*Annual Report to the Congress on Title XX of the Social Security Act, Fiscal Year 1979.* Washington, D.C.: U.S. Government Printing Office, 1980.

ANTHONY, E. J. "The Syndrome of the Psychologically Invulnerable Child." In *The Child in His Family: Children at Psychiatric Risk*, edited by E. J. Anthony and C. Koupernik. New York: Wiley, 1974, pp. 529–544.

ANTLER, JOYCE, and ANTLER, STEPHEN. "From Child Rescue to Family Protection." *Children and Youth Services Review* 1 (1979):177–204.

ANTLER, STEPHEN. "Child Protection: Small Programs for Big Problems." *Public Welfare* 36 (Fall 1978): 10–13.

——. "The Rediscovery of Child Abuse." In *The Social Context of Child Abuse and Neglect*, edited by Leroy H. Pelton. New York: Human Sciences Press, 1981.

ANTON, THOMAS J. "The New Federalism in Illinois." *Illinois Issues* 8 (Mar. 1982):6–14.

APONTE, HARRY J. "The Family–School Interview: An Ecological Approach." *Family Process* 15 (Sept. 1976a):303–311.

——. "Underorganization in the Poor Family." In *Family Therapy: Theory and Practice*, edited by Philip J. Guerin. New York: Gardner Press, 1976b, pp. 432–448.

APPELBERG, ESTHER. *A Foster Familyhood Workshop Report—The First Year.* New York: Yeshiva University, 1967.

ARIES, P. *Centuries of Childhood.* New York: Knopf, 1962.

ARMSTRONG, KATHERINE L. *How Can We Avoid Burnout?* Berkeley, Calif.: Berkeley Planning Associates, 1978.

ARNOLD, IRENE L., and GOODMAN, LAWRENCE. "Homemaker Services to Families With Young Retarded Children." *Children* 13 (July–Aug. 1966):149–152. Arvin, 1974.

ASHER, S. "Children's Peer Relations." In *Social and Personality Development*, edited by M. Lamb. New York: Holt, Rinehart, and Winston, 1978, pp. 114–130.

*Assembly Journal.* "Report and Other Papers on Subject of Laws for Relief and Settlement of Poor." Jan. 1824, pp. 386–399. In *Public Welfare Administration in the United States: Select Documents,* edited by Sophinisba P. Breckinridge. Chicago: University of Chicago Press, 1927, pp. 39–54.

AUERSWALD, EDGAR. "Interdisciplinary vs. Ecological Approach." *Family Process* 7 (Sept. 1968):202–215.

AUST, PATRICIA. "Using the Life Story Book in Treatment of Children in Placement." *Child Welfare* 60 (Sept.–Oct. 1981):535–560.

AUSTIN, J., and KRISBERG, B. "The Unmet Promise of Alternatives to Incarceration." *Crime and Delinquency* 28 (July 1982):2.

BACON, LLOYD. "Early Motherhood, Accelerated Role Transition, and Social Pathologies." *Social Forces* 52 (Mar.1974):333–341.

BAGNALL. *Textile Industries of America I.* In Edith Abbott, "A Study of the Early History of Child Labor in America." *American Journal of Sociology* 14 (Nov. 1980):115.

Bailey Scale of Infant Development. New York: The Psychological Corporation, 1969.

BAILEY, WALTER H. "A Comparison of Performance Levels between BSW and BA Social Workers." Unpublished doctoral dissertation, Catholic University of America, 1978.

BALDWIN, W. "Adolescent Pregnancy and Childbearing—Growing Concerns for Americans." *Population Bulletin* 31 (Sept. 1976):3–21.

BALDWIN, W., and CAIN, V. S. "The Children of Teenage Parents." *Family Planning Perspectives* 12 (Jan.–Feb. 1980):34–43.

BANDLER, RICHARD, and GRINDER, JOHN. *The Structure of Magic: Volume I.* Palo Alto, Calif.: Science and Behavior Books, 1975.

BANE, MARY JO. *Here to Stay: American Families in the Twentieth Century.* New York: Basic Books, 1979.

BARAN, ANNETTE; PANNOR, REUBEN; and SOROSKY, ARTHUR D. "Open Adoption." *Social Work* 21 (Mar. 1976):97–100.

BARBER, DULAN. *Unmarried Fathers.* London: Hutchinson Co., 1975.

BARRETT, MARJIE, and MCKELVEY, JANE. "Stress and Strain on the Child Care Worker: Typologies for Assessment." *Child Welfare* 59 (May 1980):277–286.

BARTOLLAS, C., and MILLER, S. *The Juvenile Offender: Control, Correction and Treatment.* Boston: Allyn and Bacon, 1978.

BATES, J. "The Concept of Difficult Temperament." *Merrill–Palmer Quarterly* 36 (Oct. 1980):299–319.

BAYH, BIRCH. "Introductory Statement." Public Law 93–415. Juvenile Justice and Delinquency Act of 1974. *Congressional Record,* Aug. 1974.

BEAN, SHIRLEY L. "The Use of Specialized Day Care in Preventing Child Abuse." In *Child Abuse: Intervention and Treatment,* edited by Nancy B. Ebeling and Deborah Hill. Acton, Mass.: Publishing Sciences Group, 1975, pp. 137–142.

BECK, A.; WEISSMAN, A.; LESTER, D.; and TRENXLER, L. "The Measurement of Pessimism: The Hopelessness Scale." *Journal of Consulting and Clinical Psychology* 42 (Dec. 1974):861–865.

BEEZLEY, PATRICIA; MARTIN, HAROLD; and ALEXANDER, HELEN. "Comprehensive Family Oriented Therapy." In *Child Abuse and Neglect: The Family and Com-*

*munity*, edited by Ray Helfer and C. Henry Kempe. Cambridge, Mass.: Ballinger, 1976, pp. 169–194.

BEKER, J. "Training and Professional Development in Child Care." In *Caring for Troubled Children: Residential Treatment in a Community Context*, edited by James K. Whittaker. San Francisco: Jossey–Bass, 1979, pp. 205–231.

BELL, R. Q. "Stimulus Control of Parent or Caretaker Behavior by Offspring." *Developmental Psychology* 4 (Jan. 1971):63–72.

––––––. "Parent, Child, and Reciprocal Influences." *American Psychologist* 34 (Oct. 1979):821–826.

BELL, R. Q., and HARPER, L. *Child Effects on Adults*. Hillsdale, N.J.: Erlbaum, 1977.

BELL, VELMA. "Special Considerations in the Adoption of the Older Child." *Social Casework* 40 (June, 1959):327–333.

BELSKY, J. "Child Maltreatment: An Ecological Integration." *American Psychologist* 35 (Apr. 1980):320–325.

BENET, MARY KATHLEEN. *The Politics of Adoption*. New York: Free Press, 1976.

BERG, W. "Effects of Job Satisfaction on Practice Decisions: A Linear Flow-Graph Analysis." *Social Work Research and Abstracts* 16 (Fall 1980):30–37.

BERGER, PETER L., and LUCKMANN, THOMAS. *The Social Construction of Reality*. Garden City, N.Y.: Doubleday, 1966.

BERGER, PETER L., and NEUHAUS, RICHARD. *To Empower People: The Role of Mediating Structures in Public Policy*. Washington, D.C.: American Enterprise Institute for Public Policy Research, 1977.

BERMANN, ERIC. *Scapegoat*. Ann Arbor: University of Michigan Press, 1973.

BERNSTEIN, BARTON E. "The Social Worker as an Expert Witness." *Social Casework* 58 (July 1977):412–417.

BESTE, HILARY M., and RICHARDSON, REBECCA G. "Developing a Life Story Book Program for Foster Children." *Child Welfare* 60 (Sept.–Oct. 1981):529–534.

BETTELHEIM, BRUNO. *The Empty Fortress*. New York: Free Press, 1967.

BIESTEK, FELIX P. *The Casework Relationship*. Chicago: Loyola University Press, 1957.

BILLINGSLEY, ANDREW. "Bureaucratic and Professional Orientation Patterns in Social Casework." *Social Service Review* 38 (Mar. 1964):400–407.

BILLINGSLEY, ANDREW, and GIOVANNONI, JEANNE M. *Children of the Storm: Black Children and American Child Welfare*. New York: Harcourt Brace Jovanovich, 1972.

BINDER, A. "The Juvenile Justice System." *American Behavioral Scientist* 22 (July–Aug. 1979):621–652.

BLANCHARD, EVELYN L., and BARSH, RUSSELL, L. "What is Best for Tribal Children? A Response to Fischler." *Social Work* 25 (Sept. 1980):350–357.

BLAU, P. "Orientation Toward Clients in a Public Welfare Agency." *Administrative Science Quarterly* 5 (Dec. 1960):341–361.

BLOMBERG, T. "Diversion's Disparate Results: An Integrative Evaluation Perspective." *Journal of Research in Crime and Delinquency* 20 (Jan. 1983):24–38.

BLOS, P. *On Adolescence.* New York: Free Press, 1962.

*Blue Cross and Blue Shield Consumer Exchange.* June 1981.

BOLTON, F. G., JR. *The Pregnant Adolescent: Problems of Premature Parenthood.* Beverly Hills, Calif.: Sage Publications, 1980.

BOND, LYNNE A., and ROSEN, JAMES C., eds. *Competence and Coping During Adulthood.* Hanover, N.H.: University Press of New England, 1980.

BONHAM, G. S., and PLACEK, P. J. "The Relationship of Maternal Health, Infant Health, and Socio-demographic Factors to Fertility." *Public Health Reports* 93 (May–June, 1978):283–291.

BORGMAN, ROBERT. "The Consequences of Open and Closed Adoption for Older Children." *Child Welfare* 61 (Apr. 1982):217–230.

BOSZORMENYI-NAGY, IVAN, and SPARK, GERALDINE. *Invisible Loyalties: Reciprocity in Intergenerational Family Therapy.* New York: Harper and Row, 1973.

BOULDING, KENNETH. "The Boundaries of Social Policy." *Social Work* 12 (Jan. 1967):3–11.

BOWEN, MURRAY. *Family Therapy in Clinical Practice.* New York: Jason Aronson, 1978.

BOWERMAN, C. E.; IRISH, D. P.; and POPE, H. "Unwed Motherhood—Personal and Social Consequences." Chapel Hill: University of North Carolina Institute for Research in the Social Sciences, 1963–1966.

BOWLBY, J. *Attachment and Loss.* Vol. I: *Attachment.* New York: Basic Books, 1969.

———. *Attachment and Loss.* Vol. II: *Loss.* New York: Basic Books, 1980.

BOWLES, SAMUEL, and GINTIS, HERBERT. *Schooling in Capitalist America.* New York: Basic Books, 1976.

BOYD, PATTYE. "They Can Go Home Again." *Child Welfare* 58 (Nov. 1979):609–615.

BOYD, LAWRENCE, and REMY, LINDA. "Is Foster Parent Training Worthwhile?" *Social Service Review* 52 (June 1978):275–296.

BOYNE, JOHN F. *Adoption of Children with Handicaps.* Westfield, N.J.: New Jersey Spaulding for Children, 1979.

BRACE, CHARLES LORING. *The Best Method of Disposing of Pauper and Vagrant Children.* New York: Wynkoop and Hallenbeck, 1859.

———. *The Dangerous Classes of New York and Twenty Years' Work Among Them.* New York: Wynkoop and Hallenback, 1872.

BRADBURY, DOROTHY E. *Four Decades of Action for Children. A Short History of the Children's Bureau.* Washington, D.C.: Children's Bureau Publication #358, 1956.

BRADEN, JOSEPHINE A. "Adopting the Abused Child: Love is Not Enough." *Social Casework* 62 (June 1981):362–367.

BRADLEY, T. *An Exploration of the Caseworker's Perception of Adoptive Applicants.* New York: Child Welfare League of America, 1966.

BRAGER, GEORGE, and BARR, SHERMAN. "Perceptions and Reality: The Poor Man's View of Social Services." In *Community Action Against Poverty,* edited by George Brager and Francis Purcell. New Haven, Conn.: College and University Press, 1967, pp. 72–80.

BRAGER, GEORGE, and HOLLOWAY, STEPHEN. *Changing Human Service Organizations: Politics and Practice.* New York: Free Press, 1978.

BRANNON, DIANE. *Enhancing the Training Role of Supervisors: A Training Monograph.* Seattle, Wa.: University of Washington, School of Social Work, Northwest Regional Child Welfare Training Center, 1982.

BRAVERMAN, HARRY. *Labor and Monopoly Capital.* New York: Monthly Review Press, 1974.

BRAZLETON, T. B. *Neonatal Behavioral Assessment Scale.* Philadelphia: Lippincott, 1973.

BREAK, GEORGE. "Intergovernmental Fiscal Relations." In *Setting National Priorities: Agenda for the 1980s,* edited by Joseph A. Pechman. Washington, D.C.: The Brookings Institution, 1981, pp. 247–281.

BREINES, WINNI; CERULLO, MARGARET; and STACYE, JUDITH. "Social Biology, Family Studies, and Anti-Feminist Backlash." *Feminist Studies* 4 (Feb. 1978).

BREMNER, ROBERT H., ed. *Children and Youth in America: A Documentary History.* Vols. I–III. Cambridge, Mass.: Harvard University Press, 1970–74.

BRENNAN, TIM; BLANCHARD, FLETCHER; HUIZINGA, DAVID; and ELLIOT, DELBERT. *Final Report: The Incidence and Nature of Runaway Behavior.* Boulder, Co.: Behavioral Research and Evaluation Corporation, May 1975.

BRIAR, KATHERINE H., and PAYNE, THELMA H. *Child and Family Welfare Project— Social Work Department.* Tacoma, Wa.: Pacific Lutheran University, n.d.

BRIELAND, DONALD, and LEMMON, JOHN. *Social Work and the Law.* St. Paul, Minn.: West Publishing, 1977.

BRIELAND, DONALD; WATSON, KENNETH; HOVDA, PHILLIP; FANSHEL, DAVID; and CAREY, JOHN J. *Differential Use of Manpower: A Team Model for Foster Care.* New York: Child Welfare League of America, 1968.

BROADHURST, DIANE D.; EDMUNDS, MARGARET; and MacDICKENS, ROBERT A. *Early Childhood Programs and the Prevention of Child Abuse and Neglect.* Washington, D.C.: U.S. Department of Health, Education and Welfare, DHEW Publication No. (OHDS) 79–30198, 1979.

BROADNAX, WALTER. "The New Federalism: Hazards for State and Local Governments?" *Policy Studies Review* 1 (Nov. 1981):231–235.

BRODKEY, HAROLD. "Largely an Oral History of My Mother." *The New Yorker* (Apr. 26, 1976):36–110.

BROOME, THOMAS H., JR., and COMER, WILLIAM S. "A Foster Parents Workshop." *Public Welfare* 29 (Spring 1971):194–201.

BROMAN, S. H.; NICHOLS, P. L.; and KENNEDY, W. A. *Preschool IQ: Prenatal and Early Developmental Correlates.* Hillsdale, N.J.: Erlbaum, 1975.

BRONFENBRENNER, U. "Contexts of Child Rearing: Problems and Prospects." *American Psychologist* 34 (Oct. 1979a):844–850.

_____. *The Ecology of Human Development.* Cambridge, Mass.: Harvard University Press, 1979b.

———. "The Isolated Generation." *Human Ecology Report* 6 (Winter 1976):6–7.

Brown, Patricia. "Racial Social Work." *Journal of Education for Social Work* 12 (Winter 1976): 28–35.

Bryant, Brad. *Special Foster Care: A History and Rationale.* New York: Child Welfare League of America, 1982.

Bryce, Marvin E., and Lloyd, June. *Placement Prevention and Family Unification: Planning and Supervising the Home Based Family Centered Program.* Iowa City: National Clearinghouse for Home Based Services to Children and Their Families, School of Social Work, University of Iowa, 1980.

Bujarski-Greene, Pamela. "A House Full of Children: A House Full of Love." *Family Circle* 91 (Dec. 1978):14–20,52.

Bumpass, L., et al. "Age and Marital Status at First Birth and the Pace of Subsequent Fertility." *Demography* 15 (Feb. 1978):75–86.

Burns, Scott. *The Household Economy.* Boston: Beacon Press, 1975.

Burt, Marvin, and Balyeat, Ralph. "A New System for Improving the Care of Neglected and Abused Children." *Child Welfare* 53 (Mar. 1974):167–179.

Bush, Malcolm, and Gordon, Andrew C. "The Case for Involving Children in Child Welfare Decisions." *Social Work* 27 (July 1982):309–314.

Bush, Sherida. "A Family Help Program That Really Works." *Psychology Today* 10 (May 1977):48, 50, 84, 86, 88.

Byler, William. "The Destruction of American Indian Families." In *The Destruction of American Indian Families,* edited by Steven Unger. New York: Association on American Indian Affairs, 1977.

Cady, Ernst, and Cady, Frank. *How To Adopt a Child.* New York: Whiteside, Inc. and William Morrow, 1956.

Caldwell, Bettye M. "Infant Day Care—The Outcast Gains Respectability." In *Child Care—Who Cares?,* edited by Pamela Roby. New York: Basic Books, 1975, pp. 20–38.

Calhoun, John A.; Grotberg, Edith H.; and Rackley, W. Ray. *The Status of Children, Youth and Families 1979.* Washington, D.C.: U.S. Department of Health and Human Services, Office of Human Development Services, Administration for Children, Youth and Families Research Demonstration and Evaluation Division, 1980.

Campbell, Angus; Converse, Philip E.; and Rogers, Willard L. *The Quality of American Life.* New York: Russell Sage Foundation, 1976.

Cannon, Lou. "Reagan Urges Another Great Revolution in Federalism." *The Washington Post* (July 31, 1981):A4.

Caplan, Robert D., et al. *Job Demands and Workers Health.* Washington, D.C.: Department of Health, Education, and Welfare, 1975.

Carbino, Rosemarie. "Developing a Parent Organization: New Roles for Parents of Children in Substitute Care." In *The Challenge of Partnership: Working with Parents of Children in Foster Care,* edited by Anthony N. Maluccio and Paula A. Sinanoglu. New York: Child Welfare League of America, 1981, pp. 165–188.

CARD, J. J., and WISE, L. L. "Teenage Mothers and Teenage Fathers: The Impact of Early Childbearing on the Parents' Personal and Professional Lives." *Family Planning Perspectives* 10 (Jul.–Aug. 1978):199–205.

CAREY, W. B. "Measurement of Infant Temperament in Pediatric Practice." In *Individual Differences in Children,* edited by J. Westman. New York: Wiley, 1973, pp. 293–306.

CARROLL, J. "Staff Burnout as a Form of Ecological Dysfunction." *Contemporary Drug Problems* 8 (Summer 1980):207–225.

CARROLL, J., and WHITE, W. "Understanding Burnout: Integrating Individual and Environmental Factors Within an Ecological Framework." *Proceedings of First National Conference on Burnout.* Philadelphia: 1981.

CARTER, E., and McGOLDRICK, M., eds. *The Family Life Cycle.* New York: Gardner Press, 1980.

CARTER, JIMMY. A Statement in New Hampshire. Aug. 1976.

CASSEL, JOHN. "Psychological Processes and 'Stress': Theoretical Formulation." *International Journal of Health Services* 4 (1974). Reprinted in Robert Kane, ed. *The Behavioral Sciences and Preventive Medicine.* Washington, D.C.: U.S. Department of Health, Education, and Welfare, DHEW Publication No. (NIH) 76–878, 1976, pp. 53–61.

CHAIKLIN, HARRIS. "Honesty in Casework Treatment." *Social Welfare Forum, 1973.* New York: Columbia University Press, 1974, pp. 266–274.

CHAMBERS, CLARKE A. *Seedtime of Reform, American Social Service and Social Action 1918–1933.* Minneapolis: University of Minnesota Press, 1963.

CHAPPELL, BARBARA. "Organizing Periodic Review in Foster Care: The South Carolina Story." *Child Welfare* 54 (July 1975):477–486.

CHAPPELL, BARBARA, and HEVENER, BARBARA. *Periodic Review of Children in Foster Care: Mechanisms for Review.* Newark, N.J.: Child Service Association of America, 1977.

CHARNLEY, JEAN. *The Art of Child Placement.* Minneapolis: University of Minnesota Press, 1955.

CHASE, ANN M.; CROWLEY, CHERYL D.; and WEINTRAUB, MILA K. "Treating the Throwaway Child: A Model for Adolescent Service." *Social Casework* 60 (Nov. 1979):538–546.

CHATTERJEE, P., and GINTER, D. "The Impact of Class Origin and Ideology on Public Welfare Workers." *Public Welfare* 31 (Fall 1973):2–8.

CHEETHAM, J. *Unwanted Pregnancy and Counselling.* London: Routledge and Kegan Paul (Boston: Henley), 1977.

CHERNISS, CARY. *Professional Burnout in Human Service Organizations.* New York: Praeger, 1980.

CHERRY, T. "The Oregon Child Study and Treatment Centers." *Child Care Quarterly* 5 (Summer 1976):146–155.

CHESTANG, LEON. "The Dilemma of Biracial Adoption." *Social Work* 17 (May 1972):100–105.

Child Welfare League of America. *Child Welfare as a Field of Social Work Practice.* Statement prepared by CWLA and Children's Bureau. Washington, D.C.: Department of Health, Education, and Welfare, 1959.

————. *Child Welfare Planning Notes* 6, 7 (Sept. 1981–Apr. 1982).

————. *Directory of Member Agencies.* New York: Child Welfare League of America, 1981.

————. *Reaching Out: A Resource Book for the Adoption of Children with Developmental Disabilities.* New York: Child Welfare League of America, 1981.

————. *Standards for Adoption Service.* Revised Edition. New York: Child Welfare League of America, 1978.

————. *Standards for Foster Family Care.* Revised Edition. New York: Child Welfare League of America, 1975.

————. *Statement on Child Advocacy.* New York: Child Welfare League of America, 1981.

*Child Welfare Reform Act: Report to the Governor and The Legislature.* New York State Department of Social Services, Jan. 1981.

"Children on Strike." *The Survey* 69 (June 1933):229.

Children's Bureau. *Child Welfare in 25 States—An Overview.* Washington, D.C.: U.S. Department of Health, Education, and Welfare, DHEW Publication No. (OHD) 77–30090, 1976.

————. *Program Guidance: Child Welfare Services Training Grants.* Washington, D.C.: U.S. Department of Health, Education, and Welfare, Office of Human Development Services, Administration for Children, Youth, and Families. Mar. 1979.

Children's Defense Fund. *A Children's Defense Fund Budget.* Washington, D.C.: Children's Defense Fund, 1983.

————. *Children and the Federal Budget: How to Influence the Budget Process.* Washington, D.C.: Children's Defense Fund, 1980.

————. *Children Without Homes: An Examination of Public Responsibility to Children in Out-of-Home Care.* Washington, D.C.: Children's Defense Fund, 1978.

Chilman, C. *Adolescent Sexuality in a Changing American Society—Social and Psychological Perspectives.* Bethesda, Md.: Department of Health, Education, and Welfare, Public Health Service, National Institute of Health, No. (NIH) 79–1426, 1979.

Chimezie, Amuzie. "Transracial Adoption of Black Children." *Social Work* 20 (July 1975):296–301.

Cicchetti, D., and Sroufe, L. "The Relationship Between Affective and Cognitive Development in Down's Syndrome Infants." *Child Development* 47 (Dec. 1976):920–929.

Clarke, A. M., and Clarke, A. B. D., eds. *Early Experience: Myth and Evidence.* New York: Free Press, 1976.

Cleckley, Betty J. "Education for Practice with Blacks." *Journal of Humanics* 8 (1980).

CLEVELAND COUNCIL ON ADOPTABLE CHILDREN. *Newsletter.* Nov. 1978.

COATES, R. B.; MILLER, A. D.; and OHLIN, L. E. *Diversity in a Youth Correctional System.* Cambridge, Mass.: Ballinger, 1978.

COBB, STANLEY. "Social Support as a Moderator of Life Stress." *Psychosomatic Medicine* 38 (Sept.–Oct. 1976):300–314.

COCHRAN, MONCRIEFF, and WOOLEVER, FRANK. "Programming Beyond the Deficit Model: The Empowerment of Parents with Information and Information Support." Unpublished manuscript. Cornell University, 1980.

CODE OF FEDERAL REGULATIONS: 45 Pub. Wel. (Revised Oct. 1, 1979), Part 80,§80.3a and 80.13f).

COHN, ANNE H. "Effective Treatment of Child Abuse and Neglect." *Social Work* 24 (Nov. 1979):513–519.

COHN, ANNE H., and COLLIGNON, FRANK C. *Evaluation of Child Abuse and Neglect Demonstration Projects, 1974–1977.* Vols. I and II. NCHSR Research Report Series, DHEW Publication No. (PHS) 79–3217–1, 1979.

COLE, ELIZABETH. "Adoption Services Today and Tomorrow." In *Child Welfare Services in the Coming Years,* edited by Alfred Kadushin. Washington, D.C.: U.S. Department of Health, Education and Welfare, Office of Human Development Services, Administration for Children, Youth and Families, Children's Bureau, DHEW Publication No. (OHDS) 78–30158, 1978, pp. 130–168.

———. "A Closer Look at Subsidized Adoption." In *Protecting Children Through the Legal System.* Edited by the staff of the National Legal Resource Center for Child Advocacy and Protection. Washington, D.C.: American Bar Association, 1981, pp. 692–704.

COLE, ELMA, ed. *Service Directory of National Voluntary Health and Social Welfare Organization.* Fourteenth Edition. New York: The National Assembly of National Voluntary Health and Social Welfare Organizations, Inc., 1980.

COLLINS, ALICE. "Helping Neighbors Intervene in Cases of Maltreatment." In *Protecting Children from Abuse and Neglect,* edited by James Garbarino and S. Holly Stocking. San Francisco: Jossey–Bass, 1980, pp. 133–172.

COLLINS, M. C. *Child Abuser: A Study of Child Abusers in Self-Help Group Therapy.* Littleton, Mass.: PSG Publishing Co., 1978.

COLÓN, FERNANDO. "The Family Life Cycle of the Multiproblem Poor Family." In *The Family Life Cycle,* edited by Elizabeth A. Carter and Monica McGoldrick. New York: Gardner Press, 1980, pp. 343–382.

———. "Family Ties and Child Placement." *Family Process* 17 (Sept. 1978):289–312.

COMMITTEE ON GOVERNMENT OPERATIONS. *A Citizen's Guide on How to Use the Freedom of Information Act and the Privacy Act in Requesting Government Documents.* Thirteenth Report. Washington, D.C.: U.S. Government Printing Office, 1977.

COMPTON, BEULAH R., and GALAWAY, BURT. *Social Work Processes.* Revised Edition. Homewood, Ill.: Dorsey Press, 1979.

CONGER, S. J. "Adolescence: A Time for Becoming." In *Social and Personality Development*, edited by M. Lamb. New York: Holt, Rinehart, and Winston, 1978, pp. 131–154.

CONLAN, TIMOTHY J. "Back in Vogue: The Politics of Block Grant Legislation." *Intergovernmental Perspective* 7 (Spring 1981):8–18.

CONNELL, E. B., and JACOBSON, J. "Pregnancy, the Teenagers, and Sex Education." *American Journal of Public Health* 61 (Sept. 1971):1840–1845.

COOMBS, J., and COOLEY, W. "Dropout in High School and After School." *American Educational Research Journal* 5 (1968):343–363.

COOMBS, L. C., and FRIEDMAN, R. "Premarital Pregnancy, Childbearing, and Later Economic Achievement." *Population Studies* 24 (1970):389.

COOMBS, L. C., ET AL. "Premarital Pregnancy and Status Before and After Pregnancy." *American Journal of Sociology* 75 (May 1970): 800–820.

COSTIN, LELA B. *Child Welfare: Policies and Practice*. Second Edition. New York: McGraw Hill, 1979.

_____. *Two Sisters for Social Justice: A Biography of Grace and Edith Abbott*. Urbana and Chicago: University of Illinois Press, 1983.

COTTRELL, LEONARD. "The Competent Community." In *Further Explorations in Social Psychiatry*, edited by B. Kaplan, R. N. Wilson, and A. Leighton. New York: Basic Books, 1976, pp. 195–209.

COUNCIL ON SOCIAL WORK EDUCATION. Commission on Educational Planning, Subcommittee on Specialization. "Specialization in the Social Work Profession." New York: Council on Social Work Education, 1979a. (Mimeograph)

_____. Commission on Educational Planning, Subcommittee on Base. "A Framework for the Explication of Base in Social Work Education." New York: Council on Social Work Education, 1979b. (Mimeograph)

COYNE, ANN. Personal communication. November, 1983.

_____. "Techniques of Recruiting Homes for Mentally Retarded Children." *Child Welfare* 67 (Feb. 1978):123–133.

COYNE, ANN, and BROWN, MARY ELLEN. "The Adoption of Children with Developmental Disabilities: A Study of Public and Private Child Placement Agencies." (For the Developmental Disabilities Project.) New York: Child Welfare League of America, 1980.

COX, FRED. "Alternative Conceptions of Community: Implications for Community Organization Practice." In *Strategies of Community Organization*, Third Edition, edited by Fred Cox, John Erlich, Jack Rothman, and John Tropman. Itasca, Ill.: F. E. Peacock, 1979, pp. 224–234.

COX, TOM. *Stress*. Baltimore: University Park Press, 1978.

CRAFT, JOHN L.; EPLY, STEPHEN W.; and THEISEN, WILLIAM M., eds. *Child Welfare Forecasting, Context, and Technique*. Springfield, Ill.: Charles C. Thomas, 1980.

CREATIVE ASSOCIATES. *Child Welfare Inservice Training Curriculum*. Washington, D.C.: Creative Associates, Inc., 1982.

CRESSEY, D., and MCDERMOTT, R. *Diversion from the Juvenile Justice System*. Ann

Arbor: University of Michigan, National Assessment of Juvenile Corrections, 1974.

CUTRIGHT, P. "Timing the First Birth—Does It Matter?" *Journal of Marriage and the Family* 35 (Mar. 1973):585–596.

CVETKOVICH, G.; GROTE, B.; BJORSETH, A.; and SARKISSIAN, J. "On the Psychology of Adolescents' Use of Contraceptives." *Journal of Sex Research* 11 (1975):256–270.

DALEY, MICHAEL R. "Burnout: Smoldering Problem in the Protective Services." *Social Work* 24 (Sept. 1979):375–379.

DANIELS, A. M. "Reaching Unwed Mothers." *American Journal of Nursing* 69 (Feb. 1969):332–335.

DANZIGER, S. "Children in Poverty: The Truly Needy Who Fell Through the Safety Net." *Children and Youth Services Review* 4:1/2 (1982):35–52.

DAVIDS, A.; RYAN, R.; and SALVATORE, P. "Effectiveness of Residential Treatment." *American Journal of Orthopsychiatry* 38 (Apr. 1968):469–475.

DAVIDS, A., and SALVATORE, P. "Residential Treatment of Disturbed Children and Adequacy of Their Subsequent Adjustment." *American Journal of Orthopsychiatry* 46 (Jan. 1967):62–73.

DAVIDSON, MARY. "Complaints and Court Cases Alleging Racial Discrimination in Child Welfare Services, 1965–1981." Unpublished paper, n. d.

DAVIDSON, MARY, and ANDERSON, GARY R. "Child Welfare and Title VI." *Social Work* 27 (Mar. 1982):147–150.

———. "Determining Title VI Discrimination." *The Journal of Intergroup Relations* IX (Autumn 1981).

———. "A Title VI View of Child Welfare Issues." *Child Welfare* 61 (Jan. 1982):49–54.

DAVIES, LINDA, and BLAND, DAVID. "The Use of Foster Parents as Role Models for Parents." *Child Welfare* 62 (June 1978):380–386.

DAVIS, ALLEN. *Spearheads for Reform: The Social Settlements and the Progressive Movement, 1890–1914.* New York: Oxford University Press, 1967.

DAY, CYRIL, and LEEDING, ALFRED. *Access to Birth Records.* London: Association of British Adoption and Fostering Agencies, May 1980.

DAY, DAWN. *The Adoption of Black Children.* Lexington, Mass.: Lexington Books, 1979.

DEAR, RONALD B., and PATTI, RINO J. "Legislative Advocacy: Seven Effective Tactics." *Social Work* 26 (July 1981):289–296.

DELANEY, ANITA J., ed. *Black Task Force Report.* New York: Family Service Association of America, 1979.

DELGADO, MELVIN. "A Hispanic Foster Parents Program." *Child Welfare* 57 (July–Aug. 1978):427–431.

DELEON, JUDY, and WESTERBERG, JUDY. "Who Adopts Retarded Children?" Westfield, N.J.: New Jersey Spaulding for Children, 1980.

DELONE, RICHARD H. *Small Futures, Children, Inequality and the Limits of Liberal Reform.* New York: Harcourt Brace Jovanovich, 1978.

DenHouter, Kathryn V. "To Silence One's Self: A Brief Analysis of the Literature on Adolescent Suicide." *Child Welfare* 60 (Jan. 1981):2–10.

Department of Health and Human Services. "Announcement of the Availability of Funds and Request for Preapplications." *Federal Register* 48:202 (Oct. 1983).

———. "Child Welfare Research Notes, #1," Washington, D.C.: DHHS, Administration for Children, Youth, and Families. Dec. 1983.

Department of Health and Human Services, Regional Resource Center. "Adoption of Children with Special Needs: A Curriculum for the Training of Adoption Workers." University of Georgia, 1982.

Derdeyn, Andre; Rogoff, Andrew; and Williams, Scott. "Alternatives to Absolute Termination of Parental Rights After Long Term Foster Care." *Vanderbilt Law Review* XXXI (Oct. 1978).

Devore, Wynetta, and Schlesinger, Elfriede G. *Ethnic-Sensitive Social Work Practice.* St. Louis: Mosby, 1981.

Dewar, D. *Orphans of the Living: A Study of Bastardy.* New York: Hilary House, 1969.

Dewey, John. *Liberalism and Social Action.* New York: G. P. Putnam's Sons, 1935.

Dickerson, Martha. *Fostering the Child with Mental Retardation.* Ypsilanti, Mi.: Foster Parent Training Project, Eastern Michigan University, 1977.

———. *Our Four Boys: Foster Parenting Retarded Teenagers.* N.Y.: Syracuse University Press, 1978.

Dille, Jeanette, and Warkov, Seymour. "Report on the Commissioners' Luncheons." Hartford, Ct.: Connecticut Child Welfare Association, 1975. (Mimeograph)

Dimock, E. T. "Youth Crisis Services: Short-term Community-based Residential Treatment." *Child Welfare* 56 (Mar. 1977):187–196.

Dinkmeyer, D., and McKay, G. D. *Systematic Training for Effective Parenting (Step).* Circle Pines, Minn.: American Guidance Service, 1976.

Dinnage, R.; Pringle, M.; and Kellmer, M. L. *Residential Care—Facts and Fallacies.* New York: Humanities Press, 1967.

Dixon, Samuel L. *Working with People in Crisis—Theory and Practice.* St. Louis: Mosby, 1979.

Donley, Kathryn. "The Mechanics of Placement." New York: New York Spaulding for Children, 1981. Unpublished manuscript.

———. *Opening New Doors.* London: Association of British Adoption Agencies, 1975.

Donzelot, Jacques. *The Policing of Families.* New York: Pantheon, 1979.

Downs, Susan Whitelaw. *Foster Care Reform in the 1970's: Final Report of the Permanency Planning Dissemination Project.* Portland, Ore.: Regional Research Institute for Human Services, Portland State University, 1981.

Downs, Susan Whitelaw, and Taylor, Catherine. *Permanent Planning for Children in Foster Care: Resources for Training.* Washington, D.C.: U.S. Government Printing Office, Department of Health and Human Services Publication No. (OHDS) 81–30790, 1980.

DREWS, K.; SALUS, M.; and DODGE, D. *Child Protective Services: In-Service Training for Supervisors.* National Center on Child Abuse and Neglect, D.H.H.S., 1981.

DRUCKER, PETER F. *Toward the Next Economics and Other Essays.* New York: Harper and Row, 1981.

DRYFOOS, J. G., and HEISLER, T. "Contraceptive Services for Adolescents: An Overview." *Family Planning Perspectives* 10 (Jul.–Aug. 1978):223–233.

DUBOS, RENÉ. *So Human an Animal.* New York: Scribners, 1968.

DUHL, FREDERICK; KANTOR, DAVID; and DUHL, BUNNY S. "Learning, Space, and Action in Family Therapy: A Primer of Sculpture." In *Techniques of Family Psychotherapy,* edited by Donald Bloch. New York: Grune & Stratton, 1973.

DUNFORD, F. W., and BRENNAN, TIM. "A Taxonomy of Runaway Youth." *Social Service Review* 4 (Sept. 1976):457–470.

DUNNETTE, MARVIN D.; CAMPBELL, JOHN P.; and HAKEL, MILTON D. "Factors Contributing to Job Satisfaction in Six Occupational Groups." *Organizational Behavior and Human Performance* 2 (May 1967):143–174.

DURKIN, R. P., and DURKIN, A. B. "Evaluating Residential Treatment Programs for Disturbed Children." In *Handbook of Evaluation Research,* Vol. 2, edited by M. Guttentag and E. L. Struening. Beverly Hills, Calif.: Sage, 1975.

DYER, EVERETT D. "Parenthood as Crisis: A Re-Study." In *Crisis Intervention: Selected Readings,* edited by Howard J. Parad. New York: Family Service Association of America, 1965.

EASTMAN, KATHLEEN SIMPSON. "The Foster Family in a Systems Theory Perspective." *Child Welfare* 58 (Nov. 1979):567–570.

EDELWICH, J., and BRODSKY, A. *Burnout: Stages of Disillusionment in the Helping Professions.* New York: Human Sciences Press, 1980.

EDWARDS, L. E.; STEINMAN, M. E.; ARNOLD, K. A.; and HAKANSON, E. Y. "Adolescent Pregnancy Prevention Services in High School Clinics." *Family Planning Perspectives* 12 (Jan.–Feb. 1980):6–14.

EINSTEIN, GERTRUDE. "The Homemaker's Role in Prevention and Treatment of Family Breakdown." *Child Welfare* 39 (May 1960):22–25.

ELIOT, MARTHA M. "The Children's Bureau: Fifty Years of Public Responsibility for Action in Behalf of Children." *American Journal of Public Health* 52 (Apr. 1962):576–591.

ELKIND, D. "Egocentrism in Adolescence." *Child Development* 38 (1967):1025–1034.

EMLEN, ARTHUR C. "Slogans, Slots, and Slander: The Myth of Day Care Need." *American Journal of Orthopsychiatry* 43 (Jan. 1973):23–36.

EMLEN, ARTHUR; L'AHTI, JANET; and DOWNS, SUSAN WHITELAW. *Overcoming Barriers to Planning for Children in Foster Care.* Washington, D.C.: U.S. Government Printing Office, 1978.

EMPEY, L. *Juvenile Justice: The Progressive Legacy and Current Reforms.* Charlottesville, Va.: University of Virginia Press, 1979.

ENGLISH, ABIGAIL. "The Foster Care System and the Role of Legal Services." *Clearinghouse Review* 14 (Apr. 1981).

Epstein, I., and Tripodi, T. *Research Techniques for Program Planning, Monitoring and Evaluation.* New York: Columbia University Press, 1977.

Erikson, Erik. *Childhood and Society.* New York: W. W. Norton, 1963.

_____. "Identity and the Life Cycle." *Psychological Issues,* Monograph 1, Vol. 1. New York: International Universities Press, 1959.

Erlanger, Howard S. "Social Class Differences in Parents' Use of Physical Punishment." In *Violence in the Family,* edited by Susan K. Steinmetz and Murray A. Strauss. New York: Dodd, Mead, 1975.

Estes, Richard, and Henry, Sue. "The Therapeutic Contract in Work with Groups: A Formal Analysis." *Social Service Review* 50 (Dec. 1976):611–622.

Etzioni, Amitai, and Doty, Pamela. *Profit in Not-For-Profit Institutions.* New York: Center for Policy Research, 1976.

Fahlberg, Vera. "Attachment and Separation." In *Project CRAFT: Training in the Adoption of Children with Special Needs.* Ann Arbor: University of Michigan School of Social Work, 1980.

_____. *Attachment and Separation: Putting the Pieces Together.* Lansing: Michigan Department of Social Services, 1979.

Falicov, Celia J., and Karrer, Betty M. "Cultural Variations in the Family Life Cycle: The Mexican–American Family." In *The Family Life Cycle,* edited by Elizabeth A. Carter and Monica McGoldrick. New York: Gardner Press, 1980, pp. 383–426.

Fallon, K. "Participatory Management: An Alternative in Human Service Delivery Systems." In *Social Administration,* edited by Simon Slavin. New York: Haworth Press, 1978.

Family Service Association of America. "Family Definition." Document 78/5–160, 1979. (Mimeograph)

_____. "FSAA Statement of Belief Concerning Families." Document 79/6–177, 1979. (Mimeograph)

Fanshel, David. "The Exit of Children from Foster Care: An Interim Research Report." *Child Welfare* 50 (Feb. 1971):65–81.

_____. *Far From the Reservation: The Transracial Adoption of American Indian Children.* Metuchen, N.J.: Scarecrow Press, 1972.

_____. "Parental Visiting of Children in Foster Care: Key to Discharge?" *Social Service Review* 49 (Dec. 1975):493–514.

Fanshel, David, and Shinn, Eugene. *Children in Foster Care—A Longitudinal Investigation.* New York: Columbia University Press, 1978.

_____. *Dollars and Sense in the Foster Care of Children: A Look at Cost Factors.* New York: Child Welfare League of America, Inc., 1972.

Farrington, Clyde. "Foster Care Programs for Formally Institutionalized Multiple Handicapped Individuals in Alaska." In *Reaching Out: A Resource Book for the Adoption of Children with Developmental Disabilities.* New York: Child Welfare League of America, 1981.

Featherstone, Helen. *A Difference in the Family: Life with a Disabled Child.* New York: Penguin Books, 1980.

FEDERAL BUREAU OF INVESTIGATION. *Uniform Crime Report: Crime in the U.S.* Washington, D.C.: U.S. Department of Justice, Oct. 1982.

FELKER, EVELYN. *Foster Parenting Young Children: Guidelines for a Foster Parent.* New York: Child Welfare League of America, 1974.

FERLEGER, BEATRICE, and COTTER, MARY JANE, eds. *Children, Families and Foster Care: New Insights from Research in New York City.* New York: Community Council of Greater New York, Dec. 1976.

FESTINGER, TRUDY. "Placement Agreements with Boarding Homes: A Survey." *Child Welfare* 53 (Dec. 1974):643–652.

FIEDLER, F. "The Leadership Game: Matching the Man to the Situation." In *Perspectives on Behavior in Organizations,* edited by J. R. Hackman, E. Lawler, and L. Porter. New York: McGraw Hill, 1977, pp. 390–397.

FIEGELMAN, WILLIAM, and SILVERMAN, ARNOLD. "Single Parent Adoptions." *Social Casework* 58 (July 1977): 418–425.

FINE, MICHELLE. "Options to Injustice." *Representation Research in Social Psychology* 10 (1 & 2, 1979):64–79.

———. "Injustice by Any Other Name." *Victimology: An International Journal* 6 (1–4, 1982):48–58.

FISCHLER, RONALD. "Protecting American Indian Children." *Social Work* 25 (Sept. 1980):341–349.

FISHER, BRUCE, and BERDIE, JANE. "Adolescent Abuse and Neglect: Issue of Incidence, Intervention and Service Delivery." *Child Abuse and Neglect* 2 (Feb. 1978):173–192.

FISHER, FLORENCE. *ALMA Christmas Album.* 1979.

———. *The Search for Anna Fisher.* New York: Arthur Fields, 1973.

FIXSEN, D. L.; PHILLIPS, E. L.; and WOLF, M. M. "The Teaching Family Model: An Example of Mission-oriented Research." In *Handbook of Behavior Analysis,* edited by C. A. Catania and T. A. Brigham. New York: Aalsted Press, 1978.

*Fletcher et al. v. Illinois,* 52 Ill.395. In *Children and Youth in America: A Documentary History.* Vols. I–III, edited by Robert Bremner. Cambridge, Mass.: Harvard University Press, 1970–74, pp. 123–124.

FLYNN, LAURIE, and HAMM, WILFRED. "Team: Parent–Agency Partnership in Adoption." *Children Today* 12 (Mar.–Apr. 1983):2–5.

FOLKS, HOMER. *The Care of Destitute, Neglected, and Delinquent Children.* New York: Macmillan, 1902.

FORD, J. M., and YOUKSTETTER, W. D. *A Study of California Children in Group Care.* Sacramento: Children's Research Institute of California, 1981.

FORSYTHE, BOBBIE J., and MARSHALL, TOMMY W. "A Group Model for Adoption Studies for Special-Needs Children." *Child Welfare* 63 (Jan.–Feb. 1984):55–61.

FOSTER PARENT RESOURCE PROJECT. *Resource Catalog for Foster Parent Education.* Manhattan, Kan.: Kansas State University, 1978.

FOX, G. L. "Family Research, Theory, and Politics: Challenges of the Eighties." *Journal of Marriage and the Family* 43 (May 1981):259–261.

————. "Sex Role Attitudes as Predictors of Contraceptive Use." Presented at the Annual Meeting of the National Council on Family Relations, Aug. 1975.

FRAIBERG, SELMA. *Clinical Studies in Infant Mental Health.* New York, Basic Books, 1980.

FRANK, HELEN. "Feeling Happy." *Journal of Family Counseling* 4 (Spring 1976):23–27.

FRASER, MARILYN. Case material. University of Connecticut School of Social Work, 1980. (Mimeograph)

————. Personal communication, 1982.

FREEDMAN, R., and COOMBS, L. "Childspacing and Family Economic Position." *American Sociological Review* 31 (Oct. 1966):631–648.

FRENCH, PAUL COMLY. "Children on Strike." *The Nation* 136 (May 31, 1933):611–612.

FRENCH, W., and BELL, C. *Organizational Development.* Englewood Cliffs, N.J.: Prentice–Hall, 1973.

FREUDENBERGER, HERBERT J. "Burn-out: Occupational Hazard of the Child Care Worker." *Child Care Quarterly* (Summer 1977).

FRIEDMAN, A. S. *Therapy with Families of Sexually Acting Out Girls.* New York: Springer, 1971.

FROMM, ERICH. *Escape From Freedom.* New York: Rinehart and Co., 1941.

————. *The Sane Society.* Greenwich, Conn.: Fawcett, 1955.

FURSTENBERG, F. F., JR. *Unplanned Parenthood: The Social Consequences of Teenage Childbearing.* New York: The Free Press, 1976.

FURSTENBERG, F. F., JR., and CRAWFORD, A. G. "Family Support: Helping Teenage Mothers to Cope." *Family Planning Perspectives* 10 (Nov–Dec. 1978):22–333.

FURSTENBERG, F. F., JR.; HERCEG-BARON, R.; and JEMAIL, J. "Bringing in the Family: Kinship Support and Contraceptive Behavior. In *Teenage Pregnancy in a Family Context: Implications for Policy,* edited by T. Ooms. Philadelphia: Temple University Press, 1981.

FURSTENBERG, F. F., JR.; LINCOLN, R.; and MENKEN, J., eds. *Crisis in American Institutions.* Fourth Edition. Philadelphia: University of Pennsylvania Press, 1981.

FUSCO, LUKE J. "Power, Authority, and Influence in Social Work Treatment and the Two-Contract Model of Practice." Paper presented at the National Association of Social Workers' Fifth Biennial Professional Symposium, San Diego, Calif., Nov. 1977.

GALINSKY, ELLEN, and HOOKS, WILLIAM. *The New Extended Family: Day Care That Works.* Boston: Houghton Mifflin, 1977.

GALPER, JEFFREY. *Social Work Practice: A Radical Perspective.* Englewood Cliffs, N.J.: Prentice-Hall, 1980.

GALVIN, J., and POLK, K. "Juvenile Justice: Time for New Direction?" *Crime and*

*Delinquency* (Special Issue: Rethinking Juvenile Justice) 29 (July 1983):325–333.

GARBARINO, JAMES. "The Human Ecology of Child Maltreatment: A Conceptual Model for Research." *Journal of Marriage and the Family* 39 (Nov. 1977):721–736.

———. "Meeting the Needs of Mistreated Youths." *Social Work* 25 (Mar. 1980):122–126.

GARBARINO, JAMES, and JACOBSON, NANCY. "Youth Helping Youth in Cases of Maltreatment of Adolescents." *Child Welfare* 57 (Sept./Oct. 1978):505–510.

GARDNER, JAMES. "The Long-Term Care for Children." Presentation at the Maryland Developmental Disabilities Council Forum on Long Term Care Opportunities for Children, Dec. 3, 1982.

GARDNER, JOHN. *Morale*. New York: W. W. Norton, 1978.

GARDNER, LESLIE. "The Gilday Center: A Method of Intervention for Child Abuse." In *Child Abuse: Intervention and Treatment*, edited by Nancy B. Ebeling and Deborah Hill. Massachusetts: Publishing Sciences Group, 1975, pp. 143–150.

GARRETT, BEATRICE. "Foster Care: America's Lost Children." *Public Welfare* 35 (Summer 1977):4–8.

*Gary W. v. State of Louisiana,* 437 F. Supp. 1209 (1976).

GAUTHIER, THOMAS. "Education and Experience Requirements for Social Work Jobs—Draft Report." Washington, D.C.: National Association of Social Workers, 1980.

GAYLIN, WILLARD; GLASSER, J.; MARCUS, STEVEN; and ROTHMAN, DAVID, eds. *Doing Good: The Limits of Benevolence*. New York: Pantheon, 1978.

GEERTZ, CLIFFORD. "Thick Description: Toward an Interpretive Theory of Culture." In *The Interpretation of Cultures*, edited by Clifford Geertz. New York: Basic Books, 1973, pp. 3–30.

GEISMAR, LUDWIG L., and WOOD, KATHERINE M. "Evaluating Practice: Science as Faith." *Social Casework* 63 (May 1982):266–275.

GELLES, RICHARD J. "Child Abuse Psychopathology: A Sociological Critique and Reformulation." *American Journal of Orthopsychiatry* 43 (July 1973):611–621.

———. "Demythologizing Child Abuse." In *Crisis in American Institutions*, Fourth Edition, edited by J. H. Skolnick and E. Currie. Boston: Little, Brown and Company, 1979.

GENERAL ACCOUNTING OFFICE. "Agencies When Providing Federal Assistance Should Ensure Compliance with Title VI, HRD–80–22." Report to the Congress by the Comptroller General, Human Resources Division. Washington, D.C.: U.S. General Accounting Office, Apr. 15, 1980.

———. "Increased Federal Efforts to Better Identify, Treat, and Prevent Child Abuse and Neglect." Report to the Congress by the Comptroller General of the United States. Washington, D.C.: U.S. General Accounting Office, Apr. 29, 1980.

GERMAIN, CAREL B. "Child Welfare in the 1980's—Will the Graduate Level Curriculum Prepare the MSW?" West Hartford, Conn.: University of Connecticut School of Social Work, New England Regional Child Welfare Training Center, 1980. (Mimeograph)

——. "The Ecological Approach to People–Environment Transactions," *Social Casework* 6 (June 1981):323–331.

——. "Introduction: Ecology and Social Work." In *Social Work Practice: People and Environments,* edited by Carel B. Germain. New York: Columbia University Press, 1979a, pp. 1–22.

——. "The Place of Community Work Within an Ecological Approach to Social Work Practice." In *Theories and Practice of Community Social Work,* edited by Robert W. Roberts and Samuel Taylor. New York: Columbia University Press, in press.

——. "Social Study: Past and Future." *Social Casework* 49 (July 1968):406–409.

——, ed. *Social Work Practice: People and Environments.* New York: Columbia University Press, 1979b.

——. "Space: An Ecological Variable in Social Work Practice." *Social Casework* 59 (Nov. 1978):515–522.

——. "Time: An Ecological Variable in Social Work Practice." *Social Casework* 57 (July 1976):419–426.

GERMAIN, CAREL B., and GITTERMAN, ALEX. *The Life Model of Social Work Practice.* New York: Columbia University Press, 1980.

GERRY, ELBRIDGE T. "The Relation of Societies for the Prevention of Cruelty to Child-Saving Work." *Proceedings of the National Conference of Charities and Corrections, 1882,* pp. 129–130.

GERSHENSON, C. P. "Residential Treatment of Children: Research Problems and Possibilities." *Social Service Review* 30 (Sept. 1956):268–275.

GIBBONS, BOYD. "Aldo Leopold: A Durable Scale of Values." *National Geographic* 160 (Nov. 1981):682–708.

GIL, DAVID G. *Beyond the Jungle.* Cambridge, Mass.: Schenkman Publishing (Boston: G. K. Hall), 1979a.

——. *The Challenge of Social Equality.* Cambridge, Mass.: Schenkman Publishing, 1976.

——, ed. *Child Abuse and Violence.* New York: AMS Press, 1979b.

——. "The Hidden Success of Schooling in the United States." *The Humanist* 39 (Nov.–Dec.) 1979c.

——. "A Holistic Perspective on Child Abuse and Its Prevention." *American Journal of Orthopsychiatry* 45 (Apr. 1975):346–356.

——. *Unravelling Social Policy.* Revised Edition. Cambridge, Mass.: Schenkman Publishing, 1981.

——. *Violence Against Children.* Cambridge, Mass.: Harvard University Press, 1970.

GILBERT, NEIL, and SPECHT, HARRY. *Dimensions of Social Welfare Policy.* Englewood Cliffs, N.J.: Prentice-Hall, 1974.

GILL, MARGARET M., and AMADIO, CAROL M. "Social Work and Law in a Foster Care/Adoption Program." *Child Welfare* 62 (Sept.–Oct. 1983):455–467.

GILMAN, DAVID. "Rethinking Juvenile Justice: The Standards Project." *Child Welfare* 59 (Mar. 1980):145–151.

GIOVANNONI, JEANNE M., and BECERRA, ROSINA. *Defining Child Abuse.* New York: Free Press, 1979.

GIOVANNONI, JEANNE M., and BILLINGSLEY, ANDREW. "Child Neglect Among the Poor: A Study of Parental Adequacy in Three Ethnic Groups." *Child Welfare* 49 (Apr. 1970):196–204.

GIOVANNONI, J. M.; CONKLIN, JOHN; and IIYAMA, PATTI. *Child Abuse and Neglect: Perspectives from Child Development Knowledge.* San Francisco: R & E Associates, 1978.

GIRALDO, Z. I., and WEATHERFORD, J. W. *Life Cycle and the American Family: Current Trends and Policy Implications.* Durham, N.C.: Center for the Study of the Family and the State, Duke University, 1978.

GLASER, JOHN. "The Stairwell Society of Public Housing." *Comparative Group Studies* 3 (Aug. 1972):159–173.

GLASSER, IRA. "Prisoners of Benevolence: Power Versus Liberty in the Welfare State." In *Doing Good: The Limits of Benevolence,* edited by Willard Gaylin, Ira Glasser, Steven Marcus, and David Rothman. New York: Pantheon, 1978.

GOLDBERG, GAIL. "Breaking the Communication Barrier: The Initial Interview with Abusive Parents." *Child Welfare* 54 (Apr. 1975):274–282.

GOLDBERG, HARRIET L., and LINDE, LLEWELLYN H. "The Case for Subsidized Adoption." *Child Welfare* 48 (Feb. 1969):96–99; 107.

GOLDBERG, S. "Social Competence in Infancy: A Model of Parent-Infant Interaction." *Merrill–Palmer Quarterly* 23 (July 1977):163–177.

GOLDSTEIN, HARRIET. "Providing Services to Children in Their Own Homes: An Approach That Can Reduce Foster Placement." *Children Today* 2 (July–Aug. 1973):2–7.

GOLDSTEIN, JOSEPH; FREUD, ANNA; and SOLNIT, ALBERT. *Beyond the Best Interests of the Child.* New York: Free Press, 1973.

GOLIEMBIEWSKI, R.; CARRIGAN, S.; MEAD, W.; MUNZENRIDER, R.; and BLUMBERG, A. "Toward Building New Work Relationships." *Journal of Applied Behavioral Science* 11 (July–Sept. 1975):317–332.

GOODMAN, JAMES A. *Dynamics of Racism in Social Work Practice.* Washington, D.C.: National Association of Social Workers, 1974.

GORDON, HENRIETTA. *Casework Services for Children: Principles and Practices.* Boston: Houghton Mifflin, 1956.

GORDON, JAMES S. "Alternative Group Foster Homes: A New Place for Young People to Live." Unpublished paper. Rockville, Md.: National Institute of Mental Health, 1974.

GORDON, WILLIAM E. "Knowledge and Value: Their Distinction and Relationship in Clarifying Social Work Practice." *Social Work* 10 (July 1965):32–39.

GRAMSCI, ANTONIO. *Prison Notebooks*. New York: International Publishers, 1971.

GRAYCAR, A., ed. *Retreat from the Welfare State*. Sydney: University of New South Wales Press, 1983.

GREENBERG, JACK. *Judicial Process and Social Change*. St. Paul, Minn.: West Publishing Co., 1977.

GREINER, L. "Patterns of Organizational Change." *Harvard Business Review*, Reprint Series, No. 21072, pp. 145–153.

GRIFFITH, NAOMI H. "A Town Learns How to Start Programs on Child Abuse." *Practice Digest* 2 (Dec. 1979):16–18.

GRINDER, JOHN, and BANDLER, RICHARD. *The Structure of Magic*. Volume II. Palo Alto, Calif.: Science and Behavior Books, 1976.

GROSSER, CHARLES F. *New Directions in Community Organization*. Expanded Edition. New York: Praeger, 1976.

GROSSER, CHARLES, and MONDROS, JACQUELINE. "Pluralism and Participation: The Political Action Approach." In *Theories and Practice of Communnity Social Work*, edited by Robert W. Roberts and Samuel Taylor. New York: Columbia University Press, 1985.

GROW, LUCILLE, and SHAPIRO, DEBORAH. *Black Children–White Parents: A Study of Transracial Adoption*. New York: Child Welfare League of America, 1974.

GRUBB, W. NORTON, and LAZERSON, MARVIN. *Broken Promises: How Americans Fail Their Children*. New York: Basic Books, 1982.

GRUBER, ALAN R. *Foster Home Care in Massachusetts*. Boston: Governor's Commission on Adoption and Foster Care, 1973.

GUERIN, PHILIP J., ed. *Family Therapy: Theory and Practice*. New York: Gardner Press, 1976.

GUERNEY, LOUISE, and WOLFGANG, G. "Long Range Evaluation of Effects on Foster Parents of a Foster Parent Skills Training Program." *Journal of Clinical Child Psychology* 10 (Spring 1981):33–37.

GULLERUD, ERNEST N., and ITZIN, FRANK H. "Continuing Education as an Effective Linkage between Schools of Social Work and the Practice Community." *Journal of Education for Social Work* 15 (Fall 1979):81–87.

GULLOTTA, THOMAS P. "Leaving Home: Family Relationships of the Runaway Child." *Social Casework* 60 (Feb. 1979):111–114.

GUSFIELD, JOSEPH P. *Symbolic Crusade: Status Politics and the American Temperance Movement*. Urbana, Ill.: University of Illinois Press, 1966.

GUTIERRES, SARA E., and REICH, JOHN W. "A Developmental Perspective on Runaway Behavior: Its Relationship to Child Abuse." *Child Welfare* 60 (Feb. 1981):89–94.

HADDOW, SUSAN, and JONES, MARY ANN. *Annual Salary Study and Survey of Selected Personnel Issues*. New York: Child Welfare League of America, 1981.

HAGE, JERALD, and AIKEN, MICHAEL. *Social Change in Complex Organizations*. New York: Random House, 1970.

HALEY, JAY. *Uncommon Therapy*. New York: W. W. Norton, 1973.

HALL, A. D., and FAGEN, R. E. "Definition of a System." In *Modern Systems Research for the Behavioral Scientists: A Sourcebook,* edited by Walter Buckley. Chicago: Aldine, 1968.

HALL, G. S. *Adolescence. Its Psychology, and Its Relation to Physiology, Anthropology, Sociology, Sex, Crime, Religion, and Education.* New York: Appleton, 1904.

HALLECK, SEYMOUR. "The Impact of Professional Dishonesty on Behavior of Disturbed Adolescents." *Social Work* 8 (Apr. 1963):48–55.

HALPER, G., and JONES, M. *Serving Families at Risk of Dissolution: Public Preventive Services in New York City.* New York: New York City Human Resources Administration, 1981.

HAMILTON, ALEXANDER. "On the Employment of Children." American State Papers, Documents, Legislative and Executive, of the Congress of the United States, from the First Session of the First to the Third Session of the Thirteenth Congress, Inclusive, Washington, D.C. 1832, Class III, Finance, Vol. I, In *The Child and the State,* edited by Grace Abbot. Chicago: University of Chicago Press, 1938, pp. 267–277.

HAMMELL, CHARLOTTE. "Preserving Family Life for Children." *Child Welfare* 48 (Dec. 1969):591–594.

HANDLER, J., and ZATZ, J., eds. *Neither Angels Nor Thieves: Studies in the Deinstitutionalization of Status Offenders.* Washington, D.C.: National Academy Press, 1982.

HARDIN, MARK. "The Erosion of Parental Rights." In *Permanent Planning for Children in Foster Care: Resources for Training,* edited by S. Downs and C. Taylor. Portland, Oregon. Regional Research Institute, Portland State University. Washington, D.C.: Government Printing Office, Department of Health and Human Services Publication No. (OHDS) 81–30790, 1980.

————, ed. *Foster Care in the Courts.* Boston: Butterworth Legal Publishers, 1983.

HAREVAN, TAMARA K. "American Families in Transition: Historical Perspective on Change." In *Normal Family Processes,* edited by Froma Walsh. New York: Guilford Press, 1982.

HARRINGTON, JOSEPH D. "The Courts Contend with Sealed Adoption Records." *Public Welfare* 38 (Spring 1980):29–43.

HARRIS, GRACE E. *Training of Public Welfare Staff in the Use of the Service Contract in Preventing and Reducing Foster Care.* Hampton, Va.: Hampton Department of Social Services, 1978.

HARRISON, W. DAVID. "Role Strain and Burnout in Child Protective Service Workers." *Social Service Review* 54 (Mar. 1980):31–44.

HART, HASTINGS H. "The Development of Child Placing in the United States." In *Foster Home Care for Dependent Children,* edited by U.S. Department of Labor, Children's Bureau, Bureau Publication No. 136. Washington, D.C.: U.S. Government Printing Office, 1924.

HARTMAN, ANN. "Anomie and Social Casework." *Social Casework* 50 (Mar. 1969):131–137.

————. "Concentrations, Specializations, and Curriculum Design in MSW and BSW Programs." *Journal of Education for Social Work* 19 (Spring 1983):16–25.

_____. "Diagrammatic Assessment of Family Relationships." *Social Casework* 59 (Oct. 1978):465–476.

_____. "The Extended Family as a Resource for Change: An Ecological Approach to Family-Centered Practice." In *Social Work Practice: People and Environments,* edited by Carel B. Germain. New York: Columbia University Press, 1979a.

_____. "The Family: A Central Focus for Practice." *Social Work* 26 (Jan. 1981):7–13.

_____. *Finding Families: An Ecological Approach to Family Assessment in Adoption.* Beverley Hills, Calif.: Sage, 1979b.

_____. *Working with Adoptive Families Beyond Placement.* New York: Child Welfare League of America, 1984.

HARTMAN, ANN, and LAIRD, JOAN. *Family-Centered Social Work Practice.* New York: Free Press, 1983.

HARTMANN, HEINZ. *Ego Psychology and the Problem of Adaptation.* New York: International Universities Press, 1958.

HASENFELD, Y., and CHEUNG, P. P. L. "The Juvenile Court as a People Processing Organization." Ann Arbor: University of Michigan CRSO Working Paper #223, 1981.

HASTINGS, JAMES. *Encyclopedia of Religion and Ethics.* New York: Scribner, 1908.

HAWLEY, AMOS H. *Human Ecology: A Theory of Community Structure.* New York: Ronald Press, 1950.

HAZEN, N. *A Bridge to Independence.* London: Blackwells, 1981.

HEARN, GORDON. "General Systems Theory and Social Work." In *Social Work Treatment,* edited by Francis Turner. New York: Free Press, 1974, pp. 364–366.

HEFFERNAN, W. JOSEPH, JR. "Political Activity and Social Work Executives." *Social Work* 9 (Apr. 1964):18–23.

HEINEMAN, MARTHA B. "The Obsolete Scientific Imperative in Social Work Research." *Social Service Review* 55 (Sept. 1981):371–397.

HEINICKE, CHRISTOPH, and STRASSMAN, LARRY. *The Effects of Day Care on Preschoolers and the Provision of Support Services for Day Care Families.* Unpublished paper, 1977.

HELFER, R. E. "The Diagnostic Process and Treatment Programs." Department of Health, Education and Welfare Publication No. (OHD) 75–69. Washington, D.C.: U.S. Government Printing Office, 1975.

HELFER, RAY E., and KEMPE, C. HENRY, eds. *The Battered Child.* Chicago: University of Chicago Press, 1968.

HENSHAW, S.; FORREST, J. D.; SULLIVAN, E.; and TIETZE, C. "Abortion in the United States, 1978–1979." *Family Planning Perspectives* 13 (Jan.–Feb. 1981):6–18.

HERMAN, MAUREEN HASSETT, and CALLANAN, BREDAN V. "Child Welfare Workers and the State Legislative Process." *Child Welfare* 52 (Jan. 1978):13–25.

HERRERA, E. G., ET AL. "A 10 Year Follow-up Study of 55 Hospitalized Adolescents." *Journal of Psychiatry* 131 (1974):769–774.

HERSHEY, P., and BLANCHARD, K. *Management of Organizational Behavior*. Englewood Cliffs, N.J.: Prentice-Hall, 1977.

HERZOG, E., and BERNSTEIN, R. "Health Services for Unmarried Mothers." Children's Bureau, Department of Health, Education and Welfare Publication No. 425. Washington, D. C., 1964.

HIGHLAND, ANNE C. "Depression in Adolescents: A Developmental View." *Child Welfare* 57 (Nov. 1979):577–585.

HILL, ROBERT B. *Informal Adoptions Among Black Families*. Washington, D.C.: National Urban League, 1977.

––––––. *The Strengths of Black Families*. New York: Emerson Hall, 1972.

HILLS, WILLIAM G.; SCURLOCK, VOYLE C.; VIAILLE, HAROLD D.; and WEST, JAMES A., eds. *Conducting the Peoples Business: The Framework and Functions of Public Administration*. Norman, Okla.: University of Oklahoma Press, 1973.

HIROSE, JOAN Y. "Diogenes Youth Services." *Journal of Alternative Human Services* 5 (Winter 1979):29–32.

HIRSCHMAN, A. *Exit, Voice, and Loyalty*. Cambridge, Mass.: Harvard University Press, 1970.

"Historical Sketch of Richmond's Oldest Chartered Charity, Memorial Homes for Girls, Formerly Female Humane Association, 1805–1928." In Emma Octavia Lundberg, *Unto the Least of These*. New York: Appleton–Century Crofts, 1947, p. 58.

HOEHN, S. R.; FRANK, J. B.; IMBER, S. D.; NASH, E. H.; STONE, A. R.; and BATTLE, C. C. "Systematic Preparation of Patients for Psychotherapy." *Journal of Psychiatric Research* 2 (1964):267–281.

HOFFMAN, DANIEL L. AND REMMEL, MARY L. "Uncovering the Precipitant in Crisis Intervention." *Social Casework* 56 (May 1975):259–267.

HOFFMAN, LYNN. *Foundations of Family Therapy*. New York: Basic Books, 1981.

HOFSTADTER, RICHARD. *Darwinism in American Thought*. Boston: Beacon Press, 1955.

HOLLIS, FLORENCE. *Casework: A Psychosocial Therapy*. New York: Random House, 1964.

HOLLIS, FLORENCE, and WOOD, MARY. *Casework: A Psychosocial Therapy*. New York: Random House, 1981.

HOLMES, PHILIP. "The Maryland State Coordinating Council for the Residential Placement of Handicapped Children: A Brief Overview as of October 1, 1983." Baltimore, Md.: 200 West Baltimore St.

*Homemaker Services in the United States: Report of the 1959 Conference*. Washington, D.C.: U.S. Government Printing Office, 1960.

HOMER, L. E. "Community-Based Resources for Runaway Girls." *Social Casework* 54 (Oct. 1973):473–479.

HORESJI, CHARLES. *Foster Family Care: A Handbook for Social Workers*. Missoula: University of Montana, 1978.

HOROWITZ, R., and DAVIDSON, H., eds. *The Legal Rights of Children*. Colorado Springs, Colo.: Shepard's/McGraw–Hill, 1984.

HOSCH, DOROTHEA. *Use of the Contract Approach in Public Social Services.* Los Angeles: Regional Research Institute in Social Welfare, University of Southern California, 1973.

*House Hearings.* Testimony of Lillian Wald before the 60th Congress, 2nd Session, Jan. 27, 1909, p. 34. In Josephine Goldmark, *Impatient Crusader.* Urbana: University of Illinois Press, 1953, p. 96.

HOWELL, MARY C.; EMMONS, E. B.; and FRANK, D. A. "Reminiscences of Runaway Adolescents." *American Journal of Orthopsychiatry* 43 (Oct. 1973):840–853.

HUBBARD, ROY S. "Child Protection." In *Social Work Yearbook, 1933,* edited by Fred A. Hall. New York: Russell Sage, 1933.

———. "Crusading for Children, 1878–1943." Boston: Massachusetts Society for the Prevention of Cruelty to Children, n. d.

HUBBELL, RUTH. *Foster Care and Families.* Philadelphia: Temple University Press, 1981.

HUBER, J. "Married Students vs. Married Dropouts." *Phi Delta Kappa* 53:2 (1970):115–116.

HUDSON, WALTER H. "Scientific Imperatives in Social Work Research and Practice." *Social Service Review* 56 (June 1982):246–258.

HUNT, E. K., and SHERMAN, HOWARD J. *Economics: An Introduction to Tradition and Radical Views.* Fourth Edition. New York: Harper and Row, 1981.

HUSBAND, CHARLES. "Culture, Context, and Practice: Racism in Social Work." In *Radical Social Work Practice,* edited by Michael Brake and Roy Baily. London: Edward Arnold Publishers, Ltd., 1980.

ILLICH, IVAN; ZOLA, IRVING; MCKNIGHT, JOHN; CAPLAN, JONATHON; and SHAIKEN, HARLEY. *Disabling Professions.* London: Marion Boyars, 1977.

INFORMATION CANADA. *Day Care: A Resource for the Contemporary Family.* Ottawa: Information Canada, 1974.

JACKSON, ARLENE, and DUNNE, MICHAEL. "Permanency Planning in Foster Care with the Ambivalent Parent." In *The Challenge of Partnership—Working with Parents of Children in Foster Care,* edited by Anthony Maluccio and Paula Sinanoglu. New York: Child Welfare League of America, 1981, pp. 151–164.

JACOBS, G. "The Reification of the Notion of Subculture in Public Welfare." *Social Casework* 49 (Nov. 1968):527–534.

JACOBS, MARC. "Foster Parent Training: An Opportunity for Skills Enrichment and Empowerment." *Child Welfare* 59 (Dec. 1980):615–623.

JAMES, H. *Children in Trouble: A National Scandal.* New York: David McKay, 1970.

JANCHILL, SISTER MARY PAUL. "People Can't Go It Alone." In *Social Work Practice: People and Environments,* edited by Carel B. Germain. New York: Columbia University Press, 1979, pp. 346–362.

JAYARATNE, S., and LEVY, R. *The Clinical-Research Model of Intervention.* New York: Columbia University Press, 1979.

JENKINS, SHIRLEY. "Child Welfare as a Class System." In *Children and Decent People,* edited by Alvin Schorr. New York: Basic Books, 1974, pp. 3–24.

_____. "Duration of Foster Care—Some Relevant Antecedent Variables." *Child Welfare* 46 (Oct. 1967):450–456.

_____. *The Ethnic Dilemma in Social Services.* New York: Free Press, 1981.

JENKINS, SHIRLEY, and NORMAN, ELAINE. *Beyond Placement: Mothers View Foster Care.* New York: Columbia University Press, 1974.

_____. *Filial Deprivation in Foster Care.* New York: Columbia University Press, 1972.

JENKINS, SHIRLEY, and SAUBER, MIGNON. *Paths to Child Placement.* New York: Community Council of Greater New York, 1966.

JENKINS, SHIRLEY; SCHROEDER, ANITA G.; and BURGDORF, KENNETH. *Beyond Intake: The First Ninety Days.* Washington, D.C.: U.S. Department of Health and Human Services, Children's Bureau, 1981. (DHHS Publication No. (OHDS) 81–30313).

JETER, HELEN R. *Children, Problems, and Services in Child Welfare Programs.* Washington, D.C.: Children's Bureau, 1963.

JEWETT, CLAUDIA. *Adopting the Older Child.* Harvard, Mass.: Harvard Common Press, 1978.

JOE, BARBARA. *Public Policies Toward Adoption.* Washington, D.C.: The Urban Institute, 1979.

JOHNS, E. A. *The Sociology of Organizational Change.* Oxford, Eng.: Pergamon Press, 1973.

JOHNSON, H. L., ET AL. "Program Evaluation in Residential Treatment." *Child Welfare* 55 (Apr. 1976):279–291.

JOHNSON, L., and REID, J. *An Evaluation of Ten Years' Work with Emotionally Disturbed Children.* Seattle, Wash.: Ryther Child Center, 1947.

JONES, A. E., and PLACEK, P. J. "Teenage Women in the United States: Sex, Contraception, Pregnancy, Fertility, and Maternal and Infant Health." In *Teenage Pregnancy in a Family Context: Implications for Policy.*, edited by Theodora Ooms. Philadelphia: Temple University Press, 1981.

JONES, E. D. "On Transracial Adoption of Black Children." *Child Welfare* 51 (Mar. 1972):156–164.

KADUSHIN, ALFRED. *Adopting Older Children.* New York: Columbia University Press, 1970.

_____. "Adopting Older Children: Summary and Implications." In *Early Experience: Myth and Evidence,* edited by A. M. Clarke and A. B. D. Clarke. New York: Free Press, 1976, pp. 205–231.

_____. "A Study of Parents of Hard to Place Children." *Social Casework* 43 (May 1962).

_____. "Child Welfare." In *Research in the Social Services,* edited by H. S. Maas. Washington, D.C.: National Association of Social Workers, 1971, pp. 49–69.

_____. *Child Welfare Services.* Third Edition. New York: Macmillan, 1980.

_____. "Child Welfare Strategy in the Coming Years: An Overview.: In *Child Welfare in the Coming Years,* edited by Alfred Kadushin. Washington, D.C.:

Department of Health, Education and Welfare, DHEW Publication No. (OHDS) 78–30158, 1978a.

_____. "Children in Foster Families and in Institutions." In *Social Service Research*, edited by Henry S. Maas. Washington, D.C.: National Association of Social Workers, 1978b., pp. 90–148.

KAGAN, J.; KEARSLEY, R. B.; and ZELAZO, P. R. *Infancy: Its Place in Human Development*. Cambridge, Mass.: Harvard University Press, 1978.

KAHN, ALFRED J. "Child Welfare." In *Encyclopedia of Social Work*. Washington, D.C.: National Association of Social Workers, 1977, pp. 100–114.

_____. *Social Policy and Social Services*. New York: Random House, 1979.

KAHN, ALFRED J., and KAMERMAN, SHEILA B. *Not for the Poor Alone*. Philadelphia: Temple University Press, 1975.

KAHN, ALFRED J.; KAMERMAN, SHEILA B.; and McGOWAN, BRENDA G. *Child Advocacy: Report of a National Baseline Study*. Washington, D.C.: U.S. Government Printing Office, 1973.

KAMERMAN, SHEILA B., and KAHN, ALFRED J. "The Day-Care Debate: A Wider View." *The Public Interest* LIV (Winter 1979):76–93.

_____. *Family Policy: Government and Famlies in Fourteen Countries*. New York: Columbia University Press, 1978.

_____. *Social Services in the United States: Policies and Programs*. Philadelphia: Temple University Press, 1976.

KANE, F. J. "Adolescent Pregnancy: A Study of Aborters and Non-Aborters." *American Journal of Orthopsychiatry* 43 (Oct. 1973):796–803.

KANTNER, J., and ZELNIK, M. "Sexual Experiences of Young Unmarried Women in the U.S." *Family Planning Perspectives* 4 (Jan.–Feb. 1972):9–17.

KANTOR, DAVID, and LEHR, WILLIAM. *Inside the Family*. New York: Harper and Row, 1975.

KAPLAN, B.; CASSEL, J.; and GORE, S. "Social Support and Health." *Medical Care*. 25:5 (1977):47–58.

KARGER, HOWARD J. "Burnout as Alienation." *Social Service Review* 55 (June 1981):270–283.

KATZ, LINDA. "Adoption Counseling as a Preventive Mental Health Specialty." *Child Welfare* 54 (Mar. 1980):161–167.

KATZ, SANFORD N. "Child Neglect Laws in America." *Family Law Quarterly* 9 (Spring 1975):1–372.

_____. "Freeing Children for Permanent Placement Through a Model Act." *Family Law Quarterly* 12 (Fall 1978):203–251.

_____. *When Parents Fail: The Law's Response to Family Breakdown*. Boston: Beacon Press, 1971.

_____, ed. *The Youngest Minority*. Washington, D.C.: American Bar Association, 1974.

KEEFE, SUSAN E.; PADILLA, AMADO M.; and CARLOS, MANUEL L. "The Mexican-American Extended Family as an Emotional Support System." *Human Organization* 38 (Summer 1979):144–152.

KELLEY, FLORENCE. *Some Ethical Gains Through Legislation.* New York: Macmillan, 1905.

KEMPE, RUTH S., and KEMPE, C. HENRY. *Child Abuse.* Cambridge, Mass.: Harvard University Press, 1978.

KENISTON, KENNETH, and the CARNEGIE COUNCIL ON CHILDREN. *All Our Children: The American Family Under Pressure.* New York: Harcourt Brace Jovanovich, 1977.

KERMISH, I., and KUSHIN, F. "Why High Turnover: Social Staff Losses in a County Welfare Agency." *Public Welfare* 27 (Apr. 1969):134–139.

KESSON, W. "The American Child and Other Cultural Inventions." *American Psychologist* 34 (Oct. 1979):815–820.

KEY, ELLEN. *The Century of the Child.* New York: G. P. Putnam's Sons, 1909.

KILGORE, GLORIA, and SALMON, GABRIEL. *Technical Notes: Summaries and Characteristics of States' Title XX Social Service Plans for Fiscal Year 1979.* Washington, D.C.: U.S. Department of Health, Education, and Welfare, Office of the Assistant Secretary for Planning and Evaluation, June 15, 1979.

KINARD, E. MILLING. "Child Abuse and Depression: Cause or Consequence." *Child Welfare* 61 (Sept.–Oct. 1982):403–413.

KING, J. L. *A Comparative Analysis of Juvenile Codes.* Champaign–Urbana: University of Illinois Community Research Forum, 1980.

KIRK, DAVID. *Shared Fate.* New York: Free Press of Glencoe, 1964.

KIRST, MICHAEL, ET AL. "States Services for Children: An Exploration of Who Governs." Unpublished report. Palo Alto: Center for Educational Research at Stanford University, Mar. 1979.

KLAUS, M. H., and KENNELL, J. S. *Maternal–Infant Bonding.* St. Louis: Mosby, 1976.

KLEIN, M. "Deinstitutionalization and Diversion of Juvenile Offenders: Litany of Impediments." In *Crime and Justice: An Annual Review of Research,* edited by N. Morris and M. Tonvy. Chicago: University of Chicago Press, 1979, pp. 101–150.

KLEIN, M., and STERN, L. "Low Birth Weight and the Battered Child Syndrome." *American Journal of Diseases of Childhood* 122 (July 1971):15–18;

KLEINKAUF, CECILIA. "A Guide to Giving Legislative Testimony." *Social Work* 26 (July 1981):297–303.

KLIBANOFF, ELTON, and KLIBANOFF, SUSAN. *Let's Talk About Adoption.* Boston: Little, Brown, 1973.

KLINE, DRAZA, and OVERSTREET, HELEN. *Foster Care of Children: Nurture and Treatment.* New York: Columbia University Press, 1972.

KLINE, LAWRENCE Y. "Some Factors in the Psychiatric Treatment of Spanish-Americans." In *Hispanic Culture and Health Care: Fact, Fiction, Folklore,* edited by Richard Arguijo. St. Louis: Mosby, 1978, pp. 205–215.

KNAPP, CAROL. *Service Contract Use in Preventing and Reducing Foster Care: Final Evaluation Report.* Hampton, Va.: Hampton Department of Social Services, 1980.

KNITZER, JANE E. "Child Advocacy: A Perspective." *American Journal of Orthopsychiatry* 46 (Apr. 1976):200–216.

———. *Unclaimed Children: The Failure of Public Responsibility to Children and Adolescents in Need of Mental Health Services.* Washington, D.C.: Children's Defense Fund, 1982.

KNITZER, J.; ALLEN, M. L.; and McGOWAN, B. *Children Without Homes: An Examination of Public Responsibility to Children in Out-of-Home Care.* Washington, D.C.: Children's Defense Fund, 1979.

KOBRIN, S., and KLEIN, M. "National Evaluation of the Deinstitutionalization of Status Offender Programs." Vols. 1 and 2. Washington, D.C.: National Criminal Justice Reference Service, 1982.

KOHLBERG, L., and TURIEL, E. "Moral Development and Moral Education." In *Psychology and Education Practice,* edited by G. Lesser. Chicago: Scott Foresman, 1971, pp. 410–465.

KOLKO, GABRIEL. *Wealth and Power in America.* New York: Praeger, 1962.

KOLLER, MARVIN R. *Families: A Multigenerational Approach.* New York: McGraw–Hill, 1974.

KOTTER, J., and SCHLESINGER, L. "Choosing Strategies for Change." *Harvard Business Review* 79 (Mar.–Apr. 1979):106–114.

KRISBERG, B., and AUSTIN, J. *The Children of Ishmael: Critical Perspectives on Juvenile Justice.* Palo Alto, Calif.: Mayfield, 1978.

KRISBERG, B., and SCHWARTZ, I. "Rethinking Juvenile Justice." *Crime and Delinquency* 29:3 (July 1983):333–364.

LADNER, JOYCE. *Mixed Families.* Garden City, N.Y.: Archer Press, 1977.

LAHTI, JANE, ET AL. *A Follow-Up Study of the Oregon Project: A Summary.* Portland, Ore.: Regional Research Institute for Human Services, Portland State University, Sept. 1978.

LAIRD, JOAN. "An Ecological Approach to Child Welfare: Issues of Family Identity and Continuity." In *Social Work Practice: People and Environments,* edited by Carel B. Germain. New York: Columbia University Press, 1979, pp. 174–209.

———. "Sorcerers, Shamans, and Social Workers: The Use of Ritual in Social Work Practice." *Social Work* 29 (Mar./Apr. 1984):123–129.

LAIRD, JOAN, and ALLEN, JO ANN. "Family Theory and Family Practice." In *A Handbook of Clinical Social Work,* edited by Aaron Rosenblatt and Diana Waldfogel. New York: Jossey–Bass, 1983, pp. 176–201.

LAIRD, JOAN, and HARTMAN, ANN. "Meanings, Beliefs, and Spirituality: The Role of Myths, Tales, and Ceremonials in Enhancing the Quality of Life." Paper presented at the American Orthopsychiatric Association conference, Toronto, Apr. 1984.

LAMB, M. "Influence of the Child on Marital Quality and Family Interaction During the Prenatal, Perinatal, and Infancy Periods." In *Child Influences on Marital and Family Interaction: A Life-Span Perspective,* edited by R. Lerner and G. Spanier. New York: Academic Press, 1978, pp. 410–465.

LANE, FRANCIS E. *American Charities and the Child of the Immigrant. A Study of the Typical Child Caring Institutions in New York and Massachusetts Between the Years 1845 and 1880.* Washington, D.C.: Catholic University of America, 1932.

LANGER, S. "Reply." *Survey* 54:5 (1925):624.

LANGSAM, MIRIAM. *Children West.* Logmarked Madison, The State Historical Archives of Wisconsin, 1964.

LASCH, CHRISTOPHER. *The Culture of Narcissism.* New York: W. W. Norton, 1979.

LASCH, CHRISTOPHER. *Haven in a Heartless World.* New York: Basic Books, 1977.

LATHROP, JULIA to Marquette Bleeker, Dec. 1, 1920, National Archives, *Children's Bureau Papers,* Drawer 408.

LATHROP, JULIA, to the Secretary of Labor, July 19, 1921. *Abbott Papers,* Box 62, Folder 6. Chicago: University of Chicago.

LAUB, J. *Trends in Juvenile Criminal Behavior, 1973–80.* Washington, D.C.: U.S. Department of Justice, Office of Justice Assistance, Research Statistics, Jan. 1983.

LAUDERDALE, MICHAEL L.; GRINNELL, RICHARD M., JR.; and McMURTRY, STEVEN L. "Child Welfare Curricula in Schools of Social Work: A National Survey." *Child Welfare* 59 (Nov. 1980):531–541.

LAWDER, ELIZABETH A. "Quasi-Adoption." *Children* 13 (Jan. 1966):11–12.

———. "Toward a More Scientific Understanding of Foster Family Care." *Child Welfare* 44 (Jan. 1964):31–41.

LAWRENCE, P. "How to Deal with Resistance to Change." *Harvard Business Review,* Reprint Series, No. 21072, pp. 145–153.

LAYZER, JEAN L., and GOODSON, BARBARA. "Impact Evaluation of Twenty Child Abuse and Neglect Demonstration, Treatment, and Innovative Projects: Client Study." Working draft, Apr. 1979.

LAZARUS, RICHARD, and LAUNIER, R. "Stress-Related Transactions Between Person and Environment." In *Perspectives in Interactional Psychology,* edited by Lewis A. Pervin and Michael Lewis. New York: Plenum Press, 1978, pp. 287–327.

LEE, JUDITH, and PARK, DANIELLE. "A Group Approach to the Depressed Adolescent Girl in Foster Care." *American Journal of Orthopsychiatry* 48 (July 1978):516–527.

———. *Walk a Mile in My Shoes—A Manual on Biological Parents for Foster Parents.* West Hartford: University of Connecticut School of Social Work, 1980.

LEE, PORTER R. "Social Work as Cause and Function." Presidential address, National Conference of Social Work, 1929. In *Social Work as Cause and Function and Other Papers.* New York: Columbia University Press, 1937.

LEE, ROBERT E., and HULL, RUTH K. "Legal, Casework, and Ethical Issues in 'Risk Adoption'." *Child Welfare* 62 (Sept.–Oct. 1983):450–454.

LEIDERMAN, P. H. "The Critical Period Hypothesis Revisited: Mother to Infant Social Bonding in the Neonatal Period." In *Early Developmental Hazards:*

*Predictions and Precautions,* edited by F. D. Horowitz. Boulder, Colo.: Westview Press, 1978, pp. 43–77.

LENNARD, HENRY L., and BERNSTEIN, ARNOLD. *The Anatomy of Psychotherapy.* New York: Columbia University Press, 1960.

LENROW, P. "The Work of Helping Strangers." *American Journal of Community Psychology* 6 (Dec. 1978):555–571.

LEONARD, MARGARET. "Mutuality as a Catalytic Power for Growth." *Social Casework* 53 (Feb. 1972):67–72.

LERMAN, P. *Deinstitutionalization and the Welfare State.* New Brunswick, N.J.: Rutgers University Press, 1982.

———. "Trends and Issues in Deinstitutionalization of Youth in Trouble." *Crime and Delinquency* 26 (Apr. 1980):281–298.

LESLIE, GERALD R. *The Family in Social Context.* New York: Oxford University Press, 1979.

LEVIN, M., and SARRI, R. *Juvenile Delinquency in the U.S.: A Comparative Analysis of Juvenile Codes.* Ann Arbor: University of Michigan, National Assessment Center of Juvenile Corrections, 1974.

LEVINGER, GEORGE. "Continuance in Casework and Other Helping Relationships: A Review of Current Research." *Social Work* 5 (July 1960):40–51.

LEVITAN, SAR A., and BELOUS, RICHARD S. *What's Happening to the American Family?* Baltimore: Johns Hopkins University Press, 1981.

LEVITON, SUSAN A., and SHUGER, NANCY. "Maryland's Exchangeable Children: A Critique of Maryland's System of Providing Services to Mentally Handicapped Children." *Maryland Law Review* 42 (1983).

LEWIN, KURT. *Field Theory in Social Science.* New York: Harper and Row, 1951.

LEWIS, MARY R. "Day Care Under the Social Security Act." *Social Service Review* XLVIII (Sept. 1974):428–437.

LEWIS, M., and ROSENBLUM, L. A. *The Effects of the Infant on Its Caregiver.* New York: Wiley, 1974.

LITTNER, NER. *Some Traumatic Effects of Separation and Placement.* New York: Child Welfare League of America, 1950.

———. "The Art of Being a Foster Parent." *Child Welfare* 57 (Jan. 1978):3–12.

LITWAK, EUGENE. "Extended Kin Relations in an Industrial Democratic Society." In *Social Structure and the Family: Generational Relations,* edited by Ethel Shanas and Gordon F. Streib. Englewood Cliffs, N.J.: Prentice–Hall, 1965.

———. "Organizational Constructs and Mega Bureaucracy." In *The Management of Human Services,* edited by Rosemary Sarri and Yeheskel Hasenfeld. New York: Columbia University Press, 1978, pp. 123–162.

LOCKE, EDWIN A. "What is Job Satisfaction?" *Organizational Behavior and Human Performance* 4 (Nov. 1969):309–336.

LOPER, NANCY F. *A Comparative Study of the Personality Factors and Social Histories of Three Groups of Adopted Adults.* Unpublished doctoral dissertation. Los Angeles: Los Angeles School of Professional Psychology, 1976.

LOPPNOW, DONALD M., and TAGGART, SARAH R. "Family and Children's Services Specialty—The Development of an Elective Concentration in a Baccalaureate Social Work Program." Ypsilanti, Mich.: Eastern Michigan University, College of Human Services, 1981.

LOUNSBURY, JOHN W., and HALL, DIANA Q. "Supervision and Consultation Conflicts in the Day-Care Licensing Role." *Social Service Review* L (Sept. 1976):515–523.

LOURIE, IRA; CAMPIGLIA, PATRICIA; JAMES, LINDA RICH; and DEWITT, JEANNE. "Adolescent Abuse and Neglect: The Role of Runaway Youth Programs." *Children Today* 8 (Nov.–Dec. 1979):27–29; 40.

LUBOVE, ROY. *The Professional Altruist: The Emergence of Social Work as a Career (1880–1930)*. New York: Atheneum, 1969.

_____. *The Struggle for Social Security, 1900–1935*. Cambridge, Mass.: Harvard University Press, 1968.

LUNDBERG EMMA O. *Unto the Least of These*. New York: Appleton–Century, 1947.

MAAS, HENRY S., and ENGLER, RICHARD E. *Children in Need of Parents*. New York: Columbia University Press, 1959.

MADISON, BERNICE, and SHAPIRO, MICHAEL. "Permanent and Long Term Foster Care as a Placement Service." *Child Welfare* 49 (Mar. 1970):131–136.

MAHAFFEY, MARY ANN. "Lobbying and Social Work." *Social Work* 17 (Jan. 1972):3–11.

MAIN, M. "Analysis of a Peculiar Form of Reunion Behavior Seen in Some Daycare Children: Its History and Sequelae in Children Who Are Home Reared." In *Social Development in Daycare*, edited by R. Webb. Baltimore: Johns Hopkins University Press, 1977.

MALONE, BEATRICE. "Help for the Child in an In-Between World." *Child Welfare* 39 (Nov. 1960):17–22.

MALUCCIO, ANTHONY N. "Beyond Permanency Planning." *Child Welfare* 59 (Nov. 1980):515–529.

_____. "Competence-oriented Social Work Practice: An Ecological Approach." In *Promoting Competence in Clients—A New/Old Approach to Social Work Practice*, edited by Anthony N. Maluccio. New York: Free Press, 1981a, pp. 1–24.

_____. "Foster Family Care Revisited: Problems and Prospects." *Public Welfare* 31 (Spring 1973):12–17.

_____. *Learning from Clients: Interpersonal Helping as Viewed by Clients and Social Workers*. New York: Free Press, 1979a.

_____. "Perspectives of Social Workers and Clients on Treatment Outcomes." *Social Casework* 60 (July 1979b):394–401.

_____. "Promoting Client and Worker Competence in Child Welfare." In *Social Welfare Forum*. New York: Columbia University Press, 1981b, pp. 136–153.

_____. *Promoting Competence in Clients*. New York: Free Press, 1981c.

_____. "Using 'A Step Toward Professionalism' in Training of Child Care Staff." *Child Welfare* 49 (Mar. 1970):165–167.

MALUCCIO, ANTHONY N., and MARLOW, WILMA D. "The Case for the Contract." *Social Work* 19 (Jan. 1974):28–35.

————. "Residential Treatment of Emotionally Disturbed Children: A Review of the Literature." *Social Service Review* 46 (June 1972):230–251.

MALUCCIO, ANTHONY N., and SINANOGLU, PAULA A., eds. *The Challenge of Partnership: Working with Parents of Children in Foster Care.* New York: Child Welfare League of America, 1981.

MANNHEIM, KARL. *Ideology and Utopia.* New York: Harcourt, Brace, and Co., 1936.

MANNINO, F., and CONANT, M. "Dropouts from Parent Education Groups." *The Family Coordinator* 18(1) (1969):54–59.

MARTIN, JUDITH A., ed. *Advanced Graduate Course Content—Children, Youth and Families: An Instructional Guide.* Pittsburgh, Penn.: University of Pittsburgh, School of Social Work, 1982.

MARX, KARL, and ENGELS, FRIEDRICH. *The German Ideology.* Moscow: The Foreign Languages Publishing House, 1964.

MARYLAND DEVELOPMENTAL DISABILITIES COUNCIL. "Position Papers 1979–1983." Baltimore, Md.

MASLACH, CHRISTINA. "Burnout." *Human Behavior* 5 (Sept. 1976):16–22.

MASLACH, CHRISTINA, and JACKSON, SUSAN E. "The Measurement of Experiences Burnout." *Journal of Occupational Behavior* 2 (Jan. 1981):99–113.

MASLACH, C., and PINES, A. "Burnout: The Loss of Human Caring." In *Experiencing Social Psychology,* edited by A. Pines and C. Maslach. New York: Knopf, 1979.

MASLOW, ABRAHAM H. *Motivation and Personality.* New York: Harper and Row, 1970. (First Edition, 1954).

————. *The Farther Reaches of Human Nature.* New York: Viking Press, 1971.

MASNICK, GEORGE, and BANE, MARY JO. *The Nation's Families, 1960–1990.* Cambridge, Mass.: Joint Center for Urban Statistics of M.I.T. and Harvard University, 1980.

*Massachusetts Records,* 1854, p. 101. In *Children and Youth in America: A Documentary History,* Vols. I and II, edited by Robert Bremner. Cambridge, Mass.: Harvard University Press, 1970–74, p. 38.

MASSACHUSETTS SOCIETY FOR THE PREVENTION OF CRUELTY TO CHILDREN. *Annual Report.* Boston: 1902; 1906.

MATAS, L.; AREND, R. A.; and SROUFE, L. A. "Continuity of Adaptation in the Second Year: The Relationship Between Quality of Attachment and Later Competence." *Child Development* 49 (Sept. 1978):547–556.

MAYER, JOHN, and TIMMS, NOEL. "Clash in Perspective between Worker and Client." *Social Casework* 50 (Jan. 1969):32–40.

MAYER, M. F., and BLUM, A., eds. *Healing Through Living: A Symposium on Residential Treatment.* Springfield, Ill.: Thomas, 1971.

MCADOO, HARRIETTE P. "Demographic Trends in People of Color." *Social Work* 27 (Jan. 1982):15–24.

MCDONALD, A., JR. "Internal-External Locus of Control and the Practice of Birth Control." *Psychology Report* 27 (Aug. 1970):206.

McFADDEN, EMILY JEAN. "Helping the Inexperienced Worker in a Public Child Welfare Agency." *Child Welfare* 54 (May 1975):319–330.

_____. "Fostering the Battered and Abused Child." *Children Today* 9 (Apr. 1980):13–15.

_____. *Working with Natural Families.* Ypsilanti, Mich.: Foster Parent Training Project, Eastern Michigan University, 1980.

McGOLDRICK, MONICA. "Normal Families: An Ethnic Perspective." In *Normal Family Processes,* edited by Froma Walsh. New York: Guilford Press, 1982, pp. 399–425.

McGOWAN, BRENDA G. "The Case Advocacy Function in Child Welfare Practice." *Child Welfare* 57 (May 1978):275–284.

_____. "Strategies in Bureaucracies." In *Working for Children,* edited by Judith Mearig. San Francisco: Jossey–Bass, 1978, pp. 155–180.

McGOWAN, BRENDA G., and MEEZAN, WILLIAM. *Child Welfare: Current Dilemmas—Future Directions.* Itasca, Ill.: F. E. Peacock, 1983.

McGOWAN, BRENDA G.; KNITZER, JANE E.; and NISHI, SETSUKO MATSUNAGA. "New York City Special Services for Children: Case Reading Study." July 1, 1976. (Mimeograph)

McINTYRE, JENNIE. "The Structure-Functional Approach to Family Study." In *Emerging Conceptual Frameworks in Family Analysis,* edited by F. Ivan Nye and Felix M. Berardo. New York: Praeger, 1981, pp. 52–78.

McLAIN, GARRY B. "The Prevention and/or Treatment of Child Abuse and Neglect in Head Start: An Eclectic, Ecologic Hypothesis." In *Proceeedings of the Second Annual National Conference on Child Abuse and Neglect,* April 17–20, 1977. Volume 2. Washington, D.C.: DHEW Pub. No. (OHDS) 78–30147, 1978, pp. 19–25.

McNEIL, J. S., and McBRIDE, M. L. "Group Therapy with Abusive Parents." *Social Casework* 60(1) (1979):36–42.

McQUISTON, MARY. "Crisis Nurseries." In *The Abused Child,* edited by Harold P. Martin. Cambridge, Mass.: Ballinger, 1976, pp. 225–234.

MEAD, MARGARET. "The Impact of Cultural Changes on the Family." In *The Family in the Urban Community.* Detroit: Merrill–Palmer School, 1953.

MEEZAN, WILLIAM. *Adoption Services in the States.* U.S. Department of Health and Human Services, Office of Human Development Services, Administration for Children, Youth and Families, Washington, D.C.: Children's Bureau, 1980.

MEEZAN, WILLIAM, ET AL. *Adoption Without Agencies.* New York: Child Welfare League of America, 1978.

MEIGS, GRACE L. *Maternal Mortality from all Conditions Connected with Childbirth in the United States and Certain Other Countries.* Children's Bureau Publications #19. Washington, D.C.: U.S. Government Printing Office, 1917.

MEISELS, S. J., and ANASTASIOW, NICHOLAS J. "The Risks of Prediction: Relationships Between Etiology, Handicapping Conditions and Developmental Outcomes." In *The Young Child: Reviews of Research,* Vol. III, edited by S.

Moore and C. Coopers. Washington, D.C.: National Association for the Education of Young Children, 1982.

MELZER, A., and HAUGH, M. "Staff Development and Differential Recruitment." *Social Work* 19 (July 1974):467–476.

MENKEN, J. "Teenage Childbearing: Its Medical Aspects and Implications for the U.S. Population." In *Demographic and Social Aspects of Population Growth*, edited by C. Westoff and R. Parks. Washington, D.C.: U.S. Government Printing Office, 1972.

MERTON, ROBERT K. *Social Theory and Social Structure.* Second Edition. New York: Free Press, 1957.

MEYER, CAROL H. *Social Work Practice*, Second Edition. New York: Free Press, 1976.

———. "What Directions for Direct Practice?" *Social Work* 24 (July 1979):267–272.

MEYER, M. F.; RICHMAN, L. H.; and BLACERZAK, E. A. *Group Care of Children, Crossroads and Transitions.* New York: Child Welfare League of America, 1977.

MICHIGAN DEPARTMENT OF SOCIAL SERVICES. *Temporary Foster Care II: Project Notebook.* Lansing, Mich.: Michigan Department of Social Services, 1979.

MILIBAND, RALPH. *The State in Capitalist Society.* New York: Basic Books, 1969.

MILLER, A. L.; OHLIN, L.; and COATES, R. *A Theory of Social Reform.* Cambridge, Mass.: Ballinger, 1978.

MILLER, WARREN B. "The Telephone in Outpatient Psychotherapy." *American Journal of Psychotherapy* 27 (Jan. 1973):15–26.

MINUCHIN, S. *Families and Family Therapy.* Cambridge, Mass.: Harvard University Press, 1974.

MIRANDY, JOAN. "Preschool for Abused Children." In *The Abused Child*, edited by Harold P. Martin. Cambridge, Mass.: Ballinger, 1976, pp. 215–224.

MIZIO, EMELICIA. "White Worker—Minority Client." *Social Work* 17 (May 1972):82–86.

———. "Impact of External Systems on the Puerto Rican Family." *Social Casework* 55 (Feb. 1974):76–83.

MNOOKIN, ROBERT. "Foster Care—In Whose Best Interests?" *Harvard Educational Review* 43 (Nov. 1973):598–638.

MONTGOMERY COUNTY (MARYLAND) ASSOCIATION FOR RETARDED CITIZENS. "A Demonstration Project for the Development of Two Community Based Residential Service Alternatives for Children Who Are Severely Developmentally Disabled." Funded by the Maryland Developmental Disabilities Council, 1983.

MOORE, EVELYN. "Day Care: A Black Perspective." In *Day Care: Scientific and Social Policy Issues.* Boston: Auburn House, 1982, pp. 413–444.

MOORE, K. A., and CALDWELL, S. B. "The Effects of Government Policies on Out-of-Wedlock Sex and Pregnancy." *Family Planning Perspectives* 9 (July–Aug. 1977):164–168.

MOORE, K. A. AND HOFFERTH, S. L. "The Consequences of Age at First Child-birth: Female Headed Families and Welfare Dependency." Working Paper 1146–05. Washington, D.C.: The Urban Institute, 1978.

MOORE, K. A., HOFFERTH, S. L., and WORTHEIMER, R. "Teenage Motherhood, Its Social and Economic Costs." *Children Today* 8 (Sept./Oct. 1979):12–16.

MOORE, K. A., ET AL. "The Consequences of Age at First Childbirth: Educational Attainment." Working Paper 1146–01. Washington, D.C.: The Urban Institute, 1978.

MOOS, R., and INSEL, P., eds. *Issues in Social Ecology.* Palo Alto, Calif.: National Press Books, 1974.

MORA, G.; TALMADGE, M.; BRYANT, F. T.; and HAYDEN, B. S. "A Residential Treatment Center Moves Toward the Community Health Model." *Child Welfare* 48 (Dec. 1969):585–590.

MORGAN, GWEN G. *The Trouble with Title XX: A Review of Child Daycare Policy.* Washington, D.C.: U.S. Department of Health, Education, and Welfare, National Institute of Education, 1977.

MORLOCK, MAUD. *Homemaker Services: History and Bibliography.* Washington, D.C.: Welfare Administration, Children's Bureau, 1964.

MORONEY, ROBERT M. *Families, Social Services, and Social Policy: The Issue of Shared Responsibility.* Rockville, Md.: U.S. Department of Health and Human Services, 1980.

MORRIS, A., and GILLER, H. *Providing Criminal Justice for Children.* London: E. Arnold, 1983.

MORRISON, SAMUEL ELIOT, ed. "Records of the Suffolk County Court, 1672–1680." CSM Publications XXX (1933):599–915. In *Children and Youth in America: A Documentary History, Vol. I, 1600–1685,* edited by Robert Bremner. Cambridge, Mass.: Harvard University Press, 1970, pp. 41–42.

MORSE, C.; SAHLER, L.; and FRIEDMAN, S. "A Three-Year Follow-Up Study of Abused and Neglected Children." *American Journal of Diseases of Children* 120 (1970):439–446.

MORSE, W. C. "The Schools and Mental Health of Children and Adolescents." In *Advocacy for Child Mental Health,* edited by I. N. Berlin. New York: Brunner/Mazel, 1975, pp. 158–198.

MOTT, F. L., and SHAW, L. *Work and Family in the School Leaving Years: A Comparison of Female High School Graduates and Dropouts.* Unpublished manuscript, Ohio State University, 1978.

MOTT, PAUL E. *Foster Care and Adoptions: Some Key Policy Issues.* Report to the Sub-Committee on Children and Youth, Committee on Labor and Public Welfare, U.S. Senate. Washington, D.C.: U.S. Government Printing Office, 1975.

MOTT, PAUL, and LUNSFORD, BILL. *Home-Based Services for Children and Their Families.* Washington, D.C.: U.S. Department of Health, Education, and Welfare, The Child Welfare Resource Information Exchange, Children's Bureau, 1979.

MOUZAKITIS, CHRIS M. "Characteristics of Abused Adolescents and Guidelines for Intervention." *Child Welfare* 63 (Mar.–Apr. 1984):149–157.

MOYNIHAN, WILLIAM. "Developing Foster Child's Identification with Agency." *Child Welfare* 42 (1963).

MURPHY, L., and MORIARITY, A. *Vulnerability, Coping and Growth.* New Haven: Yale University Press, 1976.

NADLER, D. *Feedback and Organization Development.* Reading, Mass.: Addison–Wesley, 1977.

NAGARJUNA. *The Tree of Wisdom.* Verse 79. Translated by Major W. L. Campbell, C.I.E. Calcutta: Baptist Mission Press, 1919. Quoted by R. D. Laing in *The Facts of Life—An Essay in Feelings, Facts, and Fantasy.* New York: Pantheon Books, 1976.

NATIONAL ACADEMY OF SCIENCES. *Legalized Abortion and the Public Health.* Institute of Medicine, Publication 75–02. Washington, D.C.: National Academy of Sciences, 1975.

NATIONAL ADOPTION EXCHANGE. "The Challenge of Caring." A 30-minute videotape about special needs adoption. The tape may be obtained from 1218 Chestnut Street, Philadelphia, Penn., 19107.

NATIONAL ADVISORY COMMITTEE FOR JUVENILE JUSTICE AND DELINQUENCY PREVENTION. *Standards for the Administration of Juvenile Justice.* Washington, D.C.: U.S. Department of Justice, NISS, 1980.

NATIONAL ASSOCIATION OF SOCIAL WORKERS. *"Education and Experience Requirements for Social Work Jobs—Draft Report."* National Classification Validation Project. Washington, D.C.: N.A.S.W., 1980.

*N.A.S.W. News* 26 (Jan. 1981):8.

NATIONAL CENTER ON CHILD ABUSE AND NEGLECT. *Child Abuse and Neglect in Residential Institutions.* Washington, D.C.: National Center on Child Abuse and Neglect, DHEW Pub. No. (OHDS) 78-30160, 1978.

NATIONAL CENTER FOR HEALTH STATISTICS. "Final Natality Statistics, 1976." *Monthly Vital Statistics Report* 26:12 (1978). Washington, D.C.: National Center for Health Statistics, U.S. Department of Health and Human Services.

_____. "Final Natality Statistics, 1978." *Monthly Vital Statistics Report* 29:1 (1980). Washington, D.C.: National Center for Health Statistics, U.S. Department of Health and Human Services.

NATIONAL CENTER FOR JUVENILE JUSTICE. *U.S. Estimates of Cases Processed by Courts with Juvenile Jurisdiction.* Pittsburgh, Penn.: National Center for Juvenile Justice, 1982.

NATIONAL CENTER FOR SOCIAL STATISTICS. Social and Rehabilitation Service. *Adoptions in 1975.* Washington, D.C.: U.S. Department of Health, Education, and Welfare.

_____. *Children Served by Public Welfare Agencies and Voluntary Child Welfare Agencies and Institutions.* Washington, D.C.: U.S. Department of Health, Education, and Welfare, Mar. 1972.

NATIONAL CHILD WELFARE TRAINING CENTER. *Child Welfare Trainees—Where Are They Now? Results of the National Study.* Ann Arbor: The University of Michigan School of Social Work, 1981a.

_____. *The Place of Child Welfare in Social Work Education.* Ann Arbor: The University of Michigan School of Social Work, 1982–1984.

_____. *National Follow-up Study: Child Welfare Trainees.* Ann Arbor: University of Michigan School of Social Work, 1982.

_____. *Profile One: The View from the State Offices—Administrators and Staff Development Directors Look at In-Service Training for Child Welfare.* Ann Arbor: The University of Michigan School of Social Work, 1981b.

_____. *Profile Two: Attitudes and Evaluations of In-Service Training by Local Administrators.* Ann Arbor: The University of Michigan School of Social Work, 1981c.

_____. *Profile Three: Attitudes and Evaluation of In-Service Training by Child Welfare Trainers.* Ann Arbor: The University of Michigan School of Social Work, 1981d.

_____. *Profile Four: The View from the Agency—Supervisors and Workers Look at In-Service Training for Child Welfare.* Ann Arbor: The University of Michigan School of Social Work, 1983.

NATIONAL COMMISSION ON CHILDREN IN NEED OF PARENTS. *Who Knows? Who Cares? Forgotten Children in Foster Care.* New York: Child Welfare League of America, 1979.

NATIONAL COMMISSION ON FAMILIES AND PUBLIC POLICIES. *Families and Public Policies in the United States.* Columbus, Ohio: National Conference on Social Welfare, 1978.

NATIONAL CONGRESS ON FOSTER FAMILY CARE. "Position Statement on Education and Training of Foster Parents." Interim Report. Houston, Tex.: National Congress on Foster Family Care, 1978.

NATIONAL COUNCIL FOR HOMEMAKER–HOME HEALTH AIDE SERVICES, INC. *Strengthening Family Life Through Homemaker–Home Health Aide Services.* New York: National Council for Homemaker–Home Health Aide Services, 1971.

NATIONAL FAMILY PLANNING AND REPRODUCTIVE HEALTH ASSOCIATION. "Focus on Families" (authored by Emily Moore). Washington, D.C.: National Family Planning and Reproductive Health Association, 1982.

NATIONAL HOMECARING COUNCIL. *Interpretation of the Standards.* New York: National HomeCaring Council, 1981.

NATIONAL INSTITUTE FOR ADVANCED STUDIES. *Report on Foster Care Review Systems.* Prepared for Children's Bureau, Administration for Children, Youth, and Families, Office of Human Development. Washington, D.C.: U.S. Department of Health, Education, and Welfare, 1979.

NATIONAL RESEARCH COUNCIL. *Toward a National Policy for Children and Families.* Washington, D.C. National Academy of Sciences, 1976.

NATIONAL URBAN LEAGUE. *Guide to Working with Black Families in the Adoption Process.* New York: National Urban League, 1981.

NEJILSKY, P. "Diversion: Unleashing the Hound of Heaven?" In *Pursuing Justice for the Child*, edited by M. Rosenheim. Chicago: University of Chicago Press, 1976.

NELSON, KATHERINE A. *On Adoption's Frontier: A Study of Families Who Adopted a Child with Special Needs.* Unpublished manuscript. New York: Child Welfare League of America, 1983.

NELSON, R. H.; SINGER, M. J.; and JOHNSON, L. O. "Community Considerations in the Evaluation of a Children's Residential Treatment Center." *Proceedings* 8:951–952. 81st Annual Convention, American Psychological Association, 1973.

NELSON, R. H.; SINGER, M. J.; and JOHNSON, L. O. "The Application of a Residential Treatment Evaluation Model." *Child Care Quarterly*, 7:2 (1978):164–175.

NERLOVE, MARC. "Toward a New Theory of Population and Economic Growth." In *Economics of the Family*, edited by Theodore W. Schultz. Chicago: University of Chicago Press, 1974, pp. 527–545.

NETTLER, G. "Cruelty, Dignity and Determinism." *American Sociological Review* 34 (June 1959):375–384.

NEWCOMBE, H. B., and TARENDALE, O. G. "Maternal Age and Birth Order Correlations." *Mutation Research* 1 (1964):446.

NEW YORK CITY HUMAN RESOURCES ADMINISTRATION. *The New York City Response to a Proposal by the Mayor's Task Force on Child Abuse.* New York: New York City Human Resources Administration, Nov. 1981.

*New York Sessions Laws.* "An Act to Prevent Baby Farming." 1883, Ch. 40, pp. 30–31. In *Children and Youth in America: A Documentary History*, Vol. II, edited by Robert Bremner. Cambridge, Mass.: Harvard University Press, 1970–74, pp. 195–196.

NEW YORK SOCIETY FOR THE PREVENTION OF CRUELTY TO CHILDREN. *Annual Report.* New York: 1882; 1893.

*New York Times, The.* April 10, 11, 14, 22, 27 and December 17, 1874; January 28, 1912; October 19, 1980; June 30, 1981.

*Niles Register*, XII. In Edith Abbott, "A Study of the Early History of Child Labor in America." *American Journal of Sociology* 14 (Nov. 1908):15–37.

NOBLE, LYNNE STEYER, and EUSTER, SANDRA. "Foster Parent Input: A Crucial Element in Training." *Child Welfare* 60 (Jan. 1981):35–42.

NORD, WALTER R. "Job Satisfaction Reconsidered." *American Psychologist* 32 (Dec. 1977):1026–1035.

NORTH AMERICAN COUNCIL ON ADOPTABLE CHILDREN. "Teammate." *Adoptalk* 6 (May 1981):3.

———. *Adoptalk* (May–June 1983).

OFFICE OF YOUTH DEVELOPMENT. Office of Human Development. *Youth Reporter.* Washington, D.C.: U.S. Department of Health, Education, and Welfare, Nov. 1974.

OLSEN, LENORE, and HOLMES, WILLIAM H. "Educating Child Welfare Workers: The Effects of Professional Training on Service Delivery." *Journal of Education for Social Work* 18 (Winter 1982):94–102.

O'NEIL, SISTER MARIA JOAN. "Child Welfare Education/Training for Quality Practice at the Baccalaureate Level." West Hartford, Conn.: The University of Connecticut School of Social Work, New England Regional Child Welfare Training Center, 1980. (Mimeograph)

ORTEN, JAMES D., and SOLL, SHARON K. "Runaway Children and Their Families: A Treatment Typology." *Journal of Family Issues* 1 (June 1980):249–261.

OSOFSKY, J. D., and OSOFSKY, H. S. "Teenage Pregnancy: Psychological Considerations." *Clinical Obstetrics and Gynecology* 21 (1978):1161–1173.

PAGE, M., and CLARK, M. (EDS.) *Who Cares?* London: National Children's Bureau, 1977.

PAGE, WILLIAM. "Block Grants and Budget Cuts Place States in the Middle." Unpublished paper. Florida State University, July 3, 1981.

PAKTER, J.; O'HARE, D.; NELSON, F.; and SORGAR, M. "Two Years Experience in New York City with the Liberalized Abortion Law—Progress and Problems." *American Journal of Public Health* 63 (June 1963):524–535.

PALMER, TED. "Matching Worker and Client in Corrections." *Social Work* 18 (Mar. 1973):95–103.

PANCOAST, DIANE. "Finding and Enlisting Neighbors to Support Families." In *Protecting Children from Abuse and Neglect*, edited by James Garbarino and S. Holly Stocking. San Francisco: Jossey–Bass, 1980, pp. 109–132.

PAPP, PEGGY. "Brief Therapy with Couples Groups." In *Family Therapy: Theory and Practice*, edited by Philip Guerin. New York: Gardner Press, 1976a.

———. "Family Choreography." In *Family Therapy: Theory and Practice*, edited by Philip Guerin. New York: Gardner Press, 1976b.

———. "The Greek Chorus and Other Techniques of Family Therapy." *Family Process* 19 (Mar. 1980):45–58.

PAPPENFORT, D. *The National Survey of Residential Group Care Facilities for Children and Youth: Preliminary Findings.* Unpublished paper. Chicago: University of Chicago School of Social Service Administration, Apr. 1983.

PAPPENFORT, D.; KILPATRICK, D.; and KUBY, A. *A Survey of Children's Residential Institutions, 1966.* Chicago: University of Chicago School of Social Service Administration, 1970.

PARDECK, JOHN T.; HEGAR, REBECCA L.; NANCE, KATHY NEWTON; and CHRISTY-BAKER, CYNTHIA. *Child Welfare Training and Practice—An Annotated Bibliography.* Westport, Conn.: Greenwood Press, 1982.

PARKE, ROSS D., and COLLMER, CANDACE W. "Child Abuse: An Interdisciplinary Analysis." In *Review of Child Development Research*, Volume 5, edited by Mavis Heatherington. Chicago: University of Chicago Press.

PARSONS, TALCOTT, and BALES, ROBERT F. *Family Socialization and Interaction Process.* Glencoe, Ill.: Free Press, 1955.

PASAMANICK, B., and LILIENFIELD, A. "The Association of Maternal and Fetal

Factors with the Development of Mental Deficiency: II. Relationship to Maternal Age, Birth Order, Previous Reproductive Loss, and Degree of Mental Deficiency." *American Journal of Mental Deficiency* 60 (Jan. 1956):557–569.

Pasztor, Eileen M., and Burgess, Elyse. "Finding and Keeping More Foster Parents." *Children Today* 11 (Mar.–Apr. 1982):2–5.

Patti, Rino J., and Resnick, Herman. "Changing the Agency from Within." *Social Work* 17 (1972):48–57.

Paulker, J. D. "Girls Pregnant Out of Wedlock." In *Double Jeopardy, the Triple Crisis—Illegitimacy Today.* New York: National Council on Illegitimacy, 1970.

Paulsen, M. "Court Reform and the Legal Status of Children." In *Juvenile Justice: The Progressive Legacy and Current Reforms,* edited by L. Empey. Charlottesville, Va.: University of Virginia Press, 1979.

Pawlak, E. "Differential Selection of Juveniles for Detention." *Journal of Research in Crime and Delinquency* 14:2 (1977):152–165.

Pecora, Peter J. "Outcome Evaluation in Residential Treatment: A Literature Review." Unpublished paper, N.W. Regional Child Welfare Training Center. Seattle, Wash.: University of Washington School of Social Work, 1981.

————. *Improving the Quality of Child Welfare Services: Needs Assessment for Staff Training in Alaska and Oregon.* Unpublished doctoral dissertation. Seattle, Wash.: University of Washington, July 1982.

Pecora, Peter J.; Dodson, Arthur R.; Teather, Edward C., and Whittaker, James K. "Assessing Worker Training Needs: Use of Staff Surveys and Key Informant Interviews." *Child Welfare* 62 (Sept./Oct. 1983):395–407.

Pedosuk, Leona, and Ratcliffe, Elizabeth. "Using Foster Parents to Help Foster Parents: A Canadian Experiment." *Child Welfare* 58 (July–Aug. 1979):466–470.

Pelton, Leroy H. "Child Abuse and Neglect: The Myth of Classlessness." *American Journal of Orthopsychiatry* 48 (Oct. 1978):608–617.

Pennypacker, Kathryn E. "Reaching Decisions to Initiate Court Action to Free Children in Care for Adoption." *Child Welfare* 40 (Dec. 1961):11–15.

Perlman, Helen Harris. "Intake and Some Role Considerations." *Social Casework* 41 (Apr. 1960):171–177.

————. *Persona: Social Role and Personality.* Chicago: University of Chicago Press, 1968.

————. *Relationship: The Art of Helping People.* Chicago: University of Chicago Press, 1979.

*Permanency Planning: The Black Experience—A Training Curriculum.* Knoxville, Tenn.: Office of Continuing Education, University of Tennessee, School of Social Work, 1982.

Peterson, Jean K. Unpublished Case Material. Portland, Ore.: Portland State University School of Social Work, 1980.

Pettiford, Ida; Hasenfeld, Helen; and Raney, Ann. "The Drop-In Center: Filling the Missing Link in the Neighborhood Support Network." *Journal of Clinical Child Psychology* V (Spring 1976):48–52.

Piaget, J. *The Construction of Reality in the Child.* New York: Basic Books, 1954.

_____. *Intelligence and Affectivity: Their Relationship During Child Development.* Annual Reviews Monograph. Palo Alto, Calif.: Annual Reviews, Inc., 1981.

_____. *The Moral Judgment of the Child.* Glencoe, Ill.: The Free Press, 1948.

_____. *The Origins of Intelligence in Children.* Second Edition. New York: International Universities Press, 1952.

PIERCE, MARILYN. "Epilogue." *Adoption Forum Newsletter* (Jan. 1982).

PIKE, VICTOR. "Permanent Planning for Foster Children: The Oregon Project." *Children Today* 6 (Nov./Dec. 1976):22–41.

PIKE, VICTOR; DOWNS, SUSAN; EMLEN, ARTHUR; ET AL. *Permanent Planning for Children in Foster Care: A Handbook for Social Workers.* DHEW Pub. No. (OHDS) 77–30124. Washington, D.C.: United States Government Printing Office, 1977.

PINCUS, ALLEN, and MINAHAN, ANNE. *Social Work Practice: Model and Method.* Itasca, Ill.: F. E. Peacock, 1973.

PINDERHUGHES, ELAINE. "Empowerment for Our Clients and for Ourselves." *Social Casework* 64 (June 1983): 331–338.

PINES, AYALA, and KAFRY, DISTA. "Occupational Tedium in the Social Services." *Social Work* 23 (Nov. 1978):499–507.

PIVEN, FRANCES FOX, and CLOWARD, RICHARD. *Regulating the Poor.* New York: Pantheon Books, 1971.

PLACEK, P. J., and HENDERSHOT, G. E. "Public Welfare and Family Planning: An Empirical Study of the 'Brood Sow' Myth." *Social Problems* 21 (June 1976):658–673.

PLATT, A. *The Child Savers: The Invention of Delinquency.* Chicago: University of Chicago Press, 1969. (Second Edition, 1977).

POLANSKY, NORMAN A.; BORGMAN, ROBERT D.; and DE SAIX, CHRISTINE. *The Roots of Futility.* San Francisco: Jossey–Bass, 1972.

POLANSKY, NORMAN A.; CHALMERS, MARY ANN; BUTTENWIESER, ELIZABETH; and WILLIAMS, DAVID P. *Damaged Parents: An Anatomy of Child Neglect.* Chicago: University of Chicago Press, 1981.

POLANSKY, NORMAN; HALLY, C.; and POLANSKY, NANCY. *State of Knowledge of Child Neglect.* Athens: University of Georgia Regional Institute of Social Welfare Research, School of Social Work, 1974.

POLANYI, KARL. *The Great Transformation.* Boston: Beacon Press, 1957.

POLIER, JUSTINE WISE. *A View from the Bench.* New York: National Council on Crime and Delinquency, 1964.

POPE JOHN PAUL II. *On Human Work—Laborem Exercens.* Vatican: Polyglot Press, 1981.

POULIN, J.; LEAVITT, J.; YOUNG, T.; and PAPPENFORT, D. *Juveniles in Detention Centers and Jails: An Analysis of State Variations During the Mid-1970s.* Washington, D.C.: U.S. Department of Justice, LEAA, 1980.

POWELLS, L., and POSNER, T. "Managing Change: Attitudes, Targets, Problems, and Strategies." *Group and Organizational Studies* 1 (May–June 1976):310–323.

PRESSER, H. B. "Early Motherhood: Ignorance or Bliss?" *Family Planning Perspectives* 6 (winter 1974):8–14.

_____. "Sally's Corner: Coping with Unmarried Motherhood." Paper presented at the meeting of the American Sociological Association, San Francisco, 1974.

PRESSER, J. R. "The Historical Background of the American Law of Adoption." *Journal of Family Law* 11 (Nov. 1972):488–460.

*Proceedings of the Conference on the Care of Dependent Children.* Held in Washington, D.C.: 60th Congress, 2nd Session, Jan. 25–26, 1909. S. Doc. No. 721.

PROCH, KATHLEEN O. *Adoption by Foster Parents.* Unpublished doctoral dissertation. Urbana–Champaign: University of Illinois, 1980.

_____. "Foster Parents as Preferred Adoptive Parents: Practice Implications." *Child Welfare* 60 (Nov. 1981):617–626.

PROMISLO, ESTELLE. "Confidentiality and Privileged Communication." *Social Work* 24 (Jan. 1979):10–13.

PROSSER, H. *Perspectives on Residential Child Care.* Windsor, England: National Federation for Educational Research (National Children's Bureau Reports), 1976.

PROVENCE, SALLY, and NAYLOR, AUDREY. *Working with Disadvantaged Parents and Their Children.* New Haven: Yale University Press, 1983.

PROVENCE, SALLY; NAYLOR, AUDREY; and PATTERSON, JANE. *The Challenge of Daycare.* New Haven: Yale University Press, 1977.

QUINN, ROBERT P., and SHEPPARD, LINDA J. *The 1972–73 Quality of Employment Survey.* Ann Arbor, Mich.: Institute for Social Research, 1974.

QUINN, ROBERT P., and STAINES, GRAHAM L. *The 1977 Quality of Employment Survey.* Ann Arbor, Mich.: Institute for Social Research, 1978.

RAINS, P. *Becoming an Unwed Mother.* Chicago and New York: Aldine/Atherton, 1971.

RAINWATER, L. *Family Design, Marital Sexuality, Family Size and Contraception.* Chicago: Aldine, 1965.

RAPOPORT, LYDIA. "The State of Crisis: Some Theoretical Considerations." *Social Service Review* 36 (June 1962):211–217.

RAPOPORT, R. N. "The Male's Occupation in Relation to His Decision to Marry." *Acta Sociologica* 8 (1964):68–82.

RAPOPORT, R.; RAPOPORT, R.; STRELITZ, Z.; and KEW, S. *Fathers, Mothers and Society.* New York: Vintage Books, 1980.

RAUH, K. "The Reproductive Adolescent." *Pediatric Clinics of North America* 20 (1973):1005–1020.

RAYNOR, LOIS. *The Adopted Child Comes of Age.* London: George Allen and Unwin, 1980.

REDL, FRITZ, and WINEMAN, DAVID. *The Aggressive Child.* New York: Free Press, 1957.

REID, JOSEPH. "Principles, Values and Assumptions Underlying Adoption Practice." In *Readings in Adoption,* edited by Evelyn Smith. New York: Philosophical Library, 1963, pp. 26–28.

REIN, MARTIN. *Social Policy: Issues of Choice and Change*. New York: Random House, 1970.

REISS, DAVID. *The Family's Construction of Reality*. Cambridge, Mass.: Harvard University Press, 1981.

REISTROFFER, MARY. "Participation of Foster Parents in Decision-Making: The Concept of Collegiality." *Child Welfare* 51 (Jan. 1972):25–29.

REYNOLDS, WILLIAM F.; LEVEY, CATHY; and EISNITZ, MARK. "Adoptees' Personality Characteristics and Self-Ratings of Adoptive Family Life." Paper submitted to the American Psychological Association Convention, San Franciso, Aug. 1977.

RHODES, SONYA. "Contract Negotiation in the Initial Stage of Casework Service." *Social Service Review* 51 (Mar. 1977):125–140.

RICE, ROBERT M. *American Family Policy: Content and Context*. New York: Family Service Association of America, 1977.

RICE, ROBERT M. "Exploring American Family Policy." *Marriage and Family Review* 2 (Fall 1979):1–11.

RICHMAN, H. "Social Services and Accountability." Paper presented at Columbia University, Apr. 16, 1980.

RICHMAN, LEON. "Day Care." *Encyclopedia of Social Work*. Washington, D.C.: National Association of Social Workers, 1965.

RICKETTS, S. S. *Contraceptive Use Among Teenage Mothers: Evaluation of a Family Planning Program*. Ph.D dissertation, University of Pennsylvania, 1973.

RINDFLEISCH, NOLAN J.; TOOMEY, BEVERLY G.; and SOLDANO, KITTY. *Assessing Training Needs in Children Services—How To Do It*. Columbus: The Ohio State University College of Social Work, n. d.

ROBERTS, ROBERT W., and TAYLOR, SAMUEL, eds. *Theories and Practice of Community Social Work*. New York: Columbia University Press, 1985.

ROBIN, MICHAEL. "Sheltering Arms: The Roots of Child Protection." In *Child Abuse*, edited by Eli H. Newberger. Boston: Little, Brown, 1982.

ROBINSON, NANCY D.; SHINN, EUGENE B.; ADAM, ESTHER; and MOORE, FLORENCE. *Costs of Homemaker–Home Health Aide and Alternative Forms of Service: A Survey of the Literature*. New York: National Council for Homemaker–Home Health Aide Services, Inc., 1974.

ROBY, PAMELA. "How to Look at Day-Care Programs." In *The Human Services*, edited by Ronald J. Kase. New York: AMS Press, Inc., 1979.

RODE, S. S.; CHANG, P.; FISCH, R.; and SROUFE, L. "Attachment Patterns of Infants Separated at Birth." *Developmental Psychology* 17 (Mar. 1981):188–191.

RODRIGUEZ, CAROLYN. *An Evolutionary Review of Foster Parents' Roles in the Foster Care System*. National Foster Parent Association White Paper. San Antonio, Tex.: 1982.

ROSEN, R.; HUDSON, A.; and MARTINDALE, L. "Contraception, Abortion and Self Concept." Paper presented at the meeting of the American Sociological Association, Washington, D.C., Sept. 1976.

ROSENHEIM, M. *Pursuing Justice for the Child*. Chicago: University of Chicago Press, 1976.

ROTHMAN, D. *Conscience and Convenience: The Asylum and Its Alternatives in Progressive America*. Boston: Little, Brown, 1980.

————. *The Discovery of the Asylum: Social Order and Disorder in the New Republic*. Boston: Little, Brown, 1971.

————. "The Progressive Legacy: Development of American Attitudes Toward Juvenile Delinquency." In *The Progressive Legacy and Current Reforms*, edited by L. Empey. Charlottesville: University Press of Virginia, 1979, pp. 34–68.

RUBENSTEIN, J. S., ARMENTROUT, J. A., LEVIN, S. and HERALD, D. "The Parent Therapist Program: Alternative Care for Emotionally Disturbed Children. *American Journal of Orthopsychiatry* 48 (Oct. 1978):654–662.

RUBEN, R. A., and BALOW, B. "Measures of Infant Development and Socioeconomic Status as Predictors of Later Intelligence and School Achievement." *Developmental Psychology* 15 (Mar. 1979):225–227.

RUDERMAN, FLORENCE A. *Child Care and Working Mothers: A Study of Working Mothers: A Study of Arrangements Made for Daytime Care of Children*. New York: Child Welfare League of America, 1968.

RUNYAN, ANITA, and FULLERTON, SALLY. "Foster Care Provider Training: A Preventive Program." *Children and Youth Services Review* 3 (1981):127–141.

RUOPP, RICHARD; TRAVERS, JEFFREY; GLANTZ, FREDERIC; and COELEN, CRAIG. *Children at the Center: Summary Findings and their Implications*. Cambridge, Mass.: 1979.

RUTTER, BARBARA A. *The Parents Guide to Foster Family Care: A Way of Caring*. New York: Child Welfare League of America, 1978.

RUTTER, M. "Maternal Deprivation, 1972–1978: New Findings, New Concepts, New Approaches." *Child Development* 50 (June 1979):283–305.

————. "Parent–Child Separation: Psychological Effects on the Children." In *Early Experience: Myth and Evidence*, edited by A. M. Clarke and A. B. D. Clarke. New York: Free Press, 1976, pp. 153–186.

RYAN, PATRICIA. *Issues in Fostering*. Ypsilanti: Foster Parent Training Project, Eastern Michigan University, 1979. (Available in French and Spanish)

RYAN, PATRICIA; McFADDEN, EMILY JEAN; and WARREN, BRUCE. "Foster Families: A Resource for Helping Parents." In *The Challenge of Partnership: Working with Parents of Children in Foster Care*, edited by Anthony Maluccio and Paula Sinanoglu. New York: Child Welfare League of America, 1981, pp. 189–199.

RYAN, PATRICIA, and WARREN, BRUCE. *Finding Families for the Children*. Ypsilanti: Eastern Michigan University, 1974.

RYAN, PATRICIA; WARREN, BRUCE; and McFADDEN, EMILY JEAN. *Seventeen Course Outlines for Foster Parent Training*. Ypsilanti: Foster Parent Training Project, Eastern Michigan University, 1979.

RYAN, WILLIAM. *Blaming the Victim*. New York: Random House, 1971.

————. *Equality*. New York: Pantheon Books, 1981.

SAMEROFF, A. J. "The Etiology of Cognitive Competence: A Systems Perspective." In *Infants at Risk: Assessment of Cognitive Functioning*, edited by R. B. Kearsley and I. E. Siegel. Hillsdale, N.J.: Erlbaum, 1979, pp. 115–151.

――――. "Issues in Early Reproductive and Caretaking Risk: Review and Current Status." In *Exceptional Infant: Psychosocial Risks in Infant–Environment Transactions*, Volume 4, edited by D. Sawin, et. al. New York: Brunner/Mazel, 1980, pp. 343–359.

SAMEROFF, A. J., and CHANDLER, M. J. "Reproductive Risk and the Continuum of Caretaking Casualty." In *Review of Child Development Research*, Vol. IV, edited by F. D. Horowitz. Chicago: University of Chicago Press, 1975, pp. 187–244.

SARRI, ROSEMARY. "Paradigms and Pitfalls in Juvenile Justice Diversion." In *Providing Criminal Justice for Children.*, edited by A. Morris and H. Giller. Baltimore: Edward Morris, 1983, pp. 52–73.

――――. *Under Lock and Key: A Study of Juveniles in Jail and Detention.* Ann Arbor: University of Michigan, National Assessment Center of Juvenile Corrections, 1974.

SARRI, R., and BRADLEY, P. "Juvenile Aid Panels in South Australia." *Crime and Delinquency* 26 (Jan. 1980): 42–62.

SARRI, ROSEMARY, and HASENFELD, YEHESKEL. *Brought to Justice: Juveniles, the Courts and the Law.* Ann Arbor: University of Michigan, National Assessment Center of Juvenile Corrections, 1976.

SATIR, VIRGINIA. *Conjoint Family Therapy.* Revised Edition. Palo Alto, Calif.: Science and Behavior Books, 1967.

SCARR, S. "Psychology and Children: Current Research and Practice." *American Psychologist* 34 (Oct. 1979):809–811.

SCHLOSSMAN, S. *Love and the American Delinquent.* Chicago: University of Chicago Press, 1977.

SCHMIDT, JULIANA. "The Use of Purpose in Casework Practice." *Social Work* 14 (Jan. 1969):79–84.

SCHNEIDER, A. L., and SCHRAM, D. *An Assessment of Washington's Juvenile Justice Reform: Volume X.* Eugene, Ore.: Institute of Policy Analysis, Mar. 1983.

SCHOPLER, E., and LOFTIN, J. "Thought Disorders in Parents of Psychotic Children: A Function of Test Anxiety." *Archives of General Psychology* 20 (1969):174–181.

SCHORR, ALVIN, ed. *Children and Decent People.* New York: Basic Books, 1974.

SCHOTTLAND, CHARLES I. "Government Economic Programs and Family Life." *Journal of Marriage and the Family* 29 (Feb. 1967): 71–79.

SCHRAM, M., and SCHNEIDER, J. "Establishing Uniform Sentencing Standards for Juvenile Offenders: The Experience in Washington State." Unpublished paper, Eugene, Ore.: Institute of Policy Studies, 1981.

SCHRIER, CAROL J. "Guidelines for Record-Keeping under Privacy and Open Access Laws." *Social Work* 25 (Nov. 1980):452–457.

SCHUR, E. *Radical Non-Intervention: Rethinking the Delinquency Problem.* Englewood Cliffs, N.J.: Prentice–Hall, 1973.

SCHWARTZ, WILLIAM. "Private Troubles and Public Issues: One Social Work Job or Two?" In *The Social Welfare Forum, 1969.* New York: Columbia University Press, 1969, pp. 22–43.

SCHURFIELD, RAYMOND M. "An Integrated Approach to Case Services and Social Reform." *Social Casework* 61 (Dec. 1980):610–618.

SEABERG, JAMES R. "Foster Parents as Aides to Parents." In *The Challenge of Partnership: Working with Parents of Children in Foster Care,* edited by Anthony Maluccio and Paula Sinanoglu. New York: Child Welfare League of America, 1981, pp. 209–218.

――――. "Getting There from Here: Revitalizing Child Welfare Training." *Social Work* 27 (Sept. 1982):441–447.

SEABURY, BRETT A. "The Contract: Uses, Abuses, and Limitations." *Social Work* 21 (Jan. 1976):16–21.

――――. "Negotiating Sound Contracts with Clients." *Public Welfare* 37 (Spring 1979):33–38.

SEELING, GEORGE GREGORY. "Implementation of Subsidized Adoption Programs: A Preliminary Survey." *The Journal of Family Law* 15:4 (1976–77):732–769.

SEGAL, J., and YAHRAES, H. *A Child's Journey.* New York: McGraw–Hill, 1978.

SELMAN, R. "The Development of Social Cognitive Understanding." In *Moral Development and Behavior: Theory, Research and Social Issues,* edited by T. Lickona. New York: Holt, Rinehart and Winston, 1976, pp. 299–316.

SELVINI-PALAZZOLI, MARA, ET AL. "Hypothesizing—Circularity—Neutrality: Three Guidelines for the Conductor of the Session." *Family Process* 19 (Mar. 1980):3–12.

――――. *Paradox and Counterparadox.* English translation. New York: Jason Aronson, 1978 (Italian editors, Milan: Feltrinelli Editore, 1975).

SENNETT, R. *Authority.* New York: Knopf, 1980.

SENNETT, RICHARD, and COBB, JONATHON. *The Hidden Injuries of Class.* New York: Vintage Books, 1973.

SHAFFER, G. L. *Subsidized Adoption: An Alternative to Long-Term Foster Care.* Unpublished doctoral dissertation. Urbana–Champaign: University of Illinois, 1977.

SHAMES, MIRIAM. "Use of Homemaker Service in Families That Neglect Their Children." *Social Work* 45 (Jan. 1964):12–18.

SHAPIRO, DEBORAH. *Agencies and Foster Children.* New York: Columbia University Press, 1976.

SHAPIRO, JERALD. "Commitment to the Disenfranchised." In *Handbook of Clinical Social Work,* edited by Aaron Rosenblatt and Diana Waldfogel. San Francisco: Jossey–Bass, 1983, pp. 888–902.

SHAPIRO, JOAN. *Communities of the Alone.* New York: Association Press, 1970.

SHAPIRO, NANCY. "Two Methods of Preventing Child Abuse and Neglect." *Practice Digest* 2 (Mar. 1980):15–19.

SHAPIRO, VIVIAN; ADELSON, EDNA; and TABLEMAN, B., eds. *The Introduction of Infant Mental Health Services in Michigan.* Special edition of the *Infant Mental Health Journal.* New York: Human Sciences Press, Summer 1982.

SHERIDAN, W. *Standards for Juvenile and Family Courts.* Washington, D.C.: U.S. Government Printing Office, 1967.

SHERMAN, EDMUND A.; NEUMAN, RENEE; and SHYNE, ANN W. *Children Adrift in Foster Care.* New York: Research Center, Child Welfare League of America, 1973.

SHINN, EUGENE B. *Report on Phase II of the Case Management Study.* New York: National HomeCaring Council, 1976.

———. *Report on Phase II of the Case Management Study: Case Management in Homemaker–Home Health Aide Services.* New York: National HomeCaring Council, 1979.

SHINN, M. "Burnout in Human Service Agencies: Patterns of Job Stress, Psychological Strain, and Coping Responses." In *Burnout in the Helping Professions,* edited by K. Reid. Kalamazoo: Western Michigan University, 1979.

SHIREMAN, JOAN F. and JOHNSON, PENNY R. "Single Persons as Adoptive Parents." *Social Service Review* 50 (Mar. 1976): 103–116.

SHORTER, E. *The Making of the Modern Family.* New York: Basic Books, 1977.

SHURTLEFF, NATHANIEL B., ed. *Records of Plymouth Colony,* Court Order III, Boston, 1855, pp. 71–72. In *Children in America. A Documentary History,* Vols. I and II, edited by Robert Bremner. Cambridge, Mass.: Harvard University Press, 1970.

SHYNE, ANNE W., ed. *Child Welfare Perspectives: The Selected Papers of Joseph H. Reid.* New York: Child Welfare League of America, 1979.

———. "Research on Child Caring Institutions." In *Child Caring: Social Policy and the Institution,* edited by D. M. Pappenfort, D. M. Kilpatrick, and R. W. Roberts. Chicago: Aldine, 1973.

SHYNE, ANNE W., and SCHROEDER, ANITA G. *National Study of Social Services to Children and Their Families, Overview.* Washington, D.C.: National Academy of Sciences, 1976.

———. *National Study of Social Services to Children and Their Families.* Washington, D.C.: U.S. Department of Health, Education, and Welfare, DHEW Publication No. (OHDS) 78–30150, 1978a.

———. *Public Social Services for Children and Their Families.* Maryland: Westat, 1978b.

SHYNE, ANNE W.; SHERMAN, EDMUND A.; and PHILLIPS, MICHAEL H. "Filling the Gap in Child Welfare Research: Service for Children in Their Own Homes." *Child Welfare* 51 (Nov. 1972): 572–573.

SILVERMAN, PHYLLIS R. "A Reexamination of the Intake Procedure." *Social Casework* 51 (Dec. 1970):625–634.

SIMMONS, GLADYS; SIMPERT, JOANNE; and ROTHMAN, BEULAH. "Natural Parents as Partners in Child Care Placements." *Social Casework* 54 (Apr. 1973):224–232.

SIMON, RONALD D., and SIMON, DENISE K. "The Effect of Foster Parent Selection and Training on Service Delivery." *Child Welfare* 61 (Nov./Dec. 1982):515–524.

SIPORIN, MAX. *Introduction to Social Work Practice.* New York: Macmillan, 1975.

SKOLNICK, ARLENE. *The Intimate Environment: Exploring Marriage and the Family,* Third Edition. Boston: Little, Brown and Co., 1973.

SKOLNICK, ARLENE S., and SKOLNICK, JEROME H. *Family in Transition.* Boston: Little, Brown and Co., 1971.

SMALL, RICHARD W., and WHITTAKER, JAMES K. "Residential Group Care and Home-Based Care: Toward a Continuity of Family Service." In *Home-based Services for Children and Their Families,* edited by S. Maybanks and M. Bryce. Springfield, Ill.: Charles C. Thomas, 1979.

SMITH, ADAM. *The Wealth of Nations.* Indianapolis: Bobbs–Merrill, 1961. (Originally published 1776.)

SMITH, M. BREWSTER. "Competence and Socialization." In *Socialization and Society,* edited by John A. Clausen. Boston: Little, Brown and Co., 1968.

SNYDER, C.; SHENKEL, R.; and SCHMIDT, A. "Effects of Role Perspective and Client Psychiatric History on Locus of Problems." *Journal of Consulting and Clinical Psychology* 44 (June 1976):467–472.

SOLOMON, BARBARA. *Black Empowerment: Social Work in Minority Communities.* New York: Columbia University Press, 1976.

SORICH, CAROL J., and SIEBERT, ROBERTA. "Toward Humanizing Adoption." *Child Welfare* 61 (Apr. 1982):207–216.

SOSIN, M. "Juvenile Court Commitment Rates: The Role of Organizational Factors." *Social Service Review* 55:2 (June 1981):284–299.

––––––. "Controlling Organizations through Law: Due Process Mandates and Diversion Grants in Juvenile Courts." Unpublished doctoral dissertation. University of Michigan, 1977.

SPECIAL FAMILY SERVICES PROJECT. *Final Report.* Lansing, Mi.: Michigan Department of Social Services, 1981.

SPIEGEL, JOHN P. "The Resolution of Role Conflict within the Family." In *The Patient and the Mental Hospital,* edited by Milton Greenblatt, Daniel J. Levinson, and Richard H. Williams. Glencoe. Ill.: Free Press of Glencoe, Ill., 1957.

SPERGEL, I. "Response of Organization and Community to a Deinstitutionalization Strategy." *Crime and Delinquency* 28:3 (July 1982):426–449.

SPILLANE-GRIECO, EILEEN. "Feelings and Perceptions of Parents of Runaways." *Child Welfare* 63 (Mar.–Apr. 1984):159–166.

SPINETTA, JOHN, and RIGLER, DAVID. In *Traumatic Abuse and the Neglect of Children at Home,* edited by Gertrude Williams and John Money. Baltimore: Johns Hopkins University Press, 1982.

SPREY, JETSE. "The Family as a System in Conflict." *Journal of Marriage and the Family* 31 (Nov. 1969):699–706.

SROUFE, L. A. "Wariness of Strangers and the Study of Infant Development." *Child Development* 48 (Sept. 1977):731–746.

––––––. "The Coherence of Individual Development: Early Care, Attachment, and Subsequent Developmental Issues." *American Psychologist* 34 (Oct. 1979):834–841.

SROUFE, L. A., and WATERS, E. "Attachment as an Organizational Construct." *Child Development* 48 (Dec. 1977):1184–1199.

STACK, CAROL B. *All Our Kin: Strategies for Survival in a Black Community.* New York: Harper Colophon Books, 1975.

STAMM, ALFRED M. "NASW Membership: Characteristics, Deployment, and Salaries." *Personnel Information* 12 (May 1969):34–45.

STAPLES, ROBERT, and MIRANDÉ, ALFREDO. "Racial and Cultural Variations Among American Families: A Decennial Review of the Literature on Minority Families." In *Family in Transition,* edited by Arlene S. Skolnick and Jerome H. Skolnick. Boston: Little, Brown, 1983, pp. 496–521.

STAPLETON, VAUGHN, and SMITH, E. *Court Structure as a Salient Variable.* Williamsburg, Va.: National Center for State Courts, 1980.

STAPLETON, VAUGHN, and TEITELBAUM, LEE. *In Defense of Youth: A Study of the Role of Counsel in American Juvenile Courts.* New York: Russell Sage, 1972.

STARR, RAYMOND H. ed. *Child Abuse Prediction: Policy Implications.* Cambridge, Mass.: Ballinger, 1982.

*State vs. Jones,* 95 N.C. 588. In *Children and Youth in America. A Documentary History,* Vol. II, 1866–1932, edited by Robert H. Bremner. Cambridge, Mass.: Harvard University Press, 1970, pp. 119–121.

STEIN, THEODORE J. "Child Welfare: New Directions in the Field and Their Implications for Education." *Journal of Education for Social Work* 18 (Winter 1982):103–110.

————. *Social Work Practice in Child Welfare.* Englewood Cliffs, N.J.: Prentice–Hall, 1981.

STEIN, THEODORE, and GAMBRILL, EILEEN. *Decision Making in Foster Care: A Training Manual.* Berkeley: University Extension Publications, University of California, 1976.

————. "Facilitating Decision-Making in Foster Care: The Alameda Project." *Social Service Review* 51 (Sept. 1977):502–513.

STEIN, THEODORE J.; GAMBRILL, EILEEN D.; and WILTSE, KERMIT T. *Children in Foster Homes: Achieving Continuity of Care.* New York: Praeger Special Studies, 1978.

————. "Contracts and Outcome in Foster Care." *Social Work* 22 (Mar. 1977):148–149.

————. "Foster Care: The Use of Contracts." *Public Welfare* 32 (Fall 1974):20–25.

STEIN, THEODORE J., and RZEPNICKI, TINA L. "Decision Making in Child Welfare: Current Issues and Future Directions." In *Child Welfare: Current Dilemmas— Future Directions,* edited by Brenda G. McGowan and William Meezan. Itasca, Ill.: F. E. Peacock, 1983.

STEINER, GILBERT Y. *The Children's Cause.* Washington, D.C.: The Brookings Institution, 1976.

————. *The State of Welfare.* Washington, D.C.: The Brookings Institution, 1971.

STEINFELS, MARGARET O'BRIEN. *Who's Minding the Children?* New York: Simon and Schuster, 1973.

STEINMETZ, SUZANNE, and STRAUS, MURRAY, eds. *Violence in the Family.* New York: Harper and Row, 1974.

STICKLE, G., and STICKLE, M. A. P. "Pregnancy in Adolescents, Scope of the

Problem." *Contemporary Obstetrics and Gynecology*. New York: McGraw–Hill, 1975.

STONE, HELEN D., ed. *Foster Care in Question*. New York: Child Welfare League of America, 1970.

STRAUS, MURRAY; GELLES, RICHARD; and STEINMETZ, SUZANNE. *Behind Closed Doors: Violence in the American Family*. Garden City, N.Y.: Anchor Books, 1980.

STUDT, ELIOT. "An Outline for the Study of Social Authority Factors in Casework." *Social Casework* 35 (June 1954):231–238.

_____. "Worker–Client Authority Relationships in Social Work." *Social Work* 4 (Jan. 1959):17–28.

SUDIA, CECILIA E. "What Services Do Abusive Families Need?" In *The Social Context of Child Abuse and Neglect*, edited by Leroy H. Pelton. New York: Human Sciences Press, 1981, pp. 268–290.

SUE, DERALD W. *Counseling the Culturally Different: Theory and Practice*. New York: Wiley, 1981.

SUSSMAN, MARVIN B. "Family Systems in the 1970's: Analysis, Policies and Programs." *The Annals of the American Academy*, 396 (Jul. 1971):42.

SUZUKI, MICHIO. "Title XX Program Review." Unpublished Document, U.S. Department of Health and Human Services, Office of Human Development Services, May 21, 1980.

SWENSON, CAROL. "Social Networks, Mutual Aid, and the Life Model of Practice." In *Social Work Practice: People and Environments.*, edited by Carel B. Germain. New York: Columbia University Press, 1979, pp. 213–238.

SYKES, A. KEITH. *Service Contract Use in Preventing and Reducing Foster Care: Program Progress Report*. Hampton, Va.: Hampton Department of Social Services (Dec.) 1978.

SYMONDS, M. "The 'Second Injury' to Victims." *Evaluation and Change* (1980):36–38.

TANNENBAUM, F. *Crime and the Community*. New York: Ginn & Co., 1938.

TANNENBAUM, R. and SCHMIDT, W. "How to Choose a Leadership Style." *Harvard Business Review*, Reprint Series 21072:176–186.

TARRANT, JOHN F. *Drucker: The Man Who Invented the Corporate Society*. Boston: Cahners Books, Inc., 1976.

TAWNEY, R. H. *The Acquisitive Society*. New York: Harcourt, Brace and Co., 1920.

_____. *Religion and the Rise of Capitalism*. New York: Harcourt, Brace and World, 1926.

TAYLOR, D. A., and ALPERT, S. W. *Continuity and Support Following Residential Treatment*. New York: Child Welfare League of America, 1973.

TAYLOR, HASSELTINE B. "Guardianship or 'Permanent Placement' of Children." *California Law Review* 54 (1966):741–747.

TAYLOR, JOSEPH. "The Child Welfare Agency As the Extended Family." *Child Welfare* 51 (Feb. 1972):74–83.

TERESTMAN, N. "Mood Quality and Intensity in Nursery School Children as

Predictors of Behavior Disorder." *American Journal of Orthopsychiatry* 50 (Jan. 1980):125–137.

TERKELSON, KENNETH G. "Toward a Theory of the Family Life Cycle." In *The Family Life Cycle*, edited by Elizabeth A. Carter and Monica McGoldrick. New York: Gardner Press, 1980, pp. 21–52.

TERRELL, P. "Adapting to Austerity: Human Services After Proposition 13." *Social Work* 26 (Jul. 1981):275–282.

THEIS, SOPHIE VAN SENDEN. *How Foster Children Turn Out*. New York: State Charities Aid Association, 1924.

THEODORSON, GEORGE A., and THEODORSON, ARCHILLES G. *A Modern Dictionary of Sociology*. New York: Thomas Crowell Co., 1969.

THOMAS, A., and CHESS, S. *The Dynamics of Psychological Development*. New York: Brunner/Mazel, 1980.

———. *Temperament and Development*. New York: Brunner/Mazel, 1977.

THOMAS, A.; CHESS, S.; and BIRCH, H. G. *Temperament and Behavior Disorders in Children*. New York: New York University Press, 1968.

THOMAS, G. "Debate with Authors." *Social Service Review* 54 (Dec. 1980):588–590.

THOMAS, MASON P., JR. "Child Abuse and Neglect, Part I: Historical Overview, Legal Matrix and Social Perspectives." *The North Carolina Law Review* 50 (Feb. 1972):308.

THORNBERG, H. *Teenage Pregnancy: Have They Reached Epidemic Proportions?* Phoenix: Arizona Governor's Council on Children, Youth and Families, 1979.

THURSTON, HENRY W. *The Dependent Child: A Story of Changing Aims and Methods in the Care of Dependent Children*. New York: Columbia University Press, 1930.

TIAGHA, HANNAH. "Role Analysis of the Position of the Homemaker–Home Health Aide." *Home Health Care Services Quarterly* (1982):000–000.

TIETZE, C. "Teenage Pregnancy: Looking Ahead to 1984." *Family Planning Perspectives* 10 (Jul.–Aug. 1978):205–207.

TITMUSS, RICHARD. *Social Policy: An Introduction*. New York: Pantheon Books, 1974.

TOFFLER, ALVIN. *The Third Wave*. Toronto: Bantam Books, 1981.

TOFFLER, ALVIN, and TOFFLER, HEIDI. "The Changing American Family." *Family Weekly* (March 22, 1981):8–13.

TREMITIERE, BARBARA T. "Adoption of Children with Special Needs—The Client-Centered Approach." *Child Welfare* 58 (Dec. 1979):681–686.

TRICKETT, PENELOPE K.; APFEL, NANCY H.; ROSENBAUM, LAURIE K.; and ZIGLER, EDWARD F. "A Five-Year Follow-Up of Participants in the Yale Child Welfare Research Program." In *Day Care: Scientific and Social Policy Issues*, edited by Edward F. Zigler and Edmund W. Gordon. Boston: Auburn House, 1982, pp. 200–222.

TROTSKEY, ELIAS. *Institutional Care and Placing Out*. Chicago: Marks Nathan Jewish Orphan Home, 1930.

TRUSSEL, J. "Economic Consequences of Teenage Childbearing." *Family Planning Perspectives* 8 (Jul.–Aug. 1976):184–190.

Trussel, J., and Menken, J. "Early Childbearing and Subsequent Fertility." *Family Planning Perspectives* 10 (Jul.–Aug. 1978):209–218.

Tryer, L. B.; Mazlen, R. G.; and Bradshaw, L. E. "Meeting the Special Needs of Pregnant Teenagers." *Clinical Obstetrics and Gynecology* 21 (1978):1999–2013.

United Cerebral Palsy Association, Inc. *Word from Washington* 14:8 (Aug.–Sept., 1983).

U.S. Bureau of the Census. *Children in Custody: Census of Juvenile Detention and Correctional Facilities, 1971–1979.* Washington, D.C.: U.S. Department of Justice, National Institute of Justice, 1971–1979.

U.S. Bureau of the Census. *Statistical Abstract of the United States.* Washington, D.C. Government Printing Office. (Annual Publication).

U.S. Bureau of the Census. *U.S. Census Current Population Reports,* Series 25, U.S. Government Printing Office, 1982.

U.S. Commission on Civil Rights. *Civil Rights Issues and Health Care Delivery.* Washington, D.C.: U.S. Governmental Printing Office, 1980.

———. *A Growing Crisis: Disadvantaged Women and Their Children.* Washington, D.C.: C.P. #78, May 1983.

U.S. Congress, Senate Committee on Finance. *Public Assistance Amendments of 1977.* 95th Congress, 1st Session, 1977.

U.S. Congress, House. *Adoption Assistance and Child Welfare Act of 1980.* Public Law 96–272, 96th Congress, 2nd Session, House of Representatives, 3434.

U.S. Congress. *Family Protection Act.* 96th Congress, 1st Session, Senate, 1808.

U.S. Congress, Senate. Subcommittee on Children and Youth of the Senate Committee on Labor and Public Welfare, and the House of Representatives Select Subcommittee on Education, December 1, 1975.

*U.S. Daily News,* Supplement, Section 11, V 5:228, Nov. 28, 1930.

U.S. Department of Health, Education, and Welfare. *Adoption in 1975.* SRS #77–03295, 1977.

U.S. Department of Health, Education and Welfare, Children's Bureau. *Report of the Advisory Council on Child Welfare Services.* Washington, D.C.: Government Printing Office, 1960.

———. Social Security Administration, Children's Bureau, Division of Research, Jan. 21, 1959.

U.S. Department of Health and Human Services. *Study Findings National Study of the Incidence and Severity of Child Abuse and Neglect.* Washington, D.C.: Government Printing Office, DHHS Publication No. (OHDS) 81–30325, 1981.

U.S. Department of Justice, National Institute of Justice. *Census of Juvenile Detention and Correction Facilities, 1971–1979.* Washington, D.C.: 1982.

Upton, Letitia, and Lyons, Nancy. *Basic Facts: Distribution of Personal Income and Wealth in the United States.* Cambridge, Mass.: Cambridge Institute, 1972.

Valentine, Betty Lou. *Hustling and Other Hard Work.* New York: Free Press, 1978.

VALIENTE-BARKSDALE, CLARA. "Recruiting Hispanic Families." *Children Today* 12 (Mar.–Apr. 1983):26–28.

VAN CAMP, SARAH S. "New Look in Day Care." *Day Care and Early Education* 8 (Summer 1981): 24–25.

VAN DEN HAAG, E. *Punishing Criminals.* New York: Basic Books, 1975.

VAUGHN, B. E.; EGELAND, B.; SROUFE, L. A.; and WATERS, E. "Individual Differences in Infant-Mother Attachment at 12 and 18 Months: Stability and Change in Families Under Stress." *Child Development* 50 (Dec. 1979):971–975.

VERONICO, ANTHONY. "One Church, One Child: Placing Children with Special Needs." *Children Today* 12 (Mar.–Apr. 1983):6–10.

VINTER, ROBERT; DOWNS, GEORGE; and HALL, JON. *Juvenile Corrections in the States Residential Programs and Deinstitutionalization.* Ann Arbor: University of Michigan, 1976.

VINTER, R.; KISH, R.; and NEWCOMB, T. *Time Out.* Ann Arbor: University of Michigan National Association of Juvenile Corrections, 1976.

VIRGINIA COMMISSION FOR CHILDREN AND YOUTH. *Innovative Programming for Children and Youth.* Richmond, Va.: Virginia Commission for Children and Youth, 1977.

"Virginia Comprehensive Plan of Social Services" under Title XX of the *Social Security Act,* 1980.

VON HIRSCH, ANDREW. *Doing Justice: The Choice of Punishments.* New York: Hill and Wang, 1976.

VROOM, V. "Can Leaders Learn to Lead." In *Perspectives on Behavior in Organizations,* edited by J. R. Hackman, E. Lawler, and L. Porter. New York: McGraw-Hill, 1977, pp. 398–408.

WAITE, L. J., and MOORE, K. A. "The Impact of an Early First Birth on Young Women's Educational Attainment." *Social Forces* 56:3 (1978):845–865.

WALD, LILLIAN D. *The House on Henry Street.* New York: Henry Holt and Company, 1915.

WALDINGER, GLORIA. *Subsidized Adoption: A Special Case of Paying People to Parent.* Unpublished doctoral dissertation. Los Angeles: University of California, 1979.

WALKER, DEBORAH K. *Runaway Youth: An Annotated Bibliography and Literature Overview.* Washington, D.C.: Department of Health, Education, and Welfare, 1975.

WARD, MARGARET. "Parental Bonding in Older Child Adoptions." *Child Welfare* 60 (Jan. 1981):24–34.

WASSERMAN, HARRY. "Early Careers of Professional Social Workers in a Public Child Welfare Agency." *Social Work* 15 (Jan. 1970):96.

———. The Professional Social Worker in a Bureaucracy." *Social Work* 16 (Jan. 1971):89–95.

WATERS, E.; WIPPMAN, J.; and SROUFE, L. A. "Attachment, Positive Affect, and Competence in the Peer Group: Two Studies in Construct Validation." *Child Development* 50 (Sept. 1979):821–829.

WATKINS, ELIZABETH. "So That Children May Remain in Their Own Homes." *The Child* 18 (Oct. 1953):25–29.

WATSON, KENNETH W. "Subsidized Adoption: A Crucial Investment." *Child Welfare* 51 (Apr. 1972):220–230.

WATZLAWICK, PAUL; BEAVIN, JANE; and JACKSON, DONALD. *Pragmatics of Human Communication.* New York: W. W. Norton, 1967.

WAX, JOHN. "Power Theory and Institutional Change." *Social Service Review* 45 (Sept. 1971):274–288.

WAXLER, N. E., and MISHLER, E. G. "Parental Interaction with Schizophrenic Children and Well Siblings: An Experimental Test of Some Etiological Theories." In *Annual Progress in Child Psychiatry and Child Development*, edited by S. Chess and A. Thomas. New York: Brunner/Mazel, 1972.

WAYNE, J.; EBELING, N. B.; and AVERY, N.C. "Differential Groupwork in a Protective Agency." *Child Welfare* 55 (Sept.–Oct. 1976):581–591.

WEAVER, EDWARD T. "Long-Term Foster Care: Default or Design? The Public Agency Responsibility." *Child Welfare* 47 (June 1968):339–345.

WEBER, MAX. *The Protestant Ethic and the Spirit of Capitalism.* New York: Charles Scribner's, 1958.

WEIDELL, RUTH C. "Unsealing Sealed Birth Certificates in Minnesota." *Child Welfare* 59 (Feb. 1980):113–119.

WEINTRAUB, ALEX. "Changing Population in Adolescent Residential Treatment." *American Journal of Orthopsychiatry* 44 (July 1974): 604–610.

WEISSMAN, HAROLD. *Overcoming Mismanagement in the Human Services.* San Francisco: Jossey–Bass, 1973.

WERNER, E. E., and SMITH, R. S. *Kauai's Children Come of Age.* Honolulu: University of Hawaii Press, 1977.

WERTHEIM, ELEANOR. "Family Unit Therapy and the Science and Typology of Family Systems." *Family Process* 12 (Dec. 1973):361–376.

———. "The Science and Typology of Family Systems II. Further Theoretical and Practical Considerations." *Family Process* 14 (Sept. 1975):285–309.

WHEELER, CANDACE. *Where Am I Going: Making a Life Story Book.* Juneau, Al.: Winking Owl Press, 1978.

WHEELER, ETTA ANGELL. "The Story of Mary Ellen Which Started the Child Saving Crusade Throughout the World." Albany, N.Y.: American Humane Association, Publication No. 280, circa 1910.

WHEELER, GERALD R. *Counterdeterrence.* Chicago: Nelson–Hall, 1978.

WHEELER, KATHRYN. *Tanya: The Building of a Family Through Adoption.* New York: North American Center on Adoption, Child Welfare League of America, 1979.

WHITE HOUSE CONFERENCE ON CHILDREN (1909). *Proceedings of the Conference on the Care and Protection of Dependent Children, Jan. 25–26, 1909.* Senate Document #13, 60th Congress, 1908–9. Washington, D.C.: U.S. Government Printing Office, 1909.

WHITE HOUSE CONFERENCE ON FAMILIES. *Listening to America's Families.* Washington, D.C.: U.S. Government Printing Office, 1980.

WHITE, ROBERT W. "Competence and the Psychosexual Stages of Development." In *Nebraska Symposium on Motivation*, edited by M. R. Jones. Lincoln: University of Nebraska Press, 1960.

———. *Ego and Reality in Psychoanalytic Theory.* New York: International Universities Press, 1963.

———. "Motivation Reconsidered: The Concept of Competence." *Psychological Review* 66 (Sept. 1959):297–333.

———. "Strategies of Adaptation." In *Human Adaptation*, edited by Rudolf A. Moos, Lexington, Mass.: Heath, 1976, pp. 17–32.

WHITMORE, WILLIAM HENRY. *The Law of Adoption in The United States and Especially in Massachusetts.* Albany: Joel Munsell, 1876.

WHITTAKER, JAMES K. *Caring for Troubled Children: Residential Treatment in a Community Context.* San Francisco: Jossey–Bass, 1979.

———. "Causes of Childhood Disorders: New Findings." *Social Work* 21 (Mar. 1976):91–96.

———. "The Changing Character of Residential Child Care: An Ecological Perspective." *Social Service Review* 22 (Mar. 1978):21–36.

———. "Colonial Child Care Institutions: Our Heritage of Care." *Child Welfare* 50 (July 1971a):396–400.

———. "Family Involvement in Residential Child Care: A Support System for Biological Parents." In *The Challenge of Partnership: Working with Parents in Foster Care*, edited by Anthony N. Maluccio and Paula Sinanoglu. New York: Child Welfare League of America, 1981, pp. 67–89.

———. "Mental Hygiene Influences in Children's Institutions: Organization and Technology for Treatment." *Mental Hygiene* 55 (Oct. 1971b):444–450.

WHITTAKER, JAMES; and GARBARINO, J.; and ASSOCIATES. *Social Support Networks: Informal Helping in the Human Services.* New York: Aldine, 1983.

WHITTAKER, JAMES, and PECORA, P. "The Social 'R & D' Paradigm in Child and Youth Services: Building Knowledge Convivially." *Children and Youth Services Review* 1984.

WHYTE, W. F. "A Slum Sex Code." *American Journal of Sociology* 24 (July 1943):31.

WICKENDEN, ELIZABETH. "A Perspective on Social Services: An Essay Review." *Social Service Review* 59 (Dec. 1976):574–588.

WIENER, G., and MILTON, T. "Demographic Correlates of Low Birth Weight." *American Journal of Epidemiology* 91 (1970):260.

*Wilder v. Bernstein et al.*, 499 F. Supp. 980 (1980).

*Wilder v. Sugarman et al.*, 385 F. Supp. 1013 (1974).

WILGUS, A., and EPSTEIN, I. "Group Homes for Adolescents: A Comparative Case Study." *Social Work* 23 (Nov. 1978):486–492.

WILLS, T. A. "Perceptions of Clients by Professional Helpers." *Psychological Bulletin* 85 (Sept. 1978):968–1000.

WILSON, J. A., ed. *Crime and Public Policy.* San Francisco: Institute for Contemporary Studies, 1983.

WILSON, JAMES O. *Thinking About Crime.* New York: Basic Books, 1975.

WILTSE, KERMIT J. "Current Issues and New Directions in Foster Care." In *Child*

*Welfare Strategy in the Coming Years,* edited by Alfred Kadushin. Washington, D.C.: Department of Health, Education, and Welfare, DHEW Publication No. (OHDS) 78–30158, 1978, pp. 51–89.

―――. "Education and Training for Child Welfare Practice: The Search for a Better Fit." Los Angeles: University of California–Los Angeles, School of Social Welfare, Region IX Child Welfare Training Center, 1981. (Mimeograph)

―――. "Foster Care in the 1970's: A Decade of Change." *Children Today* 8 (May–June 1979):10–14.

WILTSE, KERMIT T., and GAMBRILL, EILEEN. "Foster Care 1973: A Reappraisal." *Public Welfare* 32 (Winter 1974):7–14.

Wing, Kenneth. "Title VI and Health Facilities: Forms Without Substance." *Hastings Law Journal* 30 (Sept. 1978).

WISCONSIN COUNCIL ON DEVELOPMENTAL DISABILITIES. "State Family Support/Cash Subsidy Programs." August 1983.

WITMER, RICHARD T. "The Purpose of American Adoption Laws." In *Independent Adoption: a Follow-Up Study,* edited by Helen Witmmr, et al. New York: Russell Sage Foundation, 1963, pp. 19–43.

WITTE, EDWIN E. *The Development of the Social Security Act.* Madison: University of Wisconsin Press, 1963.

WOLFENSBERGER, W. *Normalization.* New York: National Institute on Mental Retardation, 1972.

WOLINS, M. "Observations on the Future of Institutional Care of Children in the United States." In *Child Welfare Strategy in the Coming Years,* edited by A. Kadushin. Washington, D.C.: Department of Health, Education, and Welfare, DHEW Pub. No. (OHDS) 78–30158, 1978, pp. 90–130.

WOLINS, MARTIN, and PILIAVIN, IRVING. *Institution and Foster Family: A Century of Debate.* New York: Child Welfare League of America, 1964.

WOLINS, M., and YOCHANAN, W. *Revitalizing Residential Settings.* San Francisco: Jossey–Bass, 1982.

WOLK, JAMES L. "Are Social Workers Politically Active?" *Social Work* 26 (July 1981):283–288.

WOODEN, K. *Weeping in the Playtime of Others.* New York: McGraw–Hill, 1976.

WOODS, THOMAS L. "Social Work Consultation and Student Training in Day Care Centers." *Child Welfare* 52 (Dec. 1973):663–668.

WOOLF, MICHAEL. "A Great Brodkey Novel Is Coming Slowly." *Village Voice,* Oct. 20, 1975, pp. 53–54.

YANKELOVICH, SKELLY, and WHITE, INC. *The General Mills American Family Report, 1976–1977.* Minneapolis, Minn.: General Mills, Inc., 1977.

YARROW, L. J., and PEDERSEN, F. A. "The Interplay Between Cognition and Motivation in Infancy." In *Origins of Intelligence, Infancy and Early Childhood,* edited by M. Lewis. New York: Plenum, 1976, pp. 379–399.

YELAJA, SHANKAR. *Authority and Social Work: Concept and Use.* Toronto, Canada: University of Toronto Press, 1971.

YONDORF, BARBARA, and BENKER, KAREN. "Block Grants: A New Chance for

State Legislatures to Oversee Federal Funds." Unpublished paper. National Conference of State Legislatures, Feb. 1982.

YORK, R. "Can Change Be Effectively Managed?" *Administration in Social Work* 1 (Summer 1977):187–198.

YOUNG, LEONTINE. *Wednesday's Children: A Study of Child Neglect and Abuse.* New York: McGraw–Hill, 1964.

ZABIN, L. S.; KANTNER, J. F.: and ZELNIK, M. "The Risk of Adolescent Pregnancy in the First Months of Intercourse." *Family Planning Perspectives* 11 (July–Aug. 1979):215–222.

ZELNIK, M., and KANTNER, J. F. "Sexual Activity, Contraceptive Use and Pregnancy Among Metropolitan-Area Teenagers: 1971–1979." *Family Planning Perspectives* 12 (Sept.–Oct. 1980):230–237.

———. "Contraceptive Patterns and Premarital Pregnancy Among Women Aged 15–19 in 1976." *Family Planning Perspectives* 10 (May–June 1978): 135–142.

ZIEFERT, MARJORIE. "Abuse and Neglect—The Adolescent as Hidden Victim." In *Social Work with Abused and Neglected Children,* edited by Kathleen Faller. New York: Free Press, 1981.

ZIGLER, EDWARD, and HUNSINGER, SUSAN. "Our Neglected Children." *Yale Alumni Magazine and Journal* VXLI (Feb. 1978):11–13.

ZIMMERMAN, SHIRLEY. "The Family: Building Block or Anachronism?" *Social Casework* 6 (Apr. 1980):195–204.

ZIMRING, F. *The Changing Legal World of Adolescence.* New York: Free Press, 1982.

ZINN, DEBORAH. "Reagan's Social Services Block Grant: What It Is and What You Can Do About It." Unpublished paper. Ann Arbor: University of Michigan School of Social Work, 1981.

ZWEBEN, MURRAY. *Enactment of a Law.* Washington, D.C.: U.S. Government Printing Office, 1976.

# Author Index

# Subject Index